CORPORATE TAX RATES

If taxable income is:	The tax is:
Not over $50,000	15% of taxable income
Over $50,000 but not over $75,000	$7,500 + 25% of the excess over $50,000
Over $75,000 but not over $100,000	$13,750 + 34% of the excess over $75,000
Over $100,000 but not over $335,000	$22,250 + 39% of the excess over $100,000
Over $335,000 but not over $10,000,000	$113,900 + 34% of the excess over $335,000
Over $10,000,000 but not over $15,000,000	$3,400,000 + 35% of the excess over $10,000,000
Over $15,000,000 but not over $18,333,333	$5,150,000 + 38% of the excess over $15,000,000
Over $18,333,333	$6,416,667 + 35% of the excess over $18,333,333

Visit the *Principles of Taxation for Business and Investment Planning* Online Learning Center at
www.mhhe.com/sjones2006

Principles of Taxation

for Business and Investment Planning

Principles of Taxation

for Business and Investment Planning

2006 Edition

Sally M. Jones
KPMG Professor of Accounting
McIntire School of Commerce
University of Virginia

Boston Burr Ridge, IL Dubuque, IA Madison, WI New York San Francisco St. Louis
Bangkok Bogotá Caracas Kuala Lumpur Lisbon London Madrid Mexico City
Milan Montreal New Delhi Santiago Seoul Singapore Sydney Taipei Toronto

The McGraw·Hill Companies

PRINCIPLES OF TAXATION FOR BUSINESS AND INVESTMENT PLANNING, 2006 EDITION

Published by McGraw-Hill/Irwin, a business unit of The McGraw-Hill Companies, Inc., 1221 Avenue of the Americas, New York, NY, 10020.

This book is printed on acid-free paper.

1 2 3 4 5 6 7 8 9 0 CCW/CCW 0 9 8 7 6 5

ISBN 0-07-299178-X
ISSN 1099-5587

Editorial director: *Brent Gordon*
Publisher: *Stewart Mattson*
Executive editor: *Tim Vertovec*
Managing developmental editor: *Gail Korosa*
Marketing manager: *Marc Chernoff*
Media producer: *Elizabeth Mavetz*
Project manager: *Laura Griffin*
Senior production supervisor: *Sesha Bolisetty*
Coordinator freelance design: *Artemio Ortiz Jr.*
Senior media project manager: *Rose M. Range*
Developer, Media technology: *Brian Nacik*
Cover design: *Asylum Studios*
Typeface: *10/12 Times Roman*
Compositor: *Cenveo*
Printer: *Courier Westford*

www.mhhe.com

To Zane, Ward, and Rachael

About the Author

Sally M. Jones is the KPMG Professor of Accounting at the McIntire School of Commerce, University of Virginia, where she teaches both graduate and undergraduate tax courses. Before joining the Virginia faculty in 1992, Professor Jones spent 14 years on the faculty of the Graduate School of Business, University of Texas at Austin. She received her undergraduate degree from Augusta College, her M.P.A. from the University of Texas, and her Ph.D. from the University of Houston. She is also a CPA. Professor Jones is the co-author of *Advanced Strategies in Taxation* (McGraw-Hill/Irwin) and was the first editor of *Advances in Taxation* (JAI Press) and the *PriceWaterhouse Case Studies in Taxation.* She has published numerous articles in the *Journal of Taxation, The Tax Adviser,* and the *Journal of the American Taxation Association*. Professor Jones is a frequent speaker at tax conferences and symposia, a past president of the American Taxation Association, and the 2000 recipient of the Ray M. Sommerfeld Outstanding Tax Educator Award.

Brief Contents

Contents

Chapter 4
Basic Maxims of Income Tax Planning 71

PART THREE
THE MEASUREMENT OF TAXABLE INCOME

Chapter 5
Taxable Income from Business Operations 97

Chapter 6
Property Acquisitions and Cost Recovery Deductions 129

Chapter 7
Property Dispositions 167

Chapter 8
Nontaxable Exchanges 199

PART FOUR
THE TAXATION OF BUSINESS INCOME

Chapter 9
Sole Proprietorships, Partnerships, LLCs, and S Corporations 225

PART FIVE
THE INDIVIDUAL TAXPAYER

Chapter 13
The Individual Tax Formula 349

Chapter 14
Compensation and Retirement Planning 383

Chapter 15
Investment and Personal Financial Planning 421

Chapter 16
Tax Consequences of Personal Activities 465

PART SIX
THE TAX COMPLIANCE PROCESS

Chapter 17
The Tax Compliance Process 495

Principles of Taxation for Business and Investment Planning is a unique approach to the subject of taxation. This text is designed for use in introductory tax courses included in either undergraduate or graduate business programs. Its objective is to teach students to recognize the major tax issues inherent in business and financial transactions. The text focuses on fundamental concepts, the mastery of which provides a permanent frame of reference for future study of advanced tax topics. Unlike traditional introductory texts, *Principles of Taxation for Business and Investment Planning* downplays the technical detail that makes the study of taxation such a nightmare for business students. Traditional texts are heavily compliance oriented and convince many students that the tax law is too complex and specialized to be relevant to their future careers. This text attempts to do just the opposite by convincing students that an understanding of taxation is not only relevant but critical to their success in the business world.

Principles of Taxation for Business and Investment Planning has its origin in the 1989 White Paper entitled *Perspectives on Education: Capabilities for Success in the Accounting Profession,* published jointly by the Big Eight public accounting firms. The White Paper expressed disenchantment with the narrow technical focus of undergraduate accounting curricula and called for scholastic emphasis on a broad set of business skills necessary for professional success. The Accounting Education Change Commission (AECC), operating under the aegis of the American Accounting Association, embraced the philosophy reflected in the White Paper. In September 1990, the AECC published its Position Statement No. One, entitled *Objectives of Education for Accountants.* This statement reiterated that an undergraduate business education should provide a base for lifelong learning.

Despite these calls for reform, many undergraduate tax courses are taught in a traditional manner based on a paradigm developed a half-century ago. In the modern (postwar) era of business education, the first generation of tax teachers were practitioners: accountants or attorneys hired as adjunct faculty to initiate students into the mysteries of the newly enacted Internal Revenue Code of 1954. These practitioners taught their students in the same way they trained their employees. In doing so, they created a compliance-oriented paradigm. In today's world, this traditional paradigm is an anachronism. Business students don't need to learn how to generate tax information. Instead, they must learn how to use tax information to make good business and financial decisions.

A NEW PARADIGM FOR THE INTRODUCTORY TAX COURSE

Principles of Taxation for Business and Investment Planning provides a paradigm for meeting the educational needs of tax students in the twenty-first century. This paradigm is based on three postulates:

- **Postulate 1: Students should learn the tax law as an integrated component of a complex economic environment.** They should be aware of the role taxes play in financial decision making and should understand how taxes motivate people and institutions to engage in certain transactions.
- **Postulate 2: Students should comprehend the tax law as an organic whole rather than as a fragmented collection of rules and regulations.** They should learn general tax rules rather than the myriad of exceptions that confuse rather than clarify the general rules. They should appreciate how the general rules apply to all taxpaying entities before they learn how specialized rules apply to only certain entities. Finally, they should learn how the law applies to broad categories of transactions rather than to a particular transaction.
- **Postulate 3: Students who learn fundamental concepts have a permanent frame of reference into which they can integrate the constant changes in the technical minutiae of the law.** The rapid evolution of the tax law results in a short shelf life for much of the detailed information contained in undergraduate tax texts. Yet the key elements of the law—the statutory and judicial bedrock—do not change with each new revenue act. Students who master these key elements truly are prepared for a lifetime of learning.

As a teacher with more than 30 years of experience, I know that traditional paradigms die hard and educational reform is difficult. Nevertheless, I also believe that change in the way college and university professors teach tax is both inevitable and worthwhile. Our responsibility to our students is to prepare them to cope in a business world with little tolerance for outdated skills or irrelevant knowledge. My hope is that *Principles of Taxation for Business and Investment Planning* is a tool that can help us fulfill that responsibility.

USING THIS TEXT IN A FIRST-SEMESTER TAX COURSE

Principles of Taxation for Business and Investment Planning is designed for use in a one-semester (15-week) introductory tax course. Instructors can choose which of the 17 chapters deserve a full week's coverage and which can be covered in less than a week. Instructors may even decide to omit chapters that seem less relevant to the educational needs of their students. Business students who complete a one-semester course based on this text will be well prepared to function in the modern tax environment. If they are required (or may elect) to take a second tax course, they will have a solid, theoretical foundation on which to build. The second tax course typically involves an in-depth study of the taxation of business entities: C corporations, partnerships, LLCs, and S corporations. The recommended text for the second course is *Advanced Strategies in Taxation* (Jones and Rhoades-Catanach: McGraw-Hill/Irwin). This text was written to complement *Principles of Taxation for Business and Investment Planning,* and the two textbooks provide an integrated sequence of topics that represent a complete educational package for undergraduate students.

This is the ninth annual edition of *Principles of Taxation for Business and Investment Planning*. I've been a student of the tax law far too long to believe that this edition is free from technical error or includes every relevant topic. I'm certain that adopters of the text will have many excellent suggestions as to how I can improve the next edition. I welcome any and all comments and encourage my fellow teachers to e-mail me (smj7q@virginia.edu) with their input.

Sally M. Jones

The content and organization of this text are highly compatible with the Model Tax Curriculum proposed by the American Institute of Certified Public Accountants. According to the AICPA, the introductory tax course should expose students to a broad range of tax concepts and emphasize the role of taxation in the business decision-making process. Under the model curriculum, students first learn to measure the taxable income from business and property transactions. They are then introduced to the different types of business entities and the tax considerations unique to each type. Individual taxation should be one of the last topics covered, rather than the primary focus of the course. Because *Principles of Taxation for Business and Investment Planning* reflects this recommended pedagogical approach, the text is ideal for courses based on the AICPA Model Tax Curriculum.

Part One consists of two chapters that familiarize students with the global tax environment. Chapter 1 describes the environment in terms of the legal relationship between taxes, taxpayers, and governments. Definitions of key terms are developed, and the major taxes are identified. Chapter 2 considers the tax environment from a normative perspective by asking the question: "What are the characteristics of a good tax?" Students are introduced to the notions of tax efficiency and tax equity and learn how contrasting political beliefs about efficiency and equity continue to shape the tax environment.

PART ONE

Exploring the Tax Environment

Part Two concentrates on developing a methodology for incorporating tax factors into business decisions. Chapter 3 introduces the pivotal role of net present value of cash flows in evaluating financial alternatives. Students learn how to compute tax costs and tax savings and how to interpret them as cash flows. Chapter 4 covers the basic maxims of income tax planning. The characteristics of the tax law that create planning opportunities are explained, and the generic techniques for taking advantage of those opportunities are analyzed.

PART TWO

Fundamentals of Tax Planning

Part Three focuses on the quantification of business taxable income. Chapter 5 covers the computation of income or loss from ongoing commercial activities, with special emphasis on differences between taxable income and net income for financial statement purposes. Chapters 6 and 7 explore the tax implications of acquisitions and dispositions of business property, while Chapter 8 is devoted to nontaxable exchanges.

PART THREE

The Measurement of Taxable Income

PART FOUR

The Taxation of Business Income

Part Four teaches students how to calculate the tax on business income. Chapter 9 describes the function of sole proprietorships, partnerships, LLCs, and S corporations as conduits of income, while Chapter 10 discusses corporations as taxable entities in their own right. Chapter 11 builds on the preceding two chapters by exploring the tax planning implications of the choice of business entity. Chapter 12 broadens the discussion by considering the special problems of businesses operating in more than one tax jurisdiction. This chapter introduces both multistate and international tax planning strategies.

PART FIVE

The Individual Taxpayer

Part Five concentrates on the tax rules and regulations unique to individuals. Chapter 13 presents the individual tax formula and acquaints students with the complexities of computing individual taxable income. Chapter 14 covers compensation and retirement planning. Chapter 15 covers investment and rental activities and introduces wealth transfer planning. Finally, Chapter 16 analyzes the tax consequences of personal activities, with particular emphasis on home ownership.

PART SIX

The Tax Compliance Process

Part Six consists of Chapter 17, which presents the important procedural and administrative issues confronting taxpayers. It covers the basic rules for paying tax and filing returns, as well as the penalties on taxpayers who violate the rules. Chapter 17 also describes the judicial process through which taxpayers and the IRS resolve their differences.

Tax Research is an appendix that provides a succinct overview of the tax research process and prepares students to solve the research problems included at the end of each chapter. The appendix explains the six steps in the tax research process and contains a cumulative example of the application of each step to a research case.

Learning Objectives

The chapters begin with learning objectives that preview the technical content and alert students to the important concepts to be mastered. These objectives appear again as marginal notations marking the place in the chapter where each learning objective is addressed.

Learning Objectives

After studying this chapter, you should be able to:

1. Define the terms *tax, taxpayer, incidence,* and *jurisdiction.*
2. Express the relationship between tax base, rate, and revenue as a formula.
3. Describe the types of taxes levied by local governments, state governments, and the federal government.
4. Explain why different jurisdictions compete for revenues from the same taxpayer.
5. Identify the reasons why governments modify their tax systems.
6.

SOME BASIC TERMINOLOGY

Taxes, Taxpayers, Incidence, and Jurisdiction

Objective 1
Define the terms *tax, taxpayer, incidence,* and *jurisdiction.*

Before beginning our exploration of the tax environment, we must define some minology. A **tax** can be defined as a payment to support the cost of government. fers from a fine or penalty imposed by a government because a tax is not intende or punish unacceptable behavior. On the other hand, taxes are compulsory rather untary on the part of the payer. A tax differs from a user's fee because the paymen does not entitle the payer to a specific good or service in return. In the abstract, ci ceive any number of government benefits for their tax dollars. Nevertheless, the

Examples and Cases

The chapters contain numerous examples and cases illustrating or demonstrating the topic under discussion.

Economic Nexus

Show-Me's research division recently developed a manufacturing process that the corpo patented with the federal government. Show-Me licensed this patent to a number of panies, three of which operate in South Carolina. The companies pay an annual royal use of the patent. Although Show-Me has no physical presence (tangible property o ployees) in South Carolina, it does earn revenue from marketing an intangible asset to Carolina customers. On the basis of this economic nexus, South Carolina claims jurisdict tax Show-Me's royalty income.

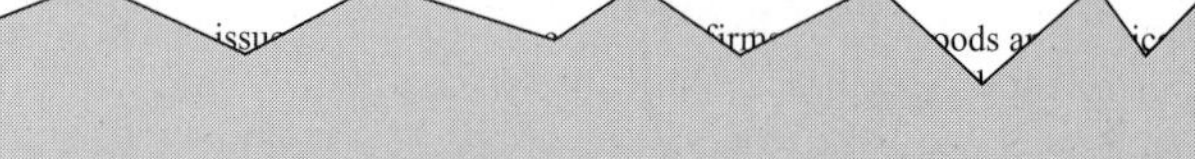

Tax Talk

Each chapter includes items of "Tax Talk." These items highlight new tax planning strategies, tax facts, legislative proposals, or innovative transactions with interesting tax implications reported in the business press.

corporations conducting business within the state. Thus, firms engaged in inter merce may be subject to tax in any number of states. Given that thousands of U. nies conduct business in more than one state, if not all 50 states, some degree o coordination is necessary to avert fiscal anarchy.

Tax Talk
The U.S. Court of Appeals for the Sixth Circuit ruled that Ohio's investment tax credit is unconstitutional because it gives preferential treatment to in-state development activities, thereby interfering with interstate commerce and hindering free trade among the states.

Article 1 of the U.S. Constitution grants the federal government the power to commerce with foreign nations, and among the several states, and with the Indi This **Commerce Clause** empowers Congress and the federal courts to establish gr for state tax laws. For a state tax to be constitutional, it must not discriminate aga state commerce. For instance, an income tax with a 3 percent rate for resident co and a 6 percent rate for nonresident corporations would be blatantly unconstitutio dition, state taxes can be levied only on businesses having nexus with the state. **Ne** the degree of contact between a business and a state necessary to establish jurisdic

The Issue of Nexus

Let's examine the concept of nexus by considering the regional business con Show-Me Inc., which is incorporated in Missouri. Show-Me's corporate headqu in St. Louis, and its two manufacturing plants are in Kansas and Arkansas. The c uses a common carrier to ship its products to customers in Missouri, Kansas, Iowa, Nebraska, and Oklahoma. Show-Me's business is illustrated in Exhibit 12.

Key Terms

Key terms are indicated in boldface in the text. A list of key terms is also listed at the end of the chapter with page references for easy review. Definitions of key terms from all the chapters are compiled in a Glossary for the text.

Key Terms

abatement 8
activity-based tax 6
ad valorem tax 7
brackets 5
Cumulative Bulletins (CBs) 17
earmarked tax 6
employment taxes 12
event- or transaction-based tax 6
excise tax 10
flat rate 5
graduated rate 5
income tax 6
Internal Revenue Bulletins (IRBs) 17
Internal Revenue Code of 1986 16
Internal Revenue Service (IRS) 16
jurisdiction 5
personalty 8
real property taxes 7
realty 7
revenue 6
revenue rulings and revenue procedu...
sales tax 9
section 16
tax 4
tax assessors 7
tax base 5
tax law 15
taxpayer 4
transfer taxes 12
Treasury regulations
unemployment tax
use tax 9
value-added tax (VA...

Sources of Book/Tax Differences

Chapters 5, 6, 7, 8, 10, 12 and 14 provide a list of the sources of book/tax differences introduced in the chapter.

Sources of Book/Tax Differences

Permanent

- Interest on state and local bonds
- Key-person life insurance proceeds and premiums
- Fines and penalties
- Political contributions and lobbying expense
- Meals and entertainment expense
- U.S. production activities deduction

Temporary

- Prepaid income
- Bad debts
- Accrued expenses failing the all-events test
- Related party accruals
- NOL carryforwards

Questions and Problems for Discussion

Challenge students to think critically about conceptual and technical issues covered in the chapter. These problems tend to be open-ended and are designed to engage students in debate. Many problems require students to integrate material from previous chapters in formulating their responses.

Questions and Problems for Discussion

1. Discuss the choice of a taxable year for the following businesses.
   a. Retail plant and garden center.
   b. French bakery.
   c. Chimney cleaning business.
   d. Moving and transport business.
   e. Software consulting business.
2. Corporation DB operates three very different lines of business. Can the corp... elect a different overall method of accounting for each line or must the corp... adopt one overall method?
3. Firm LK bought a warehouse of used furniture to equip several of its clerical o... An employee discovered a cache of gold coins in a desk drawer. A local court d...

Application Problems

Give students practice in applying the technical material covered in the chapter. Most of the problems are quantitative and require calculations to derive a numeric solution.

Application Problems

1. Mr. JK, a U.S. citizen and resident of Vermont, owns 100 percent of the stock... Services, which is incorporated under Vermont law and conducts business i... counties in the state. JK Services owns 100 percent of the stock of JK Realty, w... incorporated under Massachusetts law and conducts business in Boston.
   a. How many taxpayers are identified in the above statement of facts?
   b. Identify the governments with jurisdiction to tax each of these taxpayers.
2. In each of the following cases, determine whether the United States has jurisdic... tax Mrs. CM.
   a. Mrs. CM is a citizen of Brazil but is a permanent resident of Orlando, Florid...
   b. Mrs. CM is a citizen and resident of Brazil... owns Manha... real e...

Issue Recognition Problems

Develop students' ability to recognize the tax issues suggested by a set of facts and to state those issues as questions. The technical issues buried in these problems typically are *not* discussed in the chapter. Consequently, students must rely on their understanding of basic principles to analyze the problem, spot the tax concern or opportunity, and formulate the question to be resolved. In short, students must take the first steps in the tax research process.

Issue Recognition Problems

Identify the tax issue or issues suggested by the following situations and state each is
the form of a question.

1. Corporation DS owns assets worth $550,000 and has $750,000 outstanding debt
of DS's creditors just informed DS that it is writing off a $15,000 account rece
from DS because it believes the receivable is uncollectible. However, even wi
debt discharge, DS is insolvent and has no net worth.
2. Two years ago, a professional theater company paid $300 to an antique dealer for
oil painting that the company used as a prop. This year, the company's prop ma
was cleaning the painting and discovered an older painting hidden beneath the to
of pigment. To the company's delight, the older painting was signed by Paul C
appraisers determined that

Research Problems

Provide further opportunity for students to develop their analytic skills. These problems consist of short scenarios that suggest one or more tax issues. The scenarios conclude with explicit research questions for the students to answer. To find the answers, they need access to either a traditional or an electronic tax library. Instructors can refer their students to **Appendix C,** which provides an overview of the tax research process.

Research Problems

1. Using an electronic library such as RIA Checkpoint, CCH Tax Research NetW
Lexis-Nexis, determine how many federal tax cases decided in 2004 contain the
step transaction.
2. Select a case that discusses the step transaction doctrine in the opinion and pr
written summary (brief) of the case.
3. Using an electronic library such as RIA Checkpoint, CCH Tax Research NetW
Lexis-Nexis, find a federal tax case in which the taxpayer is found guilty of ta
sion. After reading the case, list the behaviors of the taxpayer that convinced th
that the taxpayer was evading (rather than legally avoiding) tax.

Tax Planning Cases

Give students an opportunity to integrate their tax knowledge into a business planning framework. Most cases involve taxpayers who must decide whether to undertake a certain transaction or who must choose between alternative transactions. Students must assume the role of tax adviser by recommending a course of action to maximize the after-tax value of the transaction.

Tax Planning Cases

1. Firm DFG plans to open a foreign subsidiary through which to sell its manufac
goods in the European market. It must decide between locating the subsidiary in C
try X or Country Z. If the subsidiary operates in Country X, its gross receipts
sales will be subject to a 3 percent gross receipts tax. If the subsidiary opera
Country Z, its net profits will be subject to a 42 percent income tax. However, C
try Z's tax law has a special provision to attract foreign investors: No foreign subs
is subject to the income tax for the first three years of operations.

DFG projects the following annual operating results for the two locations (in
sands of dollars).

Instructor's Manual

An **Instructor's Manual** prepared by Sally Jones includes a course outline, topics for class discussion, and teaching hints for a one-semester introductory tax course. The Instructor's Manual also provides suggested solutions to all end-of-chapter problems and cases.

Test Bank

A **Test Bank** prepared by John Barrick (Brigham Young University) contains multiple-choice, true/false, and short problems requiring analysis and written answers in a Windows platform.

Computerized Test Bank

A **Computerized Testbank** by Brownstone is available and is a user-friendly testing system that allows faculty to easily generate exams.

All the resource supplements are contained on the Instructor CD-ROM (ISBN 0072991801).

Online Learning Center

A **Web Page** (www.mhhe.com/sjones2006) includes valuable material for both instructors and students. These include relevant Internet links and Internet Research Problems for each chapter in the book prepared by James Fellows (University of South Florida). Also included are PowerPoint slides by Rebekah Heath (Emporia State University). In addition, online quizzes for students with solutions and their rationales were created by Richard Leaman (University of Denver). This Online Learning Center (OLC) can be delivered multiple ways—professors and students can access it directly through the textbook website, through PageOut, or within a course management system (i.e., WebCT, Blackboard, TopClass, or eCollege).

Acknowledgments

I want to thank the many friends and colleagues who continue to share their ideas for this textbook. I particularly want to acknowledge the contribution of Professor Pat Wilkie (George Mason University) and Professor Jim Young (Northern Illinois University). Their article entitled "Teaching the Introductory Tax Course: A Template of the Federal Income Tax Formula, Taxpayer Activities, and Taxpayer Entities" in the *Journal of the American Taxation Association* (Fall 1997) profoundly influenced my thinking and the final organization of this book. Thanks also to the following individuals who reviewed the 2004 and 2005 editions of the text. Their expert comments were invaluable, and this edition is significantly improved because of their involvement.

Reviewers

Ellen Anderson
University of Tennessee–Knoxville

Lydia Botsford
Evergreen Valley College

Julia Brennan
University of Massachusetts–Boston

Caroline Craig
Illinois State University

William Dresnack
SUNY College–Brockport

John Karayan
California State Poly University–Pomona

Barry Leibowicz
Queens College

Bruce McClain
Cleveland State University

Kenneth Milani
University of Notre Dame

Suzanne Morsfield
New York University

Mark Nixon
Bentley College

Simon Pearlman
California State University–Long Beach

Tim Peterson
Gustavus Adolphus College

John Phillips
University of Connecticut

June Roux
Salem Community College

Randy Skalberg
University of Minnesota–Duluth

Christine Todd
William Woods University

George Violette
University of Southern Maine

Scott Yetmar
Cleveland State University

I am grateful to the entire McGraw-Hill/Irwin team for their professional support. In particular, I want to acknowledge Brent Gordon, Stewart Mattson, Tim Vertovec, Marc Chernoff, Laura Griffin, Rose Range, Artemio Ortiz, Sesha Bolisetty, Elizabeth Mavetz, and Gail Korosa. Finally, I want to thank my daughter Rachael, who took over the management of the Jones household so that I could write this text.

Sally M. Jones
University of Virginia

Principles of Taxation for Business and Investment Planning explores the role that taxes play in modern life. The book is written for business students who have completed introductory courses in accounting and finance and are familiar with basic business concepts. Those of you who fit this description, regardless of your future career path, will make decisions in which you must evaluate the effect of taxes. At the most fundamental level, all business decisions have the same economic objective: maximization of long-term wealth through cash flow enhancement. The cash flow from any transaction depends on the tax consequences. Therefore, business men and women must appreciate the role of taxes before they can make intelligent decisions, whether on behalf of their firm or on their personal behalf.

Taxes as Business Costs

When businesspeople are asked to identify the common goal of all business decisions, their immediate response tends to be that the goal is to increase profits. When prompted to think past the current year, most eventually conclude that the long-term goal of business decisions is to maximize the value of the firm. In this text, a **firm** is a generic business organization. Firms include sole proprietorships, partnerships, limited liability companies, subchapter S and regular corporations, and any other arrangement through which people carry on a profit-motivated activity. Firm managers know that short-term profits and long-term value are enhanced when operating costs, including taxes, are controlled. Experienced managers never regard taxes as fixed or unavoidable costs. As you will soon discover, opportunities abound for controlling the tax cost of doing business.

The preceding paragraph suggests that tax planning means reducing tax costs to maximize the value of the firm. Firms can reduce taxes by any number of strategies. However, tax cost is only one variable that managers must consider in making business decisions. A strategy that reduces taxes may also have undesirable consequences, such as reducing revenues or increasing nontax costs. Because of nontax variables, the strategy with the least tax cost may not be the best strategy. Therefore, tax minimization in and of itself may be a short-sighted objective. This point is so elementary yet so important: *Effective tax planning must take into account both tax and nontax factors*. When faced with competing strategies, managers should implement the strategy that maximizes firm value, even when that strategy has a higher tax cost than the alternatives. In other words, managers should never let the tax tail wag the business dog.

Taxes as Household Expenditures

Principles of Taxation for Business and Investment Planning concentrates on the income taxation of business activities and organizations. This does not mean that the tax rules applying to individuals are ignored. Quite to the contrary. For income tax purposes, individuals and the profit-making activities in which they engage are entwined. As we will observe over and over again, the ultimate taxpayers in every business are the people who own and operate that business.

As you study this text, consider your own role as a lifelong taxpayer. Regardless of who you are, where you live, or how you earn and spend your money, you will pay taxes on a regular basis to any number of governments. In fact, in the United States, taxes are the single largest

Tax Bite in the Eight-Hour Day

Source: Tax Foundation.

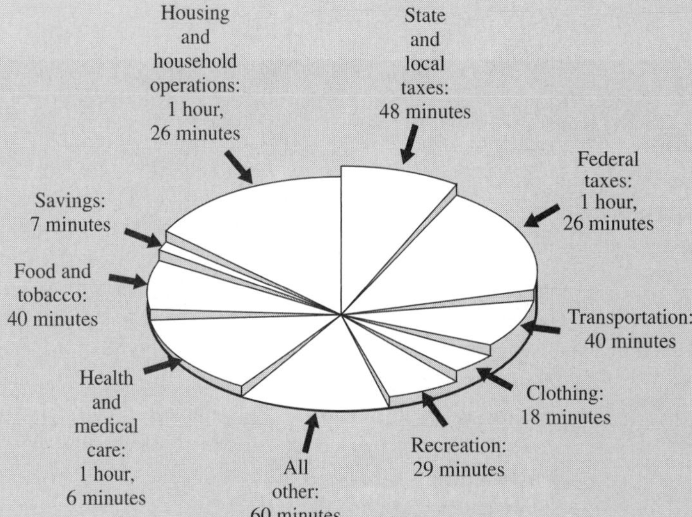

household expenditure. The above pie chart shows that a person working an eight-hour day spends almost three hours working to pay local, state, and federal taxes.

People who are clueless about taxes must take a passive role, participating in a tax system they don't understand and over which they exercise no control. In contrast, if you understand how taxes relate to your life, you can take an active role. You can take positive steps to minimize your personal tax to the fullest extent allowed by law. You can make informed financial decisions to take advantage of tax-saving opportunities. You can draw rational conclusions about the efficiency and fairness of existing tax laws and can assess the merit of competing tax reform proposals. Finally, you can change the tax system by participating as a voter in the democratic process.

The Text's Objectives

Principles of Taxation for Business and Investment Planning has three objectives that motivate the overall design of the text, the selection and ordering of topics, and the development of each topic.

Introducing Tax Policy Issues

The first objective is to acquaint you with the economic and social policy implications of the tax systems by which governments raise revenues. Most of the subject matter of the text pertains to today's tax environment and how successful businesses adapt to and take advantage of that environment. But the text also raises normative issues concerning the efficiency and equity of many features of the tax environment. You will learn how certain provisions of the tax law are intended to further the government's fiscal policy goals. You are invited to evaluate these goals and to question whether the tax system is an appropriate mechanism for accomplishing the goals.

The text identifies potentially negative aspects of the tax environment. It explains how taxes may adversely affect individual behavior or cause unintended and undesirable outcomes. You will be asked to consider whether certain provisions of the tax law favor one group of taxpayers over another and whether such favoritism is justifiable on any ethical grounds. After probing both the strengths and weaknesses of the current tax system, you can draw your own conclusions as to how the system can be improved.

Bridging the Gap between Finance and Tax

The second objective of the text is to bridge the academic gap between the study of financial theory and the study of tax law. Finance courses teach students how to make decisions on the basis of after-tax cash flows. However, these courses give only rudimentary instruction on determining the tax consequences of transactions and overlook the possibilities for controlling tax costs to maximize cash flows. In extreme cases, financial models simply ignore tax consequences by assuming that business decisions are made in a tax-free environment.

Traditional tax law courses err in the opposite direction. These courses teach students to apply statutory rules to well-defined, closed-fact situations to determine the tax consequences. Correct application of the rule is the learning objective. Students are not required to integrate the tax consequences of transactions into a business decision-making framework. In other words, they don't translate tax outcomes into cash flows. Traditional law courses may fail to encourage students to consider how closed-fact situations can be restructured to change the tax outcome and improve financial results. Consequently, students often develop the habit of analyzing transactions from a backward-looking *compliance* perspective rather than a forward-looking *planning* perspective.

The focus of *Principles of Taxation for Business and Investment Planning* is the common ground shared by financial theory and tax law. The connecting links between the two disciplines are stressed throughout the text. You will learn how effective business planning depends on an accurate assessment of relevant tax factors. Tax rules and regulations are presented and illustrated in the context of a decision-making framework. Admittedly, these rules and regulations are tough to master. Two observations should give you reassurance. First, while the tax law is extremely technical and complex, the application of its underlying principles to business decision making is relatively straightforward. Second, you can learn to appreciate tax planning strategies without becoming a tax-compliance expert.

Teaching the Framework of the Income Tax

The third objective of *Principles of Taxation for Business and Investment Planning* is to teach the framework of the federal income tax, the dominant feature of the modern tax environment. This framework has been remarkably stable over time, even though the details of the law change every year. Students who learn the framework needn't worry that their knowledge will be outdated when Congress enacts its next revenue bill.

The federal income tax system has a bad reputation as an impenetrable, intractable body of law. While the income tax law is every bit as complicated as its critics suggest, its framework consists of a manageable number of basic principles. The principles are internally consistent and underlie many technical provisions. By concentrating on these principles, you can attain a sufficient level of tax knowledge in a single introductory course. You will not be a tax expert, but you will be tax literate. You may not be capable of implementing sophisticated tax planning strategies, but you will appreciate how those strategies can improve cash flows and maximize wealth.

Because this text takes a conceptual approach to the tax law, narrowly drawn provisions, exceptions, limitations, and special cases are deemphasized. Details with the potential to confuse rather than clarify tax principles are usually relegated to footnotes. When we do examine a detailed provision of the law, the detail should illuminate an underlying concept. Or we may discuss a thorny technical rule just to emphasize the practical difficulties encountered by tax professionals who don't have the luxury of dealing with concepts.

The conceptual approach should sensitize you to the tax implications of transactions and cultivate your ability to ask good tax questions. This approach downplays the importance of the answers to these questions. Knowing the answers or, more precisely, *finding* the answers to tax questions is the job of accountants and attorneys who devote long hours in their research libraries to that end. A tax-sensitive business manager knows when to consult these experts and can help formulate the tax issues for the expert to resolve. The text's emphasis on issue recognition rather than issue resolution is reflected in the problems at the end of each chapter. Many of these problems ask you to analyze a fact situation and simply identify any tax concerns or opportunities. Other problems present you with facts suggesting tax issues with no correct solution.

A Reassuring Word to Accounting Majors

Principles of Taxation for Business and Investment Planning is an ideal introductory text for those of you who are concentrating in accounting and who may even plan to specialize in taxation. You will benefit enormously from mastering the framework of the income tax as the first step in your professional education. This mastery will be the foundation for the future study of advanced topics. You will gain a command of basic principles on which to rely as you develop an instinct for your subject—a facility for diagnosing the tax issues suggested by unfamiliar and unusual transactions.

The conceptual approach is appropriate for the first tax course because it concentrates on broad issues concerning most taxpayers instead of narrow problems encountered by only a few taxpayers. If you learn these issues, you will be well prepared to expand and deepen your tax knowledge through professional experience. You will understand that taxes are only one aspect of the economic decision-making process. Because of this understanding, those of you who become tax professionals will be equipped to serve your clients not just as tax specialists but as business advisers.

Conclusion

I hope this introduction has conveyed the message that business men and women who decide on a particular course of action without considering the tax outcomes are making an uninformed, and possibly incorrect, decision. By proceeding with the course of study contained in this text, you will learn to recognize the tax implications of a whole spectrum of transactions. On entering the business world, you will be prepared to make decisions incorporating this knowledge. You will spot tax problems as they arise and will call in a tax professional before, rather than after, a transaction with profound tax consequences. Finally, you will understand that effective tax planning can save more money than the most diligent tax compliance.

Exploring the Tax Environment

1 Types of Taxes and the Jurisdictions That Use Them

2 Tax Policy Issues: Standards for a Good Tax

Chapter **One**

Types of Taxes and the Jurisdictions That Use Them

Learning Objectives

After studying this chapter, you should be able to:

1. Define the terms *tax, taxpayer, incidence,* and *jurisdiction.*
2. Express the relationship between tax base, rate, and revenue as a formula.
3. Describe the types of taxes levied by local governments, state governments, and the federal government.
4. Explain why different jurisdictions compete for revenues from the same taxpayer.
5. Identify the reasons why governments modify their tax systems.
6. Describe the three primary sources of federal tax law.

An explorer planning a journey through unknown territory to a new destination prepares by inspecting a map of the territory. The explorer becomes familiar with topographic features such as major highways, mountain ranges, lakes and rivers, and population centers and gathers information concerning the climate of the region and the language and customs of its inhabitants. This preliminary knowledge of the environment helps the explorer chart the course and minimizes the danger that progress will be impeded by unforeseen circumstances.

For students who are just beginning their study of taxation, the tax environment in which individuals and organizations must function is unknown territory. Chapter 1 serves as a map of this territory. The chapter begins by describing the tax environment in terms of the basic relationship among taxes, taxpayers, and governments. It identifies the major types of taxes that businesses routinely encounter and examines how governments with overlapping jurisdictions compete for tax revenues. By reading the chapter, you will gain a familiarity with the tax environment that will help you in the journey toward an understanding of the role of taxes in the business decision-making process.

The chapter should alert you to two important features of the tax environment. First, taxes are *pervasive* because they are so widespread, come in so many varieties, and affect virtually every aspect of modern life. Second, taxes are *dynamic* because the tax laws change so frequently. The rate of change reflects the fact that the economic and political assumptions on which tax structures are based are constantly evolving. While these two features make the tax environment a challenging one for business managers, they also create a vitality that makes the study of tax planning so fascinating.

SOME BASIC TERMINOLOGY

Taxes, Taxpayers, Incidence, and Jurisdiction

Objective 1
Define the terms *tax, taxpayer, incidence,* and *jurisdiction.*

Before beginning our exploration of the tax environment, we must define some basic terminology. A **tax** can be defined as a payment to support the cost of government. A tax differs from a fine or penalty imposed by a government because a tax is not intended to deter or punish unacceptable behavior. On the other hand, taxes are compulsory rather than voluntary on the part of the payer. A tax differs from a user's fee because the payment of a tax does not entitle the payer to a specific good or service in return. In the abstract, citizens receive any number of government benefits for their tax dollars. Nevertheless, the value of government benefits received by any particular person is not correlated to the tax that person must pay. As the Supreme Court explained:

> A tax is not an assessment of benefits. It is . . . a means of distributing the burden of the cost of government. The only benefit to which the taxpayer is constitutionally entitled is that derived from his enjoyment of the privileges of living in an organized society, established and safeguarded by the devotion of taxes to public purposes.[1]

A **taxpayer** is any person or organization required by law to pay a tax to a governmental authority. In the United States, the term *person* refers to both natural persons (individuals) and corporations. Corporations are entities organized under the laws of one of the 50 states or the District of Columbia. These corporate entities generally enjoy the same legal rights, privileges, and protections as individuals. The taxing jurisdictions in this country uniformly regard corporations as entities separate and distinct from their shareholders. Consequently, corporations are taxpayers in their own right.

The **incidence** of a tax refers to the ultimate economic burden represented by the tax. Most people jump to the conclusion that the person or organization who makes a direct tax payment to the government bears the incidence of such tax. But in some cases, the payer can shift the incidence to a third party. Consider the following examples.

Income Tax Incidence

Government G imposes a new tax on corporate business profits. A manufacturing corporation with a monopoly on a product in great demand by the public responds to the new tax by increasing the retail price at which it sells the product. In this case, the corporation is nominally the taxpayer and must remit the new tax to the government. The economic burden of the tax falls on the corporation's customers who are indirectly paying the tax in the form of a higher price for the same product.

[1] *Carmichael* v. *Southern Coal & Coke Co.,* 301 U.S. 495, 522 (1937).

Property Tax Incidence

Mr. Blaire owns an eight-unit apartment building. Currently, the tenants living in each unit pay a $6,000 annual rent. The local government notifies Mr. Blaire that his property tax on the apartment building will increase by $2,400 for the next year. Mr. Blaire reacts by informing his tenants that their rent for the next year will increase by $300. Consequently, Mr. Blaire's total revenue will increase by $2,400. Although Mr. Blaire is the taxpayer who must remit the property tax to the government, the incidence of the tax increase is on the tenants who will indirectly pay the tax through higher rent.

The right of a government to levy tax on a specific person or organization is referred to as **jurisdiction.** Jurisdiction exists because of some rational linkage between the government and the taxpayer. For instance, our federal government has jurisdiction to tax any individual who is a U.S. citizen or who permanently resides in this country. The government also claims jurisdiction to tax individuals who are neither U.S. citizens nor residents (nonresident aliens) but who earn income from a source within the United States.

U.S. Jurisdiction over Nonresident Aliens

Mr. Kohala is a citizen of Spain and resides in Madrid. Mr. Kohala owns an interest in a partnership formed under Florida law that conducts a business within the state. Even though Mr. Kohala is a nonresident alien, the United States claims jurisdiction to tax him on his share of the partnership income because the income was earned in this country.

The Relationship between Base, Rate, and Revenue

Objective 2
Express the relationship between tax base, rate, and revenue as a formula.

Taxes are usually characterized by reference to their base. A **tax base** is an item, occurrence, transaction, or activity with respect to which a tax is levied. Tax bases are usually expressed in monetary terms.[2] For instance, real property taxes are levied on the ownership of land and buildings, and the dollar value of the property is the tax base. When designing a tax, governments try to identify tax bases that taxpayers cannot easily avoid or conceal. In this respect, real property is an excellent tax base because it cannot be moved or hidden, and its ownership is a matter of public record.

The dollar amount of a tax is calculated by multiplying the base by a tax rate, which is usually expressed as a percentage. This relationship is expressed by the following formula.

$$\text{Tax (T)} = \text{Rate (r)} \times \text{Base (B)}$$

A single percentage that applies to the entire tax base is described as a **flat rate.** Many types of taxes use a **graduated rate** structure consisting of multiple percentages that apply to specified portions or **brackets** of the tax base.

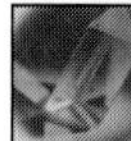

Graduated Rate Structure

Jurisdiction J imposes a tax on real property located within the jurisdiction. The tax is based on the market value of the real property and consists of three rate brackets.

Percentage Rate	*Bracket*
1%	Value from –0– to $100,000
2%	Value from $100,001 to $225,000
3%	Value in excess of $225,000

[2] A per capita, or head, tax requires each person subject to the tax to pay the same amount to the government. This antiquated type of tax does not have a monetary base.

Company C owns a tract of real property worth $500,000. The tax on this property is $11,750.

1% of $100,000 (first bracket of base)	$ 1,000
2% of $125,000 (second bracket of base)	2,500
3% of $275,000 (third bracket of base)	8,250
Total tax on $500,000 base	$11,750

The term **revenue** refers to the total tax collected by the government and available for public use. Note that in the equation $T = r \times B$, the tax is a function of both the rate and the base. This mathematical relationship suggests that governments can increase revenues by increasing either of these two variables in the design of their tax systems.

Transaction or Activity-Based Taxes

Taxes can be characterized by the frequency with which they are levied. A tax can be **event or transaction based** so that the tax is triggered only when an event occurs or a transaction takes place. A familiar example is a sales tax levied on the purchase of retail goods and services. A second example is an estate tax levied on the transfer of property from a decedent to the decedent's heirs. Taxpayers may have some degree of control over the payment of these types of taxes. By avoiding the event or transaction on which the tax is based, a person avoids the tax. With certain taxes, such as excise taxes levied on the purchase of liquor and cigarettes, people have total discretion as to whether they ever pay the tax. By choosing not to drink alcoholic beverages or not to smoke, they are also choosing not to pay the excise tax. In contrast, no individual can avoid an estate or inheritance tax levied on the transfer of property at death by indefinitely postponing the event that triggers the tax!

A tax can be described as **activity based** when it is imposed on the cumulative result of an ongoing activity. Taxpayers must maintain records of the activity, summarize the result at periodic intervals, and pay tax accordingly. An annual income tax is a prime example of an activity-based tax.

An **income tax** is imposed on the periodic inflow of wealth resulting from a person's economic activities. For persons who engage in a limited number or variety of economic transactions, the measurement of taxable income is relatively simple. For persons who engage in complex activities involving many economic transactions, the measurement of taxable income can be a complicated process.

Earmarked Taxes

Still another way to characterize taxes is to link them to specific government expenditures. The revenues from some taxes are **earmarked** to finance designated projects. For instance, revenues from local real property taxes are typically earmarked to support public school systems. Revenues generated by the federal payroll and self-employment taxes fund the Social Security system (Old-Age, Survivors, and Disability Insurance Trust Fund) and Medicare (Health Insurance Trust Fund). Revenues from so-called environmental excise taxes on businesses are appropriated to the Environmental Protection Agency's Hazardous Substance Superfund, which subsidizes the cleanup and disposal of toxic wastes. In contrast to these earmarked taxes, revenues from taxes that pour into a general fund may be spent for any public purpose authorized by the government.

THE PERVASIVE NATURE OF TAXATION

In commenting on the nature of the U.S. tax environment, Supreme Court Justice Potter Stewart made this astute observation:

> Virtually all persons or objects in this country . . . may have tax problems. Every day the economy generates thousands of sales, loans, gifts, purchases, leases, wills and the like, which suggest the possibility of tax problems for somebody. Our economy is "tax relevant" in almost every detail.[3]

Why are taxes so pervasive in our modern world? One reason is the multiplicity of jurisdictions in which people conduct business. Every firm operates in some geographic location within the taxing jurisdiction of one or more local governments. Local governments include townships, cities, municipalities, counties, and school districts, all of which have operating budgets financed by tax revenues. Local governments are subject to the authority of state governments, and state constitutions or statutes typically regulate the nature and extent of local taxation.

The governments of each of the 50 states and the District of Columbia levy taxes on firms conducting business within their geographic territory. In turn, the states' taxing jurisdiction is subject to federal constitutional and statutory constraints. The federal government represents still another jurisdiction that taxes business activities conducted within the United States. Consequently, even the smallest domestic enterprise is usually required to pay taxes to support at least three different levels of government. If a domestic enterprise conducts any business in a foreign country, the number of potential taxing jurisdictions is even higher.

Business managers who want to control tax costs must be aware of any local, state, federal, or foreign tax for which the firm is, or might become, liable. In this section of Chapter 1, we will survey the types of taxes levied by different jurisdictions to finance their governments.

Local Taxes

Objective 3
Describe the types of taxes levied by local governments.

Local governments depend heavily on real property taxes and personal property taxes, which are frequently referred to as **ad valorem taxes.** According to the most recent census data, these two taxes account for more than 75 percent of local government tax revenues.[4]

Real Property Taxes

All 50 states allow local jurisdictions to tax the ownership of real property sited within the jurisdiction. Real property or **realty** is defined as land and whatever is erected or growing on the land or permanently affixed to it. This definition encompasses any subsurface features such as mineral deposits.

Real property taxes are levied annually and are based on the market value of the property as determined by the local government itself. Elected or appointed officials called **tax assessors** are responsible for deriving the value of realty and informing the owners of the assessed value. Property owners who disagree with the assessed value of their realty may challenge the value in an administrative or judicial proceeding. A unique feature of real property taxes is that the tax rate is determined annually, based on the jurisdiction's need for revenue for that particular budget year.

[3] *United States* v. *Bisceglia,* 420 U.S. 141, 154 (1975).

[4] This and subsequent data are obtained from *Quarterly Summaries of Federal, State, and Local Tax Revenues,* Bureau of the Census, U.S. Department of Commerce.

Property Tax Rates

Springfield's city council decides that the city must raise $1.2 million of real property tax revenues during its next fiscal year. Because Springfield's tax assessor determines that the total value of real property located within the city limits is currently $23 million, the council sets the nominal tax rate for the upcoming year at 5.22 percent ($1.2 million ÷ $23 million). This rate can be adjusted each year, depending on Springfield's future revenue needs and the fluctuating value of its real property tax base.

Local governments may establish different tax rates for different classifications of property. For instance, a township may choose to tax commercial realty at a higher rate than residential realty, or a county might tax land used for agricultural purposes at a higher rate than land maintained for scenic purposes. Governments may grant permanent tax-exempt status to realty owned by charitable, religious, or educational organizations and publicly owned realty. An **abatement** is a tax exemption granted by a government for only a limited period of time. Governments usually grant abatements to lure commercial enterprises into their jurisdiction, thereby creating jobs and benefiting the local economy. From a business manager's point of view, the tax savings obtained through abatements can be significant. Consequently, firms contemplating expansion into new jurisdictions frequently negotiate for property tax abatements before acquiring or beginning construction of realty within the jurisdiction.

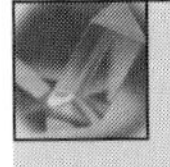

Property Tax Abatements

According to a survey conducted by the accounting firm KPMG, 51 percent of U.S. companies are receiving some form of property tax abatement or rebate from a state or local government.

Personal Property Taxes

Forty-one states permit localities to tax the ownership of **personalty,** defined as any asset that is not realty. Like real property taxes, personal property taxes are based on the value of the asset subject to tax. However, such value is not usually assessed by local government. Instead, individuals and organizations must determine the value of their taxable personalty and render (i.e., report) the value to the tax assessor.

There are three general classes of taxable personalty: household tangibles, business tangibles, and intangibles.[5] Household tangibles commonly subject to tax include automobiles and recreational vehicles, pleasure boats, and private airplanes. Taxable business tangibles include inventory, furniture and fixtures, machinery, and equipment. The most common intangible assets subject to personal property tax are marketable securities (stocks and bonds).

During the last century, personal property taxation has declined steadily as a revenue source. One reason for the decline is that this tax is much more difficult to enforce than other taxes. Personalty is characterized by its mobility; owners can easily hide their assets or move them to another jurisdiction. Any governmental attempt to actively search for personalty, particularly household tangibles, could violate individual privacy rights. Governments have responded to these practical problems by linking the payment of personal property tax to asset registration or licensing requirements.

[5] Tangible property has physical substance that can be perceived by sight or touch. Intangible property has no physical substance.

State Taxes

Objective 3
Describe the types of taxes levied by state governments.

In the aggregate, state governments rely in almost equal measure on sales taxes and income taxes as major sources of funds. These two kinds of taxes account for approximately 90 percent of total state tax revenues.

Retail Sales, Use, and Excise Taxes

Forty-five states and the District of Columbia impose a tax on in-state sales of tangible personal property and selected services. (The exceptions are Alaska, Delaware, Montana, New Hampshire, and Oregon.) Moreover, 33 states allow local governments to levy additional sales taxes. Sales taxes have been the great growth taxes of state governments during the past century.[6] In 1930, only two states had a general sales tax. During the depression era, revenue-starved states began enacting temporary sales taxes as an emergency measure. These taxes proved to be both simple and effective and soon became a permanent feature of state tax systems. Sales taxes produce about $150 billion of annual revenue, about one-third of all state tax collections. Sales taxes also have become an important revenue source for local governments, although property taxes remain their primary revenue source.

A **sales tax** is typically based on the retail sale of tangible personalty. Combined state and local tax rates range from 4 percent to 11 percent of the dollar amount of the sales transaction. Sales taxes are broad based and apply to most types of consumer goods and even to selected consumer services, such as telephone or cable television service.[7] The tax may take the form of a business tax levied on the seller or, more commonly, a consumption tax levied on the purchaser. Regardless of the form, the seller is responsible for collecting the tax at point of sale and remitting it to the state government.

Tax Talk
After the 2002 indictment of former Tyco chief executive Dennis Kozlowski on charges of evading more than $1 million of New York sales tax, New York residents became more conscientious about their use-tax obligations. In 2003, New York's revenues from voluntary use-tax filings increased by about 600 percent from prior years!

Every state with a sales tax imposes a complementary **use tax** on the ownership, possession, or consumption of tangible goods within the state. The use tax applies only if the owner of the goods did not pay the state's sales tax when the goods were purchased. A use tax acts as a backstop to a sales tax by discouraging residents from purchasing products in neighboring jurisdictions with lower sales tax rates. The one-two punch of a sales and use tax theoretically ensures that state residents are taxed on all purchases of consumer goods, regardless of where the purchase was consummated. As a result, merchants operating in high-tax states are not at a competitive disadvantage with respect to merchants operating in low-tax states.

As a general rule, consumers may take a credit for out-of-state sales taxes against their in-state use tax liability.

Use Tax Calculation

Ms. Goode is a resident of Idaho, which has a 7 percent sales and use tax. While on vacation in Hawaii, Ms. Goode purchased a diamond bracelet for $7,600 and paid $304 (4 percent) Hawaiian sales tax. Because Ms. Goode did not pay her own state's sales tax on the purchase, she owes $228 use tax to Idaho. The use tax equals $532 (7 percent of $7,600) minus a $304 credit for the Hawaiian sales tax. If Ms. Goode had vacationed in California and paid that state's 8.25 percent sales tax on her jewelry purchase, she would not owe any Idaho use tax.

[6] Hellerstein and Hellerstein, *State Taxation,* vol. II (Boston: Warren, Gorham & Lamont, 1993), p. 12–1.

[7] Many states provide sales tax exemptions for items considered necessities of life, such as food and prescription drugs.

Millions of people either are unaware of their responsibility for paying use tax on goods purchased out of state or through mail-order catalogs, or they ignore their self-assessment responsibility. States have recently become much more aggressive in collecting use taxes directly from their residents and have entered into cooperative agreements to share sales and use tax audit information. Eighteen states have added lines to their personal income tax returns on which individuals are instructed to report the use tax due on their out-of-state and catalog purchases for the year.

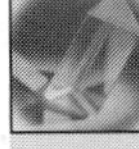

Michigan's Use Tax Initiative

In an effort to collect its use tax that has been in effect since 1937, Michigan recently added a line to its individual income tax return on which taxpayers are required to report their annual use tax. In the first year that this line was added, about 64,000 people paid use tax, resulting in more than $2.8 million of revenue for the state.

An **excise tax** is imposed on the retail sale of specific goods, such as gasoline, cigarettes, or alcoholic beverages, or on specific services, such as hotel or motel accommodations. States may impose an excise tax in addition to or instead of the general sales tax on a particular good or service. In either case, the seller is responsible for collecting and remitting the excise tax. Excise taxes can be extremely heavy. Connecticut levies a 25-cent excise tax on each gallon of gasoline, New York levies a $1.50 excise tax on one pack of cigarettes, and Tennessee levies a $4.40 excise tax per gallon of distilled liquor.

Personal Income Taxes

Forty-three states and the District of Columbia levy some form of personal income tax on individuals who reside in the state and nonresidents who earn income within the state. (The exceptions are Alaska, Florida, Nevada, South Dakota, Texas, Washington, and Wyoming.) The technical details of the computation of taxable income vary considerably from state to state, but the tax rates are uniformly modest. Currently, the maximum rates range from 2.8 percent in Pennsylvania to 9.5 percent in Vermont.

Corporate Income Taxes

Forty-five states and the District of Columbia tax corporations on their net income attributable to the state. (The exceptions are Michigan, Nevada, South Dakota, Washington, and Wyoming.) Many states allow their cities and counties to tax either the gross receipts or net income of both incorporated and unincorporated businesses operating within the locality.

The computation of corporate taxable income is prescribed by state law. Conceptually, each state could have its own unique set of computational rules, so that one corporation operating in all 46 taxing jurisdictions would be required to make 46 different calculations of taxable income. Fortunately for corporate America, differences in the computations are the exception rather than the rule. All 46 jurisdictions refer to the *federal* definition of taxable income as the starting point for calculating state taxable income. "The outstanding characteristic of State corporate net income measures is their broad conformity to the measure of the Federal corporation income tax."[8]

The major advantage of state conformity to federal income tax law is simplicity. State legislatures do not have to reinvent the wheel by enacting a comprehensive income tax statute. State agencies responsible for administering their state's income tax can refer to regulatory and judicial interpretations of the federal law. A second advantage is that state conformity to federal tax law eases the compliance burdens of corporate taxpayers. The

[8] Hellerstein, op. cit., p. 7–3.

major disadvantage is the states' lack of control over their corporate income tax revenues. Each time the U.S. Congress changes the federal definition of taxable income, the income tax base of conforming states is automatically increased or decreased.

Corporate income tax rates vary from state to state. The majority of states use a single flat rate, while the remainder use a mildly progressive graduated rate structure. Currently, the maximum rates range from 5 percent in Mississippi to 12 percent in Iowa.

Federal Taxes

Objective 3
Describe the types of taxes levied by the federal government.

The U.S. government depends almost exclusively on the income tax as a source of general revenues. The federal income tax applies to both individuals and corporations, as well as trusts and estates. The structure and operation of the federal income tax is discussed in considerable detail in Parts Three, Four, and Five of this text. At this point, suffice it to say that the federal income tax is predominant in the business environment.

History of the Income Tax

The modern income tax does not have a particularly long history in this country. The federal government enacted the first personal income tax in 1861 to raise money to support the Union armies during the Civil War. Even though Congress allowed the tax to expire in 1872, its revenue-generating capability made a lasting impression on the legislative memory. In 1894, Congress needed a permanent source of funds and decided to resurrect the personal income tax. However, in the landmark case of *Pollock* v. *Farmers' Loan and Trust Company*,[9] the Supreme Court held that the U.S. Constitution did not authorize the federal government to levy a national income tax. Determined to have its way, Congress launched a campaign to change the Constitution, a campaign that ended victoriously on February 25, 1913, when Wyoming became the 36th state to ratify the Sixteenth Amendment:

> The Congress shall have the power to lay and collect taxes on incomes from whatever source derived, without apportionment among the several states, and without regard to any census or enumeration.

Congress immediately exercised its new power by passing the Revenue Act of 1913, and the income tax became a permanent feature of American life. In 1939, Congress organized all of the federal tax laws then in effect (income and otherwise) into the first Internal Revenue Code. This compilation was substantially revised as the Internal Revenue Code of 1954 and again as the Internal Revenue Code of 1986.

The Sixteenth Amendment: Pro and Con

Supporters of the Sixteenth Amendment praised the new income tax because it applied only to the very wealthy and forced "the Carnegies, the Vanderbilts, the Morgans, and the Rockefellers" to pay while sparing the middle class from pain. But opponents of the tax warned that "When men get into the habit of helping themselves to the property of others, they cannot easily be cured of it."[10]

Employment and Unemployment Taxes

The two largest programs sponsored by the federal government are the Social Security system, which provides monthly old-age, survivors, and disability benefits to qualifying citizens and residents, and Medicare, which provides hospital insurance for the elderly and

[9] 157 U.S. 429 (1895).

[10] "Unleashing America's Potential: A Pro-Growth, Pro-Family Tax System for the 21st Century," National Commission on Economic Growth and Tax Reform, 70 *Tax Notes* 413, 418.

EXHIBIT 1.1
Fiscal Year 2003 Federal Tax Revenues

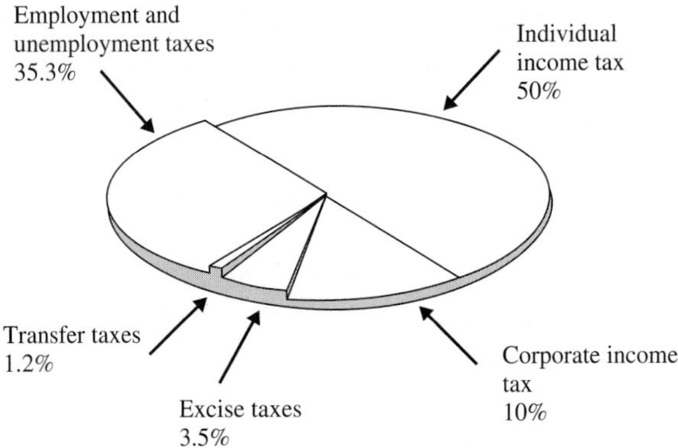

disabled. These programs are not funded from the general revenues of the income tax. Instead, the revenues from the federal **employment taxes** are earmarked to pay exclusively for Social Security and Medicare. These taxes are based on annual wages and salaries paid by employers to their employees and on the net income earned by self-employed individuals. The details of these important taxes are discussed in Chapter 9.

The federal and state governments act in coordination to provide monetary benefits to individuals who are temporarily unemployed through no fault of their own. This national unemployment insurance system is administered by the states and financed by federal and state taxes imposed directly on employers. These **unemployment taxes** are based on the annual compensation paid to employees. Virtually every business in this country pays unemployment taxes with respect to its workforce, and significant planning opportunities do exist for controlling this particular cost. Nevertheless, because of the narrow scope of the unemployment taxes, we will not discuss them further in this text.

Other Federal Taxes

The federal government raises general revenues from excise taxes imposed on the retail purchase of specific goods and services such as tobacco products, luxury automobiles, firearms, and telephone calls. The federal **transfer taxes,** which are based on the value of an individual's wealth transferred by gift or at death, are also a source of general revenues. Transfer taxes play a key role in family tax planning and are described in detail in Chapter 15. As Exhibit 1.1 shows, these two types of taxes are a minor source of federal funds. In fiscal year 2003, excise taxes accounted for only 3.5 percent of federal tax revenues, while transfer taxes accounted for just 1.2 percent.

Taxes Imposed by Foreign Jurisdictions

The types of foreign taxes that firms encounter when expanding from domestic to international operations are as varied as the languages, politics, and cultures characterizing the global environment. Many foreign taxes have a familiar structure. National governments and their political subdivisions the world over levy income taxes, property taxes, and retail sales taxes. Other taxes may have no counterpart in the United States and are therefore less familiar to domestic companies operating abroad. For instance, many industrialized nations depend heavily on some type of **value-added tax (VAT)** as a source of government revenue. Value-added taxes are levied on firms engaged in any phase of the production of goods and are based on the incremental value that the firm adds to the goods.

Value-Added Tax

Firm M and Firm W operate in a jurisdiction that imposes a 5 percent VAT. Firm M manufactures small electronic appliances. M's material cost per unit is $40, and M sells each unit to Firm W, a regional wholesaler, for $46. The $6 difference represents the incremental value that M added to the production process. Therefore, M must pay a 30-cent VAT (5 percent of $6) for each unit sold.

Firm W sells the appliances purchased from Firm M to various unrelated retailers for $50 per unit. Firm W's $4 gross profit on the sale of each unit represents the incremental value that W added to the production process by providing distribution services. Consequently, Firm W must pay a 20-cent VAT (5 percent of $4) for each unit sold.

This example is extremely simplistic because it ignores the possibility that both Firm M and Firm W can shift the economic incidence of the VAT by increasing the price at which they sell their product to the next business in the production sequence. To the extent that a VAT is shifted along the entire production sequence to the final purchaser (the customer who buys the product for personal consumption), the VAT resembles a retail sales tax.

Value-added taxes can be powerful revenue raisers. Even so, Michigan is the only domestic jurisdiction that uses this type of tax. The Michigan Single Business Tax, enacted in 1976 to replace the state's corporate income tax, is a modified VAT applying to both incorporated and unincorporated businesses operating within the state.

Jurisdictional Competition

Objective 4
Explain why different jurisdictions compete for revenues from the same taxpayer.

Domestic businesses that span territorial borders pay tax to multiple state and local governments, as well as to the federal government. International businesses pay tax to any number of foreign jurisdictions. Governments understand that their taxing jurisdictions frequently overlap and that, as a result, they are competing for revenues from the same businesses. They also understand that taxpayers are mobile, and that business managers make location decisions with an eye on comparative tax costs. Thus, jurisdictional competition creates an interesting tension. On the one hand, a government that fails to protect its jurisdictional turf may lose revenues to more assertive taxing authorities. On the other hand, a government that is overly aggressive may drive businesses away from its jurisdiction.

In the United States, the competing levels of government have traditionally accommodated each other by relying on different taxes as their primary source of funding. As we learned earlier in the chapter, property taxes are the mainstay of local governments, while retail sales taxes are used almost exclusively by state governments. Our federal government does not levy either property taxes or a national sales tax, but instead relies on income and employment taxes for its revenues.

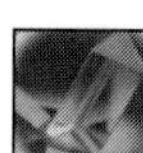

Ready for a National Sales Tax?

A group of business executives organized as Americans for Fair Taxation are publicly campaigning to replace the federal income tax, Social Security and Medicare employment taxes, and transfer taxes with a 23 percent national sales tax. The tax would apply to retail purchases of all goods and services, including food, medicine, and housing. According to AFT, this new tax would raise the same federal revenue as existing taxes, while stimulating economic growth.

Corporations conducting business in more than one state face particularly difficult problems of duplicative taxation. The jurisdictional concerns of corporations engaged in interstate commerce are discussed more fully in Chapter 12. Of course, the potential for jurisdictional conflict is greatest when corporations operate on a global scale. Industrialized nations assume that it is in their self-interest to promote the growth of international business operations. These nations understand that if they fail to adapt their tax systems to the needs of the worldwide marketplace, their economies will be at a competitive disadvantage. Consequently, the industrialized nations have created a network of bilateral and multilateral tax treaties to minimize friction among their respective tax systems and to reduce duplicative taxation of international businesses. The role of these treaties and other unique features of international tax planning are covered in Chapter 12.

DYNAMIC NATURE OF TAXATION

Objective 5
Identify the reasons why governments modify their tax systems.

Business managers must understand that taxes are not only pervasive in the modern world but that tax systems are in a constant state of flux. Tax systems are dynamic because they must be attuned to the fiscal condition of their respective jurisdictions. In every jurisdiction, individual citizens and institutions continually reevaluate the nature and level of services they want from their governments. Governments, in turn, must reassess the tax systems that pay for those services.

Tax Base Changes

Any government dependent on a tax system that no longer raises sufficient revenues will sooner or later be forced to change the system. The loss of revenue-generating power is often attributable to an eroding tax base. For instance, cities that depend on real property taxes experience a decline in revenues when their populations decrease. As families and businesses move away from urban areas, residential and commercial properties located within the city lose value. Owners can no longer afford to maintain the properties and, in extreme cases, they may simply abandon them. Cities only worsen this cycle of deterioration if they raise their property tax rates. The only solution may be to identify an alternative tax base or a source of nontax revenue.

Tax Talk
States often devote gambling revenues to popular public services. A congressman recently boasted that Oregon residents "are gambling for education, salmon restoration, parks, and economic activity. It's an amazing phenomenon."

Legalized Gambling

One controversial source of nontax revenue is legalized gambling. About 40 years ago, a few states experimented with lotteries as a means of raising money. Lotteries proved so lucrative that 39 states and the District of Columbia are now sponsoring these betting games. In the late 1980s, states in the Midwest and the South decided to shore up their tax bases by going into the casino business and gave private gambling corporations legal monopolies to operate within the state. Today, casinos are legal in more than half the states, and all but two states (Hawaii and Utah) depend on some form of gambling as a source of revenue.

A Gambler's Worst Bet

According to a report by the National Gambling Impact Study Commission, state lotteries pay back only 50 percent of the money received from ticket sales—the smallest share of the take of any legal gambling game. In contrast, slot machines, which offer the worst odds of any private casino game, pay back 85 percent of the money fed into them.

Sales Tax Expansion

State and local governments are aggressive in exploiting new tax bases that develop in the economy. Historically, state sales taxes applied to retail purchases of tangible property but not to purchases of retail services. Because of the dramatic growth in the service sector over the last several decades, an increasing number of states are adding selected services, such as cable television, parking, and theater tickets, to their sales tax base. In 1987, Florida expanded its general sales tax to apply to a broad range of consumer services, and Massachusetts followed suit in 1991. Public reaction was so negative that both states repealed the sales tax on services within a year.

States are trying to find a way to force mail-order and Internet companies to collect tax on sales made to residents. Millions of consumers have discovered the ease of shopping by catalog and online. Quite naturally, states take the position that their residents who do so should bear the same tax burden as residents who patronize retail stores located within the state. In 1992, the Supreme Court ruled that state laws requiring companies with no *physical* presence in a state to collect sales tax were unconstitutional, regardless of the volume of business in the state.[11] State governments were infuriated with this decision and have been lobbying Congress ever since to enact federal legislation permitting states to require sales tax collection on mail-order and Internet transactions.

Taxes and the Political Process

The political process by which tax law is made contributes to the dynamic nature of taxes. In this country, local, state, and federal tax laws are the result of democratic systems in which elected or appointed representatives decide on the appropriate tax structure. These representatives are naturally sensitive to the political climates of their respective constituencies. As these climates change over time, representatives may decide that the tax structure should change as well. Many of these changes have little to do with revenues. Instead, the changes are philosophic in nature, reflecting a shift in the public attitude concerning the proper role of taxes in society.

Special interest groups have a significant effect on the tax legislative process. Thousands of organizations have pet provisions in the existing law or wish lists of proposals for new provisions. These organizations use their own emissaries or hire professional lobbyists to communicate their point of view to government officials. The constant pressure from powerful organizations with competing and even conflicting political objectives certainly adds to the vibrant nature of the tax law.

Regardless of the type of tax or the jurisdiction levying the tax, people don't like paying it. In fact, individuals and businesses devote considerable money and effort to finding ways to avoid taxes. Each time taxpayers or their advisers devise a new tactic to reduce their tax burdens, governments respond by enacting a new rule to render the tactic ineffective. This constant gamesmanship is yet another reason why the tax environment is dynamic. As humorist Dave Barry explains, "[Tax laws] are constantly changing as our elected representatives seek new ways to ensure that whatever tax advice we receive is incorrect."

SOURCES OF FEDERAL TAX LAW

Objective 6
Describe the three primary sources of federal tax law.

Throughout this text, we will constantly refer to the **tax law.** For modern tax systems, this term encompasses three basic sources of authority: statutory law, administrative pronouncements, and judicial decisions. In combination, these sources provide the rules of the game by which both taxpayers and governments must abide. This final section of Chapter 1 describes the primary sources of authority that comprise our federal tax law. In subsequent

[11]*Quill Corporation* v. *North Dakota,* 504 U.S. 298 (1992).

chapters of the text, you will encounter much technical information originating from this body of law. You should have a much easier time understanding this information if you are familiar with the underlying sources from which the information is derived.

Statutory Authority

In its narrowest sense, federal tax law means the **Internal Revenue Code of 1986,** the voluminous compilation of statutory rules enacted by Congress. The Internal Revenue Code itself is a dynamic document; almost every year Congress passes legislation that adds to, deletes from, or modifies its provisions.

The Vanishing Tax Act

President Bush signed the Economic Growth and Tax Relief Reconciliation Act into law on June 7, 2001. This act, which made hundreds of changes to the tax system, is a nightmare of complexity because many of the changes are phased in over a number of years. Perhaps the most controversial feature of the 2001 act is its "sunset provision" under which the entire act will expire on December 31, 2010. In other words, unless Congress takes further action, the federal tax law will revert to its pre-2001 act status for 2011 and subsequent years. While Congress probably will not allow the entire 2001 act to expire, it will certainly revise or repeal many of its provisions before they even go into effect.

The Internal Revenue Code consists of numerically ordered **sections,** beginning with Section 1 and ending (at last count) with Section 9833. Each section contains an operational, definitional, or procedural rule relating to one of the federal taxes. Code section numbers have become the language in which tax experts communicate, and accountants and lawyers have incorporated many of them into their professional jargon. (Bob, I think our client has a real Section 469 problem.) Sections are divided into subsections, paragraphs, subparagraphs, and so on. In the footnotes to the text, a reference such as §469(f)(3)(B) is citing the precise statutory rule under discussion.

Administrative Authority

The Department of the Treasury is responsible for writing regulations that interpret and illustrate the rules contained in the Internal Revenue Code. These **Treasury regulations** provide tremendous guidance to taxpayers and their advisers. Every week the Treasury publishes new regulations or amends existing regulations to keep abreast of legislative developments. While Treasury regulations carry great authority as the government's official explanation of the law, they are not laws in and of themselves. On rare occasions, taxpayers have convinced the federal courts that a regulation was an incorrect interpretation of statute and was therefore invalid.[12]

The citation to a Treasury regulation consists of a sequence of numbers, the first of which identifies the type of federal tax under consideration. For instance, a regulation beginning with 1 is an income tax regulation. The next number identifies the Code section to which the regulation relates. The last number in the sequence is the number of the regulation itself. The cite Reg. §1.469–4 refers to the fourth Treasury regulation relating to Section 469 of the Internal Revenue Code. Some sections have only one regulation while others have dozens, and some Code sections have no interpretive regulations at all!

The **Internal Revenue Service (IRS),** the subdivision of the Treasury responsible for the enforcement of the law and collection of tax, provides still more guidance in the form of **revenue rulings and revenue procedures.** These pronouncements explain how the IRS

[12]The Internal Revenue Code occasionally empowers the Treasury to write regulations that have the force and effect of law. These so-called legislative regulations have the same authority as statutory law.

applies the tax law to a particular set of facts and circumstances. While they carry much less authority than the Code and regulations, these pronouncements do represent the IRS's official position and provide valuable insight on specific issues. Rulings and procedures are published in weekly **Internal Revenue Bulletins (IRBs)** that are compiled into semiannual **Cumulative Bulletins (CBs).** Footnote references such as Rev. Rul. 2005-46, 2005-29 IRB 117, or Rev. Proc. 89-17, 1989-1 CB 118, are citing these sources of authority.

Judicial Authority

The third primary source of tax law is the federal judicial system. Taxpayers who disagree with the IRS's interpretation of the law as it applies to their own situations may take their cases to federal court. The hundreds of legal decisions handed down every year clarify the correct implementation of the tax law. The weight of authority of a particular case depends on the court that rendered the verdict. Trial court verdicts have less authority than verdicts by an appellate court. A Supreme Court verdict is the equivalent of law and becomes the final word in any tax dispute. Chapter 17 discusses the process by which a federal judge or jury resolves a controversy between a taxpayer and the IRS. When this text refers to a judicial decision, an accompanying footnote provides the complete legal cite. You can use the cite to locate the decision in any law library or commercial tax service.

Conclusion

Business managers engaged in effective tax planning take into account the wide variety of taxes existing in the modern economic environment. When making strategic decisions, managers must consider their firm's total tax burden rather than any tax in isolation. A strategy that minimizes the cost of one tax could easily increase the cost of another. The primary focus of this text is the federal income tax; as a result, other taxes that affect business and investment decisions will be mentioned only occasionally. Even so, many income tax planning strategies are valid in other tax contexts. Decision makers should remember that every tax represents a controllable cost of conducting business.

As increasing numbers of U.S. firms expand their operations across territorial boundaries, jurisdictional tax planning becomes crucial. Managers must determine which tax systems result in favorable business climates and which systems are inhospitable to foreign investors. They must be aware of differences between competing tax regimes and how those differences can be exploited to the firm's advantage. In today's tax environment, successful tax planning must be conducted on a global scale.

Key Terms

Questions and Problems for Discussion

1. How do tax payments differ from other payments that people or organizations make to governmental agencies?
2. The Green River, which is heavily polluted by industrial waste, flows through State S. Eighty-five companies operate manufacturing facilities that border the river. State S recently enacted legislation requiring each company to pay $50,000 annually into a special fund to clean up Green River. Does this payment meet the definition of a tax?
3. Custer County is considering raising revenues by imposing a $25 fee on couples who obtain a marriage license within the county. Does this fee meet the definition of a transaction-based tax?
4. Mr. P owns a residential apartment complex in a suburban area. This year, the local jurisdiction increased the property tax rate on the apartment complex. To offset this additional cost, Mr. P decreased the amount he usually spends on maintaining the exterior of the building and the landscaping. Who bears the incidence of the increased property tax?
5. Mr. and Mrs. K pay $18,000 annual tuition to a private school for their three children. They also pay $2,300 property tax on their personal residence to support the local public school system. Should Mr. and Mrs. K be exempt from this property tax?
6. A local government imposed a new 2 percent tax on the gross receipts of businesses operating within its jurisdiction. XYZ Company, which manufactures soap and other toiletries, responded to the tax by reducing the size of its bars of soap and purchasing a cheaper grade of ingredients. By making these changes, XYZ maintained its before-tax level of profits. Who bears the incidence of the new gross receipts tax?
7. Why is real property a better tax base than personal property?
8. Many local jurisdictions apply a low property tax rate to land owned by privately operated golf courses. What is the economic justification for such a preferential rate?
9. University K is located in a small town that depends on real property taxes for revenue. Over the past decade, University K has expanded by purchasing a number of commercial buildings and personal residences and converting them to classrooms and dormitories. In what way could this expansion result in a decline in the town's revenues?
10. Why can people avoid paying an excise tax more readily than they can avoid paying a sales tax?
11. The Internal Revenue Code and Treasury regulations are two major sources of federal tax law. Differentiate between the Code and the regulations in terms of their relative weight of authority.
12. A city government increased its local sales tax from 1 percent to 2 percent of the dollar value of consumer goods purchased in the city. However, the city's sales tax revenues increased by only 30 percent after the doubling of the tax rate. What factors might account for this result?
13. Both the federal government and many states impose so-called sin taxes: excise taxes levied on the retail sale of liquor and cigarettes. Discuss the reasons why sales of these particular items make a good tax base.
14. Does the federal income tax or the federal payroll tax have the broader tax base?
15. Differentiate between a property tax and a transfer tax.
16. One way for the federal government to increase tax revenues would be to enact either a VAT or a national retail sales tax. The U.S. sales tax could be collected in the same

manner and at the same time as state and local sales taxes. Which tax would be less costly for the federal government to implement and administer? Which tax would be less likely to cause jurisdictional conflict?

Application Problems

1. Mr. JK, a U.S. citizen and resident of Vermont, owns 100 percent of the stock of JK Services, which is incorporated under Vermont law and conducts business in four counties in the state. JK Services owns 100 percent of the stock of JK Realty, which is incorporated under Massachusetts law and conducts business in Boston.
   a. How many taxpayers are identified in the above statement of facts?
   b. Identify the governments with jurisdiction to tax each of these taxpayers.
2. In each of the following cases, determine whether the United States has jurisdiction to tax Mrs. CM.
   a. Mrs. CM is a citizen of Brazil but is a permanent resident of Orlando, Florida.
   b. Mrs. CM is a citizen and resident of Brazil. She owns Manhattan real estate that generates $100,000 net rental income annually.
   c. Mrs. CM is a citizen and resident of Brazil. She owns no property and conducts no business in the United States.
   d. Mrs. CM is a U.S. citizen but is a permanent resident of São Paulo, Brazil.
3. This year, Company LI built a light industrial facility in County G. The assessed property tax value of the facility is $20 million. To convince Company LI to locate within its jurisdiction, the county abated its 4 percent property tax for the year. Because of the local economic boom created by the new facility, the aggregate assessed value of County G's property tax base (including the LI facility) increased by $23 million. Calculate the net effect on County G's current year tax revenue from the abatement.
4. This year, Jurisdiction A raised revenues by increasing its general sales tax rate from 5 percent to 6 percent. Because of the increase, the volume of taxable sales declined from $800 million to $710 million. In contrast, Jurisdiction Z raised revenues from its 5 percent sales tax by expanding the tax base to include certain retail services. The volume of services subject to tax was $50 million. Compute the additional revenue raised by Jurisdiction A and by Jurisdiction Z.
5. Firm H operates its business in Jurisdiction H, which levies a 6 percent sales and use tax. This year, the firm purchased $600,000 tangible property in Jurisdiction K and paid $18,000 sales tax to the jurisdiction. It also purchased $750,000 tangible property in Jurisdiction L and paid $48,750 sales tax to the jurisdiction. Firm H transported both items of property into Jurisdiction H for use in its business.
   a. Compute the use tax that Firm H owes to Jurisdiction H for the property purchased in Jurisdiction K.
   b. Compute the use tax that Firm H owes to Jurisdiction H for the property purchased in Jurisdiction L.
6. Firm L, which operates a mail-order clothing business, is located in State L. This year, the firm shipped $18 million of merchandise to customers in State R. State R imposes a 6 percent sales and use tax on the purchase and consumption of retail goods within the state.
   a. Do State R residents who purchased Firm L merchandise owe use tax on their purchases?

b. If State R could legally require Firm L to collect a 6 percent tax on mail-order sales made to residents of the state, how much additional revenue would the state collect? Explain the reasoning behind your answer.

7. Mr. and Mrs. CS operate a hardware store in a jurisdiction that levies both a sales tax on retail sales of tangible personalty and an annual personal property tax on business tangibles. The personal property tax is based on book value as of December 31. This year, Mr. and Mrs. CS purchased $840,000 inventory for their store.
   a. Are Mr. and Mrs. CS required to pay sales tax on the purchase of the inventory?
   b. How can Mr. and Mrs. CS minimize their personal property tax by controlling the timing of their inventory purchases?
8. Firm Q and Firm R conduct business in a jurisdiction that imposes a 3 percent VAT. Firm Q produces entertainment videos at a $6 cost per unit and sells the videos to Firm R for $9 per unit. Firm R sells the videos at retail for $10 per unit. This year, the combined efforts of Firm Q and Firm R resulted in sales of 12.4 million videos to the public. Compute the VAT for each firm.

Issue Recognition Problems

Identify the tax issue or issues suggested by the following situations, and state each issue in the form of a question.

1. A local government levies an annual real property tax on the personal residence located at 123 Maple Drive. This tax is assessed on a calendar year basis, and the homeowner must pay the tax before December 31. In November, Mr. and Mrs. J received the annual tax bill for $2,900. The couple purchased the home on October 6.
2. Company F operates in a jurisdiction that levies real property tax but no personal property tax. This year, the company spent $6 million to add an exterior lighting system and security fences to the parking lot adjacent to its corporate headquarters.
3. Company B, which has offices in six states, owns an airplane that company executives use to travel from office to office. When the plane is not in use, it is stored in a hangar located in a jurisdiction that does not levy a personal property tax on business tangibles. When the plane is in use, it is stored on a temporary basis in hangars located in jurisdictions that tax business tangibles.
4. For the past 22 years, Mrs. O contributed part of her salary to a retirement plan sponsored by her corporate employer. Under federal law, Mrs. O did not pay tax on the income so contributed. She will, however, pay federal income tax on the distributions from the plan when she retires. Mrs. O has resided in State A for her entire life. Because State A's personal income tax is based on taxable income for federal purposes, Mrs. O never paid State A tax on her retirement contributions. This year, Mrs. O retires and moves to State K, which has no personal income tax.
5. Business Q orders $500,000 of office furniture from Vendor V, which ships the furniture by rail from its manufacturing facility in State V to Business Q's corporate headquarters in State Q. State V imposes a 6.5 percent sales tax while State Q imposes only a 4 percent sales tax.
6. Acme Corporation was formed under the laws of State X and has its corporate headquarters in that state. Acme operates a manufacturing plant in State Y and sells goods to customers in States X, Y, and Z. All three states have a corporate income tax. This year, Acme's net profit from its tristate operation was $14 million.

7. Mr. W is a professional golfer who played 23 tournaments in 14 different states and earned $893,000 total prize money for the year. When he is not traveling, Mr. W lives with his family in Tucson, Arizona.
8. Eighteen months ago, BBB Company opened a manufacturing facility in County K. As an incentive for BBB to locate within its jurisdiction, County K abated all local property taxes for the first two years of operation. BBB recently announced that it will shut down the facility before the end of the year.
9. Dempsey Corporation is organized under Canadian law and has its corporate headquarters in Montreal. This year, Dempsey sold $28 million of goods to customers who live in the United States. However, Dempsey does not maintain any type of office in the United States.
10. Mr. KW, age 72, has lived in Los Angeles his entire life. His net worth is estimated at $95 million. Mr. KW is considering renouncing his U.S. citizenship, selling his home in Los Angeles, and permanently relocating to the Cayman Islands. The Cayman Islands impose no tax of any sort on their residents.

Research Problems

1. Visit the website for the Federation of Tax Administrators (**www.taxadmin.org**) to find out if your state has either an individual or corporate income tax. If so, what is the maximum tax rate?
2. Visit the website for the Internal Revenue Service **(www.irs.gov)**. What is the name of the Commissioner of the IRS, and how many employees work for the IRS?
3. Conduct a search on the Internet to find a brief description of the flat tax. Write a short paragraph describing the flat tax and explaining how it differs from the federal individual income tax.
4. The next time you buy groceries in a supermarket, study your receipt. Which items that you purchased were subject to your state's sales tax, and which items were exempt from sales tax?

Tax Planning Cases

1. The management of WP Company must decide between locating a new branch office in foreign Jurisdiction F or foreign Jurisdiction G. Regardless of location, the branch operation will use tangible property (plant and equipment) worth $10 million and should generate annual gross receipts of $2 million. Jurisdiction F imposes an annual property tax of 4 percent of the value of business property and a 15 percent gross receipts tax. Jurisdiction G imposes no property tax but imposes a 30 percent gross receipts tax. Solely on the basis of these facts, should WP locate its new branch in Jurisdiction F or Jurisdiction G?
2. KTR Company earns a $10 profit on each unit of manufactured goods, and it sells 20 million units each year. KTR's income tax rate is 20 percent. However, the jurisdiction in which KTR operates just increased the tax rate to 22 percent for next year. KTR's owners are considering two alternatives. They could simply accept the $4 million tax increase as a reduction in their after-tax profit, or they could raise the price of each unit by 20 cents, thereby increasing the profit per unit to $10.20. However, the marketing department estimates that the price increase could reduce annual sales to 19 million units. Which alternative is better for KTR's owners?

Chapter Two

Tax Policy Issues: Standards for a Good Tax

Learning Objectives

After studying this chapter, you should be able to:

1. Explain the concept of sufficiency of a good tax.
2. Differentiate between the income effect and the substitution effect of a tax rate increase.
3. Describe the characteristics of a convenient tax.
4. Contrast the concept of tax neutrality with the concept of taxes as a fiscal policy tool.
5. Define horizontal and vertical equity.
6. Differentiate between a regressive, a proportionate, and a progressive rate structure.
7. Explain the difference between marginal and average tax rates.
8. Discuss distributive justice as a tax policy objective.

In Chapter 1, we identified the various taxes that exist in the modern tax environment. In this chapter, we will consider a more qualitative dimension of the environment as we identify the *normative* standards by which politicians, economists, social scientists, and individual taxpayers evaluate the merit of a tax.

Governments are cognizant of and influenced by these standards as they formulate tax policy. **Tax policy** can be defined as a government's attitude, objectives, and actions with respect to its tax system. Presumably, tax policy reflects the normative standards that the government deems most important. After reading this chapter, you can draw your own conclusions as to the relative importance of the standards by which tax systems are judged. You will be able to evaluate the current federal tax system in light of these standards. When you are asked as a voter to choose between competing tax policy proposals, the material covered in this chapter will help you make an informed decision.

Business managers and their tax advisers share a keen interest in tax policy. They know that many complex rules in the Internal Revenue Code have an underlying policy rationale. If they can understand this rationale, the rule itself is easier to interpret and apply. Moreover, business managers know that today's policy issues shape tomorrow's tax environment. By paying close attention to the current policy debate, managers can anticipate developments that might affect their firm's long-term strategies. Their familiarity with policy issues helps them assess the probability of changes in the tax law and develop contingent strategies to deal with such changes.

STANDARDS FOR A GOOD TAX

The American jurist Oliver Wendell Holmes is quoted as saying, "I like to pay taxes. With them I buy civilization." Few people in modern society seem to share this sentiment. In fact, many people regard taxes as a necessary evil and consider the notion of a good tax as a contradiction in terms. Nonetheless, theorists maintain that every tax can and should be evaluated on certain basic standards.[1] These standards can be summarized as follows:

- A good tax should be sufficient to raise the necessary government revenues.
- A good tax should be convenient for the government to administer and for people to pay.
- A good tax should be efficient in economic terms.
- A good tax should be fair.

In Chapter 2, we will discuss these four standards in detail. We will also identify the reasons why standards that are easy to describe in the abstract can be so difficult to put into practice.

TAXES SHOULD BE SUFFICIENT

Objective 1
Explain the concept of sufficiency of a good tax.

The first standard by which to evaluate a tax is its **sufficiency** as a revenue raiser. A tax is sufficient if it generates enough funds to pay for the public goods and services provided by the government. After all, the reason that governments tax their citizens in the first place is to raise revenues needed for specific purposes. If a tax (or combination of taxes) is sufficient, a government can balance its budget. Tax revenues equal government spending, and the government has no need to raise additional funds.

What is the consequence of an insufficient tax system? The government must make up its revenue shortfall (the excess of current spending over tax receipts) from some other source. In Chapter 1, we learned that state governments now depend heavily on legalized gambling as an alternative source of funds. Governments may own assets or property rights that they can lease or sell to raise money. For example, the U.S. government raises minuscule revenues by selling energy generated by federally owned dams and mineral and timber rights with respect to federal lands.

Another option is for governments to borrow money to finance their operating deficits. In the United States, the federal, state, and local governments sell debt obligations in the capital markets. By selling both short-term instruments (such as U.S. Treasury bills) and long-

[1] Adam Smith, author of *The Wealth of Nations,* was one of the first economists to suggest such standards. Smith's four canons were that a good tax should be equitable, certain in application, convenient for people to pay, and economical for the government to collect.

term bonds, governments with insufficient tax systems can make ends meet. Debt financing is not a permanent solution to an insufficient tax system. Like other debtors, governments must pay interest on borrowed funds. As the public debt increases, so does the annual interest burden. At some point, a government may find itself in the untenable position of borrowing new money not to provide more public goods and services but merely to pay the interest on existing debt. In a worst-case scenario, a government may be forced to default on its debt obligations, damaging its credibility and creating havoc in its capital markets.

Tax Talk
The Brookings Institution released a study describing three different strategies for balancing the federal budget by 2014. All three strategies include tax increases, and one calls for raising tax revenues by $629 billion over 10 years. The study warns that deficit spending is "out of control" and that "there is no end in sight to this tide of red ink."

The National Debt

According to Congressional Budget Office data, the federal government operated at a deficit for every fiscal year from 1970 through 1999. After generating small surpluses in 2000 and 2001, the government returned to deficit spending in 2002. In 1970, the national debt was about $380 billion and interest payments totaled $14 billion. In 2004, the debt approached $7.5 trillion and interest payments on this debt totaled $322 billion.

These data suggest that our federal tax system is insufficient to support the level of government spending. Yet politicians continue to tell their constituencies that taxes are too high, and few people seem inclined to disagree. But the arithmetic is inescapable. If we want to pay less tax and at the same time curb the growth of the national debt, the federal government must cut spending. If we want our government to maintain its level of spending without incurring additional debt, we should be prepared to pay the necessary federal tax.[2]

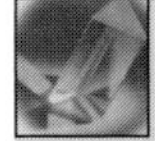

How Much Deficit?

For fiscal year 2004, the federal government operated at a $415 billion deficit. This deficit, however, included a $153 billion Social Security Trust Fund surplus, which is earmarked to fund retirement benefits to future Social Security recipients. If Social Security is excluded from the budget, the 2004 operating deficit was $568 billion.

How to Increase Tax Revenues

Taxing jurisdictions can attempt to increase revenues in at least three ways. One way is to exploit a new tax base. For instance, the legislature of one of the seven states without a personal income tax could enact such a tax. Another way is to increase the rate of an existing tax. A jurisdiction with a 5 percent corporate income tax could increase the rate to 7 percent. Still a third way is to enlarge an existing tax base. A jurisdiction with a retail sales tax applying to tangible goods could expand the tax to apply to selected personal services, such as haircuts or dry cleaning. A jurisdiction that exempts land owned by private charities from real property tax could simply eliminate the exemption.

From a pragmatic perspective, the enactment of a tax on a new base is the most radical and politically sensitive way to increase revenues. Consequently, elected officials tend to favor the less drastic alternative of enhancing the revenue-raising capability of a tax that people are accustomed to paying. In this situation, an increase in the percentage rate is the more obvious strategy and therefore is likely to anger the greatest number of voters. In contrast, an expansion of the tax base is more subtle and less likely to attract public attention. It is hardly surprising that many significant tax increases in recent years have been accomplished through the base-expansion method.

[2] As another author so eloquently describes the situation, "Elected representatives must eventually confront the political reality of an electorate with an apparently insatiable appetite for 'public goods' that at the same time harbors a deep-rooted intolerance for the levels of taxation sufficient to support its own proclivities." Sheldon D. Pollack, "The Failure of U.S. Tax Policy: Revenue and Politics," 73 *Tax Notes* 341, 348.

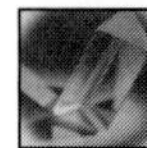

Social Security Tax Increases

The 6.2 percent rate for the federal Social Security payroll tax has not changed since 1990. However, the tax base (the annual amount of wages or salary subject to tax) increases every year. In 1990, this wage base was $51,300. In 2004, the base was $87,900. In 1990, an employee with a $90,000 salary paid $3,181 Social Security tax (6.2 percent of $51,300). In 2004, that employee paid $5,450 Social Security tax (6.2 percent of $87,900).

Static versus Dynamic Forecasting

In Chapter 1, we expressed the amount of tax as an arithmetic function of the tax rate and base: $T = r \times B$. This equation suggests that an increase in the rate should increase government revenues by a proportionate amount. For instance, if the tax rate is 5 percent and the base is $500,000, a rate increase of one percentage point should generate $5,000 additional tax. This straightforward math represents a **static forecast** of the incremental revenue resulting from a change in the rate structure. The forecast is static because it assumes that B, the base variable in the equation, is unrelated to r, the rate variable. Accordingly, a change in the rate has no effect on the tax base.

Economic theory suggests that in many cases the two variables in the equation $T = r \times B$ are correlated. In other words, a change in the rate actually causes a change in the base.

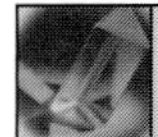

Effect of a Rate Change on Base

For the last 10 years, the city of Fairview has levied a hotel occupancy tax equal to 10 percent of the price of a room. In the prior fiscal year, this tax yielded $800,000 revenue.

Total annual hotel receipts subject to tax	$8,000,000
Prior year rate	.10
Prior year revenue	$ 800,000

At the beginning of the fiscal year, the city increased the tax rate to 12 percent. On the basis of a static forecast, the city expected revenue to increase to $960,000.

Forecasted hotel receipts subject to tax	$8,000,000
Current year rate	.12
Forecasted current year revenue	$ 960,000

Unfortunately, business travelers and tourists reacted to the additional cost represented by the higher room tax by purchasing fewer accommodations from Fairview hotels. Occupancy rates fell, and annual hotel receipts declined by $500,000. Consequently, the room tax yielded only $900,000 current year revenue.

Actual hotel receipts subject to tax	$7,500,000
Current year rate	.12
Actual current year revenue	$ 900,000

In the above example, the increase in the tax rate caused a decrease in the tax base. Because the city of Fairview failed to anticipate this effect, it overestimated the incremental revenue from the rate increase.

If a jurisdiction can predict the extent to which a change in tax rates will affect the tax base, it can incorporate the effect into its revenue projections. These projections, which assume a correlation between rate and base, are called **dynamic forecasts.** The accuracy of dynamic forecasts depends on the accuracy of the assumptions about the correlation. In a complex economic environment, a change in tax rates may be only one of many factors contributing to an expansion or contraction of the tax base. Economists may be unable to isolate the effect of the rate change or to test their assumptions empirically. Consequently, governments usually rely on static forecasting to estimate the revenues gained or lost because of a tax rate change.

Behavioral Responses to Rate Changes

Objective 2
Differentiate between the income effect and the substitution effect of a tax rate increase.

In the case of an income tax, the incremental revenue generated by a rate increase depends on whether (and to what extent) the increase affects the aggregate amount of income subject to tax. Specifically, the increment depends on the ways that individuals modify their economic behavior in response to higher tax rates.

The Income Effect

An increase in income tax rates might induce people to engage in more income-producing activities. Consider the case of Mr. Spivey, who earns $25,000 a year as a factory worker and pays 20 percent of that income ($5,000) in tax. Mr. Spivey spends every penny of his $20,000 after-tax income to make ends meet. How might Mr. Spivey react if the government increases the tax rate to 30 percent, thereby reducing his disposable income to $17,500? He might decide to work more hours or even take a second job to increase his before-tax income to at least $28,600. Under the new rate structure, Mr. Spivey will pay $8,580 tax on this income, leaving him with $20,020 and the same disposable income he enjoyed before the rate increase. This reaction (akin to running faster just to stay in the same place) has been labeled the **income effect** of a rate increase.[3]

If Mr. Spivey responds to the higher tax rate by working longer to generate more income, the government will enjoy a revenue windfall. A static forecast indicates that the government should collect an additional $2,500 revenue from Mr. Spivey because of the 10 percent rate increase.

Static Forecast	
Revenue after rate increase	
(30% × $25,000 base)	$7,500
Revenue before rate increase	
(20% × $25,000 base)	(5,000)
Additional revenue from Mr. Spivey	$2,500

However, if Mr. Spivey reacts by increasing his income from $25,000 to $28,600, the government will actually collect $3,580 additional revenue.

[3] Musgrave and Musgrave, *Public Finance in Theory and Practice,* 3rd ed. (New York: McGraw-Hill, 1980), p. 663.

Income Effect	
Revenue after rate increase (30% × $28,600 base)	$8,580
Revenue before rate increase (20% × $25,000 base)	(5,000)
Additional revenue from Mr. Spivey	$3,580

The Substitution Effect

If we change the financial circumstances of our hypothetical taxpayer, we might expect a different behavioral response to an income tax rate increase. Assume Ms. Hoover works 60 hours a week as a self-employed management consultant, earning $350,000 annual income. At a 20 percent tax rate, her after-tax income is $280,000—more than enough to support her comfortable lifestyle. If the government increases the tax rate to 30 percent, Ms. Hoover may devote less time and effort to her income-producing activity. Such a reaction makes sense if the after-tax value of an hour of additional labor is now worth less to her than an additional hour of leisure. This behavioral reaction to a rate increase is called the **substitution effect.**[4]

If Ms. Hoover responds to the higher tax rate by working fewer hours and generating less income, the government will suffer a revenue shortfall. On the basis of a static forecast, the government is anticipating an additional $35,000 revenue from Ms. Hoover.

Static Forecast	
Revenue after rate increase (30% × $350,000 base)	$105,000
Revenue before rate increase (20% × $350,000 base)	(70,000)
Additional revenue from Ms. Hoover	$ 35,000

If Ms. Hoover's income falls to $325,000 because the tax increase dampened her entrepreneurial spirit, the additional revenue from Ms. Hoover will be only $27,500.

Substitution Effect	
Revenue after rate increase (30% × $325,000 base)	$97,500
Revenue before rate increase (20% × $350,000 base)	(70,000)
Additional revenue from Ms. Hoover	$27,500

The probability of a substitution effect varies across taxpayers. The degree of personal control that individuals exercise over their careers determines the extent to which they can replace an hour of work with an hour of relaxation. Consequently, the substitution effect is

[4] Ibid.

more potent for self-employed persons than for salaried employees with rigid 9 A.M. to 5 P.M. schedules. The financial flexibility necessary to curtail work effort is more characteristic of a family's secondary wage earner than of the primary wage earner. Finally, ambitious career-oriented people who are highly motivated by nonmonetary incentives such as prestige and power may be impervious to the substitution effect.

Whether an income tax will goad a person to extra effort or whether it will be a disincentive to work depends on that person's economic circumstances. Theoretically, the income effect is most powerful for lower-income taxpayers who may already be at a subsistence standard of living and don't have the luxury of choosing leisure over labor. The substitution effect becomes stronger as an individual's disposable income rises and the financial significance of each additional dollar declines. From a macroeconomic viewpoint, these contradictory behavioral reactions have important tax policy implications. Conventional wisdom suggests that governments needing more revenue should increase the tax rate on people with the highest incomes. But if the tax rate climbs too high, the substitution effect may become so strong that the projected revenues never materialize as more and more people are discouraged from working because the after-tax return on their labor is too small.

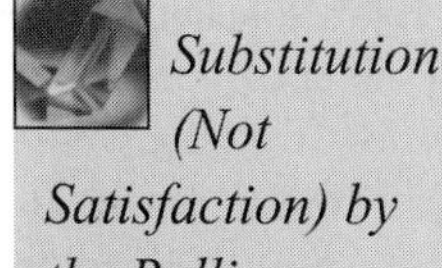

Substitution (Not Satisfaction) by the Rolling Stones

According to an article in the *London Daily Telegraph,* the Rolling Stones canceled plans for four British rock-and-roll concerts because of the high tax rates in Great Britain. Lead singer Mick Jagger is quoted as saying "I was tempted to bite the bullet [and pay the high taxes], but I am not the only one affected. A Rolling Stones world tour is a two-year project and there are over 200 people involved." The article concluded that "one knows a rock band is getting old when it cancels a tour for tax reasons."[5]

Supply-Side Economics

Faith in the substitution effect is the foundation for **supply-side economic theory,** which holds that a decrease in the highest income tax rates should ultimately result in an increase in government revenues. The logic underlying this theory is that a rate cut increases the value of income-generating activities (work and investment) relative to the value of nonincome-generating activities (leisure and consumption). Accordingly, people who benefit directly from the rate reduction will invest their tax windfall in new commercial ventures rather than simply spend it. This influx of private capital will stimulate economic growth and job creation. An expanding economy will result in prosperity across the board so that everyone, regardless of income level, indirectly benefits from the tax rate reduction. People will earn more income for the government to tax, and revenues attributable to this enlarged tax base will swell.

Does this supply-side theory hold true? In 1981, the Reagan administration, acting on its belief in the theory, convinced Congress to enact the Economic Recovery Tax Act. This legislation lowered the highest marginal individual tax rates from 70 percent to 50 percent on ordinary income and from 28 percent to 20 percent on capital gains. The Tax Reform Act of 1986 went even further by reducing the highest marginal rate for individuals to 28 percent. These deep rate cuts were just one of many dramatic factors affecting the U.S. economy during the 1980s. The price of oil dropped by half, and the double-digit inflation of the late 1970s fell to less than 4 percent. Federal spending on many domestic programs declined, but defense spending soared. Congress increased the federal payroll tax rates significantly to keep pace with the explosive growth in Social Security and Medicare outlays.

[5] "Rolling Stones Protest Taxes, Cancel Gigs," *Journal of Taxation,* July 1998.

The government borrowed money at an unprecedented rate, creating deficits of record peacetime magnitude.[6]

Economists have engaged in nonstop debate as to whether the supply-side experiment of the 1980s (dubbed Reaganomics by the press) was a success or a failure. Some believe that the Reagan tax cuts fueled the rising level of employment, expansion of the small business sector, and steady growth in the gross domestic product over the last two decades. Others maintain that the cuts were a financial windfall to the wealthiest American families but did little for the middle- and lower-income classes. There is only one point on which economists agree: Untangling the stimulative effect of the tax cuts from the web of other factors that shaped the Reagan economic era is an impossible task.

TAXES SHOULD BE CONVENIENT

Objective 3
Describe the characteristics of a convenient tax.

Our second standard for evaluating a tax is **convenience.** From the government's viewpoint, a good tax should be convenient to administer. Specifically, the government should have a method for collecting the tax that most taxpayers understand and with which they routinely cooperate. The collection method should not overly intrude on taxpayers' privacy but should offer minimal opportunity for noncompliance. States that levy retail sales taxes use a collection method under which sellers are responsible for collecting the tax from buyers at point of sale and remitting the tax to the state. This method is effortless for buyers and offers them no opportunity to evade the tax. States can concentrate their enforcement efforts on retail businesses, which are much easier to audit than individual consumers. In contrast, states have yet to develop a workable collection mechanism for use taxes; consequently, these taxes generate almost no revenue.

A good tax should be economical for the government. The administrative cost of collecting and enforcing the tax should be reasonable in comparison with the total revenue generated. At the federal level, the Internal Revenue Service (IRS) is the agency responsible for administering the income, payroll, excise, and transfer taxes. For its 2003 fiscal year, the IRS operated at a cost of $9.4 billion and collected $1,953 billion tax revenue. Thus, the federal government's cost of collecting $100 tax was a modest 48 cents.[7]

From the taxpayer's viewpoint, a good tax should be convenient to pay. The convenience standard suggests that people can compute their tax with reasonable certainty. Moreover, they do not have to devote undue time or incur undue costs in complying with the tax law. A retail sales tax receives high marks when judged by these criteria. People can easily compute the sales tax on a purchase and can pay the tax as part of the purchase price with no effort whatsoever!

In contrast, the federal income tax is denounced as both uncertain and costly. Because the income tax laws are so complex and change with such frequency, even tax professionals may be unsure how the law should apply to a particular transaction. Millions of Americans are bewildered by the income tax and have no confidence in their ability to compute the amount they owe. As a result, the majority pay someone else to prepare their income tax returns. By any measure, the cost to society of complying with the federal tax law is high; according to IRS estimates, taxpayers devote almost 6 billion hours each year to this inconvenient task. In dollar terms, the annual private sector cost of federal tax compliance is estimated at $100 billion.[8]

[6] Isabel V. Sawhill, "Reaganomics in Retrospect: Lessons for a New Administration," *Challenge,* May–June 1989, p. 57.

[7] IRS 2003 Data Book.

[8] Scott Moody, "The Cost of Tax Compliance," The Tax Foundation, February 2002.

TAXES SHOULD BE EFFICIENT

Our third standard for a good tax is economic **efficiency.** Tax policymakers use the term *efficiency* in two different ways. Sometimes the term describes a tax that does not interfere with or influence taxpayers' economic behavior. At other times, policymakers describe a tax as efficient when individuals or organizations react to the tax by deliberately changing their economic behavior. In this section of the chapter, we will compare these two competing concepts of efficiency.

The Classical Standard of Efficiency

Objective 4
Contrast the concept of tax neutrality with the concept of taxes as a fiscal policy tool.

Policymakers who believe that competitive markets result in the optimal allocation of scarce resources within a society define an efficient tax as one that is *neutral* in its effect on the free market. From this perspective, a tax that causes people to modify their economic behavior is inefficient because it distorts the market and may result in suboptimal allocations of goods and services.

The classical economist Adam Smith believed that taxes should have as little impact as possible on the economy. In his 1776 masterwork, *The Wealth of Nations,* Smith concluded the following:

> A tax . . . may obstruct the industry of the people, and discourage them from applying to certain branches of business which might give maintenance and employment to great multitudes. While it obliges the people to pay, it may thus diminish, or perhaps destroy, some of the funds which might enable them more easily to do so.

The laissez-faire system favored by Adam Smith theoretically creates a level playing field on which individuals and organizations, operating in their own self-interest, freely compete. When governments interfere with the system by taxing certain economic activities, the playing field tilts against the competitors engaging in those activities. The capitalistic game is disrupted, and the outcome may no longer be the best for society.

Of course, every modern economy has a tax system, and firms functioning within the economy must adapt to that system. Business managers become familiar with the existing tax laws and make decisions based on those laws. To return to the sports metaphor, these managers have adjusted their game plan to suit the present contours of the economic playing field.

When governments change their tax structures, firms are forced to reevaluate their tax situations in light of the change. Some may find that they benefit from the change, while others may conclude that the new tax structure puts them at a competitive disadvantage. Managers must reassess how the tax laws affect their particular business operations. They may discover that traditional planning strategies no longer work, while the efficacy of new strategies is uncertain. In short, every time the government changes its tax structure, the contours of the economic playing field shift. Because these shifts are both costly and unsettling to the business community, many economists conclude that "an old tax is a good tax."

Taxes as an Instrument of Fiscal Policy

The British economist John Maynard Keynes disagreed with the classical notion that a good tax should be neutral. Keynes believed that free markets are effective in organizing production and allocating scarce resources but lack adequate self-regulating mechanisms for maintaining economic stability.[9] According to Keynes, governments should protect their

[9] John Maynard Keynes, *The General Theory of Employment, Interest and Money* (New York: Harcourt, Brace, 1936).

citizens and institutions against the inherent instability of capitalism. Historically, this instability caused cycles of high unemployment, severe fluctuations in prices (inflation or deflation), and uneven economic growth. Lord Keynes believed that governments could counteract these problems through *fiscal policies* to promote full employment, price-level stability, and a steady rate of economic growth.

In the Keynesian schema, tax systems are a primary tool of fiscal policy. Rather than trying to design a neutral tax system, governments should deliberately use taxes to move the economy in the desired direction. If an economy is suffering from sluggish growth and high unemployment, the government could reduce taxes to transfer funds from the public to the private sector. The tax cut should both stimulate demand for consumer goods and services and increase private investment. As a result, the economy should expand and new jobs should be created. Conversely, if an economy is overheated so that wages and prices are in an inflationary spiral, the government could raise taxes. People will have less money to spend, the demand for consumer and investment goods should soften, and the upward pressure on wages and prices should be relieved.

The U.S. government formally embraced its fiscal policy responsibilities when Congress enacted the Employment Act of 1946. This legislation charged the Executive Branch with promoting full employment and a stable dollar and resulted in the formation of the President's Council of Economic Advisers. Since 1946, both political parties have regarded the federal income tax as a legitimate instrument of fiscal policy and have advocated changes in that system to further their respective economic agendas. Changes that have the intended macroeconomic effect are applauded as enhancing the efficiency of the tax system, while changes that have no effect on the national economy are branded as inefficient. Certainly, this Keynesian concept of efficiency is far removed from the classic concept of economic neutrality.

Taxes and Behavior Modification

Modern governments use their tax systems to address not only macroeconomic concerns but also social problems. Many such problems could be alleviated if people or institutions could be persuaded to alter their behavior. Governments can promote behavioral change by writing tax laws to penalize undesirable behavior or reward desirable behavior. The penalty takes the form of a higher tax burden, while the reward is some type of tax relief.

Some of the social problems that the federal income tax system tries to remedy are byproducts of the free enterprise system, which economists refer to as **negative externalities.** One of the most widely recognized is environmental pollution. The tax system contains provisions that either pressure or entice companies to clean up their act, so to speak. One example of a provision that discourages environmentally unfriendly behavior is the excise tax on ozone-depleting chemicals manufactured in or exported into the United States.[10] An example of a provision that encourages the private sector to be more environmentally responsible is the lucrative tax break for the construction of pollution control facilities such as wastewater purification plants.[11]

Tax systems may also promote activities that are undervalued by the free market but that the government believes are socially desirable. By bestowing a tax benefit on the activity, the government is providing a financial "carrot." This carrot should induce more taxpayers to engage in the activity and thus result in a greater level of the activity across society. An

[10] §4681.

[11] §169.

example of an activity that the federal government promotes is the rehabilitation of historic buildings. The law allows firms to reduce their annual tax bill by a percentage of the cost of renovating a certified historic structure.[12] Without this tax break, firms might find it cheaper to build or purchase modern buildings than to invest in historic structures requiring extensive renovation. At the margin, the tax break could make the investment in the historic structure the more cost-effective business decision.

Governments use tax breaks to subsidize targeted activities, thereby making those activities less costly or more profitable. An excellent example of such a subsidy is the provision in the Internal Revenue Code making the interest paid on state and local debt obligations nontaxable.[13] Because investors pay no tax on the income generated by these tax-exempt bonds, they are willing to accept a lower before-tax interest rate than if the interest was taxable. Consequently, state and local governments can pay less interest than other debtors and still compete in the financial markets. By providing this tax break, the federal government subsidizes state and local governments by reducing their cost of borrowed capital.

Income Tax Preferences

Provisions in the federal income tax system designed as incentives for certain behaviors or as subsidies for targeted activities are described as **tax preferences.** These provisions do not contribute to the accurate measurement of the tax base or the correct calculation of the tax. Tax preferences do not support the primary function of the law, which is to raise revenues. In fact, tax preferences do just the opposite. Because they allow certain persons or organizations to pay less tax, preferences lose money for the Treasury. In this respect, preferences are indirect government expenditures.

Like any other government outlay, a tax preference is justifiable only if the intended result has merit and deserves public support. But a tax preference should be subject to a second level of scrutiny: Is a tax incentive or subsidy the best way to accomplish the intended result, or would direct government support be more effective? This question can be hard to answer in any objective manner. Preferences are based on assumptions about how taxpayers react to the law. In a complex economy consisting of well over 100 million taxpayers, measuring the aggregate reaction to a tax preference is extremely difficult.

The Tax Expenditures Budget

Opponents of tax preferences maintain that they are too well hidden within the Internal Revenue Code and, as a result, their cost to the government is easily overlooked. In response to this criticism, Congress publishes an annual **Tax Expenditures Budget** that quantifies the revenue loss from each major tax preference.[14] For example, the government loses about $68 billion each year because individuals can deduct their home mortgage interest payments and another $17 billion because they can deduct local property taxes on their homes.

The Tax Expenditures Budget sheds much needed light on the cost of specific preferences and their aggregate cost to the government. However, tax expenditures are not

[12] §47.

[13] §103.

[14] A tax expenditure is measured by the difference between tax liability under present law and the tax liability that would result from a recomputation of tax without benefit of the tax expenditure. This measurement is static because taxpayer behavior is assumed to remain unchanged for tax expenditure estimate purposes. Joint Committee on Taxation, *Estimates of Federal Tax Expenditures for Fiscal Years 1998–2002,* December 15, 1997.

included in the calculation of any federal operating deficit. Another troubling aspect of tax preferences is that they add enormously to the length and complexity of the tax law. If the Internal Revenue Code could be stripped of every provision that is not necessary to measure taxable income and compute tax, it would be far simpler to understand and apply.

TAXES SHOULD BE FAIR

The fourth standard by which to evaluate a tax is whether the tax is fair to the people who must pay it. While no economist, social scientist, or politician would ever argue against fairness as a norm, there is precious little agreement as to the exact nature of tax equity. Many people nurture the belief that their tax burden is too heavy, while everyone else's burden is too light. As former U.S. Senator Russell Long expressed it, the attitude of the man on the street concerning tax equity is "Don't tax you, don't tax me; tax the fellow behind the tree." Clearly any meaningful discussion of the standard of fairness must rise above this sentiment.

Ability to Pay

A useful way to begin our discussion of equity is with the proposition that each person's contribution to the support of government should reflect that person's **ability to pay.** In the tax policy literature, ability to pay refers to the economic resources under a person's control. Each of the major taxes used in this country is based on some dimension of ability to pay. For instance, income taxes are based on a person's inflow of economic resources during the year. Sales and excise taxes are based on a different dimension of ability to pay: a person's consumption of resources represented by the purchase of goods and services. Real and personal property taxes complement income and sales taxes by focusing on a third dimension of ability to pay: a person's accumulation of resources in the form of property. Transfer taxes capture a fourth dimension: the accumulated wealth that a person gives to others during life or at death.

Horizontal Equity

Objective 5
Define horizontal equity.

If a tax is designed so that persons with the same ability to pay (as measured by the tax base) owe the same amount of tax, that system can be described as horizontally equitable. The structure of certain taxes guarantees their **horizontal equity.** In a jurisdiction with a 6 percent sales tax, every consumer who buys a taxable good with a $50 retail price pays the same $3 sales tax. The horizontal equity of taxes with more complex structures may not be so easy to analyze.

Taxable Income and Ability to Pay

In the federal income tax system, the tax base is annual taxable income. Consequently, the income tax is horizontally equitable if the taxable income calculation accurately reflects ability to pay. Let's explore this notion in more depth by comparing two people, Ms. Buell and Mr. Deetz, both unmarried, both earning a $40,000 annual salary. Neither has any additional inflows of economic resources. Do Ms. Buell and Mr. Deetz have the same ability to pay an income tax? If we consider only their identical marital status and salaries, the answer must be yes, and the two should pay an equal tax.

But what additional facts might be relevant in measuring ability to pay? Suppose that Ms. Buell suffers from a chronic illness and has $7,000 of uninsured medical expenses for the year while Mr. Deetz is in perfect health. Suppose that Mr. Deetz pays $4,500 annual alimony to a former spouse while Ms. Buell has no such legal obligation. On the basis of this new evidence, should we still conclude that Ms. Buell and Mr. Deetz have the same ability to pay an income tax? To ask the question another way, should medical expenses and alimony enter into the computation of taxable income? Certainly our two individuals would argue that it is only fair to consider these variables.

The horizontal equity of the income tax is enhanced by refining the calculation of taxable income to include the significant variables affecting a person's economic circumstances. But perfecting the tax base has its price: Every refinement adds another page to the Internal Revenue Code. Increased precision in the measurement of ability to pay may improve the horizontal equity of the income tax, but it also increases the complexity of the law.

Annual versus Lifetime Horizontal Equity

Federal taxable income is computed on a 12-month basis. This annual measurement of ability to pay may bear little or no relationship to a person's lifetime ability to pay.

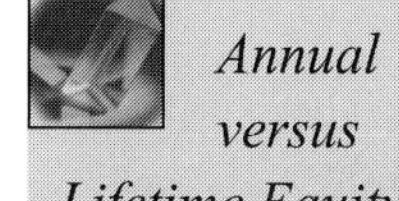

Annual versus Lifetime Equity

This year, a blue-collar laborer wins a $200,000 lottery jackpot and, as a result, has the same taxable income as the scion of a wealthy family who lives off the interest and dividends from a trust fund. Prior to his lucky year and for the rest of his working life, the laborer's taxable income averages $25,000 while the trust fund beneficiary's income averages $200,000. Nevertheless, both individuals owe the same tax this year.

Tax Preferences and Horizontal Equity

In the previous section of this chapter, we introduced the concept of tax preferences. These income tax provisions are designed as incentives or subsidies and favor people who arrange their affairs to take advantage of the preference. Consequently, the tax benefit represented by preferences is not distributed impartially across taxpayers.

Preferences and Equity

Two unrelated individuals, Mr. Malone and Ms. Olaf, invested in two different businesses this year. Both businesses earned a $20,000 profit for their respective investors. Mr. Malone's business qualifies for several tax preferences. As a result, Mr. Malone must report only $14,000 of the profit on his income tax return. In contrast, Ms. Olaf must report her entire profit. Their businesses increased our two individuals' economic ability to pay by the same $20,000. But because of the tax preferences with respect to his business, Mr. Malone's taxable income is $6,000 less than Ms. Olaf's.

This example suggests that tax preferences can distort the horizontal equity of the income tax. Certainly the public perception is that the law is riddled with preferences that allow a privileged few to avoid paying their fair share of tax. We will examine the validity of this perception in later chapters of the text. Even if the perception is false and preferences do not undermine horizontal equity, the perception nonetheless erodes civic confidence in the fairness of the income tax system.

Vertical Equity

Objective 5
Define vertical equity.

A tax system is vertically equitable if persons with a greater ability to pay owe more tax than persons with a lesser ability to pay. While horizontal equity is concerned with a rational and impartial measurement of the tax base, **vertical equity** is concerned with a fair rate structure by which to calculate the tax.

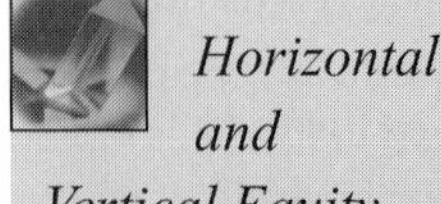

Horizontal and Vertical Equity

A local government enacted a real property tax and established a board of assessors to determine the market values of the properties in its jurisdiction. The board completes its task in a conscientious manner so that each resident's tax base (assessed value of their real property) is accurate. The property tax system has a two-bracket rate structure.

Percentage Rate	*Bracket*
2%	Assessed value from –0– to $1 million
1%	Assessed value in excess of $1 million

Mr. Foley owns real property with an assessed value of $500,000; his property tax is $10,000 (2 percent of $500,000). Ms. Lennon owns real property with an assessed value of $1.5 million; her property tax is $25,000 (2 percent of $1 million + 1 percent of $500,000).

This property tax is horizontally equitable because the base is fairly measured, and taxpayers with the same base (assessed value) bear an equal tax burden. The tax is also vertically equitable because taxpayers with a greater base (such as Ms. Lennon) owe more tax than taxpayers with a lesser base (such as Mr. Foley).

Objective 6
Differentiate between a regressive, a proportionate, and a progressive rate structure.

Regressive Taxes

The property tax described in the preceding example meets a strict definition of vertical equity because Ms. Lennon pays more tax than Mr. Foley: her $25,000 to his $10,000. However, Ms. Lennon's average tax rate is less than Mr. Foley's average tax rate.

Ms. Lennon: $25,000 tax ÷ $1,500,000 base = 1.667% average tax rate
Mr. Foley: $10,000 tax ÷ $500,000 base = 2% average tax rate

This inversion in average rates occurs because the property tax has a **regressive rate structure:** graduated rates that decrease as the base increases. Tax policymakers agree that regressive rates violate the standard of equity because they place a proportionally greater tax burden on persons with smaller tax bases. However, the regressive nature of a tax is not always obvious from its rate structure.

Retail sales taxes consist of only a single rate and therefore are not explicitly regressive. Even so, many economists criticize these taxes as regressive in operation, bearing most heavily on people with the least economic resources.

Regressive Sales Tax Rates

Mr. James and Mr. Kim live in Maryland, which has a 5 percent sales tax on all retail purchases. Mr. James earns $20,000 annual disposable income and spends this entire amount on taxable purchases. Mr. James pays $1,000 sales tax, and his average tax rate (with respect to disposable income) is 5 percent.

Mr. James: $1,000 tax ÷ $20,000 base = 5% average tax rate

In contrast, Mr. Kim earns $100,000 annual disposable income, spends only $75,000, and invests the remaining $25,000. Mr. Kim pays $3,750 sales tax, and his average tax rate is 3.75 percent.

Mr. Kim: $3,750 tax ÷ $100,000 base = 3.75% average tax rate

A 1988 study concluded that "sales and excise taxes everywhere are regressive, often shockingly so; they can create unconscionable hardships for people living in poverty, they represent real financial burdens for middle-income families, and they let the rich, particularly the super-rich, off the hook almost entirely."[15] The majority of states mitigate the inherent regressivity of sales taxes by legislating broad exemptions for groceries purchased for home consumption, prescription medicines, and residential utilities.

Income Tax Rate Structures

In an income tax system, the simplest rate structure consists of a single rate applied to taxable income. To illustrate this **proportionate rate structure,** consider a group of three individuals, A, B, and C, who have respective incomes of $20,000, $45,000, and $100,000. A proportionate 10 percent income tax results in the following tax for each individual.

Proportionate Rate (10%)

	Taxable Income	Tax
Taxpayer A	$ 20,000	$ 2,000
Taxpayer B	45,000	4,500
Taxpayer C	100,000	10,000
		$16,500

Under this rate structure, individual C, who has the most taxable income and presumably the greatest ability to pay, owes the most tax, while B, who has more income than A, owes more tax than A. Despite this result, many theorists believe that a single rate fails to fairly apportion the tax burden across people with different incomes. They argue that the 10 percent tax is relatively less of a hardship on C than on A and B. Although the tax rate is proportionate, the economic sacrifice is disproportionate.

This argument is based on the theory of the **declining marginal utility of income.** This theory presumes that the financial importance of each dollar of income diminishes as total income increases. In other words, people value the subsistence income spent on necessities, such as food and shelter, more than they value incremental income spent on luxury items. According to this theory, a **progressive rate structure** in which the rates increase as income increases results in an equality of sacrifice across taxpayers.[16]

Assume that our individuals A, B, and C compute their income tax under a progressive rate structure consisting of three rate brackets.

Percentage Rate	Bracket
5%	Income from –0– to $20,000
10%	Income from $20,001 to $50,000
16%	Income in excess of $50,000

[15] *Citizens for Tax Justice,* "Nickels and Dimes: How Sales and Excise Taxes Add Up in the 50 States," March 1988.

[16] See Walter J. Blum and Harry Kalven, Jr., *The Uneasy Case for Progressive Taxation* (Chicago: University of Chicago Press, 1953), for a provocative analysis of the arguments for and against progressive tax rates.

This rate structure results in the following.

Progressive Rates

	Taxable Income	Tax Computation	Tax
Taxpayer A	$ 20,000	5% of 20,000	$ 1,000
Taxpayer B	45,000	5% of 20,000 +10% of 25,000	3,500
Taxpayer C	100,000	5% of 20,000 +10% of 30,000 +16% of 50,000	12,000
			$16,500

Note that this rate structure raises the same $16,500 revenue as the 10 percent proportionate rate structure, and the aggregate tax burden is unchanged. However, A and B are paying fewer dollars while C's tax has increased by $2,000.

Is the proportionate or the progressive rate structure the more equitable for our three individuals? And if the progressive rate structure seems fairer than the proportionate structure, would a more progressive structure—perhaps with a top rate of 25 percent—be even fairer? There are no objective answers to these questions. Progressivity has an intuitive appeal to many people, and the U.S. income tax has always used a progressive rate structure. Nonetheless, while it may be plausible that individuals value income less as their economic resources increase, this proposition cannot be tested empirically. To refer back to our illustration, the taxing authorities have no idea how A, B, or C personally values income, or whether the economic sacrifices they make by paying tax are even remotely comparable. Until economists discover how to measure the utility of income and to compare utilities across individuals, the extent to which any progressive rate structure achieves equality of sacrifice is a matter of opinion.

Objective 7
Explain the difference between marginal and average tax rates.

Marginal and Average Tax Rates

Before leaving the subject of income tax rate structures, we must distinguish between marginal and average tax rates. The **marginal rate** is the rate that applies to the *next* dollar of income. In the progressive rate structure in our example, individual C with $100,000 taxable income owed $12,000 tax. If C earns one more dollar, that dollar is subject to a 16 percent tax rate. Nevertheless, the fact that C is in the 16 percent marginal tax bracket does not mean she is paying 16 percent of her income to the government. Her $12,000 tax divided by $100,000 taxable income is an **average rate** of only 12 percent. Similarly, individual B has a 10 percent marginal rate, but her average rate is 7.8 percent ($3,500 tax divided by $45,000 taxable income).

Under a proportionate rate structure, the marginal and average rates are the same for all levels of taxable income. Under a progressive rate structure, the marginal rate is higher than the average rate for incomes in excess of the first rate bracket. The graphs in Exhibit 2.1 illustrate the relationship between marginal and average rate for the proportionate and progressive tax structures in our examples. In both graphs, the marginal rate is represented by a solid line, and the average rate is represented by a broken line.

Distributive Justice

In a social sense, a tax is equitable if it redresses economic inequities existing in a capitalistic system. A vastly uneven distribution of private wealth across households, character-

EXHIBIT 2.1A
Marginal and Average Tax Rates under Proportionate Rate Structure

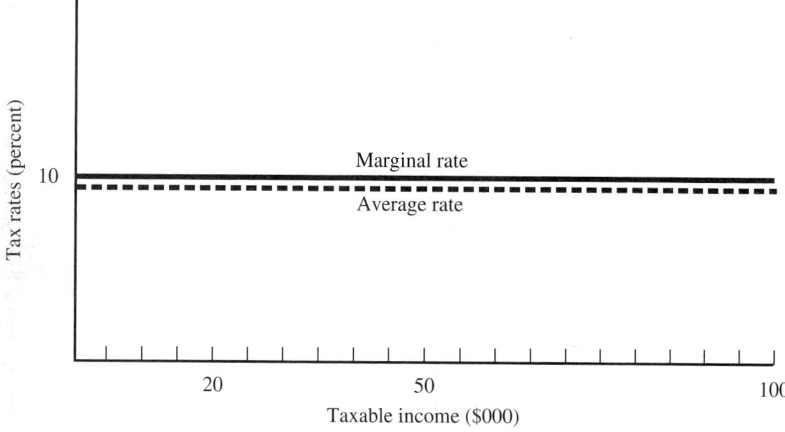

EXHIBIT 2.1B
Marginal and Average Tax Rates under Progressive Rate Structure

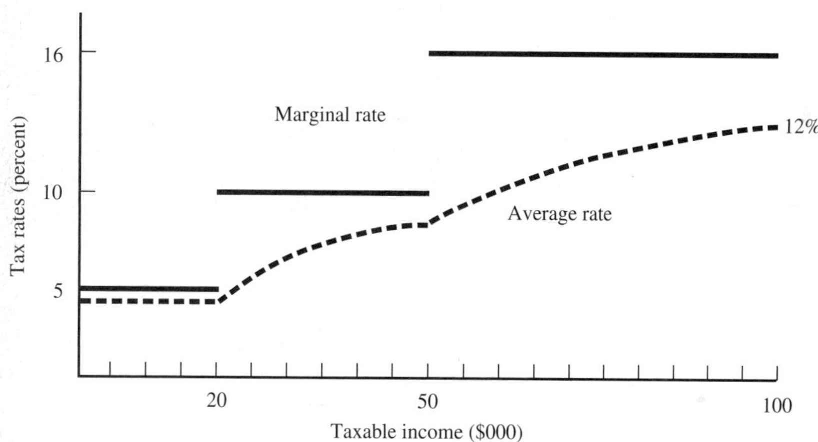

Objective 8
Discuss distributive justice as a tax policy objective.

ized by extremes of poverty and affluence, is one such inequity. By definition, taxes appropriate private wealth for public use, and they appropriate more from the rich than from the poor. Consequently, taxes become mechanisms for the redistribution of wealth across society. Wealth transfer taxes, such as the federal estate and gift taxes, are prime examples of taxes with strong distributional implications. These taxes were enacted early in this century to allow the government to tap into the immense personal fortunes amassed during America's "gilded age." Some policymakers believe that the justification for a progressive income tax is its potential for rectifying distributive inequity. "The case for drastic progression in taxation must be rested on the case against inequality—on the ethical or aesthetic judgment that the prevailing distribution of wealth and income reveals a degree (and/or kind) of inequality that is distinctly evil or unlovely."[17]

Many social commentators view the current distribution of wealth across American households as unjust.[18] These commentators suggest that the federal government could combat this injustice by making the income tax rate structure more progressive. But once

[17] Henry Simons, *Personal Income Taxation* (Chicago: University of Chicago Press, 1938), pp. 18–19.

[18] In 1989, the United States had 66 billionaires and 31.5 million people living below the official poverty line. In 1999, the number of billionaires increased to 268 while the number of people living in poverty increased to 34.5 million. Currently, the top 1 percent of U.S. households own more wealth than the bottom 95 percent. "Divided Decade: Economic Disparity at the Century's Turn," published by United For A Fair Economy, December 15, 1999.

Tax Talk
According to a Federal Reserve study, pretax income of the top 10 percent of American families grew by 19.3 percent between 1998 and 2001, compared with only 11.9 percent growth for the remaining 90 percent of families.

again the nagging question arises: How much more progressivity is desirable? Only the most fanatic egalitarian would argue that the tax system should result in a perfectly equal distribution of wealth across households. Although many people agree (to a greater or lesser extent) with the concept of distributive justice, many also oppose the notion of Uncle Sam playing Robin Hood. In the final analysis, the degree of progressivity in the income tax system remains a value judgment—a matter of political taste rather than of natural law.

The Perception of Inequity

The most widespread complaint against the federal income tax system is that it is unfair. Of course, no government has been or ever will be capable of designing a tax that people enjoy paying. As Edmund Burke, the English parliamentarian and social scientist, observed, "To tax and to please, no more than to love and be wise, is not given to man." Nevertheless, the public perception that the federal income tax is unfair has increased in recent decades.

This perception of inequity has many negative consequences. Research has shown that individuals who believe that the income tax system is unfair are more likely to deliberately underreport their incomes than individuals who believe the system is fair. This result suggests that as public confidence in the equity of the federal tax system erodes, the level of compliance will decline. As greater numbers of citizens regard tax evasion as acceptable, and even rational, behavior, the tax system will place an increasingly unfair burden on the honest remainder who comply with the law.

> Taxpayer morale ultimately depends on the belief that taxes are fair. If the basis for this belief comes under suspicion, voluntary compliance with the tax laws is jeopardized. Thus, the perceived lack of fairness of the income tax may be as important as actual complexities, economic distortions, and inequities.[19]

Many individuals believe that the income tax system is unfair because it is so complicated. They are convinced that the system is full of exotic loopholes benefitting only the rich who can afford expert legal advice. As you will learn, this conviction is unfounded. Many of the complexities of the law were designed to ensure that high-income taxpayers cannot manipulate the system to unwarranted advantage. Affluent individuals undeniably use the tax planning strategies discussed throughout this text on a routine basis to maximize the net present value of their business and investment transactions. However, most of these strategies derive from commonplace features of the law rather than from closely guarded secrets known only to tax professionals.

Conclusion

Jack Kemp, the 1996 Republican vice-presidential candidate, provides this summary description of a good tax.

> Surely, a tax code which is simple and fair must generate sufficient revenue so that the federal government may carry out its legitimate tasks. Second, it must not place a tax burden on those members of society least able to bear one. And, perhaps most important of all, it must not restrict the innovative and entrepreneurial capacities of Americans upon which rising living standards and our general prosperity so greatly depend.[20]

This summary touches on the four normative standards discussed in Chapter 2: sufficiency, convenience, efficiency, and equity. In our discussions, we learned that people interpret these standards in different ways and hold different opinions as to how each should be implemented.

[19] Department of the Treasury, *Tax Reform for Fairness, Simplicity, and Economic Growth,* vol. 1 (Washington, D.C.: U.S. Government Printing Office, 1984), p. 9.

[20] "Unleashing America's Potential: A Pro-Growth, Pro-Family Tax System for the 21st Century," National Commission on Economic Growth and Tax Reform, 70 *Tax Notes* 413, 415.

The standards for a good tax are not necessarily in harmony, and reconciling them can be a tricky proposition. A government's attempt to improve the sufficiency of its tax system by raising rates or expanding the base could make the tax less efficient in terms of its economic impact. The introduction of a preferential rule to enhance economic efficiency might damage the equity of the tax. Conversely, the enactment of a provision making a tax more fair may create complexity that makes it more difficult to administer. Tax policymakers are well aware of the frictions between the standards for a good tax. They know that trade-offs may be necessary in the design and implementation of the tax system that best serves the needs of their governments.

Key Terms

ability to pay *34*
average rate *38*
convenience *30*
declining marginal utility of income *37*
dynamic forecast *27*
efficiency *31*
horizontal equity *34*
income effect *27*
marginal rate *38*
negative externality *32*
progressive rate structure *37*
proportionate rate structure *37*
regressive rate structure *36*
static forecast *26*
substitution effect *28*
sufficiency *24*
supply-side economic theory *29*
Tax Expenditures Budget *33*
tax policy *23*
tax preferences *33*
vertical equity *35*

Questions and Problems for Discussion

1. Identify the tax policy issue that you believe is the most important in today's society.
2. What evidence suggests that the federal tax system receives a low grade when evaluated on the standard of sufficiency?
3. Identify three ways that governments can alter their tax system to increase revenues.
4. National governments have the authority to print their own currency. Why might governments be reluctant to finance an operating deficit (excess of spending over revenues) by simply printing more money?
5. In each of the following cases, discuss how the taxpayers might respond to a tax rate increase in a manner consistent with the income effect.
   a. Mr. E earns $32,000 a year as an employee, and Mrs. E doesn't work.
   b. Mr. F earns $22,000 a year as an employee, and Mrs. F earns $10,000 a year as a self-employed worker.
   c. Mr. G earns $22,000 a year as an employee, and Mrs. G earns $10,000 a year as an employee.
6. In each of the following cases, discuss how the taxpayers might respond to a tax rate increase in a manner consistent with the substitution effect.
   a. Mr. H earns $125,000 a year as a salaried employee, and Mrs. H doesn't work.
   b. Mr. J earns $125,000 a year as a salaried employee, and Mrs. J earns $20,000 a year as a salaried employee.
   c. Ms. K is single and earns $125,000 a year as a self-employed consultant.
7. Ms. V resides in a jurisdiction with a 35 percent income tax. Ms. V has $40,000 that she could invest in bonds paying 12 percent annual interest. She is also considering spending the $40,000 on a new luxury automobile. Ms. V is having a hard time deciding between these two alternatives. Why might her decision be easier if the jurisdiction increases its income tax rate to 50 percent?

8. What nonmonetary incentives affect the amount of time and energy people devote to income-generating activities?
9. The U.S. Congress has occasionally considered enacting a federal tax on the sale of consumer goods and services. This national sales tax would be in addition to any state and local sales tax. Would this new source of federal revenue affect the revenues of state and local governments?
10. The federal government levies a gift tax on the value of property that people give away during their life and an estate tax on the value of property that people transfer at death. From the government's perspective, which tax is more convenient?
11. Discuss the tax policy implications of the saying "an old tax is a good tax."
12. Jurisdiction R and Jurisdiction S both impose a personal income tax on their residents. Under Jurisdiction R's system, employers are required to withhold income tax from their employees' paychecks and remit the tax to the government. Jurisdiction S's system has no such withholding requirement. Instead, residents must compute their income tax and pay the tax directly on a monthly basis. Which tax system is more convenient for the government and for the taxpayer?
13. The federal income tax is criticized as being both inequitable across individuals and overly complicated. Discuss why equity and simplicity can be considered conflicting tax policy goals.
14. Jurisdiction W has decided to enact a personal income tax on its residents. Policymakers are considering the following alternatives.
    a. No tax on income up to $35,000, and a 15 percent tax on all income in excess of $35,000.
    b. A 10 percent tax on all income.
    c. A 15 percent tax on all income up to $80,000, and no tax on any income in excess of $80,000.

    Identify the rate structure of each of the three alternatives.
15. Corporation R and Corporation T conduct business in Jurisdiction Q. The corporations' financial records for last year show the following.

	Corporation R	*Corporation T*
Gross receipts from sales	$5,000,000	$5,000,000
Cost of goods sold	(3,200,000)	(3,670,000)
Gross profit	$1,800,000	$1,330,000
Annual operating expenses	(1,000,000)	(400,000)
Charitable contributions	–0–	(300,000)
Net profit	$ 800,000	$ 630,000

    Jurisdiction Q decided to enact a tax on corporations conducting business within its jurisdiction but has not decided on the tax base. Identify four different tax bases suggested by the corporations' financial records and discuss each base in terms of horizontal equity.
16. Jurisdiction E spends approximately $7 million each winter on snow removal. The jurisdiction is considering adding a new income tax provision that would allow people to deduct the cost of snow removal equipment purchased during the year.

a. Does this proposed change in Jurisdiction E's tax law meet the definition of a tax preference? Explain briefly.

b. Jurisdiction E forecasts that the proposed change will decrease its annual tax revenues by $250,000 but will improve the jurisdiction's financial condition by $300,000. On what assumptions is this forecast based?

17. Ms. P is considering investing $20,000 in a new business. She projects that this investment should generate $3,000 income each year. In estimating her tax on this future income stream, should Ms. P use her marginal or her average tax rate?

Application Problems

1. Mrs. C, a single taxpayer, earns a $28,000 annual salary and pays 15 percent in state and federal income tax. If tax rates increase so that Mrs. C's annual tax rate is 20 percent, how much additional income must she earn to maintain her after-tax standard of living?
2. Mr. and Mrs. J own a florist business that generates $100,000 taxable income each year. For the past few years, the couple's federal tax rate on this income has been 30 percent. Congress recently increased the tax rate for next year to 40 percent.

   a. Based on a static forecast, how much additional revenue will the federal government collect from Mr. and Mrs. J next year?

   b. How much additional revenue will the government collect if Mr. and Mrs. J respond to the rate increase by working harder and earning $118,000 next year?

   c. How much additional revenue will the government collect if Mr. and Mrs. J respond to the rate increase by working less and earning only $90,000 next year?
3. Government G levies an income tax with the following rate structure.

Percentage Rate	*Bracket*
6%	Income from –0– to $30,000
10	Income from $30,001 to $70,000
20	Income from $70,001 to $200,000
28	Income in excess of $200,000

   a. Taxpayer A's annual income is $83,000. Compute A's tax and average tax rate. What is A's marginal tax rate?

   b. Taxpayer B's annual income is $310,000. Compute B's tax and average tax rate. What is B's marginal tax rate?
4. Refer to Government G's rate structure described in the preceding problem. Taxpayer O earns $50,000 annually during years 1 through 10. Taxpayer P earns $20,000 annually during years 1 through 5 and $80,000 annually during years 6 through 10.

   a. How much total income does each taxpayer earn over the 10-year period?

   b. Compute each taxpayer's average tax rate for the 10-year period.
5. Jurisdiction Z levies an excise tax on retail purchases of jewelry and watches. The tax equals 3 percent of the first $1,000 of the purchase price plus 1 percent of the purchase price in excess of $1,000.

   a. Individual C purchases a watch for $500. Compute C's excise tax and average excise tax rate.

b. Individual D purchases a watch for $5,000. Compute D's excise tax and average excise tax rate.

c. Is Jurisdiction Z's excise tax vertically equitable? Explain briefly.

Issue Recognition Problems

Identify the tax issue or issues suggested by the following situations, and state each issue in the form of a question.

1. County M imposes a 1 percent tax on the gross receipts earned by firms operating within its jurisdiction. For the last year, gross receipts subject to tax totaled $400 million. The county government is considering raising the tax rate to 2 percent because it needs $400,000 additional revenue to improve its road system.
2. The Internal Revenue Code allows individuals to deduct state income tax payments in the computation of federal taxable income. However, state sales tax payments are not deductible. Mrs. F resides in a state with a 5 percent personal income tax and a 3 percent sales tax. Mrs. L resides in a state with no personal income tax and a 7 percent sales tax. Last year, both women paid $8,000 state tax.
3. Four years ago, the citizens of Country C complained that the national tax system was too uncertain because the government changed the tax laws so frequently. In response to this criticism, the government enacted a 10-year moratorium on change: No existing tax law can be modified and no new tax law can be enacted for a decade. This year, Country C is experiencing a severe recession. Economic growth is at a standstill, and the national unemployment rate is 18 percent.
4. Two years ago, the government of State P decided to improve the horizontal equity of its individual income tax by allowing families to deduct the cost of heating and air conditioning their homes. This modification necessitated an additional tax form and three additional pages of instructions. For the past two years, only one-third of the families eligible for the deduction actually claimed it on their returns.
5. Jurisdiction J decides to clean up its streets, parks, and waterways by providing a tax break for businesses that assign employees to pick up trash for a minimum number of hours each month. The annual revenue loss from this tax break is $1.9 million.
6. Country O imposes just two taxes on its citizens. The first tax is a 20 percent excise tax on motor fuel and motor oil. This tax is earmarked for Country O's Highway Improvement Trust Fund, and the revenues cannot be spent for any other purpose. The second tax is a 10 percent general sales tax on consumer goods and services (excluding retail purchases of motor fuel and motor oil). Sales tax revenues can be spent for any authorized public purpose. This year, Country O collected $185 million in excise tax and spent only $77 million from the Highway Improvement Trust Fund. It collected $718 million in sales tax and spent $800 million for public purposes.

Research Problems

1. Visit the website for the Congressional Budget Office (**www.cbo.gov**) and look up the most current Monthly Budget Review. What is the CBO's estimate of the U.S. government's total budget surplus or deficit for fiscal year 2005? Does this estimate include or exclude the surplus in the Social Security Trust Fund?
2. Visit the website for the Tax Foundation (**www.taxfoundation.org**). How does the Tax Foundation describe itself on its home page? Visit the Tax Bites page to research the following:
   a. What and when was Tax Freedom Day in 2004?
   b. When was Tax Freedom Day in 1950?

3. Visit the U.S. Treasury's Public Debt website (**www.publicdebt.treas.gov**) to find out today's national debt to the penny!

Tax Planning Case

Jurisdiction B's tax system consists of a 6.5 percent general sales tax on retail goods and selected services. Over the past decade, the average annual volume of sales subject to this tax was $500 million. The jurisdiction needs to increase its tax revenues by approximately $5 million each year to finance its spending programs. The taxing authorities are considering two alternatives: a 1 percent increase in the sales tax rate or a new 2 percent tax on the net income of corporations doing business in the jurisdiction. Based on recent economic data, the annual net income subject to the new tax would be $275 million. However, the jurisdiction would have to create a new agency responsible for enforcing and collecting the income tax. The estimated annual cost of the agency is $500,000. Jurisdiction B borders four other taxing jurisdictions, all of which have a general sales tax and two of which have a corporate income tax.

1. Based on a static forecast, how much incremental revenue would Jurisdiction B raise under each alternative?
2. Assume that the taxing authorities in Jurisdiction B want a dynamic forecast of the incremental revenues under each alternative. What additional facts would be important in making such a forecast and why?

Fundamentals of Tax Planning

Chapter Three

Taxes as Transaction Costs

Learning Objectives

After studying this chapter, you should be able to:

1. Compute the tax cost of an income item and the tax savings from a deduction.
2. Integrate tax costs and savings into NPV calculations of after-tax cash flows.
3. Identify the reasons why assumptions about future tax costs and savings are uncertain.
4. Explain why a business strategy that minimizes tax costs may not be the optimal strategy.
5. Explain why the parties to a private market transaction should consider the tax consequences to both parties.
6. Distinguish between arm's-length and related party transactions.

In the introduction to *Principles of Taxation for Business and Investment Planning,* we established the premise that the overall objective of business decisions is to maximize the value of the firm. The premise is relevant to managers who are employed to make decisions on behalf of the owners of the firm. Managers who make good decisions that increase the value of owners' equity can expect to be well compensated for their success. Managers who make bad decisions that decrease value can expect to lose their jobs. A variation of the premise holds true for individuals acting in their own economic self-interest. Individuals want to make personal financial decisions that further their goal of wealth maximization.

In Chapter 3, we will explore the business decision-making process. The chapter begins with a review of the concept of net present value of cash flows as the cornerstone of this process. The chapter then focuses on how the tax consequences of business transactions affect net present value and how these consequences must be integrated into the decision-making framework. We will consider how managers can structure transactions to control tax consequences and maximize net present value. The chapter concludes by discussing the extent to which the various parties to a business transaction can negotiate to reduce the tax burden on the transaction and to share the tax savings among themselves.

THE ROLE OF NET PRESENT VALUE IN DECISION MAKING

Every business operation consists of a series of transactions intended to generate profit and create value for the owners of the firm. Business managers need a method for evaluating whether an isolated transaction or an integrated sequence of transactions will contribute to or detract from the profitability of the operation. The method should be useful to managers who must choose between alternative transactions that accomplish the same functional result for the firm.

Quantifying Cash Flows

Financial theorists agree that the first step in evaluating a business transaction is to quantify the cash flows from the transaction. Some transactions result in the receipt of cash by the firm. The sale of merchandise to a customer or the rental of property to a lessee are examples of transactions generating cash inflows. Other transactions require the firm to disburse cash. The purchase of business assets and the hiring of employees are common transactions requiring cash outflows. Of course, many transactions involve both inflows and outflows and must be evaluated on the basis of **net cash flow** (the difference between cash received and cash disbursed).

The various revenue-generating transactions in which firms engage typically result in positive net cash flows that increase the value of the firm. If managers must choose between alternative revenue-generating opportunities, they should choose the opportunity with the greatest positive net cash flow. The various costs that firms incur can be expressed as negative net cash flows. Viewed in isolation, negative net cash flows decrease the value of the firm. However, costs are essential components of an integrated business operation and contribute to short-term and long-term profitability. If managers conclude that a particular cost is unnecessary because it does not enhance profitability, the cost should be eliminated. If a cost is justified, managers should reduce the negative net cash flow associated with the cost as much as possible.

In summary, managers want to make decisions that enhance profitability by increasing revenues and controlling costs. More precisely, *managers want to make decisions that maximize the value of the firm by maximizing positive cash flow or minimizing negative cash flow.*

The Concept of Present Value

When cash flows from a transaction occur at different times, the quantification of net cash flow should take into account the **time value of money.** Time value refers to the fact that a dollar available today is worth more than a dollar available tomorrow because the current dollar can be invested to start earning interest immediately.[1] A dollar available today has a present value of a dollar. The present value of a dollar available in the future is based on a **discount rate**—the after-tax rate of interest on invested funds for the deferral period. A transaction's **net present value (NPV)** is the sum of the present values of cash inflows and outflows from the transaction.

The next several paragraphs review the mathematical derivation of present value. If you are already familiar with this material, please feel free to jump ahead to the issue of risk on page 52.

[1] This proposition is considered the first basic principle of finance. Richard A. Brealey and Stewart C. Myers, *Principles of Corporate Finance,* 5th ed. (New York: McGraw-Hill, 1996).

Present Value

The algebraic expression of the present value (PV) of a dollar available at the end of one period based on the discount rate (r) for that period is:

$$PV(\$1) = \frac{1}{1 + r}$$

PV Calculation

At an annual 10 percent discount rate, the present value of $1 to be received at the end of one year is $.9091.

$$\$.9091 = \frac{1}{1.10}$$

If the availability of the dollar is deferred for a number of periods (n) over which the discount rate is constant, the algebraic expression of present value is:

$$PV(\$1) = \frac{1}{(1 + r)^n}$$

PV Calculation

At an annual 10 percent discount rate, the present value of $1 to be received at the end of three years is $.7513.

$$\$.7513 = \frac{1}{1.331} = \frac{1}{(1.10)^3}$$

In other words, $.7513 invested today to earn 10 percent compounded annually will accumulate to $1 at the end of three years.

Present Value of an Annuity

A cash flow consisting of a constant dollar amount available at the end of the period for a specific number of periods is called an **annuity.** Examples include monthly rent payments over the term of a lease agreement and equal annual payments to retire the principal of an outstanding loan. The algebraic expression of the present value (PV) of an annuity of one dollar for a number of periods (n) based on the discount rate (r) over the period is:

$$PV(\$1 \text{ for n periods}) = \frac{1}{r} - \frac{1}{r(1 + r)^n}$$

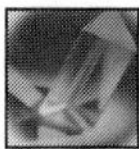

PV of an Annuity

At a 10 percent annual discount rate, the present value of $1 to be received at the end of years 1 through 4 is $3.1699.

$$PV(\$1 \text{ for 4 years}) = \frac{1}{.10} - \frac{1}{.10(1.10)^4}$$

$$PV(\$1 \text{ for 4 years}) = 10 - \frac{1}{.10(1.4641)}$$

$$\$3.1699 = 10 - 6.8301$$

The present value of the annuity is the sum of the present values of the four $1 payments. Note that this formula works only for a series of *equal* payments.

Present Value Tables

The algebraic formulas in the preceding paragraphs can be used to derive tables of discount factors for computing the present value of cash receipts or payments deferred for any given number of periods. Appendix A of this text is a table of discount factors for computing the present value of $1 available at the end of 1 through 20 years at annual discount rates ranging from 3 percent to 20 percent. Appendix B is a table of discount factors for computing the present value of a $1 annuity for a period of 1 through 20 years at annual discount rates ranging from 3 percent to 20 percent. Throughout the text, computations of the net present value of cash flows are based on factors from these tables.

The net present value of cash flows can also be computed by using a financial calculator or a spreadsheet computer program such as Microsoft Excel or Lotus 1-2-3. Remember that discount factor tables, calculators, and electronic spreadsheets are all means to the same end. Business managers can use whichever tool is the most convenient for computing net present value.

The Issue of Risk

The quantification of cash flows and calculation of their net present value are based on assumptions concerning future events. In projecting the cash inflows and outflows from a proposed transaction, business managers research pertinent industry and economic data, consult professionals who have expertise relevant to the transaction, and rely on their experience with past transactions of a similar nature. Nonetheless, even the most carefully developed projections can be inaccurate, and unexpected events can dramatically alter the actual cash flows from a transaction.

Financial forecasters must accept the possibility that one or more of the assumptions on which their cash flow projections are based will be wrong. Of course, some assumptions are more certain than others. The assumption that the U.S. government will pay the interest on its debt obligations is more certain than the assumption that the value of an initial public offering (IPO) of stock will double in value over the next 12 months. This difference in certainty makes a decision to invest in U.S. Treasury bills less risky than a decision to invest in the IPO.

Business managers must be sensitive to the uncertainties and the resultant degree of risk inherent in any transaction. When calculating net present value, they should invoke the financial principle that a safe dollar is worth more than a risky dollar. In other words, the present value of a highly speculative future dollar should be based on a higher discount rate than the present value of a guaranteed future dollar.

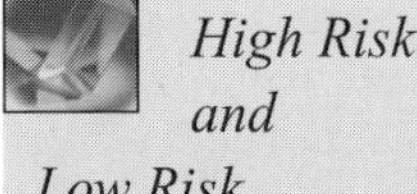

High Risk and Low Risk

Firm Z has the opportunity to invest $200,000 in a new business venture. The promoters of the venture provide Firm Z with a 10-year projection of net cash flows. Firm Z determines that the venture has a high degree of risk and therefore decides to use a 15 percent discount rate to calculate the net present value of the projected cash flows. With the high discount rate, the net present value is a *negative* number. Consequently, Firm Z decides not to make the investment. In contrast, assume that Firm Z determines that the venture has a low degree of risk and uses a 7 percent discount rate to calculate net present value. With the lower discount rate, the net present value is a positive number and Firm Z decides to make the investment.

Because this text concentrates on the tax aspects of business decisions, the cash flow examples throughout the text incorporate two simplifying assumptions about financial risk. First, they assume that the discount rate in the example accurately reflects the risk of the transaction under consideration. Second, the examples assume that such risk is stable over time so that the appropriate discount rate does not change from period to period.

A Basic Net Present Value Example

Let's summarize our discussion of net present value and its role in business decision making by working through a simple example. Suppose a consulting firm must decide between two engagements, either of which would require the firm's complete attention for two years. Engagement 1 will generate $150,000 of revenues in each of the two years. The firm estimates that this engagement will require $90,000 of expenses in the current year and $10,000 of expenses in the next year. Engagement 2 will generate $200,000 of revenues in the current year and $125,000 of revenues in the next year. The firm estimates that Engagement 2 will require $65,000 of annual expenses. Based on a 10 percent discount rate and *without considering the effect of any type of tax,* the net present values of the competing engagements are computed as follows.

	Engagement 1	Engagement 2
Current year:		
Cash revenues	$150,000	$200,000
Cash expenses	(90,000)	(65,000)
Net cash flow	$ 60,000	$135,000
Next year:		
Cash revenues	$150,000	$125,000
Cash expenses	(10,000)	(65,000)
Net cash flow	$140,000	$ 60,000
Present value of current year cash flow	$ 60,000	$135,000
Present value of next year cash flow (cash flow × .909 discount factor)	127,260	54,540
NPV	$187,260	$189,540

The firm now has a rational basis for choosing between the two consulting opportunities. It should accept Engagement 2 because Engagement 2 has a greater net present value than Engagement 1.

In the above example, the net cash flow received in the current year was not discounted, and the net cash received in the next year was discounted for one period. This treatment is based on an assumption that cash flows attributable to the current year (year 0) are available immediately and are not discounted. Cash flows attributable to the next year (year 1) are available one year hence and are discounted for one period, and so forth. *This assumption is used consistently throughout the NPV examples in the text and for the solutions to the problems and cases at the end of each chapter.*

TAXES AND CASH FLOWS

Calculations of net present value must reflect all cash flows including any tax costs or tax savings resulting from the transaction. In the business decision-making process, cash flows before tax have no relevance.

Objective 1
Compute the tax cost of an income item and the tax savings from a deduction.

Tax Costs

If a transaction results in an increase in any tax for any period, the increase (**tax cost**) is a cash outflow. A tax cost may be incremental to a nontax cost. For instance, a firm that purchases machinery may pay a sales tax; the cash outflow from the transaction includes both the purchase price and the tax. In the context of an income tax, tax cost can be a direct result of the receipt of taxable income; the cash outflow represented by the tax is linked to any cash inflow represented by the income item.

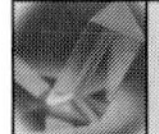

Income Tax Cost

Firm F sells a unit of inventory for $50 cash. If the unit cost was $40, the sales transaction generates $10 taxable income. If the firm is subject to a 30 percent income tax, the tax cost of the transaction is $3. The sales transaction generates both $50 cash inflow and $3 cash outflow, resulting in positive net cash flow of $47.

Tax Savings

If a transaction results in a decrease in any tax for any period, the decrease (**tax savings**) is a cash inflow. In the income tax system, tax liability is based on net business profits rather than gross revenues. Accordingly, many business expenditures can be subtracted, or deducted, in the computation of taxable income. The **deduction** reduces taxable income and causes a corresponding reduction in tax. Hence, the deductible expenditure results in a tax savings.[2]

Income Tax Savings

Firm F leases office space for $1,000 monthly rent. Each $1,000 expenditure is deductible in computing the firm's taxable income; in other words, the expenditure shields $1,000 income from tax. If the firm is subject to a 30 percent tax rate, the deduction causes a $300 tax savings. The monthly rent transaction involves both a $1,000 cash outflow and a $300 cash inflow, resulting in negative net cash flow of $700.

Note that in both of the above examples, the tax cost or tax savings from a transaction is treated as a cash flow *in the year that the transaction occurs.* This timing of the cash flow reflects the reality that taxpayers must pay the tax on their current income *during the current year* and not when they file their tax return in the following year. (The tax payment requirements for corporations are discussed in Chapter 10, and the tax payment requirements for individuals are discussed in Chapter 13.) If a taxpayer engages in a transaction with tax consequences in 2005, the taxpayer's tax cost or savings is a 2005 cash flow.

The Significance of Marginal Tax Rate

The income tax cost or savings from a particular transaction is a function of the firm's marginal tax rate. In Chapter 2, we defined marginal rate as the rate that applies to the next dollar of taxable income. When analyzing transactions that either increase or decrease taxable income, the marginal rate is the rate at which the increase or decrease would be taxed. If this rate is constant over the increase or decrease, the computation of the tax cost or savings from the transaction is simple.

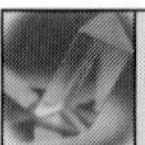

Constant Marginal Rate

Firm F is subject to a progressive income tax consisting of two rates: 15 percent on the first $50,000 taxable income and 30 percent on taxable income in excess of $50,000. The firm's taxable income to date is $100,000. If Firm F engages in a transaction that generates $10,000 additional income, the entire increment is subject to a 30 percent tax rate. Therefore, the transaction has a $3,000 tax cost.

[2] In the accounting and finance literature, the tax savings from deductible business expenditures are often described as *tax shields.*

The computation of tax cost or savings is more complex if the marginal tax rate is not constant over the change in taxable income.

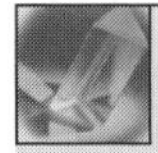

Changing Marginal Rate

Firm G is subject to a progressive income tax consisting of two rates: 15 percent on the first $50,000 taxable income and 30 percent on taxable income in excess of $50,000. The firm's taxable income to date is $44,000. If Firm G engages in a transaction that generates $10,000 additional income, the marginal rate on the first $6,000 increment is 15 percent and on the next $4,000 increment is 30 percent. Thus, the transaction has a $2,100 tax cost.

If Firm G engages in a transaction that generates a $10,000 deduction, the marginal tax rate on the entire income shielded by the deduction is 15 percent. Thus, the transaction results in a $1,500 tax savings.

Obviously, managers must know their firm's marginal tax rate to accurately compute the tax cost or savings from a transaction.

Net Present Value Example Revisited

Objective 2
Integrate tax costs and savings into NPV calculations of after-tax cash flows.

Let's integrate income tax consequences into the net present value example developed earlier in the chapter. Remember that our consulting firm must choose between two engagements with different revenues and expenses over a two-year period. Now assume that the revenues are taxable, the expenses are deductible, and the income tax rate is 40 percent. Based on these assumptions, the net present values of the competing engagements are computed as follows.

	Engagement 1	**Engagement 2**
Current year:		
Taxable revenues	$150,000	$200,000
Deductible expenses	(90,000)	(65,000)
Before-tax cash flow/taxable income	$ 60,000	$135,000
Income tax cost at 40%	(24,000)	(54,000)
After-tax cash flow	$ 36,000	$ 81,000
Next year:		
Taxable revenues	$150,000	$125,000
Deductible expenses	(10,000)	(65,000)
Before-tax cash flow/taxable income	$140,000	$ 60,000
Income tax cost at 40%	(56,000)	(24,000)
After-tax cash flow	$ 84,000	$ 36,000
Present value of current year cash flow	$ 36,000	$ 81,000
Present value of next year cash flow (after-tax cash flow × .909 discount factor)	76,356	32,724
NPV	$112,356	$113,724

The introduction of an income tax reduced the NPV of each engagement but did not change the proportionate difference between the values. With or without the tax, the NPV of Engagement 1 is only 98.80 percent of the NPV of Engagement 2. Because the income tax applies in the same manner to each engagement and because the marginal rate doesn't change over the two-year period, the tax is neutral. In other words, income tax consequences are not a factor affecting the decision as to which engagement to accept. Now let's consider two examples in which the income tax consequences become an important factor in the decision-making process.

Different Tax Treatments across Transactions

Tax costs are not neutral if the income tax law applies differentially to the two engagements. Assume that the law allows the firm to deduct 100 percent of the expenses of Engagement 1, but only 75 percent of the expenses of Engagement 2. Observe how the NPV computations change.

	Engagement 1		Engagement 2	
Current year:				
Taxable revenues		$150,000		$200,000
Deductible expenses		(90,000)		(48,750)
Nondeductible expenses		–0–		(16,250)
Before-tax cash flow		$ 60,000		$135,000
Income tax cost:				
Taxable income	$ 60,000		$151,250	
	.40		.40	
Tax cost		(24,000)		(60,500)
After-tax cash flow		$ 36,000		$ 74,500
Next year:				
Taxable revenues		$150,000		$125,000
Deductible expenses		(10,000)		(48,750)
Nondeductible expenses		–0–		(16,250)
Before-tax cash flow		$140,000		$ 60,000
Income tax cost:				
Taxable income	$140,000		$ 76,250	
	.40		.40	
Tax cost		(56,000)		(30,500)
After-tax cash flow		$ 84,000		$ 29,500
Present value of current year cash flow		$ 36,000		$ 74,500
Present value of next year cash flow (after-tax cash flow × .909 discount factor)		76,356		26,816
NPV		$112,356		$101,316

The fact that the tax law limits the deduction for the Engagement 2 expenses increases the tax cost of the engagement and decreases after-tax cash flow. As a result, the NPV of Engagement 2 is less than that of Engagement 1, and Engagement 1 is the superior opportunity. In this case, tax consequences are a factor in the decision.

Different Tax Rates over Time

Calculations of net present value are sensitive to changes in tax rates over time. To illustrate this point, modify the example again by returning to the initial assumption that the firm can deduct 100 percent of the expenses of both engagements. But now assume that Congress recently enacted legislation reducing the income tax rate from 40 percent in the current year to 25 percent in the next year.

	Engagement 1	Engagement 2
Current year:		
Taxable revenues	$150,000	$200,000
Deductible expenses	(90,000)	(65,000)
Before-tax cash flow/taxable income	$ 60,000	$135,000
Income tax cost at 40%	(24,000)	(54,000)
After-tax cash flow	$ 36,000	$ 81,000
Next year:		
Taxable revenues	$150,000	$125,000
Deductible expenses	(10,000)	(65,000)
Before-tax cash flow/taxable income	$140,000	$ 60,000
Income tax cost at 25%	(35,000)	(15,000)
After-tax cash flow	$105,000	$ 45,000
Present value of current year cash flow	$ 36,000	$ 81,000
Present value of next year cash flow (after-tax cash flow × .909 discount factor)	95,445	40,905
NPV	$131,445	$121,905

The fact that a lower tax rate applies next year decreases the tax cost for that year relative to the tax cost for the current year. Engagement 1 generates more of its total taxable income in the next year than Engagement 2. Consequently, Engagement 1 has a lower overall tax cost and a greater NPV than Engagement 2 and is the superior opportunity.

The Uncertainty of Tax Consequences

Objective 3
Identify the reasons why assumptions about future tax costs and savings are uncertain.

A net present value calculation is incomplete unless it includes cash flows attributable to the current and future tax consequences of the proposed transaction. However, assumptions concerning tax consequences have their own unique uncertainties.

Audit Risk

Oftentimes the correct application of the tax law to a proposed transaction is unclear or unresolved. In such case, business managers must decide on the most probable tax consequences to incorporate into their net present value calculations. Whenever a firm enters into a transaction involving ambiguous tax issues, it runs the risk that the Internal Revenue Service (or state and local tax authorities) will challenge the tax treatment on audit. The IRS may conclude that the transaction resulted in a greater tax cost or a smaller tax savings than the manager originally projected. The firm can dispute the unfavorable result of the audit in court.[3] But even if the firm wins its case, the cost of litigation can be substantial. Accordingly, actual cash flows from a contested transaction may vary from the estimated cash flows in the NPV calculation.

[3] Historically, the burden of proof in a federal tax case was on the taxpayer, not the government. In other words, taxpayers had to convince the court that the IRS was wrong in its conclusions. In the IRS Reform and Restructuring Act of 1998, Congress modified this long-standing rule. Section 7491(a) provides that the burden of proof with *respect to any factual issue* shifts to the IRS if the taxpayer introduces credible evidence concerning the facts, meets any statutory substantiation requirements, and has cooperated with the IRS in establishing the facts of the case. Corporations, trusts, and partnerships with net worth in excess of $7 million are ineligible for the benefits of the burden-shifting provision.

Managers can reduce the risk of an IRS challenge by engaging a tax professional, such as a CPA or an attorney, to analyze questionable transactions and render an expert opinion as to the proper tax treatment. Managers can even ask the IRS to analyze a proposed transaction and to conclude how the tax law should be applied. The IRS will communicate its conclusion in the form of a **private letter ruling** to the firm. Obtaining a private letter ruling can be expensive; firms typically require professional help in drafting a ruling request, and the IRS currently charges a $6,000 fee for a ruling.[4] Despite the cost, a private letter ruling can be invaluable when thousands or even millions of tax dollars are at stake. If a firm reports the tax consequences of a transaction in accordance with a private letter ruling, it has a guarantee that the consequences will not be challenged by the IRS upon subsequent audit.[5]

Tax Law Uncertainty

A second source of uncertainty is the possibility that tax laws may change during the time period of the NPV computation. Of course, the potential for change varies greatly with the particular tax under consideration. The federal income tax system is notorious for the frequency with which Congress changes the rules of the game. But even within this volatile tax system, some provisions are quite stable. The tax consequences of a proposed transaction to which a stable tax provision applies are more predictable than the consequences of a transaction subject to a provision that Congress modifies every year. As a result, the NPV of the former transaction can be calculated with greater certainty than the NPV of the latter.

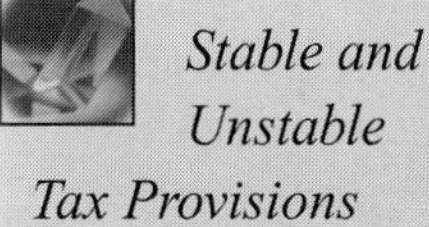

Stable and Unstable Tax Provisions

The Internal Revenue Code allows firms to deduct "all interest paid or accrued within the taxable year on indebtedness." This provision was included in the Internal Revenue Code of 1939 and has been substantially unchanged for more than 60 years. In contrast, the provision requiring corporations to pay an alternative minimum tax in addition to regular income tax was added to the Internal Revenue Code in 1986, then amended in 1988, 1990, 1992, 1993, 1996, 1997, 1998, 2001, 2002, and 2003.

Marginal Rate Uncertainty

The estimated tax cost or savings from a transaction are a function of the firm's projected marginal tax rate. This marginal rate may change in future years because the government changes the statutory rates for all taxpayers. The marginal rate may also change because of a change in the firm's circumstances. In the income tax context, marginal rate depends on the amount of annual taxable income. If taxable income for a future year is significantly more or less than anticipated, the actual marginal rate for that year may vary from the projected rate. If the actual rate is higher than projected, the tax cost or savings in that year will be more than expected. Conversely, if the rate is lower than projected, the tax cost or savings will be less than expected.

Marginal Rate Increase

Last year, Company N had to choose between two business opportunities in different tax jurisdictions. The company projected that Opportunity 1 would generate $100,000 income taxed at 30 percent, while Opportunity 2 would generate $90,000 income taxed at 20 percent.

[4] Rev. Proc. 2004-1, Appendix A, 2004-1 IRB 1.

[5] A taxpayer may rely on a ruling unless the ruling request misstated or omitted material facts concerning the proposed transaction or the actual transaction differs substantially from the proposed transaction. No taxpayer may rely on a ruling issued to another taxpayer. Rev. Proc. 2004-1, Section 11, 2004-1 IRB 1.

Company N chose Opportunity 2 because its $72,000 projected after-tax income ($90,000 − $18,000 tax) exceeded the $70,000 projected after-tax income ($100,000 − $30,000 tax) from Opportunity 1. Because of an unexpected change in circumstances, the marginal tax rate on the income from Opportunity 2 increased to 25 percent this year. As a result, Company N's after-tax income was only $67,500 ($90,000 − $22,500), and in retrospect, Opportunity 2 was the wrong choice.

STRUCTURING TRANSACTIONS TO REDUCE TAXES

The tax consequences of business transactions depend on the legal and financial structure of the transaction. Firms often can change the tax consequences by changing the structure. For instance, a firm that needs an additional worker to perform a certain task could hire a part-time employee. As a result of this employment transaction, the firm is liable for federal and state payroll taxes on the salary paid to the employee.[6] Alternatively, the firm could engage an independent contractor to perform the same task. The firm is not liable for payroll taxes on the fee paid to the independent contractor. Thus, by changing the legal structure of the transaction, the firm eliminates the payroll tax cost of adding personnel.

Let's add some numbers to compute the after-tax cost of each alternative.

Cost of Employee

Firm W plans on hiring an employee to perform a certain task. The firm would pay a $15,000 salary and $1,250 payroll tax on the salary. Both the salary and the payroll tax are deductible in computing taxable income. If the firm's marginal income tax rate is 35 percent, the after-tax cost of the transaction is $10,562.

Cash flows:	
Salary	$(15,000)
Payroll tax cost	(1,250)
Income tax savings	
($16,250 × 35%)	5,688
Net cash flow	$(10,562)

Cost of Independent Contractor

If Firm W engages an independent contractor to perform the task and pays the contractor a $15,000 fee, the after-tax cost of the transaction is only $9,750.

Cash flows:	
Fee	$(15,000)
Income tax savings	
($15,000 × 35%)	5,250
Net cash flow	$ (9,750)

[6] An independent contractor is a self-employed individual who performs services for compensation. Unlike an employee, an independent contractor significantly controls the manner in which the services are performed.

In this simple example, Firm W can eliminate the payroll tax cost without affecting any nontax cash flow. The income tax applies in the same manner to both alternatives and thus is a neutral consideration. Consequently, Firm W can minimize the after-tax cost of the transaction by engaging an independent contractor instead of hiring an employee.

An Important Caveat

Objective 4
Explain why a business strategy that minimizes tax costs may not be the optimal strategy.

Business managers who decide to change the structure of a transaction to reduce tax costs must consider the effect of the change on nontax factors. If a change that saves tax dollars adversely affects other factors, the change may be a bad idea. In financial terms, a strategy that minimizes the tax cost of a transaction may not maximize net present value and may not be the optimal strategy for the firm.

To demonstrate this important point, reconsider the example in which Firm W can either hire an employee or engage an independent contractor to perform a task. The firm can hire the employee for a $15,000 salary and an after-tax cost of $10,562. But what if the independent contractor demands a $17,500 fee to do the job?

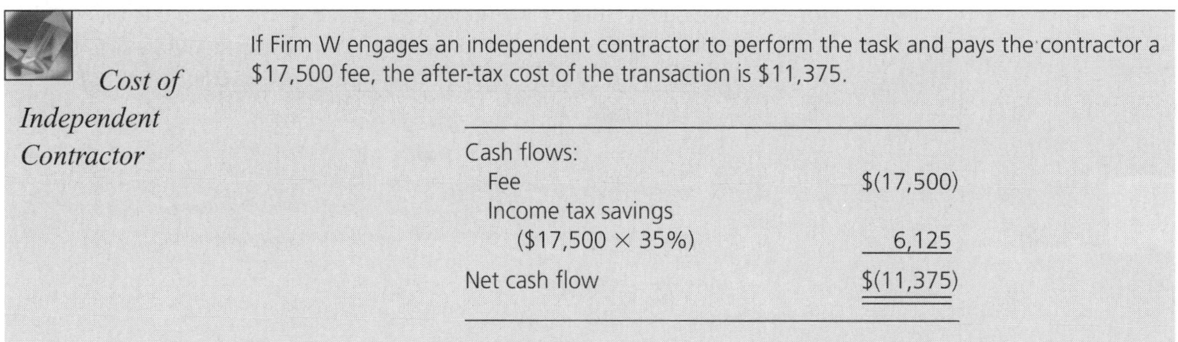

Cost of Independent Contractor

If Firm W engages an independent contractor to perform the task and pays the contractor a $17,500 fee, the after-tax cost of the transaction is $11,375.

Cash flows:	
Fee	$(17,500)
Income tax savings ($17,500 × 35%)	6,125
Net cash flow	$(11,375)

Now the alternative that eliminates the payroll tax cost increases the compensation that Firm W must pay. As a result, the after-tax cost of engaging an independent contractor ($11,375) exceeds the after-tax cost of hiring an employee ($10,562). Firm W should hire the employee, even though this alternative does not minimize the payroll tax cost of the transaction.

Transactional Markets

The extent to which managers can control the tax consequences of transactions depends on the nature of the market in which the transaction occurs. A **market** is a forum for commercial interaction between two or more parties for the purpose of exchanging goods or services. One or both parties may want to customize the terms of the exchange to obtain a certain tax result. Their ability to do so depends on the flexibility of the particular market.

Private Market Transactions

Objective 5
Explain why the parties to a private market transaction should consider the tax consequences to both parties.

Many business transactions involve private parties who deal directly with each other. The parties have flexibility in designing a transaction that accommodates the needs of both. The legal and financial characteristics of the transaction are specified in the contract to which both parties finally agree. In negotiating such **private market** transactions, each party can evaluate the tax consequences not only to itself but also to the other party. By doing so, the parties can work together to minimize the aggregate tax cost of the transaction and share the tax savings between them.

To illustrate this bilateral approach to tax planning, consider the case of Firm M and key employee Mr. Grant, and their negotiation of a new employment contract. For simplicity's sake, the case disregards payroll tax costs and focuses on the income tax consequences of the contract. Firm M and Mr. Grant have respective marginal income tax rates of 35 percent and 30 percent. Salary payments are deductible by Firm M and taxable to Mr. Grant.

Initial Compensation Package

Firm M and Mr. Grant begin their negotiation by analyzing the consequences of a $120,000 salary payment. The firm's after-tax cost of the $120,000 payment would be $78,000.

Cash flows:	
Salary	$(120,000)
Income tax savings ($120,000 × 35%)	42,000
Net cash flow	$ (78,000)

Mr. Grant's after-tax cash flow would be $84,000.

Cash flows:	
Salary	$120,000
Income tax cost ($120,000 × 30%)	(36,000)
Net cash flow	$ 84,000

Firm M knows that Mr. Grant spends $10,000 each year to pay the premiums on his family's health insurance policy. Mr. Grant can't deduct this expense in computing taxable income; therefore, the premium payments don't result in any tax savings to him.[7] After this expense, Mr. Grant's after-tax cash flow is only $74,000.

Cash flows:	
Salary	$120,000
Income tax cost ($120,000 × 30%)	(36,000)
Insurance premium	(10,000)
Net cash flow	$ 74,000

Both parties know that Firm M could pay a $5,000 premium for comparable health insurance for Mr. Grant under its group plan. Moreover, Firm M could deduct the premium payment. The compensatory fringe benefit (employer-provided health insurance) would be nontaxable to Mr. Grant.[8] On the basis of this mutual knowledge, the parties agree to a final compensation package.

[7] The tax consequences of an individual's personal expenses are discussed in Chapter 16.

[8] Nontaxable employee fringe benefits are discussed in Chapter 14.

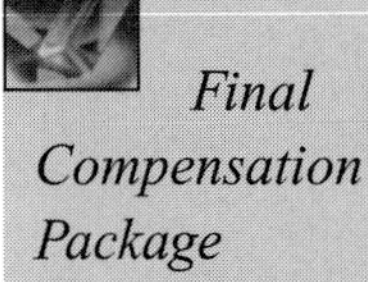

Final Compensation Package

Firm M agrees to pay Mr. Grant a $110,000 salary and provide health insurance coverage under its group plan. The firm's after-tax cost of this compensation package is $74,750.

Cash flows:	
Salary	$(110,000)
Insurance premium	(5,000)
Income tax savings ($115,000 × 35%)	40,250
Net cash flow	$ (74,750)

Based on this compensation package, Mr. Grant's after-tax cash flow is $77,000.

Cash flows:	
Salary	$110,000
Income tax cost ($110,000 × 30%)	(33,000)
Insurance premium	-0-
Net cash flow	$ 77,000

By considering the tax consequences to both parties, Firm M and Mr. Grant structured their contract to improve both their after-tax positions. Specifically, Firm M decreased the after-tax cost of employing Mr. Grant by $3,250, and Mr. Grant increased his after-tax cash flow by $3,000.

The Arm's-Length Presumption

An important presumption about market transactions is that the parties are negotiating at arm's length. In other words, each party is dealing in its own economic self-interest, trying to obtain the most advantageous terms possible from the other party. In an **arm's-length transaction,** the parties' consideration of the mutual tax consequences is just one element of their bargaining strategy. If one party suggests a modification to the transaction that directly improves its tax outcome, the other party may not agree unless it can indirectly capture some part of the tax benefit for itself. To do so, the other party might demand more favorable terms with respect to another aspect of the transaction.

This *quid pro quo* is exemplified in the employment contract between Firm M and Mr. Grant. The fact that Mr. Grant's compensation package includes a nontaxable fringe benefit (the insurance coverage) results in a direct tax savings to him. However, the firm captures part of this tax savings by paying less salary to Mr. Grant. In the final analysis, Firm M agreed to a compensation package that includes the fringe benefit because the package minimizes its after-tax cost, not because the package saves income tax for Mr. Grant.

The only interested party worse off because of the final terms of the employment contract is the federal government. The inclusion of a nontaxable fringe benefit in the compensation package costs the Treasury $1,250 in revenue.

Tax Cost to Government		*Initial Compensation Package*	*Final Compensation Package*	*Increase (Decrease) in Tax Revenue*
	Firm M's tax savings	$42,000	$40,250	$ 1,750
	Mr. Grant's tax cost	36,000	33,000	(3,000)
	Net decrease in tax revenue			$(1,250)

In spite of potential revenue loss, the IRS (and state and local tax authorities) generally accept the tax consequences of arm's-length transactions because those consequences reflect economic reality. The IRS understands that parties negotiate to further their respective business objectives and that any favorable tax outcomes are legitimate by-products of these negotiations.

Public Market Transactions

Some business transactions occur in **public markets** that are too large, too impersonal, or too regulated to allow parties to communicate privately and to customize their transactions. Firms entering such markets must accept the terms dictated by the market. For instance, if a firm decides to invest excess working capital in short-term U.S. government bonds, it must purchase the bonds through a federal bank for the prevailing market price. The firm can't negotiate with the selling party (the government) to buy the bonds at a different price. Similarly, the financial characteristics of the bonds such as the interest rate and maturity date are nonnegotiable.

Firms have limited flexibility in tailoring public market transactions to control the tax results. Because buyers and sellers are not involved in direct negotiation, they can't develop a bilateral strategy to improve their joint tax consequences. Any tax planning that does occur must be one-sided.

Fictitious Markets: Related Party Transactions

Objective 6
Distinguish between arm's-length and related party transactions.

The arm's-length presumption is unreliable for transactions between related parties, such as family members or subsidiary corporations owned by the same controlling parent corporation. **Related party transactions** lack the economic tension characteristic of transactions between unrelated parties. In commercial dealings, unrelated parties typically have competing objectives; related parties may have compatible objectives or even share a single objective. Unrelated parties are motivated by self-interest to drive the hardest possible bargain; related parties may be eager to accommodate each other in their negotiations.

If related parties are not dealing at arm's length, no true market exists, and any transaction between them may not reflect economic reality. In this fictitious market setting, related parties are unconstrained by many of the financial considerations that normally drive arm's-length transactions. As a result, they enjoy significant flexibility in controlling the tax consequences of their transactions. The IRS is well aware that related party transactions lack arm's-length rigor and regards the tax consequences with suspicion. If the IRS concludes that a transaction is bogus, it may disallow any favorable tax outcome claimed by the related parties.

Let's examine a related party transaction with a favorable tax outcome.

Related Party Transaction

Mr. and Mrs. Bowen are business owners with a 35 percent marginal tax rate. The couple has a 17-year-old son who is interested in taking over the business at some future date. Mr. and Mrs. Bowen decide to give their son some experience by hiring him as a full-time employee. If Mr. and Mrs. Bowen pay their son a $20,000 annual salary, this deductible payment saves them $7,000 a year in federal income tax.[9] Because the son has so little taxable income, his marginal tax rate is only 10 percent. Consequently, his tax cost of the salary is only $2,000. As a result of this related party transaction, the Bowen family saves $5,000 income tax.

While the federal tax laws don't explicitly prohibit Mr. and Mrs. Bowen from deducting the salary payment to their son, the IRS will carefully scrutinize the employment transaction if it audits the parents' tax return. The familial relationship of the transacting parties suggests that the salary was not negotiated at arm's length. If the IRS examines all the relevant facts, it may discover that the son did not actually perform any valuable services whatsoever for his parents' business. In this extreme case, the employment transaction had no purpose other than tax avoidance, and the IRS may recast the $20,000 payment from parents to child as a gift.[10] Consequently, Mr. and Mrs. Bowen lose their $20,000 tax deduction, the son has no salary income, and the family's anticipated income tax savings disappear.

On the other hand, the relevant facts may indicate that the son is a genuine employee and that his salary is comparable to the salary an unrelated person could have negotiated at arm's length. In this case, the IRS should respect the transaction and accept the favorable tax consequences of the $20,000 salary payment. Whatever the outcome, the lesson from this example should be clear. Whenever related parties transact, they must be aware that the tax authorities may challenge the validity of the transaction. If the related parties can't offer convincing evidence that the terms of the transaction approximate an arm's-length standard, they may forfeit control of the tax consequences altogether.

Conclusion

Estimating cash flows and calculating the net present value of those cash flows are central to the business decision-making process. A manager's ability to determine after-tax cash flows depends on his or her skill in quantifying the tax cost or savings from the transaction. Managers must be familiar with current tax law and must be prepared to make informed assumptions concerning how that law might change in future periods. Managers involved in business negotiations should evaluate the tax implications for all parties to the transaction in formulating an optimal tax strategy.

While managers should view all business taxes as controllable costs, they should understand that the transaction with the least tax cost may not maximize net present value. Business transactions consist of any number of interrelated tax and nontax variables, all of which must be considered in the decision-making process. In the next chapter, we will concentrate on strategies that manipulate the income tax variable. But as we focus on tax planning ideas, remember the basic lesson of this chapter. Cash flows can't be analyzed in a meaningful way until they are stated as after-tax numbers.

[9] Federal payroll taxes are not an issue in this example because such taxes are not levied on wages paid by parents to their children under the age of 18. §3121(b)(3)(A).

[10] When a related party transaction is a blatant tax avoidance scheme, the IRS may impose monetary penalties on the taxpayers. See the discussion of taxpayer negligence and fraud in Chapter 17.

Key Terms

Questions and Problems for Discussion

1. Does the NPV of future cash flows increase or decrease as the discount rate increases?
2. Explain the relationship between the degree of financial risk associated with future cash flows and the discount rate used to compute NPV.
3. Does the after-tax cost of a deductible expense increase or decrease as the taxpayer's marginal income tax rate increases?
4. Firm A and Firm Z are in the same business. Both firms considered spending $10,000 for the exact same reason. The expenditure would be a current deduction for both firms. Firm A decided that the expenditure was worthwhile and spent the money, but Firm Z rejected the expenditure. Can you provide a tax reason to explain these apparently inconsistent decisions?
5. In what circumstance is the before-tax cost of an expenditure equal to its after-tax cost?
6. Corporation N must decide between two opportunities that will generate different cash flows over a five-year period. Describe the circumstances in which the tax cost of the opportunities is a neutral factor in the corporation's decision-making process.
7. Which assumption about the tax consequences of a future transaction is more uncertain: an assumption based on a provision that has been in the Internal Revenue Code for 25 years or an assumption based on a provision that Congress added to the Code two years ago?
8. Which type of tax law provision should be more stable and less uncertain as to its future application: a provision relating to the proper measurement of taxable income or a provision designed to encourage individual taxpayers to engage in a certain economic behavior?
9. In the U.S. system of criminal justice, a person is innocent until proven guilty. Does this general rule apply to disputes between a taxpayer and the IRS?
10. Identify two reasons why a firm's actual marginal tax rate for a year could differ from the projected marginal tax rate for that year.
11. Firm F is negotiating to purchase a multimillion-dollar computer system from the manufacturer. Under applicable state law, Firm F is exempt from sales tax on the purchase. Because the manufacturer discovered this fact, it increased its selling price for the system by $25,000. Is this transaction taking place in a private or a public market?
12. Corporation P owns 85 percent of the outstanding stock of Corporation R. This year, employees of Corporation R performed extensive management services for Corporation P. In return for the services, Corporation P paid a $250,000 fee to Corporation R, which Corporation P reported as a deductible business expense.
    a. Is the consulting arrangement an arm's-length transaction?
    b. If the IRS challenges the validity of Corporation P's deduction, what facts might the corporation offer as evidence of the validity of the payment?

Application Problems

1. Using the present value tables included in Appendix A and Appendix B, compute the NPV of each of the following cash inflows.
   a. $89,000 received at the end of six years. The discount rate is 12 percent.
   b. $3,400 received annually at the end of each of the next 15 years. The discount rate is 9 percent.
   c. A 10-year annuity of $5,000 per annum. The first $5,000 payment is due immediately. The discount rate is 6 percent.
   d. $20,000 received annually at the end of years 1 through 5 followed by $13,000 received annually at the end of years 6 through 10. The discount rate is 15 percent.
2. Taxpayer Y, who has a 15 percent marginal tax rate, invested $50,000 in a bond that pays 9 percent annual interest. Compute Y's annual net cash flow from this investment assuming that:
   a. The interest is tax-exempt income.
   b. The interest is taxable income.
3. Taxpayer D has $100,000 in an investment paying 12 percent taxable interest per annum. Each year D incurs $1,500 of expenses relating to this investment. Compute D's annual net cash flow assuming the following.
   a. D's marginal tax rate is 15 percent, and the annual expense is deductible.
   b. D's marginal tax rate is 35 percent, and the annual expense is deductible.
   c. D's marginal tax rate is 25 percent, and the annual expense is not deductible.
   d. D's marginal tax rate is 35 percent, and only $1,000 of the annual expense is deductible.
4. Firm E must choose between two alternative transactions. Transaction 1 requires a $9,000 cash outlay that would be nondeductible in the computation of taxable income. Transaction 2 requires a $13,500 cash outlay that would be a deductible expense. Determine which transaction has the lesser after-tax cost, assuming that:
   a. Firm E's marginal tax rate is 20 percent.
   b. Firm E's marginal tax rate is 40 percent.
5. Firm Q is about to engage in a transaction with the following cash flows over a three-year period.

	Year 0	Year 1	Year 2
Taxable revenue	$10,000	$12,500	$18,000
Deductible expenses	(3,400)	(5,000)	(7,000)
Nondeductible expenses	(800)	(1,100)	–0–

   If the firm's marginal tax rate over the three-year period is 35 percent and its discount rate is 10 percent, compute the NPV of the transaction.
6. Corporation ABC invested in a project that will generate $60,000 annual after-tax cash flow in years 0 and 1 and $40,000 annual after-tax cash flow in years 2, 3, and 4. Compute the NPV of these cash flows assuming that:
   a. ABC uses a 7 percent discount rate.
   b. ABC uses a 10 percent discount rate.
   c. ABC uses a 12 percent discount rate.

7. Firm W has the opportunity to invest $150,000 in a new venture. The projected cash flows from the venture are as follows.

	Year 0	*Year 1*	*Year 2*	*Year 3*
Initial investment	$(150,000)			
After-tax cash flow		$11,000	$16,000	$ 18,000
Return of investment				150,000
Net cash flow	$(150,000)	$11,000	$16,000	$168,000

Determine if Firm W should make the investment, assuming that:

a. It uses a 15 percent discount rate to compute NPV.

b. It uses a 9 percent discount rate to compute NPV.

8. Firm X has the opportunity to invest $200,000 in a new venture. The projected cash flows from the venture are as follows.

	Year 0	*Year 1*	*Year 2*	*Year 3*
Initial investment	$(200,000)			
Revenues		$40,000	$40,000	$ 40,000
Expenses		(25,000)	(7,000)	(7,000)
Return of investment				200,000
Before-tax net cash flow	$(200,000)	$15,000	$33,000	$233,000

Firm X uses an 8 percent discount rate to compute NPV, and its marginal tax rate over the life of the venture will be 35 percent. Determine if Firm X should make the investment, assuming that:

a. The revenues are taxable income, and the expenses are deductible.

b. The revenues are taxable income, but the expenses are nondeductible.

9. Firm E operates in a jurisdiction that levies an income tax with the following rate structure.

Percentage Rate	*Bracket*
7%	Income from –0– to $75,000
10	Income from $75,001 to $150,000
15	Income in excess of $150,000

Firm E has the opportunity to invest in a project that should generate $20,000 additional taxable income for the year. Compute the tax cost of this additional income assuming that:

a. Firm E's taxable income before considering the additional income is $130,000.

   b. Firm E's taxable income before considering the additional income is $2 million.
   c. Firm E has an $8,000 loss before considering the additional income.

10. Refer to the facts in the preceding problem. Now assume that Firm E incurs an $18,000 deductible expense. Compute the current year tax savings from the deduction assuming that:
    a. Firm E's taxable income before considering the additional deduction is $50,000.
    b. Firm E's taxable income before considering the additional deduction is $160,000.
    c. Firm E has a $4,000 loss before considering the additional deduction.
11. Company DL must choose between two business opportunities. Opportunity 1 will generate $14,000 before-tax cash in years 0 through 3. The annual tax cost of Opportunity 1 is $2,500 in years 0 and 1 and $1,800 in years 2 and 3. Opportunity 2 will generate $14,000 before-tax cash in year 0, $20,000 before-tax cash in years 1 and 2, and $10,000 before-tax cash in year 3. The annual tax cost of Opportunity 2 is $4,000 in years 0 through 3. Which opportunity should Company DL choose if it uses a 10 percent discount rate to compute NPV?
12. M&B must choose between two business opportunities. Opportunity 1 will generate an $8,000 deductible loss in year 0, $5,000 taxable income in year 1, and $20,000 taxable income in year 2. Opportunity 2 will generate $5,000 taxable income in years 0 through 2. The income and loss reflect before-tax cash inflow and outflow. M&B uses a 12 percent discount rate to compute NPV and has a 40 percent marginal tax rate over the three-year period.
    a. Which opportunity should M&B choose?
    b. Would your answer change if M&B's marginal tax rate over the three-year period is 15 percent?
    c. Would your answer change if M&B's marginal tax rate is 40 percent in year 0 but only 15 percent in years 1 and 2?

Issue Recognition Problems

Identify the tax issue or issues suggested by the following situations, and state each issue in the form of a question.

1. Mr. and Mrs. J's taxable income from their business has been stable for the last five years, and their average federal income tax rate has ranged between 22 and 24 percent. Because of a boom in the local economy, the couple estimates that their business will generate an additional $100,000 taxable income next year. In making their cash flow projections, they estimate that their federal income tax cost with respect to this incremental income will be $24,000.
2. Firm V must choose between two alternative investment opportunities. On the basis of current tax law, the firm projects that the NPV of Opportunity 1 is significantly less than the NPV of Opportunity 2. The provisions in the tax law governing the tax consequences of Opportunity 1 have been stable for many years. In contrast, the provisions governing the tax consequences of Opportunity 2 are extremely complicated and have been modified by Congress several times during the last five years.
3. Company WB is evaluating a business opportunity with uncertain tax consequences. If the company takes a conservative approach by assuming the least beneficial tax consequences, the tax cost is $95,000. If the company takes an aggressive approach by assuming the most beneficial tax consequences, the tax cost is only $86,000. If the company takes the aggressive approach, the IRS will certainly challenge the approach on audit.

4. Refer to the facts in Problem 3. Company WB is considering engaging a CPA to prepare a request for a private letter ruling from the IRS concerning the tax consequences of the business opportunity.
5. Ms. O is the chief financial officer for Firm XYZ. The marketing department requested approval for an $80,000 cash expenditure. The request points out that the expenditure would be deductible. Therefore, the marketing department concludes that Ms. O should approve the expenditure because it would reduce XYZ's tax cost.
6. Earlier in the year, Mrs. G, a business manager for Company RW, evaluated a prospective opportunity that could generate $20,000 additional taxable income. Mrs. G determined that the company's marginal tax rate on this income would be 25 percent. Later in the year, a different manager evaluated another opportunity that could generate $100,000 additional taxable income. This manager referred to Mrs. G's earlier evaluation and used the same 25 percent marginal rate in his analysis of after-tax cash flows.
7. Firm UW is about to enter into a venture that will generate taxable income for the next six to eight years. The director of tax has come up with an idea to restructure the venture in a way that will reduce tax costs by at least 5 percent.
8. DLT's chief operating officer is negotiating the acquisition of a controlling interest in the stock of AA Inc. from Mr. and Mrs. A. The director of tax suggested that the acquisition be structured as a nontaxable transaction to Mr. and Mrs. A. The CEO rejected the suggestion by saying, "Since DLT is the purchaser, our negotiating team doesn't really care if the structure of the acquisition saves taxes for the seller."
9. Ms. S is the sole shareholder and chief executive officer of SMJ Corporation. Ms. S's college roommate recently lost her job, is in financial difficulty, and has asked Ms. S for a loan. Instead of a loan, Ms. S offered the roommate a job with SMJ at a $35,000 annual salary.

Tax Planning Cases

1. Firm B wants to hire Mrs. X to manage its advertising department. The firm offered Mrs. X a three-year employment contract under which it will pay her an $80,000 annual salary in years 0, 1, and 2. Mrs. X projects that her salary will be taxed at a 25 percent rate in year 0 and a 40 percent rate in years 1 and 2. Firm B's tax rate for the three-year period is 34 percent.
   a. Assuming an 8 percent discount rate for both Firm B and Mrs. X, compute the NPV of Mrs. X's after-tax cash flow from the employment contract and Firm B's after-tax cost of the employment contract.
   b. To reduce her tax cost, Mrs. X requests that the salary payment for year 0 be increased to $140,000 and the salary payments for years 1 and 2 be reduced to $50,000. How would this revision in the timing of the payments change your NPV computation for both parties?
   c. Firm B responds to Mrs. X's request with a counterproposal. It will pay her $140,000 in year 0 but only $45,000 in years 1 and 2. Compute the NPV of Firm B's after-tax cost under this proposal. From the firm's perspective, is this proposal superior to its original offer ($80,000 annually for three years)?
   d. Should Mrs. X accept the original offer or the counterproposal? Support your conclusion with a comparison of the NPV of each offer.
2. Firm D is considering investing $400,000 cash in a three-year project with the following cash flows.

	Year 0	*Year 1*	*Year 2*
Investment/ return of investment	$(400,000)	–0–	$400,000
Revenues	80,000	$ 65,000	35,000
Expenses	(25,000)	(25,000)	(10,000)
Before-tax net cash flow	$(345,000)	$ 40,000	$425,000

Under each of the following assumptions, determine if Firm D should make the investment. In each case, use a 10 percent discount rate to compute NPV.

a. The revenue is taxable, the expenses are deductible, and the marginal tax rate is 15 percent.

b. The revenue is taxable, the expenses are deductible, and the marginal tax rate is 40 percent.

c. The revenue is taxable, only one-half the expenses are deductible, and the marginal tax rate is 15 percent.

d. Firm D can deduct the expenses in the year paid (against other sources of income) but can defer recognizing the $180,000 total income until year 2. (It will *collect* the revenues as indicated in years 0, 1, and 2 so that before-tax cash flows do not change.) The marginal tax rate is 40 percent.

Chapter Four

Basic Maxims of Income Tax Planning

Learning Objectives

After studying this chapter, you should be able to:

1. Differentiate between tax avoidance and tax evasion.
2. List the four variables that determine the tax consequences of a transaction.
3. Explain why an income shift or a deduction shift between entities can improve NPV.
4. Explain how the assignment of income doctrine constrains income-shifting strategies.
5. Identify the circumstances in which a strategy that defers tax may not improve NPV.
6. Contrast the tax character of ordinary income and capital gain.
7. Distinguish between an explicit tax and an implicit tax.
8. Summarize the four basic tax planning maxims.
9. Describe the three tax law doctrines that the IRS can use to challenge a tax planning strategy.

In the preceding chapter, we learned that the concept of net present value (NPV) plays a key role in the business decision-making process and that the computation of NPV incorporates tax costs as cash outflows and tax savings as cash inflows. With these lessons in mind, we begin Chapter 4 by defining **tax planning** as the structuring of transactions to reduce tax costs or increase tax savings to maximize the NPV of the transaction.

Why does the structure of a business transaction matter in the tax planning process? Specifically, what are the variables that determine the tax outcome of the transaction? These questions are addressed in the first section of the chapter. Our study of the variables leads to the development of *income tax planning maxims*—basic principles that are the foundation for many planning techniques discussed in subsequent chapters. We will analyze how these maxims improve the tax outcomes of business transactions. We will also identify the major limitations on their use in the planning process. In the final section of the chapter, we will consider how managers use the maxims to develop tax strategies for their firms and why managers must be cognizant of how the Internal Revenue Service (IRS) may react to their strategies.

TAX AVOIDANCE—NOT EVASION

Objective 1
Differentiate between tax avoidance and tax evasion.

Tax Talk
Several years ago, Black & Decker Corporation implemented a tax plan that saved over $57 million in tax. The IRS challenged the plan in federal court because the purpose of the plan was obviously to reduce tax. The court agreed that the plan was motivated primarily by tax avoidance. However, the plan was perfectly legal and had economic substance, so the court ruled that Black & Decker was entitled to its tax savings.

Our discussion in this and subsequent chapters is restricted to tax planning ideas that are entirely legal. Legitimate means of reducing taxes are described as **tax avoidance;** illegal means to the same end constitute **tax evasion.** Tax evasion is a federal crime—a felony offense punishable by severe monetary fines and imprisonment.[1] The qualitative difference between avoidance and evasion is in the eye of the beholder. Many aggressive tax plans involve major questions of judgment. Taxpayers eager to implement these plans run the risk that the IRS will conclude that the plan crosses the line between a good faith effort to reduce tax and a willful attempt to defraud the U.S. government. Business managers should always exercise caution and consult a tax professional before engaging in any transaction with profound tax consequences.

Even if tax avoidance strategies are legal, are they ethical? In 1947, federal judge Learned Hand answered this question in the following way:

> Over and over again courts have said that there is nothing sinister in so arranging one's affairs as to keep taxes as low as possible. Everybody does so, rich or poor; and all do right, for nobody owes any public duty to pay more than the law demands: taxes are enforced exactions, not voluntary contributions. To demand more in the name of morals is mere cant.[2]

This spirited defense of tax planning makes the point that every person has the civic responsibility of paying the legally required tax and not a penny more. Business managers should be reassured that when they engage in effective tax planning, they are engaging in proper behavior from the perspective of their firm, their government, and society.

WHAT MAKES INCOME TAX PLANNING POSSIBLE?

The federal income tax system applies to every entity conducting a business activity in the United States. If the tax law applied uniformly to every commercial transaction by every entity in every time period, it would be neutral and therefore irrelevant in the business decision-making process. However, as we will observe over and over again, the income tax is anything but neutral. The tax system is replete with rules affecting only particular transactions, entities, or time periods. In every case in which the law applies differentially to a certain dollar of business profit or cost, a planning opportunity is born.

The tax consequences of a transaction depend on the interaction of four variables common to all transactions.

Objective 2
List the four variables that determine the tax consequences of a transaction.

1. The entity variable: Which entity undertakes the transaction?
2. The time period variable: During which tax year or years does the transaction occur?
3. The jurisdiction variable: In which taxing jurisdiction does the transaction occur?
4. The character variable: What is the tax character of the income from the transaction?

We will focus on each variable in turn to learn why the variable matters and how it can be manipulated to change the tax outcome of the transaction.

[1] The civil and criminal penalties for tax evasion are discussed in Chapter 17.

[2] *Commissioner* v. *Newman*, 159 F.2d 848, 850 (CA-2, 1947).

THE ENTITY VARIABLE

In the federal tax system, individuals and corporations are the two primary entities that pay tax on business income. While trusts and estates are also taxable entities, they don't routinely engage in the active conduct of a business. For this reason, this text doesn't address the specialized rules governing the income taxation of trusts and estates. Businesses can be organized as sole proprietorships, partnerships, LLCs, or S corporations, but these organizational forms are not taxable entities. Income generated by a proprietorship, partnership, LLC, or S corporation is taxed to the proprietor, partners, members, or shareholders. The operation of these passthrough entities is examined in detail in Chapter 9.

For the most part, the provisions in the Internal Revenue Code governing the computation of taxable income apply uniformly across organizational forms.[3] In other words, the *amount of taxable income* from a business activity does not depend on the type of entity conducting the business; the tax law is essentially neutral across entities with respect to the tax base. So why do the tax consequences of business transactions depend on which entity undertakes the transaction? The answer lies in the potential difference between applicable *tax rates*.

Section 1 of the Internal Revenue Code provides the tax rate structure for individuals, which currently consists of six income brackets with rates ranging from 10 percent to 35 percent. Section 11 provides a completely different rate structure for corporations; the corporate rates range from 15 percent to 39 percent. (The rates for both individuals and corporations are printed on the inside front cover of the text.) Both the individual and corporate rate structures are progressive, so that the tax on a given dollar of business income depends on the marginal rate of the entity earning that dollar.[4] An entity with a lower marginal rate will pay less tax on a dollar of income than an entity with a higher marginal rate. Consequently, the after-tax value of the dollar is greater to the low-tax entity than to the high-tax entity.

Tax Rate Differential

Entity H has a 39 percent marginal tax rate while Entity L has a 15 percent marginal tax rate. Both receive $100 cash that represents taxable income. The after-tax cash available to each entity is computed as follows.

	Entity H	*Entity L*
Cash received	$100	$100
Tax cost ($100 income × marginal rate)	(39)	(15)
After-tax cash	$ 61	$ 85

A comparison of the tax consequences to Entities H and L suggests our first income tax planning maxim: *Tax costs decrease (and cash flows increase) when income is generated by an entity subject to a low tax rate.*

This maxim is especially important when entrepreneurs are starting a new venture and must decide which organizational form to adopt. The choice of organizational form determines whether the business income will be taxed at the individual rates or the corporate

[3] The few special provisions applying only to businesses operated in the corporate form are discussed in Chapter 10.

[4] A complete discussion of the intricacies of the corporate rate structure is included in Chapter 10.

rates. Chapter 11 provides an in-depth discussion of the tax implications of the choice of organizational form for new businesses.

Income Shifting

Objective 3
Explain why an income shift or a deduction shift between entities can improve NPV.

The first maxim implies that the tax on business income can be reduced if that income is shifted from an entity with a high tax rate to an entity with a low tax rate. Assume that Entity H in the previous example could redirect its $100 cash receipt (and the income represented by the cash) to Entity L.

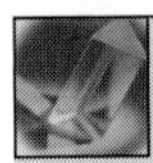

Income Shift

Entity H and Entity L both expect to receive $100 cash that represents taxable income. Entity H arranges to shift its $100 to Entity L. The after-tax cash available to each entity is computed as follows.

	Entity H	*Entity L*
Cash received	–0–	$200
Tax cost (taxable income × marginal rate)	–0–	(30)
After-tax cash	–0–	$170

This income shift reduces the tax on the shifted $100 from $39 to $15 and increases the after-tax cash from $61 to $85. However, that after-tax cash now belongs to Entity L rather than to Entity H. From Entity H's perspective, the income shift *reduces* its after-tax cash flow from $61 to zero. On the presumption that Entity H makes rational decisions, this transaction makes sense only if Entity H controls, enjoys, or benefits from the shifted cash in some manner. One possible explanation is that Entity L is a corporation and Entity H is its sole shareholder. In such case, any cash shifted from Shareholder H to Corporation L increases the value of Corporation L's stock and still belongs indirectly to Shareholder H. Although Shareholder H holds less cash, Shareholder H's wealth (which includes the value of Corporation L stock) increases by the $24 tax savings from the income shift.

Deduction Shifting

Entities with different marginal rates can save tax not only by shifting income but also by shifting deductible expenses. To illustrate a deduction shift, let's use Entities H and L again.

Deduction Shift

Entity L expects to pay an $80 expense that is fully deductible in computing taxable income. Because Entity L is in a 15 percent marginal tax bracket, the $80 deduction would save $12 in tax, and the after-tax cost of the payment is $68.

Cash expended by Entity L	$(80)
Tax savings ($80 deduction × 15%)	12
After-tax cost	$(68)

If Entity H could make the $80 payment on behalf of Entity L and claim the $80 deduction on its own tax return, the tax savings would increase to $31 and the after-tax cost would decrease to $49:

Cash expended by Entity H	$(80)
Tax savings ($80 deduction × 39%)	31
After-tax cost	$(49)

Because the deduction is shifted from the entity with the low tax rate to the entity with the high tax rate, the cash outflow with respect to the expense decreases by $19. But the shift actually increases Entity H's cash outflow by $49. Entity H would never agree to this strategy unless it derives some indirect economic benefit from the tax savings.

Constraints on Income Shifting

Because income-shifting transactions involve transfers of value from one party to another, they usually occur between related parties. After the income shift, the parties *in the aggregate* are financially better off by the tax savings from the transaction. Congress has long recognized that income-shifting techniques lose revenue for the Treasury. Many effective techniques that were once widely used by related parties have been abolished by legislation; in subsequent chapters, we will consider a number of powerful statutory restrictions on income shifting. The IRS is vigilant in policing related party transactions involving beneficial income shifts. If a transaction serves no genuine purpose besides tax avoidance, the IRS may disallow the tax consequences intended by the parties.

Assignment of Income Doctrine

Objective 4
Explain how the assignment of income doctrine constrains income-shifting strategies.

The federal courts have consistently held that our income tax system cannot tolerate artificial shifts of income from one taxpayer to another. Almost 75 years ago, the Supreme Court decided that income must be taxed to the person who earns it, even if another person has a legal right to the wealth represented by the income.[5] Thus, a business owner who receives a $10,000 check in payment for services rendered to a client can't avoid reporting $10,000 income by simply endorsing the check over to his daughter. In the picturesque language of the Court, the tax law must disregard arrangements "by which the fruits are attributed to a different tree from that on which they grew."

The Supreme Court elaborated on this theme in the case of a father who detached negotiable interest coupons from corporate bonds and gave the coupons to his son as a gift.[6] When the coupons matured, the son collected the interest and reported it as income on his own tax return. The Court concluded that the interest income was taxable to the father because he continued to own the underlying asset (the bonds) that created the right to the interest payments. The holdings in these two cases have melded into the **assignment of income doctrine:** Income must be taxed to the entity that renders the service or owns the capital with respect to which the income is paid. Over the years, the IRS has frustrated many creative income-shifting schemes by invoking this simple, but potent, doctrine.

[5] *Lucas* v. *Earl*, 281 U.S. 111 (1930).

[6] *Helvering* v. *Horst*, 311 U.S. 112 (1940).

THE TIME PERIOD VARIABLE

Because both federal and state income taxes are imposed annually, the tax costs or savings from a transaction depend on the year in which the transaction occurs. In Chapter 3, we learned that these costs and savings are a function of the firm's marginal tax rate. If that rate changes from one taxable year to the next, the tax costs and savings fluctuate accordingly. We've also discussed the fact that the technical details of the federal and state income tax systems change periodically. A tax benefit available in one year may disappear in the next. Conversely, a statutory restriction causing a tax problem this year may be lifted in the future. Managers must be aware of annual changes in the tax laws pertaining to their business operations. By controlling the timing of transactions, they may reduce the tax cost or increase the tax savings for their firm.

Even if marginal tax rates and the tax law were absolutely stable over time, the tax costs and savings from transactions would still vary with the time period during which the transaction occurs. This variation is because of the time value of money. In present value terms, a tax dollar paid this year costs more than a tax dollar paid in a future year. Conversely, a tax dollar saved this year is worth more than a tax dollar saved in the future. Consider a transaction that takes place over two taxable years. In the first year (year 0), Firm R receives \$120 revenues and pays \$40 expenses. In the next year (year 1), it receives \$180 revenues and pays \$80 expenses. If the revenues are taxable when received and the expenses are deductible when paid, Firm R has \$80 taxable income in the first year and \$100 taxable income in the next year. If it has a 35 percent tax rate for the two-year period and uses a 12 percent discount rate, the NPV of the cash flows is \$110.

		Year 0		Year 1
Revenues		\$120		\$180
Expenses		(40)		(80)
Income tax cost:				
Taxable income	\$80		\$100	
	.35		.35	
Tax cost		(28)		(35)
After-tax net cash flow		\$ 52		\$ 65
Present value of year 0 cash flow		\$ 52		
Present value of year 1 cash flow (\$65 × .893 discount factor)		58		
NPV		\$110		

Now assume that Firm R could restructure the transaction in a way that *doesn't affect before-tax cash flows* but allows it to report the entire \$180 taxable income (and pay the \$63 tax thereon) in year 1.[7]

[7] For purposes of computing NPV, before-tax cash flows, tax costs, and tax savings in the same taxable year are assumed to occur at the same point in time.

		Year 0		Year 1
Revenues		$120		$180
Expenses		(40)		(80)
Income tax cost:				
Taxable income	–0–		$180	
			.35	
Tax cost		–0–		(63)
After-tax net cash flow		$ 80		$ 37
Present value of year 0 cash flow		$ 80		
Present value of year 1 cash flow ($37 × .893 discount factor)		33		
NPV		$113		

The NPV of Firm R's restructured transaction is $3 more than that of the original transaction. This entire increase is attributable to the deferral of a $28 tax cost for one year. The only difference in the transactions is one of timing. This observation suggests our second income tax planning maxim: *In present value terms, tax costs decrease (and cash flows increase) when a tax is deferred until a later taxable year.*

Income Deferral and Opportunity Costs

The restructured transaction in the preceding example represents an ideal situation in which a firm defers the payment of tax without affecting before-tax cash flows from the transaction. Realistically, firms can defer tax only by deferring the taxable income generated by the transaction, which may be difficult to do without affecting cash flows. A tax deferral strategy that does affect before-tax cash flows may not improve NPV. To illustrate this possibility, assume that Firm R avoids taxable income in year 0 by delaying the receipt of $80 revenues until year 1. Let's recompute the NPV of the transaction based on this assumption.

		Year 0		Year 1
Revenues		$ 40		$260
Expenses		(40)		(80)
Income tax cost:				
Taxable income	–0–		$180	
			.35	
Tax cost		–0–		(63)
After-tax net cash flow		–0–		$117
Present value of year 0 cash flow		–0–		
Present value of year 1 cash flow ($117 × .893 discount factor)		$104		
NPV		$104		

In this transaction, the NPV is $6 *less* than that of the original transaction. While Firm R defers a $28 tax cost for one year, it also delays the receipt of $80 cash. The net result is that Firm R loses the use of $52 for one year at an opportunity cost of $6 ($52 − [$52 × .893 discount factor]).

Instead of delaying the receipt of revenues, what if Firm R could defer taxable income by paying all the expenses in the first year?

		Year 0		Year 1
Revenues		$120		$180
Expenses		(120)		–0–
Income tax cost:				
Taxable income	–0–		$180	
			.35	
Tax cost		–0–		(63)
After-tax net cash flow		–0–		$117
Present value of year 0 cash flow		–0–		
Present value of year 1 cash flow ($117 × .893 discount factor)		$104		
NPV		$104		

This alternative method for deferring taxable income has exactly the same negative effect on NPV. By deferring a $28 tax cost and accelerating the payment of $80 expenses, Firm R deprives itself of the use of $52 for one year at an opportunity cost of $6. In both transactions, the advantage of tax deferral is overwhelmed by a disadvantageous change in before-tax cash flows. Consequently, we can conclude that our second tax planning maxim holds true only when a tax payment can be deferred independently of before-tax cash flows or when the value of the deferral exceeds any opportunity cost of a coinciding change in before-tax cash flows.

Income Deferral and Rate Changes

Objective 5
Identify the circumstances in which a strategy that defers tax may not improve NPV.

The deferral of taxable income into future years creates uncertainty as to the marginal rate that will apply to that income. The value of the deferral could be reduced if Congress were to increase the statutory rates or if the firm were to move unexpectedly into a higher tax bracket. The risk that deferred income will be taxed at a higher rate escalates with the length of the deferral period. To illustrate this problem, assume that Firm N, which is in a 35 percent marginal tax bracket, generates $30,000 profit on a transaction. It has the choice of reporting the entire profit as current year income or reporting the profit as income ratably over the next three years at no opportunity cost. Firm N chooses the deferral strategy based on the following projection (which uses a 9 percent discount rate).

	Year 0	Year 1	Year 2	Year 3
Without deferral:				
Taxable income	$30,000	–0–	–0–	–0–
Tax cost at 35%	$10,500	–0–	–0–	–0–
NPV of tax costs	$10,500			

With deferral:				
Taxable income	–0–	$10,000	$10,000	$10,000
Tax cost at 35%	–0–	$ 3,500	$ 3,500	$ 3,500
Discount factors		.917	.842	.772
		$ 3,210	$ 2,947	$ 2,702
NPV of tax costs	$ 8,859			

Now assume that Firm N's marginal tax rate in years 1 through 3 jumps to 45 percent because of a change in the tax law. As a result, the tax costs in years 1 through 3 are much higher than projected.

	Year 0	Year 1	Year 2	Year 3
Taxable income	–0–	$10,000	$10,000	$10,000
Tax cost at 45%	–0–	$ 4,500	$ 4,500	$ 4,500
Discount factors		.917	.842	.772
		$ 4,127	$ 3,789	$ 3,474
Actual NPV of tax costs	$11,390			

Because the value of deferring the tax cost is insufficient to compensate for the higher rate at which the deferred income is actually taxed, Firm N's choice to defer the income *increased* the tax cost of the transaction by $890 in present value terms.

Actual NPV of tax costs	$ 11,390
NPV of tax cost without deferral	(10,500)
	$ 890

THE JURISDICTION VARIABLE

Every domestic business is subject to the taxing jurisdiction of the federal government. Therefore, the geographic location of a firm within the United States is a neutral factor in the computation of its federal income tax. However, most states and the District of Columbia also tax business income. Because of the differences in state tax systems, a firm's aggregate income tax liability (federal, state, and local) is very much a function of the jurisdictions in which it conducts business.

Consider two domestic firms that each receive $5,000 cash, all of which is taxable income. Firm Y operates in State Y, which imposes a flat 4 percent tax on business income. Firm Z operates in State Z, which imposes a flat 10 percent tax on business income. For federal purposes, state income tax payments are deductible in the computation of taxable income.[8] Both firms face a 39 percent federal tax rate. Under these facts, Firms Y and Z have the following after-tax cash flows.

[8] §164(a).

	Firm Y	Firm Z
Before-tax cash/income	$5,000	$5,000
State income tax cost	(200)	(500)
Federal taxable income	$4,800	$4,500
Federal tax cost		
(Taxable income × 39%)	(1,872)	(1,755)
After-tax cash flow	$2,928	$2,745

A comparison of these after-tax cash flows gives us our third income tax planning maxim: *Tax costs decrease (and cash flows increase) when income is generated in a jurisdiction with a low tax rate.*

The comparison between the after-tax cash flows of Firms Y and Z would be more complex if these firms operate in any foreign country that taxes business income. Clearly, managers must be aware of the income tax laws of every locality in which their firm operates or plans to operate in the future. Managers should appreciate that they can often minimize the total tax burden by conducting business in jurisdictions with favorable tax climates. The intricacies of tax planning in a multijurisdictional setting are the subject of Chapter 12.

THE CHARACTER VARIABLE

The fourth variable that determines the tax consequences of transactions is the tax character of the income generated by the transaction. The tax character of any item of income is determined strictly by law; it is not intuitive and may bear no relationship to any financial or economic attribute of the income. In addition, the character of income and the ramifications of that characterization can change with each new tax bill passed by Congress or each new regulation published by the Treasury. Because the character variable is artificial, it is the hardest one to discuss in a generalized manner.

Objective 6
Contrast the tax character of ordinary income and capital gain.

Every item of income is ultimately characterized for tax purposes as either **ordinary income** or **capital gain.** The income generated by routine sales of goods or services to customers or clients is ordinary income. The yield on invested capital, such as interest, dividends, and rents, is also ordinary in character. As the label implies, ordinary income is typically taxed at the regular individual or corporate rates. The sale or exchange of certain types of property, referred to as capital assets, gives rise to capital gain. The term *capital asset* is defined in detail in Chapter 7. Historically, capital gain has enjoyed favorable treatment under the federal tax law, usually in the form of a preferential tax rate. Currently, individuals (but not corporations) pay tax on their capital gains at a 28, 25, 15, or 5 percent rate.[9]

Many items of ordinary income and capital gain have additional characteristics that affect the tax on the income. For instance, the ordinary income earned by a U.S. firm conducting business both in the United States and foreign countries is characterized as either U.S. source income or foreign source income. As we will discuss in Chapter 12, this characterization is crucial in determining how much federal income tax the firm must pay on its ordinary income.

[9] The preferential rates apply only to long-term capital gains. The Jobs and Growth Tax Relief Reconciliation Act of 2003 extended the 15 percent and 5 percent preferential rates to dividend income. Chapter 15 includes a detailed discussion of the individual preferential rates.

To demonstrate the effect of the character variable, let's compare the cash flow consequences of three different items of income received by Mr. Thompson, who has a 35 percent regular marginal tax rate. Each item consists of $1,000 cash. The first item is ordinary income with no other special characteristic; the second item is capital gain eligible for the 15 percent rate; and the third item is interest on a bond issued by the City of New York. While interest generically is ordinary income, municipal bond interest has a very special characteristic—it is exempt from federal income tax. In other words, municipal bond interest is taxed at a preferential rate of zero.

	Ordinary Income	Capital Gain	Tax-Exempt Income
Before-tax cash/income	$1,000	$1,000	$1,000
Tax cost	(350)	(150)	–0–
After-tax cash flow	$ 650	$ 850	$1,000

The fact that the character of income determines whether the income is taxed at the regular rate or at a special rate suggests our fourth tax planning maxim: *Tax costs decrease (and cash flows increase) when income is taxed at a preferential rate because of its character.*

Determining the Value of Preferential Rates

The value of a preferential rate to a particular taxpayer can be quantified only by reference to that taxpayer's regular marginal rate. In the above example, the $200 difference between the after-tax cash flow from the ordinary income and the capital gain is due to the 20 percentage point spread between Mr. Thompson's 35 percent regular tax rate and the 15 percent preferential rate on the capital gain. If Mr. Thompson's marginal rate on ordinary income is only 28 percent, the 13 percentage point spread between the regular rate and the preferential rate results in only a $130 difference in after-tax cash flow.

	Ordinary Income	Capital Gain
Before-tax cash/income	$1,000	$1,000
Tax cost (28% regular rate)	(280)	(150)
After-tax cash flow	$ 720	$ 850

Constraints on Conversion

For many years, taxpayers and their advisers have heeded the fourth tax planning maxim by structuring transactions to result in capital gain rather than ordinary income. The more aggressive have devised ingenious techniques for converting the potential ordinary income from a transaction to capital gain. In response, Congress has worked hard to protect the integrity of the distinction between the two types of income. The Internal Revenue Code contains dozens of prohibitions against artificial conversions of ordinary income into capital gain, many of which we will examine in later chapters. In fact, the preferential treatment of capital gains is responsible for more complexity in the federal income tax system than any other feature. Why then does Congress persist in maintaining the capital gains preference? This intriguing tax policy question is addressed in Chapter 15.

Implicit Taxes

Objective 7
Distinguish between an explicit tax and an implicit tax.

The decision to engage in a transaction generating income taxed at a preferential rate should be based on the NPV of the transaction rather than the fact of the preferential rate. The tax cost may not be the only cash flow affected by the tax-favored character of the income. Suppose that Ms. Crowe has $20,000 to invest in either a tax-exempt municipal bond or a corporate bond of identical risk. The interest from the latter would be ordinary income taxed at 33 percent. Let's make an initial assumption that both bonds pay 10 percent interest per annum. A comparison of the annual after-tax cash flows indicates that the municipal bond is the superior investment.

	Corporate Bond Interest	Municipal Bond Interest
Before-tax cash/income	$2,000	$2,000
Tax cost	(660)	–0–
After-tax cash flow	$1,340	$2,000

The assumption that the two bonds offer identical before-tax yields is unrealistic. State and local governments take advantage of the tax-exempt status of their debt obligations by offering lower interest rates than their competitors in the capital markets. They know that many investors will accept the lower rate because of the tax-favored status of the bonds. Let's change our example by assuming that the municipal bond would pay only 8 percent interest on Ms. Crowe's $20,000 investment.

	Corporate Bond Interest	Municipal Bond Interest
Before-tax cash/income	$2,000	$1,600
Tax cost	(660)	–0–
After-tax cash flow	$1,340	$1,600

While the municipal bond is still a better investment than the corporate bond, the value of the preferential tax rate to Ms. Crowe has decreased because of the difference in the bonds' respective before-tax yields. While Ms. Crowe would pay no direct **explicit tax** on the interest from the municipal bond, she must accept a reduced market rate of return to take advantage of the tax preference. In the tax literature, this reduction is referred to as an **implicit tax.**[10]

What if the municipal bond would pay only 6.5 percent interest on the $20,000 investment?

[10] This term was popularized by Myron S. Scholes and Mark A. Wolfson in *Taxes and Business Strategy: A Planning Approach* (Englewood Cliffs, N.J.: Prentice Hall, 1992).

	Corporate Bond Interest	Municipal Bond Interest
Before-tax cash/income	$2,000	$1,300
Tax cost	(660)	-0-
After-tax cash flow	$1,340	$1,300

Now the $700 implicit tax that Ms. Crowe would incur by purchasing the municipal bond (the reduction in the before-tax yield) is greater than the $660 explicit tax on the interest from the corporate bond. Consequently, the after-tax cash generated by the corporate bond exceeds the after-tax cash generated by the tax-favored municipal bond, and Ms. Crowe should invest accordingly.

Municipal bond interest has no inherent financial characteristic that creates a natural immunity to taxation.[11] Congress granted tax-exempt status to this type of income to help state and local governments compete in the capital markets. The loss in revenues attributable to the tax preference represents an indirect federal subsidy to these governments. Whether this tax preference (or any other preference) is worth anything to a given investor depends on the investor's marginal tax rate and any implicit tax on the investment.

DEVELOPING TAX PLANNING STRATEGIES

Our analysis of the variables that determine the tax consequences of transactions resulted in the following maxims.

Objective 8
Summarize the four basic tax planning maxims.

- *Tax costs decrease (and cash flows increase) when income is generated by an entity subject to a low tax rate.*
- *In present value terms, tax costs decrease (and cash flows increase) when a tax is deferred until a later taxable year.*
- *Tax costs decrease (and cash flows increase) when income is generated in a jurisdiction with a low tax rate.*
- *Tax costs decrease (and cash flows increase) when income is taxed at a preferential rate because of its character.*

Tax planning strategies that enhance cash flows typically reflect at least one of these maxims. Many strategies combine two or more maxims working together to minimize taxes. Other strategies may adhere to one maxim but violate another. In such cases, business managers must carefully assess the overall tax consequences to determine if the strategy improves NPV. The following example demonstrates the problem of conflicting maxims.

Conflicting Maxims

Firm MN operates as two separate taxable entities, Entity M and Entity N. The firm is negotiating a transaction that will generate $25,000 cash in year 0 and $60,000 cash in year 1. If Entity M undertakes the transaction, taxable income will correspond to cash flow (i.e., Entity M will report $25,000 and $60,000 taxable income in years 0 and 1). If Entity N undertakes the transaction, it must report the entire $85,000 taxable income in year 0. Entity M has a 30

[11] For state income tax purposes, interest on state and local bonds is generally taxable.

percent marginal tax rate while Entity N has a 25 percent marginal tax rate. Firm MN uses a 9 percent discount rate to compute NPV.

	Entity M		*Entity N*	
Year 0:				
Before-tax cash flow		$25,000		$25,000
Taxable income	$25,000		$85,000	
	.30		.25	
Tax cost		(7,500)		(21,250)
After-tax cash flow		$17,500		$ 3,750
Year 1:				
Before-tax cash flow		$60,000		$60,000
Taxable income	$60,000		-0-	
	.30			
Tax cost		(18,000)		-0-
After-tax cash flow		$42,000		$60,000
Present value of year 0 cash flow		$17,500		$ 3,750
Present value of year 1 cash flow (.917 discount factor)		38,514		55,020
NPV		$56,014		$58,770

On the basis of an NPV comparison, Firm MN should undertake the transaction through Entity N. This strategy adheres to the tax planning maxim that cash flows increase when income is generated by an entity with a low tax rate. However, the strategy accelerates the entire tax on the transaction into year 0, thus violating the maxim that calls for tax deferral.

Additional Strategic Considerations

The four tax planning maxims offer general guidance to the tax planning process. Like all generalizations, each one is subject to conditions, limitations, and exceptions depending on the exact nature of the tax strategy under consideration. Even though the maxims focus on the reduction of tax costs, managers should remember that their strategic goal is not tax minimization per se but NPV maximization. Consequently, they must consider key factors other than tax costs in formulating a winning strategy. One obvious factor is the expense of implementing the strategy. Firms may require professional advice in designing, executing, and monitoring a sophisticated tax plan, and the cost of the advice must be weighed against the potential tax savings from the strategy.

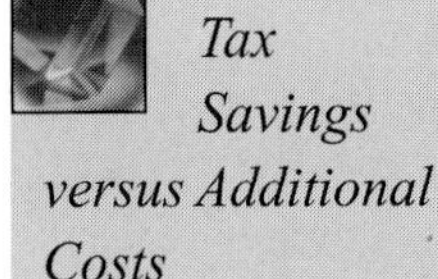

Tax Savings versus Additional Costs

Firm B has a choice between two strategies for reducing its tax with respect to a line of business. The simpler of the two strategies would reduce the annual tax by $50,000 and would not cost anything to implement. The more complex of the two strategies would reduce the annual tax by $70,000 but would require additional legal and accounting fees with an after-tax cost of $25,000. Firm B should choose the simpler strategy because it has the greater value even though it saves less tax.

Managers must consider the economic consequences of tax strategies to all parties. In Chapter 3, we learned that firms negotiating in private markets can work together to maximize the after-tax value of the transaction to both parties. A manager intent on implementing a unilateral tax strategy may miss an opportunity for effective multilateral planning. Even worse, if a manager fails to consider the repercussions of a strategy on other interested parties, those parties might retaliate in ways that diminish the overall value of the strategy to the firm.

Multilateral Planning

Corporation F and Corporation D plan to form a joint venture to conduct a new business. Corporation F's tax cost would be minimized if the business is conducted in Germany. Corporation D's tax cost would be minimized if the business is conducted in the United States. Corporation F agrees to locate the business in the United States, provided that it receives 60 percent of the profit and Corporation D receives only 40 percent. This compromise increases Corporation F's tax cost and decreases Corporation D's before-tax profit. Nevertheless, the corporations agree to the compromise because it maximizes the after-tax value of the joint venture to both corporations.

Tax strategies must be evaluated on the basis of flexibility: the extent to which the strategy can be adapted to unforeseen circumstances. Every strategy's anticipated effect on cash flows is based on assumptions about the future. The more uncertain the assumptions, the greater the risk that the strategy could backfire and have a detrimental effect on cash flows. If the firm can quickly modify or even reverse a failed strategy at minimal cost, this risk may be slight. But if the strategy is irreversible or would be extremely expensive to fix, the cost of potential failure may outweigh the benefit of success.

The Flexibility Factor

Four years ago, Firm D formed a Brazilian corporation to operate its business in South America. Firm D selected the corporate form to take advantage of generous tax preferences available only to Brazilian corporations. This year, Brazil repealed the preferences and substantially increased its corporate tax rate. If Firm D had not formed the corporation, it could easily avoid the tax increase by restructuring its South American operation. But Firm D cannot dissolve the Brazilian corporation without incurring prohibitively high legal and political costs. With hindsight, Firm D would have maximized the after-tax value of its South American operation by choosing a more flexible tax strategy.

Tax Law Doctrines

Objective 9
Describe the three tax law doctrines that the IRS can use to challenge a tax planning strategy.

Managers must be confident that they have identified the correct tax consequences of the strategies implemented by their firm. If a manager makes a technical error in applying the tax law to a critical transaction and the IRS discovers the error on audit, the planning strategy could unravel, with disastrous effects on cash flows. Even when managers believe that a strategy is technically sound, they must consider the government's reaction to the overall propriety of the strategy. Over the years, both the IRS and the federal courts have made taxpayers adhere not only to the letter but also to the spirit of the law. Consequently, three important legal doctrines have evolved in the tax planning area. The IRS can invoke these doctrines when a firm seems to be bending the rules to gain an unjustified tax advantage.

The **business purpose doctrine** holds that a transaction should not be effective for tax purposes unless it has a genuine business purpose other than tax avoidance. The lack of any business purpose by the participants can render a transaction meaningless, at least from the perspective of the IRS, even if the transaction literally complies with the law.[12]

[12] This doctrine originated with the case of *Gregory* v. *Helvering*, 293 U.S. 465 (1935).

Lack of Business Purpose

Mr. Early decided to sell an investment asset. He calculated that the sale would generate a $45,000 gain on which he would pay tax at a 25 percent rate. Mr. Early planned to invest the after-tax cash from the sale in his family business. Instead of selling the asset directly, Mr. Early formed a new corporation to which he contributed the asset. The corporation immediately sold the asset and paid tax on the $45,000 gain at a 15 percent rate. The corporation then made a long-term loan of the after-tax cash from the sale to Mr. Early's family business. If the IRS concludes that Mr. Early had no business purpose for creating the new corporation other than to reap the benefit of the lower corporate tax rate, it could disregard the incorporation transaction. As a result, the IRS would treat Mr. Early as the seller of the asset and require him to pay tax on the gain at his 25 percent rate.[13]

The **substance over form doctrine** holds that the IRS can look through the legal formalities to determine the economic substance (if any) of a transaction. If the substance differs from the form, the IRS will base the tax consequences of the transaction on the reality rather than the illusion.[14]

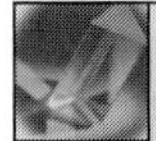

Substance over Form

The sole shareholder and president of Corporation JKL negotiated a leasing contract with a local businessman. Under the terms of the contract, JKL paid $35,000 for the use of equipment for one year and deducted this payment as a business expense. The revenue agent who audited JKL's tax return uncovered two additional facts. First, the local businessman who received the $35,000 was a candidate for state political office and was enthusiastically endorsed by JKL's owner. Second, the corporation had no apparent need for the leased equipment. If these facts convince the agent that the substance of the leasing arrangement was a disguised political contribution (which is completely nondeductible), JKL may lose its $35,000 deduction and the tax savings therefrom.

The **step transaction doctrine** allows the IRS to collapse a series of intermediate transactions into a single transaction to determine the tax consequences of the arrangement in its entirety.[15] The IRS applies the doctrine when transactions are so obviously interdependent that the parties involved would not have consummated the first transaction without anticipating that the whole series of transactions would occur. Transactions occurring within a short period of time are more vulnerable to the step transaction doctrine than those occurring over a longer interval. As a rule of thumb, the IRS considers transactions occurring within a 12-month period as suspect.[16] Transactions separated in time by more than 12 months are presumed to be independent. In tax parlance, the first transaction is "old and cold" with no connection to the second transaction.

Potential Step Transactions

ABC Corporation sells property to an unrelated purchaser who subsequently resells the property to ABC's wholly owned subsidiary. If these two sales occur within the same month, the IRS would certainly question their autonomy. Unless ABC could present evidence to the contrary, the IRS could collapse the two transactions into a direct sale of property from ABC to its subsidiary and recast the tax consequences of this related party transaction. On the other hand, if the first sale occurs five years before the second sale, the substantial length of time between the sales should make them immune to the step transaction doctrine.

[13] *Paymer* v. *Commissioner*, 150 F.2d 334 (CA-2, 1945).

[14] *Commissioner* v. *Danielson*, 378 F.2d 771 (CA-3, 1967), *cert. denied* 389 U.S. 858 (1967).

[15] *Helvering* v. *Alabama Asphaltic Limestone Co.*, 315 U.S. 179 (1942).

[16] Treas. Reg. §1.368-2(c).

Tax Talk
A federal judge ruled that Long-Term Capital Management, the now-defunct hedge fund, used sham transactions with no economic substance to avoid federal taxes and must pay $75 million in taxes, interest, and penalties.

There is considerable overlap in the scope of these three doctrines, and the IRS frequently uses them in combination to challenge an offending transaction. Of course, the courts may or may not uphold the IRS's challenge. Judges or juries may side with the taxpayer by concluding that a transaction has an independent business purpose and an economic substance to match its form. Business managers should understand that the doctrines seem to be the exclusive property of the IRS; taxpayers cannot invoke them to undo the consequences of their own ill-fated tax strategies.[17] Managers should be aware that the IRS's application of these doctrines is extremely subjective. Given the threat of the business purpose, substance over form, and step transaction doctrines, managers can never be absolutely certain that a creative tax plan will work, even if it seems to comply with the letter of the law.

Conclusion

Now that you've completed Part Two of *Principles of Taxation for Business and Investment Planning*, you should appreciate how tax planning strategies can reduce tax costs and increase the NPV of business transactions. The framework for a thorough understanding of the tax planning process is in place. Parts Three and Four of the text build on this framework by presenting the basics of the income tax law: how firms compute annual taxable income and the federal tax on that income. As you integrate this legal knowledge into your understanding of taxes as financial costs, your appreciation of the tax planning process will progress from the abstract to the specific.

Key Terms

assignment of income doctrine *75*
business purpose doctrine *85*
capital gain *80*
explicit tax *82*
implicit tax *82*
ordinary income *80*
step transaction doctrine *86*
substance over form doctrine *86*
tax avoidance *72*
tax evasion *72*
tax planning *71*

Questions and Problems for Discussion

1. For each of the following situations, discuss whether the individual is engaging in tax avoidance or tax evasion.
   a. Mr. L performed minor construction work for a number of individuals who paid him in cash. Because Mr. L knows that there is almost no chance that the IRS could learn of these payments, he reports only half the payments as income on his federal tax return.
   b. Mr. P, who is in the 35 percent tax bracket, recently had the opportunity to invest $50,000 in a new business that should yield an annual return of at least 17 percent. Rather than invest himself, Mr. P gave $50,000 cash to his son, who then made the investment. The son's marginal tax rate is only 15 percent.
   c. Mrs. Q sold an asset during January. Her $12,000 profit on the sale is ordinary income. After preparing her income tax return for the prior year, Mrs. Q realized that her marginal tax rate for that year was 28 percent. She also realized that her marginal rate for this year will be 35 percent. Mrs. Q decides to report the profit on her prior year return to take advantage of the lower tax rate.

[17] *Durkin*, TC Memo 1992-325.

2. Assume that Congress amends the tax law to provide for a maximum 18 percent rate on rental income generated by single-family residences. What effect might this preferential rate have on the market value of this category of real estate?
3. Tax planners often tell their clients that "a tax delayed is a tax not paid." Can you provide a more formal explanation of this bit of wisdom?
4. Mrs. K is about to begin a new business activity and asks you if she can reduce taxable income by operating the activity as a corporation rather than as a sole proprietorship. How do you answer Mrs. K?
5. Is every business organization a taxable entity for federal income tax purposes? Explain briefly.
6. Based on the rates printed on the inside of the front cover, determine the marginal tax rate for:
   a. A corporation with $23,000 taxable income.
   b. A corporation with $250,000 taxable income.
   c. A single (unmarried) individual with $75,000 taxable income.
   d. A single (unmarried) individual with $250,000 taxable income.
7. Assume that the U.S. Congress replaces the current individual and corporate income tax rate structures with a proportionate rate that applies to both types of taxpayers. Discuss the effect of this change in the federal law on tax strategies based on:
   a. The entity variable.
   b. The time period variable.
   c. The jurisdiction variable.
   d. The character variable.
8. Compare the potential tax savings of an income shift from one entity to another if the entities are subject to:
   a. A progressive income tax system with rates from 5 percent to 19 percent.
   b. A progressive income tax system with rates from 10 percent to 50 percent.
   c. A 20 percent proportionate income tax system.
9. Why do income shifts and deduction shifts usually occur between taxpayers who are related parties?
10. Corporation P owns a controlling stock interest in Subsidiary S and Subsidiary T. Corporation P's marginal tax rate is 25 percent. It engages in one transaction that shifts $10,000 income to Subsidiary S and a second transaction that shifts a $15,000 deduction to Subsidiary T. Based on these facts, what conclusions can you draw about marginal tax rates of the two subsidiaries?
11. Firm A expects to receive a $25,000 item of income in August and a second $25,000 item of income in December. The firm could delay the receipt of both items until January. As a result, it would defer the payment of tax on $50,000 income for one full year. Firm A decides to receive the August payment this year (and pay current tax on $25,000 income) but delay the receipt of the December payment. Can you offer an explanation for this decision?
12. Identify the reasons why managers should evaluate the flexibility of a tax planning strategy before implementing the strategy.
13. In June, Congress enacts legislation that increases income tax rates for all entities effective for the next calendar year.
    a. Why might such legislation result in an increase in federal tax revenues for this year?

b. In what way would this legislation create a conflict between tax planning maxims?

14. Mr. T is considering a strategy to defer $10,000 income for five years with no significant opportunity cost. Discuss the strategic implications of the following independent assumptions.
    a. Mr. T is age 24. He graduated from law school last month and accepted a position with a prominent firm of attorneys.
    b. Mr. T is age 63. He plans to retire from business at the end of this year and devote his time to volunteer work and sailing.

Application Problems

1. Refer to the corporate rates schedule printed on the inside of the front cover of the text.
    a. What is the tax liability, the marginal tax rate, and the average tax rate for a corporation with $35,000 taxable income?
    b. What is the tax liability, the marginal tax rate, and the average tax rate for a corporation with $400,000 taxable income?
    c. What is the tax liability, the marginal tax rate, and the average tax rate for a corporation with $17,690,000 taxable income?
    d. What is the tax liability, the marginal tax rate, and the average tax rate for a corporation with $58,632,000 taxable income?
2. Refer to the individual rates schedules printed on the inside of the front cover of the text.
    a. What is the tax liability, the marginal tax rate, and the average tax rate for a married couple filing jointly with $40,000 taxable income?
    b. What is the tax liability, the marginal tax rate, and the average tax rate for a single individual with $175,000 taxable income?
    c. What is the tax liability, the marginal tax rate, and the average tax rate for a head of household with $620,000 taxable income?
3. Ms. JK recently made a gift to her 19-year-old daughter, Alison. Ms. JK's marginal income tax rate is 35 percent and Alison's marginal income tax rate is 15 percent. In each of the following cases, compute the annual income tax savings resulting from the gift.
    a. The gift consisted of a corporate bond paying $7,500 annual interest to its owner.
    b. The gift consisted of the $7,500 interest payment on a corporate bond owned by Ms. JK.
    c. The gift consisted of rental property generating $8,300 annual rental income to its owner.
    d. The gift consisted of an $8,300 rent check written by the tenants who lease rental property owned by Ms. JK.
4. Firm A has a 15 percent marginal tax rate, and Firm Z has a 35 percent marginal tax rate. Firm A owns a controlling interest in Firm Z. The owners of Firm A decide to incur a $40,000 deductible expense that will benefit both firms. Compute the after-tax cost of the expense assuming that:
    a. Firm A incurs the expense.
    b. Firm Z incurs the expense.
5. Firm M and Firm N are related parties. For the past several years, Firm M's marginal tax rate has been 34 percent, and Firm N's marginal tax rate has been 25 percent. Firm M is evaluating a transaction that will generate $10,000 income in each of the next three years. Firm M could restructure the transaction so that the income would shift to Firm N. Because of the restructuring, the annual income would decrease to $9,000. Should Firm M restructure the transaction?

6. Assume that Congress amends the tax law to provide for a maximum 20 percent rate on royalty income. Calculate the annual tax savings from this new preferential rate to each of the following taxpayers.
   a. Mrs. A, who is in a 35 percent marginal tax bracket and receives $70,000 royalty income each year.
   b. Mr. B, who is in a 28 percent marginal tax bracket and receives $15,000 royalty income each year.
   c. Ms. C, who is in a 33 percent marginal tax bracket and receives $8,000 royalty income each year.
   d. Mr. D, who is in a 15 percent marginal tax bracket and receives $3,000 royalty income each year.
7. Firm Q has a 30 percent marginal tax rate and uses a 9 percent discount rate to compute NPV. The firm started a venture that will yield the following before-tax cash flows: year 0, $3,000; year 1, $6,500; year 2, $7,000; year 3, $6,000.
   a. If the before-tax cash flows represent taxable income in the year received, compute the NPV of the cash flows.
   b. Compute the NPV if Firm Q can defer the receipt of years 0 and 1 cash flows/income until year 2. (It would receive no cash in years 0 and 1 and would receive $16,500 cash in year 2.)
   c. Compute the NPV if Firm Q can defer paying tax on years 0 and 1 cash flows until year 2. (It would receive $7,000 cash in year 2 but would pay tax on $16,500 income.)
8. Firm H has the opportunity to engage in a transaction that will generate $100,000 cash flow (and taxable income) in year 0. How does the NPV of the transaction change if the firm could restructure the transaction in a way that does not change before-tax cash flow but results in no taxable income in year 0, $50,000 taxable income in year 1, and the remaining $50,000 taxable income in year 2? Assume a 10 percent discount rate and a 34 percent marginal tax rate for the three-year period.
9. What is the effect on the NPV of the restructured transaction in Problem 8 if Firm H's marginal tax rate in year 2 increases to 39 percent?
10. Mr. G has $15,000 to invest. He is undecided about putting the money into tax-exempt municipal bonds paying 7 percent annual interest or corporate bonds paying 9.5 percent annual interest. The two investments have the same risk.
    a. Which investment should Mr. G make if his marginal tax rate is 33 percent?
    b. Would your conclusion change if Mr. G's marginal tax rate is only 15 percent?
11. At the beginning of the year, Mr. L put $50,000 cash into an investment. At the end of the year, he received a check for $5,000, representing his annual return on the investment. Mr. L's marginal tax rate on ordinary income is 28 percent. However, his return on this particular investment is a capital gain taxed at 15 percent. Compute the value of the preferential rate to Mr. L.
12. Refer to the facts in the preceding problem. At the beginning of the year, Mr. L could have invested his $50,000 in a business with a 12 percent annual return. However, this return would have been ordinary income rather than capital gain.
    a. Considering the fact that Mr. L could have invested in this business, how much implicit tax did he pay with respect to the investment described in the preceding problem?
    b. Did Mr. L make the correct investment decision?
13. Firm L has $500,000 to invest and is considering two alternatives. Investment A would pay 13 percent ($65,000 annual before-tax cash flow). Investment B would pay 9.5 per-

cent ($47,500 annual before-tax cash flow). The return on Investment A is taxable, while the return on Investment B is tax exempt. Firm L forecasts that its 35 percent marginal tax rate will be stable for the foreseeable future.

a. Compute the explicit tax and implicit tax that Firm L will pay with respect to Investment A and Investment B.

b. Which investment results in the greater annual after-tax cash flow?

14. Firm W, which has a 34 percent marginal tax rate, plans to operate a new business that should generate $40,000 annual cash flow/ordinary income for three years (years 0, 1, and 2). Alternatively, Firm W could form a new taxable entity (Entity N) to operate the business. Entity N would pay tax on the three-year income stream at a 25 percent rate. The nondeductible cost of forming Entity N would be $5,000. If Firm W uses a 6 percent discount rate, should it operate the new business directly or form Entity N to operate the business?

Issue Recognition Problems

Identify the tax issue or issues suggested by the following situations, and state each issue in the form of a question.

1. Mr. and Mrs. TR own an investment yielding a 7.2 percent after-tax return. Their friend Ms. K is encouraging them to sell this investment and invest the proceeds in her business, which takes advantage of several favorable tax preferences. Consequently, Ms. K's after-tax return is 8.4 percent.
2. Company QP must decide whether to build a new manufacturing plant in Country B or Country C. Country B has no income tax. However, its political regime is unstable and its currency has been devalued four times in three years. Country C has both a 20 percent income tax and a stable democratic government.
3. Dr. P is a physician with his own medical practice. For the last several years, his marginal income tax rate has been 35 percent. Dr. P's daughter, who is a college student, has no taxable income. During the last two months of the year, Dr. P instructs his patients to remit their payments for his services directly to his daughter.
4. Mrs. Y owns 1,800 shares of Acme common stock, which she purchased for $10 per share in 1990. In October, she decides to sell her Acme stock for the market price of $27 per share, the highest price at which the stock has traded in the last 22 months. A friend advises her to hold onto the Acme stock until next January so that her gain from the sale will be taxed next year rather than this year.
5. In November, Corporation Q negotiated to sell a tract of land to an unrelated buyer. The buyer refused to close the sale until February. Corporation Q wanted to close the sale by year-end so that the gain would be taxed at its current 25 percent rate. Corporation Q's rate for next year will be 39 percent. In December, Corporation Q sold the land to its wholly owned subsidiary. In February, the subsidiary sold the land to the unrelated buyer.
6. Mr. and Mrs. K own rental property that generates $4,000 monthly revenue. The couple is in the highest marginal tax bracket. For Christmas, Mr. and Mrs. K give the uncashed rent checks for October, November, and December to their 19-year-old grandson as a gift.
7. Firm Z is considering implementing a long-term tax strategy to accelerate the deduction of certain business expenses. The strategy has an opportunity cost because it decreases before-tax cash flows, but the tax savings from the strategy should be greater than this opportunity cost. The strategy is aggressive, and the IRS might disallow the intended tax outcome if it audits Firm Z's tax returns.

8. Ms. LG plans to structure a transaction as a legal sale of property, even though the economic substance of the transaction is a lease of the property. In her current position, the tax consequences of a sale are much more favorable than those of a lease. Ms. LG believes that if her position unexpectedly changes so that she would prefer a lease to a sale, she can ignore the legal formalities and report the transaction as a lease.
9. Firm HR is about to implement an aggressive long-term strategy consisting of three phases. It is crucial to the success of the strategy that the IRS accepts Firm HR's interpretation of the tax consequences of each distinct phase. The firm could implement the first phase in November 2005 and the second phase in August 2006. Alternatively, it could delay the second phase until January 2007.

Research Problems

1. Using an electronic library such as RIA Checkpoint, CCH Tax Research NetWork, or Lexis-Nexis, determine how many federal tax cases decided in 2004 contain the phrase *step transaction.*
2. Select a case that discusses the step transaction doctrine in the opinion and prepare a written summary (brief) of the case.
3. Using an electronic library such as RIA Checkpoint, CCH Tax Research NetWork, or Lexis-Nexis, find a federal tax case in which the taxpayer is found guilty of tax evasion. After reading the case, list the behaviors of the taxpayer that convinced the court that the taxpayer was evading (rather than legally avoiding) tax.

Tax Planning Cases

1. Firm DFG plans to open a foreign subsidiary through which to sell its manufactured goods in the European market. It must decide between locating the subsidiary in Country X or Country Z. If the subsidiary operates in Country X, its gross receipts from sales will be subject to a 3 percent gross receipts tax. If the subsidiary operates in Country Z, its net profits will be subject to a 42 percent income tax. However, Country Z's tax law has a special provision to attract foreign investors: No foreign subsidiary is subject to the income tax for the first three years of operations.

   DFG projects the following annual operating results for the two locations (in thousands of dollars).

	Country X	*Country Z*
Gross receipts from sales	$110,000	$110,000
Cost of sales	(60,000)	(60,000)
Operating expenses	(22,000)	(15,000)
Net profit	$ 28,000	$ 35,000

   DFG projects that it will operate the foreign subsidiary for 10 years (years 0 through 9) and that the terminal value of the operation at the end of this period will be the same regardless of location. Assuming a 10 percent discount rate, determine which location maximizes the NPV of the foreign operation.
2. Mr. A, who is in a 35 percent marginal tax bracket, must decide between two investment opportunities, both of which require a $50,000 initial cash outlay in year 0. Investment 1 will yield $8,000 before-tax cash flow in years 1, 2, and 3. This cash represents ordinary taxable income. In year 3, Mr. A can liquidate the investment and recover his $50,000 cash outlay. He must pay a nondeductible $200 annual fee (in years 1, 2, and 3) to maintain Investment 1.

Investment 2 will not yield any before-tax cash flow during the period over which Mr. A will hold the investment. In year 3, he can sell Investment 2 for $75,000 cash. His $25,000 profit on the sale will be capital gain taxed at 15 percent.

Assuming a 9 percent discount rate, determine which investment has the greater NPV.

3. Mrs. O is negotiating to purchase a tract of land from DC Company, which is a calendar year taxpayer. DC bought this land six years ago for $480,000. According to a recent appraisal, the land is worth $800,000 in the current real estate market. According to DC's director of tax, the company's profit on the sale will be taxed at 30 percent if the sale occurs this year. However, this tax rate will definitely increase to 40 percent if the sale occurs next year. Mrs. O is aware of DC's need for haste and offers to pay $785,000 for the land with a guarantee that the sale will close by December 31. Should DC accept Mrs. O's offer?

The Measurement of Taxable Income

Chapter **Five**

Taxable Income from Business Operations

Learning Objectives

After studying this chapter, you should be able to:

1. Describe the relationship between business operating cycle and taxable year.
2. Identify the methods of accounting that a firm can use for tax purposes.
3. Explain why tax policy objectives affect the computation of taxable income.
4. Apply the cash method of accounting to compute taxable income.
5. Contrast the principles of conservatism reflected by GAAP and by the tax law.
6. Differentiate between a permanent and a temporary book/tax difference.
7. Explain the difference between tax expense per books and tax payable.
8. Apply the general tax accounting rules for prepaid income and accrued expenses.
9. Explain how the NOL deduction smooths taxable income over time.

The keynote of the text to this point has been the role of taxes in the business decision-making process. We've been concerned with income and deductions only in the generic sense and have worked through a series of hypothetical transactions demonstrating how income and deductions result in tax costs and tax savings. We have incorporated these costs and savings into cash flow models for computing the net present value (NPV) of the transactions.

In Part Three, our attention turns to the statutory, regulatory, and judicial rules governing the measurement of taxable income. Chapter 5 examines the effect of a firm's choice of a taxable year and a method of accounting on the measurement process, with emphasis on the differences between the computation of financial statement income and taxable income. In contrast to earlier chapters, this chapter contains numerous references to the Internal Revenue Code and Treasury regulations and to court cases pertaining to the computation of taxable income. We will analyze this new technical material in terms of its effect on cash flows and its relevance to the tax planning process. In doing so, we will accomplish one of the main objectives of *Principles of Taxation for Business and Investment Planning*—bridging the gap between finance courses that assume away knowledge of the tax law and traditional law courses that ignore the role of taxes in the larger context of financial decision making.

BUSINESS PROFIT AS TAXABLE INCOME

The base for the federal income tax is **taxable income,** defined as gross income minus allowable deductions.[1] The Internal Revenue Code defines **gross income** by stating that "gross income means all income from whatever source derived."[2] In the business context, gross income consists primarily of revenues from the sale of goods or performance of services in the regular course of a commercial activity. Gross income also includes revenues generated by invested capital, such as interest, dividends, and rents. The concept of gross income is broad enough to encompass other, less commonplace increases in net worth from business transactions.

Discharge of Debt Income

Firm C had an $80,000 overdue account payable to a major supplier. The supplier knew that Firm C was having severe cash flow problems and was eager to settle the account as quickly and as advantageously as possible. After some negotiation, Firm C paid $60,000 cash to the supplier in full settlement of the account payable. Because Firm C extinguished an $80,000 liability with only $60,000 of assets, its net worth increased by $20,000, an increase that Firm C must account for as gross income.

Firms can deduct most of their routine operating expenses in the computation of taxable income.[3] They can also deduct the various state, local, and foreign taxes incurred in carrying on their business activities.[4] Firms can even deduct the cost of assets acquired for long-term use in their business; these cost recovery deductions (such as depreciation) are typically spread over some extended period of years. Cost recovery deductions are discussed in detail in Chapter 6. Because the tax law allows firms to deduct expenses and costs incurred in revenue-generating activities, the federal income tax is imposed on *net profit* rather than gross receipts.

THE TAXABLE YEAR

A firm must measure its taxable income every year and pay tax on an annual basis. Firms have considerable latitude with respect to the 12-month period over which to measure income. A firm's taxable year generally corresponds to its annual accounting period for financial statement purposes.[5] If a firm keeps its financial books and records on a **calendar year,** it measures taxable income over the same January through December period. If a firm keeps its financial records on a **fiscal year** (any 12-month period ending on the last day of any month except December), it uses this fiscal year as its taxable year.[6]

Objective 1
Describe the relationship between business operating cycle and taxable year.

The choice of a calendar or fiscal year is usually dictated by the firm's operating cycle; firms want to close their books and calculate their profit at the end of a natural cycle of business activity. A retail clothing store might find that a February 28 fiscal year-end most

[1] §63(a).

[2] §61.

[3] "There shall be allowed as a deduction all the ordinary and necessary expenses paid or incurred during the taxable year in carrying on any trade or business." §162(a).

[4] §164(a). Firms may forgo a deduction for foreign income taxes paid to claim a credit for these taxes against their federal income tax liability. The foreign tax credit is discussed in Chapter 12.

[5] §441(b) and (c).

[6] Firms may also use a 52–53-week year for financial statement and tax return purposes. A 52–53-week year is an annual period that is either 52 or 53 weeks long and that always ends on the same day of the week. §441(f).

accurately reflects an operating cycle that peaks during the holiday season and reaches its lowest point before the beginning of the spring season. A ski resort might use a May 31 fiscal year-end so that its financial statements reflect the profit from a business cycle that ends when the snow finally melts off the slopes.

Changing a Taxable Year

As a general rule, a new business entity establishes its taxable year by filing an initial tax return on the basis of such year.[7] The initial return reflects taxable income or loss from the date business began until the end of the year. As a result, an initial return typically reflects a short period of less than 12 months. After establishing a taxable year, a firm can't change its year unless it formally requests and receives permission to do so from the IRS.[8] This requirement has particular significance when an individual begins a new business as a sole proprietor and wants to keep records on a fiscal year basis. In all likelihood, the individual has always filed a calendar year tax return. Although the business itself is new, the taxable entity (the owner) is already established as a calendar year taxpayer. Consequently, the individual must request permission from the IRS to change to a fiscal year conforming to the sole proprietorship's accounting records.

When a firm has a convincing business reason for changing its annual accounting period, the IRS usually grants permission for the firm to change its taxable year. If the firm lacks a convincing reason, the IRS may withhold permission for the change. In those cases in which the IRS grants permission, the firm files a **short-period return** to accomplish the change.

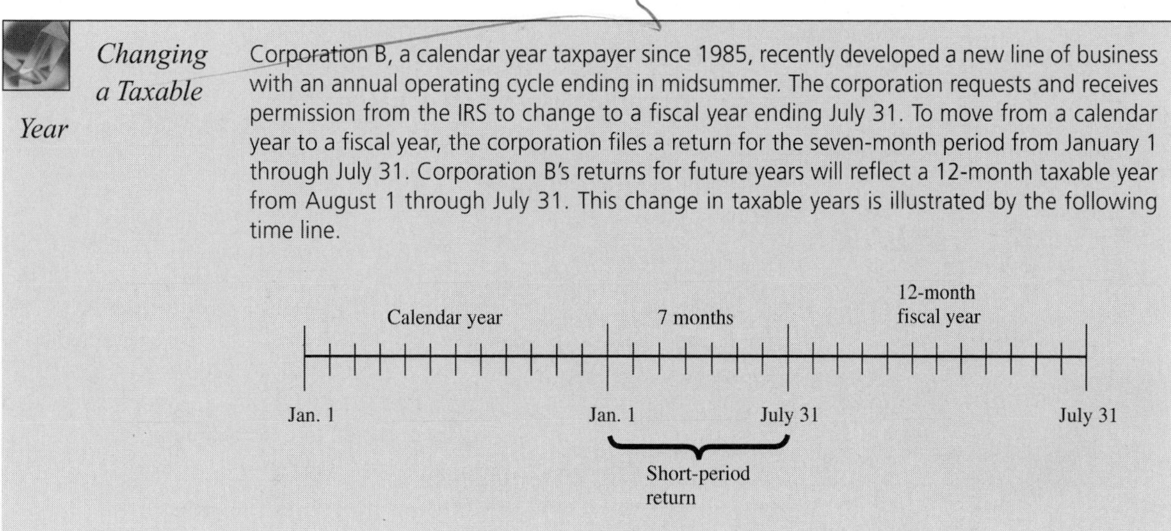

Changing a Taxable Year

Corporation B, a calendar year taxpayer since 1985, recently developed a new line of business with an annual operating cycle ending in midsummer. The corporation requests and receives permission from the IRS to change to a fiscal year ending July 31. To move from a calendar year to a fiscal year, the corporation files a return for the seven-month period from January 1 through July 31. Corporation B's returns for future years will reflect a 12-month taxable year from August 1 through July 31. This change in taxable years is illustrated by the following time line.

Annualizing Income on a Short-Period Return

Because a short-period return reflects less than a full year of income, the tax on that income might be abnormally low. To demonstrate this possibility, assume that Corporation B in the previous example generates $10,000 monthly income. In a 12-month year, the corporation's average tax rate is 25.04 percent. However, in a taxable year consisting of only seven months, the average tax rate falls to 17.86 percent.

[7] Reg. §1.441-1T(b)(2).

[8] §442. Rev. Proc. 2002-37, 2002-1 CB 1030, provides that certain corporations that have not changed their taxable year within a 48-month period ending with the close of the proposed year can change their year without IRS approval.

	12-Month Year	7-Month Year
Taxable income	$120,000	$70,000
Tax on:		
First $50,000 at 15%	$ 7,500	$ 7,500
Next $25,000 at 25%	6,250	5,000
Next $25,000 at 34%	8,500	
Next $20,000 at 39%	7,800	
Total tax	$ 30,050	$12,500

12-month year: $30,050 tax ÷ $120,000 taxable income = 25.04%
7-month year: $12,500 tax ÷ $ 70,000 taxable income = 17.86%

The 7.18 percent rate reduction would result in a $5,026 permanent tax savings ($70,000 × 7.18 percent) to Corporation B. The savings results from the application of progressive rates to a truncated tax base.

The federal tax law prevents this result when a firm files a short-period return to change its taxable year. The taxable income reported on the return must be **annualized**—mathematically inflated to reflect 12 months of business operations.[9] The tax is calculated on the inflated base, then deflated to reflect the actual number of months covered by the return. Let's annualize Corporation B's taxable income on its short-period return and see what happens.

	7-Month Year
Taxable income	$ 70,000
Multiplied by inflation factor (12 months ÷ 7 months)	1.7143
Annualized income	$120,000
Tax on annualized income	$ 30,050
Multiplied by deflation factor (7 months ÷ 12 months)	.5833
Total tax	$ 17,528

$17,528 tax ÷ $70,000 taxable income = 25.04%

Corporation B's average tax rate on the short-period return is 25.04 percent, the same rate at which it pays tax on a normal 12-month basis. Because of the annualization requirement, firms reap no tax benefit when they file a short-period return because of a change in their taxable year. The requirement is inapplicable to short-period returns filed because the taxable entity was *in existence* for only a portion of a taxable year.[10] Accordingly, the short-period income reported on the first return filed by a new business entity or the last return filed by an entity going out of business may be taxed at a bargain rate.

[9] §443(b).
[10] Reg. §1.443-1(a)(2).

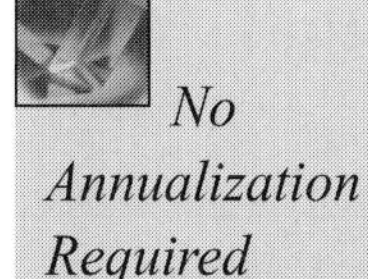

No Annualization Required

Corporation W, a calendar year taxpayer since 1985, ceased operations and dissolved under state law on March 31. For the last 20 years, the corporation's average tax rate on annual income was 34 percent. On its last federal tax return, Corporation W reported $96,200 taxable income earned from January 1 through March 31. Because it was in existence for only three months, the corporation was not required to compute its tax on an annualized basis, and its tax on the short-period return was $20,958.

Tax on:	
First $50,000 at 15%	$ 7,500
Next $25,000 at 25%	6,250
Next $21,200 at 34%	7,208
Total tax	$20,958

Consequently, Corporation W's average tax rate for its last year was only 21.79 percent ($20,958 tax ÷ $96,200 taxable income).

METHODS OF ACCOUNTING

Objective 2
Identify the methods of accounting that a firm can use for tax purposes.

After establishing its taxable year, a firm must assign the items of income and deduction from its transactions to a particular year. To do this, the firm must adopt a **method of accounting:** a consistent system for determining the point in time at which items of income and deduction are *recognized* (taken into account) for tax purposes. The Internal Revenue Code permits firms to use the cash receipts and disbursements (cash) method, the accrual method, or a combined (hybrid) method as their overall method of computing taxable income.[11] We will discuss each of these three methods later in the chapter. The Code also provides specialized methods of accounting that apply only to particular transactions. For example, firms that contract to manufacture an item of property that will take more than 12 months to complete (an oceangoing oil tanker, for example) must use the Section 460 percentage-of-completion method of accounting to measure the annual taxable income from the contract.

The tax law acknowledges that "no uniform method of accounting can be prescribed for all taxpayers. Each taxpayer shall adopt such forms and systems as are, in his judgment, best suited to his needs."[12] Moreover, a taxpayer engaged in more than one business may use a different method of accounting for each business.[13] This permissive attitude is tempered by a caveat: "No method of accounting is acceptable unless, in the opinion of the Commissioner [of the IRS], it clearly reflects income."[14] Thus, the IRS has the right to satisfy itself that a firm's method of income **recognition** accurately measures its ability to pay federal tax.

When related parties enter into business transactions, the IRS has particular reason to scrutinize the methods of accounting used to report the tax consequences, and it has broad authority to challenge these methods. Section 482 of the Internal Revenue Code states that in the case of two or more businesses under common ownership or control, the IRS may "distribute, apportion, or allocate gross income, deduction, credits, or allowances" among the businesses to clearly reflect the income of each.

[11] §446(c).

[12] Reg. §1.446-1(a)(2).

[13] §446(d).

[14] Reg. §1.446-1(a)(2).

The IRS typically invokes Section 482 when it determines that a method of accounting results in a beneficial shift of income between related parties. The following example illustrates this situation.

Using an Accounting Method to Shift Income

ABC Inc. and XYZ Inc. are owned by the same group of investors. ABC operates a manufacturing business, and XYZ is a regional wholesaler that purchases its inventory from a number of suppliers, including ABC. ABC's marginal tax rate is 35 percent, and XYZ's marginal tax rate is only 15 percent. As a result, the owners have an incentive to shift income from ABC to XYZ. They accomplish this shift by having ABC sell its product to XYZ at cost instead of the market price charged to unrelated wholesalers. When XYZ sells ABC's product to its customers, the entire profit with respect to the manufacture and sale of the product is included in XYZ's income.

In the above example, ABC's method of accounting for sales to XYZ distorts the taxable income of both corporations. If a revenue agent discovers the questionable accounting method during an audit, the IRS could use its Section 482 authority to allocate income from XYZ to ABC to correct the distortion.

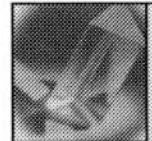

Section 482 Allocation

During its audit of ABC Inc.'s 2002 tax return, the IRS determined that ABC would have recognized $670,000 more gross income if it had charged an arm's-length market price for the inventory sold to XYZ Inc. Accordingly, the IRS allocated $670,000 gross income from XYZ to ABC to accurately measure the 2002 taxable income of both corporations.

Once a firm adopts a method of accounting, it may not change the method unless it formally requests and receives permission to do so from the IRS.[15] The request must state the reason why the firm wants to change and provide a detailed description of its present and proposed method of accounting. The IRS does not rubber-stamp these requests. When the IRS does grant permission, it carefully monitors the change to make sure that the firm does not omit income or duplicate deductions in the year of conversion to the new method of accounting.[16]

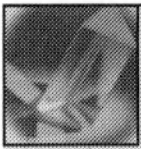

A Request Denied

In 1987, American Express requested the IRS's permission to change its method of accounting for the annual fees received from credit card holders. Until 1987, American Express recorded these fees as income in the month that they were billed. It requested a change to a "ratable inclusion" method under which fees would be recorded as income in equal monthly portions over the 12-month period beginning on the date of billing. The IRS took the position that the proposed method did not clearly reflect the corporation's taxable income and denied permission to make the change. American Express took its case to federal court, but after 14 years of litigation, the U.S. Court of Appeals held for the government. As a result, American Express incurred $199 million additional tax in 1987.[17]

Tax Policy Objectives That Transcend Income Measurement

Objective 3
Explain why tax policy objectives affect the computation of taxable income.

The accurate measurement of taxable income is not the sole objective of the tax law. Congress wants the law to be consistent with public policy and political concerns, and the tax rules that achieve this consistency have nothing to do with income measurement. For instance, contributions to political parties or candidates for public office and federal or state

[15] §446(e).

[16] §481(a).

[17] *American Express Company* v. *United States*, 262 F.3d 1376 (CA FC, 2001), *aff'm* 47 Fed Cl 127 (2000).

lobbying expenses are not deductible.[18] Firms certainly must record these expenses in their accounting records, but because Congress does not want to subsidize political activities, these expenses do not reduce taxable income. Similarly, firms cannot deduct illegal business bribes or kickbacks or fines or penalties paid to any government for a violation of law because Congress does not want to subsidize bad behavior with a tax deduction.[19]

The tax treatment of business meals and entertainment expenses is based on political concerns. Many firms incur these expenses to improve their relationships with customers, clients, investors, and employees. While these expenses may have a good business purpose, they may also result in personal enjoyment for the participants. The "three-martini lunch" has become a catchphrase for lavish meals and entertainment that involve more pleasure than business. In response to criticism that the tax law should not underwrite such activities, Congress allows firms to deduct only 50 percent of most meal and entertainment expenses.[20]

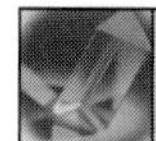

Nondeductible Expenses

Firm PLW operates a manufacturing business. This year, PLW paid a $2,000 fine to the city of Memphis for violating a local zoning law, contributed $3,500 to a candidate for state office, and spent $8,200 on meals and entertainment. While these items were recorded as business expenses on PLW's books, the fine and political contribution were nondeductible and only $4,100 of the meals and entertainment expense was deductible.

Tax Preferences

The tax law contains many provisions to encourage certain economic behaviors or activities. In Chapter 4, we learned that the interest paid on state and local debt obligations is exempt from federal income tax. Firms that earn tax-exempt interest record it as revenue on their books but do not recognize it as gross income for tax purposes. The law provides a similar preference for the proceeds of life insurance policies: the proceeds are excluded from the recipient's gross income.[21] Many firms insure the lives of their officers and top-level management to protect against business disruption if one of these essential personnel dies. The firm itself (rather than the insured employee's family) is the beneficiary of such **key-person life insurance policies.** When a key person dies and the firm receives payment from the insurance company, the payment is recorded as revenue but is not taxable.

A corollary to the tax-exempt status of municipal bond interest and key-person life insurance proceeds is that expenses related to these income items are nondeductible. Accordingly, a firm can't deduct the interest paid on a debt if the borrowed funds were used to purchase or carry tax-exempt bonds.[22] Nor can a firm deduct the annual premiums paid on key-person life insurance policies.[23]

Key-Person Life Insurance

OKD owns insurance policies on the lives of its CEO and five other corporate officers and paid $14,300 premiums on these policies this year. In November, the CEO was killed in a boating accident, and OKD received $750,000 of insurance proceeds. OKD cannot deduct the $14,300 premium expense, and it does not include the $750,000 proceeds in gross income.

[18] §276 and §162(e).

[19] §162(c) and (f).

[20] §274(n). Section 274 includes many complicated restrictions on the deduction of business travel and entertainment expenses.

[21] §101(a).

[22] §265(a)(2).

[23] §264(a).

As part of the American Jobs Creation Act of 2004, Congress enacted a major tax preference: the deduction for income attributable to domestic production activities.[24] This deduction is available in tax years beginning after December 31, 2004. For 2005, the amount of the deduction generally equals three percent of a firm's net income from sales of property "manufactured, produced, grown, or extracted" within the United States. Here is a simple example.

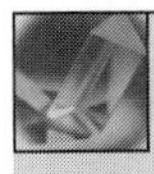

U.S. Production Activities Deduction

For its 2005 taxable year, Firm K earned the following manufacturing income:

Net income from U.S. manufacturing	$500,000
Net income from foreign manufacturing	600,000

Its U.S. production activities deduction is $15,000 (3 percent × $500,000 net income from U.S. manufacturing). Thus, Firm K's taxable income from its U.S. manufacturing operation is only $485,000.

According to Congress, this new **U.S. production activities deduction** indirectly reduces the tax rate on *domestic* manufacturing income. The threefold purpose of this preferential rate is to help U.S. businesses compete in the global marketplace, encourage investment in domestic manufacturing facilities, and create and preserve U.S. manufacturing jobs. The new deduction is discussed in greater detail in Chapter 10.

THE CASH METHOD

Objective 4
Apply the cash method of accounting to compute taxable income.

Under the **cash method of accounting,** firms record revenue from the sale of goods or the performance of services in the year that payment is received, regardless of when the sale occurred or the services were performed.

Cash Method for Revenues

Firm CM, a calendar year, cash basis consulting business, completed an engagement late in the year. On December 12, the firm mailed a bill to the client for its $20,000 consulting fee. If CM does not receive a check in payment before year-end, it does not record revenue for the year, even though the services were performed during the year. CM will record $20,000 revenue when it receives payment in the following year.

Under the cash method, firms record expenses in the year the expense is paid, regardless of when the liability for the expense was incurred.

Cash Method for Expenses

Firm CM hired a temporary employee to help the secretarial staff with year-end paperwork. The temp completed the assignment on December 28, but CM didn't issue his $950 paycheck until January 15. CM incurred the $950 liability when the employee completed the job in a satisfactory manner. Even so, it will record the $950 expense when it makes payment in the following year.

[24] §199.

The Cash Method and Cash Flows

The term *cash method* should not be taken too literally. In the first place, the receipt of noncash forms of payment creates revenue equal to the value of the payment. The fact that no money is received is irrelevant.

Noncash Receipts

Firm CM billed a client for a $12,000 consulting fee, and the client settled the bill by transferring $12,000 worth of marketable securities to the firm. CM records $12,000 revenue on the receipt of the securities, even though the transaction did not involve the receipt of money.

As this example suggests, the net income computed under the cash method does not equate to net cash flows. In other words, the terms *income* and *cash* are not synonymous, even for a cash-basis taxpayer.

Income and Cash Flow

Firm CM lends $25,000 to an unrelated party at a 10 percent annual interest rate. Three years later, the debtor pays $33,275 ($25,000 principal + $8,275 interest) to CM in satisfaction of the debt. CM's income, expense, and cash flow from this transaction are as follows.

	Income/Expense	*Cash Flow*
Year of loan	–0–	$(25,000)
Year of repayment	$8,275	33,275

Constructive Receipt

Under the cash method of accounting, income is received when a person has unrestricted access to and control of the income, even if it is not in the person's actual possession. Treasury regulations state that this doctrine of **constructive receipt** applies when income is credited to a taxpayer's account, set apart for him, or otherwise made available so the taxpayer can draw on it during the taxable year.[25] For instance, interest accumulating in a savings account is constructively received on the day the owner has the right to withdraw the interest. The owner doesn't avoid income recognition merely because she declines to make the withdrawal.

In litigation between cash basis firms and the IRS, the courts have generally concluded that constructive receipt occurred if no substantial barrier to the firm's control and possession of the income existed. In other words, a calendar year, cash basis firm can't defer income from one year to the next by holding the checks received from its customers in December and cashing the checks the following January.[26]

The Lost Check

Horace and Donna Walter used the cash method to account for the income from their cattle ranch. During an audit of the Walters' 1996 tax records, an IRS agent found the top half of a business document indicating that Mr. Walter sold 115 steers to a customer for $77,442. The document apparently had been attached to a check from the customer. However, the Walters' bank records did not show a deposit of $77,442 during 1996. Mr. Walter contacted the customer, who advised him that the check issued in 1996 had never been cashed. The

[25] Reg. §1.451-2(a).

[26] *C. F. Kahler*, 18 TC 31 (1952).

customer then issued a new check, which Mr. Walter received and deposited in 1998. The Walters argued that they were not in constructive receipt of the income represented by the original check in 1996 because they had obviously lost the check instead of cashing it. The IRS contended that the fact that the Walters failed to cash the check was irrelevant, and they must include the $77,442 payment in 1996 income. The federal court that decided the case agreed with the IRS, stating, "Losing the check was a restriction on collection imposed by the Walters, the payees. No tax case has recognized an exception to the rule that receipt of a check is constructive receipt of the income when the restrictions on the disposition of the proceeds were the payees' own."[27]

Prepaid Expenses and Interest

Under the cash method of accounting, an expense is recorded in the year when payment is made. Cash basis firms can accelerate a deduction by paying an expense before the year in which the expense contributes to the generation of revenues. If the tax savings from the deduction is greater than the opportunity cost of the early payment, the firm has implemented a successful tax-planning strategy. This strategy is limited by the well-established principle that any expenditure creating a benefit with a useful life extending substantially beyond the close of the year is not deductible but must be capitalized and amortized over its useful life.[28] The tax law provides a "12-month rule" for determining whether an expenditure is currently deductible or must be capitalized to an asset account. If the expenditure results in a benefit with a duration of 12 months or less *and* that benefit does not extend beyond the end of the taxable year *following* the year of payment, the expenditure is deductible in the year of payment. If the expenditure results in a benefit with a duration of more than 12 months, it must be capitalized.[29]

Prepaid Insurance

On November 28, 2005, Firm L, a calendar year, cash basis taxpayer, paid a $9,930 premium to acquire a casualty insurance policy on its business equipment.

- If the insurance policy has a one-year term from December 1, 2005, through November 30, 2006, its benefit has a duration of only 12 months and does not extend beyond 2006. Therefore, Firm L can deduct the $9,930 premium in 2005.
- If the insurance premium has a one-year term from February 1, 2006, through January 31, 2007, its benefit has a duration of only 12 months, but this benefit extends beyond 2006. Therefore, Firm L must capitalize the $9,930 premium. It can amortize and deduct $9,103 (11/12 × $9,930) of the cost in 2006 and $827 (1/12 × $9,930) of the cost in 2007.
- If the insurance premium has a three-year term from January 1, 2006, through December 31, 2008, its benefit has a three-year duration. Therefore, Firm L must capitalize the $9,930 premium and can amortize and deduct $3,310 (1/3 × $9,930) of the cost in 2006, 2007, and 2008.

For many years, cash basis firms with excess liquidity toward the end of the year could generate a deduction by prepaying interest expense to cooperative creditors. Congress forestalled this planning technique by enacting a statutory requirement that prepaid interest be

[27] *Walter* v. *United States*, 148 F.3d 1027 (CA-8, 1996).

[28] *Welch* v. *Helvering*, 290 U.S. 111 (1933).

[29] Reg. §1.263(a)-4. This regulation applies to expenditures paid or incurred on or after December 31, 2003.

capitalized and deducted in the future year or years for which the interest is actually charged.[30]

Prepaid Interest

On October 1, Firm W, a calendar year, cash basis taxpayer, borrowed $100,000 from a local bank at 8.2 percent interest per annum. On December 19, the firm paid $8,200 to the bank for the first year's interest on the loan. Even though Firm W is a cash basis taxpayer, it can deduct only $2,050 (the interest for October, November, and December). The $6,150 interest for January 1 through September 30 of the following year is deductible in the following year.

Merchandise Inventories

Firms that sell merchandise to their customers must use the accrual method to account for purchases and sales of the merchandise.[31] In other words, they must capitalize the cost of merchandise as an inventory asset and can expense only the cost of inventory sold during the year. Moreover, they must record revenue from the sale of inventory when the sale occurs instead of when payment is received. Firms that sell merchandise can use an overall **hybrid method of accounting** in which they account for purchases and sales of inventories under the accrual method and all other transactions under the cash method.

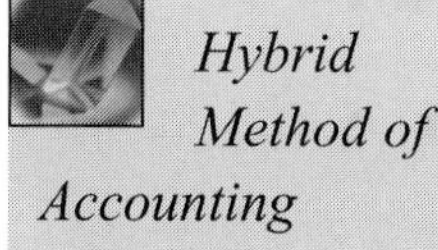

Hybrid Method of Accounting

LWT Company, a retail sporting goods store, uses a hybrid method of accounting under which it accounts for all transactions that don't involve inventory under the cash method. It accounts for inventory transactions under the accrual method by capitalizing all merchandise purchases to inventory, performing a physical count at year-end to determine ending inventory and cost of goods sold, and recording revenues from inventory sales when the sales occur.

Many firms that provide services to clients may also sell tangible products as a secondary component of their principal service activity. For example, landscaping companies usually provide both design services and the plant materials necessary to implement the designs. Plumbing contractors usually provide both installation and repair services and any plumbing parts and fixtures incidental to the services. These firms may have inventories of the products sold in conjunction with their service activities. Under the general rule for inventories, they must account for purchases and sales of these products under the accrual method. However, the law provides a simplified cash method of accounting for service firms with average annual gross receipts of $10 million or less. These small businesses do not have to use the accrual method to account for their sales of products. However, they must account for their product inventory on hand at year-end as an asset.[32]

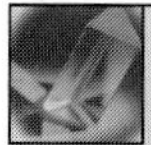

Small Service Business Exception

Jamestown Animal Hospital's principal business activity is the provision of veterinarian services, but it also sells pet supplies to its patients' owners. Jamestown's average annual gross receipts are $3 million. Consequently, it can use the cash method to account for its sales of both services and supplies. During the last month of this taxable year, Jamestown purchased $65,800 of pet supplies to restock its shelves. At year-end, it had $41,100 of these supplies on hand, so it could deduct only $24,700 of the cost this year. Jamestown can deduct the $41,100 capitalized cost in the year when it sells the supplies.

[30] §461(g). This capitalization requirement does not apply to prepaid interest (points) on certain home mortgages.

[31] Regs. §1.446-1(a)(4)(i) and §1.471-1.

[32] Rev. Proc. 2002-28, 2002-1 CB 815.

Limitations on Use of the Cash Method by Corporations

The cash method of accounting is both simple and objective because the measurement of taxable income is based on cash receipts (bank deposits) and disbursements (checks written). The cash method also provides some control over the timing of income recognition.

Year-End Tax Planning under the Cash Method

Firm E is a calendar year, cash basis service business. At the end of each year, the firm delays billing its clients for work performed in December until the following January to defer taxable income. It also prepays as many expenses as possible to accelerate tax deductions.

Because the cash method can be manipulated to defer income and accelerate deductions, the tax law limits its use by large corporations. Corporations that average more than $5 million annual gross receipts cannot use the cash method for tax purposes.[33] This prohibition extends to partnerships with corporate partners. However it does not apply to **personal service corporations,** defined as corporations that offer professional services (medical, legal, accounting, etc.) performed by individual shareholder/employees for the corporate clients. Any corporation, no matter how large, that is a personal service corporation can use the cash method to compute taxable income.

THE ACCRUAL METHOD

According to **generally accepted accounting principles (GAAP),** only the accrual method of accounting accurately measures annual income.[34] Firms that provide audited financial statements to external users are typically required to use the accrual method. The Security and Exchange Commission (SEC) requires every publicly held corporation to prepare accrual basis financial statements in accordance with GAAP.

Under the **accrual method of accounting,** firms record revenue when the revenue is realized. **Realization** occurs when the earnings process with respect to the provision of goods or services is complete, regardless of when payment for the goods or services is received.

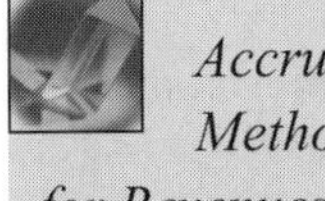

Accrual Method for Revenues

Firm ADM, a calendar year, accrual basis consulting business, performed client services during October and November and billed the client for $9,200 on December 8. ADM recorded a $9,200 account receivable and $9,200 revenue even though it did not receive payment from the client until January 10 of the following year.

Accrual basis firms match expenses against revenue in the year the liability for the expense is incurred, regardless of when payment of the expense is made.

Accrual Method for Expenses

Firm ADM hired a plumber to repair some leaky pipes in the executive washroom. The plumber completed his repairs on December 19 and submitted his bill for $550. ADM recorded a $550 account payable and a $550 expense even though it did not pay the bill until January 20 of the following year.

[33] §448.

[34] Generally accepted accounting principles are developed by the Financial Accounting Standards Board (FASB) and adhered to by the public accounting profession.

If a firm uses the accrual method for both financial accounting (book) purposes and tax purposes, doesn't its annual income per books equal its taxable income? The answer to this question is usually no. For most accrual basis firms, book income and taxable income are different numbers. Discrepancies between the two income computations occur because certain transactions are treated one way under GAAP and another way for tax accounting purposes. One explanation for the inconsistent treatment is the contrast in perspectives on income measurement that shape financial accounting principles and the tax law.

Contrasting Perspectives on Income Measurement

Objective 5
Contrast the principles of conservatism reflected by GAAP and by the tax law.

Business managers have one attitude toward income measurement for financial statement purposes and a different attitude toward income measurement for tax purposes. Managers have incentives to report as much book income as possible. Their compensation and even their job security may depend on the level of earnings reported to existing and potential investors. However, GAAP is based on a principle of conservatism: When in doubt, financial statements should delay the realization of income and accelerate the realization of losses.[35] In theory at least, GAAP curbs any tendency of management to *inflate* book income by overstating revenues or understating expenses.

In contrast to their expansive attitude toward book income, managers want to *deflate* the taxable income (and resultant tax cost) reported to the government. Congress and the Treasury are well aware of this measurement bias. Consequently, the federal tax law also embraces a principle of conservatism, but one that operates to prevent managers from understating gross income and overstating deductions. The contrasting principles of conservatism reflected by GAAP and the federal tax law lead to many of the book/tax differences described in Part Three of the text. To help readers keep track, a list of the sources of book/tax differences introduced in each chapter is provided at the end of the chapter.

Permanent versus Temporary Differences

Objective 6
Differentiate between a permanent and a temporary book/tax difference.

Differences between book income and taxable income are either permanent or temporary. A **permanent difference** results when income or gain is realized for book purposes but *never* recognized for tax purposes. Tax-exempt interest is an example of this type of permanent difference. Permanent differences also result when an expense or loss is realized for book purposes but *never* recognized for tax purposes. Nondeductible fines and penalties are good examples. Finally, permanent differences result when the tax law provides for a deduction that *never* corresponds to a book expense or loss. The new U.S. production activities deduction described on page 104 and the dividends-received deduction that we will study in Chapter 10 are prime examples. Firms that have permanent book/tax differences never recoup the tax cost or repay the tax savings attributable to the differences.

Permanent Book/Tax Differences

Kalvoni, an accrual basis business, earned $114,000 tax-exempt interest, incurred $386,400 nondeductible expenses, and was allowed a $767,000 U.S. production activities deduction this year. If these were Kalvoni's only book/tax differences and its book income before tax was $4,712,000, its taxable income is computed as follows:

[35] Jamie Pratt, *Financial Accounting*, 2nd ed. (Cincinnati, OH: South-Western Publishing, 1994), p. 192.

Book income before tax	$4,712,000
Income never recognized	(114,000)
Expenses never deducted	386,400
Deduction never expensed	(767,000)
Taxable income	$4,217,400

Kalvoni's $494,600 permanent excess of book income over taxable income represents a $168,164 permanent tax saving ($494,600 excess × 34 percent) for the business.

A permanent book/tax difference affects only the year in which it occurs. Consequently, income tax expense *for financial statement purposes* is based on book income adjusted for all permanent differences.

Tax Expense per Books

Kalvoni's audited financial statements must include its federal income tax expense for the year. The tax expense per books is based on Kalvoni's book income adjusted for its permanent book/tax differences.

Book income before tax	$4,712,000
Income never recognized	(114,000)
Expenses never deducted	386,400
Deductions never expensed	(767,000)
Adjusted book income	$4,217,400
Tax rate	.34
Tax expense per books	$1,433,916

Temporary differences occur when an item of income, gain, expense, or loss is taken into account in a different year (or years) for book purposes than for tax purposes. Any excess of taxable income over book income from a temporary difference turns around to become an excess of book income over taxable income in some future year, and vice versa. The tax cost or tax savings from temporary differences are recouped or repaid in the future year in which the difference reverses.

Reversal of Temporary Book/Tax Difference

In year 1, Corporation QZ engages in a transaction that generates $100,000 income for financial accounting purposes. For tax purposes, the transaction generates $60,000 income in year 1, $35,000 income in year 2, and $5,000 income in year 3. The following table shows the computation of the book/tax difference each year and the tax savings (cost) at a 34 percent rate.

	Book Income	*Taxable Income*	*Difference*	*Tax Savings (Cost)*
Year 1	$100,000	$ 60,000	$40,000	$13,600
Year 2	–0–	35,000	(35,000)	(11,900)
Year 3	–0–	5,000	(5,000)	(1,700)
Total	$100,000	$100,000	–0–	–0–

Tax Expense versus Tax Payable

Objective 7
Explain the difference between tax expense per books and tax payable.

When a firm has temporary book/tax differences, the tax expense reported on the income statement is based on book income (after adjustment for permanent book/tax differences) rather than taxable income. Consequently, federal tax expense per books is either less than or more than the federal tax the firm must actually pay. The difference between the two tax numbers is recorded as a **deferred tax asset** or a **deferred tax liability** on the balance sheet.

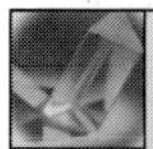

Deferred Taxes

In year 1, Corporation QZ's tax expense per books with respect to the transaction described in the prior example is based on $100,000 book income; at a 34 percent rate, the tax expense is $34,000. However, QZ pays only $20,400 tax in year 1 with respect to the transaction (34 percent of $60,000 taxable income). The $13,600 excess of tax expense over tax payable is reported on QZ's balance sheet as a deferred tax liability. In years 2 and 3, QZ has no tax expense per books with respect to the transaction. The tax payments in those years are charged against the deferred tax liability, which is reduced to zero by the end of the three-year period.

	Tax Expense	*Tax Payable*	*Deferred Tax Liability*
Year 1	$34,000	$20,400	$13,600
Year 2	–0–	11,900	(11,900)
Year 3	–0–	1,700	(1,700)
Total	$34,000	$34,000	–0–

The deferred tax liability reflects QZ's tax savings in year 1 from the deferral of $40,000 taxable income. QZ repays this tax savings in years 2 and 3 when taxable income exceeds financial statement income by $40,000.

Permanent and Temporary Book/Tax Differences

Corporation XYZ engages in many transactions that result in permanent and temporary differences between book income and taxable income. This year, XYZ's financial records show the following.

Book income before tax	$712,000
Net permanent differences	(19,000)
Net temporary differences	63,000
Taxable income	$756,000

XYZ's tax expense for financial statement purposes is $235,620.

Book income before tax	$712,000
Permanent differences	(19,000)
	$693,000
Tax rate	.34
Tax expense per books	$235,620

XYZ's tax payable is $257,040.

Taxable income	$756,000
Tax rate	.34
Tax payable	$257,040

The $21,420 excess of tax payable over tax expense represents a net increase in the deferred tax assets on XYZ's balance sheet.

Temporary Book/Tax Accounting Differences

Prepaid Income

Objective 8
Apply the general tax accounting rules for prepaid income and accrued expenses.

According to GAAP, income from the sale of goods or performance of services is realized in the year the goods or services are provided to customers or clients, even if the customers or clients prepay in an earlier year. For tax purposes, income is recognized when all the events have occurred that fix the right to receive such income and the amount can be determined with reasonable accuracy.[36] The IRS has interpreted this accounting rule to mean that accrual basis firms must recognize many types of prepaid income in the year of receipt.[37]

Prepaid Rent

Firm CRO, an accrual basis taxpayer, leases real estate to a tenant for $30,000 annual rent. At the beginning of the year, CRO received a $90,000 payment from the tenant for three years' rent. For financial statement purposes, it reported $30,000 rent revenue on its income statement and $60,000 deferred revenue as a liability on its balance sheet. For tax purposes, CRO must recognize the entire $90,000 prepayment as income. The $60,000 excess of taxable income over book income is a temporary difference that will reverse over the next two years.[38]

Accrued Expenses

At the close of the year, GAAP requires firms to identify any unpaid expenses incurred during the year and accrue their liability for the expense. The tax law allows a deduction for such accrued expenses only if the expense meets the **all-events test.** This test has two basic requirements. First, the liability for the expense must be fixed because all the events that established the liability have already occurred. Second, the amount of the liability must be determinable with reasonable accuracy.[39] If the accrued expense meets these two requirements and is a recurring item that the firm treats in a consistent manner every year, the expense is deductible.[40]

Tax Talk
The Tax Court recently held that Westpac Pacific Foods, an accrual basis food distribution company, could not defer recognition of income from cash prepayments from manufacturers for multiyear distribution contracts. Although Westpac recorded the prepayments as liabilities (unearned revenue), it had to include them in gross income in the year received.

[36] Reg. §1.451-1(a).

[37] Prepaid income for services is subject to a special tax rule. If the recipient is required by contract to perform the services by the end of the year following the year of receipt, the recipient recognizes the income in the year earned (i.e., under the GAAP rule). If the recipient can delay performing the services until after the following year, it must recognize the prepaid income in the year of receipt. Rev. Proc. 71-21, 1971-2 CB 549.

[38] Reg. 1.61-8(b).

[39] Reg. §1.461-1(a)(2)(i).

[40] Such recurring items generally must be paid within 8½ months after the close of the taxable year per §461(h)(3)(A)(ii).

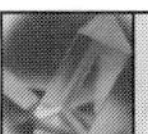

Passing the All-Events Test I

MQP is an accrual basis, calendar year taxpayer that leases machinery for $27,500 monthly rent that is payable within 15 days after the end of the month. MQP did not pay its December rent until January 11. Consequently, it accrued a $27,500 rent expense and a $27,500 liability (rent payable) for financial statement purposes. Because MQP's liability to pay this recurring expense is fixed and the $27,500 amount is certain, it can deduct the accrued expense this year.

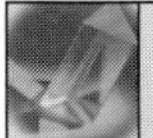

Passing the All-Events Test II

MQP used over 100 temporary employees during the last two weeks of December but did not receive a bill for their wages from the employment agency before year-end. On the basis of its record of the hours worked, MQP estimated that the December wages were $111,500. Consequently, MQP accrued a $111,500 wage expense and a $111,500 liability (wages payable) for financial statement purposes. Because MQP's liability to pay the wages is fixed and the $111,500 amount is determinable with reasonable accuracy, it can deduct the accrued expense this year.

Failing the All-Events Test I

SFL, an accrual basis taxpayer, provides a medical reimbursement plan for its 4,800 employees. At the end of each year, SFL estimates the reimbursable expenses incurred during the year for which employees have not yet filed written claims. On the basis of this estimate, SFL accrues a medical reimbursement expense and a corresponding liability for financial statement purposes. However, SFL cannot deduct this recurring expense because it fails the first requirement of the all-events test: SFL's liability for the estimated reimbursements is not fixed until the employees actually file written claims.[41]

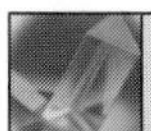

Failing the All-Events Test II

MHY Airlines, an accrual basis taxpayer, routinely issues travel vouchers to customers who voluntarily surrender their reserved seats on overbooked flights. The vouchers are for a stated dollar amount and can be used by customers against the purchase price of future tickets. The vouchers are valid for only one year, and many vouchers expire without being used. At the end of the year, MHY accrues an estimated travel voucher expense and a corresponding liability for financial statement purposes. However, MHY cannot deduct this recurring expense because it fails the first requirement of the all-events test: MHY's liability for the vouchers is not fixed until the customers actually use them to purchase tickets.[42]

For many year-end accruals that are required by GAAP to properly match expenses against revenues, the all-events test for deductibility consists of only the two requirements described in the preceding paragraphs. However, for a few types of accrued expenses, the all-events test has a third requirement: no deduction is allowed until **economic performance** occurs.[43] In many instances, economic performance is equivalent to *payment* of the accrued liability, and this third requirement simply puts the firm on the cash basis for the expense. Expenses that are deductible only in the year of payment include legal settlements resulting from any tort, breach of contract, or violation of law; customer rebates or refunds; awards, prizes, or jackpots; and state income taxes.[44]

[41] *United States* v. *General Dynamics Corp.*, 481 U.S. 239 (1987).

[42] IRS Letter Ruling 200203004 (January 18, 2002).

[43] §461(h).

[44] Reg. §1.461-4(g).

Economic Performance

XMP, an accrual basis taxpayer, was sued in 2001 by an employee who was injured on the job as a result of XMP's alleged negligence. XMP's auditors required it to accrue a $2 million contingent liability as a 2001 expense for financial statement purposes. XMP could not deduct the accrued expense because it failed the first requirement of the all-events test (no fixed liability). XMP and the employee agreed to a $1.7 million out-of-court settlement in 2003, and XMP paid the settlement in 2004. Although the expense met the two basic requirements of the all-events test in 2003 (the liability became fixed and the amount was determinable), XMP could not deduct the expense until 2004 when economic performance (payment) occurred.

Related Party Accruals

The parties to a transaction may use different methods to account for the tax consequences of the transaction. As a result, the two sides of the transaction may be reported in different years.

Different Accounting Methods: Arm's-Length Transaction

Company AB, an accrual basis taxpayer, hires Firm CB, a cash basis taxpayer, to provide professional services. Firm CB performs the services in year 1 and bills Company AB for $10,000. Company AB pays this bill in year 2. For financial statement purposes, the two parties record the following.

	Year 1	*Year 2*
Company AB's accrued expense	$(10,000)	–0–
Firm CB's realized income	–0–	$10,000

If Company AB and Firm CB are not related parties, the tax consequences of the transaction are consistent with the financial accounting treatment. Company AB reaps the tax savings from a $10,000 deduction in year 1, while Firm CB bears the tax cost of $10,000 income in year 2. In present value terms, the tax savings exceed the tax cost, even if both parties have the same marginal tax rate. Although the Treasury is being whipsawed because of the difference in the parties' accounting methods, the tax law tolerates the result because it arises from an arm's-length transaction.

Now assume that Firm CB owns a controlling interest in Company AB. Because the transaction occurs between related parties, the tax law does not allow Company AB to deduct the accrued expense in year 1. Instead, Company AB must defer the $10,000 deduction until year 2 when Firm CB recognizes $10,000 income from the transaction.[45]

Different Accounting Methods: Related Parties

If Company AB and Firm CB are related parties, Company AB accrues the $10,000 expense in year 1 but reports a $10,000 deduction in year 2.

	Year 1	*Year 2*
Company AB's:		
Accrued expense	$(10,000)	–0–
Tax deduction	–0–	$(10,000)
Firm CB's realized income	–0–	10,000

[45] §267(a)(2). Under this section, a controlling interest is generally more than a 50 percent ownership interest.

Business Bad Debts

When an accrual basis firm sells goods or services and the purchaser doesn't pay cash at the point of sale, the firm records an account receivable for the sales price. Firms anticipate that some portion of their accounts receivable will never be collected because of defaults by customers to whom the firm extended credit. According to GAAP, firms should use the **allowance method** to account for bad debts. Under this method, firms estimate the portion of their accounts receivables that will be uncollectible and establish a bad debt allowance or reserve for this portion. The annual addition to the allowance is recorded as a bad debt expense and matched against sales revenue.

The tax law does not allow deductions based on allowances or reserves. Accordingly, firms must use the **direct write-off method** to account for bad debts. Under this method, firms can deduct accounts receivable (and any other business debts) actually written off as uncollectible during the year.[46]

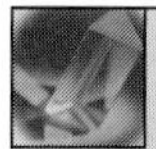

Accounting for Bad Debts

ABC, an accrual basis corporation, began the year with a $298,000 balance in its allowance for bad debts. During the year, it wrote off $155,000 uncollectible accounts receivable against this allowance. On the basis of ABC's year-end accounts receivable, the independent auditors determined that a $173,000 addition to the bad debt allowance was necessary. As a result, the year-end balance in the allowance increased to $316,000.

Beginning allowance for bad debts	$298,000
Actual write-offs during the year	(155,000)
Addition to allowance	173,000
Ending allowance for bad debts	$316,000

ABC's income statement shows a bad debt expense of $173,000, while its tax return shows a bad debt deduction of only $155,000. If ABC's book income before tax is $6,700,000 and it has no other book/tax differences, its taxable income is computed as follows.

Book income before tax	$6,700,000
Nondeductible bad debt expense	173,000
Deductible bad debt write-offs	(155,000)
Taxable income	$6,718,000

NET OPERATING LOSSES

In this chapter, we've learned that firms must choose a method of accounting to divide a continuous stream of income into 12-month segments. The choice of accounting method has very little to do with the measurement of taxable income *over the life* of a firm, but everything to do with the measurement of income for each taxable year. The final section of this chapter focuses on one possible outcome of this annual measurement process: a net operating loss.

[46] §166(a).

The Problem of Excess Deductions

If a taxpayer's annual business operation results in an excess of deductible expenses over gross income, this excess is labeled a **net operating loss (NOL).** Because the taxpayer reports no taxable income, it obviously incurs no tax cost in the year of the NOL. But a more subtle fact is that the excess deductions yield no current tax savings; the taxpayer has the same zero tax cost with or without these deductions. If the excess deductions are wasted because they never yield any tax savings, the taxpayer's average tax rate *over time* could be distorted.

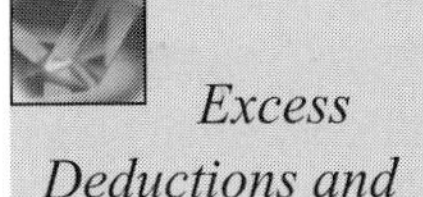

Excess Deductions and Average Tax Rate

TUV Inc. conducts a business with a 24-month operating cycle. Its most recent operating cycle generated $300,000 profit.

	Year 1	*Year 2*	*Total*
Gross income	$100,000	$625,000	$725,000
Deductible expenses	(300,000)	(125,000)	(425,000)
Profit			$300,000

If TUV had to report its income and pay tax based on strict 12-month intervals, it would report a $200,000 NOL for year 1 and $500,000 taxable income for year 2. At a 34 percent rate, it would owe no tax in year 1 and $170,000 tax in year 2. Thus, TUV's overall tax rate on its profit would be 56.67 percent.

$170,000 tax ÷ $300,000 profit = 56.67%

This inflated rate reflects the fact that $200,000 of TUV's deductible expenses (year 1 NOL) generated no tax savings for the corporation.

Solution: The NOL Deduction

Objective 9
Explain how the NOL deduction smooths taxable income over time.

The tax law prevents the rate distortion that could result from an inflexible one-year reporting period by permitting taxpayers to smooth income over time by deducting excess deductions in one year against income in another. Specifically, a taxpayer may carry an NOL back as a deduction against taxable income reported in the two years immediately before the loss year; the deduction must be used in chronological order beginning with the earlier year in the carryback period.[47] Any NOL in excess of the previous two years' income may be carried forward as a deduction to the next 20 taxable years.

NOL Carryback and Carryforward

In 1999, Corporation Q generated a $612,000 NOL. The following schedule shows the years in which it used the NOL as a deduction against taxable income.

	1997	*1998*	*2000*	*2001*	*2002*	*2003*
Taxable income before NOL deduction	$165,000	$110,000	$138,000	$99,000	$54,000	$125,000
NOL deduction	(165,000)	(110,000)	(138,000)	(99,000)	(54,000)	(46,000)
Taxable income	–0–	–0–	–0–	–0–	–0–	$ 79,000

[47] §172.

Corporation Q used $275,000 of the 1999 NOL to reduce 1997 and 1998 taxable income to zero. It used the remaining $337,000 NOL as carryforward deductions in 2000 through 2003.

A taxpayer reports an **NOL carryback** by filing a one-page form with the IRS showing the NOL deducted against prior year income and the recomputed prior year tax.[48] After processing the form, the IRS refunds the tax overpayment. A taxpayer reports an **NOL carryforward** as a deduction on future tax returns until the NOL has been fully utilized or until it expires.

Let's incorporate an NOL deduction into the earlier example involving TUV Inc.

NOL Deduction

Assuming that year 1 was TUV's first taxable year, the NOL in year 1 is carried forward as a deduction into year 2. TUV's tax returns for the two years show the following.

	Year 1	*Year 2*
Gross income	$ 100,000	$625,000
Deductible expenses	(300,000)	(125,000)
NOL	$(200,000)	
NOL carryforward deduction		(200,000)
Taxable income		$300,000

At a 34 percent rate, TUV owes $102,000 tax in year 2. Because of the NOL carryforward, TUV's taxable income in year 2 equals the $300,000 profit for the 24-month operating cycle, and TUV's tax rate on this profit is 34 percent.

Valuing an NOL Deduction

The value of a deduction equals the tax savings from the deduction. In the case of an NOL deduction, the tax savings (and cash flows) depend on the year (or years) in which the taxpayer takes the deduction against taxable income. If the NOL can be deducted against prior years' income, the taxpayer enjoys the savings immediately in the form of a cash refund.

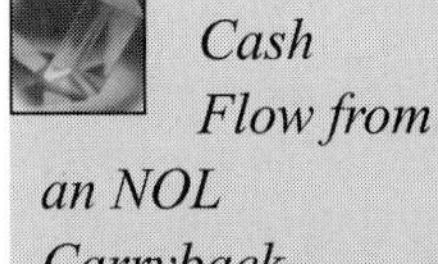

Cash Flow from an NOL Carryback

Corporation C, which has operated profitably since 1985, experienced a severe business downturn during 2004 and closed the year with a $900,000 loss. The corporation carried this loss back as an NOL deduction to 2002 and 2003.

	2002	*2003*
Taxable income on original return	$430,000	$1,600,000
NOL carryback from 2004	(430,000)	(470,000)
Recomputed taxable income	–0–	$1,130,000
Tax on original return*	$146,200	$ 544,000
Recomputed tax	–0–	(384,200)
Refund due to Corporation C	$146,200	$ 159,800

*Tax computations are based on the corporate rate schedule.

[48] See Form 1139 (Corporation Application for Tentative Refund).

Corporation C received a $306,000 refund of 2002 and 2003 tax resulting in an *after-tax* loss of $594,000 ($900,000 operating loss minus $306,000 tax savings). In other words, the NOL *deduction* was worth $306,000 to Corporation C.

Now let's modify the example so that 2004 is Corporation C's first taxable year. Consequently, the corporation can use its $900,000 NOL deduction only on a carryforward basis. In this case, the present value of the deduction depends on the corporation's projection of its future income stream.

NPV of an NOL Carryforward

Corporation C projects that it will generate $350,000 annual income over the next three years. Based on a 9 percent discount rate, the value in 2004 of the NOL carryforward is only $268,958.

	2005	2006	2007
Projected income	$350,000	$350,000	$350,000
NOL carryforward from 2004	(350,000)	(350,000)	(200,000)
Taxable income	–0–	–0–	$150,000
Tax on projected income*	$119,000	$119,000	$119,000
Actual tax	–0–	–0–	(41,750)
Tax savings from NOL	$119,000	$119,000	$ 77,250
Present value of tax savings	$109,123	$100,198	$ 59,637
NPV of tax savings	$268,958		

*Tax computations are based on the corporate rate schedule.

Because the tax savings from the NOL deduction are deferred into future years, the present value of the deduction decreases. In the carryforward example, Corporation C's after-tax loss is $631,042 ($900,000 − $268,958). Clearly, the longer the period of time over which a taxpayer deducts an NOL carryforward, the less present value the deduction has.

Giving Up an NOL Carryback

An interesting feature of the NOL deduction is that taxpayers can elect to give up the carryback and keep the entire loss as a prospective deduction for future years.[49] In most cases, taxpayers are eager to use an NOL carryback deduction to create immediate cash flow in the form of a tax refund. However, if a taxpayer determines that its marginal tax rate during the two-year carryback period was significantly lower than its projected rate for future years, a decision to forgo the carryback may maximize the value of the NOL deduction.

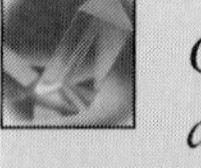

Giving Up an NOL Carryback

Corporation JM incurs a $20,000 NOL this year, which it could carry back as a deduction against prior year income. However, the marginal tax rate in the carryback year was only 25 percent. JM projects that its marginal tax rate next year will be 39 percent. If JM uses a 7 percent discount rate, the NOL deduction is worth $2,293 more as a carryforward than as a carryback.

[49] §172(b)(3). This election is irrevocable.

Present value of NOL carryforward ($20,000 × 39% × .935 discount factor)	$7,293
Present value of NOL carryback ($20,000 × 25%)	(5,000)
	$2,293

Accounting for NOLs

A firm that incurs an operating loss for financial statement purposes obviously reports no tax expense for the year. However, according to GAAP, the firm reports the tax *benefit* of the loss carryback or carryforward on its income statement. If the loss is carried back, the firm realizes the benefit immediately as a tax refund receivable.

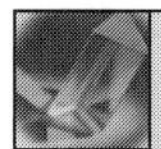

Accounting for NOL Carryback

Herold Inc., a calendar year, accrual basis taxpayer, generated a $783,000 operating loss for both book and tax purposes in 2004. Herold carried the loss back to 2002 as an NOL deduction, which entitled the corporation to a $266,220 refund ($783,000 × 34 percent) of 2002 tax. Herold accounted for the tax effect of its operating loss by recording a $266,220 tax refund receivable on its 2004 balance sheet and a $266,220 tax benefit (negative tax expense) on its 2004 income statement.

If a firm cannot (or elects not to) carry back an NOL, it will realize the tax benefit of the loss in the future year or years in which the loss carryforward is deductible. Nonetheless, according to GAAP, the firm reports the tax benefit of the carryforward in the year the loss occurs. Instead of a tax refund receivable, the future tax saving expected from the carryforward is reported as a deferred tax asset.[50]

Accounting for NOL Carryforward

Groh Inc., a calendar year accrual basis taxpayer, generated a $492,000 operating loss for both book and tax purposes in 2004. Because 2004 was Groh's first taxable year, the corporation can only carry the loss forward as a future deduction. Groh accounted for the tax effect of its operating loss by recording a $167,280 deferred tax asset ($492,000 × 34 percent) on its 2004 balance sheet and a $167,280 tax benefit (negative tax expense) on its 2004 income statement.

Groh Inc. generated $1,316,000 book and taxable income in 2005. Its tax expense per books was $447,440 ($1,316,000 × 34 percent), and its tax payable was $280,160 [($1,316,000 – $492,000 NOL deduction) × 34 percent]. Groh accounted for the $167,280 difference between tax expense and tax payable by removing the deferred tax asset from its balance sheet.

[50] If the realization of a deferred tax asset is questionable, the asset may be reduced by a valuation allowance on the balance sheet.

Conclusion

The computation of business taxable income depends on the taxable year and the method of accounting adopted by the firm. Firms often use the same overall method for both financial reporting and tax purposes. Even so, many discrepancies exist between the computations of book and taxable income. In subsequent chapters, we'll encounter many more of these book/tax differences. To make sense of these differences, it may help to keep the following in mind. The goal of generally accepted accounting principles (and financial statements prepared in accordance with GAAP) is to provide useful and pertinent information to management, shareholders, creditors, and other business decision makers. In contrast, the primary (but certainly not the only) goal of the Internal Revenue Code (and the responsibility of the IRS) is to generate and protect federal tax revenues.

Sources of Book/Tax Differences

Permanent

- Interest on state and local bonds
- Key-person life insurance proceeds and premiums
- Fines and penalties
- Political contributions and lobbying expense
- Meals and entertainment expense
- U.S. production activities deduction

Temporary

- Prepaid income
- Bad debts
- Accrued expenses failing the all-events test
- Related party accruals
- NOL carryforwards

Key Terms

accrual method of accounting *108*
all-events test *112*
allowance method *115*
annualized income *100*
calendar year *98*
cash method of accounting *104*
constructive receipt *105*
deferred tax asset *111*
deferred tax liability *111*
direct write-off method *115*
economic performance *113*
fiscal year *98*
generally accepted accounting principles (GAAP) *108*
gross income *98*
hybrid method of accounting *107*
key-person life insurance policies *103*
method of accounting *101*
net operating loss (NOL) *116*
NOL carryback *117*
NOL carryforward *117*
permanent difference *109*
personal service corporations *108*
realization *108*
recognition *101*
short-period return *99*
taxable income *98*
temporary difference *110*
U.S. production activities deduction *104*

Questions and Problems for Discussion

1. Discuss the choice of a taxable year for the following businesses.
   a. Retail plant and garden center.
   b. French bakery.
   c. Chimney cleaning business.
   d. Moving and transport business.
   e. Software consulting business.
2. Corporation DB operates three very different lines of business. Can the corporation elect a different overall method of accounting for each line or must the corporation adopt one overall method?
3. Firm LK bought a warehouse of used furniture to equip several of its clerical offices. An employee discovered a cache of gold coins in a desk drawer. A local court declared

Firm LK the rightful owner of the coins, which have a $72,000 FMV. Does Firm LK recognize income because of this lucky event?

4. Discuss the various circumstances in which a firm is required to prepare financial statements in accordance with GAAP.
5. Firm NB, which uses the cash method of accounting, recently received two cases of French wine from a client in settlement of a $1,300 bill. Does Firm NB avoid income recognition because it received a noncash item as payment?
6. For many years, Mr. K, the president of KJ Inc., took the corporation's most important clients to lunch at Al's Steak House several times a week. However, since the tax law was amended to disallow a deduction for 50 percent of the cost of business meals, Mr. K and his clients patronize this restaurant only once or twice a month. What does this scenario suggest about the incidence of the indirect tax increase represented by the meals and entertainment disallowance rule?
7. If a corporation purchases insurance on the life of its chief executive officer and the corporation is named the policy beneficiary, the premium payments are nondeductible. If the officer's spouse and children are named as beneficiaries, the premium payments are deductible. Can you provide a reason for this inconsistent tax treatment?
8. Describe the contrasting treatment of prepaid income under GAAP and under the tax law and explain how each treatment reflects a different principle of conservatism.
9. Describe the book/tax difference resulting from each of the following transactions.
   a. Firm A spent $110 on a business dinner attended by the firm's vice president and a potential client.
   b. Firm B borrowed $50,000 and invested the loan proceeds in tax-exempt City of Los Angeles bonds. This year, Firm B paid $2,800 interest on the loan and earned $3,500 interest on the bonds.
   c. Firm C sent its president and several other key employees to Washington, D.C., to lobby a group of senators to enact legislation that would be extremely beneficial for the firm's business. The cost of this trip was $7,400. While in the capital city, the president attended a "$10,000 a plate" fund-raising dinner sponsored by one senator's reelection committee.
10. The manager of Firm Z, a new business that anticipates a steady growth in profits over the next decade, must decide between the cash method and the accrual method as the overall method for tax purposes. She understands that the difference between the two methods is essentially one of timing and that, over the life of the firm, either method should result in the same taxable income. What she doesn't understand is why the cash method might improve the NPV of the firm's cash flows over the next decade. Can you provide an explanation?
11. Net operating losses can be carried forward for 20 years, after which time they expire. Why is it unusual for a firm to experience the expiration of an NOL?
12. Why do tax preferences often result in differences between book income and taxable income? Would a book/tax difference from a tax preference be a permanent difference or a timing difference? Which type of difference is more valuable in NPV terms?

Application Problems

1. PT Inc., which has been in business since 1980, uses a fiscal year ending June 30. The shareholders recently voted to dissolve the corporation under state law. PT ceased operations in September and distributed its remaining assets to its shareholders in October. PT's final tax return for the year beginning on July 1 and ending on October 31 reported $80,000 taxable income.

a. Compute PT's tax for its last year using the corporate tax rates.
b. Assume that PT operates an ongoing business and filed the short-period return described above because the IRS granted permission to change from a fiscal year ending June 30 to a fiscal year ending October 31. How does this change in fact affect the tax computation?

2. Firm B uses the calendar taxable year and the cash method of accounting. On December 31, 2004, Firm B made the following cash payments. To what extent can it deduct the payment in 2004?
   a. $3,000 compensation to a consultant who spent three weeks in January 2005 analyzing B's internal control system.
   b. $5,000 to purchase a new refrigerator for the employees' lounge. The refrigerator was delivered on January 8, 2005.
   c. $16,900 property tax to the local government for the first six months of 2005.

   d. $50,000 for a two-year office lease beginning on February 1, 2005.
   e. $23,700 of inventory items held for sale to customers.
3. RTY is a calendar year corporation. On December 12, RTY billed a client $17,800 for services rendered during October and November. It had not received payment by December 31. On December 10, RTY received a $4,000 check from a tenant that leases office space from the corporation. The payment was for next year's January and February rent.
   a. If RTY is a cash basis taxpayer, how much income should it recognize from the above transactions this year?
   b. If RTY is an accrual basis taxpayer, how much income should it recognize from the above transactions this year?
4. Firm B, a calendar year, cash basis taxpayer, leases lawn and garden equipment. During December, it recorded the following cash receipts. To what extent does each payment represent current taxable income to Firm B?
   a. $2,000 deposit from a customer who rented mechanical equipment. Firm B must return the entire deposit when the customer returns the undamaged equipment.
   b. $1,260 prepaid rent from the same customer. The rent is $12 per day for the 105-day period from December 17 through March 31.
   c. $25,000 short-term loan from a local bank. Firm B gave the bank a written note to repay the loan in one year at 9 percent interest.
   d. $1,045 repayment of a loan from an employee. Firm B loaned $1,000 to the employee six months ago, and the employee repaid the loan with interest.
5. Firm F, a calendar year taxpayer, owes an $800,000 long-term debt to an unrelated creditor. In December, it paid $72,000 to the creditor as interest for the 12-month period from the prior September 1 through August 31 of the following year. Compute the deduction for this payment assuming that:
   a. Firm F uses the accrual method of accounting for tax purposes.
   b. Firm F uses the cash method of accounting for tax purposes.
6. Company N, an accrual basis taxpayer, owes $50,000 to Creditor K. At the end of 2004, Company N accrued $4,100 interest payable on this debt. It didn't pay this liability until March 3, 2005. Both Company N and Creditor K are calendar year taxpayers. For each of the following cases, determine the year in which Company N can deduct the $4,100 interest expense.
   a. Creditor K is a cash basis taxpayer, and Company N and Creditor K are unrelated parties.

b. Creditor K is an accrual basis taxpayer, and Company N and Creditor K are related parties.

c. Creditor K is a cash basis taxpayer, and Company N and Creditor K are related parties.

7. Acme is an accrual basis corporation. Mrs. T, Acme's chief financial officer, is a cash basis individual. In December 2004, Acme's board of directors decided that Mrs. T should receive a $20,000 bonus as additional compensation. Acme paid the $20,000 bonus to Mrs. T on January 12, 2005. In which year can Acme deduct the $20,000 bonus assuming that:

   a. Mrs. T owns no Acme stock?

   b. Mrs. T owns 63 percent of Acme stock?

8. MG is an accrual basis corporation. In 2004, it wrote off a $65,000 account receivable as uncollectible. In 2005, it received a $65,000 check from the creditor in full payment of this receivable.

   a. What was the effect of the write-off on MG's 2004 financial statement income and taxable income?

   b. What was the effect of the collection of the receivable on MG's 2005 financial statement income and taxable income?

9. Firm F is a cash basis legal firm. In 2004, it performed services for a client, mailed the client a bill for $2,900, and recorded a $2,900 receivable. In 2005, Firm F discovered that the client was under criminal indictment and had fled the country. After learning this news, it wrote off the receivable.

   a. What was Firm F's tax basis in the $2,900 account receivable?

   b. What was the effect of the write-off on Firm F's taxable income?

10. Assuming a 35 percent marginal tax rate, compute the after-tax cost of the following business expenses.

   a. $25,000 political contribution.

   b. $12,000 client entertainment.

   c. $5,600 premium on business property and casualty insurance.

   d. $3,700 premium on key-person life insurance.

   e. $10,000 fine paid to Oregon for violation of a state law.

11. EFG, an accrual basis calendar year corporation, reported $500,000 net income before tax on its financial statements prepared in accordance with GAAP. EFG's records reveal the following information.

   - The allowance for bad debts as of January 1 was $58,000. Write-offs for the year totaled $13,800, and the addition to the allowance for the year was $12,500. The allowance as of December 31 was $56,700.
   - EFG paid a $17,500 fine to the state of Delaware for a violation of state pollution control laws.
   - EFG was sued by a consumers group for engaging in false advertising practices. Although EFG's lawyers are convinced that the suit is frivolous, its independent auditors insisted on establishing a $50,000 allowance for contingent legal liability and reporting a $50,000 accrued expense on the income statement.

   Compute EFG's taxable income.

12. GT Inc.'s net income before tax on its financial statements was $700,000, and its taxable income was $810,000. The $110,000 difference is the aggregate of temporary book/tax differences. GT's tax rate is 34 percent.

a. Compute GT's tax expense for financial statement purposes.
b. Compute GT's tax payable.
c. Compute the net increase in GT's deferred tax assets or deferred tax liabilities (identify which) for the year.

13. Corporation H's auditors prepared the following reconciliation between book and taxable income. H's tax rate is 34 percent.

Net income before tax	$600,000
Permanent book/tax differences	15,000
Temporary book/tax differences	(76,000)
Taxable income	$539,000

a. Compute Corporation H's tax expense for financial statement purposes.
b. Compute Corporation H's tax payable.
c. Compute the net increase in Corporation H's deferred tax assets or deferred tax liabilities (identify which) for the year.

14. PSD, an accrual basis corporation, reported $320,000 net income before tax on its financial statements prepared in accordance with GAAP. PSD's records reveal the following information.
    - PSD earned $215,600 net income from its U.S. manufacturing activity and $75,400 from its foreign manufacturing activity.
    - Late in the year, PSD entered into a five-year licensing agreement with an unrelated firm. The agreement entitles the firm to use a PSD trade name in marketing its own product. In return, the firm will pay PSD an annual royalty of 1 percent of gross revenues from sales of the product. The firm paid a $40,000 advanced royalty to PSD on the day the agreement was finalized. For financial statement purposes, this prepayment was credited to a deferred revenue account.
    - At its final meeting for the year, PSD's board of directors authorized a $15,500 salary bonus for the corporation's president to reward him for an outstanding performance. PSD paid the bonus on January 12. The president does not own enough PSD stock to make him a related party for federal tax purposes.
    - PSD was incorporated last year. On its first tax return, it reported a $13,600 net operating loss.

    Compute PSD's taxable income.

15. NC Company, a retail hardware store, began business in August and elected a calendar year for tax purposes. From August through December, NC paid $589,000 for inventory to stock the store. According to a physical inventory count on December 31, NC had $272,300 of inventory on hand. Compute NC's cost of goods sold for its first year assuming:

    a. NC adopted the cash method as its overall method of accounting.
    b. NC adopted the accrual method as its overall method of accounting.

16. On November 1, NC Company prepaid $1,800 rent for office equipment. The rental agreement entitled NC to use the equipment from November 1 until October 31 of the following year. How much of the prepayment can NC deduct this year assuming:

    a. NC adopted the cash method as its overall method of accounting?
    b. NC adopted the accrual method as its overall method of accounting?

17. KLP, a calendar year corporation, sponsored a contest for its customers with a grand prize of $100,000 cash. Contestants could enter the contest from June 1 through November 30. KLP selected the winner and announced her name on December 20. However, it did not present a $100,000 check to the winner until January 13. In which year can KLP deduct the $100,000 payment assuming:
    a. KLP uses the cash method of accounting?
    b. KLP uses the accrual method of accounting?
18. In 2003, AS, an accrual basis corporation, contracted with a nationally prominent artist to paint a mural in the lobby of the new corporate headquarters under construction. The artist's commission was $180,000, payable on completion of the mural. The artist finished her work and received the $180,000 commission in 2005. AS has a 35 percent marginal tax rate and uses a 7 percent discount rate to compute NPV.
    a. Compute AS's after-tax cost of the commission if it can deduct the $180,000 accrued liability in 2003.
    b. Compute AS's after-tax cost of the commission if the economic performance requirement delays the deduction until 2005.
19. TRW Inc. began business in 1997 and was profitable for its first three years. In 2000, it generated an $819,000 net operating loss. The following table shows TRW's taxable income *before consideration of this NOL.*

	1997	1998	1999	2000	2001	2002	2003	2004
Taxable income	$20,000	$138,000	$81,000	($819,000)	$21,000	$398,000	$687,000	$905,000

Recompute TRW's taxable income for this eight-year period assuming that it did not elect to give up the NOL carryback.

Issue Recognition Problems

Identify the tax issue or issues suggested by the following situations and state each issue in the form of a question.

1. Corporation DS owns assets worth $550,000 and has $750,000 outstanding debts. One of DS's creditors just informed DS that it is writing off a $15,000 account receivable from DS because it believes the receivable is uncollectible. However, even with this debt discharge, DS is insolvent and has no net worth.
2. Two years ago, a professional theater company paid $300 to an antique dealer for an old oil painting that the company used as a prop. This year, the company's prop manager was cleaning the painting and discovered an older painting hidden beneath the top coat of pigment. To the company's delight, the older painting was signed by Paul Cézanne. Two independent appraisers determined that the painting is worth at least $250,000.
3. BL Inc. has been in business since 1990. This year BL's new CPA discovered that it is using an incorrect accounting method for a certain expense. BL is willing to change to the correct accounting method recommended by the CPA.
4. Company A, a calendar year taxpayer, has always used the cash method of accounting. It completed an engagement for a major client in November 2004 and submitted a bill for its $160,000 fee. Because Company A did not receive payment before year-end, it recognized no income from the engagement on its 2004 tax return. In January 2005,

Company A received permission from the IRS to change from the cash method to the accrual method. This change is effective for 2005. On February 2, 2005, Company A received a $160,000 check from the client in payment of the bill.

5. Mr. RJ owns a consulting firm that uses a calendar year and the cash method. In November, Mr. RJ billed a client $3,500 for services performed in September. After waiting several weeks, he called the client to remind her of the bill. The embarrassed client promised to telephone Mr. RJ as soon as she prepared a check for $3,500. Mr. RJ left his business office on December 23 and did not return until January 2. A message on his answering machine said that he could pick up his check from the client's receptionist. The message was dated December 30.
6. Masterson Inc., an accrual basis, calendar year corporation, operates exclusively in Missouri and pays that state's corporate income tax. Masterson filed its 2004 Missouri tax return on March 7, 2005, and enclosed a check for $119,200, which was the balance due of its 2004 state tax liability.
7. ABC Partnership owns 100 percent of the stock of two corporations, HT (an advertising firm) and LT (a commercial real estate development firm). HT is in a 35 percent marginal tax bracket. LT has an NOL carryforward deduction and will pay no tax this year. HT recently developed a new advertising campaign for LT and charged $75,000 for its services.
8. In 2004, Firm K paid $129,000 real property tax to Jurisdiction J and deducted the payment. In 2005, it successfully contested the property tax assessment. As a result, Jurisdiction J refunded $18,000 of the property tax.
9. In October 2003, Firm G completed a consulting engagement and received a $200,000 cash payment for its services. In December, the client notified Firm G that it was not satisfied with the work and demanded that Firm G refund $50,000 of the payment. Firm G refused and referred the matter to its attorney. In 2005, Firm G settled the dispute by paying the client $30,000. Firm G's 2003 marginal tax rate was 39 percent and its 2005 marginal tax rate was 34 percent.
10. Corporation WJ began business in 2002 and reported taxable income in both 2002 and 2003. In 2004, WJ incurred a $25,000 net operating loss. It wants to carry the NOL back as a deduction against 2003 taxable income because its 2003 marginal tax rate was higher than its 2002 marginal tax rate.
11. BL and TM are both calendar year corporations. On January 1, 2005, BL purchased TM's entire business (all TM's balance sheet assets), and TM's shareholders dissolved the corporation under state law. On January 1, TM had a $190,000 NOL carryforward. BL's business for 2005 (which includes the business purchased from TM) generated $600,000 taxable income.

Research Problems

1. Bontaine Publications, an accrual basis, calendar year corporation, publishes and sells weekly and monthly magazines to retail bookstores and newsstands. The sales agreement provides that the retailers may return any unsold magazines during the one-month period after purchase. Bontaine will refund one-half of the purchase price of each returned magazine. During December 2004, Bontaine recorded $919,400 of magazine sales. During January 2005, Bontaine refunded $82,717 to retailers that returned magazines purchased during December. Can Bontaine reduce its 2004 income by the refund?
2. CheapTrade, an accrual basis, calendar year corporation, operates a discount securities brokerage business. CheapTrade accepts orders to buy or sell marketable securities for

its customers and charges them a commission fee for effecting the transaction in a timely, low-cost manner. CheapTrade executes an order on the "trade" date, but title to the securities is not legally transferred and payment to or from the customer is not due until the "settlement date." In the normal five-day interval between the trade and settlement dates, CheapTrade performs administrative and accounting functions to record the transaction. During the last week of 2004, CheapTrade effected over 18,000 transactions with a trading date in 2004 but a settlement date in 2005. CheapTrade's commission from these transactions was $1,712,400. In which year should CheapTrade recognize this income?

3. Moleri, an accrual basis corporation with a fiscal taxable year ending on July 31, owns real estate on which it pays annual property tax to Madison County, Texas. The county assesses the tax for the upcoming calendar year on January 1, and the tax becomes a lien on the property as of the assessment date. Property owners have until March 31 to pay the tax without penalty. Moleri paid its 2005 property tax of $29,820 on March 11, 2005. How much of this tax payment is deductible on Moleri's tax return for the fiscal year ending July 31, 2005?
4. Jetex, an accrual basis, calendar year corporation, engages in the business of long-distance freight hauling. Every year, Jetex is required to purchase several hundred permits and licenses from state and local governments in order to legally operate its fleet of trucks. During 2005, the cost of these permits and licenses totaled $1,119,200. Even though none of the permits and licenses was valid for more than 12 months, a substantial number of them did not expire until sometime in 2006. If fact, Jetex calculated that $612,000 of the total cost incurred in 2005 actually benefited the company in 2006. For financial statement purposes, Jetex capitalized this amount as an asset and expensed only the $507,200 remainder on its 2005 income statement. As an accrual basis taxpayer, is Jetex limited to a $507,200 deduction in 2005?

Tax Planning Cases

1. Company Y began business in February 2005. By the end of the calendar year, it had billed its clients for $3.5 million of services and had incurred $800,000 of operating expenses. As of December 31, it had collected $2.9 million of its billings and had paid $670,000 of its expenses. It expects to collect the remaining outstanding bills and pay the remaining expenses by March 2006. Company Y adopted a calendar year for federal tax purposes. It may use either the cash method or the accrual method of accounting on its first tax return, and has asked you to quantify the value of using the cash method for the first year. In doing so, assume Company Y uses a 7 percent discount rate to compute NPV.
2. Corporation VB's tax returns for 2001, 2002, and 2003 provide the following information.

	2001	2002	2003
Gross income	$150,000	$1,890,000	$7,810,000
Deductions	(190,000)	(1,830,000)	(7,700,000)
Taxable income or (NOL)	$ (40,000)	$ 60,000	$ 110,000

a. On the basis of the above data, did VB derive any tax benefit from its 2001 NOL? Explain your conclusions.

b. VB generated a $350,000 net operating loss for 2004. It projects that it will continue to operate at a loss through 2005 but should generate at least $1 million taxable income in 2006. On the basis of this projection, compute the value of the 2004 NOL, assuming that VB deducts it as a carryback and carryforward to the extent possible. In making your calculations, refer to the corporate tax rate schedule to compute VB's tax in 2002 and 2003 and use a 7 percent discount rate to compute NPV.

c. Should VB elect to give up the carryback of its 2004 NOL and use the entire NOL as a carryforward deduction? Support your conclusion with calculations.

Chapter Six

Property Acquisitions and Cost Recovery Deductions

Learning Objectives

After studying this chapter, you should be able to:

1. Describe the factors that determine whether a business expenditure is deducted or capitalized.
2. Define the terms *tax basis* and *adjusted basis.*
3. Explain how leverage can reduce the after-tax cost of purchased assets.
4. Compute cost of goods sold for tax purposes.
5. Describe the relationship between recovery period, depreciation method, and depreciation convention in the MACRS computation.
6. Apply the Section 179 expensing election.
7. Incorporate depreciation deductions into the computation of NPV.
8. Explain how a firm recovers the cost of purchased intangibles through amortization.
9. Distinguish between cost depletion and percentage depletion.

In Chapter 5, we learned that taxable income equals the excess of gross income over allowable deductions. We also learned that firms are allowed to deduct their expenditures over the period of time that the expenditures create value for the firm. If an expenditure benefits the firm only in the current year, the expenditure is generally allowed as a current deduction. If an expenditure will benefit the firm for more than one taxable year, the deduction for the expenditure must be properly matched against future gross income.

In Chapter 6, we address this timing issue: In which taxable year or years can a firm deduct its business expenditures? The chapter begins with a discussion of the tax rules that distinguish between deductible expenditures and expenditures that must be capitalized. The discussion then turns to the concept of capitalized costs as the tax basis of business assets.

The relationship between basis and cost recovery deductions is explored, and the effect of cost recovery deductions on cash flows is examined. The second part of the chapter focuses on the various methods by which firms recover basis as cost of goods sold or through depreciation, amortization, and depletion deductions.

DEDUCTIBLE EXPENSE OR CAPITALIZED COST?

When a firm expends resources as part of its income-generating activity, the financial cost of the expenditure is reduced by any tax savings resulting from the expenditure. In present value terms, tax savings are usually maximized (and after-tax cost is minimized) if the expenditure is deductible in the current year. The present value of the tax savings decreases if the firm must capitalize the expenditure and postpone its deduction until some future year. For tax accounting purposes, **capitalization** means that an expenditure is recorded as an asset on the balance sheet rather than as a current expense. If the firm is never allowed any tax deduction for the capitalized expenditure, the before-tax cost of the expenditure equals its after-tax cost.

Absent any restrictions, firms would immediately deduct every business expenditure. However, a basic premise of the federal income tax is that *no expenditure is deductible* unless the Internal Revenue Code authorizes the deduction. The Supreme Court has elaborated on this premise by observing that "an income tax deduction is a matter of legislative grace" and "the burden of clearly showing the right to the claimed deduction is on the taxpayer."[1] These observations are consistent with the tax law's conservative attitude toward the measurement of taxable income.

The Internal Revenue Code does allow firms to deduct all "ordinary and necessary expenses paid or incurred during the taxable year in carrying on any trade or business."[2] Because of this generic rule, firms deduct routine operating expenses in the year incurred under the firm's method of accounting. But the Code also prohibits a deduction for payments for "permanent improvements or betterments made to increase the value of any property."[3] As we will learn later in this chapter, the law relaxes this prohibition by allowing firms to recover many capital expenditures in the form of *future* deductions. In these cases, the difference in the tax consequences of current expenses and capitalized costs is the timing of the deduction for each. Even so, in cash flow terms, future deductions are worth less than current deductions, and firms minimize their cost of operations by deducting expenditures as soon as possible.

Objective 1
Describe the factors that determine whether a business expenditure is deducted or capitalized.

What factors determine whether a particular business expenditure is treated as a current deduction or a capital cost? If the expenditure creates or enhances an identifiable asset with a useful life substantially beyond the current year, the expenditure must be capitalized.[4] Even if the expenditure does not create or enhance a specific asset, the expenditure must be capitalized if it results in a significant long-term benefit to the firm.[5] Moreover, if the tax treatment of an expenditure is uncertain, capitalization is the norm while deductibility is the exception.[6]

The following example quantifies the difference between deduction and capitalization in cash flow terms.

[1] *Interstate Transit Lines* v. *Commissioner*, 319 U.S. 590, 593 (1943).

[2] §162(a).

[3] §263(a).

[4] Reg. §1.263(a)-2(a) and *Commissioner* v. *Lincoln Savings & Loan Assn.*, 403 U.S. 345 (1971).

[5] *Indopco Inc.* v. *Commissioner*, 503 U.S. 79 (1992).

[6] Ibid.

Current Deduction versus Capitalized Cost

This year, Corporation M raised $1 million of new capital by issuing preferred stock to a group of private investors.[7] The corporation incurred $40,000 of legal and other professional fees related to this transaction. Corporation M's marginal tax rate is 35 percent. Compare the after-tax cash flows under two different assumptions concerning the tax treatment of the $40,000 expenditure.

	Current Deduction	*Capitalized Cost*
Proceeds of stock issue	$1,000,000	$1,000,000
Professional fees	(40,000)	(40,000)
Tax savings ($40,000 deduction × 35%)	14,000	–0–
After-tax cash flow	$ 974,000	$ 960,000

In this example, the $40,000 expenditure did not create or enhance a new asset for Corporation M. However, the federal courts have consistently ruled that expenses related to raising capital or reorganizing a firm's capital structure benefit the firm for the duration of its existence and are not deductible.[8] Based on this rule of law, Corporation M must charge the $40,000 expenditure against the proceeds of the stock sale, which nets $960,000 for the corporation on an after-tax basis.

Repairs and Cleanup Costs

Every firm that owns tangible operating assets must make incidental repairs and perform routine maintenance to keep the assets in good working order. Repair and maintenance costs that are regular and recurring in nature and do not materially add to either the value or the useful life of an asset are deductible.[9] In contrast, expenditures that substantially increase the value or useful life of an asset are nondeductible capital improvements. Similarly, the expense of adapting an existing asset to a new or different use must be capitalized to the cost of the asset.[10] The distinction between a repair and a capital improvement is not always obvious and is frequently a matter of dispute between taxpayers and the Internal Revenue Service.

Repair or Capital Improvement

Out of concern for earthquake safety, the city of San Francisco required the Fairmont Hotel to either remove or replace the concrete parapets and cornices that had decorated the hotel's exterior since 1907. The hotel spent $3 million to replace the old parapets and cornices with replicas made of lightweight fiberglass. The Fairmont Hotel deducted the expenditure as a repair. The IRS concluded that the expenditure was a capital improvement to the building and disallowed the deduction. In court, the Fairmont's owners argued that the $3 million expenditure was necessary to maintain the classical appearance of the building and to preserve its identity as a "grand hotel of the world." Moreover, the expenditure was not voluntary but was required by city ordinance. In spite of these arguments, the court agreed with the IRS that the expenditure materially prolonged the life and increased the value of the Fairmont Hotel and was not deductible.[11]

[7] Corporations do not recognize gain on the receipt of cash in exchange for stock. §1032.

[8] See *General Bancshares Corp.* v. *Commissioner*, 326 F.2d 712 (CA-8, 1964) and *Mills Estate, Inc.* v. *Commissioner*, 206 F.2d 244 (CA-2, 1953).

[9] Reg. §1.162-4.

[10] Reg. §1.263(a)-1(b).

[11] *Swig Investment Co.* v. *United States*, 98 F.3d 1359 (CA-FC, 1996).

The business community and the IRS are presently debating the proper treatment of environmental cleanup costs. Many firms, either voluntarily or because of government mandate, are spending millions of dollars to clean up pollutants, toxic wastes, and other dangerous substances unleashed on the environment as industrial by-products. The firms argue that cleanup costs should be currently deductible, while the IRS maintains that many such costs must be capitalized.

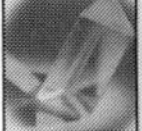

Cleanup Costs

Company NM replaced the asbestos insulation in all its manufacturing equipment with nonhazardous insulation and deducted the replacement expense. The company justified the deduction because the replacement was made to protect the health of its employees and did not improve the operating efficiency or increase the value of the equipment. Furthermore, the replacement expense remedied a historic problem and was not related to the generation of future income. Upon audit, the IRS concluded that the asbestos replacement did, in fact, result in a long-term benefit to Company NM by permanently improving the work environment. Therefore, the IRS required the company to capitalize the replacement expense to the cost of the reinsulated equipment.[12]

As part of the Tax Reform Act of 1997, Congress enacted a provision allowing firms to elect to deduct (rather than capitalize) expenditures to abate or control hazardous substances at targeted contamination sites, commonly described as "brownfields."[13] This provision was intended to encourage firms to undertake environmental remediation of these sites by reducing the after-tax cost of the remediation.

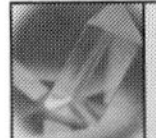

Environmental Remediation

In 2005, AVC Inc. purchased a manufacturing plant situated on 25 acres of land qualifying as a targeted contamination site. AVC spent $80,000 to rid the property of toxic chemical substances. Because AVC was in a 35 percent marginal tax bracket and elected to deduct its environmental remediation expenditure, the after-tax cost of the expenditure was $52,000 ($80,000 − $28,000 tax savings from the deduction).

Current Deductions of Capital Expenditures as Subsidies

The tax law contains special rules permitting firms to deduct expenditures that clearly are capital in nature. These preferential rules reduce the firm's after-tax cost of the expenditure and thereby represent an indirect federal subsidy. For instance, firms may deduct the first $15,000 of the annual cost of the removal of architectural and transportation barriers from buildings or transportation equipment to make such facilities more accessible to handicapped or elderly people.[14] A more significant preference is the deduction for **research and experimental expenditures.** This deduction is available even if the research leads to the development of an identifiable asset with an extended useful life to the firm.[15] This valuable preference reflects the federal government's belief that basic research is crucial to economic growth and should be encouraged through the tax law.

Self-Created Patent

CPT's research laboratory spent $2 million in the development of a chemical process that eliminates cholesterol from dairy products. CPT applied for and received a patent on the process from the U.S. Patent Office. The patent gave CPT the exclusive right to exploit the process for

[12] This example is based on IRS Letter Ruling 9240004 (July 29, 1992).

[13] §198.

[14] §190.

[15] §174(a).

commercial purposes for 17 years. Even though the patent is an identifiable asset with long-term value, CPT deducted the $2 million cost of this "self-created asset" as a research and experimental expenditure. Consequently, its capitalized cost of the patent is zero.

Many preferential deductions benefit only certain industries. For instance, farmers are allowed to deduct soil and water conservation expenditures, which include the cost of leveling, grading, and terracing land, constructing drainage ditches and earthen dams, and planting windbreaks to inhibit soil erosion.[16] Farmers get a second tax break in the form of a deduction for the cost of fertilizers or other materials used to enrich farmland.[17]

Oil and gas producers can deduct **intangible drilling and development costs (IDC)** associated with locating and preparing wells for production.[18] Expenditures such as wages, fuel, repairs to drilling equipment, hauling, and supplies that contribute to the development of a productive well undeniably result in a long-term benefit to the producer and are usually captialized for financial statement purposes. By allowing a deduction for such IDC, the tax law provides an incentive for producers to undertake new drilling projects.

Advertising costs are deductible, even though a firm's successful advertising campaign can increase its market share and improve its competitive position for years to come.[19] While the IRS acknowledges that the advertising of a particular product or advertising intended to promote name recognition or goodwill may enhance a firm's profitability, it does not require capitalization of advertising costs except in unusual circumstances.[20]

Graphic Design Costs

R.J. Reynolds Tobacco Company deducted $2.2 million of graphic design costs related to its cigarette packs and cartons. Graphic design comprises the verbal information, styles of print, pictures or drawings, shapes, patterns, and colors displayed on the packs and cartons. The IRS disallowed the deduction because the design costs created intangible "brand equity" assets that were distinguishable from the goodwill created by advertising. In court, R.J. Reynolds argued that its graphic designs fit the textbook definition of advertising as any "presentation and promotion of ideas, goods, or services by an identified sponsor, which involves the use of mass media." The judge accepted this argument and held that R.J. Reynolds could deduct the graphic design costs as advertising expenses.[21]

THE CRITICAL ROLE OF TAX BASIS

Objective 2
Define the terms *tax basis* and *adjusted basis*.

When a firm capitalizes an expenditure to a new asset account, the amount of the expenditure becomes the firm's **tax basis** in the asset. Basis can be defined as a taxpayer's investment in any asset or property right—the measure of *unrecovered dollars* represented by the asset. An asset's basis plays a key role in the calculation of cash flows because taxpayers are entitled to recover this basis at no tax cost. This recovery occurs either through a series of future deductions or when the taxpayer disposes of the asset. Cost recovery deductions are covered in this chapter, while the tax consequences of asset dispositions are the subject of Chapter 7.

[16] §175. This preferential deduction may not exceed 25 percent of the gross income derived from farming during the taxable year.

[17] §180.

[18] §263(c).

[19] Regs. §1.162-1(a) and §1.162-20(a)(2).

[20] Rev. Rul. 92-80, 1992-2 CB 57.

[21] *RJR Nabisco Inc.*, TC Memo 1998-252.

Basis, Cost Recovery, and Cash Flow

When a firm is allowed a deduction for a portion of the capitalized cost of an asset, the deduction has two consequences. The first consequence is that the asset's initial tax basis is reduced by the deduction.[22] The reduced basis is called the asset's **adjusted basis.** The second consequence is that the deduction generates a tax savings that reduces the after-tax cost of the asset.

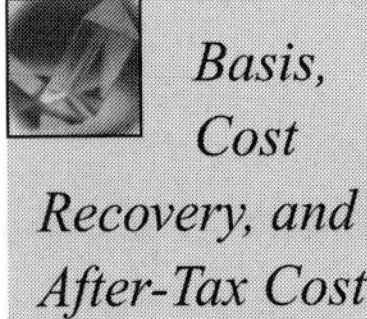

Basis, Cost Recovery, and After-Tax Cost

Firm J pays $5,000 cash for a business asset. The tax law allows Firm J to deduct the capitalized cost of the asset ratably over five years. In the year of purchase and in each of the four subsequent years, the firm deducts $1,000 and reduces its basis in the asset by this deduction. If the firm has a 35 percent marginal tax rate and uses a 7 percent discount rate to compute net present value (NPV), the after-tax cost of the asset (NPV of cash flows) is $3,464.

			Cash Flows			
Year	*Year-End Adjusted Basis*	*Annual Deduction*	*Initial Payment*	*Tax Savings from Deduction*	*Discount Factor*	*NPV*
0	$4,000	$(1,000)	$(5,000)	$350		$(4,650)
1	3,000	(1,000)		350	.935	327
2	2,000	(1,000)		350	.873	306
3	1,000	(1,000)		350	.816	286
4	–0–	(1,000)		350	.763	267
						$(3,464)

Firm J's adjusted basis in its asset at the end of each year is the $5,000 cost less the accumulated cost recovery deductions. By the end of the fifth year, the firm has recovered its entire investment in the asset, leaving the asset with a zero tax basis. A zero tax basis does not imply anything about the *value* of the asset to the firm; it simply indicates that Firm J has deducted the entire $5,000 expenditure that created the asset.

The difference between Firm J's $5,000 before-tax cost and $3,464 after-tax cost results from the stream of tax savings generated by the cost recovery deductions. If the firm could have recovered its tax basis over a shorter period of time, the present value of this stream would increase and the after-tax cost of the asset would decrease. Conversely, if the recovery period were longer, the present value of the tax savings would decrease and the after-tax cost of the asset would increase.[23]

Cost Basis

The majority of assets reported on a firm's balance sheet have an initial **cost basis**—the price paid to acquire the asset. Cost basis includes any sales tax paid by the purchaser and any incidental costs related to putting the asset into production.[24] While firms acquire many assets in straightforward cash transactions, they also acquire assets in exchange for

[22] §1016(a)(2).

[23] This calculation of after-tax cost implies that the asset has no residual value after five years. If the firm could sell the asset for cash, the present value of this after-tax cash would reduce the after-tax cost of the asset. The cash flow implications of asset sales are addressed in the next chapter.

[24] See, for example, Rev. Rul. 69-640, 1969-2 CB 211.

property or services. In such case, the cost basis of the asset equals the fair market value (FMV) of the property surrendered or the services performed.[25]

Cost Basis of Asset Acquired in Exchange for Property

BT Corporation, a manufacturer of heavy equipment, sold inventory to an unrelated land developer. BT agreed to let the developer pay for the inventory by transferring five acres of land to the corporation. The inventory has a FMV of $139,000. BT's cost basis in its new asset (the land) is $139,000, the FMV of the inventory that BT exchanged for the asset.

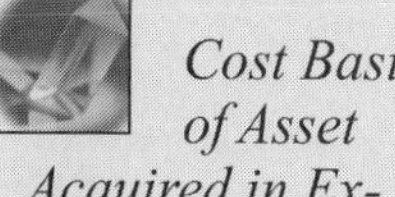

Cost Basis of Asset Acquired in Exchange for Note

Modify the previous example by assuming that BT sold the inventory for the developer's written, interest-bearing note to pay $139,000 in three years' time. BT's cost basis in its new asset (the note receivable) is $139,000, the FMV of the inventory that BT exchanged for the asset.

Cost Basis of Property Acquired in Exchange for Services

Firm C, a consulting business, performed professional services for an unrelated corporation and billed the corporation for $17,500. The corporation paid its bill by issuing 1,000 shares of its own common stock to the firm. Firm C recognizes $17,500 gross income and takes a $17,500 cost basis in its new asset (1,000 shares of corporate stock). This basis represents Firm C's investment in these shares—the dollar amount that the firm can recover tax free when it disposes of the stock.

Leveraged Cost Basis

When a firm acquires an asset through debt financing, the cost basis of the asset equals its entire cost, not just the firm's equity in the asset. Refer back to the example on page 132 in which Firm J purchased a business asset for $5,000. Assume that the firm financed the purchase by paying $1,500 from its bank account and borrowing $3,500 from a commercial lender. Firm J gave the lender a lien on the asset to secure the debt. Although the firm's initial investment in the asset is only $1,500, its cost basis is the full $5,000 purchase price.[26] The firm's repayment of the debt will create additional equity in the asset but will have no effect on the tax basis of the asset.

Objective 3
Explain how leverage can reduce the after-tax cost of purchased assets.

Tax planners refer to the use of borrowed funds to create tax basis as **leverage.** The use of leverage can reduce the purchaser's after-tax cost of the asset. Let's expand on the Firm J example to demonstrate how the after-tax cost of the $5,000 asset is reduced by the use of borrowed funds.

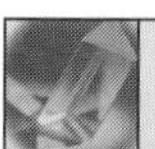

After-Tax Cost of Leveraged Purchase

Under the terms of its agreement with the commercial lender, Firm J must pay $315 interest (9 percent) at the beginning of each year and repay the $3,500 principal amount at the beginning of the fifth year. The annual interest payments are deductible expenses, while the principal payment is charged against (and retires) the firm's $3,500 debt. The following table

[25] Fair market value is the price at which property or services would change hands between a willing buyer and a willing seller, neither being under any compulsion to buy or to sell and both having reasonable knowledge of the relevant facts. Reg. §20.2031-1(b). Although this definition is in the estate tax regulations, it is the accepted definition for income tax purposes.

[26] *Crane* v. *Commissioner*, 331 U.S. 1 (1947).

reflects each year's net cash flows related to the asset purchase using Firm J's 35 percent marginal tax rate and 7 percent discount rate.

			Tax Savings From				
Year	*Initial Payment/ Debt Repayment*	*Interest Payment*	*Cost Recovery Deduction*	*Interest Deduction*	*Net Cash Flow*	*Discount Factor*	*NPV*
0	$(1,500)		$350		$(1,150)		$(1,150)
1		(315)	350	110	145	.935	136
2		(315)	350	110	145	.873	127
3		(315)	350	110	145	.816	118
4	(3,500)	(315)	350	110	(3,355)	.763	(2,560)
							$(3,329)

By leveraging its purchase of the asset, Firm J reduced the after-tax cost from $3,464 to $3,329. The cash flow data explain this result. Firm J's initial cash outflow to buy the asset was only $1,500. By borrowing the balance of the purchase price, it deferred paying $3,500 cash until the fifth year. This beneficial change in cash flows did not affect the firm's $5,000 tax basis in the asset, its annual cost recovery deductions, or the timing of the stream of tax savings from those deductions. The annual cost of the leverage was $205, which is the after-tax interest on the note ($315 interest payment – $110 tax savings). However, even considering this additional cost, the leverage saved the firm $135.[27]

INTRODUCTION TO COST RECOVERY METHODS

The topics covered in the first part of this chapter all relate to a key tax planning concept: The after-tax cost of a capitalized expenditure depends on the time period over which the firm can recover the expenditure as a deduction. The remainder of the chapter examines the four basic methods of periodic cost recovery: cost of goods sold, depreciation, amortization, and depletion. If none of these recovery methods is applicable, a cost is recoverable only when the firm disposes of the asset or when that asset ceases to exist.

INVENTORIES AND COST OF GOODS SOLD

In Chapter 5, we learned that firms maintaining inventories of goods for sale to customers must account for their inventory on the accrual basis. In other words, firms can't deduct the cost of manufactured or purchased inventory but must capitalize the cost to an asset account. At the end of each year, the firm ascertains how much inventory is still on hand and how much has been sold during the year. The cost of the inventory on hand is carried on the

[27] The leverage was beneficial in this example because Firm J's after-tax interest rate on borrowed funds was 5.85 percent ($205 after-tax interest ÷ $3,500 debt), while its discount rate was 7 percent. If Firm's J's after-tax interest rate was higher than its discount rate, the leverage would be detrimental and would increase the after-tax cost of the asset in NPV terms.

balance sheet, while the **cost of goods sold** is deducted.[28] The following formula summarizes this accounting procedure:

Cost of inventory on hand at the beginning of the year
Cost of inventory manufactured or purchased during the year

Total cost of inventory available for sale
(Cost of inventory on hand at the end of the year)

Cost of goods sold

Objective 4
Compute cost of goods sold for tax purposes.

This formula is based on two assumptions. The first assumption is that all expenditures that contributed to the value of inventory are capitalized to the inventory account. The second assumption is that the total cost of inventory is properly allocated between the inventory on hand at the end of the year and the inventory sold during the year. Let's examine the basic tax rules underlying each of these assumptions.

The Unicap Rules

Firms typically prefer to treat expenditures as deductible *period costs* rather than *product costs* that must be capitalized to inventory. Not surprisingly, the tax law contains explicit rules about the expenditures that must be included in inventory. These **uniform capitalization (unicap) rules** are as strict as they are complicated.[29] Under unicap, firms must capitalize all direct costs of manufacturing, purchasing, or storing inventory (direct materials and direct labor) and any indirect costs that "benefit or are incurred by reason of the performance of production or resale activities."[30] Examples of indirect costs that must be capitalized *to the extent they relate to a firm's production or resale function* include:[31]

- Officer's compensation.
- Pension, retirement, and other employee benefits.
- Rents paid on buildings and equipment used in a manufacturing process.
- Premiums paid to carry property insurance on production assets.
- Repair and maintenance of production assets.
- Cost recovery deductions for the cost of production assets.

The unicap rules may require indirect costs that were expensed for financial statement purposes to be capitalized for tax purposes. The resulting book/tax difference is temporary and will reverse in the year in which the capitalized costs are deducted as cost of goods sold.

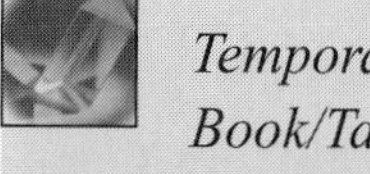

Temporary Book/Tax Difference for Unicap

In 2003, Company MN constructed an inventory item that was on hand at year-end. It incurred $100,000 direct and indirect costs in the construction process. For financial statement purposes, Company MN capitalized $80,000 as inventory product costs and expensed $20,000 as period costs. Under the unicap rules, it had to capitalize $88,000 to inventory and could deduct only $12,000 on its tax return. In 2004, Company MN sold the inventory item. For the two-year period, the difference in accounting methods resulted in the following:

[28] Technically, cost of goods sold is subtracted from gross receipts to compute gross income. Reg. §1.61-3(a).

[29] The unicap rules are found in §263A and the accompanying regulations.

[30] Reg. §1.263A-1(e)(3)(i).

[31] Reg. §1.263A-1(e)(3)(ii).

	Book		Tax		
2003	*Expense*	*Inventory Cost*	*Deduction*	*Inventory Cost*	*Taxable Income over Book Income*
	$20,000	$80,000	$12,000	$88,000	$8,000
2004	*Cost of Goods Sold*		*Cost of Goods Sold*		*Book Income over Taxable Income*
	$80,000		$88,000		$8,000

Allocating Costs between Inventory and Cost of Goods Sold

The allocation of costs between ending inventory and cost of goods sold is based on the method of accounting by which a firm tracks the flow of inventory items through its system. If a firm knows the actual cost of each item, it can use the **specific identification method** to value ending inventory and compute cost of goods sold. Real estate developers and antique dealers are good examples of businesses in which specific identification of inventory is possible.

For manufacturing and retail businesses that deal with thousands, if not millions, of inventory items, specific identification of each item is impossible. These firms must use a costing convention that is not based on the physical movement of inventory through the system. The two most commonly used costing conventions are **FIFO** (first-in, first-out) and **LIFO** (last-in, first-out).

A firm's selection of an inventory costing convention may have a substantial effect on annual taxable income. During a period of rising prices, it is generally to a firm's advantage to adopt LIFO because the convention assumes that the last goods manufactured or purchased are the first goods sold. In an inflationary economy, the most recently acquired goods are the most expensive. If a firm assumes these goods are the first to be sold, it maximizes the cost of goods sold and minimizes the cost of ending inventory. While the LIFO convention can offer substantial tax savings, its popularity is diminished by the fact that any firm electing LIFO for tax purposes must also use it to prepare financial statements.[32] Because of this forced conformity, any reduction in taxable income attributable to LIFO is mirrored by a reduction in accounting income and earnings per share reported to the firm's investors.

DEPRECIATION OF TANGIBLE BUSINESS ASSETS

Book and Tax Concepts of Depreciation

Under generally accepted accounting principles (GAAP), firms write off, or *depreciate,* the capitalized cost of tangible assets over their estimated useful lives.[33] As a result, the cost of an asset is expensed over the years in which it contributes to the firm's revenue-generating activity. The concept of **depreciation** applies only to wasting assets that:

[32] §472(c).

[33] The depreciable cost is reduced by the asset's estimated residual or salvage value.

- Lose value over time because of wear and tear, physical deterioration, or obsolescence.
- Have a reasonably ascertainable useful life.

Nonwasting tangible assets that lack these characteristics, such as land and works of art acquired for display, are nondepreciable. For financial statement purposes, firms may calculate their annual depreciation expense under a variety of methods and may choose the method that results in the best matching of the cost of an asset against revenue.

Before 1981, depreciation for tax purposes was also based on the estimated useful life of business property. Because the probable useful life of any asset is a matter of conjecture, taxpayers and the IRS were constantly wrangling over the question of asset lives. Firms argued for the shortest life over which to recover the tax basis of their depreciable assets, while the IRS asserted that a longer recovery period was more realistic. In 1981, Congress enacted a radically new cost recovery system to replace the old depreciation rules. In 1986, Congress refined this system into the **Modified Accelerated Cost Recovery System (MACRS),** which is in effect today.[34] Under MACRS, the estimated useful life of an asset is irrelevant in the computation of tax depreciation. Because the MACRS computation is independent of the computation of book depreciation, the depreciation deduction on a firm's tax return and depreciation expense on its financial statements are usually different numbers.

The MACRS Framework

Objective 5
Describe the relationship between recovery period, depreciation method, and depreciation convention in the MACRS computation.

This section of Chapter 6 presents the MACRS framework: the general rules for computing depreciation for federal tax purposes. Business managers who understand this framework can appreciate the role of MACRS in the tax planning process. They do not need to master the system's fine technical points; consequently, many of the details of MACRS are omitted from our discussion.

Recovery Periods

MACRS applies to both depreciable realty (buildings, improvements, and other structures permanently attached to the land) and personalty (any tangible asset not part of a building or other permanent structure) used in a trade, business, or income-producing activity. Every depreciable asset is assigned to one of 10 **recovery periods.** Table 6.1 lists these periods and gives examples of assets assigned to each. For the most part, the MACRS recovery period for an asset is shorter than the asset's estimated useful life. The shortened time frame over which firms may deduct their investment in operating assets reduces the after-tax cost of the assets and acts as an incentive for firms to make capital acquisitions.

Depreciation Methods

The method by which annual depreciation is calculated is a function of the recovery period. Assets with a 3-year, 5-year, 7-year, or 10-year recovery period are depreciated using a 200 percent (i.e., double) declining-balance method. Assets with a 15-year or 20-year recovery period are depreciated using a 150 percent declining-balance method. In each case, the depreciation method switches to straight line when a straight-line computation over the remaining recovery period results in a greater deduction than the declining-balance method. For these six classes of business personalty, MACRS lives up to its name—depreciation deductions are indeed accelerated into the early years of the recovery period. Such front-end loading of tax depreciation further reduces the after-tax cost of tangible personalty.[35]

[34] §168.

[35] Under §168(b)(5), taxpayers may elect the straight-line method (rather than an accelerated method) for any class of property placed in service during the year.

TABLE 6.1
Recovery Periods for Tangible Business Assets

MACRS Recovery Period	Assets Included
3 years	Small manufacturing tools, racehorses and breeding hogs, special handling devices used in food manufacturing
5 years	Cars, trucks, buses, helicopters, computers, typewriters, duplicating equipment, breeding and dairy cattle, and cargo containers
7 years	Office furniture and fixtures, railroad cars and locomotives, most machinery and equipment
10 years	Single-purpose agricultural and horticultural structures, assets used in petroleum refining, vessels, barges, and other water transportation equipment, fruit- or nut-bearing trees and vines
15 years	Land improvements such as fencing, roads, sidewalks, bridges, irrigation systems, and landscaping; telephone distribution plants; pipelines; billboards; and service station buildings
20 years	Certain farm buildings
25 years	Commercial water treatment facilities, municipal sewers
27.5 years	Residential rental real property (duplexes and apartments)
39 years	Nonresidential real property (office buildings, factories, and warehouses)
50 years	Railroad grading or tunnel bore

Before 1987, buildings and other types of realty could also be depreciated using accelerated declining-balance methods. Since 1987, properties with a 25-year, 27.5-year, 39-year, or 50-year recovery period must be depreciated using the straight-line method. For real property, MACRS is an accelerated cost-recovery system in name only.

Depreciation Conventions

The depreciation computation requires some assumption as to how much depreciation is allowed in the year of an asset's acquisition or disposition. Under MACRS, all personalty (assets with recovery periods from 3 to 20 years) are assumed to be placed in service or disposed of exactly halfway through the year. This **half-year convention** means that in the first year of the recovery period, six months of depreciation is allowed, regardless of when the asset was actually placed in service. The same convention applies in the year in which an asset is disposed of. Regardless of the actual date of disposition, the firm may claim six months of depreciation.[36]

The half-year convention is subject to an important exception. If more than 40 percent of the depreciable personalty acquired during a taxable year is placed in service during the last three months of the year, the firm must use a **midquarter convention** with respect to *all* personalty placed in service during the year. Under this convention, assets placed in service during any quarter (three months) of the year are assumed to be placed in service midpoint (one and one-half months) through the quarter. When an asset subject to this convention is disposed of, the disposition is treated as occurring at the midpoint of the quarter in which the disposition occurs.

[36] No MACRS depreciation is allowed for property placed in service and disposed of in the same year. Reg. §1.168(d)-1(b)(3)(ii).

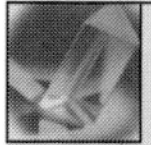

Half-Year and Midquarter Conventions

During its calendar taxable year, Company P purchased the following depreciable personalty.

Date Placed in Service	*Depreciable Basis*
February 27	$ 68,000
July 8	20,000
November 19	55,000
	$143,000

Only 38 percent of the depreciable personalty was placed in service during the last three months of the year. Therefore, Company P uses the half-year convention and calculates six months of depreciation for each asset.

Now assume that Company P purchases a $19,000 depreciable asset on December 4. In this case, 46 percent of the depreciable personalty ($74,000 ÷ $162,000) was placed in service in the last three months of the year. For this reason, Company P must use the midquarter convention with the following result.

Quarter Placed in Service	*Depreciable Basis*	*Months of Depreciation Allowed*
First quarter	$ 68,000	10.5 months
Second quarter	–0–	7.5
Third quarter	20,000	4.5
Fourth quarter	74,000	1.5
	$162,000	

A **midmonth convention** applies to the year in which depreciable realty (assets with recovery periods of 25, 27.5, 39, or 50 years) is placed in service or disposed of. Under this convention, realty placed in service (or disposed of) during any month is treated as placed in service (or disposed of) midway through the month.

Midmonth Convention

Company RS placed three buildings into service during its calendar taxable year. It can claim the following months of depreciation for each building.

	Date Placed in Service	*Months of Depreciation Allowed*
Building 1	April 2	8.5 months
Building 2	July 30	5.5 months
Building 3	December 18	.5 month

Comprehensive Examples

The next two examples illustrate the calculation of the MACRS depreciation deduction.

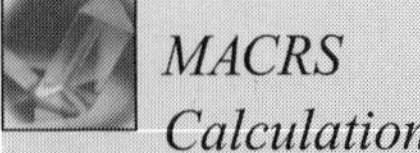

MACRS Calculation

Firm P, a calendar year taxpayer, buys a computer for $38,000 and places it in service on September 19. The computer has a five-year recovery period, and the firm uses the 200 percent declining-balance method to compute depreciation. Under this method, the straight-line rate of depreciation (20 percent) is doubled, and the resulting rate (40 percent) is applied each year to the unrecovered basis of the asset. Firm P will depreciate the computer according to the following schedule.

Year	Unrecovered Basis at Beginning of Year	Recovery Method	Convention	MACRS Depreciation
1	$38,000	40% DB	Half-year	$ 7,600
2	30,400	40% DB		12,160
3	18,240	40% DB		7,296
4	10,944	40% DB		4,378
5	6,566	SL*		4,378
6	2,188	SL		2,188
				$38,000

*$364.78 per month.

- Because only one-half year of depreciation is allowed in year 1, one-half year of depreciation is necessary in year 6 to complete the five-year recovery period.
- The declining-balance method is changed to the straight-line method in year 5 so that the $6,566 unrecovered basis is depreciated ratably over the remaining one and one-half years (18 months) in the recovery period.
- The basis of the computer is reduced to zero. For MACRS purposes, depreciable assets are assumed to have no residual value.

MACRS Calculation in Year of Sale

Refer to the facts in the previous example but assume that Firm P sells the computer on May 3 in year 4. In this case, the half-year convention also applies in the year of disposition.

Year	Unrecovered Basis at Beginning of Year	Recovery Method	Convention	MACRS Depreciation
1	$38,000	40% DB	Half-year	$ 7,600
2	30,400	40% DB		12,160
3	18,240	40% DB		7,296
4	10,944	40% DB	Half-year	2,189

The computer's adjusted basis immediately prior to sale is $8,755 ($10,944 unrecovered basis at beginning of year 4 − $2,189 depreciation in year 4).

IRS Depreciation Tables

To allow taxpayers to avoid the MACRS math process, the IRS publishes a set of convenient tables incorporating the MACRS computational rules. The tables consist of a series of annual percentages that are multiplied against the *initial undepreciated* basis of the asset to result in depreciation for the year. Table 6.2 contains the annual percentages for the

TABLE 6.2
MACRS for Business Personalty (Half-Year Convention)

	Recovery Period					
	3-Year	5-Year	7-Year	10-Year	15-Year	20-Year
Year	Depreciation Rate					
1	33.33%	20.00%	14.29%	10.00%	5.00%	3.750%
2	44.45	32.00	24.49	18.00	9.50	7.219
3	14.81	19.20	17.49	14.40	8.55	6.677
4	7.41	11.52	12.49	11.52	7.70	6.177
5		11.52	8.93	9.22	6.93	5.713
6		5.76	8.92	7.37	6.23	5.285
7			8.93	6.55	5.90	4.888
8			4.46	6.55	5.90	4.522
9				6.56	5.91	4.462
10				6.55	5.90	4.461
11				3.28	5.91	4.462
12					5.90	4.461
13					5.91	4.462
14					5.90	4.461
15					5.91	4.462
16					2.95	4.461
17						4.462
18						4.461
19						4.462
20						4.461
21						2.231

six recovery periods for business personalty. By referring to this table, Firm P can compute its annual depreciation deductions for its $38,000 computer as follows:

MACRS Tables

Year	Initial Basis	Table Percentage	MACRS Depreciation
1	$38,000	20.00%	$ 7,600
2	38,000	32.00	12,160
3	38,000	19.20	7,296
4	38,000	11.52	4,378
5	38,000	11.52	4,378
6	38,000	5.76	2,188
			$38,000

Note that the table percentage in year 1 is one-half of the declining-balance rate. In other words, the half-year convention for the year of acquisition is built into this table. However, the table percentages for the remaining years reflect a full year of depreciation. If an asset is disposed of before it is fully depreciated, the MACRS deduction for the year is only one-half of the amount indicated by the table. The IRS tables that provide the annual percentages for personalty depreciated under a midquarter convention are included in Appendix 6A.

Tables 6.3 and 6.4 are abridged versions of the IRS tables for computing annual depreciation for 27.5-year and 39-year recovery property. Because these real properties are

TABLE 6.3 MACRS for Residential Real Property (27.5-year property)

	Month Placed in Service											
Year	**1**	**2**	**3**	**4**	**5**	**6**	**7**	**8**	**9**	**10**	**11**	**12**
	Depreciation Rate											
1	3.485%	3.182%	2.879%	2.576%	2.273%	1.970%	1.667%	1.364%	1.061%	0.758%	0.455%	0.152%
2–27	3.636	3.636	3.636	3.636	3.636	3.636	3.636	3.636	3.636	3.636	3.636	3.636
28	1.970	2.273	2.576	2.879	3.182	3.458	3.636	3.636	3.636	3.636	3.636	3.636
29	0.000	0.000	0.000	0.000	0.000	0.000	0.152	0.455	0.758	1.061	1.364	1.667

TABLE 6.4 MACRS for Nonresidential Real Property (39-year property)

	Month Placed in Service											
Year	**1**	**2**	**3**	**4**	**5**	**6**	**7**	**8**	**9**	**10**	**11**	**12**
	Depreciation Rate											
1	2.461%	2.247%	2.033%	1.819%	1.605%	1.391%	1.177%	0.963%	0.749%	0.535%	0.321%	0.107%
2–39	2.564	2.564	2.564	2.564	2.564	2.564	2.564	2.564	2.564	2.564	2.564	2.564
40	0.107	0.321	0.535	0.749	0.963	1.177	1.391	1.605	1.819	2.033	2.247	2.461

depreciated by the straight-line method, the tables are really helpful only for the year of acquisition in which the midmonth convention applies.

MACRS Depreciation for Commercial Building

Bulona Company, a calendar year taxpayer, purchased commercial real property for $3 million and allocated $200,000 cost to the land and $2.8 million to the building. The property was placed in service on June 4. According to the IRS table, Bulona can recover the $2.8 cost of the building as follows.

Year 1 ($2.8 million × 1.391 percent)	$38,948
Years 2–39 ($2.8 million × 2.564 percent)	71,792
Year 40 ($2.8 million × 1.177 percent)	32,956

Under a straight-line calculation, Bulona's annual depreciation on the building is $71,795 ($2.8 million cost ÷ 39 years), which corresponds to the rounded number generated by the IRS table for years 2 through 39. In year 1, Bulona can deduct only 6.5 months of depreciation, while in year 40, it can deduct the residual 5.5 months of depreciation.

MACRS and FMV

It is important to understand that MACRS deductions do not represent cash outflows. Neither do these deductions correlate to any decline in the FMV of the depreciable asset. While operating assets typically lose value as they age, the annual MACRS deduction in no way reflects such loss. Moreover, firms may claim depreciation deductions for assets that may actually appreciate in value over time.[37] The adjusted tax basis in a business asset is the capitalized cost that the firm has not yet deducted and conveys no information concerning FMV.

[37] *Noyce,* 97 TC 670 (1991).

Depreciation for an Appreciating Asset?

Richard and Fiona Simon purchased two 100-year-old antique violin bows for a total cost of $51,500. The couple used the bows in their business as professional violinists and claimed depreciation deductions based on a five-year recovery period. The IRS denied the deductions because the bows were treasured works of art that had actually appreciated in value since they were acquired by the Simons. A federal court concluded that the violin bows met the definition of depreciable property because they suffered "wear and tear" in the taxpayers' business activity. Thus, the Simons could recover their cost and reduce their tax basis in the violin bows to zero even though the bows continued to increase in value.[38]

Limited Depreciation for Passenger Automobiles

The tax law contains a major exception to MACRS for depreciation allowed for passenger automobiles held for business use.[39] **Passenger automobiles** are defined as four-wheeled vehicles manufactured primarily for use on public roads with an unloaded gross vehicle weight of 6,000 pounds or less. Vehicles directly used in the business of transporting people or property for compensation, such as taxicabs, limousines, hearses, ambulances, and delivery vans and trucks, are excluded from the definition of passenger automobiles.

The annual depreciation deduction for passenger automobiles may not exceed the limits provided under a special schedule, which is adjusted annually for inflation. For automobiles placed in service during 2004, annual depreciation was limited to the following:

2004	$2,960
2005	4,800
2006	2,850
2007 and subsequent years	1,675

Passenger Automobile Depreciation

In 2004, WRP Inc. paid $23,000 for a passenger automobile for exclusive business use by its employees. For MACRS purposes, automobiles are five-year recovery property. The following schedule contrasts MACRS depreciation with the limited depreciation schedule for a passenger automobile costing $23,000.[40]

Year	*MACRS Depreciation*	*Limited Depreciation*
2004	$4,600	$2,960
2005	7,360	4,800
2006	4,416	2,850
2007	2,650	1,675
2008	2,650	1,675
2009	1,324	1,675
2010		1,675
2011		1,675
2012		1,675
2013		1,675
2014		665
	$23,000	$23,000

[38] *Simon,* 103 TC 247 (1994).

[39] §280F(a).

[40] This example assumes that the automobile did not qualify for the first-year bonus depreciation allowed in 2004.

Because MACRS depreciation would exceed the annual limits, WRP must use the limited depreciation schedule with respect to its new automobile. Consequently, WRP will recover its $23,000 cost over eleven years rather than over the normal six years in the MACRS recovery period.

Tax Talk

Since 2003, business owners could treat a luxury SUV, such as the Cadillac Escalade, as qualifying property under Section 179 and deduct the first $100,000 of the cost. The American Jobs Creation Act of 2004 reduced the limited dollar amount to $25,000. The consumer group Public Citizen stated: "$25,000 is better than $100,000, but we don't think Congress should encourage people to buy these big, fuel-inefficient vehicles."

Firms that use passenger automobiles in their business cannot circumvent the limitation on depreciation by leasing automobiles rather than purchasing them. The tax law provides that business deductions for lease payments on passenger automobiles must be limited in a manner that is "substantially equivalent" to the depreciation limitation.[41] IRS Publication 463, *Travel, Entertainment, Gift, and Car Expenses,* includes the complicated procedure by which firms compute their limited deduction for lease payments on passenger automobiles.

The Section 179 Expensing Election

Section 179 allows firms to elect to expense (rather than capitalize) a limited dollar amount of the cost of certain property placed in service during the year. Congress has been tinkering with the limited dollar amount for the past several years. For 2002, the amount was $25,000, but Congress increased it to $100,000 for 2003. For 2004, this amount was increased by an inflation adjustment to $102,000, and for 2005, it was increased again to $105,000. However, according to current law, the limited dollar amount will revert back to $25,000 in 2007.[42]

Objective 6

Apply the Section 179 expensing election.

Property that qualifies for the **Section 179 election** includes tangible depreciable personalty and off-the-shelf computer software the cost of which is amortizable over 36 months.[43] The Section 179 election allows many small firms to simply deduct the cost of their newly acquired assets and avoid the burden of maintaining depreciation or amortization schedules. Firms that purchase qualifying property with an aggregate cost in excess of the limited dollar amount may expense part of the cost of a specific asset or assets. The unexpensed cost is capitalized and recovered through depreciation or amortization.[44]

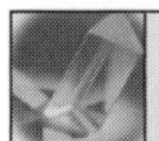

Section 179 Expensing

In July 2005, Firm B purchased two new items of tangible personalty. Item 1 was seven-year recovery property costing $78,200, and item 2 was five-year recovery property costing $48,000. These were the only items that qualified for the Section 179 election. Firm B elected to expense the entire $78,200 cost of item 1 (because of its longer recovery period) and $26,800 of the cost of item 2. Firm B's 2005 total cost recovery deduction for item 2 is $31,040.

		Recovery Deductions
Initial cost	$48,000	
Section 179 expense	(26,800)	$26,800
Adjusted basis for MACRS	$21,200	
Percentage from Table 6.2	20.00%	
MACRS depreciation	$ 4,240	4,240
		$31,040

[41] §280F(c)(3).

[42] §179(b).

[43] §179(d)(1).

[44] In the case of passenger automobiles, any Section 179 expense is treated as depreciation subject to the limitations of §230F(a).

Firm B's 2005 cost recovery deductions for 2005 items 1 and 2 total $109,240 ($78,200 for item 1 + $31,040 for item 2). At the end of 2005, the firm's adjusted tax basis in item 1 is zero, and its adjusted tax basis in item 2 is $16,960 ($48,000 – $31,040).

The Section 179 expense election has two limitations. If a firm purchases more than a threshold amount of qualifying property in a year ($410,000 in 2004 and $420,000 in 2005), the annual dollar amount is reduced by the excess of the total cost of the property over the threshold.[45] Because of this *excess property limitation,* a firm that purchases more than $512,000 of qualifying property in 2004 or $525,000 of qualifying property in 2005 cannot benefit from a Section 179 election because its limited dollar amount is reduced to zero.

Excess Section 179 Property Limitation

During 2005, Firm R purchased $468,000 of equipment. Consequently, its excess amount of qualifying property was $48,000 ($468,000 – $420,000 threshold). Because of the excess property limitation, Firm R may expense only $57,000 of the cost of its qualifying property ($105,000 limited dollar amount – $48,000). It must capitalize the remaining $411,000 cost and recover it through MACRS depreciation.

Once a firm has elected to expense the cost of qualifying property, its deduction for such expense is limited to taxable business income computed without regard to the deduction. Any expense that is disallowed as a deduction under this *taxable income limitation* is carried forward to succeeding taxable years.[46]

Taxable Income Limitation

Firm X purchased $47,800 of tangible personalty in 2004 and elected to expense the entire cost. Its 2004 taxable income before consideration of this expense was $29,600. Because of the taxable income limitation, Firm X may deduct only $29,600 of the expense, thereby reducing its taxable income to zero. The $18,200 expense that Firm X could not deduct carries forward.

Firm X purchased $41,200 of tangible personalty in 2005 and elected to expense the entire cost. Its 2005 taxable income before consideration of this expense was $395,000. Firm X's deduction is $59,400 ($41,200 + $18,200 carryforward from 2004), and its 2005 taxable income is $335,600.

The carryforward of an expense to a succeeding taxable year does not increase the limited dollar amount for such year. Assume that Firm X in the above example purchased $91,000 of qualifying property in 2005. In this case, Firm X's Section 179 expense deduction for 2005 is limited to $105,000 ($91,000 + $14,000 carryforward from 2004), and the firm has a $4,200 expense carryforward to 2006.

Purchase versus Leasing Decision

Objective 7
Incorporate depreciation deductions into the computation of NPV.

Business managers routinely make decisions concerning the acquisition of operating assets. One of the more common decisions is whether the firm should purchase an asset or lease it. Both options provide the firm with the use of the asset over time, but the cash flows associated with each option are different. Managers should choose the option that minimizes the after-tax cost of the acquisition in present value terms. The following example illustrates how depreciation deductions are incorporated into a cash flow analysis.

[45] §179(b)(2).

[46] §179(b)(3) and Reg. §1.179-3.

Purchase versus Leasing

SGM must acquire a piece of heavy machinery for use in its construction business. SGM could purchase the machine for $75,000 cash. The machine would be seven-year recovery property. SGM's engineers estimate that the machine would actually last for 10 years, after which time it would have no residual value. Alternatively, SGM could lease the machine for 10 years for $11,300 annual rent. SGM is in a 35 percent marginal tax bracket and uses a 7 percent discount rate to compute NPV. To decide whether to purchase or to lease the machine, SGM must calculate and compare the after-tax cost of each option.

Purchase Option

Purchase price	$(75,000)
Present value of tax savings from depreciation (see following table)	22,193
After-tax cost of purchase option	$(52,807)

Year	*MACRS Depreciation*	*Tax Savings at 35%*	*Discount Factor*	*Present Value of Tax Savings*
0	$10,717	$3,751	—	$3,751
1	18,367	6,428	.935	6,010
2	13,118	4,591	.873	4,008
3	9,367	3,278	.816	2,675
4	6,698	2,344	.763	1,788
5	6,690	2,342	.713	1,670
6	6,698	2,344	.666	1,561
7	3,345	1,171	.623	730
	$75,000			$22,193

Lease Option

Annual lease payment	$(11,300)
Tax savings ($11,300 deduction × 35%)	3,955
After-tax annual payment	$ (7,345)
Present value of year 0 payment	$ (7,345)
Present value of years 1–9 payment ($7,345 × 6.515 discount factor)	(47,853)
After-tax cost of rent option	$(55,198)

A comparison of after-tax cash flows provides SGM with the information necessary to make its decision. SGM should purchase the machine (after-tax cost $52,807) rather than lease it (after-tax cost $55,198) to minimize after-tax cost.

AMORTIZATION OF INTANGIBLE ASSETS

Objective 8
Explain how a firm recovers the cost of purchased intangibles through amortization.

Firms may own a variety of assets that have no physical substance but that represent a valuable property right or economic attribute. The tax basis in such intangible assets may be recoverable under some type of **amortization** method authorized by the Internal Revenue Code. As a general rule, amortization is permitted only if the intangible asset has a determinable life.[47] For instance, a firm that purchases a patent or copyright can deduct the cost ratably over the number of months during which the patent or copyright confers an exclusive legal right on the owner.

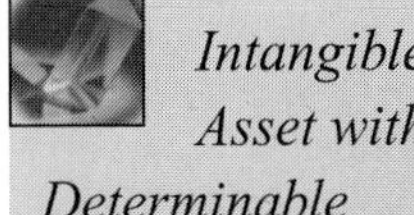

Intangible Asset with Determinable Life

Refer back to the example beginning on page 132 in which CPT patented a chemical process that eliminates cholesterol from dairy products. Hanover, a manufacturer of frozen foods, wanted to use the process to develop a new line of healthy ice cream. Thus, Hanover purchased the patent from CPT for $10 million. At date of purchase, the patent had a remaining legal life of 157 months. Hanover must capitalize the cost of the patent and can amortize the cost at the rate of $63,694 per month ($10 million ÷ 157 months).

The cost basis in an intangible asset with an indeterminable life is not amortizable but can be recovered only upon disposition of the asset.

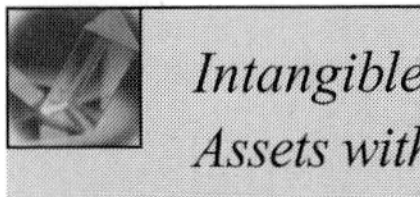

Intangible Assets with Indeterminable Life

This year, Firm FG purchased 16,000 shares of common stock in ABC Inc. and a 10 percent interest in KLM Partnership. Firm FG must capitalize the cost of both these intangible equity interests. Because the interests represent permanent investments, Firm FG cannot recover the capitalized costs through amortization.

In the following paragraphs, we will analyze three types of intangible assets subject to cost recovery through amortization: organizational and start-up costs, leasehold costs, and purchased intangibles.

Organizational and Start-Up Costs

The tax law contains a specific rule for the tax treatment of the **organizational costs** of forming a partnership or corporation. These costs include legal and accounting fees attributable to the formation and any filing or registration fees required under state or local law. A new partnership or corporation can deduct the *lesser* of its actual organizational costs or $5,000. This $5,000 maximum is reduced by the amount by which total costs exceed $50,000. The entity must capitalize any nondeductible organizational cost and may elect to amortize such cost over a 180-month period starting with the month in which business begins.[48]

The tax law includes a similar rule for the **start-up expenditures** of any new business, regardless of organizational form. Start-up expenditures include both the up-front costs of investigating the creation or purchase of a business and the routine expenses incurred during the preoperating phase of a business. This preoperating phase ends only when the business has matured to the point that it can generate revenues. A firm may deduct the *lesser* of its actual start-up expenditures or $5,000 (reduced by the amount by which total expenditures exceed $50,000).The firm must capitalize any nondeductible start-up expenditures and may elect to amortize the capitalized cost over a 180-month period starting with the month in which business begins.[49]

[47] Reg. §1.167(a)-3.

[48] §709 and §248.

[49] §195. According to §195(c)(1), interest expense, taxes, and research and experimentation costs are not start-up expenditures and may be deducted even if incurred during the preoperating phase of a business venture.

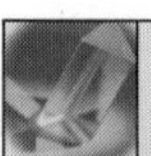

Organizational and Start-Up Costs

Mr. Dugan and Mrs. Guffman went into partnership to start a new business. Their first step was to engage an attorney to draft a partnership agreement and a CPA to set up an accounting system for the business. The total cost of these professional services was $10,580. DG Partnership spent three months locating and renting suitable office space, hiring and training staff, publicizing the new business on radio and television, and applying for the operating license required under local law. These preoperating expenses totaled $61,200. The partnership received an operating license in late August and opened its doors for business on September 8.

DG Partnership can deduct $5,000 of its organizational costs and must capitalize the $5,580 remainder. Because its start-up expenditures exceeded $55,000, its deduction for these expenditures is reduced to zero, and it must capitalize the entire $61,200. On its first Form 1065 (U.S. Partnership Return of Income), the partnership makes a written election to amortize the $66,780 total of these capitalized costs over 180 months.[50] If the partnership reports on a calendar year basis, its amortization deduction for its first taxable year is $1,284.

$66,780 ÷ 180 months = $371 monthly amortization

$371 × four months (September through December) = $1,484

DG Partnership will amortize the $65,296 remaining capitalized costs over the next 176 months.

The capitalization requirement for start-up expenditures does not apply to the **expansion costs** of an existing business.[51] Once DG Partnership in the above example begins operations, it has established an active business. If DG Partnership expands to a second location, it will repeat the process of renting a facility, hiring and training additional staff, and advertising the new location. Although the expenses with respect to these activities are functionally identical to the $61,200 start-up expenditures, DG Partnership can deduct these expenses because they are incurred in the conduct of an existing business.

Business Start-Up or Expansion?

TresChic Company manufactures and imports perfumes, cosmetics, clothing, and accessories. For many years, TresChic sold its goods only at wholesale. However, three years ago, the company decided to move into the retail market and opened its first "BeBe Boutique." The success of the first boutique prompted the company to open 11 more boutiques nationwide. The boutiques operate in exactly the same manner, have a standardized décor, and carry the same merchandise. TresChic handles the accounting, financing, management, purchasing, and advertising for all the boutiques. The IRS ruled that TresChic's retail operation is a substantially different activity than its wholesale operation. Consequently, the first BeBe Boutique represented a new business, and TresChic had to capitalize its start-up expenditures accordingly. However, the next 11 boutiques represented the expansion of TresChic's existing retail operation. Therefore, TresChic could deduct all the operating expenses associated with each new boutique in the year incurred.[52]

Leasehold Costs and Improvements

When a firm rents tangible property for use in its business, it may incur up-front costs to acquire the lease on the property. Such **leasehold costs** must be capitalized and amortized over the term of the lease.[53] In contrast, if a firm pays for physical improvements to leased

[50] The two partners, not the partnership itself, will pay tax on the income generated by the partnership business. Nevertheless, the partnership is required to file an information return on which any elections that affect the computation of taxable income are made. See §703(b).

[51] §195(c)(1)(B).

[52] This example is based on IRS Letter Ruling 9331001 (April 23, 1993).

[53] §178

property, the cost of the **leasehold improvements** must be capitalized to an asset account, assigned to a MACRS recovery period, and depreciated under the MACRS rules. This cost recovery rule applies even when the term of the lease is shorter than the MACRS recovery period.[54]

Leasehold Costs and Improvements

Early in the year, VB Corporation entered into a lease agreement for commercial office space. VB's cost of negotiating the lease was $3,120, and it also spent $28,000 to construct cabinets, bookshelves, and lighting fixtures to conform the leased space to its needs. The term of the lease is 48 months, beginning on May 1. VB Corporation must capitalize the $3,120 lease acquisition cost and amortize it over 48 months ($65 per month for a current year amortization deduction of $520). It must also capitalize the $28,000 cost of the leasehold improvements. These improvements qualify as seven-year recovery property, and VB will recover its cost basis through MACRS depreciation.[55]

Purchased Intangibles

A firm that purchases an entire business is usually buying more than just the monetary and operating assets recorded on the business's balance sheet. A substantial portion of the value of the business may consist of intangible assets that do not appear on the balance sheet. If the purchaser pays a lump-sum price for the business, it must allocate a portion of the price to each balance sheet asset acquired. The price allocated to each asset equals that asset's FMV and becomes the purchaser's cost basis in the asset.[56]

If the lump-sum price exceeds the value of the balance sheet assets, the excess is allocated to the unrecorded intangible assets of the business. Such assets include **goodwill** (value created by the expectancy that customers will continue to patronize the business) and **going-concern value** (value attributable to the synergism of business assets working in coordination). Other common purchased intangibles are:

- Information-based intangibles such as accounting records, operating systems or manuals, customer lists, and advertiser lists.
- Customer-based or supplier-based intangibles such as favorable contracts with major customers or established relationships with key suppliers.
- Know-how intangibles such as designs, patterns, formulas, and other intellectual properties.
- Workforce intangibles such as the specialized skills, education, or loyalty of company employees and favorable employment contracts.
- Covenants not to compete and similar arrangements with prior owners of the business.
- Franchises, trademarks, trade names, licenses, and permits.

For tax purposes, firms recover the cost of purchased intangibles over a 15-year period, regardless of the actual length of time that the intangible is expected to yield any commercial benefit.[57] Amortization begins in the month in which the intangible asset is acquired.

[54] §168(i)(8).

[55] Unless VB Corporation renews its lease on the commercial office space after 48 months, it will not have recovered its entire cost basis in the leasehold improvements when it surrenders the space back to the lessor. The tax consequences of this situation are discussed in the next chapter.

[56] Reg. §1.1060-1T.

[57] §197. The 15-year amortization rule does not apply to equity interests in other businesses, debt instruments, existing leases of tangible property, and computer software available for purchase by the general public. Under §167(f)(1), the cost of such off-the-shelf software is amortizable over 36 months.

The tax treatment of purchased goodwill is very different from the treatment under GAAP. Before 2002, firms were required to amortize purchased goodwill over a realistic period not to exceed 40 years. Beginning in 2002, firms are not required to amortize goodwill for financial reporting purposes. Instead, they must test the goodwill annually for impairment and revalue the goodwill as necessary.[58]

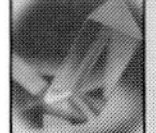

Amortization of Purchased Intangibles

On March 9, BV Company (a calendar year taxpayer) paid $2 million to buy a business from Mr. Lopez. The sales contract stated that $1.7 million of the lump-sum price was attributable to the appraised value of monetary and tangible operating assets. An additional $50,000 was attributable to the business's trade name, $150,000 was attributable to goodwill, and $100,000 was attributable to a convenant not to compete. Under this covenant, Mr. Lopez agreed not to engage in a similar business for the next three years. BV Company must capitalize the $300,000 cost of the purchased intangibles and amortize the cost over 15 years at a rate of $1,667 per month. Its amortization deduction in the year of purchase is $16,670 ($1,667 for 10 months).

Patents and copyrights are included in the category of purchased intangibles *only if* they are acquired as part of the purchase of an *entire business*. In such case, the purchaser must amortize the cost allocated to the patent or copyright over 15 years, regardless of the remaining legal life of the asset.

Patent as Purchased Intangible

Refer back to the example on page 149 in which Hanover purchased a patent for a chemical process for use in its manufacturing business. This year, Crown Food purchased Hanover's entire business operation. Consequently, Crown Food acquired all Hanover's tangible and intangible assets, including the patent. At date of purchase, the patent had a remaining legal life of only eight years (96 months). But because the patent is included as one of Crown Food's purchased intangibles, it must recover its cost allocated to the patent over a 15-year amortization period.

Comprehensive Example of a Lump-Sum Purchase

Firms that pay a lump-sum price to purchase a business must determine the cost basis of each tangible and intangible asset included in the purchase as well as any cost recovery method allowed for each asset. The next example illustrates this important process.

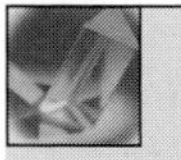

Firm RT's Lump-Sum Purchase

Firm RT purchased the business operated by SW Inc. for a lump-sum price of $1 million. At date of purchase, the appraised values of SW's business assets were:

	Appraised FMV
Accounts receivable	$120,000
Supplies	25,000
Inventory	325,000
Furniture and fixtures	360,000
Lease on real property (8-year remaining term)	40,000
	$870,000

[58] SFAS No. 142, *Goodwill and Other Intangible Assets* (2000).

RT was willing to pay $1 million because the business has such an excellent reputation in the local community. The cost basis in each of its newly acquired business assets is:

	Initial Cost Basis
Accounts receivable	$ 120,000
Supplies	25,000
Inventory	325,000
Furniture and fixtures	360,000
Lease on real property	40,000
Purchased goodwill	130,000
	$1,000,000

- RT will recover its basis in the accounts receivable as the receivables are collected.
- RT will recover its basis in the supplies as a deduction when the supplies are consumed.
- RT will recover its basis in the inventory through cost of goods sold.
- RT will recover its basis in the furniture and fixtures through MACRS depreciation.
- RT will recover its basis in the lease through amortization deductions over the eight-year remaining term of the lease.
- RT will recover its basis in the goodwill through amortization deductions over 15 years.

DEPLETION OF NATURAL RESOURCES

Firms engaged in the business of extracting minerals, oil, gas, and other natural deposits from the earth incur a variety of up-front costs to locate, acquire, and develop their operating mines and wells. Some of these costs must be capitalized and recovered over the period of years that the mine or well is productive.[59] The method for recovering a firm's investment in an exhaustible natural resource is called **cost depletion.** The annual cost depletion deduction is based on the following formula.

$$\frac{\text{Units of production sold during the year}}{\text{Estimated total units in the ground at the beginning of the year}^{60}} \times \text{Unrecovered basis in the mine or well}$$

Cost Depletion

Company M, which operates a mining business, spent $500,000 for geological surveys, mineral rights, and excavation costs, all of which were capitalized as the basis of a new copper mine. At the beginning of the first year of production, the company's engineers estimated that the mine should produce 80,000 tons of copper ore. During the first year, 20,000 tons of ore were extracted and sold. The company's cost depletion deduction was $125,000.

$$\frac{20{,}000 \text{ tons}}{80{,}000 \text{ tons}} \times \$500{,}000 \text{ initial basis} = \$125{,}000$$

[59] Oil and gas producers may deduct many intangible drilling and development costs, thereby minimizing the capitalized basis of productive wells.

[60] §611.

At the beginning of the second year, the engineers revised their estimate of the mine's remaining productivity to 65,000 tons; during the second year, 32,000 tons of copper ore were extracted and sold. The cost depletion deduction was $184,615.

$$\frac{32{,}000 \text{ tons}}{65{,}000 \text{ tons}} \times \$375{,}000 \text{ unrecovered basis} = \$184{,}615$$

By the year in which the copper deposit is exhausted and the mine is no longer productive, Company M will have recovered its entire $500,000 tax basis through cost depletion deductions.

Percentage Depletion

Objective 9
Distinguish between cost depletion and percentage depletion.

To encourage the high-risk activity of exploration and extraction, Congress invented **percentage depletion,** an annual deduction based on the gross income generated by a depletable property multiplied by an arbitrary depletion rate. For instance, the statutory depletion rate for sulfur and uranium is 22 percent; the rate for gold, silver, copper, iron ore, and crude oil is 15 percent; and the rate for asbestos, coal, and lignite is 10 percent. In any year, a firm is allowed to deduct the *greater* of the cost depletion or percentage depletion attributable to its properties.[61]

Let's highlight the relationship of cost depletion and percentage depletion by returning to our example of Company M and its copper mine.

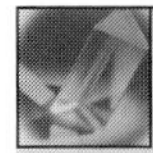

Percentage Depletion

Company M can sell its copper ore for $40 per ton, and its percentage depletion equals 15 percent of gross income from sales of the ore. The following table shows the computation of the annual depletion deduction (indicated by bold type).

Year	*Estimated Tons/ Beginning of Year*	*Tons Sold during Year*	*Gross Income*	*Unrecovered Basis/ Beginning of Year*	*Cost Depletion*	*Percentage Depletion**
1	80,000	20,000	$ 800,000	$500,000	**$125,000**	$120,000
2	65,000	32,000	1,280,000	375,000	184,615	**192,000**
3	30,000	17,000	680,000	183,000	**103,700**	102,000
4	15,000	18,500	740,000	79,300	79,300	**111,000**
5	5,000	4,000	160,000	-0-	-0-	**24,000**
6	2,500	2,000	80,000	-0-	-0-	**12,000**

*15 percent of gross income.

Note that in years 1 through 4, Company M deducted the *greater* of cost depletion or percentage depletion and reduced the tax basis in the mine accordingly, But in year 4, a curious thing occurred. Company M claimed a $111,000 depletion deduction that exceeded its unrecovered basis in the mine by $31,700! In years 5 and 6, it deducted $36,000 percentage depletion even though it had a zero basis in the copper mine.

The magic of the percentage depletion deduction is that it is not limited to the capitalized cost of the mine or well. Percentage depletion is available in every year that the property generates gross income, regardless of the fact that the tax basis has been reduced to zero. In such cases, percentage depletion is not a cost recovery deduction at all but an indirect preferential tax rate on the income earned by the extractive industries.

[61] §613(a) and (b).

Not surprisingly, this highly beneficial deduction is subject to restrictions. Annual percentage depletion may not exceed 50 percent of the taxable income from the depletable property (100 percent for oil and gas property).[62] In the oil and gas industry, only independent producers and royalty owners are entitled to percentage depletion. This tax break is denied to the giant integrated companies that extract, refine, and sell oil and gas to retail customers.[63] Even with these restrictions, percentage depletion is a valuable government subsidy.

Conclusion

The after-tax cost of a business expenditure is a function of the time period over which the firm can deduct the expenditure. If an expenditure is not deductible in the current year but must be capitalized to an asset account, its after-tax cost depends on the method (if any) by which the firm can compute cost recovery deductions with respect to the asset. Exhibit 6.1 summarizes the tax treatment of business expenditures and should help you appreciate the key roles that cost of goods sold, depreciation, amortization, and depletion play in the tax planning process.

[62] Ibid.

[63] §613A(c).

EXHIBIT 6.1
Tax Treatment of Business Expenditures

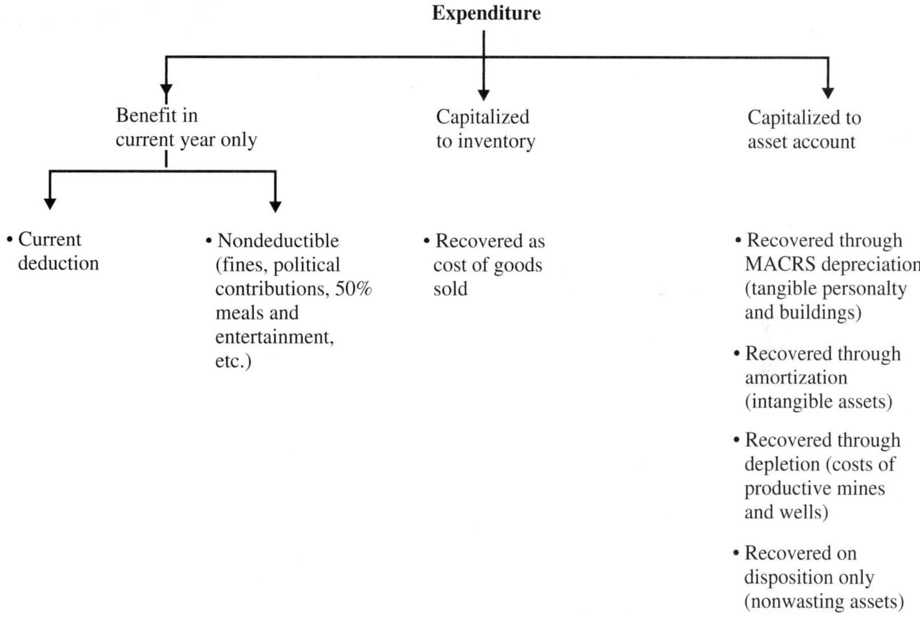

Sources of Book/Tax Differences

Permanent

- Percentage depletion in excess of cost depletion

Temporary

- Intangible drilling costs (IDC)
- Inventory costs capitalized under UNICAP
- MACRS depreciation
- Section 179 expense election
- Amortization of organizational and start-up costs
- Amortization of purchased intangibles (goodwill)

Key Terms

- adjusted basis *134*
- amortization *148*
- capitalization *130*
- cost basis *134*
- cost depletion *153*
- cost of goods sold *137*
- depreciation *138*
- expansion costs *150*
- FIFO *138*
- going-concern value *151*
- goodwill *151*
- half-year convention *140*
- intangible drilling and development costs (IDC) *133*
- leasehold costs *150*
- leasehold improvements *151*
- leverage *135*
- LIFO *138*
- midmonth convention *141*
- midquarter convention *140*
- Modified Accelerated Cost Recovery System (MACRS) *139*
- organizational costs *149*
- passenger automobiles *145*
- percentage depletion *154*
- recovery period *139*
- research and experimental expenditures *132*
- Section 179 election *146*
- specific identification method *138*
- start-up expenditures *149*
- tax basis *133*
- uniform capitalization (unicap) rules *137*

Questions and Problems for Discussion

1. How is the principle of conservatism reflected in the tax law's premise concerning the deductibility of business expenditures?
2. Assume that Congress enacted legislation requiring firms to capitalize advertising costs and amortize them over 20 years. Discuss the potential effects of such legislation on the amount of advertising that firms purchase and the price that advertising companies charge for their product.
3. Discuss the relationship between cost recovery deductions and cash flows.
4. To what extent do cost recovery deductions based on the capitalized cost of a tangible asset reflect a decline in the economic value of that asset?
5. Can a firm have a negative tax basis in an asset?
6. If the tax law did not allow farming businesses to deduct soil and water conservation expenditures but required capitalization of these costs, in what year or years would farmers recover these costs?
7. Corporation J is engaged in the manufacture of electrical appliances. Corporation K provides architectural services. During the year, both corporations paid $56,000 annual premiums to carry fire and casualty insurance on their tangible assets. Corporation J was required to capitalize the $56,000 cost for tax purposes while Corporation K was allowed a $56,000 deduction. Can you explain this difference in tax treatment between the two corporations?
8. Identify the tax and nontax issues that firms must consider in adopting the LIFO method of accounting for inventories.
9. Identify four possible differences in the computation of depreciation expense for financial statement purposes and MACRS depreciation.
10. What is the purpose of the MACRS half-year, midquarter, and midmonth conventions?
11. Why do the MACRS tables published by the IRS incorporate a depreciation convention for the first year during an asset's recovery period but not for the year of disposition?
12. Discuss the reasons why the Section 179 election is more valuable to small firms than to large firms.
13. Firm O purchased two items of business personalty this year. The first item cost $135,000 and has a five-year recovery period, and the second item cost $116,500 and has a seven-year recovery period. Firm O wants to make the Section 179 election for one of its new assets. Which asset should the firm choose and why?

14. Discuss the strengths and weaknesses of the tax rule providing for 15-year amortization of any asset meeting the statutory definition of purchased intangible.
15. Describe the difference in tax treatment between start-up costs of a new business and expansion costs of an existing business.
16. On February 1, Mr. B purchased a business from Mr. and Mrs. S for a lump-sum price of $750,000. The business consisted of the following balance sheet assets.

	Appraised FMV
Accounts receivable	$ 27,600
Inventory	195,000
Office supplies (4 months' worth)	8,500
Furniture and fixtures	395,000

By buying the business, Mr. B acquired a favorable lease on office space with a remaining term of 31 months; he estimates that the value of this lease is $20,000. The purchase contract stipulates that Mr. and Mrs. S will not engage in a competitive business for the next 36 months. Discuss how Mr. B can recover the cost of each of the business assets acquired in this purchase.

17. Firm W and Firm X both have goodwill and going-concern value worth approximately $1 million. However, only Firm X reports an amortization deduction with respect to its goodwill and going-concern value on its tax return. Can you explain this difference in tax treatment between the two firms?
18. Under what circumstances is percentage depletion not a true cost recovery deduction?

Application Problems

1. In 2004, Firm A paid $40,000 cash to purchase a tangible business asset. In 2004 and 2005, it deducted $2,800 and $5,600 depreciation with respect to the asset. Firm A's marginal tax rate in both years was 35 percent.
   a. Compute Firm A's net cash flow attributable to the asset purchase in each year.
   b. Compute Firm A's adjusted basis in the asset at the end of each year.
2. Refer to the facts in Problem 1. Now assume that Firm A borrowed $40,000 to purchase the asset. In each year, it paid $3,600 annual interest on the debt. The interest payments were deductible.
   a. How does this change in facts affect Firm A's net cash flow attributable to the asset purchase in each year?
   b. How does this change in facts affect Firm A's adjusted basis in the asset at the end of each year?
3. In year 0, Company L paid $80,000 for an overhaul of a tangible operating asset. Company L has a 34 percent marginal tax rate and uses an 8 percent discount rate to compute NPV.
   a. Compute the after-tax cost of the overhaul if Company L can deduct the $80,000 payment as a repair in year 0.
   b. Compute the after-tax cost of the overhaul if Company L must capitalize the $80,000 payment to the asset account and can recover it on a straight-line basis in years 0, 1, 2, and 3.
4. Company XYZ manufactures a tangible product and sells the product at wholesale. In its first year of operations, XYZ manufactured 1,000 units of product and incurred

$200,000 direct material cost and $130,000 direct labor costs. For financial statement purposes, XYZ capitalized $85,000 indirect costs to inventory. For tax purposes, it had to capitalize $116,000 indirect costs to inventory under the unicap rules. At the end of its first year, XYZ held 260 units in inventory. Compute XYZ's cost of goods sold for book purposes and for tax purposes.

5. Refer to the facts in Problem 4. In its second year of operations, XYZ manufactured 2,000 units of product and incurred $410,000 direct material cost and $275,000 direct labor costs. For financial statement purposes, XYZ capitalized $139,000 indirect costs to inventory. For tax purposes, it had to capitalize $193,000 indirect costs to inventory under the unicap rules. At the end of its second year, XYZ held 300 items in inventory. Compute XYZ's cost of goods sold for book purposes and for tax purposes assuming that:
   a. XYZ uses the FIFO costing convention.
   b. XYZ uses the LIFO costing convention.
6. Firm L purchased only one asset during its calendar taxable year. The asset cost $650,000 and has a three-year recovery period. Compute Firm L's MACRS depreciation with respect to this asset over the recovery period assuming that:
   a. The asset was placed in service on September 29.
   b. The asset was placed in service on October 2.
7. In 2005, Firm L purchased machinery costing $68,500 and elected to expense the entire cost under Section 179. How much of the expense can Firm L deduct in each of the following cases?
   a. Its taxable income before the deduction was $1,367,000.
   b. Its taxable income before the deduction was $20,400.
   c. Its net operating loss (NOL) before the deduction was $4,420.
8. In 2004, Company W elected under Section 179 to expense $89,300 of the cost of qualifying property. However, it could deduct only $65,000 of the expense because of the taxable income limitation. In 2005, Company W's taxable income before any Section 179 expense deduction was $812,000. Compute Company W's 2005 Section 179 expense deduction if:
   a. The total cost of its qualifying property purchased in 2005 was $55,000.
   b. The total cost of its qualifying property purchased in 2005 was $87,700.
9. At the beginning of its 2005 taxable year, Firm HG owned the following business assets.

	Date Placed in Service	*Initial Cost*	*Accumulated Depreciation*	*Recovery Period*	*Depreciation Convention*
Furniture	6/19/03	$25,000	$ 9,696	7-year	Half-year
Equipment	5/2/02	70,000	49,840	5-year	Half-year
Machinery	9/30/02	58,000	41,296	5-year	Half-year

On July 8, Firm HG sold its machinery. On August 18, it purchased and placed in service tools costing $123,000; these tools are three-year recovery property. These were its only capital transactions for the year. Compute HG's cost recovery deduction for 2005. In making your computation, assume that taxable income before depreciation exceeds $500,000.

10. BTN, a calendar year taxpayer, paid $164,000 for machinery (seven-year recovery property) that was placed in service on September 9, 2005.
    a. Assuming that the machinery was the only tangible property placed in service during the year, compute BTN's maximum cost recovery deduction.
    b. How would your computation change if BTN paid $457,500 for the machinery?
    c. How would your computation change if BTN paid $675,000 for the machinery?
11. AP constructed a new manufacturing plant for a total cost of $7,615,000 and placed it in service on March 2. To finance the construction, AP took out a $6 million, 30-year mortgage on the property. Compute AP's MACRS depreciation for the manufacturing plant for the first, second, and third years of its operation.
12. EDI Company, a calendar year taxpayer, purchased equipment for $800,000 and placed it in service on March 1. EDI's chief engineer determined that the equipment had an estimated useful life of 120 months and a $50,000 residual value. For financial statement purposes, EDI uses the straight-line method to compute depreciation.
    a. Compute EDI's book depreciation expense for the year.
    b. Assuming that the equipment has a seven-year recovery period and is subject to the half-year convention, compute EDI's MACRS depreciation for the year.
    c. Compute EDI's book basis and tax basis in the equipment at the beginning of next year.
13. QQ Inc. was formed on April 25 and elected a calendar year for tax purposes. QQ paid $3,480 to the attorney who drew up the articles of incorporation and $5,100 to the CPA who advised the corporation concerning the accounting and tax implications of its organization. QQ began business operations on June 15. To what extent can QQ deduct its $8,580 organizational costs on its first tax return?
14. Mr. and Mrs. FB, a retired couple, decided to open a family restaurant. During March and April, they incurred the following expenses.

Prepaid rent on commercial real estate ($2,100 per month from April through December)	$18,900
Prepaid rent on restaurant equipment ($990 per month from April through December)	8,910
Advertising of upcoming Grand Opening	900
Staff hiring and training	11,500
	$40,210

    Mr. and Mrs. FB served their first meal to a customer on May 1. Determine the tax treatment of the above expenses on their tax return.
15. Firm DEF is a calendar year taxpayer. On July 1, DEF signed a 36-month lease on 2,100 square feet of commercial office space. It paid a $3,240 fee to the real estate agent who located the space and negotiated the lease and $4,400 to install new overhead lighting in the office space. Lighting equipment is seven-year recovery property. Compute DEF's first-year cost recovery deduction with respect to the $7,640 cost relating to the lease space.
16. On April 23, 2005, Mrs. Y purchased a taxi business from Mr. M for a lump-sum price of $60,000. The business consisted of a two-year-old taxicab worth $19,000, Mr. M's license to operate a taxi business in Baltimore, his list of regular customers, and his

registered business name "On Time Any Time Taxi." Mrs. Y operated the business from April 24 through the end of the year.

a. Compute Mrs. Y's 2005 taxable income from the taxi business if her taxable income *before consideration of any cost recovery deductions* was $36,890.

b. Compute Mrs. Y's 2005 taxable income from the taxi business if her taxable income *before consideration of any cost recovery deductions* was $17,100.

17. ZEJ, a calendar year corporation, reported $619,300 net income before tax on its financial statements prepared in accordance with GAAP. The corporation's records reveal the following information.
    - ZEJ incurred $75,000 of research costs that resulted in a new 17-year patent for the corporation. ZEJ expensed these costs for book purposes.
    - ZEJ's depreciation expense per books was $98,222, and its MACRS depreciation deduction was $120,000.
    - ZEJ was organized two years ago. For its first taxable year, it capitalized $27,480 start-up costs and elected to amortize them over 180 months. For book purposes, it expensed the costs in the year incurred.

    Compute ZEJ's taxable income.

18. A&Z incurred $450,000 of capitalized costs to develop a uranium mine. The corporation's geologists estimated that the mine would produce 900,000 tons of ore. During the year, 215,000 tons were extracted and sold. A&Z's gross revenues from the sales totaled $689,000, and its operating expenses for the mine were $200,000. Calculate A&Z's depletion deduction.

Issue Recognition Problems

Identify the tax issue or issues suggested by the following situations and state each issue in the form of a question.

1. Corporation J paid $500,000 for six acres of land on which it plans to build a new corporate headquarters. Four months after the purchase, Corporation J paid $20,000 to a demolition company to tear down an old warehouse located on the land and haul away the rubble from the demolition site.
2. Mr. R lived in a two-bedroom, one-bath residence until August when he moved to a new home and converted his old residence into residential rent property. He had no trouble finding tenants who signed a one-year lease and moved in on September 1. As of this date, the market value of the old residence was $120,000. Mr. R purchased the residence six years ago for $180,000.
3. Mrs. K owns her own consulting firm, and her husband, Mr. K, owns a printing business. This year, Mrs. K's consulting business generated $89,000 taxable income. Mr. K's business operated at a loss. In July, Mr. K bought new office furniture for $16,000. This was the only purchase of tangible business personalty by either spouse for the year. Mr. and Mrs. K always file a joint tax return.
4. ROJ Inc. purchased a 20-acre industrial complex consisting of three warehouses and two office buildings surrounded by parking lots. About 12 acres of the land is undeveloped. ROJ paid a lump-sum purchase price of $19.4 million.
5. Firm PY purchased industrial equipment from a Canadian vendor. The firm paid $12,800 to transport the equipment to its manufacturing plant in Florida and a $1,700 premium for insurance against casualty or theft of the equipment while en route.

6. WRT owns a chain of retail bookstores. It recently decided to add coffee bars in each store to sell gourmet coffee drinks and pastries to the bookstore customers. WRT has not yet obtained the necessary licenses required under local law to serve food to the public. However, it has incurred almost $30,000 in up-front expenditures on the coffee bars.
7. In 2003, Firm Z elected to expense the $8,000 cost of a machine, which it reported as the only item of business equipment placed in service that year. This year, the IRS audited Firm Z's 2003 return and discovered that it had incorrectly deducted a $10,000 expenditure. According to the IRS, Firm Z should have capitalized this expenditure as the cost of depreciable equipment with a 5-year recovery period.
8. Company JJ, a calendar year corporation, bought an airplane for use in its oil and gas business in December. The manufacturer delivered the plane to the company's hangar on December 19. Because of severe winter weather, JJ's pilot was unable to fly the plane on company business until February 16 of the next year.
9. TCJ bought a 10-acre tract of undeveloped land that it intends to improve and subdivide for sale to real estate customers. This year, TCJ paid $4,300 to a local company to clean up the land by hauling away trash, cutting down dead trees, and spraying for poison ivy.
10. Firm D paid a $500,000 lump-sum price for a commercial office building. A local consulting company approached Firm D with a proposal. For a $15,000 fee, the company will analyze the components of the building (shelving, lighting fixtures, floor coverings, plumbing, etc.) to determine how much of the $500,000 price is attributable to five-year or seven-year recovery property rather than to the building itself.

Research Problems

1. Elsworthy Company operates a number of public golf courses in Florida. This year, Elsworthy constructed six new greens of a type described as "modern" greens. Modern greens contain sophisticated drainage systems that include subsurface drainage tiles and interconnected pipes. These tiles and pipes require replacement about every 20 years. The cost of each modern green was $115,000: $30,000 for earthmoving, grading, and shaping of the land in preparation for construction and $85,000 for construction of the green itself. What is the correct tax treatment of the total cost of each modern green?
2. On January 1 of every year since 1993, Lanier Corporation has paid a $35,000 retainer fee to the law firm of Myer and Weeble (MW). MW specializes in structuring corporate mergers and acquisitions. In return for the annual payment, MW guarantees that it will represent Lanier for one year. Moreover, MW will not provide legal assistance to any business that Lanier attempts to acquire during the year. MW is entitled to keep the annual retainer regardless of the actual amount of legal work performed for Lanier. On January 1, Lanier paid the annual $35,000 retainer to MW. In August, MW structured Lanier's acquisition of Carstron Manufacturing. MW sent Lanier a bill for $100,000 of additional legal fees in connection with this acquisition.

   The tax law clearly requires Lanier to capitalize the $100,000 additional legal fees as part of the cost of Carstron Manufacturing. But can Lanier deduct (rather than capitalize) the $35,000 retainer paid in January?
3. Last year, Manabee Inc. leased a computer system from ICS Company for five years. After using the system for only 10 months, Manabee realized that it was no longer adequate for its expanding business needs. As a result, Manabee negotiated with ICS to terminate the original lease and enter into a new five-year lease under which ICS

would provide Manabee with an expanded, upgraded computer system. ICS would not agree to the arrangement unless Manabee paid a $200,000 lease cancellation fee. Can Manabee deduct this fee as a current expense, or must Manabee capitalize the fee as a leasehold cost and amortize it over the five-year term of the new lease?

4. Peter Nelson is employed full time as an accountant by an insurance company. In his spare time, he operates a secondary business as a self-employed wedding photographer. On January 3, 2005, Peter purchased new video recording equipment for $14,500. During 2005, he used this equipment for personal enjoyment (filming his family members on holidays and during vacations). He also used the equipment for business purposes when a client wanted video coverage of a wedding. Peter did not purchase any other property for business use during 2005.

   Peter kept a careful written record of the time that he used the video recording equipment for either personal or business reasons during 2005. This record substantiates that he used the equipment 59 percent of the time for personal reasons and 41 percent of the time for business reasons. Is Peter allowed any amount of cost recovery deduction with respect to the video recording equipment?

Tax Planning Cases

1. MRT, a calendar year corporation, placed the following assets in service this year.

Asset	*Initial Cost*	*Recovery Period*	*Date Placed in Service*
Manufacturing equipment	$219,000	7 years	April 23
Furniture and fixtures	16,000	7 years	May 2
Transportation equipment	195,000	5 years	September 3
Office equipment	120,000	7 years	December 1

   a. Compute MRT's MACRS depreciation with respect to the assets placed in service this year.

   b. In December, MRT decided to purchase $200,000 of additional equipment. The corporation could buy the equipment and place it in service before year-end, or it could postpone the purchase until January. What effect does this decision have on MRT's depreciation with respect to the assets already in service?

2. Company C has a 34 percent marginal tax rate and uses an 8 percent discount rate to compute NPV. The company must decide whether to lease or purchase an item of equipment to use for years 0 through 7. It could lease the equipment for $21,000 annual rent, or it could purchase the equipment for $100,000. The seller would require no money down and would allow Company C to defer payment until year 4 at 11.5 percent simple interest ($11,500 interest payable in years 1, 2, 3, and 4). The equipment would be seven-year MACRS recovery property with no residual value. Should Company C lease or purchase the equipment to minimize the after-tax cost of the use of the property for eight years?

3. MG, a corporation in the 34 percent marginal tax bracket, owns equipment that is fully depreciated. This old equipment is still operating and should continue to do so for four

years (years 0, 1, 2, and 3). MG's chief financial officer estimates that repair costs for the old equipment will be $1,400 in year 0, $1,400 in year 1, $1,500 in year 2, and $1,600 in year 3. At the end of year 3, the equipment will have no residual value.

MG could junk the old equipment and buy new equipment for $5,000 cash. The new equipment will have a three-year MACRS recovery period, should not require any repairs during years 0 through 3, and will have no residual value at the end of year 3.

a. Assume MG cannot make a Section 179 election to expense the $5,000 cost of the new equipment. Which option (keep old or buy new) minimizes MG's after-tax cost? In making your calculations, use a 10 percent discount rate.

b. Assume MG can make a Section 179 election to expense the entire $5,000 cost of the new equipment. Under this change in facts, which option (keep old or buy new) minimizes MG's after-tax cost?

4. KP Inc. is negotiating a 10-year lease for three floors of space in a commercial office building. KP can't use the space unless a security system is installed. The cost of the system is $50,000, and it will qualify as seven-year recovery property under MACRS. The building's owner has offered KP a choice. The owner will pay for the installation of the security system and charge $79,000 annual rent. Alternatively, KP can pay for the installation of the security system, and the owner will charge only $72,000 annual rent. Assuming that KP has a 35 percent marginal tax rate, cannot make a Section 179 election to expense the $50,000 cost, and uses a 9 percent discount rate to compute NPV, which alternative should it choose?

Appendix 6–A

Midquarter Convention Tables

Midquarter Convention for Business Personalty Placed in Service in Fourth Quarter

	Depreciation Rate for Recovery Period					
Year	**3-Year**	**5-Year**	**7-Year**	**10-Year**	**15-Year**	**20-Year**
1	58.33%	35.00%	25.00%	17.50%	8.75%	6.563%
2	27.78	26.00	21.43	16.50	9.13	7.000
3	12.35	15.60	15.31	13.20	8.21	6.482
4	1.54	11.01	10.93	10.56	7.39	5.996
5		11.01	8.75	8.45	6.65	5.546
6		1.38	8.74	6.76	5.99	5.130
7			8.75	6.55	5.90	4.746
8			1.09	6.55	5.91	4.459
9				6.56	5.90	4.459
10				6.55	5.91	4.459
11				0.82	5.90	4.459
12					5.91	4.460
13					5.90	4.459
14					5.91	4.460
15					5.90	4.459
16					0.74	4.460
17						4.459
18						4.460
19						4.459
20						4.460
21						0.557

Midquarter Convention for Business Personalty Placed in Service in Second Quarter

	Depreciation Rate for Recovery Period					
Year	**3-Year**	**5-Year**	**7-Year**	**10-Year**	**15-Year**	**20-Year**
1	41.67%	25.00%	17.85%	12.50%	6.25%	4.688%
2	38.89	30.00	23.47	17.50	9.38	7.148
3	14.14	18.00	16.76	14.00	8.44	6.612
4	5.30	11.37	11.97	11.20	7.59	6.116
5		11.37	8.87	8.96	6.83	5.658
6		4.26	8.87	7.17	6.15	5.233
7			8.87	6.55	5.91	4.841
8			3.33	6.55	5.90	4.478
9				6.56	5.91	4.463
10				6.55	5.90	4.463
11				2.46	5.91	4.463
12					5.90	4.463
13					5.91	4.463
14					5.90	4.463
15					5.91	4.462
16					2.21	4.463
17						4.462
18						4.463
19						4.462
20						4.463
21						1.673

Midquarter Convention for Business Personalty Placed in Service in Third Quarter

	Depreciation Rate for Recovery Period					
Year	**3-Year**	**5-Year**	**7-Year**	**10-Year**	**15-Year**	**20-Year**
1	25.00%	15.00%	10.71%	7.50%	3.75%	2.813%
2	50.00	34.00	25.51	18.50	9.63	7.289
3	16.67	20.40	18.22	14.80	8.66	6.742
4	8.33	12.24	13.02	11.84	7.80	6.237
5		11.30	9.30	9.47	7.02	5.769
6		7.06	8.85	7.58	6.31	5.336
7			8.86	6.55	5.90	4.936
8			5.53	6.55	5.90	4.566
9				6.56	5.91	4.460
10				6.55	5.90	4.460
11				4.10	5.91	4.460
12					5.90	4.460
13					5.91	4.461
14					5.90	4.460
15					5.91	4.461
16					3.69	4.460
17						4.461
18						4.460
19						4.461
20						4.460
21						2.788

Midquarter Convention for Business Personalty Placed in Service in Fourth Quarter

	Depreciation Rate for Recovery Period					
Year	**3-Year**	**5-Year**	**7-Year**	**10-Year**	**15-Year**	**20-Year**
1	8.33%	5.00%	3.57%	2.50%	1.25%	0.938%
2	61.11	38.00	27.55	19.50	9.88	7.430
3	20.37	22.80	19.68	15.60	8.89	6.872
4	10.19	13.68	14.06	12.48	8.00	6.357
5		10.94	10.04	9.98	7.20	5.880
6		9.58	8.73	7.99	6.48	5.439
7			8.73	6.55	5.90	5.031
8			7.64	6.55	5.90	4.654
9				6.56	5.90	4.458
10				6.55	5.91	4.458
11				5.74	5.90	4.458
12					5.91	4.458
13					5.90	4.458
14					5.91	4.458
15					5.90	4.458
16					5.17	4.458
17						4.458
18						4.459
19						4.458
20						4.459
21						3.901

Chapter **Seven**

Property Dispositions

Learning Objectives

After studying this chapter, you should be able to:

1. Distinguish between gain or loss realization and recognition.
2. Describe the installment sale method of accounting.
3. Explain why the tax law disallows losses on related party sales.
4. Identify the two components of the capital gain or loss definition.
5. Apply the limitation on the deductibility of capital losses.
6. Apply the Section 1231 netting process.
7. Incorporate the recapture rules into the Section 1231 netting process.
8. Describe the tax consequences of property dispositions that don't involve a sale or exchange.

Chapter 7 continues our investigation of the tax consequences of property transactions. In this chapter, we will discuss how firms account for gains or losses from property dispositions. This discussion centers on three basic tax questions:

- What is the gain or loss recognized on the disposition of property?
- In what taxable year does the recognition occur?
- What is the tax character of the recognized gain or loss?

The answers to these questions determine the tax cost or savings and, in turn, the after-tax cash flows from the property disposition.

COMPUTATION OF GAIN OR LOSS RECOGNIZED

Realization and Recognition of Gains or Losses

The Internal Revenue Code specifies that gross income includes "gains derived from dealings in property"[1] and allows a deduction for "any loss sustained during the taxable year and not compensated for by insurance or otherwise."[2] These two rules of law mean that firms

[1] §61(a)(3).

[2] §165(a).

account for gains and losses from property transactions in the computation of taxable income. The **realized gain or loss** from the disposition of property is computed as follows:[3]

Amount realized on disposition
(Adjusted tax basis of property)
Realized gain or (loss)

This computation reflects the realization principle of accounting. Under this principle, increases or decreases in the value of assets are not accounted for as income. Such increases or decreases are not taken into account until an asset is converted to a different asset through an external transaction with another party. As a simple illustration of this principle, suppose that Firm F bought an asset four years ago for $25,000. Although the market value of the asset has steadily increased, the firm has not reported any of this accrued economic gain on either its financial statements or tax returns. This year, Firm F sells the asset for $60,000 cash, finally realizing a $35,000 gain.

Objective 1
Distinguish between gain or loss realization and recognition.

A third general rule of law is that the gain or loss realized on a property disposition is taken into account for tax purposes.[4] In other words, realized gain or loss becomes **recognized gain or loss** for the year.

Amount realized on disposition
(Adjusted tax basis of property)
Realized gain or (loss)
↓
Recognized gain or (loss)

Most of the property transactions examined in Chapter 7 reflect this linkage between realization and recognition. In Chapter 8, we will explore the exceptions to the general rule: transactions in which realized gain or loss is not recognized in the same year.

The realization principle has important planning implications because it gives property owners some control over the timing of gain or loss recognition. Owners of appreciated property can defer gain recognition and the related tax cost for as long as they hold the property. Owners of devalued property can accelerate the deduction of loss and the related tax savings by disposing of the property as soon as possible.

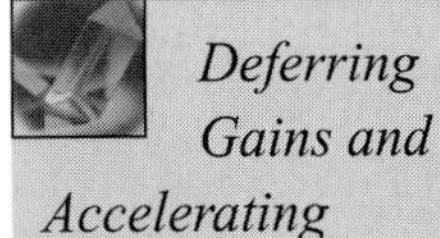

Deferring Gains and Accelerating Losses

Firm K has a $15,000 basis in Asset A and a $141,000 basis in Asset B. Near the end of its taxable year, Firm K has the opportunity to sell each asset for $100,000. It decides to hold Asset A to avoid recognizing its $85,000 economic gain and sell Asset B to recognize its $41,000 economic loss. Firm K can deduct this loss against income that would be taxed at 35 percent. Thus, the loss results in a $14,350 tax savings this year.

The amount of gain or loss that a taxpayer recognizes for tax purposes may not be the same amount reported on the taxpayer's financial statements. If an asset's adjusted tax basis does not equal its book basis, the tax gain or loss realized on disposition will not equal the book gain or loss.

[3] §1001(a).

[4] §1001(c).

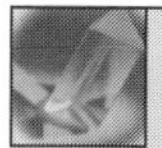

Book/Tax Difference on Asset Disposition

Orlof Inc. purchased a depreciable asset four years ago for $87,400 and sold it this year for $72,000. Orlof's book and tax gain on the sale is computed as follows:

	Book	Tax
Initial cost basis	$87,400	$87,400
Accumulated depreciation	(18,000)	(33,900)
Adjusted basis at date of sale	$69,400	$53,500
Amount realized on sale	$72,000	$72,000
Adjusted basis	(69,400)	(53,500)
Gain realized	$ 2,600	$18,500

The $15,900 excess tax gain over book gain is a reversal of the temporary differences between Orlof's book income and taxable income caused by excess tax depreciation over book depreciation during the four years that Orlof held the asset.

Sales and Exchanges

Owners can dispose of property through a sale for cash (including the purchaser's obligation to pay cash in the future) or through an exchange for other property. The owner's **amount realized** on the disposition equals any cash received plus the fair market value (FMV) of any property received.[5] For example, if Company J exchanges equipment for marketable securities and the securities are worth $50,000, Company J's amount realized is $50,000. While the amount realized equals the value of the cash and/or property received by the seller, the amount realized also equals the value of the property surrendered. In our example, both parties to the transaction must agree that the equipment is also worth $50,000. Why is this so? In an economic setting, no rational person would sell property for less than its value, nor would any purchaser pay more than the property's value. The private market created between seller and purchaser establishes the equal values of the properties changing hands.

Relief of Debt as Amount Realized

In Chapter 6, we learned that the tax basis of property includes any amount that the owner borrowed to acquire the property. In other words, tax basis encompasses both the owner's equity in the property and any debt to which the property is subject. If the owner sells the property and is relieved of debt in the transaction, the owner must include the debt relief in the amount realized on sale.

Relief of Debt

TG Corporation purchased investment land 15 years ago for $450,000. It put $100,000 of its own money into the investment and borrowed the remaining $350,000 from a bank, which took a mortgage on the property. TG's cost basis in the land is $450,000. Each year as TG paid down the principal of the mortgage, the payments increased its equity in the land but had no effect on TG's basis. This year, TG sold the land for $875,000. The purchaser assumed the $200,000 principal balance of the mortgage and paid the $675,000 remaining sales price in cash. TG's realized gain is computed as follows:

[5] §1001(b). The amount realized is reduced by selling costs such as sales commissions and title transfer fees.

Amount realized on sale:	
Cash received	$675,000
Relief of debt	200,000
	$875,000
Basis of land	(450,000)
Realized gain	$425,000

Tax-Free Recovery of Basis and Cash Flow

On a sale or exchange of property, only the excess of amount realized over adjusted basis is taxable income. Accordingly, sellers recover their investment in the property at no tax cost.

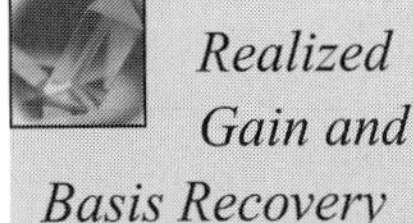

Realized Gain and Basis Recovery

Firm R owns an asset with a $5,000 basis. If it sells the asset for $8,000 cash, it realizes a taxable gain of only $3,000. The first $5,000 cash received represents a nontaxable recovery of Firm R's investment in the asset. Assuming that Firm R has a 35 percent marginal tax rate, the sale generates $6,950 cash flow.

	Tax Result	*Cash Flow*
Amount realized on sale	$8,000	$8,000
Basis	(5,000)	
Gain realized	$3,000	
	.35	
Tax cost of gain	$1,050	(1,050)
After-tax cash flow		$6,950

If a seller realizes a loss on a sale or exchange, the entire amount realized is a tax-free recovery of the seller's investment. Moreover, the seller may be allowed to deduct the *unrecovered* investment (realized loss) in the computation of taxable income.

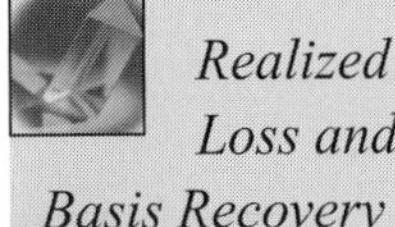

Realized Loss and Basis Recovery

Refer to the facts in the preceding example. If Firm R sells the asset for only $4,000, it realizes a $1,000 loss. *Assuming that this loss is fully deductible,* the firm recovers its $5,000 investment in the asset in the form of $4,000 cash plus a $1,000 deduction. Because of the tax savings from the deduction, the sale generates $4,350 cash flow.

	Tax Result	*Cash Flow*
Amount realized on sale	$ 4,000	$4,000
Basis	(5,000)	
Loss realized	$(1,000)	
	.35	
Tax savings from loss	$ (350)	350
After-tax cash flow		$4,350

In these two examples, the realized gain or loss does not enter into the computation of Firm R's net cash flow. Only the tax cost or savings resulting from the gain or loss are cash items.

Taxation of Inflationary Gains

As the preceding examples demonstrate, taxpayers who sell property can recover their basis at no tax cost. In financial terms, a return of investment does not represent income. Only the amount realized in excess of the investment—a return *on* investment—should be recognized as income. This return is overstated if the value of the dollar has changed between the date an asset is purchased and the date that asset is sold. In a period of inflation, the dollars that the taxpayer invested in the asset were worth more in terms of purchasing power than the dollars the taxpayer receives on sale.

Inflationary Gain

Refer to the first example in which Firm R sells an asset with a $5,000 cost basis for an $8,000 amount realized. Because of inflation, a dollar in the year the firm acquired the asset was worth $1.25 of today's dollars. In current dollar terms, Firm R's investment in its asset is $6,250 ($5,000 basis × $1.25), and its economic gain on sale is only $1,750 ($8,000 amount realized − $6,250 inflation-adjusted basis). However, because the tax system fails to account for changes in the dollar's purchasing power over time, Firm R pays tax on a $3,000 gain, $1,250 of which is not economic income but a return of its original investment.[6]

Seller-Financed Sales

In many sale transactions, the seller accepts the purchaser's debt obligation (note) as part of the sale price. Such note represents the purchaser's promise to pay cash to the seller over a specified future period rather than on the date of sale. In an arm's-length **seller-financed sale,** the seller charges the purchaser a market rate of interest on the note. As a general rule, the seller includes the principal amount of the purchaser's note in the amount realized on sale and computes gain or loss accordingly.

Seller-Financed Sale

Company Q sold property with a $195,000 basis for $300,000. The purchaser paid $30,000 cash on the date of sale and gave Company Q a note for the $270,000 balance of the price. The note obligated the purchaser to pay the $270,000 principal over the next 10 years and carried a 9.2 percent annual interest rate. Company Q realized a $105,000 gain on this seller-financed sale, even though it received only $30,000 cash in the year of sale.

Installment Sale Method

Objective 2
Describe the installment sale method of accounting.

Taxpayers may use a statutory method of accounting for gains realized on seller-financed sales of certain types of property. Under the **installment sale method,** the seller does not recognize the entire realized gain in the year of sale. Instead, gain recognition is linked to the seller's receipt of cash over the term of the purchaser's note.[7] The seller calculates the gain recognized in the year of sale and each subsequent year by multiplying the cash received during the year by a **gross profit percentage.** This percentage is calculated by dividing the gain realized by the sale price.

[6] Congress and the Treasury are well aware of this problem. The theoretically sound solution is to allow taxpayers to adjust the basis in their assets for inflation. Lawmakers have been reluctant to enact this solution into law because of the potential revenue loss and the enormous complexity it would add to the computation of basis, cost recovery deductions, and recognized gains and losses.

[7] §453.

Installment Sale Method

In year 1, Firm B sold a five-acre tract of investment land with a $150,000 basis for $214,500. The purchaser paid $14,500 cash on the date of sale and gave Firm B a note for the $200,000 balance of the price. The note provides for annual principal payments of $50,000 in years 2 through 5 plus 6 percent annual interest on the unpaid balance. Firm B's realized gain and gross profit percentage are computed as follows:

Amount realized on sale:	
Cash received	$ 14,500
Purchaser's note	200,000
	$214,500
Basis of land	(150,000)
Realized gain	$ 64,500

$$\frac{\$64{,}500 \text{ realized gain}}{\$214{,}500 \text{ sale price}} = 30.07 \text{ gross profit percentage}$$

Firm B will recognize the following taxable gain each year:

Year	*Cash Received*	*Gross Profit Percentage*	*Taxable Gain Recognized*
1	$14,500	30.07%	$ 4,360
2	50,000	30.07	15,035
3	50,000	30.07	15,035
4	50,000	30.07	15,035
5	50,000	30.07	15,035
			$64,500

Note that the annual interest payments that Firm B receives on the installment note do not enter into the computation of recognized gain. The firm must recognize these payments as ordinary income under its regular method of accounting.

Taxpayers can use the installment sale method to defer gain recognition on the sale of many types of business and investment property. (The method has no application to realized losses.) However, the method does not apply to gains realized on the sale of stocks or securities traded on an established market.[8] Nor does the method apply to gains realized on the sale of inventory to customers in the ordinary course of the seller's business.[9]

Installment Sale of Inventory

Refer to the preceding example. If Firm B is a real estate developer that buys and sells land in the ordinary course of business, it cannot use the installment sale method to account for the gain realized on sale of the five-acre tract. Thus, Firm B would recognize the entire $64,500 gain in the year of sale.

[8] §453(k)(2)(A). Established securities markets include the New York Stock Exchange (NYSE), the American Stock Exchange (AMEX), and Nasdaq.

[9] §453(b)(2)(A).

Taxpayers generally benefit from the use of the installment sale method to defer gain recognition. In cases in which deferral is not beneficial, taxpayers may make a written election *not* to use the installment sale method.[10] For taxpayers preparing their financial statements according to GAAP, use of the installment sale method results in a favorable temporary difference between book income and taxable income. The difference originates in the year of sale and reverses over the years when the taxpayer receives principal payments on the purchaser's note.

Book/Tax Difference from Installment Sale Method

Assume that Firm B in our original example prepares its financial statements in accordance with GAAP. In the year of the land sale, Firm B included its entire $64,500 realized gain in book income but only $4,360 recognized gain in taxable income. This $60,140 excess of book income over taxable income will reverse over the next four years as Firm B recognizes taxable income on receipt of the $50,000 annual principal payments on the purchaser's note.

Seller's Basis in Purchaser's Note

When a seller receives the purchaser's note in a seller-financed sale, the seller generally takes a basis in the note equal to its face value. This basis represents the dollars that the seller will recover as tax-free principal payments.

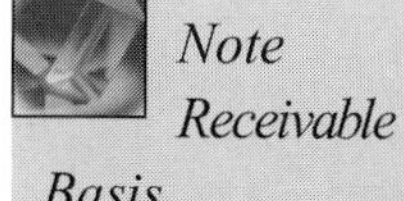

Note Receivable Basis

Refer back to the example on page 171 in which Company Q sold property for $300,000, accepted the purchaser's note for $270,000, and realized a $105,000 gain. If Company Q recognized the entire gain in the year of sale, its basis in the note receivable is the note's $270,000 face value. The principal payments that Company Q will receive over the next 10 years will reduce both the face value and tax basis of this note to zero.

In the case of an installment sale, the seller is not entitled to a tax-free recovery of the dollars represented by the purchaser's note. Instead, the seller will recognize a percentage of every dollar received as taxable income. Consequently, the seller's tax basis in the installment note is reduced by the deferred gain represented by the note.[11]

Note Receivable Basis—Installment Sale Method

Refer back to the example on page 172 in which Firm B sold a five-acre tract of land for $214,500, accepted the purchaser's note for $200,000, and used the installment sale method to defer gain recognition. Firm B's basis in the note receivable is only $139,860 ($200,000 face value − $60,140 deferred gain). As Firm B receives each $50,000 principal payment, it will recognize a portion of the deferred gain and reduce the face value and tax basis of the note according to the following schedule.

Year	*Note Receivable Face Value*	*Deferred Gain*	*Note Receivable Basis*
1	$200,000	$60,140	$139,860
2	150,000	45,105	104,895
3	100,000	30,070	69,930
4	50,000	15,035	34,965
5	-0-	-0-	-0-

[10] §453(d).

[11] §453B(b).

If a taxpayer converts a note receivable to cash, the taxpayer must immediately recognize any deferred gain represented by the note.[12] Assume that Firm B in the preceding example collected only two $50,000 principal payments, then sold the note to a financial institution for its $100,000 face value. Because Firm B accelerated its receipt of cash from the installment sale, it must recognize the remaining $30,070 deferred gain. What if Firm B tried the more subtle technique of pledging the note as collateral for a $100,000 loan from the financial institution? In this case, Firm B still owns the note. Nonetheless, Firm B must recognize the $30,070 deferred gain. The installment sale rules stipulate that a pledge of an installment note is treated as a disposition of the note for cash.[13]

Disallowed Losses on Related Party Sales

Earlier in the chapter, we focused on the general rule that the entire gain or loss realized on a property disposition is recognized for tax purposes. Consequently, firms can usually deduct losses realized on the sale of business assets. One important exception to the general rule is that losses realized on the sale or exchange of property between related parties are nondeductible.[14] For purposes of this exception, the Internal Revenue Code defines related parties as people who are members of the same family, an individual and a corporation if the individual owns more than 50 percent of the value of the corporation's outstanding stock, and two corporations controlled by the same shareholders.[15]

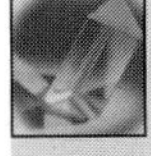

Disallowed Loss

Firm M sold a business asset to Purchaser P for $75,000. Firm M's basis in the asset was $90,000, and it reported a $15,000 realized loss on its financial statements. Firm M and Purchaser P are related parties for federal tax purposes. Consequently, Firm M may not deduct the $15,000 loss in the computation of taxable income. Even though Firm M's loss is disallowed, Purchaser P takes a $75,000 cost basis in the asset.

Objective 3
Explain why the tax law disallows losses on related party sales.

This disallowance rule is based on the theory that a related party loss may not represent an economic loss to the seller. For instance, when a corporation realizes a loss on the sale of an asset to an unrelated purchaser, the loss corresponds to the corporation's unrecovered investment in the asset—a permanent reduction in net worth. If the corporation sells that asset to its controlling shareholder, the underlying ownership of the asset doesn't change. If the value of the asset increases after the sale, the shareholder may eventually recover the corporation's entire investment. In this case, the corporation's loss has no economic substance and should not be deductible in computing taxable income.

A second explanation for the disallowance rule is that related party transactions occur in a fictitious market in which seller and purchaser may not be negotiating at arm's length. Because of this possibility, the government has no assurance that the sale price equals the market value at which the asset would change hands between unrelated parties. If the price is unrealistically low, the seller's loss is inflated and results in an unwarranted tax deduction. Because of this possibility, the loss disallowance rule applies to every related party sale, regardless of the actual bargaining stance between the parties. For instance, if a brother realizes a loss on the sale of a business asset to his sister, the loss is nondeductible, even if the brother can prove that the siblings have been estranged for years, and the transaction between them was strictly at arm's length.

[12] §453B.

[13] §453A(d).

[14] §267(a)(1).

[15] §267(b)(1), (2), and (3). A person's family includes a spouse, brothers and sisters, ancestors, and lineal descendants. §267(c)(4).

Offset of Gain by Previously Disallowed Loss

From the seller's perspective, the loss disallowance rule causes a permanent difference between loss realized and loss recognized on the sale of property. Thus, the seller never receives the benefit of a tax deduction for the disallowed loss. However, in the right set of circumstances, the *purchaser* may receive some or all of the benefit. If the purchaser subsequently sells the property acquired in the related party transaction and realizes a gain, the purchaser can offset this gain by the previously disallowed loss.[16]

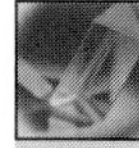

Use of Seller's Disallowed Loss by Purchaser

Refer to the preceding example in which Firm M realized a $15,000 disallowed loss on the sale of an asset to Purchaser P. Assume that the asset was nondepreciable in P's hands. Several years after the related party transaction, Purchaser P sells the asset to an *unrelated* buyer. The tax consequences based on three different assumptions as to the sale price are presented in the following table.

	Assumption 1	*Assumption 2*	*Assumption 3*
Amount realized on sale	$93,000	$81,000	$70,000
Basis of asset	(75,000)	(75,000)	(75,000)
Gain (loss) realized	$18,000	$ 6,000	$ (5,000)
Previously disallowed loss	(15,000)	(6,000)	-0-
Gain (loss) recognized	$ 3,000	-0-	$ (5,000)

This example demonstrates that Purchaser P can use Firm M's previously disallowed loss only to *reduce* the gain recognized on a subsequent sale of the asset. The disallowed loss cannot *create* a recognized loss or *increase* the recognized loss on a subsequent sale.

TAX CHARACTER OF RECOGNIZED GAINS AND LOSSES

Objective 4
Identify the two components of the capital gain or loss definition.

Taxpayers must compute the gain or loss realized on a property disposition and determine the taxable year (or years) in which the gain or loss is recognized. In addition, they must determine the character of the recognized gain or loss. In the tax world, every gain or loss is ultimately characterized as either ordinary or capital. A **capital gain or loss** results from the sale or exchange of a capital asset.[17] Any gain or loss that does not meet this definition is **ordinary** in character.[18]

The capital gain/loss definition has two distinct components. First, the transaction resulting in the gain or loss must be a sale or exchange. Second, the asset surrendered must be a capital asset. If a firm disposes of a capital asset in some way other than a sale or exchange, the realized gain or loss is ordinary in character. Several of these dispositions are discussed later in the chapter. At this point, let's focus our attention on the second component of the capital gain/loss definition: the capital asset requirement.

Capital Asset Defined

The Internal Revenue Code defines the term **capital asset** by exception.[19] For tax purposes, *every* asset is a capital asset unless it falls into one of eight categories:

[16] §267(d).

[17] §1222.

[18] §64 and §65.

[19] §1221.

1. Inventory items or property held by the taxpayer primarily for sale to customers in the ordinary course of business.
2. Accounts or notes receivable acquired in the ordinary course of business (i.e., acquired through the sale of inventory or the performance of services).
3. Supplies used or consumed in the ordinary course of business.
4. Real or depreciable property used in a business (including rental real estate) and intangible business assets subject to amortization.[20]
5. A copyright; literary, musical, or artistic composition; a letter or memorandum; or similar property held by a taxpayer whose personal efforts created the property or a person to whom the property was gifted by the creator.
6. Certain publications of the U.S. government.
7. Commodities derivative financial instruments held by a dealer.
8. Hedging transaction properties.

While the last three categories of capital assets are listed for the sake of completeness, they are not discussed in this text.

Capital asset status is not determined by the intrinsic nature of the asset itself but by the use for which the asset is held by its owner.

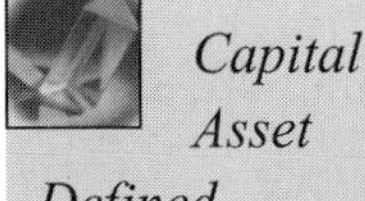

Capital Asset Defined

Ms. Helm, a professional sculptor, purchased $50 worth of clay and created a work of art that she sold for $5,000 to BVC Corporation. BVC uses the sculpture as decoration in the lobby of its corporate headquarters. The work of art is not a capital asset in the hands of its creator, so Ms. Helm's $4,950 gain recognized on the sale is ordinary income. In contrast, the sculpture is a capital asset to BVC because it is not a *depreciable* business asset. As a result, if the corporation ever sells the sculpture, its recognized gain or loss will be capital in character.

Capital Loss Limitation

Objective 5
Apply the limitation on the deductibility of capital losses.

The federal income tax system contains a subset of rules applying to capital gains and losses. One logical way to analyze these rules is to begin with the limitation on capital losses: *Capital losses can be deducted only to the extent of capital gains.*[21] In other words, if the combined result of all sales and exchanges of capital assets during the year is a net loss, the net loss is nondeductible. If the combined result is a net gain, the net gain is included in taxable income. The following diagram depicts the result of this netting process.

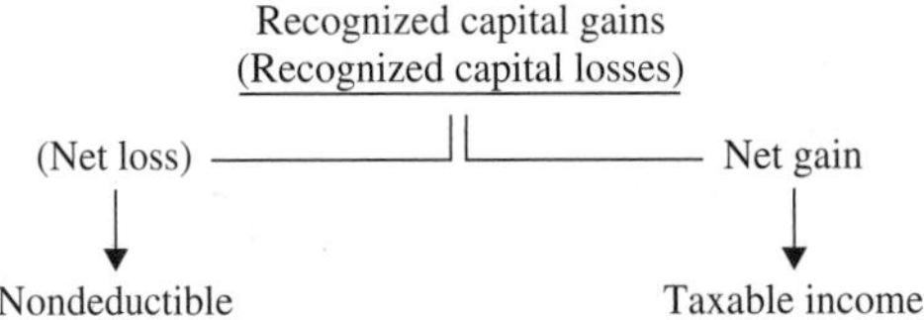

The capital loss limitation has a major effect on the tax savings generated by a capital loss. The next three examples demonstrate this effect.

[20] Reg. §1.167(a)-3 and §197(f)(7).

[21] §1211. This strict limitation is relaxed very slightly for individual taxpayers. See the discussion of individual capital losses in Chapter 15.

Fully Deductible Capital Loss

Firm SD sold a capital asset with a $100,000 basis for $25,000. If the firm's marginal tax rate is 25 percent, how much tax savings does this $75,000 capital loss generate? If Firm SD recognized at least $75,000 capital gain during the year, the capital loss generates $18,750 current tax savings, and the after-tax loss on the sale is $56,250.

Loss on sale of capital asset	$(75,000)
Current tax savings ($75,000 deductible loss × 25%)	18,750
After-tax loss	$(56,250)

Partially Deductible Capital Loss

Assume that Firm SD recognized only $40,000 capital gain during the year. In this case, the firm can deduct only $40,000 capital loss; its $35,000 **net capital loss** (excess of current year capital loss over capital gain) is nondeductible.[22] The current tax savings generated by the capital loss decreases to $10,000, and the after-tax loss increases to $65,000.

Loss on sale of capital asset	$(75,000)
Current tax savings ($40,000 deductible loss × 25%)	10,000
After-tax loss	$(65,000)

Nondeductible Capital Loss

In the worst-case scenario, Firm SD recognized no capital gains during the year. Consequently, none of the $75,000 net capital loss is deductible, and the before-tax and after-tax loss are both $75,000.

Loss on sale of capital asset	$(75,000)
Current tax savings	–0–
After-tax loss	$(75,000)

Loss Carrybacks and Carryforwards

The above examples are incomplete because they show the effect of the capital loss limitation only for an isolated year. If a taxpayer has a net capital loss for the year, the law provides a mechanism by which the loss can be deducted in a previous or future year. For no obvious policy reason, the tax law differentiates between capital losses incurred by individuals and those incurred by corporations.

- A net capital loss incurred by an *individual* is carried forward indefinitely.[23] In any future year in which the individual recognizes net capital gain (excess of capital gain over capital loss), the loss carryforward is deductible to the extent of such gain.
- A net capital loss incurred by a *corporation* is carried back three years and forward five years, but only as a deduction against net capital gains recognized during this eight-year period.[24]

[22] Net capital losses are reported for financial statement purposes and result in a difference between book income and taxable income.

[23] §1212(b)(1).

[24] §1212(a)(1).

Let's look at an example of the corporate rule.

Capital Loss Carryback

RO, a corporation with a 35 percent marginal tax rate, sold two capital assets in 2004, recognizing a $50,000 gain on the first sale and an $85,000 loss on the second. RO included the $50,000 gain in gross income and deducted $50,000 of the loss on its 2004 tax return; its nondeductible net capital loss is $35,000. RO's taxable income for the three previous years is as follows.

	2001	2002	2003
Ordinary income	$600,000	$400,000	$730,000
Net capital gain	–0–	10,000	12,000
Taxable income	$600,000	$410,000	$742,000

- Because RO had no net capital gain in the earliest year of its carryback period, it can't deduct any of its 2004 net capital loss against 2001 income.
- RO may deduct $10,000 and $12,000 of the 2004 loss against the taxable income reported in 2002 and 2003, recompute its tax accordingly, and file for a tax refund.
- RO will carry the $13,000 remaining net capital loss forward for five years to deduct against future capital gains.

Taxation of Capital Gains

Under the federal income tax system, capital gains have the unique capacity to absorb capital losses. As a result, both corporate and individual taxpayers always prefer capital gains to ordinary income. In a year in which a taxpayer recognizes a net capital gain (excess of capital gain over capital loss), the net gain is included in taxable income. If the taxpayer is a corporation, this net gain is taxed at the same rates as ordinary income. If the taxpayer is an individual, the net capital gain may be taxed at a preferential rate of 5, 15, 25, or 28 percent.[25] Given that the highest marginal rate on ordinary income is 35 percent, the preferential rates on capital gains are extremely valuable to high-income individuals. The details of the preferential rate structure are discussed in Chapter 15.

Capital Asset Definition Revisited

Now that you understand the special tax consequences of capital gains and losses, you can appreciate why gain and loss characterization is so important in the tax planning process. As a general rule, taxpayers prefer capital gains to ordinary income, and they prefer ordinary losses to capital losses. As we discussed earlier in this section, the characterization of gain and loss depends on whether the property was a noncapital or a capital asset in the hands of the seller. More specifically, does the property fit into one of the categories of noncapital assets listed in the Internal Revenue Code? If the property does not fit into one of these eight categories, the property is a capital asset.[26] This classification scheme is presented in the following diagram.

[25] §1(h). These rates apply only to long-term capital gains, which are derived from the sale of assets held for more than one year. See §1222.

[26] *Arkansas Best Corp.* v. *Commissioner*, 485 U.S. 212 (1988).

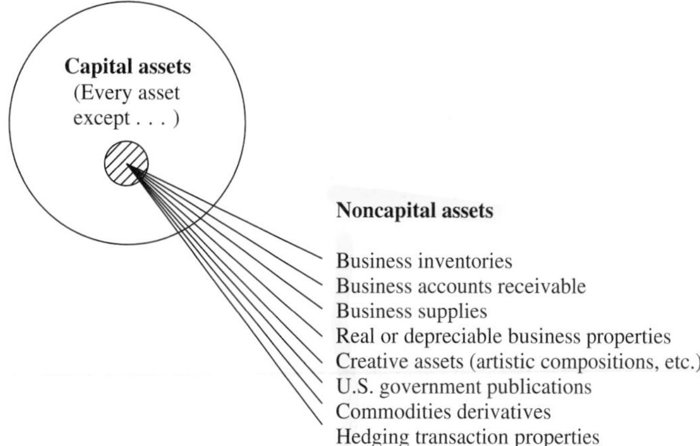

DISPOSITIONS OF NONCAPITAL ASSETS

The expansive definition of a capital asset as every asset except for those specifically excepted may be misleading. In the business context, capital assets are the exception rather than the rule. Most properties listed on a firm's balance sheet fall into one of the first four categories of noncapital assets. In this section of the chapter, we will analyze the tax consequences of the dispositions of these noncapital business assets.

What types of business properties are capital in character? Any asset held by a firm for long-term investment rather than for active business or commercial use is a capital asset. Similarly, equity and creditor interests in other firms, such as stocks, bonds, and partnership interests, are capital in character. Self-created intellectual properties such as copyrights, trademarks, and patents are capital assets.[27] Finally, the goodwill and going-concern value *created* by a profitable business is a capital asset.[28]

Inventory

The first category of noncapital assets includes any property held as inventory or primarily for sale to customers. When firms sell inventory assets as part of their everyday operations, the recognized gain or loss is the quintessence of ordinary income or loss. For firms engaged in the manufacture, production, wholesaling, distribution, or retailing of tangible goods, the identification of inventory assets is fairly straightforward. Disputes between taxpayers and the IRS concerning the status of property as inventory most frequently arise when the asset in question is land.

Real Estate

If a taxpayer sells a tract of land at a profit, the taxpayer usually prefers to categorize the tract as an investment asset and the profit as capital gain. The IRS might challenge this result if it believes that the taxpayer acquired and held the land primarily for sale to customers rather than as a long-term investment. From this perspective, the profit from the sale is ordinary income. The federal courts have been called on many times to resolve this particular difference of opinion. In cases in which the land sale was an unusual or isolated

[27] §1221(a)(3) and §1235.

[28] See IRS Letter Ruling 200243002 (October 25, 2002). *Purchased* goodwill/going-concern value is not a capital asset to the purchaser. Purchased intangibles fall into the fourth category of noncapital assets, and the tax consequences of their disposition are governed by the specialized rules of §197(f)(1).

occurrence, the courts have tended to side with the taxpayer. In cases in which the taxpayer sold other tracts of land on a regular and continual basis, subdivided and improved the land prior to sale, or advertised the availability of the land to the general public, the courts have tended to agree with the IRS that the land was an inventory asset.

Business Accounts Receivable and Supplies

The second category of noncapital assets includes business accounts receivable from the sale of goods or performance of services. Accrual basis firms realize ordinary income from the transactions that create their receivables. Therefore, the tax basis in their accounts receivable equals face value. Cash basis firms do not realize ordinary income until they collect their receivables. Therefore, the tax basis in their *unrealized* accounts receivable is zero. Firms usually either collect their receivables or write off any uncollectible accounts as bad debts. In an unusual case, a firm that needs immediate cash might sell or *factor* its accounts receivable to a third party (typically a financial institution). The difference between the amount realized and the tax basis of the receivables is ordinary income or loss.

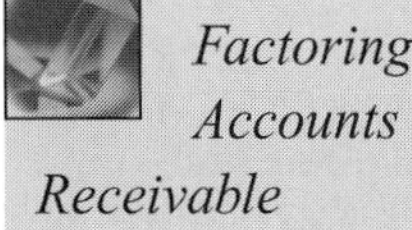

Factoring Accounts Receivable

SP Company has $400,000 accounts receivable that it expects to collect over the next 120 days. To meet a cash emergency, SP factors the receivables with First City Bank for $383,000. If SP uses the accrual method of accounting, it has a $400,000 basis in its accounts receivable and recognizes a $17,000 ordinary loss on their disposition. If SP uses the cash method of accounting, it has a zero basis in its accounts receivable and recognizes $383,000 ordinary income on their disposition.

The third category of noncapital assets includes business supplies. Depending on their method of accounting, firms deduct the cost of supplies either in the year of purchase or in the year in which the supplies are consumed. In an unusual case, a firm with unneeded or excess supplies on hand might sell the supplies to a third party. The difference between the amount realized and the tax basis of the supplies is ordinary income or loss.

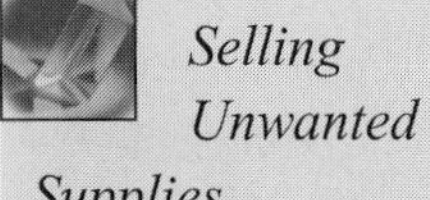

Selling Unwanted Supplies

Firm EQP is moving its home office to a new location and does not want to transport its stock of office supplies for which it paid $6,000. EQP sells the supplies to a neighboring business for $5,600. If EQP deducted the $6,000 cost, it has a zero basis in the supplies and recognizes $5,600 ordinary income on their disposition. If EQP capitalized the $6,000 cost, it recognizes a $400 ordinary loss on their disposition.

Section 1231 Assets

The fourth category of noncapital assets includes real or depreciable property used in a business (including rental real estate) and intangible business assets subject to amortization (such as *purchased* goodwill). In other words, the operating assets on a balance sheet are noncapital assets. The tax consequences of a sale of an operating asset depends on the length of time the seller held the asset. If the holding period is a year or less, gain or loss recognized on sale is ordinary in character. If the holding period exceeds one year, the gain or loss is subject to a complex set of characterization rules.

Objective 6
Apply the Section 1231 netting process.

These rules are found in Section 1231 of the Internal Revenue Code; consequently, the assets subject to the rules are called **Section 1231 assets.** The basic rule of Section 1231 is simple. If the *combined result* of all sales and exchanges of Section 1231 assets during the year is a net loss, the loss is an ordinary loss. On the other hand, if the result is a net gain, the gain is treated as a capital gain.[29] The following diagram depicts the Section 1231 netting process and the two possible results.

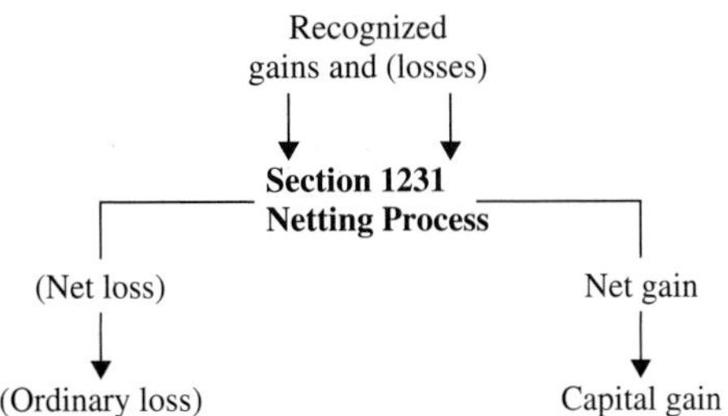

Note that this asymmetric rule offers the best of both worlds to the business community—ordinary loss or capital gain on the sale of operating assets. Let's work through two examples of the basic Section 1231 netting process.

Section 1231 Net Loss

During 2005, Company RC sold three Section 1231 assets with the following result.

	Gain or (Loss) Recognized
Asset sale 1	$ 45,000
Asset sale 2	(35,000)
Asset sale 3	(16,000)
Section 1231 net loss	$ (6,000)

Company RC's $6,000 Section 1231 net loss is an ordinary loss, fully deductible in the computation of taxable income.

Section 1231 Net Gain

Assume that asset sale 2 generated only a $5,000 (rather than a $35,000) loss for Company RC. In this case, the company has a net gain on the sale of its Section 1231 assets.

	Gain or (Loss) Recognized
Asset sale 1	$ 45,000
Asset sale 2	(5,000)
Asset sale 3	(16,000)
Section 1231 net gain	$ 24,000

Under the basic rule of Section 1231, Company RC treats the $24,000 gain as a capital gain. Consequently, the company can deduct up to $24,000 of capital losses or capital loss carryforwards. If the company's capital loss deduction is less than $24,000, the excess Section 1231 gain is treated as net capital gain. If the company's income is taxed at the individual rates (for example, if Company RC is a sole proprietorship), this gain is taxed at the preferential capital gains rates.

[29] §1231(a)(1).

Recapture of Previous Year Ordinary Losses

Objective 7
Incorporate the recapture rules into the Section 1231 netting process.

Before Company RC can treat its Section 1231 net gain as a capital gain, it must consider an exception to the basic characterization rule. This exception applies if a taxpayer has a Section 1231 net gain in the current year but had a Section 1231 net loss in any of the five previous taxable years. In such case, the taxpayer must **recapture** the previous year loss (which was deductible as ordinary loss) by treating an equivalent amount of current year gain as ordinary income.[30] The next diagram incorporates this recapture rule.

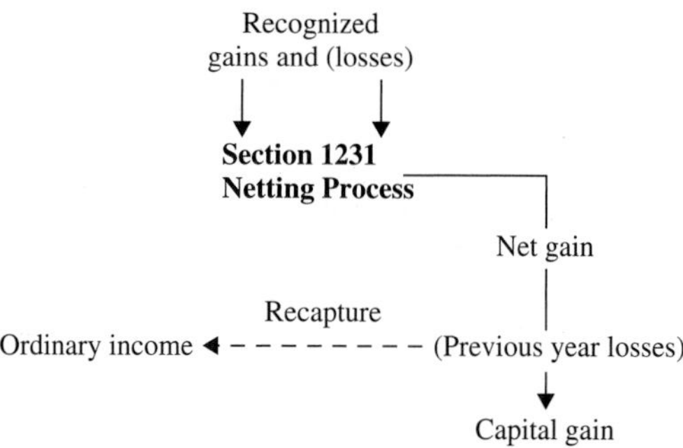

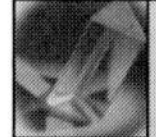

Recapture of Previous Year Loss

Company RC did not sell any Section 1231 assets in 2000 through 2002 or in 2004. However, in 2003, it recognized a $7,100 Section 1231 net loss, which it deducted in the computation of 2003 taxable income. In 2005, Company RC recognized a $24,000 Section 1231 net gain. It must recapture the 2003 loss by reporting $7,100 of this gain as ordinary income. The $16,900 remaining Section 1231 net gain is treated as capital gain.

Once a taxpayer has recaptured a previous year Section 1231 net loss, the loss is not recaptured again. If Company RC has a Section 1231 net gain in 2004, the entire gain is treated as capital gain because the company has no *unrecaptured* Section 1231 losses for the previous five-year period.

Depreciation Recapture

The pro-business rule of Section 1231 is modified when applied to gains recognized on the sale of depreciable or amortizable property. The modification requires that gain attributable to previous year depreciation or amortization deductions be characterized as ordinary income rather than Section 1231 gain.[31] This **depreciation recapture** rule has three components: full recapture, partial recapture, and 20 percent recapture. Before analyzing each component, let's add the basic recapture rule to our diagram.

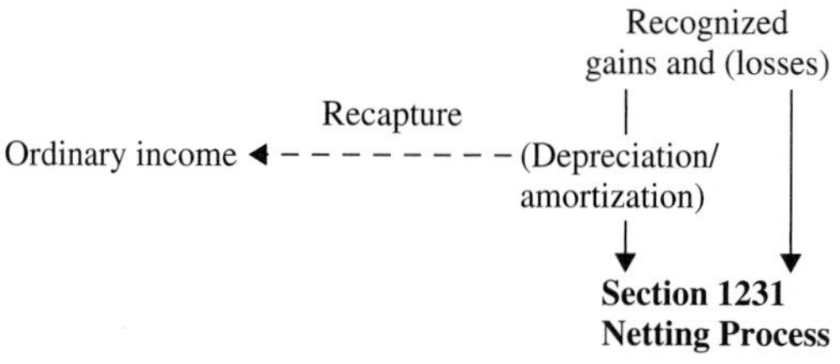

[30] §1231(c).

[31] The ordinary income created by any of the depreciation recapture rules is not eligible for installment sale treatment and must be recognized in the year of sale. §453(i).

Full Recapture Rule

The full recapture rule applies to gains recognized on sales of depreciable personalty and amortizable intangibles. Under this rule, an amount of gain equal to accumulated depreciation or amortization through date of sale is recharacterized as ordinary income.[32] The rationale for this recapture requirement can best be explained through a numeric example.

Rationale for Recapture

Firm D purchased a tangible asset several years ago for $100,000 and has accumulated $40,000 MACRS depreciation through date of sale. As a result, its adjusted basis in the asset is $60,000. If the firm sells the asset for $100,000, it recognizes a $40,000 gain. *Absent a recapture requirement,* this gain is a Section 1231 gain with the potential (subject to the Section 1231 netting process) for capital gain treatment. However, the entire gain is attributable to previous years' cost recovery deductions, which reduced the firm's *ordinary income* in those years by $40,000.

The recapture requirement prevents this conversion of ordinary income into capital gain. In our example, Firm D must characterize its $40,000 gain as ordinary income. If we modify the example by changing the amount realized on sale, the amount of recaptured ordinary income also changes. The following table illustrates the recapture computation based on four different amounts realized.

		Assumption 1	**Assumption 2**	**Assumption 3**	**Assumption 4**
Amount realized		$100,000	$ 90,000	$105,000	$ 48,000
Cost of asset	$100,000				
Depreciation	(40,000)				
Adjusted basis		(60,000)	(60,000)	(60,000)	(60,000)
Gain (loss) recognized		$ 40,000	$ 30,000	$ 45,000	$ (12,000)
Gain recaptured as ordinary income		$ 40,000	$ 30,000	$ 40,000	-0-
Section 1231 gain (loss)		-0-	-0-	5,000	$ (12,000)
		$ 40,000	$ 30,000	$ 45,000	$ (12,000)

- Assumption 1 reflects the original facts in the Firm D example. The $40,000 gain recognized equals the $40,000 accumulated depreciation, and the entire gain is recaptured as ordinary income.
- Under Assumption 2, the $30,000 gain recognized *is less than* accumulated depreciation. In this case, the entire gain is recaptured as ordinary income.
- Under Assumption 3, the $45,000 gain *is more than* accumulated depreciation. In this case, only $40,000 of the gain (an amount equal to accumulated depreciation) is recaptured, and the remaining $5,000 gain (appreciation in the value of the asset) is Section 1231 gain.
- Under Assumption 4, Firm D recognizes a $12,000 loss on the sale. This is a Section 1231 loss; the recapture rules don't apply to losses.

[32] §1245 and §197(f)(7).

Partial Recapture Rule for Realty

The recapture rule applying to gains recognized on sales of depreciable realty (buildings, improvements, and other permanent attachments to land) is less stringent than the full recapture rule.[33] Although Congress has changed the details of this rule many times over the past decades, the essential concept is that only *accelerated depreciation in excess of straight-line depreciation* is recaptured. In the preceding chapter, we learned that real property placed in service after 1986 and subject to MACRS must be depreciated under the straight-line method. Therefore, the partial recapture rule applies only to realty placed in service before 1987.

Partial Depreciation Recapture

Company NB sold a residential apartment complex for $1 million: $200,000 for the underlying land and $800,000 for the building. NB purchased the property in 1986 for $1,120,000 and allocated $170,000 and $950,000 of this cost basis to the land and building, respectively. NB deducted $600,000 accelerated depreciation with respect to the building through date of sale. Straight-line depreciation over the same period would have been only $325,000; consequently, NB deducted $275,000 *excess* accelerated depreciation. The computation of NB's recognized gain on sale and characterization of that gain is as follows:

	Land		*Building*	
Amount realized		$ 200,000		$800,000
Cost of asset	$170,000		$ 950,000	
Depreciation	–0–		(600,000)	
Adjusted basis		(170,000)		(350,000)
Gain recognized		$ 30,000		$450,000
Gain recaptured as ordinary income (excess accelerated depreciation)		–0–		$275,000
Section 1231 gain		$ 30,000		175,000
		$ 30,000		$450,000

Twenty Percent Recapture by Corporations

Corporate taxpayers must contend with a special recapture rule applying to gain recognized on sales of depreciable realty.[34] Corporations must compute the excess of the gain that would have been characterized as ordinary income under the full recapture rule over the gain characterized as ordinary income under the partial recapture rule. The corporation must then recapture 20 percent of this excess as additional ordinary income.

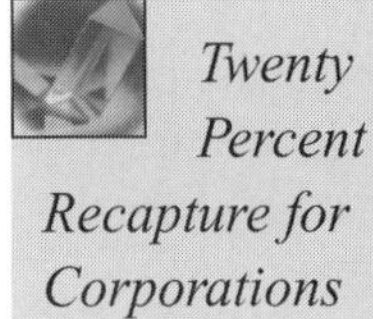

Twenty Percent Recapture for Corporations

If Company NB in the preceding example is a corporation, the 20 percent rule has the following result:

[33] §1250. Nonresidential realty (commercial buildings, warehouses, and so on) placed in service after 1980 and before 1987 and depreciated under an accelerated method is subject to the full recapture rule. See §1245(a)(5) prior to its amendment by the Tax Reform Act of 1986.

[34] §291(a)(1).

	Land	Building
Ordinary income under full recapture (entire gain recognized)	–0–	$450,000
Ordinary income under partial recapture (excess accelerated depreciation)	–0–	(275,000)
Excess	–0–	$175,000
		.20
Additional recapture	–0–	$ 35,000

Summary of Gain Characterization

	Land	Building
Ordinary income under full recapture rule	–0–	–0–
Ordinary income under partial recapture rule	–0–	$275,000
Ordinary income under 20 percent rule	–0–	35,000
Section 1231 gain	$30,000	140,000
	$30,000	$450,000

The 20 percent recapture rule has particular significance for real property placed in service after 1986. Because firms must use the straight-line method to compute MACRS depreciation for these properties, the partial recapture rule is inapplicable. Even so, *corporations* that sell these properties must recapture 20 percent of the amount that would have been ordinary income if the property were subject to the full recapture rule.

Summary

Exhibit 7.1 provides a summary of the ordinary income recapture rules. Remember that recapture only applies to recognized gain on sale of a Section 1231 asset. If a Section 1231 asset is sold at a loss, the entire loss is recognized as a Section 1231 loss subject to the Section 1231 netting process.

EXHIBIT 7.1
Summary of Recapture Rules

Recognized GAIN on Sale or Exchange of Section 1231 Asset	Basic Recapture Rule
• Nondepreciable property [land]	No recapture
• Tangible personalty	Full recapture of depreciation
• Purchased intangibles	Full recapture of amortization
• Depreciable realty [buildings] placed in service before 1987	Partial recapture [accelerated depreciation over SL] and 20% recapture by corporations
• Depreciable realty [buildings] placed in service after 1986	20% recapture by corporations

Comprehensive Example

The tax rules governing the character of gains and losses recognized on the sale or exchange of business operating assets are quite difficult. Before leaving this subject, let's review the rules by working through a comprehensive example.

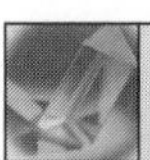

Characterizing Gains and Losses

In 2004, BC, a calendar year corporation, recognized a $145,000 capital loss on the sale of marketable securities. The corporation did not sell any other capital assets during the year. Therefore, BC cannot deduct any of the capital loss *unless* it recognized a Section 1231 net gain for the year.

BC recognized the following gains and losses on 2004 sales of operating assets. The column headed *Accumulated Depreciation* reflects the correct MACRS depreciation through date of sale.

	Date Placed in Service	*Date Sold*	*Initial Basis*	*Accumulated Depreciation*	*Sale Price*	*Gain (Loss)*
Office equipment	11/3/03	2/14	$ 8,200	$ 2,300	$ 5,100	$ (800)
Copying equipment	8/16/00	5/14	4,000	3,650	2,350	2,000
Furniture	12/19/02	5/31	18,000	4,900	20,400	7,300
Hauling equipment	2/12/03	8/28	32,000	12,000	19,250	(750)
Real property:						
Land	4/12/00	11/3	100,000	–0–	125,000	25,000
Building	4/12/00	11/3	500,000	62,000*	550,000	112,000

*Straight-line.

These gains and losses are characterized as follows:

	Gain (Loss)	*Ordinary Income or (Loss)*	*Section 1231 Gain or (Loss)*
Office equipment	$ (800)	$ (800)	
Copying equipment	2,000	2,000	
Furniture	7,300	4,900	$ 2,400
Hauling equipment	(750)		(750)
Real property:			
Land	25,000		25,000
Building	112,000	12,400	99,600
		$18,500	$126,250

- BC owned the office equipment for less than a year. Therefore, this asset is neither a capital asset nor a Section 1231 asset, and the loss recognized on sale is ordinary.
- Gain recognized on sale of the copying equipment is less than accumulated depreciation. Therefore, the entire gain is recaptured as ordinary income.
- Gain recaptured as ordinary income on sale of the furniture is limited to accumulated depreciation. The rest of the gain is Section 1231 gain.
- Loss recognized on sale of the hauling equipment is Section 1231 loss.
- Gain recognized on sale of the land is Section 1231 gain.
- Gain recognized on sale of the building is subject to the 20 percent recapture rule. Therefore, $12,400 (20 percent of $62,000 accumulated depreciation) is recaptured as ordinary income. The rest of the gain is Section 1231 gain.

BC's tax returns for the previous five years show $8,400 unrecaptured Section 1231 net losses. Thus, the final step in characterizing the corporation's gains and losses is to recapture this loss.

	Ordinary Income or (Loss)	*Section 1231 Gain or (Loss)*
Current year totals	$18,500	$126,250
Previous loss recapture	8,400	(8,400)
	$26,900	$117,850

In summary, BC's sales of operating assets generated $26,900 ordinary income and $117,850 Section 1231 gain. BC treats the Section 1231 gain as capital gain. As a result, the corporation can deduct $117,850 of its $145,000 capital loss from the security sale. The $27,150 nondeductible capital loss can be deducted only on a carryback or carryforward basis.

OTHER PROPERTY DISPOSITIONS

Objective 8
Describe the tax consequences of property dispositions that don't involve a sale or exchange.

To this point in the chapter, our consideration of the tax consequences of property dispositions has been limited to the consequences of sales and exchanges. While sales and exchanges are the most common ways to dispose of assets, they are not the only ways. In this section, we consider three other property dispositions and their effect on taxable income.

Abandonment and Worthlessness

If a firm formally relinquishes its ownership interest in an asset, any unrecovered basis in the asset represents an **abandonment loss.**[35] An abandonment loss is an ordinary deduction even if the abandoned asset is a capital asset because the loss is not realized on a sale or exchange. To claim a loss, a firm must take overt action to indicate that it has no intention of reviving its interest or reclaiming the asset in the future.[36]

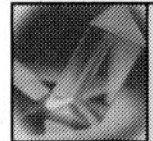

Abandonment Loss

Firm WB occupied leased office space for eight years. During this time, it capitalized the cost of several leasehold improvements to an asset account. This year, WB had a serious dispute with its landlord, broke its lease, and relocated to a new office. Unfortunately, the leasehold improvements were not portable so WB had to leave them behind. WB's adjusted basis in these improvements was $28,200, so it can claim a $28,200 abandonment loss as an ordinary deduction.

Firms typically don't abandon property unless the property no longer has any value and is worthless to the firm. The Internal Revenue Code contains a special rule for *securities* that become worthless during the taxable year.[37] The owner must treat the securities as if they were sold on the last day of the year for a price of zero. This fictitious sale triggers a realized loss equal to the owner's basis in the securities. If the securities were capital assets in the owner's hands, the loss is characterized as a capital loss because it resulted from a deemed sale. For purposes of this rule, securities include corporate stocks and bonds, debentures, or other corporate or government debt instruments that bear interest coupons or are in registered form.

[35] Regs. §1.165-1(b), §.165-2, and §1.167(a)-8.

[36] *Echols* v. Commissioner, 950 F.2d 209 (CA-5, 1991).

[37] §165(g)(1).

An important modification to the worthless securities rule applies if a corporation owns worthless securities in an affiliated corporation.[38] An **affiliated corporation** is any 80 percent or more controlled domestic subsidiary that has always derived more than 90 percent of its annual gross receipts from the conduct of an active business. In this case, the corporation can treat the securities as a noncapital asset. Accordingly, the corporation's loss is not subject to the capital loss limitation but is fully deductible.

Worthless Securities

BGH, a calendar year corporation, owns XYZ bonds with a $290,000 tax basis. BGH also owns 90 percent of the outstanding stock of Subsidiary S, a domestic corporation deriving all its gross receipts from a manufacturing business. BGH's basis in this stock is $500,000. Both the bonds and the stock are capital assets.

This year, BGH's chief financial officer determined that the XYZ bonds and the Subsidiary S stock are worthless. For tax purposes, BGH recognizes a loss as if it sold both securities on December 31 for an amount realized of zero. The $290,000 loss from the deemed bond sale is a capital loss. However, the $500,000 loss from the deemed stock sale qualifies as an ordinary loss because Subsidiary S qualifies as an affiliated corporation.

Foreclosures

If a firm owns property that is collateral for a debt, the firm will lose the property if it fails to service the debt and the creditor forecloses. The tax consequences of a foreclosure depend on whether the debt is recourse or nonrecourse in nature. A **recourse debt** is one for which the debtor is personally liable; the debtor is obligated to repay the debt out of any and all of its assets. A **nonrecourse debt** is secured by only the specific property pledged as collateral; the debtor is not personally liable for repayment of the debt.

Recourse Debt Foreclosure

Company T owned a tract of land for which it paid $400,000 and which was subject to a $275,000 recourse mortgage. Because of financial difficulties, Company T failed to make the required payments on the mortgage. As a result, the creditor foreclosed and took possession of the land. As part of the foreclosure proceedings, Company T and the creditor agreed that the FMV of the land was $240,000.[39] Therefore, Company T was obligated to pay $35,000 cash to the creditor in full satisfaction of the $275,000 recourse mortgage.

For tax purposes, Company T treats the foreclosure as if it sold the land for its $240,000 FMV, thereby realizing a $160,000 loss.[40] The character of the loss depends on Company T's use of the land. If Company T operates a real estate business and held the land as inventory, the loss is ordinary. If it used the land in the operation of its business, the loss is a Section 1231 loss. If it held the land as an investment, the loss is a capital loss.

Now change the facts in the preceding example by assuming that Company T is in such poor financial condition that it could not pay the $35,000 cash to fully satisfy the mortgage. If the creditor decides not to pursue its legal claim to such payment, Company T must recognize $35,000 ordinary cancellation-of-debt income.[41] This subsequent development does not affect the tax consequences of the land foreclosure itself.

[38] §165(g)(3).

[39] FMV is frequently established by the creditor's subsequent sale of the property at public auction.

[40] Reg. §1.1001-2(c), Example 8.

[41] §61(a)(12). If Company T is insolvent, only the cancellation-of-debt income in excess of the insolvency is taxable. If Company T is involved in bankruptcy proceedings, none of the cancellation-of-debt income is taxable. §108(a). For a recent case, see *Frazier,* 111 TC No. 11 (1998).

Non-recourse Debt Foreclosure

Refer to the facts in the preceding example but assume that the $275,000 mortgage on the land was a nonrecourse debt. The creditor's only right when Company T defaulted on the debt was to foreclose on the land. From the creditor's perspective, it received an asset worth only $240,000 in full settlement of a $275,000 debt and, as a result, incurred a $35,000 bad debt loss. Company T treats the foreclosure as a deemed sale for an amount realized of $275,000—the full amount of the nonrecourse debt—and recognizes a $125,000 loss.[42]

Tax Talk

The IRS announced tax relief for small businesses hurt by the 2005 hurricanes. Commissioner Everson stated "The severity of this hurricane season in Florida, compounded by multiple storms hitting the same counties, leads us to provide a longer period of tax relief than usual."

Casualties and Thefts

In this uncertain world, firms may dispose of assets involuntarily because of a sudden, destructive event such as a fire, flood, earthquake, or other act of nature, or through some human agency such as theft, vandalism, or riot. If a firm is adequately insured, the reimbursement from the insurance company should compensate for the economic loss from such casualties. If the insurance reimbursement is less than the adjusted basis of the destroyed property, the firm can claim the unrecovered basis as an ordinary deduction.[43] If the reimbursement exceeds the adjusted basis, the firm must recognize the excess as taxable income unless it takes advantage of a deferral opportunity discussed in the next chapter.

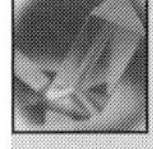

Casualty Loss

Firm JBJ recently suffered a casualty loss when a flood destroyed four automobiles used in its business. The firm carried property insurance and received a $42,000 reimbursement after filing a claim with its insurance company. The adjusted basis of the four automobiles was $53,800. JBJ can deduct its $11,800 unrecovered basis as an ordinary loss in the computation of taxable income.

Conclusion

The rules governing the tax consequences of property transactions are among the most complicated in the tax law. Nevertheless, business managers must understand how these rules operate to determine the taxable gain or deductible loss triggered by sales, exchanges, and other dispositions of assets. The rules relate both to the timing of gain or loss recognition and the character of the gain or loss. The critical distinction between ordinary and capital gain or loss can result in significant differences in tax cost or tax savings. Managers who do not understand this distinction may miss tax planning opportunities that can dramatically improve after-tax cash flows from asset dispositions. In the next chapter, we continue our discussion of property transactions by examining still another type of asset disposition—a nontaxable exchange.

[42] Reg. §1.1001-2(c), Example 7, and *Commissioner* v. *Tufts,* 461 U.S. 300 (1983).

[43] Reg. §1.165-7(b). This general statement disregards the complex casualty gain/loss netting rule of §1231(a)(4)(C).

Sources of Book/Tax Differences

Permanent

- Loss on related party sale

Temporary

- Disposition of asset with different book/tax basis
- Seller-financed sale eligible for installment sale method
- Net capital loss

Key Terms

Questions and Problems for Discussion

1. BBB Company, which manufactures industrial plastics, owns the following assets. Characterize each asset as either a capital, ordinary, or Section 1231 asset.
   a. A computer system used in BBB's main office.
   b. A 50 percent interest in a business partnership organized to conduct a mining operation in Utah.
   c. Heavy equipment used to mold BBB's best-selling plastic item.
   d. BBB's customer list developed over 12 years of business.
   e. BBB's inventory of raw materials used in the manufacturing process.
   f. An oil painting of BBB's founder and first president that hangs in the board room.
   g. A patent developed by BBB's research and development department.
   h. BBB's company airplane.
2. For tax purposes, what is the difference between a sale of property and an exchange of property?
3. Under what circumstances could a taxpayer have an amount realized on the disposition of an asset without any inflow of cash or property?
4. Under what circumstances would a taxpayer elect not to use the installment sale method of reporting gain?
5. Does the characterization of gain or loss as either ordinary or capital have any effect on the computation of net income per books?
6. Distinguish between a firm's tax basis in an asset and its equity in that asset.
7. Corporation A and Corporation Z both have business goodwill worth approximately $1 million. The goodwill is a capital asset to Corporation A and a Section 1231 asset to Corporation Z. Can you explain this apparently inconsistent tax characterization?
8. Company W, a calendar year, cash basis business, paid $2,700 for office supplies in November. The following March, the company moved its office location. Rather than transport the office supplies still on hand, it sold them to a neighboring business for $500 cash. What is the amount and character of the gain or loss recognized on this sale?
9. Two years ago, Firm OP bought a tract of land for $600,000, paying $50,000 down and borrowing the balance of the purchase price from a commercial lender. The land is the collateral for OP's debt. To date, OP has not repaid any of the loan.
   a. If the debt is recourse, to what extent do OP and the commercial lender bear the risk of loss if the FMV of the land decreases to $475,000?
   b. How does your answer change if the debt is nonrecourse?
10. Mr. K realized a loss on the sale of an asset to Mr. P, his best friend for 20 years. Does this sale represent an arm's-length transaction? Are Mr. K and Mr. P related parties for tax purposes?
11. Why do both corporate and noncorporate taxpayers prefer capital gains to ordinary income? Why is the preference stronger for noncorporate taxpayers?

12. Why is the partial recapture rule inapplicable to sales of realty subject to MACRS depreciation?
13. Does a taxpayer always realize a loss on the involuntary disposition of property because of a casualty or a theft?
14. Firm F's adjusted basis in operating asset A is $75,000. If the firm carries $75,000 of property insurance on this asset, is it adequately protected against risk of loss?

Application Problems

1. Firm CS performed consulting services for Company P. The two parties agreed that Company P would pay for the services by transferring investment securities to Firm CS. At date of transfer, the securities had a FMV of $50,000. Company P's tax basis in the securities was $47,000.
   a. How much income must Firm CS recognize on receipt of the securities? What is the character of this income? What is Firm CS's tax basis in the securities?
   b. How much income must Company P recognize on disposition of the securities? What is the character of the income?
   c. Does disposition of the securities result in a deduction for Company P? If so, what is the amount of the deduction?
2. Company L sold an inventory item to Firm M for $50,000. Company L's marginal tax rate is 35 percent. In each of the following cases, compute Company L's after-tax cash flow from the sale.
   a. Firm M's payment consisted of $50,000 cash. Company L's basis in the inventory item was $12,000.
   b. Firm M's payment consisted of $10,000 cash and its note for $40,000. The note is payable two years from the date of sale. Company L's basis in the inventory item was $12,000.
   c. Firm M's payment consisted of $50,000 cash. Company L's basis in the inventory item was $54,000.
   d. Firm M's payment consisted of $10,000 cash and its note for $40,000. The note is payable two years from the date of sale. Company L's basis in the inventory item was $54,000.
3. KNB sold real property to Firm P for $15,000 cash and Firm P's assumption of the $85,000 mortgage on the property.
   a. What is KNB's amount realized on sale?
   b. Compute KNB's after-tax cash flow from the sale if its adjusted basis in the real property is $40,000, and its marginal tax rate is 34 percent.
4. In 2002, LM sold investment land with a $50,000 tax basis for $95,000. Payment consisted of $15,000 cash down and the purchaser's note for $80,000. The note is being paid in 10 annual installments of $8,000, beginning in 2003.
   a. Compute LM's recognized gain under the installment sale method in 2002 and 2003.
   b. In 2005, LM pledges the note as partial collateral for a $75,000 bank loan. The unpaid principal at date of pledge is $56,000. Determine the tax consequences of this transaction to LM.
5. Refer to the facts in the preceding problem but assume that LM's basis in the investment land was $100,000 rather than $50,000.
   a. Compute LM's recognized loss in 2002.
   b. In 2005, LM pledges the note received from the purchaser as partial collateral for a $75,000 bank loan. The unpaid principal at date of pledge is $56,000. Determine the tax consequences of this transaction to LM.

6. Corporation S sold investment land to Corporation P for $100,000 cash. Corporation S's basis in the land was $167,000. Mr. and Mrs. J own 100 percent of the stock of both corporations.

   a. What is Corporation P's tax basis in the land purchased from Corporation S?
   b. Corporation P holds the land as an investment for seven years before selling it to an unrelated buyer. Compute the gain or loss recognized by Corporation P if the amount realized on sale is (1) $175,000, (2) $120,000, or (3) $95,000.

7. Firm J, an accrual basis taxpayer, recorded a $40,000 account receivable on the sale of an asset on credit. Its basis in the asset was $33,000. Two months after the asset sale, Firm J sold the receivable to a local bank for $38,000.

   a. Assuming that the asset was an inventory item, determine the amount and character of Firm J's gain or loss recognized on sale of (1) the asset and (2) the receivable.
   b. Assuming that the asset was a capital asset, determine the amount and character of Firm J's gain or loss recognized on sale of (1) the asset and (2) the receivable.

8. This year, PRS Corporation generated $300,000 income from the performance of consulting services for its clients. It sold two assets during the year, recognizing a $20,000 gain on the first sale and a $31,000 loss on the second sale. Compute PRS's taxable income assuming that:

   a. Both the $20,000 gain and the $31,000 loss were capital.
   b. Both the $20,000 gain and the $31,000 loss were ordinary.
   c. The $20,000 gain was capital, and the $31,000 loss was ordinary.
   d. The $20,000 gain was ordinary, and the $31,000 loss was capital.

9. This year, Zeron Company generated $87,200 income from the performance of services for its clients. It also sold several assets during the year. Compute Zeron's taxable income under each of the following assumptions about the tax consequences of the asset sales.

   a. Zeron recognized $1,000 recaptured ordinary income, a $2,400 net Section 1231 gain, and a $7,000 capital loss.
   b. Zeron recognized a $6,600 net Section 1231 loss and a $1,700 capital loss.
   c. Zeron recognized $3,900 recaptured ordinary income, a $1,510 net Section 1231 gain, and a $1,200 capital gain.
   d. Zeron recognized a $10,300 net Section 1231 loss and a $4,000 capital gain.
   e. Zeron recognized a $2,800 net Section 1231 gain, a $5,200 capital gain, and a $6,300 capital loss.

10. This year, Firm GH generated $430,000 income from its routine business operations. In addition, it sold the following assets, all of which were held for more than 12 months. Compute GH's taxable income.

	Initial Basis	***Acc. Depr.****	***Sale Price***
Office equipment	$ 22,400	$ 18,600	$ 4,500
Construction equipment	175,000	121,700	50,000
Furniture	6,000	1,500	4,750
Transportation equipment	83,200	26,000	55,000

*Through date of sale.

11. This year, Corporation JK generated $980,000 income from its routine business operations. In addition, the corporation sold the following assets, all of which were held for more than 12 months.

	Initial Basis	***Acc. Depr.****	***Sale Price***
Investment securities	$144,000	–0–	$ 64,000
Production equipment	76,000	$76,000	13,000
Business realty:			
Land	85,000	–0–	100,000
Building	200,000	58,300	210,000

*Through date of sale.

a. Compute JK's taxable income assuming that it used the straight-line method to calculate depreciation on the building and has no unrecaptured Section 1231 losses.
b. Recompute taxable income assuming that JK sold the securities for $150,000 rather than $64,000.

12. EzTech, a calendar year accrual basis corporation, generated $1,219,400 ordinary income from its business this year. It also sold the following assets, all of which had been owned for more than 12 months.

	Initial Basis	***Acc. Depr.****	***Sale Price***
Machinery	$118,000	$60,160	$ 90,500
Office equipment	50,000	12,470	57,500
Warehouse	163,500	21,620	125,000
Investment securities	72,700	n/a	83,100
Investment land	200,000	n/a	178,000

*Through date of sale.

EzTech used the straight-line method to calculate depreciation on the warehouse and has no unrecaptured Section 1231 losses.
a. Compute EzTech's taxable income.
b. Recompute taxable income assuming that EzTech used the land in its business instead of holding it for investment.

13. Corporation Q, a calendar year taxpayer, has incurred the following Section 1231 net gains and losses since its formation in 2001.

	2001	***2002***	***2003***
Section 1231 gains	$ 15,000	$ 7,600	–0–
Section 1231 losses	(13,000)	(9,000)	$(5,000)
Net gain or (loss)	$ 2,000	$(1,400)	$(5,000)

a. In 2004, Corporation Q sold only one asset and recognized a $3,900 Section 1231 gain. How much of this gain is treated as capital gain and how much is ordinary?
b. In 2005, Corporation Q recognized a $16,700 Section 1231 gain on the sale of one asset and a $3,000 Section 1231 loss on the sale of a second asset. How much of the $13,700 net gain is treated as capital gain and how much is ordinary?

14. In 1996, TYR Inc. purchased a warehouse for $295,000. This year, the corporation sold the warehouse to Firm D for $80,000 cash and D's assumption of a $225,000 mortgage. Through date of sale, TYR deducted $72,000 straight-line depreciation on the warehouse.
    a. Compute TYR's gain recognized on sale of the warehouse.
    b. What is the character of this gain?
    c. Would your answers change if TYR is a noncorporate business?
15. Firm P, a noncorporate taxpayer, purchased residential realty in 1984 for $1 million. This year it sold the realty for $450,000. Through date of sale, Firm P deducted $814,000 accelerated depreciation on the realty. Straight-line depreciation would have been $625,000.
    a. Determine the amount and character of Firm P's recognized gain on sale.
    b. How would your answer change if Firm P was a corporation?
16. Six years ago, Corporation CN purchased a business and capitalized $200,000 of the purchase price as goodwill. Through this year, CN has deducted $74,000 amortization with respect to this goodwill. At the end of the year, CN sold the business for $2 million, $250,000 of which was allocable to goodwill. Determine the amount and character of CN's gain from its sale of goodwill.
17. Firm L owns a commercial building that is divided into 23 offices. Several years ago, it leased an office to Company K. As part of the lease agreement, Firm L spent $29,000 to construct new interior walls to conform the office to Company K's specifications. It capitalized this expenditure to an asset account and has deducted $6,200 depreciation with respect to the asset. Early this year, Company K broke its lease and vacated the office. Firm L has found a prospective tenant that wants Firm L to demolish the interior walls before it will sign a lease. What are the tax consequences to Firm L if it agrees to the demolition?
18. Firm R owned depreciable real property subject to a $300,000 nonrecourse mortgage. The property's FMV is only $250,000. Consequently, the firm surrendered the property to the creditor rather than continue to service the mortgage. At date of surrender, Firm R's adjusted basis in the property was $195,000. Determine Firm R's cash flow consequences of the disposition, assuming that the gain recognized is taxed at 25 percent.
19. A fire recently destroyed a warehouse owned by Company J. Its adjusted basis in the warehouse was $489,000. However, the warehouse's replacement value (cost to rebuild) was $610,000. Determine the tax consequences of this property disposition assuming that:
    a. The building was insured, and Company J received a $450,000 reimbursement from the insurance company.
    b. The building was uninsured.
20. ZEJ Inc. reported $270,000 net income before tax on this year's financial statements prepared in accordance with GAAP. The corporation's records reveal the following information.
    - Depreciation expense per books was $41,900, and MACRS depreciation was $39,200.
    - ZEJ sold business equipment for $100,000 cash. The original cost of the equipment was $125,000. Book accumulated depreciation through date of sale was $48,000, and MACRS accumulated depreciation through date of sale was $63,000.
    - ZEJ sold investment land to Coroda, a corporation owned by the same person that owns ZEJ. The amount realized on sale was $250,000, and ZEJ's basis in the land was $285,000.

- ZEJ sold marketable securities to its sole shareholder. The amount realized on sale was $60,000, and ZEJ's basis in the securities was $42,000.

Compute ZEJ's taxable income.

21. St. George Inc. reported $711,800 net income before tax on this year's financial statement prepared in accordance with GAAP. The corporation's records reveal the following information.
    - Four years ago, St. George realized a $283,400 gain on sale of investment property and elected the installment sale method to report the sale for tax purposes. Its gross profit percentage is 36.91, and it collected $62,000 principal and $14,680 interest on the installment note this year.
    - Five years ago, St. George purchased investment property for $465,000 cash from an LLC. Because St. George and the LLC were related parties, the LLC's $12,700 realized loss on sale was disallowed for tax purposes. This year, St. George sold the property to an unrelated purchaser for $500,000.
    - A flood destroyed several antique carpets that decorated the floors of corporate headquarters. Unfortunately, St. George's property insurance does not cover damage caused by rising water, so the loss was uninsured. The carpets' adjusted book basis was $32,400, and their adjusted tax basis was $18,090.

    Compute St. George's taxable income.

22. Ms. D sold a business that she had operated as a sole proprietorship for 18 years. On date of sale, the business balance sheet showed the following assets.

	Tax Basis
Accounts receivable	$ 32,000
Inventory	125,000
Furniture and equipment:	
Cost	45,800
Accumulated depreciation	(38,000)
Leasehold improvements:	
Cost	29,000
Accumulated depreciation	(5,100)

    The purchaser paid a lump-sum price of $300,000 cash for the business. The sales contract stipulates that the FMV of the business inventory is $145,000, and the FMV of the remaining balance sheet assets equals adjusted tax basis. Assuming that Ms. D's marginal tax rate on ordinary income is 35 percent and her rate on capital gain is 15 percent, compute the net cash flow from the sale of her business.

23. Five years ago, Firm SJ purchased land for $100,000 with $10,000 of its own funds and $90,000 borrowed from a commercial bank. The bank holds a recourse mortgage on the land. For each of the following independent transactions, compute SJ's positive or negative cash flow. Assume that SJ is solvent, any recognized loss is fully deductible, and SJ's marginal tax rate is 35 percent.
    a. SJ sells the land for $33,000 cash and the buyer's assumption of the $80,000 principal balance of the mortgage.
    b. SJ sells the land for $113,000 cash and pays off the $80,000 principal balance of the mortgage.
    c. SJ sells the land for $82,000 cash and pays off the $80,000 principal balance of the mortgage.

d. SJ defaults on the $80,000 mortgage. The bank forecloses and sells the land at public auction for $64,000. The bank notifies SJ that it will not pursue collection of the $16,000 remaining debt.

e. SJ defaults on the $80,000 mortgage. The bank forecloses and sells the land at public auction for $64,000. The bank requires SJ to pay off the $16,000 remaining debt.

Issue Recognition Problems

Identify the tax issue or issues suggested by the following situations, and state each issue in the form of a question.

1. On March 1, DS Company, a calendar year taxpayer, recognized a $15,000 loss on sale of marketable securities. On May 12, it recognized an $85,000 Section 1231 gain on sale of an office building. In forecasting current taxable income, DS's chief financial officer plans to deduct the $15,000 loss against the $85,000 gain.
2. Firm LD, a calendar year taxpayer, owns 20,000 shares of MXP stock with a $160,000 basis. In November, LD's chief financial officer learned that MXP had just declared bankruptcy. The CFO was unable to determine if MXP's board of directors intend to try to save the corporation or dissolve it under state law.
3. A fire damaged industrial equipment used by Firm L in its manufacturing process. Immediately before the fire, the equipment was worth $40,000. After the fire, the equipment was worth only $15,000. Firm L's adjusted basis in the equipment was $14,000, and it received only $10,000 insurance reimbursement for its loss.
4. Company LR owns a commercial office building. Four years ago, LR entered into a long-term lease with Lessee M for 2,400 square feet of office space. LR spent $13,600 to finish out the space to meet Lessee M's requirements. The leasehold improvements included several interior walls and special purpose electrical wiring. This year, Lessee M terminated the lease and moved out of the office space. To make the space more marketable, LR tore down the interior walls and removed the special purpose wiring.
5. Two years ago, Corporation M loaned $80,000 to its employee Mr. E. The corporation received Mr. E's properly executed note in which he promised to repay the loan at the end of seven years and to pay annual interest of 9 percent (the market interest rate on the date of the loan). This year, when interest rates were 6 percent, Corporation M sold the $80,000 note to an unrelated party for $92,700.
6. In its second taxable year, Corporation NM generated a $25,000 net operating loss and recognized an $8,000 net capital loss. The corporation's tax return for its first year reported $15,000 taxable income, $10,000 of which was capital gain.
7. Firm WD sold depreciable realty for $225,000. The firm purchased the realty 12 years earlier for $350,000 and deducted $155,000 MACRS depreciation through date of sale. During an audit of the tax return on which the sale was reported, the IRS determined that WD had incorrectly computed its depreciation with respect to the realty. The correct depreciation through date of sale should have been $200,000.
8. Corporation AD operates four antique dealerships. Last year, it sold a 200-year-old desk to its sole shareholder, Mr. C, for $35,000. AD reported its $2,700 gain as ordinary income from the sale of inventory. This year, Mr. C sold the desk to an unrelated collector for $60,000 and reported a $25,000 capital gain on his tax return.
9. Mr. V sold his sole proprietorship to an unrelated party for a lump-sum price of $900,000. The contract of sale specifies that $100,000 is for a covenant not to compete—Mr. V's promise not to operate a similar business anywhere in the state for the next four years.

10. Corporation TJ ceased business operations and was dissolved under state law. On the last day of its existence, TJ's balance sheet showed $2,200 unamortized organizational costs and $12,000 unamortized goodwill.
11. At the beginning of the year, Firm GH owned 8,200 shares of common stock in LSR, a publicly held corporation. GH's basis in these shares was $290,000. On a day when LSR stock was trading at $1.14 per share, GH delivered the 8,200 shares to its broker with a letter stating that it was formally abandoning ownership of its LSR equity interest.

Research Problems

1. Four years ago, Delta Fabrics paid $3.5 million to purchase a 45-acre tract of land on which it planned to build a new manufacturing facility. Unfortunately, Delta's construction crew discovered that the soil and ground water were contaminated with hazardous chemical waste, so Delta spent $130,000 to clean up the contamination. Because the tract of land was a "qualified contaminated site" for federal tax purposes, Delta was allowed to deduct the $130,000 expenditure rather than capitalizing it to the cost of the land. This year, Delta decided not to build the new facility and sold the 45 acres to an unrelated purchaser for $3.7 million. What is the character of Delta's $200,000 gain recognized on sale?
2. Six years ago, Graham Inc., an accrual basis corporation, sold investment land (basis $562,250) to Jervil LLC and accepted Jervil's note for the entire $865,000 sale price. The land was the collateral for the note, and Graham used the installment sale method of reporting its taxable gain on sale. This year, Jervil defaulted on the note, and Graham repossessed the land. At the date of repossession, the principal of the note was $644,000. Graham also had $40,800 accrued interest receivable on the note. How much gain must Graham recognize on repossession, and what is its new tax basis in the repossessed land?
3. In 1988, Big Skye Partnership paid $695,500 for a Christmas tree farm in northern Arizona. In 1991, over 300 farms and ranches in the area were granted allocations of water from a newly completed irrigation project funded by the U.S. Department of the Interior. This year, Big Skye Partnership discontinued its tree farming operation and converted the property to a sheep ranch. Because the property no longer needed irrigation, Big Skye sold its federal water rights to a neighboring farm for $175,000. What is the amount and character of Big Skye's gain or loss on disposition of its water rights?
4. The BPL Corporation is considering selling investment land to Kaier Partnership for the land's independently appraised FMV of $1.2 million. BPL purchased the land in 1993 for $1.32 million cash. Mr. Larry Bass is the largest shareholder in BPL; he owns 892 of 2,000 BPL shares outstanding. Larry's sister, Mrs. Ann Olsen, owns 165 BPL shares, and various investors who are unrelated to Larry and Ann own the remaining shares outstanding. Ann is a limited partner in Kaier Partnership; she owns a 35 percent interest in Kaier's profits and capital. Ann's daughter, Suzanne Olsen, owns a 22 percent limited interest in Kaier's profits and capital. Ann and Suzanne are unrelated to any other Kaier partner and are not involved in any aspect of the management of the partnership. If BPL sells its land to Kaier Partnership, can it recognize the $120,000 loss that it will realize on the sale?

Tax Planning Cases

1. Firm Z, a corporation with a 35 percent tax rate, has $100,000 to invest in year 0 and two investment choices. Investment 1 will generate $12,000 taxable cash flow annually for years 1 through 5. In year 5, the firm can sell the investment for $100,000. Investment 2 will not generate any taxable income or cash flow in years 1 through 5, but in year 5, the firm can sell Investment 2 for $165,000.

a. Assuming a 6 percent discount rate, which investment has the greater NPV?
b. Would your answer change if Firm Z is a noncorporate taxpayer with a 35 percent tax rate, and the gain on sale of Investment 2 is eligible for the 15 percent capital gains rate?

2. Mr. RH purchased 30 acres of undeveloped ranch land 10 years ago for $935,000. He is considering subdividing the land into one-third-acre lots and improving the land by adding streets, sidewalks, and utilities. He plans to advertise the 90 lots for sale in a local real estate magazine. Mr. RH projects that the improvements will cost $275,000 and that he can sell the lots for $20,000 each. He is also considering an offer from a local corporation to purchase the 30-acre tract in its undeveloped state for $1.35 million. Assuming that Mr. RH makes no other property dispositions during the year and has a 35 percent tax rate on ordinary income and a 15 percent tax rate on capital gain, which alternative (develop or sell as is) maximizes his cash flow?
3. For its first four years of operation, Corporation Y reported the following taxable income.

	2001	*2002*	*2003*	*2004*
Ordinary income	$12,000	$ 6,000	$150,000	$600,000
Net capital gain	–0–	19,000	4,000	–0–
Taxable income	$12,000	$25,000	$154,000	$600,000

In 2005, Corporation Y has generated $900,000 ordinary income and recognized a $20,000 loss on the sale of a capital asset. It is considering selling a second capital asset before the close of 2005. This sale would generate a $21,000 capital gain that would allow the corporation to deduct its entire capital loss. Alternatively, it could carry its $20,000 net capital loss back to 2002 and 2003 and receive a tax refund. Which course of action do you recommend and why?

Chapter Eight

Nontaxable Exchanges

Learning Objectives

After studying this chapter, you should be able to:

1. Compute the substituted basis of qualifying property received in a nontaxable exchange.
2. Compute gain recognized when boot is received in a nontaxable exchange.
3. Identify the types of property that qualify for like-kind exchange treatment.
4. Describe the effect of the relief and assumption of debt in a like-kind exchange.
5. Compute gain recognized and the basis of replacement property in an involuntary conversion.
6. Explain the tax consequences of the exchange of property for an equity interest in a corporation or a partnership.
7. Describe the tax consequences of a wash sale.

In our analysis of property dispositions thus far, we've been working under the premise that any realized gain or loss is recognized (taken into account for tax purposes) in the year of disposition. In Chapter 8, we will examine a number of transactions that trigger gain or loss realization but do not result in current recognition of some or all of that gain or loss. These transactions are called **nontaxable exchanges,** and each one is authorized by a provision of the Internal Revenue Code. Congress enacted these provisions for particular tax policy reasons, which we will discuss as we look at the details of selected provisions.

TAX NEUTRALITY FOR ASSET EXCHANGES

The nontaxable exchange provisions are extremely useful because they allow taxpayers to convert property from one form to another without a tax cost. In other words, a nontaxable exchange provision makes the tax law *neutral* with respect to certain business and investment decisions.

Neutrality of Nontaxable Exchange

Firm T, which has a 35 percent marginal tax rate, owns an investment asset with a $50,000 basis and a $110,000 fair market value (FMV). The asset generates $6,600 annual income, which represents a 6 percent return on FMV. Firm T is considering selling this asset and reinvesting the proceeds in a new venture that promises a 7 percent return on capital. If the sale of the investment asset is taxable, Firm T will have only $89,000 after-tax proceeds to reinvest.

Amount realized on sale	$110,000
Basis in investment asset	(50,000)
Gain realized and recognized	$ 60,000
	.35
Tax cost	$ 21,000
After-tax cash ($110,000 − $21,000)	$ 89,000

The annual income from an $89,000 investment at a 7 percent rate of return is only $6,230. Therefore, Firm T should not undertake the sale/reinvestment because of the front-end tax cost.

On the other hand, if the conversion of the investment to an equity interest in the new venture can be accomplished with no front-end tax cost, the new investment is superior to the old, and Firm T should undertake the sale/reinvestment.

Unfortunately for taxpayers in the same strategic position as Firm T, tax neutrality for asset exchanges is the exception rather than the rule. An asset exchange is taxable unless it meets the requirements of one of the nontaxable exchange provisions scattered throughout the Internal Revenue Code. These requirements vary substantially across provisions. Some nontaxable exchange provisions are mandatory, while others are elective on the part of the taxpayer. Some apply only to realized gains, while others apply to both realized gains and losses. Certain provisions require a direct exchange of noncash assets, while others allow the taxpayer to be in a temporary cash position. Nevertheless, all the nontaxable exchanges share several characteristics. We begin the chapter by analyzing these common characteristics in the context of a generic exchange. By doing so, we can focus on the structure of nontaxable exchanges before considering the details of any particular exchange.

A GENERIC NONTAXABLE EXCHANGE

Exchanges of Qualifying Property

Every nontaxable exchange transforms one property interest into another. The type of property that can be swapped tax free depends on the unique qualification requirements of the operative statutory provision. But only the disposition and receipt of **qualifying property** can be a nontaxable exchange. Consider the diagram of a nontaxable exchange between Firm A and Firm B in Exhibit 8.1 on page 201. Given that the exchange involves only qualifying property, it is nontaxable to both firms. What else do we know about this exchange? Assuming that Firms A and B are unrelated parties dealing at arm's length, they must have agreed that the properties are of equal value.

To quantify the respective tax consequences of the exchange to each firm, we must know the FMV of the property received and the tax basis in the property surrendered. This

EXHIBIT 8.1

EXHIBIT 8.2

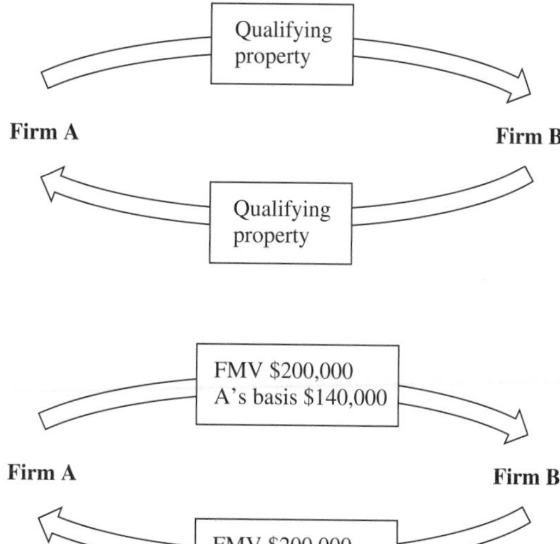

information is presented in Exhibit 8.2 above. Because Firm A disposed of property with a $140,000 basis in return for property worth $200,000, it realized a $60,000 gain. Because the exchange involved qualifying property, Firm A does not recognize any gain in the current year. Similarly, Firm B's disposition of qualifying property with a $185,000 basis in return for qualifying property worth $200,000 resulted in a $15,000 realized but unrecognized gain.

The Substituted Basis Rule

Objective 1
Compute the substituted basis of qualifying property received in a nontaxable exchange.

The nontaxable exchange label is a misnomer. The tax law does not intend that gains and losses realized on nontaxable exchanges should escape recognition permanently. Instead, the exchange provisions are designed so that unrecognized gains and losses are merely deferred until some future year in which the qualifying property is disposed of in a taxable transaction. This deferral is accomplished through the rule for calculating the tax basis of qualifying property acquired in the exchange: The basis of this property equals the basis of the qualifying property surrendered. In the Firm A/Firm B exchange, each firm expended $200,000 (FMV of the property surrendered) to acquire their new properties. Because the exchange was nontaxable, the firms did not take a cost basis. Instead, Firm A's basis in its new property is $140,000, while Firm B's basis in its new property is $185,000.

This **substituted basis** rule causes the unrecognized gain or loss on a nontaxable exchange to be embedded in the basis of the qualifying property acquired. The gain or loss remains dormant as long as the taxpayer holds the property.[1] If and when the taxpayer makes a taxable disposition of the property, the deferral ends, and the unrecognized gain or loss on the nontaxable exchange is finally recognized.

To demonstrate this important concept, return to the facts in the Firm A/Firm B exchange. If Firm A eventually sells its new property for $200,000 cash, it will recognize a $60,000 gain, even though the property has not appreciated in value since Firm A acquired it. Similarly, if Firm B sells its new property for $200,000, it will recognize the $15,000 gain deferred on the exchange. This observation suggests an alternate method for computing the

[1] If the qualifying property is depreciable or amortizable, the embedded gain or loss is recognized over the recovery period for the substituted basis.

basis of qualifying property acquired in a nontaxable exchange: Basis equals the property's FMV *minus* deferred gain or *plus* deferred loss on the exchange. The substituted basis rule for nontaxable exchanges is summarized as follows.

Basis of property surrendered = Basis of qualifying property acquired

Alternate method: FMV of qualifying property acquired
− Deferred gain or
+ Deferred loss
Basis of qualifying property acquired

The Effect of Boot

The facts of our generic exchange between Firm A and Firm B are contrived because the FMVs of the properties are equal. A more realistic scenario is that the FMVs of the properties qualifying for nontaxable exchange treatment are unequal. In this case, the party owning the property of lesser value must transfer additional value in the form of cash or nonqualifying property to make the exchange work.

Objective 2
Compute gain recognized when boot is received in a nontaxable exchange.

In tax parlance, any cash or nonqualifying property included in a nontaxable exchange is called **boot.** The presence of boot does not disqualify the entire exchange. Instead, the party receiving the boot must recognize a portion of realized gain equal to the FMV of the boot. Refer to Exhibit 8.3 in which the FMV of the property surrendered by Firm B was only $192,000. For Firm A to agree to the exchange, Firm B had to pay $8,000 cash so that Firm A received $200,000 total value in exchange for its asset worth $200,000. In this case, Firm A received $8,000 boot and must recognize $8,000 of its $60,000 realized gain.

EXHIBIT 8.3

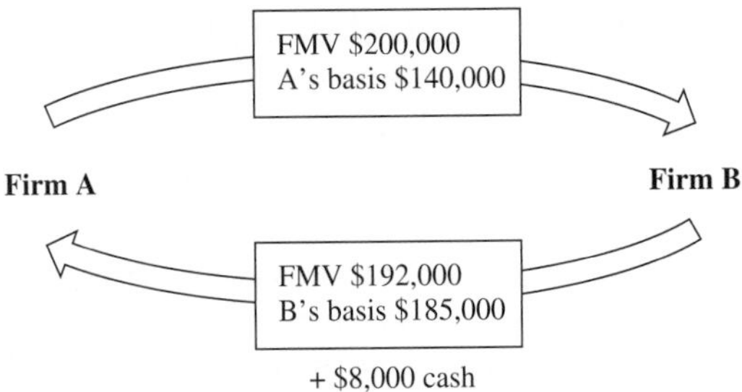

Because Firm A must recognize an $8,000 gain, it can increase its basis in its new assets by this amount. In other words, Firm A's investment in the new assets has increased to $148,000 ($140,000 basis in the surrendered property plus $8,000 gain recognized). Firm A must allocate this $148,000 basis between the two assets acquired: $8,000 cash and the qualifying property. Cash always takes a basis equal to monetary value. Consequently, only $140,000 of basis is allocated to the qualifying property. This $140,000 basis can also be derived by subtracting Firm A's $52,000 deferred gain from the $192,000 FMV of the qualifying property. The modification to the substituted basis rule when boot is *received* in a nontaxable exchange is summarized as follows.

Basis of qualifying property surrendered
+ Gain recognized
− FMV of boot received
Basis of qualifying property acquired

The fact that Firm B *paid* boot in the exchange did not cause it to recognize gain. Firm B surrendered property with an aggregate basis of $193,000 ($8,000 cash + $185,000 basis of surrendered property) to acquire property worth $200,000. As a result, Firm B realized a $7,000 gain, none of which is recognized. Firm B's basis in the new property is $193,000, the aggregate basis of the cash and property surrendered. This $193,000 basis equals the $200,000 FMV of the new property less $7,000 deferred gain. The substituted basis rule when boot is *paid* in a nontaxable exchange is summarized as follows.

Basis of qualifying property surrendered
+ FMV of boot paid
Basis of qualifying property acquired

Two more facts concerning boot should be mentioned. First, the receipt of boot can never trigger recognition of more gain than the recipient realized on the exchange. For example, if Firm A received $70,000 cash and qualifying property worth $130,000, the receipt of $70,000 boot would trigger recognition of the entire $60,000 gain realized. (After all, Firm A would recognize only $60,000 gain if it sold the property for $200,000 cash!) In this case, Firm A's basis in the qualifying property would be $130,000 ($140,000 basis of qualifying property surrendered + $60,000 gain recognized − $70,000 boot received).

Second, the receipt of boot does not trigger loss recognition. Consider the new set of facts in Exhibit 8.4 in which Firm A surrendered qualifying property with a $230,000 basis in exchange for $8,000 cash and qualifying property worth $192,000. As a result, it realized a $30,000 loss, none of which is recognized. Firm A's $230,000 basis in the surrendered property must be allocated between the $8,000 cash received and the new property. Because the cash absorbed $8,000 of the substituted basis, Firm A's basis in the qualifying property is $222,000 ($230,000 basis of qualifying property surrendered − $8,000 boot received). This basis can also be derived by *adding* Firm A's $30,000 deferred loss to the $192,000 FMV of the property.

EXHIBIT 8.4

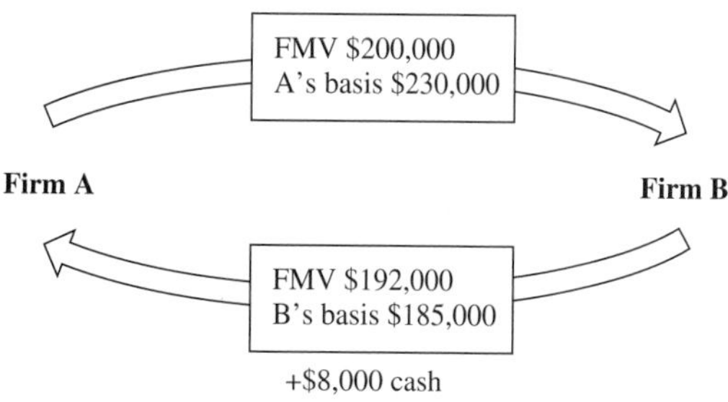

Book/Tax Difference from Nontaxable Exchange

For financial reporting purposes, gains and losses realized on property exchanges are generally included in book income. Therefore, nontaxable exchanges can cause a difference between book income and taxable income. The book basis of the property received in the exchange (the property's FMV) is different than the property's tax basis. Consequently, the book/tax difference caused by the exchange is temporary and will reverse as the newly acquired property is depreciated or when it is disposed of in a taxable transaction.

Book/Tax Difference from Nontaxable Exchange

Hogan Inc. exchanged old property ($138,200 adjusted book and tax basis) for new property ($210,000 FMV). Hogan's $71,800 realized gain was included in book income but was not recognized as taxable income because the old and new properties qualified for nontaxable exchange treatment. Hogan's depreciable book basis in the new property is $210,000, and its depreciable tax basis is only $138,200. Therefore, the $71,800 excess of book income over taxable income resulting from the exchange will reverse as future excesses of book depreciation over MACRS depreciation.

Summary

The Internal Revenue Code contains an assortment of nontaxable exchange provisions with different definitional and operational rules. Nonetheless, these provisions share the following generic characteristics.

- The exchange must involve qualifying property, as defined in the provision.
- The gain or loss realized on the exchange is deferred.
- The basis of the qualifying property received equals the basis of the qualifying property surrendered (substituted basis rule).
- The receipt of boot triggers gain recognition to the extent of the boot's FMV.

The remainder of the chapter focuses on four nontaxable exchanges with particular relevance in the business world: like-kind exchanges, involuntary conversions, formations of business entities, and wash sales. Before proceeding, refer back to the diagram on page 168 that links gain or loss realization and gain or loss recognition. Let's expand the diagram to include the possibility of gain or loss deferral on a nontaxable exchange.

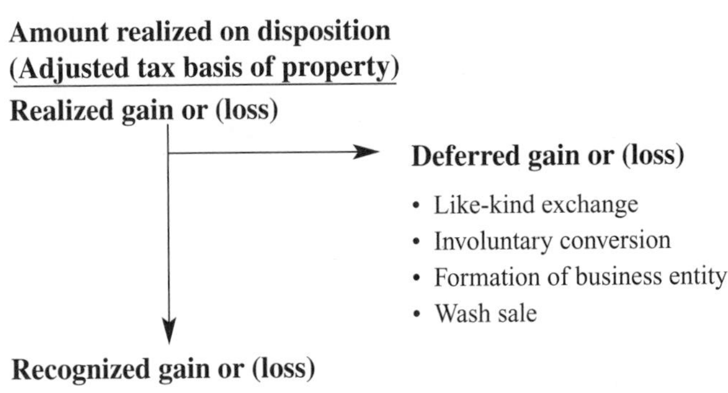

LIKE-KIND EXCHANGES

Objective 3
Identify the types of property that qualify for like-kind exchange treatment.

No gain or loss is recognized on the exchange of business or investment property for property of a like kind.[2] This rule allows firms to convert one asset to another asset with the same function or purpose at no tax cost. The rule's scope, however, is limited: It does not apply to exchanges of inventory property, equity or creditor interests (stocks, bonds, notes, etc.), or partnership interests.

Like-Kind Personalty

The definition of **like-kind property** for tangible personalty is determined under a detailed IRS classification system.[3] Under this system, automobiles and taxis constitute one class of

[2] §1031.

[3] Reg. §1.1031(a)-2(b)(1) and Rev. Proc. 87-56, 1987-2 CB 674.

Tax Talk
The IRS recently announced that the exchange of a business automobile for a minivan or SUV to be used in the taxpayer's business qualifies as an exchange of like-kind properties.

like-kind property, while buses constitute another. Accordingly, the exchange of a business automobile for another automobile is nontaxable, while the exchange of an automobile for a bus is taxable. Airplanes and helicopters are like-kind properties, while airplanes and tugboats are not. The logic of the classification system is not always apparent. Office furniture and copying equipment are like-kind properties, while copying equipment and computers are not. Livestock of the same sex are like-kind properties, while livestock of different sexes are not.[4] If a rancher swaps a bull held for breeding purposes for another bull, the exchange is nontaxable, but if he swaps the bull for a breeding heifer, the exchange is taxable. Clearly, firms that want to dispose of business personalty through a nontaxable exchange should consult their tax advisers to determine exactly which assets qualify as like-kind.[5]

Like-Kind Realty

In contrast to the narrow rules defining like-kind personalty, virtually all types of business and investment real estate are considered like-kind. As a result, any swap of realty for realty can be structured as a nontaxable exchange.[6]

EXHIBIT 8.5

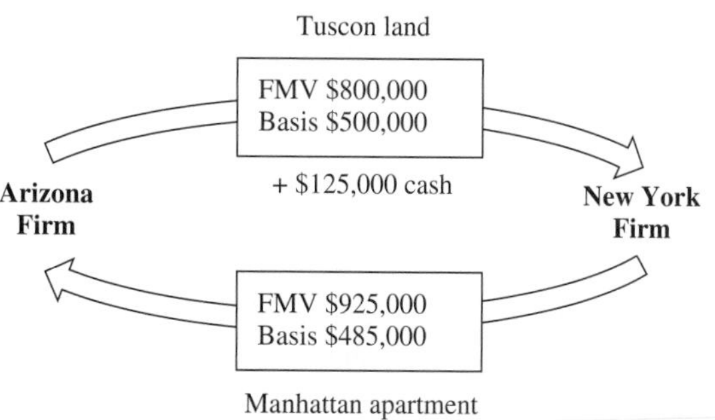

Like-Kind Realty Exhange

An Arizona firm that owned undeveloped investment land in Tucson negotiated with a New York firm that owned an apartment in Manhattan to trade their properties. This exchange is diagrammed in Exhibit 8.5. The investment land has an $800,000 FMV, while the apartment has a $925,000 FMV. As a result, the Arizona firm paid $125,000 cash to the New York firm to equalize the values exchanged. The tax consequences of this exchange are summarzied as follows:

	Arizona Firm	New York Firm
Amount realized:		
FMV of realty acquired	$925,000	$800,000
Boot received	–0–	125,000
	$925,000	$925,000
Basis of property surrendered:		
Realty	(500,000)	(485,000)
Boot paid	(125,000)	–0–
Gain realized	$300,000	$440,000

[4] §1031(e).

[5] There are no published IRS guidelines for intangible assets. Whether intangible assets are like-kind depends on the nature of the legal right represented by the asset. For example, copyrights on two different novels are like-kind, but a copyright on a novel and a copyright on a song are not. Reg. §1.1031(a)-2(c)(3), Examples 1 and 2.

[6] Reg. §1.1031(a)-1(b).

Gain recognized*	–0–	$125,000
Gain deferred	$300,000	315,000
	$300,000	$440,000

*Lesser of FMV of boot received or gain realized.

The final step in the analysis of this like-kind exchange is to determine each party's basis in its newly acquired realty.

	Arizona Firm	New York Firm
Basis of realty surrendered	$500,000	$485,000
Boot paid	125,000	–0–
Gain recognized	–0–	125,000
Boot received	–0–	(125,000)
Basis of realty acquired	$625,000	$485,000

Note that the Arizona firm's basis in its Manhattan property equals the $925,000 FMV less the $300,000 gain deferred in the exchange. The New York firm's basis in its Tucson property equals the $800,000 FMV less the $315,000 gain deferred in the exchange.

The above example suggests a practical question. How did the Arizona firm and the New York firm find each other? Most like-kind exchanges of realty are arranged by *qualified intermediaries:* real estate professionals who specialize in *three-party* exchanges. In a prototype three-party exchange, a taxpayer that wants to sell property without recognizing gain and a prospective buyer use a qualified intermediary to locate replacement property that is suitable to the seller. The seller relinquishes its property to the intermediary who transfers it to the buyer, the buyer transfers cash to the intermediary, and the intermediary uses the cash to purchase the replacement property for the seller. The tax law governing like-kind exchanges is flexible enough so that the seller is treated as exchanging the relinquished property directly for the replacement property.[7]

Three-Party Exchange

Talmadge Partnership wants to dispose of rent property with a $900,000 FMV, and Vernon Inc. is willing to buy the property for cash. However, Talmadge's tax basis in the property is only $100,000, and it does not want to recognize gain on the disposition. Talmadge and Vernon work through a qualified intermediary to facilitate a three-party exchange. Talmadge relinquishes its property to the qualified intermediary who transfers it to Vernon for $900,000 cash. The intermediary then uses the cash to purchase replacement property on Talmadge's behalf. For tax purposes, Talmadge has made a nontaxable exchange of the relinquished property for the replacement property.

Exchanges of Mortgaged Properties

Objective 4
Describe the effect of the relief and assumption of debt in a like-kind exchange.

Many real property interests involved in like-kind exchanges are subject to mortgages that are transferred along with the property and become the legal liability of the new owner. As we learned in Chapter 7, a taxpayer that is relieved of debt on a property disposition must treat the relief as an amount realized from the disposition. In the like-kind exchange context, a party that surrenders mortgaged property receives boot equal to the debt relief. In other words, the relief of debt is treated exactly like cash received in the exchange, while the assumption of debt is treated as cash paid.

[7] Reg. §1.1031(b)-2 and Reg. §1.1031(k)-1(g)(4). The various steps in a three-party exchange must be completed within a 180-day time period.

EXHIBIT 8.6

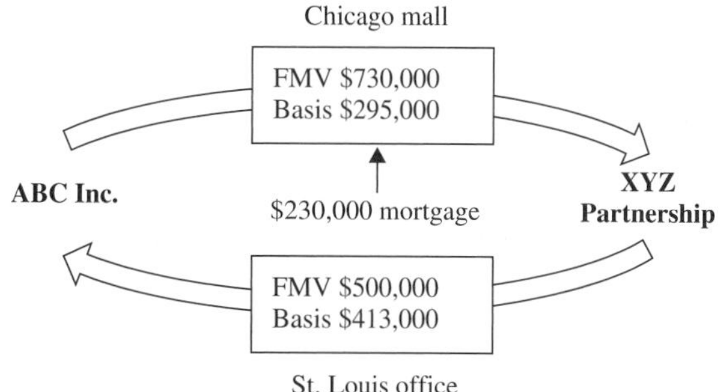

Exchange of Mortgaged Property

ABC Inc. and XYZ Partnership exchanged a Chicago shopping mall and a commercial office building located in St. Louis. This exchange is diagrammed in Exhibit 8.6. The net value of the shopping mall is $500,000 ($730,000 FMV − $230,000 mortgage), and the FMV of the office building is $500,000. The tax consequences of this exchange are summarized as follows:

	ABC Inc.	XYZ Partnership
Amount realized:		
FMV of realty acquired	$500,000	$730,000
Boot received (debt relief)	230,000	–0–
	$730,000	$730,000
Basis of property surrendered:		
Realty	(295,000)	(413,000)
Boot paid (debt assumed)	–0–	(230,000)
Gain realized	$435,000	$ 87,000
Gain recognized*	$230,000	–0–
Gain deferred	205,000	$ 87,000
	$435,000	$ 87,000
Basis of realty surrendered	$295,000	$413,000
Boot paid	–0–	230,000
Gain recognized	230,000	–0–
Boot received	(230,000)	–0–
Basis of realty acquired	$295,000	$643,000

*Lesser of FMV of boot received or gain realized.

In a like-kind exchange in which both properties are subject to a mortgage so that both parties are relieved of debt, only the *net* amount of debt is treated as boot given and boot received.[8]

Net Debt Relief as Boot

Firm O and Firm R entered into a like-kind exchange of realty. The property surrendered by Firm O was subject to a $120,000 mortgage, and the property surrendered by Firm R was subject to a $100,000 mortgage. Firm O was relieved of a $20,000 net amount of debt and therefore received $20,000 boot in the exchange. Firm R assumed a $20,000 net amount of debt and therefore paid $20,000 boot in the exchange. Consequently, Firm O must recognize $20,000 of realized gain, while Firm R has a totally nontaxable exchange.

[8] Reg. §1.1031(b)-1(c).

INVOLUNTARY CONVERSIONS

Objective 5
Compute gain recognized and the basis of replacement property in an involuntary conversion.

Firms generally control the circumstances in which they dispose of property. Occasionally, a disposition is involuntary; property may be stolen or destroyed by a natural disaster such as a flood or a fire. If the property is not insured or if the insurance proceeds are less than the property's adjusted basis, the owner can deduct the unrecovered basis as an ordinary casualty loss. However, if the property is insured and the insurance proceeds are more than the adjusted basis, the disposition actually results in a realized gain. Another example of an **involuntary conversion** is a condemnation of private property by a government agency that takes the property for public use. If a government has the right of eminent domain, it can compel an owner to sell property to the agency for its FMV. If the condemnation proceeds exceed the basis of the condemned property, the owner realizes a gain.

A taxpayer that realizes a gain on the involuntary conversion of property can elect to defer the gain if two conditions are met.[9] First, the taxpayer must reinvest the amount realized on the conversion (the insurance or condemnation proceeds) in **property similar or related in service or use.** This condition requires taxpayers to replace their original property to avoid paying tax on the realized gain.[10] Both the IRS and the courts have been strict in their interpretation of the concept of similar or related property. For instance, the IRS ruled that a taxpayer who owned a bowling alley that was destroyed by fire and who used the insurance proceeds to purchase a billiard parlor was ineligible for nonrecognition treatment because the properties were not similar in function.[11]

The second condition is that replacement of the involuntarily converted property must occur within the two taxable years following the year in which the conversion took place. Thus, taxpayers making the deferral election usually have ample time to locate and acquire replacement property.

If the cost of replacement property equals or exceeds the amount realized on an involuntary conversion, none of the taxpayer's realized gain is recognized. If the taxpayer does not reinvest the entire amount realized in replacement property (i.e., the taxpayer uses some of the insurance or condemnation proceeds for other purposes), the amount not reinvested is treated as boot, and the taxpayer must recognize gain accordingly. In either case, the basis of the replacement property is its cost less unrecognized gain. As a result, unrecognized gain is deferred until the taxpayer disposes of the replacement property in a future taxable transaction.

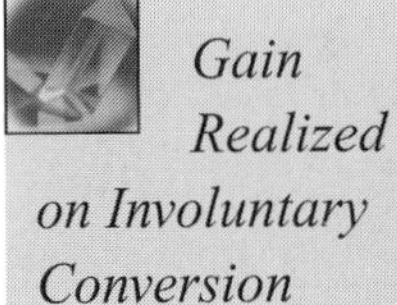

Gain Realized on Involuntary Conversion

Company UL owned equipment that was completely destroyed in the most recent California earthquake. The equipment's adjusted basis was $80,000. The company collected $100,000 of insurance proceeds, thereby realizing a $20,000 gain on the involuntary conversion. Company UL purchased identical equipment in the year after the disaster. The following table shows the tax consequences under four different assumptions about the cost of the replacement property.

Insurance Proceeds	*Cost of Replacement Property*	*Unreinvested Proceeds*	*Gain Recognized*	*Gain Deferred*	*Basis of Replacement Property**
$100,000	$135,000	–0–	–0–	$20,000	$115,000

[9] §1033.

[10] If real property held for business or as an investment is condemned by a government agency, the owner may replace it with like-kind property (any realty held for business or as an investment) rather than realty similar or related in service or use to the property so condemned. §1033(g).

[11] Rev. Rul. 83-93, 1983-1 CB 364.

100,000	100,000	-0-	-0-	20,000	80,000
100,000	92,000	$ 8,000	$ 8,000	12,000	80,000
100,000	77,000	23,000	20,000	-0-	77,000

*Cost less gain deferred.

The involuntary conversion rule provides relief to taxpayers deprived of property through circumstances beyond their control and who want nothing more than to return to the status quo by replacing that property. The rule applies to the involuntary conversion of any type of asset.[12] Moreover, the rule is elective; taxpayers that would benefit by recognizing the entire gain realized on an involuntary conversion may do so.

FORMATIONS OF BUSINESS ENTITIES

Objective 6
Explain the tax consequences of the exchange of property for an equity interest in a corporation or a partnership.

In the early days of the federal income tax, Congress decided that the tax law should be neutral with respect to the formation of business entities. If entrepreneurs wanted to organize a new business as a corporation or partnership for legal or financial reasons, they should not be discouraged from doing so because of a front-end tax cost. Congress achieved this neutrality with a pair of nontaxable exchange provisions that the business community has relied on for decades. These provisions allow organizers to transfer assets to a corporation or a partnership in exchange for an equity interest without the recognition of gain. In this section of the chapter, we will examine the basic operation of these two extremely useful nontaxable exchanges.

Corporate Formations

No gain or loss is recognized when property is transferred to a corporation solely in exchange for that corporation's stock if the transferors of property are in control of the corporation immediately after the exchange.[13] In this context, the term *property* is defined broadly to include cash, tangible, and intangible assets. Personal services are not property; individuals who perform services in exchange for corporate stock must recognize the FMV of the stock as compensation income. To satisfy the control requirement for this nontaxable exchange, the transferors of property *in the aggregate* must own at least 80 percent of the corporation's outstanding stock immediately after the exchange.[14]

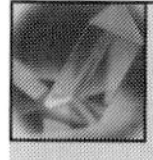

Corporate Formation

Mr. Jiang and Ms. Kirt each owned a business. The two individuals combined forces by transferring their respective operating assets to newly incorporated J&K Inc. Based on recent appraisals, Mr. Jiang's assets have a $375,000 FMV, and Ms. Kirt's assets have a $250,000 FMV. Therefore, the corporation's beginning balance sheet reflected operating assets with a $625,000 total FMV. The articles of incorporation authorize J&K to issue 100 shares of voting common stock. These shares were issued in proportion to the FMV of the contributed assets: 60 shares to Mr. Jiang and 40 shares to Ms. Kirt. This corporate formation is diagrammed in Exhibit 8.7 on page 210.

[12] The involuntary conversion rules apply to business and investment assets, as well as assets owned by individuals and used for personal enjoyment and consumption.

[13] §351.

[14] More precisely, the transferors must own stock possessing at least 80 percent of the voting power represented by all outstanding voting shares and at least 80 percent of the total number of shares of all nonvoting classes of stock. §368(c) and Rev. Rul. 59-259, 1959-2 CB 115.

EXHIBIT 8.7

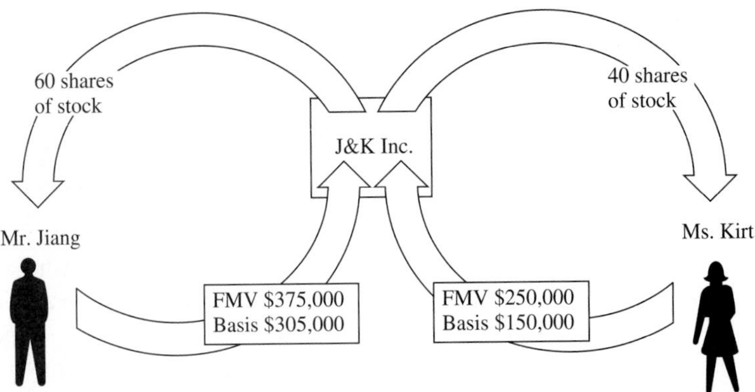

Tax Consequences of Formation

Mr. Jiang's adjusted basis in the assets transferred to J&K was $305,000. Ms. Kirt's adjusted basis in the assets transferred to J&K was $150,000. Consequently, the two transferors realized the following gains on the exchange of property for stock.

	Mr. Jiang	*Ms. Kirt*
Amount realized (FMV of stock)	$ 375,000	$ 250,000
Basis of property transferred	(305,000)	(150,000)
Gain realized	$ 70,000	$ 100,000

Because Mr. Jiang and Ms. Kirt *in the aggregate* own 100 percent of J&K's stock immediately after the exchange, neither recognizes any gain. Each takes a substituted basis in the shares of stock ($305,000 stock basis for Mr. Jiang and $150,000 stock basis for Ms. Kirt).[15] Thus, their unrecognized gains on the corporate formation are deferred until they dispose of the stock in a taxable transaction.

The nontaxable exchange provision governing corporate formations also applies to transfers of property to an existing corporation. However, if the transferor fails to satisfy the 80 percent control requirement, the exchange of property for stock is taxable.

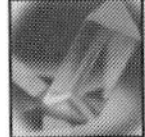

Taxable Exchange of Property for Stock

Two years after J&K is formed, a third individual, Mr. Larkin, contributes real property with a $285,000 FMV and a $240,000 adjusted basis in exchange for 50 shares of newly issued stock. Immediately after the exchange, Mr. Larkin (the only transferor in the transaction) owns only 33 percent of J&K's stock. Because he does not satisfy the control requirement, Mr. Larkin must recognize the $45,000 gain realized on the exchange. Because the exchange is taxable, Mr. Larkin takes a $285,000 cost basis in his J&K shares.

Tax Consequences to the Corporation

Corporations that issue stock in exchange for property never recognize gain or loss on the exchange, regardless of whether the exchange is nontaxable or taxable to the transferor of the property.[16] However, a corporation's tax basis in the property received does depend on

[15] §358(a)(1).

[16] §1032.

whether the exchange is nontaxable or taxable to the transferor. If the exchange is nontaxable (because the transferor satisfies the 80 percent control requirement), the corporation's basis in the property received equals the transferor's basis.[17] In other words, the corporation takes a **carryover basis** in the property.

Carryover Basis of Property

Refer back to the example diagrammed on page 210 in which Mr. Jiang and Ms. Kirt transferred operating assets to J&K Inc. in exchange for stock. This exchange was nontaxable to the two transferors because they satisfied the control requirement immediately after the exchange. The exchange also was a nontaxable event to J&K. The corporation's carryover tax basis in the assets received from Mr. Jiang is $305,000, and its carryover tax basis in the assets received from Ms. Kirt is $150,000.

For financial reporting purposes, J&K Inc. recorded the assets received in the exchange at FMV. Consequently, the corporation has a $375,000 book basis in the assets received from Mr. Jiang, and a $250,000 book basis in the assets received from Ms. Kirt. The difference in J&K's book and tax basis will be eliminated over time as the corporation depreciates or amortizes the assets or when it disposes of the assets.

If a corporation issues stock in exchange for property and the exchange is taxable to the transferor (because the transferor does not satisfy the 80 percent control requirement), the corporation takes a cost basis in the property.[18]

Cost Basis of Property

Refer back to the example on page 210 in which Mr. Larkin transfers real property to J&K Inc. in exchange for stock. The exchange is taxable to Mr. Larkin because he does not satisfy the control requirement immediately after the exchange. However, J&K does not recognize any gain on the issuance of its stock in exchange for Mr. Larkin's real property. The corporation's tax basis in the real property is its $285,000 cost (FMV of the shares issued to Mr. Larkin), which equals the book basis of the property for financial reporting purposes.

Partnership Formations

The tax law treats partnership formations in the same way that it treats corporate formations. Specifically, neither the partners nor the partnership recognizes gain or loss when property is exchanged for an equity interest in the partnership.[19] If Mr. Jiang and Ms. Kirt in our earlier example had decided to become partners, they could have transferred their appreciated assets to J&K Partnership in exchange for a 60 percent and 40 percent interest without recognizing gain. Mr. Jiang's basis in his partnership interest would be a $305,000 substituted basis, and Ms. Kirt's basis in her partnership interest would be a $150,000 substituted basis.[20] The partnership would take a carryover basis in their contributed assets of $305,000 and $150,000, respectively.[21]

While this nontaxable exchange provision is clearly a first cousin to the corporate provision, it lacks any control requirement and is more flexible. For example, if our third individual, Mr. Larkin, wants to become a partner in some future year, he can do so without recognizing gain. If he contributes appreciated real property ($285,000 FMV and $240,000 adjusted basis) for a one-third equity interest in J&K Partnership, the transaction qualifies

[17] §362(a).

[18] Reg. §1.1032-1(d).

[19] §721.

[20] §722.

[21] §723.

as a nontaxable exchange, and his $45,000 realized gain escapes current taxation. Of course, Mr. Larkin's substituted basis in his new interest and the partnership's carryover basis in its new property would be only $240,000.

WASH SALES

Objective 7
Describe the tax consequence of a wash sale.

The **wash sale** rule is a nontypical nontaxable exchange provision because it defers only the recognition of *losses* realized on certain sales of marketable securities.[22] A wash sale occurs when an investor sells securities at a loss and reacquires substantially the same securities within 30 days before or 30 days after the sale. This rule prohibits investors from selling securities to generate a tax loss, while simultaneously buying the stock back to keep their investment portfolio intact. If the wash sale rule applies, the cost of the reacquired securities is increased by the unrecognized loss realized on the sale.

Wash Sale

BNJ Company owns 10,000 shares of Acme stock with an $85,000 basis. The stock is trading at $6 per share so that the BNJ's holding is worth only $60,000. BNJ believes that the stock is an excellent long-term investment and that the depression in the market price is temporary. Nonetheless, it sells the stock on July 13 to trigger a $25,000 tax loss. If BNJ purchases 10,000 shares of Acme stock during the period beginning on June 13 and ending on August 12, it cannot recognize the $25,000 loss. If BNJ paid $61,000 for the replacement shares, its basis in these shares is $86,000 ($61,000 cost + $25,000 unrecognized loss).

Taxpayers who sell stock at a loss can easily avoid the wash sale rule by waiting for more than 30 days to reestablish their investment position. The risk, of course, is that in the time between sale and repurchase, the market value of the securities rebounds and the taxpayer must pay a higher price for the same securities. This additional cost could easily exceed the tax benefit of the recognized loss.

Conclusion

Business managers may defer the recognition of gain realized on the conversion of property from one form to another by structuring the conversion as a nontaxable exchange. The deferral reduces the tax cost of the conversion and increases the value of the transaction. While the advantages offered by the various nontaxable exchange provisions are considerable, these transactions require careful planning and a respect for the technical nuances differentiating one from the other.

Chapter 8 is the final chapter in Part Three in which we focused on the measurement of taxable income from business operations. You've learned how firms account for their routine activities and how that accounting can differ under generally accepted accounting principles (GAAP) and the tax law. You've been introduced to the tax consequences of asset acquisitions and dispositions and determined how property transactions affect taxable income. In Part Four of the text, we turn to the next issue: how the tax on that income is calculated and paid to the federal government.

[22] §1091.

Sources of Book/Tax Differences

Permanent	Temporary
None	• Like-kind exchange • Involuntary conversion • Nontaxable exchange of property for equity • Wash sale of securities

Key Terms

Questions and Problems for Discussion

1. Four years ago, Company PJ acquired 1,000 acres of undeveloped land. On the date of the exchange, the land's FMV was $700,000. During the past four years, the land appreciated in value by $600,000; a recent appraisal indicated that it is worth $1.3 million today. However, if Company PJ sells the land for $1.3 million, the taxable gain will be $825,000. Can you explain this result?
2. In a nontaxable exchange between unrelated parties, are the amounts realized by the parties always equal?
3. In a nontaxable exchange, do the tax consequences to one party in any way depend on the tax consequences to the other party?
4. Is the substituted basis of the qualifying property received in a nontaxable exchange more or less than the cost of that property?
5. Determine if each of the following transactions qualifies as a nontaxable exchange.
   a. Firm A exchanges a 2 percent interest in MG Partnership for a 10 percent interest in KLS Partnership.
   b. Mr. B exchanges investment land for common stock in RV Inc. Immediately after the exchange, Mr. B owns 42 percent of RV's outstanding stock.
   c. Corporation C exchanges business equipment for a 25 percent interest in a residential apartment complex.
   d. Company D exchanges 15,000 units of inventory for a new computer system.
6. Firm Q, a real estate broker, exchanged 16 acres of land for a commercial warehouse owned by Company M. Company M, a light industrial business, plans to hold the land as a long-term investment. Is this exchange nontaxable to Firm Q and Company M?
7. Company W exchanged the following assets for Blackacre, investment land worth $2 million.

	Company W's Basis	*FMV*
Real property used in Company W's business	$800,000	$1,750,000
Marketable securities	30,000	250,000

   Does Company W recognize any gain on this exchange?
8. Under what conditions can the destruction of property by casualty or theft result in an economic loss but a realized gain?
9. In what way is the nontaxable exchange rule for partnership formations more flexible than the nontaxable exchange rule for corporate formations?
10. Explain the difference between a substituted basis in an asset and a carryover basis in an asset.
11. If a corporation engages in a nontaxable exchange of assets, could the transaction result in a book/tax difference? Is this difference a permanent or a temporary difference?
12. When a taxpayer transfers appreciated property to a corporation in exchange for newly issued stock and the exchange is nontaxable, the gain deferred on the exchange actually doubles. Can you explain this?

13. Why doesn't Congress extend the wash sale rule to apply to realized gains?
14. This year, Firm B recognized a $100,000 capital gain on the sale of investment land. Toward the end of the year, the firm plans to sell stock from its investment portfolio to generate a $100,000 capital loss. It has two blocks of stock that are candidates for sale (basis exceeds FMV by $100,000). However, Firm B plans to reacquire whichever block it sells on the 31st day after the sale. How should it decide which block of stock to sell and reacquire?
15. Why is the label "nontaxable exchange" a misnomer?

Application Problems

1. Firm A exchanged an old asset with a $20,000 tax basis for a new asset with a $32,000 FMV. Under each of the following assumptions, apply the generic rules to compute A's realized gain, recognized gain, and tax basis in the new asset.
   a. Old asset and new asset are not qualified property for nontaxable exchange purposes.
   b. Old asset and new asset are qualified property for nontaxable exchange purposes.
   c. Old asset and new asset are not qualified property for nontaxable exchange purposes. To equalize the values exchanged, Firm A paid $1,700 cash to the other party.
   d. Old asset and new asset are qualified property for nontaxable exchange purposes. To equalize the values exchanged, Firm A paid $1,700 cash to the other party.
   e. Old asset and new asset are not qualified property for nontaxable exchange purposes. To equalize the values exchanged, Firm A received $4,500 cash from the other party.
   f. Old asset and new asset are qualified property for nontaxable exchange purposes. To equalize the values exchanged, Firm A received $4,500 cash from the other party.
2. Firm Q exchanged old property with an $80,000 tax basis for new property with a $65,000 FMV. Under each of the following assumptions, apply the generic rules to compute Q's realized loss, recognized loss, and tax basis in the new property.
   a. Old property and new property are not qualified property for nontaxable exchange purposes.
   b. Old property and new property are qualified property for nontaxable exchange purposes.
   c. Old property and new property are not qualified property for nontaxable exchange purposes. To equalize the values exchanged, Firm Q paid $2,000 cash to the other party.
   d. Old property and new property are qualified property for nontaxable exchange purposes. To equalize the values exchanged, Firm Q paid $2,000 cash to the other party.
   e. Old property and new property are not qualified property for nontaxable exchange purposes. To equalize the values exchanged, Firm Q received $8,000 cash from the other party.
   f. Old property and new property are qualified property for nontaxable exchange purposes. To equalize the values exchanged, Firm Q received $8,000 cash from the other party.
3. Company T exchanged an old asset with a $30,000 tax basis and a $40,000 FMV for a new asset worth $37,500 and $2,500 cash.
   a. If the exchange is nontaxable, compute Company T's realized and recognized gain and tax basis in the new asset.
   b. How would your answers change if the new asset were worth only $26,000, and Company T received $14,000 cash in the exchange?

4. CC Company exchanged a depreciable asset with a $17,000 initial cost and a $10,000 adjusted basis for a new asset priced at $16,000.
   a. Assuming that the assets do not qualify as like-kind property, compute the amount and character of CC's recognized gain and its basis in the new asset.
   b. Assuming that the assets qualify as like-kind property, compute the amount and character of CC's recognized gain and its basis in the new asset.
5. XYZ exchanged old equipment for new like-kind equipment. XYZ's adjusted basis in the old equipment was $13,000 ($30,000 initial cost – $17,000 accumulated depreciation), and its FMV was $20,000. Because the new equipment was worth $28,500, XYZ paid $8,500 cash in addition to the old equipment.
   a. Compute XYZ's realized gain and determine the amount and character of any recognized gain.
   b. Compute XYZ's basis in its new equipment.
6. RTY exchanged old furniture for new like-kind furniture. RTY's adjusted basis in the old furniture was $41,000 ($60,000 initial cost – $19,000 accumulated depreciation), and its FMV was $55,000. Because the new furniture was worth only $52,500, RTY received $2,500 cash in addition to the new furniture.
   a. Compute RTY's realized gain and determine the amount and character of any recognized gain.
   b. Compute RTY's basis in its new furniture.
7. Firm ML, a noncorporate taxpayer, exchanged residential rental property plus $15,000 cash for 20 acres of investment land with a $200,000 FMV. ML used the straight-line method to compute depreciation on the rental property.
   a. Assuming that ML's exchange was negotiated at arm's length, what is the FMV of the rental property?
   b. If the adjusted basis of the rental property is $158,000, compute ML's realized and recognized gain. What is the character of the recognized gain?
   c. Compute ML's basis in the 20 acres of investment land.
8. Refer to the facts in the preceding problem, but assume that ML exchanged the residential rental property for the 20 acres of investment land plus $22,000 (i.e., ML *received* cash in the exchange).
   a. Assuming that ML's exchange was negotiated at arm's length, what is the FMV of the rental property?
   b. If the adjusted basis of the rental property is $158,000, compute ML's realized and recognized gain. What is the character of the recognized gain?
   c. Compute ML's basis in the 20 acres of investment land.
9. Firm PO and Corporation QR exchanged the following business real estate.

	Marvin Gardens (exchanged by PO)	***Boardwalk (exchanged by QR)***
FMV	$800,000	$250,000
Mortgage	(550,000)	–0–
Equity	$250,000	$250,000

   a. If PO's adjusted basis in Marvin Gardens was $310,000, compute PO's realized gain, recognized gain, and basis in Boardwalk.
   b. If QR's adjusted basis in Boardwalk was $60,000, compute QR's realized gain, recognized gain, and basis in Marvin Gardens.

10. Company B and Firm W exchanged the following business real estate.

	Blackacre (exchanged by B)	Whiteacre (exchanged by W)
FMV	$400,000	$525,000
Mortgage	(100,000)	(225,000)
Equity	$300,000	$300,000

a. If B's adjusted basis in Blackacre was $240,000, compute B's realized gain, recognized gain, and basis in Whiteacre.
b. If W's adjusted basis in Whiteacre was $100,000, compute W's realized gain, recognized gain, and basis in Blackacre.

11. On June 2, 2004, a tornado destroyed the building in which FF operated a fast-food franchise. FF's adjusted basis in the building was $214,700. In each of the following cases, determine FF's recognized gain or loss on this property disposition and FF's basis in the replacement building. Assume that FF would elect to defer gain recognition to the extent possible.
a. On September 8, 2004, FF received a $250,000 reimbursement from its insurance company. On August 10, 2005, it completed construction of a replacement building for a total cost of $300,000.
b. On September 8, 2004, FF received a $200,000 reimbursement from its insurance company. On August 10, 2005, it completed construction of a replacement building for a total cost of $300,000.

12. On January 10, 2003, a fire destroyed a warehouse owned by NP Company and used to store inventory. NP's adjusted basis in the warehouse was $530,000. On March 12, 2003, NP received a $650,000 reimbursement from its insurance company. In each of the following cases, determine NP's recognized gain on this property disposition. Assume that NP would elect to defer gain recognition to the extent possible.
a. NP's board of directors decided not to replace the warehouse.
b. On July 8, 2005, NP paid $700,000 to acquire a warehouse to store its inventory.
c. On February 8, 2006, NP paid $700,000 to acquire a warehouse to store its inventory.

13. RP owned residential real estate with a $680,000 adjusted basis that was condemned by City Q because it needed the land for a new convention center. RP received $975,000 condemnation proceeds for the real estate. Assume that RP would elect to defer gain recognition to the extent possible.
a. What are the tax consequences if RP spent $200,000 of the proceeds to expand its inventory and the remaining $775,000 to purchase new residential real estate? What is RP's basis in the inventory and the new real estate?
b. How would your answer change if RP's basis in the condemned real estate was $850,000 rather than $680,000?
c. How would your answer change if RP invested the entire condemnation proceeds plus an additional $100,000 cash in new residential real estate?

14. PV Inc. transferred the operating assets of one of its business divisions into newly incorporated SV Inc. in exchange for 100 percent of SV's stock. PV's adjusted basis in the operating assets was $4 million, and their FMV was $10 million.

a. Discuss the business reasons why a parent corporation like PV operates a business through a subsidiary like SV.
b. Compute PV's realized gain, recognized gain, and basis in its SV stock.

15. Mr. ZJ owns a sole proprietorship. The business assets have a $246,000 aggregate adjusted basis. According to an independent appraisal, the business is worth $400,000. Mr. ZJ transfers his business to ZJL Corporation in exchange for 1,000 shares of ZJL stock. In each of the following cases, compute Mr. ZJ's recognized gain on the exchange of business assets for stock.
    a. Immediately after the exchange, ZJL has 20,000 shares of outstanding stock of which Mr. ZJ owns 1,000 shares.
    b. Immediately after the exchange, ZJL has 1,500 shares of outstanding stock of which Mr. ZJ owns 1,000 shares.
    c. Immediately after the exchange, ZJL has 1,200 shares of outstanding stock of which Mr. ZJ owns 1,000 shares.
16. Refer to the facts in the preceding problem. Assume that Mrs. L, who is Mr. ZJ's business colleague, transfers $200,000 cash to ZJL Corporation in exchange for 500 shares of ZJL stock. Mr. ZJ and Mrs. L's transfers occur on the same day, and after the exchange ZJL has 1,500 shares of outstanding stock (1,000 owned by Mr. ZJ and 500 owned by Mrs. L).
    a. Compute Mr. ZJ's recognized gain on the exchange of assets for stock.
    b. Compute Mr. ZJ and Mrs. L's tax basis in their ZJL stock.
    c. Compute ZJL's tax basis in the assets transferred from Mr. ZJ.
17. KAI, a calendar year corporation, reported $500,000 net income before tax on its financial statements prepared in accordance with GAAP. The corporation's records reveal the following information.
    - KAI received an $80,000 insurance reimbursement for the theft of equipment with a $62,000 book basis and a $58,000 adjusted tax basis. KAI used $75,000 to replace the equipment and the remaining $5,000 to pay Christmas bonuses.
    - KAI exchanged investment real estate with a $250,000 book and tax basis for commercial real estate with a $600,000 FMV.

    Compute KAI's taxable income. In making your computation, assume that the corporation defers the recognition of gain whenever possible.
18. Corporation A and Corporation Z go into partnership to develop, produce, and market a new product. The two corporations contribute the following properties in exchange for equal interests in AZ Partnership.

	Corporation A	***Corporation Z***
Cash	$100,000	$50,000
Business equipment (FMV)	30,000	80,000

Corporation A's adjusted basis in the contributed equipment is $34,000, and Corporation Z's adjusted basis in the contributed equipment is $12,000.

a. Compute each corporation's realized and recognized gain or loss on the formation of AZ Partnership.
b. Compute each corporation's basis in its half interest in AZ Partnership.

c. Compute the partnership's basis in the equipment contributed by each corporate partner.

19. In 1998, SW purchased 1,000 shares of Delta stock. On May 20, 2004, it sold these shares for $90 per share. In each of the following cases, compute SW's recognized gain or loss on this sale.
    a. SW's cost basis in the 1,000 shares was $104 per share. It did not purchase any other Delta shares during 2004.
    b. SW's cost basis in the 1,000 shares was $104 per share. It purchased 1,200 shares of Delta on May 1, 2004, for $92 per share and held these 1,200 shares throughout the remainder of the year.
    c. SW's cost basis in the 1,000 shares was $104 per share. It purchased 1,200 shares of Delta on June 8, 2004, for $92 per share and held these 1,200 shares throughout the remainder of the year.
    d. SW's cost basis in the 1,000 shares was $79 per share. It purchased 1,200 shares of Delta on June 8, 2004, for $92 per share and held these 1,200 shares throughout the remainder of the year.
20. Refer to the facts in the preceding problem. In each case in which SW purchased 1,200 Delta shares in 2004, compute its tax basis in the shares.

Issue Recognition Problems

Identify the tax issue or issues suggested by the following situations, and state each issue in the form of a question.

1. ST Inc. and Firm WX are negotiating an exchange of the following business properties.

	Office Building (owned by ST)	*Warehouse (owned by WX)*
FMV	$2,000,000	$1,700,000
Mortgage	(450,000)	–0–

   ST agrees to pay $150,000 cash to WX to equalize the value of the exchange. ST's adjusted basis in the office building is $700,000, and WX's adjusted basis in the warehouse is $500,000.

2. Company JK disposed of the following items of business equipment in a like-kind exchange.

	Initial Cost	*Acc. Depr.*	*FMV*
Item 1	$75,000	$38,000	$45,000
Item 2	30,000	16,000	10,000

   In exchange for the two items, JK received like-kind equipment worth $50,000 and $5,000 cash.

3. NBV, a California corporation, exchanged commercial real estate located in San Francisco for commercial real estate located in Tokyo, Japan. NBV's gain realized was $16.3 million.

4. FM Inc. operates a dairy farm. The local government required the corporation to destroy 150 head of cattle because the herd had been exposed to mad cow disease. None of the cattle displayed any symptoms of the disease before they were destroyed. The local government paid $150,000 to FM as compensation for the loss. FM's adjusted basis in the herd was $105,000.
5. Company T operated a drive-in movie theater from 1980 through 2003. The company ceased operations because so few people were attending the outdoor facility. This year, the entire facility (movie screen, projection building, snack bar, 15 picnic tables, and playground equipment) was destroyed by a tornado. Company T received a $360,000 insurance reimbursement. The aggregate adjusted basis in the destroyed properties was $200,000. Four months after the twister, Company T purchased a new four-screen movie theater complex located in an urban shopping mall.
6. In 2002, an office building owned by Firm F was completely destroyed by fire. F's adjusted basis in the building was $485,000, and its insurance reimbursement was $550,000. On its 2002 tax return, F elected to defer the $65,000 gain realized on the involuntary conversion. In 2003, F invested $560,000 in another office building. In 2005, F settled a dispute with its insurance company concerning the 2002 claim. Pursuant to the settlement, it received an additional reimbursement of $25,000.
7. In 2002, an industrial plant owned by Company C, a calendar year taxpayer, was destroyed in a flood. C's adjusted basis in the plant was $1.65 million, and the company received a $2 million insurance reimbursement. On its 2002 tax return, C elected to defer the gain realized on the involuntary conversion. C promptly began construction of a new plant on the site of the old. However, because of unexpected delays, construction was not completed until January 2005, and C did not place the new industrial plant into service until March 2005. The total construction price was $3 million.
8. In 2003, transportation equipment owned by Corporation ABC was stolen. The adjusted basis in the equipment was $105,000, and ABC received a $400,000 insurance reimbursement. It immediately paid $440,000 for replacement transportation equipment. On its 2003 tax return, ABC elected to defer the $295,000 gain realized on the involuntary conversion. In 2004, ABC generated a $7 million net operating loss—the first in its history. ABC's aggregate taxable income on its 2002 and 2003 returns was $3.2 million.
9. Mr. P, a professional architect, entered into an agreement with Partnership M under which he designed three buildings for the partnership and transferred a copyright for design software to the partnership. Mr. P had no tax basis in this software. In exchange for the services and computer software, Mr. P received a 35 percent interest in Partnership M.
10. On May 19, WJ realized a $48,000 loss on the sale of 10,000 shares of voting common stock in XZY Corporation. On May 30, WJ purchased 3,200 shares of XZY nonvoting preferred stock.

Research Problems

1. Kiley Communication Inc. owns and operates radio and television stations that broadcast throughout the northwestern United States. This year, Kiley entered into an agreement with another broadcasting company under which Kiley surrendered one AM and two FM radio station licenses in Oregon for one television station license in California. Kiley realized a $3.9 million gain on the exchange. Must it recognize this gain for tax purposes?
2. Mr. Bryan Olgivie owned an indoor roller-skating rink as a sole proprietorship. On April 9, a flood completely destroyed the rink. Mr. Olgivie's adjusted basis in the rink

was $833,400. On May 15, he received a check for $1.1 million from his insurance company in complete settlement of his damage claim. Mr. Olgivie is planning to use the entire insurance settlement to purchase 100 percent of the outstanding stock of IceMagic Inc., a corporation that owns an indoor ice-skating rink. Can he defer the recognition of gain on the involuntary conversion of his roller-skating rink by purchasing the IceMagic stock?

3. On February 2, Mr. Eugene Pomeroy transferred all the assets of his sole proprietorship (Pomeroy's Ski Shop) to a newly created corporation, Pomeroy Ski Inc. In exchange for the business assets, Mr. Pomeroy received all 1,000 shares of the corporation's newly issued voting common stock. On February 3, Mr. Pomeroy gave 100 shares of this stock to each of his five children and three grandchildren, leaving him with 200 shares. Does Mr. Pomeroy's exchange of business assets for corporate stock qualify as a nontaxable exchange even though he reduced his ownership interest from 100 percent to only 20 percent on the day after Pomeroy Ski Inc. was incorporated?
4. On April 1, 2005, Bullen Company transferred machinery used in its business to Eaton Inc. in exchange for Eaton common stock. Both Bullen and Eaton use the calendar year for tax purposes. Bullen's exchange of property for stock qualified as a nontaxable exchange under Section 351. Consequently, Bullen's adjusted tax basis in the machinery carried over to become Eaton's tax basis. Bullen purchased the machinery in 2003 for $413,000 cash. The machinery was seven-year recovery property, and Bullen deducted a total of $160,161 MACRS depreciation in 2003 and 2004. Compute the 2005 MACRS depreciation deduction with respect to the machinery allowed to Bullen Company and to Eaton Inc.

Tax Planning Cases

1. Firm NS owns 90 percent of the outstanding stock of Corporation T. NS also owns business realty that T needs for use in its business. The FMV of the realty is $4 million, and NS's adjusted basis is $5.6 million. Both NS and T are in the 35 percent marginal tax bracket. Discuss the tax implications of each of the following courses of action, and decide which course you would recommend to NS.
   a. NS could exchange the realty for newly issued shares of T stock worth $4 million.
   b. NS could sell the realty to T for $4 million cash.
   c. NS could lease the realty to T for its annual fair rental value of $600,000.
2. Firm K, a noncorporate taxpayer, has owned investment land with a $600,000 basis for four years. Two unrelated parties want to acquire the land from K. Party A has offered $770,000 cash, and Party B has offered another tract of land with a $725,000 FMV. If K accepts Party B's offer, it would hold the new land for no more than two years before selling it. The FMV of this land should appreciate 10 percent annually. K's tax rate on capital gain is 15 percent, and it uses a 7 percent discount rate to compute NPV. Which offer should K accept to maximize the NPV of the transaction?
3. This year, Corporation EF decides to replace old, outmoded business equipment (adjusted basis $50,000) with new, improved equipment. The corporation has two options.
   - Sell the old equipment for $120,000 cash and use the cash to purchase the new equipment. This option has no transaction cost.
   - Exchange the old equipment for the new like-kind equipment. This exchange has a $6,000 transaction cost that EF could deduct in the current year.

   The new equipment has a MACRS recovery period of five years, and EF will use the half-year convention. EF cannot make a Section 179 election for the cost of the new equipment. Which option should EF choose? In making your computations, assume a 35 percent tax rate and a 6 percent discount rate.

4. DM Inc. incurred a $25,000 net capital loss in 2000 that has carried forward into 2005. During 2005, a hurricane destroyed business assets with a $120,000 basis. DM received a $150,000 insurance reimbursement which it immediately used to purchase replacement assets. The new assets have a three-year MACRS recovery period. Should DM elect to defer the gain recognized on the involuntary conversion?

Comprehensive Problems for Part Three

1. Croyden is a calendar year, accrual basis corporation. Mr. and Mrs. Croyden (cash basis taxpayers) are the sole corporate shareholders. Mr. Croyden is president and Mrs. Croyden is vice president of the corporation. Croyden's financial records, prepared in accordance with GAAP, show the following information for the year.

Revenues from sales of goods	$12,900,000
Cost of goods sold (LIFO)	(9,260,000)
Gross profit	$ 3,640,000
Bad debt expense	$ 24,000
Administrative salaries and wages	612,000
State and local business taxes	135,000
Interest expense	33,900
Advertising	67,000
Property insurance premiums	19,800
Life insurance premiums	7,300
Depreciation expense	148,800
Repairs, maintenance, utilities	81,000

Croyden's records reveal the following facts.

- Under the UNICAP rules, Croyden had to capitalize $142,800 of administrative wages to inventory. These wages were expensed for financial statement purposes.
- Because of the UNICAP rules, Croyden's cost of goods sold for tax purposes exceeds cost of goods sold for financial statement purposes by $219,000.
- Bad debt expense equals the addition to the corporation's allowance for bad debts. Actual write-offs of uncollectible accounts during the year totaled $31,200.
- Administrative salaries include an accrued $50,000 year-end bonus to Mr. Croyden and an accrued $20,000 year-end bonus to Mrs. Croyden. These bonuses were paid on January 17 of the following year.
- The life insurance premiums were on key-person policies for Mr. and Mrs. Croyden. The corporation is the policy beneficiary.
- Croyden disposed of two assets during the year. (These dispositions are *not* reflected in the financial statement information shown above.) It sold office furnishings for $45,000. The original cost of the furnishings was $40,000, and accumulated MACRS depreciation through date of sale was $12,700. It also exchanged transportation equipment for a 15 percent interest in a partnership. The original cost of the transportation equipment was $110,000, and accumulated MACRS depreciation through date of exchange was $38,900.

- MACRS depreciation for assets placed in service in prior years (including the office furnishings and transportation equipment disposed of this year) is $187,600. The only asset acquired this year was new equipment costing $275,000. The equipment has a seven-year recovery period and was placed in service on February 11.
- Croyden's prior year tax returns show no unrecaptured Section 1231 losses and a $7,400 capital loss carryforward.

Solely on the basis of the above facts, compute Croyden's taxable income.

2. LN Consulting is a calendar year, cash basis unincorporated business. The business is not required to provide audited financial statements to any external user. LN's accounting records show the following.

Cash receipts:	
Revenues from service contracts	$292,000
Proceeds from sale of mutual fund shares	18,000
Insurance reimbursement for fire loss	7,000
Cash disbursements:	
Administrative salaries	$ 32,000
Professional fees	800
Business meals and entertainment	1,090
State and local business taxes	5,000
Interest expense	7,600
Advertising	970
Office expense	1,200
Office rent	14,400
New office equipment	8,300

LN's records reveal the following facts.

- In December, the bookkeeper prepaid $1,500 interest on a business debt. This interest is related to the next taxable year.
- LN disposed of two assets during the year. It exchanged computer equipment for office furniture. (These assets are not like-kind for federal tax purposes.) The original cost of the computer equipment was $13,000, and accumulated MACRS depreciation through date of exchange was $9,700. The office furniture has a $6,000 FMV. It sold 1,200 shares in a mutual fund for $18,000. LN purchased the shares as a short-term investment of excess working capital. The cost of the shares was $16,600.
- An electrical fire completely destroyed a company car. The adjusted basis of the car was $9,100, and LN's property insurance company paid $7,000 in complete settlement of its damage claim. LN used the insurance money to pay various operating expenses.
- MACRS depreciation for assets placed in service in prior years (including the computer equipment and company car) is $4,600. The only asset acquired this year (in addition to the office furniture) was office equipment costing $8,300. The equipment was placed in service on August 19.

On the basis of the above facts, compute the taxable income generated by LN Consulting's activities.

The Taxation of Business Income

Chapter Nine

Sole Proprietorships, Partnerships, LLCs, and S Corporations

Learning Objectives

After studying this chapter, you should be able to:

1. Compute net profit or loss from a sole proprietorship.
2. Compute the FICA payroll taxes and the federal SE tax.
3. Differentiate between a distributive share of partnership income and cash flow.
4. Adjust the tax basis in a partnership interest.
5. Apply the basis limitation on the deduction of partnership losses.
6. Explain how limited liability companies (LLCs) are treated for federal tax purposes.
7. Determine if a corporation is eligible to be an S corporation.
8. Contrast the basis limitation for S corporation losses with the basis limitation for partnership losses.

In Part Three of *Principles of Taxation for Business and Investment Planning*, we learned that taxable income from business transactions and activities equals gross income minus allowable deductions.[1] In Part Four of the text, we will learn how to compute the tax on business income. Throughout Part Three, we used the labels *firm* and *company* to refer to business organizations. We could get by with these generic labels because we were concentrating on the *measurement of taxable income*. The measurement process does not depend on the type of legal entity operating the business. As stated in Chapter 4, the tax law is essentially neutral across business entities with respect to the tax base. But to make the actual *tax computation*, we must focus on the specific organizational form of the business.

For tax purposes, business organizations fall into one of two categories. The first category consists of organizations that are not taxable entities. The income generated by the organization is taxed directly to the owners. This category includes sole proprietorships, partnerships, limited liability companies (LLCs), and S corporations, all of which are discussed in Chapter 9. The second category consists of corporations (often referred to as

[1] §63(a).

regular or C corporations), which are both persons under the law and taxpayers in their own right. Corporations pay tax on their income at the entity level. If a corporation distributes after-tax earnings to its owners, the distributed income is taxed a second time at the owner level. This potential for double taxation, as well as other characteristics of corporate taxpayers, is examined in detail in Chapter 10. Exhibit 9.1 contrasts the two categories of business organizations in terms of the identity of the taxpayer.

EXHIBIT 9.1
Categories of Business Organization

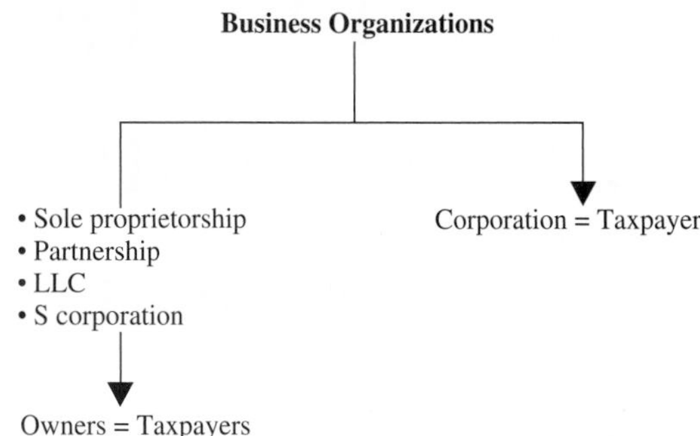

Part Four includes two more chapters that complete our discussion of the taxation of business income. Chapter 11 compares the tax advantages and disadvantages of the various business entities and identifies tax planning strategies unique to each. Finally, Chapter 12 introduces the complexities that develop when business entities operate in more than one taxing jurisdiction.

SOLE PROPRIETORSHIPS

The simplest form of business organization is a **sole proprietorship,** defined as an unincorporated business activity owned by one individual.[2] A sole proprietor owns the business assets in his or her own name and is personally liable for the business debts. In other words, the business has no legal identity separate from that of its owner. Sole proprietorships are the most common form of business entity in the United States. According to recent Internal Revenue Service data, over 18 million nonfarm sole proprietorships operate in this country, and three of every four businesses that report to the IRS are operated by sole proprietors.[3]

Overview of Schedule C

Objective 1
Compute net profit or loss from a sole proprietorship.

The taxable income from a sole proprietorship is reported on Schedule C (Profit or Loss from Business) of the proprietor's Form 1040 (U.S. Individual Income Tax Return).[4] This schedule is the proprietorship's income statement for the year. Gross income from the sale of goods to customers or performance of services for clients is accounted for in Part I. The proprietorship's deductible operating expenses and cost recovery deductions are listed in Part II. An excess of gross income over deductions is reported as net profit, while an excess of deductions over gross income is reported as net loss.

[2] This definition includes businesses in which the owner's spouse has an equity interest in the business under state property law.

[3] IRS Statistics of Income Bulletin, Spring 2003.

[4] Agricultural business operations are reported on Schedule F (Profit or Loss from Farming).

Faux Antique—Sole Proprietorship

Mr. Tom Owen owns and operates a firm that manufactures reproductions of antique furniture. The business name for this sole proprietorship is Faux Antique. For 2004, the business records reflect the following items of revenue and expense.

Revenue from furniture sales		$1,117,300
Sales returns		(21,000)
Expenses:	Advertising	6,200
	Accounts written off as uncollectible	8,800
	Attorney and CPA fees	2,150
	Business license tax	2,500
	Cost of goods sold	599,700
	Interest to Credit Union	7,300
	MACRS depreciation	3,600
	Payroll taxes	9,250
	Property and liability insurance	5,600
	Rent on workroom	23,200
	Repairs to tools and equipment	17,900
	Supplies	18,000
	Utilities	14,000
	Wages	73,200

Mr. Owen used the above information to prepare the Schedule C included in his Form 1040. Page 1 of this Schedule C is shown as Exhibit 9.2. The $304,900 net profit reported on Schedule C was included in Mr. Owen's 2004 taxable income.

Note that the tax on net profit is not computed on Schedule C. Instead, the net profit carries to the first page of Form 1040 as ordinary income and is combined with all other income items recognized during the year. Consequently, the individual's business income is just one component of total income on which tax is computed. Similarly, if the sole proprietorship operated at a loss, the loss carries to the first page of Form 1040 to be deducted against other income for the year. If the business loss exceeds other income, the individual can carry the excess loss back two years and forward 20 years as a net operating loss (NOL) deduction.

Individual Net Operating Loss

Mr. Zeller reported the following items on his Form 1040 for 2004.

Salary from employer	$21,600
Interest and dividend income from investments	1,200
Business loss from sole proprietorship	(26,810)
Net operating loss	$ (4,010)

Mr. Zeller can use his $4,010 net operating loss as a carryback deduction (to 2002 and 2003) or as a carryforward deduction for the next 20 years.[5]

[5] This example ignores many technical details that complicate the computation of the individual NOL deduction.

EXHIBIT 9.2

SCHEDULE C (Form 1040)
Department of the Treasury
Internal Revenue Service

Profit or Loss From Business
(Sole Proprietorship)
▶ Partnerships, joint ventures, etc., must file Form 1065 or 1065-B.
▶ Attach to Form 1040 or 1041. ▶ See Instructions for Schedule C (Form 1040).

OMB No. 1545-0074
2004
Attachment Sequence No. 09

Name of proprietor: Tom G. Owen
Social security number (SSN): 497 : 45 : 9058

A Principal business or profession, including product or service (see page C-2 of the instructions): manufacturing - furniture
B Enter code from pages C-7, 8, & 9: ▶ 337000
C Business name. If no separate business name, leave blank.: Faux Antique
D Employer ID number (EIN), if any: 26 : 1147131
E Business address (including suite or room no.) ▶ 1012 East Main
City, town or post office, state, and ZIP code: Widener Kentucky 42714
F Accounting method: (1) ☐ Cash (2) ☒ Accrual (3) ☐ Other (specify) ▶
G Did you "materially participate" in the operation of this business during 2004? If "No," see page C-3 for limit on losses ☒ Yes ☐ No
H If you started or acquired this business during 2004, check here ▶ ☐

Part I Income

		Line	Amount
1	Gross receipts or sales. **Caution.** If this income was reported to you on Form W-2 and the "Statutory employee" box on that form was checked, see page C-3 and check here ▶ ☐	1	1,117,300
2	Returns and allowances	2	21,000
3	Subtract line 2 from line 1	3	1,096,300
4	Cost of goods sold (from line 42 on page 2)	4	599,700
5	**Gross profit.** Subtract line 4 from line 3	5	496,600
6	Other income, including Federal and state gasoline or fuel tax credit or refund (see page C-3)	6	
7	**Gross income.** Add lines 5 and 6 ▶	7	496,600

Part II Expenses. Enter expenses for business use of your home **only** on line 30.

		Line	Amount			Line	Amount
8	Advertising	8	6,200	19	Pension and profit-sharing plans	19	
9	Car and truck expenses (see page C-3)	9		20	Rent or lease (see page C-5):		
				a	Vehicles, machinery, and equipment	20a	
10	Commissions and fees	10		b	Other business property	20b	23,200
11	Contract labor (see page C-4)	11		21	Repairs and maintenance	21	17,900
12	Depletion	12		22	Supplies (not included in Part III)	22	18,000
13	Depreciation and section 179 expense deduction (not included in Part III) (see page C-4)	13	3,600	23	Taxes and licenses	23	11,750
				24	Travel, meals, and entertainment:		
				a	Travel	24a	
				b	Meals and entertainment		
14	Employee benefit programs (other than on line 19)	14		c	Enter nondeductible amount included on line 24b (see page C-5)		
15	Insurance (other than health)	15	5,600				
16	Interest:						
a	Mortgage (paid to banks, etc.)	16a		d	Subtract line 24c from line 24b	24d	
b	Other	16b	7,300	25	Utilities	25	14,000
17	Legal and professional services	17	2,150	26	Wages (less employment credits)	26	73,200
18	Office expense	18		27	Other expenses (from line 48 on page 2) bad debts	27	8,800

		Line	Amount
28	**Total expenses** before expenses for business use of home. Add lines 8 through 27 in columns ▶	28	191,700
29	Tentative profit (loss). Subtract line 28 from line 7	29	304,900
30	Expenses for business use of your home. Attach **Form 8829**	30	
31	**Net profit or (loss).** Subtract line 30 from line 29. • If a profit, enter on **Form 1040, line 12,** and **also** on **Schedule SE, line 2** (statutory employees, see page C-6). Estates and trusts, enter on Form 1041, line 3. • If a loss, you **must** go to line 32.	31	304,900

32 If you have a loss, check the box that describes your investment in this activity (see page C-6).
• If you checked 32a, enter the loss on **Form 1040, line 12,** and **also** on **Schedule SE, line 2** (statutory employees, see page C-6). Estates and trusts, enter on Form 1041, line 3.
• If you checked 32b, you **must** attach **Form 6198.**
32a ☐ All investment is at risk.
32b ☐ Some investment is not at risk.

For Paperwork Reduction Act Notice, see Form 1040 instructions. Cat. No. 11334P **Schedule C (Form 1040) 2004**

Cash Flow Implications

The after-tax cash generated by a sole proprietorship belongs to the individual owner. The individual can retain the cash for use in the business, spend it for personal consumption, or invest it in other income-producing property. In the latter case, earnings from the owner's investments (interest, dividends, rents, etc.) are not considered business income and are not reported on Schedule C.[6]

Dispositions of Business Assets

Only the results of the sole proprietorship's routine operations are reported on Schedule C. If the owner disposes of assets used in the business, recognized gains and losses are

[6] Chapter 15 discusses the taxation of investment income earned by an individual taxpayer.

Tax Talk
The IRS estimates that the annual "tax gap" (taxes that people legally owe but don't pay) equals $300 billion. About $80 billion of the gap is attributable to sole proprietors who understate their revenue (often received in cash) or overstate their deductions.

reported on Form 4797 (Sales of Business Property). The tax consequences of the disposition are based on the rules discussed in Chapters 7 and 8. For instance, if the owner sells business equipment at a gain, he must report depreciation recapture as ordinary income and any additional gain as Section 1231 gain. If he sells the equipment at a loss, the loss is a Section 1231 loss.

Interest Expense

If an individual borrows money for a business purpose relating to her sole proprietorship, the interest paid on the debt is deductible on Schedule C. The deductibility of business interest is in sharp contrast to the tax treatment of other types of interest expense. For example, individuals can't deduct the interest paid on debt incurred to purchase consumer goods such as a family car or a new wardrobe. If the sole proprietorship fails to generate enough cash to service the business debt, the individual owner is personally liable for repayment, and the business creditors can look to the owner's nonbusiness assets for satisfaction.

Home Office Deduction

If an individual uses a portion of his personal residence as an office for his sole proprietorship, the expenses allocable to the home office may qualify as a business deduction.

Home Office Deduction

Mrs. Greer, a self-employed consultant, uses one room of her home as a business office. This room represents 15 percent of the home's square footage. This year, Mrs. Greer incurred the following expenses in connection with her home.

Home mortgage interest	$18,000
Property tax on residence	4,300
Homeowner's insurance	2,950
Utilities	3,600
House cleaning service	2,400
Repairs	1,900
	$33,150

If Mrs. Greer's office meets the tax law requirements, she can deduct $4,973 (15 percent of the total expenses) as a business deduction on her Schedule C.[7] She can also claim a MACRS depreciation deduction based on 15 percent of the cost of the residence.

The possibility of deducting some percentage of monthly household expenses might prompt the conversion of many a spare bedroom into a home office—even if the use of such office is extraneous to the conduct of the homeowner's business. The tax law limits the potential for abuse through a set of tough requirements for qualifying a portion of a residence as a home office. Essentially, the office must be *exclusively* used on a regular basis as the principal place of any business operated by the homeowner or as a place to meet with patients, clients, or customers.[8] A home office used exclusively for administrative or management activities qualifies as a principal place of business if the taxpayer has no other fixed location where such activities are conducted.

[7] Mrs. Greer can deduct the remainders of her home mortgage interest and property tax as itemized deductions. See Chapters 13 and 16.

[8] §280A(c)(1).

Principal Place of Business

Dr. Milby is a self-employed obstetrician who treats patients at three different urban hospitals. Although Dr. Milby spends more than 12 hours during an average week at each hospital, he does not maintain an office in any of the hospitals. He does all his medical reading, patient billing and record keeping, and other administrative tasks in his home office where he spends two to three hours each day. Patient treatment is the most significant aspect of Dr. Milby's business, and he spends more hours working at the hospitals than in his home office. Nevertheless, his home office qualifies as Dr. Milby's principal place of business, and he can deduct the expenses allocable to the office.

Even when an individual meets the requirements for a home office, the home office deduction is limited to the taxable income of the business before consideration of the deduction.[9] In other words, the home office deduction can't create or increase a net loss. A sole proprietor who claims a home office deduction must isolate the deduction on line 30, Schedule C, and attach a separate Form 8829 to show the detailed computation of the deduction. Clearly, the IRS is very sensitive about home office deductions. Sole proprietors who are entitled to the deduction should carefully document the underlying expenses and be prepared to justify the necessity of a home office if their tax return is audited.

Employment Taxes

A sole proprietor may be the only person working in the business or the proprietor may have any number of employees. In the latter case, the sole proprietor must obtain an **employer identification number** from the IRS and comply with the state and federal employment tax requirements imposed on every business organization.

Unemployment and FICA Tax

Objective 2
Compute the FICA payroll taxes and the federal SE tax.

Employers must pay both a state and federal unemployment tax based on the compensation paid to their employees during the year.[10] As we discussed in Chapter 1, these taxes fund the national unemployment benefits program. Employers must also pay the tax authorized by the Federal Insurance Contribution Act (FICA) that funds our national Social Security and Medicare systems. This **employer payroll tax** has two components: a Social Security tax of 6.2 percent of a base amount of compensation paid to each employee and a Medicare tax of 1.45 percent of the employee's total compensation.[11] Congress adjusts the Social Security base each year: In 2004, the base was \$87,900, and in 2005, the base is \$90,000.

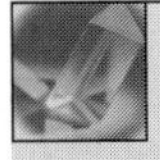

Employer Payroll Tax

Mr. Carr has a full-time employee, Mrs. Stroh, who manages Mr. Carr's sole proprietorship. Mrs. Stroh's 2004 salary was \$98,500, and Mr. Carr's employer payroll tax on this salary was \$6,878.

Social Security tax (6.2% × \$87,900)	\$5,450
Medicare tax (1.45% × \$98,500)	1,428
Employer payroll tax	\$6,878

[9] §280A(c)(5). *Michael H. Visin*, TC Memo 2003-246.

[10] §3301.

[11] §3111.

In addition to paying unemployment and payroll taxes, employers must collect the FICA tax levied on their employees.[12] This **employee payroll tax** is computed in exactly the same manner as the employer payroll tax.

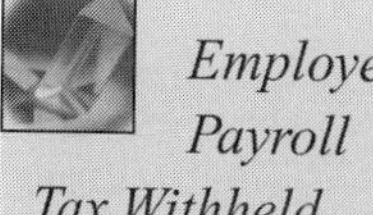

Employee Payroll Tax Withheld by Employer

Based on the facts in the preceding example, Mrs. Stroh's 2004 employee payroll tax was also $6,878.[13] Mr. Carr withheld this tax from Mrs. Stroh's salary and remitted it along with his employer payroll tax to the U.S. Treasury for a total payment of $13,756. Thus, Mr. Carr is the collection agent for the federal government with respect to the employee payroll tax.

Employers should take their responsibility to collect and remit employee payroll tax seriously. If an employer fails to remit the proper FICA tax for an employee, the federal government may collect both halves of the tax (the employer and the employee portions) from the employer.[14]

Income Tax Withholding on Employee Compensation

Employers are required to withhold federal income tax (and possibly state income tax) from the compensation paid to their employees.[15] Employers must remit the withholding to the U.S. Treasury periodically throughout the year. The withholding for each employee is based on the information on the employee's Form W-4 (Employee's Withholding Allowance Certificate) and computed by reference to withholding tables provided by the IRS.

Gross and Net Compensation

During 2004, Mr. Carr also withheld $18,000 federal income tax from Mrs. Stroh's $98,500 gross salary. Therefore, Mrs. Stroh received only $73,622 after-tax (net) compensation.

Gross salary	$98,500
FICA tax withheld	(6,878)
Federal income tax withheld	(18,000)
Net salary received	$73,622

Tax Talk

Increasing enforcement of employment tax withholding is high on the list of the IRS's priorities. The IRS is carefully but aggressively looking at cases where the employer uses the taxes withheld from his employees for a "yacht or second home" instead of remitting the taxes to the government.

At the end of each year, employers are required to provide information concerning the gross wages or salary paid to each employee during the year and the payroll and income tax withheld from that gross income. This information is summarized on the familiar Form W-2 (Wage and Tax Statement).

Income Tax Consequences to the Employer

Business organizations can deduct the gross amount of compensation paid to their employees.[16] They can also deduct state and federal unemployment taxes and the employer payroll

[12] §3102.

[13] §3101. The employee payroll tax is nondeductible for federal income tax purposes.

[14] The employer is not technically liable for an employee's payroll tax. However, an employer that fails to "collect, truthfully account for, and pay over" this tax is subject to a penalty equal to 100 percent of such tax. In other words, the penalty on the employer equals the uncollected employee tax. §6672. This penalty has been described as the "iron fist" of the FICA tax system.

[15] §3402.

[16] Unless some or all the compensation must be capitalized to inventory under the uniform capitalization (unicap) rules.

tax because these taxes are ordinary and necessary expenses incurred in the conduct of an active business.[17] Let's summarize the relationship between these deductible expenses, the employer's withholding requirements, and the net compensation paid to employees by referring back to Mr. Carr's sole proprietorship.

Compensation and Cash Disbursements

For 2004, Mr. Carr paid $98,500 compensation to Mrs. Stroh and $6,878 employer payroll tax on that compensation. He withheld $24,878 employee payroll tax and income tax from Mrs. Stroh's compensation and remitted $31,756 total tax to the U.S. Treasury.

		Cash Disbursed to:	
	Deductible Business Expense	**Mrs. Stroh**	**U.S. Treasury**
Salary	$ 98,500	$73,622	$24,878
Employer FICA tax	6,878		6,878
	$105,378	$73,622	$31,756

Self-Employment Tax

While sole proprietors are responsible for collecting and remitting payroll and income taxes from their employees, sole proprietors themselves are not employees and do not receive a salary from the business. Sole proprietors are self-employed and must pay the federal **self-employment (SE) tax** on their business income.[18] Refer to Schedule C in Exhibit 9.2 and note how line 31 instructs the sole proprietor to carry net profit to Schedule SE. The self-employment tax is computed on this schedule and paid along with the individual's income tax for the year.

The SE tax has two components: a Social Security tax of 12.4 percent of a base amount of net earnings from self-employment and a Medicare tax of 2.9 percent of total net earnings. In 2004, the Social Security base was $87,900, and in 2005, it is $90,000. Note that the SE tax rates equal the *combined* employer/employee payroll tax rates and the Social Security base is the same for both taxes. The SE tax was enacted to complement the FICA tax; the federal government collects the same tax on a sole proprietor's self-employment income as it would collect on an identical amount of compensation. To complete the parallel, sole proprietors can claim one-half of their SE tax (the equivalent of the employer payroll tax) as an income tax deduction.[19]

In calculating after-tax business income, sole proprietors must factor in both the income tax and the SE tax levied on that income.

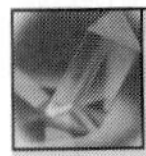

Self-Employment Tax

Mr. Carr's sole proprietorship generated $200,000 net profit in 2004. If his marginal income tax rate was 33 percent, the after-tax income from the business was $120,426.

[17] See Rev. Rul. 80-164, 1980-1 CB 109.

[18] §1401. Self-employed individuals are not eligible to receive unemployment benefits and, therefore, are not subject to state and federal unemployment taxes.

[19] §164(f).

Schedule C net profit		$200,000
Self-employment tax:		
Net earnings from self-employment[20]	$184,700	
Social Security tax (12.4% × $87,900)	10,900	
Medicare tax (2.9% × $184,700)	5,356	
Total SE tax		(16,256)
Income tax:		
Schedule C net profit	$200,000	
One-half SE tax	(8,128)	
	$191,872	
	.33	
		(63,318)
After-tax business income		$120,426

Note that the SE tax is not a progressive tax because the combined 15.3 percent rate applies to the first dollar of self-employment income. For sole proprietors who earn modest incomes, the SE tax can be a heavier burden than the income tax.

PARTNERSHIPS

Entrepreneurs who pool their resources by becoming co-owners of a business can organize the business as a partnership. **Partnerships** are unincorporated entities created by contractual agreement among two or more business associates.[21] Such associates can be individuals, corporations, and even other partnerships. All 50 states and the District of Columbia have enacted statutes (generally patterned after the Revised Uniform Partnership Act and the Revised Uniform Limited Partnership Act) to define the characteristics and requirements for partnerships operating within their jurisdiction.

Forming a Partnership

The first step in the formation of a partnership is the drafting of an agreement by the prospective partners.[22] A partnership agreement is a legal contract stipulating both the rights and obligations of the partners and the percentage of profits and losses allocable to each. The agreement gives the partners flexibility to customize their business arrangement to suit their unique situation. The partners can agree to share all profits and losses equally, or they can decide on different sharing ratios for special items of income, gain, deduction, or loss. Ideally, a partnership agreement should be drafted by an attorney, should be in writing, and should be signed by all the partners. However, even oral partnership agreements have been respected as binding contracts by the courts.[23]

[20] The statutory base for the SE tax is "net earnings from self-employment." Net earnings equals net profit minus a deduction equal to 7.65 percent of such profit. §1402(a)(12). Schedule SE builds this deduction into its computation of net earnings by defining that number as 92.35 percent of Schedule C net profit.

[21] The term *partnership* encompasses syndicates, groups, pools, joint ventures, or any other unincorporated business organization. §761(a).

[22] See the discussion of organizational and start-up costs in Chapter 6.

[23] See, for example, *Elrod*, 87 TC 1046 (1986) and *Kuhl* v. *Garner*, 894 P.2d 525 (Oregon, 1995).

A partnership can be a **general partnership** in which all partners have unlimited personal liability for debts incurred by the partnership. Alternatively, a partnership can be a **limited partnership** in which one or more limited partners are liable for partnership debt only to the extent of their capital contributions to the partnership. Limited partnerships must have at least one general partner. A limited partner's role is restricted to that of a passive investor; state law typically prohibits limited partners from active involvement in the partnership business. Limited partners who violate this prohibition may forfeit their limited liability for the partnership's debts.

Individuals who perform professional services for patients or clients, such as doctors, attorneys, and CPAs, often form **limited liability partnerships (LLPs).** General partners in an LLP are not personally liable for malpractice-related claims arising from the professional negligence of any other partner. However, they are personally liable for other debts of the LLP.[24]

Limited Liability Partnership

Doctors Jeff Batson, Susan Lloyd, and Cary Carew formed an LLP to conduct their medical practice. The three doctors are general partners. This year, the LLP is the defendant in two lawsuits.

The first lawsuit was initiated by a former LLP employee who claims that she was fired from her job because of age discrimination. Consequently, the ex-employee is suing the LLP for $600,000 damages. The second lawsuit was initiated by the family of a patient who died shortly after Dr. Carew performed a routine surgical procedure. Because the family believes that Dr. Carew was grossly negligent, it is suing the LLP for $1.2 million damages.

If the LLP loses the first lawsuit, the three general partners are personally liable for any portion of the $600,000 settlement not covered by the LLP's insurance. If the LLP loses the second lawsuit, only Dr. Carew is personally liable for any portion of the $1.2 million settlement not covered by the LLP's or his own malpractice insurance.

Tax Basis in Partnership Interests

Partnerships are both legal entities (title to property can be held and conveyed in the partnership name) and accounting entities (financial books and records are maintained by the partnership). An equity interest in a partnership is an intangible asset, the value of which depends on the underlying value of the partnership business. Partnership interests are considered illiquid assets because partnership agreements usually prevent partners from disposing of their interests without the consent of the other partners. A partner's initial tax basis in a partnership interest equals the cash plus the adjusted basis of any property transferred to the partnership in exchange for the equity interest.[25]

As legal entities, partnerships can borrow money in their own name. Nonetheless, general partners have unlimited liability for repayment of debt to the partnership's creditors. If the partnership business does not generate enough cash to service its debts, the general partners must contribute funds to satisfy any unpaid liabilities.[26] As a result, a partner's economic investment consists of the initial investment of cash or property *plus* the share of partnership debt for which the partner may ultimately be responsible. The tax law acknowledges this responsibility by providing that a partner's share of partnership debt is included in the basis in her partnership interest.[27]

[24] The Big Four public accounting firms are LLPs.

[25] The exchange of property for a partnership interest is nontaxable to both the partner and the partnership. §721. See the discussion of partnership formations in Chapter 8.

[26] In this respect, a general partner's risk with respect to the partnership business is equivalent to a sole proprietor's business risk.

[27] §752(a).

Basis in Partnership Interest

Three individuals each contributed $10,000 cash to a new partnership in which they are equal general partners. The partnership immediately borrowed $24,000 from a local bank and used the money to purchase equipment and supplies. Each partner's basis in his partnership interest is $18,000: the initial cash contribution plus an equal share of partnership debt.[28]

Partnership Reporting Requirements

The Internal Revenue Code states that "a partnership as such shall not be subject to the income tax . . . Persons carrying on a business as partners shall be liable for income tax only in their separate or individual capacities."[29] Although partnerships are not taxable entities, they are required to file an annual Form 1065 (U.S. Partnership Return of Income) with the IRS.[30]

The taxable income generated by partnership activities is measured and characterized at the entity level. All items of gross income and deduction relating strictly to business operations are reported on page 1 of Form 1065. The net of these items is reported on line 22 as ordinary income or loss. This income or loss is allocated among the partners according to the sharing ratio specified in the partnership agreement. The partners report their share of income or loss on their respective returns and include it in the calculation of taxable income. Accordingly, net profit from a partnership business is taxed directly to the partners; the tax rate depends on whether the partner is an individual or a corporation.[31] Because partnerships serve only as conduits of income, they are described as **passthrough entities.**

Faux Antique—Partnership

Refer back to our earlier example in which Mr. Tom Owen operates a furniture business (Faux Antique) as a sole proprietorship. Let's change the facts by assuming that Mr. Owen and two co-owners organized Faux Antique as a partnership. Mr. Owen owns a 60 percent equity interest as a general partner. Faux Antique generated $304,900 ordinary business income for 2004. Page 1 of the partnership's Form 1065 is shown as Exhibit 9.3.

Partnerships frequently recognize items of income, gain, expense, or loss that don't relate to business operations. For example, a partnership might invest excess cash in marketable securities that pay dividends and interest. The partnership might recognize gain or loss on the sale of one of these securities. Or the partnership could make a contribution to a local charity. These items are not included in the calculation of ordinary business income or loss. Instead, they are reported on Schedule K of Form 1065 and allocated to the partners for inclusion on the partners' returns.[32] These **separately stated items** retain their tax character as they pass through to the partners.[33]

[28] The regulatory rules for calculating a partner's share of partnership debt are extremely complex. The simplest summary of these rules is that recourse debt is shared only by general partners based on their relative loss-sharing ratios and nonrecourse debt is shared by all partners based on their profit-sharing ratios. Reg. §1.752-2 and Reg. §1.752-3.

[29] §701.

[30] As a general rule, partnerships are required to use the same taxable year as that used by their partners. Under this rule, a partnership consisting of individual partners who are calendar year taxpayers files its Form 1065 on a calendar year basis. §706(b).

[31] If partnership income is allocated to a partner that is a passthrough entity (another partnership, LLC, or S corporation), the income is passed through again until it is finally allocated to a taxable entity (an individual or corporation).

[32] More specifically, Reg. §1.702-1(a)(8)(ii) explains that each partner must be able to take into account separately his or her distributive share of any partnership item that results in an income tax liability different from that which would result if the item were not accounted for separately.

[33] §702(b).

EXHIBIT 9.3

Form **1065** Department of the Treasury Internal Revenue Service

U.S. Return of Partnership Income

For calendar year 2004, or tax year beginning ...., 2004, and ending ...., 20....
▶ See separate instructions.

OMB No. 1545-0099

2004

A Principal business activity: Manufacturing	Name of partnership: Faux Antique	D Employer identification number: 81 : 1138419
B Principal product or service: Furniture	Number, street, and room or suite no. If a P.O. box, see page 14 of the instructions.: 1012 East Main	E Date business started: 1990
C Business code number: 337000	City or town, state, and ZIP code: Widner Kentucky 42714	F Total assets (see page 14 of the instructions): $ N/a

Use the IRS label. Otherwise, print or type.

G Check applicable boxes: (1) ☐ Initial return (2) ☐ Final return (3) ☐ Name change (4) ☐ Address change (5) ☐ Amended return

H Check accounting method: (1) ☐ Cash (2) ☒ Accrual (3) ☐ Other (specify) ▶

I Number of Schedules K-1. Attach one for each person who was a partner at any time during the tax year ▶ 3

Caution: *Include **only** trade or business income and expenses on lines 1a through 22 below. See the instructions for more information.*

Income	1a	Gross receipts or sales	1a	1,117,300		
	b	Less returns and allowances	1b	21,000	1c	1,096,300
	2	Cost of goods sold (Schedule A, line 8)			2	599,700
	3	Gross profit. Subtract line 2 from line 1c			3	496,600
	4	Ordinary income (loss) from other partnerships, estates, and trusts *(attach schedule)*			4	
	5	Net farm profit (loss) *(attach Schedule F (Form 1040))*			5	
	6	Net gain (loss) from Form 4797, Part II, line 17			6	
	7	Other income (loss) *(attach statement)*			7	
	8	**Total income (loss).** Combine lines 3 through 7			8	496,600
Deductions (see page 16 of the instructions for limitations)	9	Salaries and wages (other than to partners) (less employment credits)			9	73,200
	10	Guaranteed payments to partners			10	
	11	Repairs and maintenance			11	17,900
	12	Bad debts			12	8,800
	13	Rent			13	23,200
	14	Taxes and licenses			14	11,750
	15	Interest			15	7,300
	16a	Depreciation *(if required, attach Form 4562)*	16a	3,600		
	b	Less depreciation reported on Schedule A and elsewhere on return	16b		16c	3,600
	17	Depletion **(Do not deduct oil and gas depletion.)**			17	
	18	Retirement plans, etc.			18	
	19	Employee benefit programs			19	
	20	Other deductions *(attach statement)* prof. fees 2,150 supplies 18,000 advertising 6,200 insurance 5,600 utilities 14,000			20	45,950
	21	**Total deductions.** Add the amounts shown in the far right column for lines 9 through 20			21	191,700
	22	**Ordinary business income (loss).** Subtract line 21 from line 8			22	304,900

Sign Here

Under penalties of perjury, I declare that I have examined this return, including accompanying schedules and statements, and to the best of my knowledge and belief, it is true, correct, and complete. Declaration of preparer (other than general partner or limited liability company member) is based on all information of which preparer has any knowledge.

▶ Signature of general partner or limited liability company member manager ▶ Date

May the IRS discuss this return with the preparer shown below (see instructions)? ☐ Yes ☐ No

Paid Preparer's Use Only

Preparer's signature	Date	Check if self-employed ▶ ☐	Preparer's SSN or PTIN
Firm's name (or yours if self-employed), address, and ZIP code ▶		EIN ▶	
		Phone no. ( )	

For Privacy Act and Paperwork Reduction Act Notice, see separate instructions. Cat. No. 11390Z Form **1065** (2004)

Separately Stated Items

For several years, Faux Antique partnership has invested any excess cash in a mutual fund. In 2004, the partnership received a $1,680 dividend from the fund. The partnership made a $2,500 donation to the United Way during the year. Neither the dividend nor the donation was included in the computation of ordinary income. As a 60 percent partner, Tom Owen was allocated a $1,008 share of the dividend and a $1,500 share of the donation. Because these shares retained their tax character, Mr. Owen reported his share of the dividend as investment income (instead of business income) and his share of the donation as a personal charitable contribution (instead of a business expense) on his Form 1040.

Tax Consequences to Partners

Distributive Shares and Cash Flows

Objective 3
Differentiate between a distributive share of partnership income and cash flow.

After the close of its taxable year, a partnership issues a Schedule K-1 (Partner's Share of Income, Credits, Deductions, etc.) to each partner. Schedule K-1 provides detailed information concerning the partner's **distributive share** of the partnership's ordinary business income or loss and any separately stated items. The schedule tells individual partners how and where to include each item on their tax return. For instance, a partner's distributive share of ordinary income or loss is reported on Schedule E of Form 1040.

Partners must pay tax on their distributive share of partnership income, regardless of the cash flow from the partnership during the year. In an extreme case, partners may decide to retain all available cash in the partnership. As a result, each partner must find another source of funds to pay the tax on his distributive share of partnership income. Alternatively, partners may decide to withdraw enough cash to pay their taxes. Another possibility is that the partners withdraw all available cash for personal consumption. The important point is that the cash flow is irrelevant in determining the partners' taxable income.

Partnership Schedule K-1

Each partner in Faux Antique received a 2004 Schedule K-1 reporting that partner's distributive share of ordinary business income, dividend income, and charitable donation. Tom Owen's Schedule K-1 is shown as Exhibit 9.4. On the basis of the information on this schedule, Mr. Owen included $182,940 (60 percent of the partnership's $304,900 business income) and $1,008 (60 percent of the partnership's $1,680 dividend income) in his taxable income. He included a $1,500 donation (60 percent of the $2,500 partnership donation) in his total charitable contributions for the year.[34] According to line 19 of Schedule K-1, the partnership distributed $150,000 cash to Mr. Owen during 2004. This cash flow is irrelevant to the computation of his taxable income.

Guaranteed Payments

The personal involvement of individual partners in the partnership business can vary greatly across partners. Limited partners, by definition, do not actively participate in the day-to-day operation of the business and, at most, may take part in major management decisions. General partners may have different levels of participation; some may be sporadically involved, while others may devote 100 percent of their workweek to the business.

Partners who work for the partnership on a continual basis expect to be compensated. These partners typically receive **guaranteed payments** from the partnership based on the value of their work. Guaranteed payments to partners are analogous to the salaries paid to partnership employees. The partnership deducts guaranteed payments in computing ordinary income, and partners report guaranteed payments as ordinary income.[35] However, partners can't be employees of their partnerships any more than individuals can be employees of their sole proprietorships. Because a guaranteed payment is not a salary, neither the partnership nor the partner pays FICA payroll tax. Nor does the partnership withhold any federal income tax from the guaranteed payment. If a partner earns a $10,000 monthly guaranteed payment, that partner receives $10,000 cash each month. At the end of the year, the partnership does not issue a Form W-2 to the partner. Instead, the total guaranteed payments are reported as an ordinary income item on the partner's Schedule K-1.

[34] The tax consequences of personal charitable contributions are discussed in Chapter 16.

[35] §707(c).

EXHIBIT 9.4

6511

☐ Final K-1 ☐ Amended K-1 OMB No. 1545-0099

Schedule K-1 (Form 1065) **2004**

Department of the Treasury Internal Revenue Service

Tax year beginning Jan. 1, 2004 and ending Dec. 31, 2004

Partner's Share of Income, Deductions, Credits, etc. ▶ See back of form and separate instructions.

Part I Information About the Partnership

A Partnership's employer identification number: 81 1138419

B Partnership's name, address, city, state, and ZIP code: Faux Antique, 1012 East Main, Widner Kentucky 42714

C IRS Center where partnership filed return: Cincinnati

D ☐ Check if this is a publicly traded partnership (PTP)

E ☐ Tax shelter registration number, if any

F ☐ Check if Form 8271 is attached

Part II Information About the Partner

G Partner's identifying number: 497-45-9058

H Partner's name, address, city, state, and ZIP code: Tom G. Owen, 330 Aspen Lane, Widner Kentucky 42714

I ☒ General partner or LLC member-manager ☐ Limited partner or other LLC member

J ☐ Domestic partner ☐ Foreign partner

K What type of entity is this partner? individual

L Partner's share of profit, loss, and capital:

	Beginning	Ending
Profit	60 %	60 %
Loss	60 %	60 %
Capital	60 %	60 %

M Partner's share of liabilities at year end:

Nonrecourse	$
Qualified nonrecourse financing	$ 13,612
Recourse	$ 21,050

N Partner's capital account analysis:

Beginning capital account	$ 25,000
Capital contributed during the year	$
Current year increase (decrease)	$ 182,448
Withdrawals & distributions	$(150,000)
Ending capital account	$ 57,448

☐ Tax basis ☐ GAAP ☒ Section 704(b) book ☐ Other (explain)

Part III Partner's Share of Current Year Income, Deductions, Credits, and Other Items

1 Ordinary business income (loss) 182,940	15 Credits & credit recapture
2 Net rental real estate income (loss)	
3 Other net rental income (loss)	16 Foreign transactions
4 Guaranteed payments	
5 Interest income	
6a Ordinary dividends 1,008	
6b Qualified dividends 1,008	
7 Royalties	
8 Net short-term capital gain (loss)	
9a Net long-term capital gain (loss)	17 Alternative minimum tax (AMT) items
9b Collectibles (28%) gain (loss)	
9c Unrecaptured section 1250 gain	
10 Net section 1231 gain (loss)	18 Tax-exempt income and nondeductible expenses
11 Other income (loss)	
	19 Distributions
12 Section 179 deduction	cash 150,000
13 Other deductions charitable contribution 1,500	20 Other information
14 Self-employment earnings (loss) 182,940	

*See attached statement for additional information.

For IRS Use Only

For Privacy Act and Paperwork Reduction Act Notice, see Instructions for Form 1065. Cat. No. 11394R Schedule K-1 (Form 1065) 2004

Self-Employment Income

Individual general partners are considered to be self-employed. Consequently, any guaranteed payments plus their distributive share of ordinary business income are net earnings from self-employment subject to SE tax.[36] Limited partners are not considered self-employed and are not required to pay self-employment tax on their distributive share of ordinary income.[37]

[36] §1402(a).

[37] §1402(a)(13).

EXHIBIT 9.4
(concluded)

Schedule K-1 (Form 1065) 2004 Page **2**

This list identifies the codes used on Schedule K-1 for all partners and provides summarized reporting information for partners who file Form 1040. For detailed reporting and filing information, see the separate Partner's Instructions for Schedule K-1 and the instructions for your income tax return.

1. **Ordinary business income (loss).** You must first determine whether the income (loss) is passive or nonpassive. Then enter on your return as follows:

	Enter on
Passive loss	See the Partner's Instructions
Passive income	Schedule E, line 28, column (g)
Nonpassive loss	Schedule E, line 28, column (h)
Nonpassive income	Schedule E, line 28, column (j)
2. **Net rental real estate income (loss)**	See the Partner's Instructions
3. **Other net rental income (loss)**	
Net income	Schedule E, line 28, column (g)
Net loss	See the Partner's Instructions
4. **Guaranteed payments**	Schedule E, line 28, column (j)
5. **Interest income**	Form 1040, line 8a
6a. **Ordinary dividends**	Form 1040, line 9a
6b. **Qualified dividends**	Form 1040, line 9b
7. **Royalties**	Schedule E, line 4
8. **Net short-term capital gain (loss)**	Schedule D, line 5, column (f)
9a. **Net long-term capital gain (loss)**	Schedule D, line 12, column (f)
9b. **Collectibles (28%) gain (loss)**	28% Rate Gain Worksheet, line 4 (Schedule D Instructions)
9c. **Unrecaptured section 1250 gain**	See the Partner's Instructions
10. **Net section 1231 gain (loss)**	See the Partner's Instructions
11. **Other income (loss)**	
Code	
A Other portfolio income (loss)	See the Partner's Instructions
B Involuntary conversions	See the Partner's Instructions
C Sec. 1256 contracts & straddles	Form 6781, line 1
D Mining exploration costs recapture	See Pub. 535
E Cancellation of debt	Form 1040, line 21 or Form 982
F Other income (loss)	See the Partner's Instructions
12. **Section 179 deduction**	See the Partner's Instructions
13. **Other deductions**	
A Cash contributions (50%)	Schedule A, line 15
B Cash contributions (30%)	Schedule A, line 15
C Noncash contributions (50%)	Schedule A, line 16
D Noncash contributions (30%)	Schedule A, line 16
E Capital gain property to a 50% organization (30%)	Schedule A, line 16
F Capital gain property (20%)	Schedule A, line 16
G Deductions—portfolio (2% floor)	Schedule A, line 22
H Deductions—portfolio (other)	Schedule A, line 27
I Investment interest expense	Form 4952, line 1
J Deductions—royalty income	Schedule E, line 18
K Section 59(e)(2) expenditures	See Partner's Instructions
L Amounts paid for medical insurance	Schedule A, line 1 or Form 1040, line 31
M Educational assistance benefits	See the Partner's Instructions
N Dependent care benefits	Form 2441, line 12
O Preproductive period expenses	See the Partner's Instructions
P Commercial revitalization deduction from rental real estate activities	See Form 8582 Instructions
Q Penalty on early withdrawal of savings	Form 1040, line 33
R Pensions and IRAs	See the Partner's Instructions
S Reforestation expense deduction	See the Partner's Instructions
T Other deductions	See the Partner's Instructions

14. **Self-employment earnings (loss)**

Note. *If you have a section 179 deduction or any partner-level deductions, see the Partner's Instructions before completing Schedule SE.*

A Net earnings (loss) from self-employment	Schedule SE, Section A or B
B Gross farming or fishing income	See the Partner's Instructions
C Gross non-farm income	See the Partner's Instructions
15. **Credits & credit recapture**	
A Low-income housing credit (section 42(j)(5))	Form 8586, line 5
B Low-income housing credit (other)	Form 8586, line 5
C Qualified rehabilitation expenditures (rental real estate)	Form 3468, line 1
D Qualified rehabilitation expenditures (other than rental real estate)	Form 3468, line 1
E Basis of energy property	Form 3468, line 2
F Qualified timber property	Form 3468, line 3
G Other rental real estate credits	See the Partner's Instructions
H Other rental credits	See the Partner's Instructions

Code	*Enter on*
I Undistributed capital gains credit	Form 1040, line 69, box a
J Work opportunity credit	Form 5884, line 3
K Welfare-to-work credit	Form 8861, line 3
L Disabled access credit	Form 8826, line 7
M Empowerment zone and renewal community employment credit	Form 8844, line 3
N New York Liberty Zone business employee credit	Form 8884, line 3
O New markets credit	Form 8874, line 2
P Credit for employer social security and Medicare taxes	Form 8846, line 5
Q Backup withholding	Form 1040, line 63
R Recapture of low-income housing credit (section 42(j)(5))	Form 8611, line 8
S Recapture of low-income housing credit (other)	Form 8611, line 8
T Recapture of investment credit	See Form 4255
U Other credits	See the Partner's Instructions
V Recapture of other credits	See the Partner's Instructions
16. **Foreign transactions**	
A Name of country or U.S. possession	Form 1116, Part I
B Gross income from all sources	Form 1116, Part I
C Gross income sourced at partner level	Form 1116, Part I
Foreign gross income sourced at partnership level	
D Passive	Form 1116, Part I
E Listed categories	Form 1116, Part I
F General limitation	Form 1116, Part I
Deductions allocated and apportioned at partner level	
G Interest expense	Form 1116, Part I
H Other	Form 1116, Part I
Deductions allocated and apportioned at partnership level to foreign source income	
I Passive	Form 1116, Part I
J Listed categories	Form 1116, Part I
K General limitation	Form 1116, Part I
Other information	
L Total foreign taxes paid	Form 1116, Part II
M Total foreign taxes accrued	Form 1116, Part II
N Reduction in taxes available for credit	Form 1116, line 12
O Foreign trading gross receipts	Form 8873
P Extraterritorial income exclusion	Form 8873
Q Other foreign transactions	See the Partner's Instructions
17. **Alternative minimum tax (AMT) items**	
A Post-1986 depreciation adjustment	See the Partner's Instructions and the Instructions for Form 6251
B Adjusted gain or loss	
C Depletion (other than oil & gas)	
D Oil, gas, & geothermal—gross income	
E Oil, gas, & geothermal—deductions	
F Other AMT items	
18. **Tax-exempt income and nondeductible expenses**	
A Tax-exempt interest income	Form 1040, line 8b
B Other tax-exempt income	See the Partner's Instructions
C Nondeductible expenses	See the Partner's Instructions
19. **Distributions**	
A Cash and marketable securities	See the Partner's Instructions
B Other property	See the Partner's Instructions
20. **Other information**	
A Investment income	Form 4952, line 4a
B Investment expenses	Form 4952, line 5
C Fuel tax credit information	Form 4136
D Look-back interest—completed long-term contracts	Form 8697
E Look-back interest—income forecast method	Form 8866
F Dispositions of property with section 179 deductions	See the Partner's Instructions
G Recapture of section 179 deduction	
H Special basis adjustments	
I Section 453(l)(3) information	
J Section 453A(c) information	
K Section 1260(b) information	
L Interest allocable to production expenditures	
M CCF nonqualified withdrawals	
N Information needed to figure depletion—oil and gas	
O Amortization of reforestation costs	
P Unrelated business taxable income	
Q Other information	

Self-Employment Income

Refer to Mr. Owen's Schedule K-1 from the Faux Antique partnership (Exhibit 9.4). Line 14 shows that Mr. Owen's $182,940 distributive share of business income represents net earnings from self-employment. Mr. Owen must report these earnings on a Schedule SE and compute his SE tax accordingly.

Comprehensive Example

To summarize our discussion of the tax consequences of partnerships, consider the case of ABC Partnership. This business is owned by three individual partners. Ms. Alton and Mr. Bach are general partners who work in the business, and Ms. Cole is a limited partner. The partnership agreement provides that Ms. Alton and Mr. Bach are each allocated 40 percent of income or loss, while Ms. Cole is allocated the remaining 20 percent. ABC pays a $3,000 monthly guaranteed payment to Ms. Alton and a $1,100 monthly guaranteed payment to Mr. Bach. For 2001, ABC's ordinary business income (after deducting the guaranteed payments) was $90,800. ABC also earned $3,300 interest income from a mutual bond fund investment. On December 24, ABC distributed $20,000 cash to its partners ($8,000 to Ms. Alton and Mr. Bach and $4,000 to Ms. Cole). ABC reported the following information on each partner's 2001 Schedule K-1.

ABC Partnership 2001 Schedule K-1s

	Ms. Alton	Mr. Bach	Ms. Cole
Guaranteed payments	$36,000	$13,200	–0–
Distributive shares:			
Ordinary business income	36,320	36,320	$18,160
Interest income	1,320	1,320	660
Net earnings from self-employment	72,320	49,520	–0–
Cash distribution	8,000	8,000	4,000

The partners included their guaranteed payments and their share of business and interest income in 2001 taxable income, and Ms. Alton and Mr. Bach paid SE tax on their net earnings from self-employment. Assuming that Ms. Alton was in a 28 percent marginal tax bracket and both Mr. Bach and Ms. Cole were in a 31 percent marginal tax bracket, each partner's after-tax cash flow from ABC is computed as follows.

ABC Partner Cash Flows

	Ms. Alton	Mr. Bach	Ms. Cole
Guaranteed payments	$36,000	$13,200	–0–
Cash distribution	8,000	8,000	$ 4,000
SE tax*	(10,218)	(6,997)	–0–
Income tax	(19,189)	(14,676)	(5,834)
After-tax cash flow	$14,593	$ (473)	$ (1,834)
Income tax calculation:			
Guaranteed payments	$36,000	$13,200	–0–
Ordinary business income	36,320	36,320	$18,160
Interest income	1,320	1,320	660
One-half SE tax	(5,109)	(3,499)	–0–
Taxable income	$68,531	$47,341	$18,820
	.28	.31	.31
Income tax	$19,189	$14,676	$ 5,834

*Self-employment tax based on 92.35 percent of net earnings from self-employment. See footnote 19.

Ms. Alton had positive cash flow from the partnership, but both Mr. Bach and Ms. Cole had negative cash flows. This cash flow information reflects the fact that the three partners paid tax on partnership profits that they did not withdraw as cash from the business.

Adjusting the Basis of a Partnership Interest

Objective 4
Adjust the tax basis in a partnership interest.

When a partner is allocated a share of partnership income but does not receive a cash distribution of that income, the partner is making an additional investment in the partnership. The partner should be entitled to recover this investment tax-free at some future date. When a partner receives a cash distribution, the distribution is treated as a nontaxable return of investment.[38] These investment increases and decreases are captured as positive and negative year-end adjustments to the tax basis in the partner's interest in the partnership.[39] Let's continue the comprehensive example by computing the ABC partners' basis adjustments for 2001.

ABC Partner Basis Adjustments for 2001*

	Ms. Alton	Mr. Bach	Ms. Cole
Adjusted basis on January 1	$35,000	$60,000	$100,000
Increased by:			
Ordinary business income	36,320	36,320	18,160
Interest income	1,320	1,320	660
Decreased by:			
Cash distribution	(8,000)	(8,000)	(4,000)
Adjusted basis on December 31	$64,640	$89,640	$114,820

*This comprehensive example ignores any changes in partnership liabilities that would affect the partners' basis.

When a partnership generates an ordinary business loss or a separately stated loss, each partner's share of the loss represents a decrease in the partner's investment that is captured as a negative basis adjustment. Year-end basis adjustments for losses are made after any adjustments for income items or cash distributions.[40]

To illustrate the negative basis adjustment for losses, assume that ABC Partnership generated a $99,200 operating loss (after deducting Ms. Alton's and Mr. Bach's guaranteed payments) in 2002. ABC earned $2,400 interest income and recognized a $19,600 capital loss on the sale of mutual fund shares. The partnership made no cash distributions to its partners. ABC reported the following information on each partner's 2002 Schedule K-1.

ABC Partnership 2002 Schedule K-1s

	Ms. Alton	Mr. Bach	Ms. Cole
Guaranteed payments	$36,000	$13,200	–0–
Distributive shares:			
Ordinary business loss	(39,680)	(39,680)	$(19,840)
Interest income	960	960	480
Capital loss	(7,840)	(7,840)	(3,920)
Net earnings from self-employment	(3,680)	(26,480)	–0–
Cash distribution	–0–	–0–	–0–

[38] §731(a) and §733. If a partner receives a cash distribution that exceeds the partner's basis, the excess distribution is recognized as capital gain.

[39] §705(a). Basis is also increased for a partner's distributive share of tax-exempt income.

[40] Reg. §1.705-1(a). Basis is also decreased by a partner's distributive share of nondeductible expenses.

The partners included their guaranteed payments and their share of interest income in 2002 taxable income. They also deducted their share of ordinary business loss and included their share of ABC's capital loss in their net capital gain or loss for 2002.[41] Because Ms. Alton and Mr. Bach had negative earnings from self-employment, they paid no SE tax for the year.

ABC Partner Basis Adjustments for 2002

	Ms. Alton	Mr. Bach	Ms. Cole
Adjusted basis on January 1	$64,640	$89,640	$114,820
Increased by:			
Interest income	960	960	480
Decreased by:			
Ordinary business loss	(39,680)	(39,680)	(19,840)
Capital loss	(7,840)	(7,840)	(3,920)
Adjusted basis on December 31	$18,080	$43,080	$ 91,540

Basis Limitation on Loss Deductions

Objective 5
Apply the basis limitation on the deduction of partnership losses.

As a general rule, partners may deduct their distributive share of partnership losses for the year. However, they must reduce the basis in their partnership interest by their share of losses, and the basis cannot be reduced below zero. If a partner's share of losses exceeds basis, the excess is not deductible in the current year.[42] The partner can carry the nondeductible loss forward indefinitely and can deduct it in a future year in which basis in the partnership interest is restored.

Suppose that ABC Partnership had another bad year in 2003. The partnership did not make any guaranteed payments to Ms. Alton or Mr. Bach. Even with this frugality, ABC's business generated a $160,000 operating loss. ABC did earn $3,000 interest income from its mutual fund and reported the following information on each partner's 2003 Schedule K-1.

ABC Partnership 2003 Schedule K-1s

	Ms. Alton	Mr. Bach	Ms. Cole
Guaranteed payments	–0–	–0–	–0–
Distributive shares:			
Ordinary business loss	$(64,000)	$(64,000)	$(32,000)
Interest income	1,200	1,200	600
Net earnings from self-employment	(64,000)	(64,000)	–0–
Cash distribution	–0–	–0–	–0–

Ms. Alton's and Mr. Bach's deduction for their share of loss is limited to the adjusted basis in their partnership interest immediately before the negative basis adjustment for the loss.

[41] This example assumes that the §465 at-risk limitation and the §469 passive activity loss limitation are inapplicable for all three partners. These limitations are discussed in Chapter 15.

[42] §704(d).

ABC Partner Basis Adjustments for 2003

	Ms. Alton	Mr. Bach	Ms. Cole
Adjusted basis on January 1	$ 18,080	$ 43,080	$ 91,540
Increased by:			
Interest income	1,200	1,200	600
Decreased by:			
Deductible loss	(19,280)	(44,280)	(32,000)
Adjusted basis on December 31	–0–	–0–	$ 60,140
Nondeductible loss carryforward	$(44,720)	$(19,720)	–0–

In 2003, all three partners must include their share of ABC's interest income in taxable income. Ms. Cole can deduct her entire $32,000 share of ABC's ordinary business loss. Ms. Alton can deduct only $19,280 and Mr. Bach can deduct only $44,280 of their share of loss. Ms. Alton and Mr. Bach can carry their nondeductible loss into future taxable years, but they must restore basis in their partnership interests to deduct the carryforward. These partners could easily create basis by investing more money in ABC Partnership. But if the partnership's business is failing (as the 2002 and 2003 losses suggest), Ms. Alton and Mr. Bach could lose their additional investment. In such case, they would have made the mistake of throwing good money after bad to secure a tax deduction. Of course, if ABC's business becomes profitable again, the partners' shares of future income will create basis against which Ms. Alton and Mr. Bach can deduct their loss carryforwards.

Let's complete our comprehensive example with one more year of ABC Partnership's operations. In 2004, the partnership generated $64,400 ordinary business income after deducting an $18,000 guaranteed payment to Ms. Alton and a $6,600 guaranteed payment to Mr. Bach. ABC earned $3,400 interest income and recognized an $11,000 capital gain on the sale of mutual fund shares. ABC reported the following information on each partner's 2004 Schedule K-1.

ABC Partnership 2004 Schedule K-1s

	Ms. Alton	Mr. Bach	Ms. Cole
Guaranteed payments	$18,000	$ 6,600	–0–
Distributive shares:			
Ordinary business income	25,760	25,760	$12,880
Interest income	1,360	1,360	680
Capital gain	4,400	4,400	2,200
Net earnings from self-employment	43,760	32,360	–0–
Cash distribution	–0–	–0–	–0–

The partners included their guaranteed payments and their share of business, interest, and capital gain in 2004 taxable income, and Ms. Alton and Mr. Bach paid SE tax on their net earnings from self-employment. The partners increased the basis in their partnership interests by their share of income, and, as a result, Ms. Alton could deduct $31,520 and Mr. Bach could deduct $19,720 of their 2003 loss carryforwards in the computation of 2004 taxable income. Ms. Alton has a $13,200 remaining loss carryforward that she can deduct to the extent of future increases in the basis in her ABC interest.

ABC Partner Basis Adjustments for 2004

	Ms. Alton	Mr. Bach	Ms. Cole
Adjusted basis on January 1	–0–	–0–	$60,140
Increased by:			
Ordinary business income	$25,760	$25,760	12,880
Interest income	1,360	1,360	680
Capital gain	4,400	4,400	2,200
	$ 31,520	$31,520	$75,900
Decreased by:			
Deductible loss carryforward	(31,520)	(19,720)	–0–
Adjusted basis on December 31	–0–	$11,800	$75,900
Remaining loss carryforward	$(13,200)	–0–	–0–

Limited Liability Companies

Objective 6
Explain how limited liability companies (LLCs) are treated for federal tax purposes.

Business owners often prefer the partnership form to the corporate form because partnership income is not taxed at the entity level but only at the owner level. The partnership form also provides the greatest flexibility in the manner in which business income can be divided among the co-owners. The major disadvantage of the partnership form is the unlimited personal liability of the general partners for business debt.

Every state (and the District of Columbia) permits business owners to organize as a **limited liability company (LLC)** as an alternative to a general or limited partnership. An LLC is an unincorporated legal entity owned by one or more *members.* In contrast to a partnership, every member has limited liability for the LLC's debts. This limited liability protects even those members who are actively involved in the LLC's business. State laws do not limit the number of members nor the type of entity that can be a member in an LLC. Thus, an LLC's membership can include individuals, partnerships, corporations, and even other LLCs.

Under Treasury regulations that classify business entities for federal tax purposes (the check-the-box regulations), an LLC with two or more members is classified as a partnership.[43] Consequently, income earned by an LLC is not taxed at the entity level but passes through to the various members. An LLC with only one member (i.e., one owner) is a *disregarded entity* for federal tax purposes. If the single member is an individual, the LLC is treated as a sole proprietorship. If the single member is an entity, the LLC is treated as a division or branch of the entity.

LLCs offer business owners a terrific combination: one owner-level tax on income and limited liability for business debt. Moreover, LLCs are not subject to many of the bothersome restrictions that apply to S corporations (our next topic). As a result, LLCs are an attractive option for business ventures. However, because LLCs are a relatively new organizational form, many tax questions concerning their operation have yet to be resolved. Business owners and their advisers must consider this element of uncertainty in making the decision to organize an LLC.

One major unresolved issue is the extent to which members are subject to self-employment tax on their LLC income. The self-employment tax statute was written before the advent of

[43] Reg. §301.7701-3(b)(1). Under this regulation, an LLC can elect to be classified as a corporation for federal tax purposes. There is no obvious reason why a domestic LLC would make such an election.

LLCs and is silent as to whether distributive shares of LLC business income are net earnings from self-employment. In 1997, the Treasury attempted to resolve this issue through proposed regulations.[44] The regulations contain elaborate rules for determining whether an LLC member may be regarded as a limited partner. If so, the member's share of LLC income is not self-employment income. If a member may not be regarded as a limited partner, both guaranteed payments and any share of LLC income are self-employment income. The tax professional community's reaction to these proposed regulations was extremely critical. Congress responded to the criticism by issuing a moratorium that prevented the Treasury from finalizing the 1997 regulations. To date, the Treasury has declined to make a second attempt to resolve this issue.

Self-Employment Income or Not?

Mrs. Miller is a member in Wooster LLC. She does not work for Wooster on a daily basis and does not receive any guaranteed payments. However, last year she worked about 175 hours during October and November on a special marketing campaign for Wooster. Mrs. Miller's share of Wooster's ordinary business income last year was $38,170. Since she is not involved in Wooster's business on a regular basis, Mrs. Miller could argue that she should be regarded as a limited partner and should not pay SE tax on her share of LLC income. However, the IRS could argue that Mrs. Miller did perform substantial personal services for the LLC and therefore should treat her LLC income as earned income subject to SE tax.

SUBCHAPTER S CORPORATIONS

Before the advent of LLCs, business owners who wanted to avoid both the corporate income tax and the risk of unlimited personal liability had only one choice: the **subchapter S corporation.** This form of business organization is a corporate entity, organized as such under state law.[45] A predominant characteristic of corporations is the limited liability of their shareholders. If a corporation gets into financial trouble and can't pay its debts, the corporate creditors have no claim against the personal assets of the shareholders. Thus, the shareholders' risk is limited to their investment in the corporation.

For federal tax purposes, a subchapter S corporation is a passthrough entity; its business income is allocated and taxed directly to the corporation's shareholders.[46] The statutory rules providing for this passthrough are almost identical to the partnership rules. The ordinary income or loss generated by an S corporation's business is reported on page 1 of Form 1120S (U.S. Income Tax Return for an S Corporation). This income or loss is allocated among the shareholders based on their percentage ownership of the corporation's outstanding stock.[47]

Faux Antique— S Corporation

Refer back to our earlier example involving Mr. Tom Owen and his antique furniture restoration business. Let's change the facts again by assuming that Mr. Owen and his two co-owners incorporated the business as Faux Antique, Inc., which is an S corporation for federal tax purposes. Tom Owen owns 60 percent of the outstanding stock. Faux Antique, Inc., generated $304,900 ordinary business income in 2004. Page 1 of the S corporation's Form 1120 is shown as Exhibit 9.5.

[44] Prop. Reg. §1.1402(a)-2(h).

[45] While a partnership must have at least two co-owners as partners, a corporation may be owned by one shareholder.

[46] §1363(a) and §1366.

[47] §1377(a).

EXHIBIT 9.5

Form **1120S** — Department of the Treasury, Internal Revenue Service

U.S. Income Tax Return for an S Corporation

▶ Do not file this form unless the corporation has timely filed Form 2553 to elect to be an S corporation.
▶ See separate instructions.

OMB No. 1545-0130 — **2004**

For calendar year 2004, or tax year beginning , 2004, and ending , 20

A Effective date of S election: 1990	Name: Faux Antique Inc.	C Employer identification number: 81 : 1138419
B Business code number (see pages 36–38 of the Insts.): 337000	Number, street, and room or suite no. (If a P.O. box, see page 12 of the instructions.): 1012 East Main	D Date incorporated: 1990
	City or town, state, and ZIP code: Widner Kentucky 42714	E Total assets (see page 12 of instructions): $ N/a

Use the IRS label. Otherwise, print or type.

F Check applicable boxes: (1) ☐ Initial return (2) ☐ Final return (3) ☐ Name change (4) ☐ Address change (5) ☐ Amended return
G Enter number of shareholders in the corporation at end of the tax year ▶ 3

Caution: *Include* ***only*** *trade or business income and expenses on lines 1a through 21. See page 13 of the instructions for more information.*

Income	1a	Gross receipts or sales 1,117,300 b Less returns and allowances 21,000 c Bal ▶		1c	1,096,300
	2	Cost of goods sold (Schedule A, line 8)		2	599,700
	3	Gross profit. Subtract line 2 from line 1c		3	496,600
	4	Net gain (loss) from Form 4797, Part II, line 17 *(attach Form 4797)*		4	
	5	Other income (loss) *(attach schedule)*		5	
	6	**Total income (loss).** Add lines 3 through 5 ▶		6	496,600
Deductions (see page 14 of the instructions for limitations)	7	Compensation of officers		7	
	8	Salaries and wages (less employment credits)		8	73,200
	9	Repairs and maintenance		9	17,900
	10	Bad debts		10	8,800
	11	Rents		11	23,200
	12	Taxes and licenses		12	11,750
	13	Interest		13	7,300
	14a	Depreciation *(attach Form 4562)*	14a 3,600		
	b	Depreciation claimed on Schedule A and elsewhere on return	14b		
	c	Subtract line 14b from line 14a		14c	3,600
	15	Depletion **(Do not deduct oil and gas depletion.)**		15	
	16	Advertising		16	6,200
	17	Pension, profit-sharing, etc., plans		17	
	18	Employee benefit programs. Prof. Fees. 2,150 supplies 18,000		18	
	19	Other deductions *(attach schedule)* utilities. 14,000 insurance 5,600		19	39,750
	20	**Total deductions.** Add the amounts shown in the far right column for lines 7 through 19 ▶		20	191,700
	21	Ordinary business income (loss). Subtract line 20 from line 6		21	304,900
Tax and Payments	22	**Tax:** a Excess net passive income tax *(attach schedule)*	22a		
	b	Tax from Schedule D (Form 1120S)	22b		
	c	Add lines 22a and 22b (see page 18 of the instructions for additional taxes)		22c	
	23	**Payments: a** 2004 estimated tax payments and amount applied from 2003 return	23a		
	b	Tax deposited with Form 7004	23b		
	c	Credit for Federal tax paid on fuels *(attach Form 4136)*	23c		
	d	Add lines 23a through 23c		23d	
	24	Estimated tax penalty (see page 18 of instructions). Check if Form 2220 is attached ▶☐		24	
	25	**Tax due.** If line 23d is smaller than the total of lines 22c and 24, enter amount owed		25	
	26	**Overpayment.** If line 23d is larger than the total of lines 22c and 24, enter amount overpaid		26	
	27	Enter amount of line 26 you want: **Credited to 2005 estimated tax** ▶ **Refunded** ▶		27	

Sign Here — Under penalties of perjury, I declare that I have examined this return, including accompanying schedules and statements, and to the best of my knowledge and belief, it is true, correct, and complete. Declaration of preparer (other than taxpayer) is based on all information of which preparer has any knowledge.

Signature of officer | Date | Title

May the IRS discuss this return with the preparer shown below (see instructions)? ☐ **Yes** ☐ **No**

Paid Preparer's Use Only — Preparer's signature | Date | Check if self-employed ☐ | Preparer's SSN or PTIN
Firm's name (or yours if self-employed), address, and ZIP code | EIN | Phone no. ( )

For Privacy Act and Paperwork Reduction Act Notice, see the separate instructions. Cat. No. 11510H Form **1120S** (2004)

If an S corporation recognizes items of income, gain, deduction, or loss that don't relate to ordinary business operations, these items are separately stated on Schedule K of Form 1120S and retain their tax character as they flow through to the shareholders.

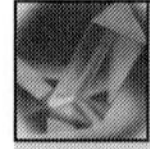

Separately Stated Items

Faux Antique, Inc., received a $1,680 dividend and made a $2,500 United Way donation in 2004. (These are the two separately stated items included in the earlier partnership example.) Assume also that the S corporation recognized a $3,710 gain on the sale of mutual funds shares acquired four years ago. None of these items is included in the computation of ordinary business income.

Eligible Corporations

Objective 7
Determine if a corporation is eligible to be an S corporation.

Only domestic corporations formed under the law of one of the 50 states or the District of Columbia are eligible to be S corporations for federal tax purposes. Eligibility is based on three statutory requirements.[48]

1. Only individuals, estates, certain trusts, and tax-exempt organizations may be shareholders, and nonresident aliens (persons who are neither citizens nor permanent residents of the United States) cannot be shareholders. This requirement ensures that the S corporation's income is taxed at the individual rates.
2. The number of shareholders is limited to 100. A family may elect for all family members to be treated as one shareholder.
3. The corporation can have only a single class of outstanding common stock; an S corporation cannot include preferred stock in its capital structure. Because of this requirement, shares of stock in an S corporation carry identical rights to corporate profits and assets. This requirement is not violated if the outstanding shares have different voting rights.

There are no statutory limits on an S corporation's invested capital, volume of sales, or number of employees. Consequently, S corporations can be very large corporate enterprises.

Subchapter S Election

An eligible corporation becomes an S corporation by the unanimous election of its shareholders.[49] The election is permanent for the life of the corporation unless shareholders owning a majority of the stock revoke the election.[50] The election is immediately terminated if the corporation loses its eligibility. For example, if a shareholder sells shares to a partnership (an ineligible shareholder), the election terminates as of the date of sale.[51] The corporation is no longer a passthrough entity and is subject to the corporate income tax.

The inadvertent termination of an S election can be a tax planning disaster for the shareholders. Moreover, they generally cannot make a new election for five years.[52] Because of the potential severity of the problem, the tax law provides a relief measure. If shareholders discover that an inadvertent termination has occurred and take immediate steps to correct the situation (repurchase the corporate stock from the partnership in our example), the IRS may allow the original S election to remain in effect.[53]

Tax Basis in S Corporation Stock

A shareholder's initial tax basis in stock issued by an S corporation equals the cash plus the adjusted basis of any property transferred to the corporation in exchange for the stock.[54] When an S corporation incurs a debt, no shareholder has any personal liability.

[48] §1361. Corporations that have been operating as regular corporations and that meet the eligibility requirements can be converted to S corporations. Converted S corporations are subject to several troublesome corporate level taxes that don't apply to original S corporations. See §1374 and §1375.

[49] §1362(a). To document consent to the election, each shareholder must file a signed Form 2553 with the IRS.

[50] §1362(d)(1).

[51] §1362(e)(1).

[52] §1362(g).

[53] §1362(f).

[54] The transfer of property to a corporation in exchange for stock is nontaxable to the transferors if they have at least 80 percent control of the corporation immediately after the transfer. §351. See the discussion of corporate formations in Chapter 8.

Accordingly, no S corporation debt is included in a shareholder's stock basis, even if the shareholder has guaranteed the debt.

Basis in S Corporation Stock

Three individuals each contributed $10,000 cash to form a new S corporation. Each individual received 100 shares of the 300 shares of outstanding stock. The S corporation immediately borrowed $24,000 from a local bank and used the money to purchase equipment and supplies. The bank required the shareholders to personally guarantee repayment of the loan. Each shareholder's basis in her S corporation stock is $10,000: the initial cash contribution to the corporation.

Tax Consequences to Shareholders

After the close of its taxable year, an S corporation issues a Schedule K-1 (Shareholder's Share of Income, Credits, Deductions, etc.) to each shareholder. The Schedule K-1 has the same function as a partnership Schedule K-1; it informs the owners of their share of business income or loss as well as their share of any separately stated item.

The S corporation shareholders must incorporate the information on Schedule K-1 into their individual tax returns. Thus, the corporate income is taxed at the individual rates, and the shareholders pay the tax. The cash (if any) that the shareholders received from the corporation is irrelevant in determining their taxable income.

S Corporation Schedule K-1

Each shareholder in Faux Antique, Inc., received a Schedule K-1 reporting a share of ordinary business income, dividend income, charitable donation, and capital gain. As a 60 percent shareholder, Tom Owen had a $182,940 share of ordinary business income, a $1,008 share of the dividend, a $1,500 share of the donation, and a $2,226 share of the capital gain. Mr. Owen's Schedule K-1 is shown as Exhibit 9.6. According to line 16, the S corporation distributed $150,000 cash to Mr. Owen during 2004. This cash from the business is irrelevant to the computation of his taxable income.

Salary Payments

A significant difference between partnerships and S corporations is that an owner (shareholder) can be an employee of the corporation. Shareholders who work in the corporate business receive salaries as compensation for their services. Both the corporation and the employee pay the FICA payroll tax on the salary, and the corporation withholds federal income tax. At the end of the year, the corporation issues a Schedule K-1 and a Form W-2 to any shareholder/employee. S corporation shareholders are not considered to be self-employed. Therefore, their share of corporate business income is not subject to self-employment tax.

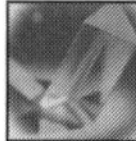

Payments to Shareholder/ Employees

Milo Todd owns 20 percent of the stock in Sussex Inc., a calendar year S corporation, and is employed as the corporation's CEO. This year, Milo's salary from Sussex was $75,000, from which Sussex withheld both employee FICA tax and state and local income tax. Sussex's ordinary business income (after deduction of all employee compensation) was $984,000, and Milo's share of this income was $196,800. Milo received a $160,000 cash distribution from Sussex with respect to his stock. Milo must include $271,800 ($75,000 salary + $196,800 share of corporate income) in taxable income. The $160,000 cash distribution has no effect on Milo's taxable income.

EXHIBIT 9.6

6711

☐ Final K-1 ☐ Amended K-1 OMB No. 1545-0130

Schedule K-1 (Form 1120S) **2004**

Department of the Treasury
Internal Revenue Service

Tax year beginning Jan. 1, 2004 and ending Dec. 31, 2004

Shareholder's Share of Income, Deductions, Credits, etc. ▶ See back of form and separate instructions.

Part I Information About the Corporation

A Corporation's employer identification number
81 1138419

B Corporation's name, address, city, state, and ZIP code
Faux Antique Inc.
1012 East Main
Widner Kentucky
42714

C IRS Center where corporation filed return
Cincinnati

D ☐ Tax shelter registration number, if any

E ☐ Check if Form 8271 is attached

Part II Information About the Shareholder

F Shareholder's identifying number
497-45-9058

G Shareholder's name, address, city, state and ZIP code
Tom G. Owen
330 Aspen Lane
Widner Kentucky
42714

H Shareholder's percentage of stock ownership for tax year . . . . 60 %

For IRS Use Only

Part III Shareholder's Share of Current Year Income, Deductions, Credits, and Other Items

1 Ordinary business income (loss)	182,940	13 Credits & credit recapture	
2 Net rental real estate income (loss)			
3 Other net rental income (loss)			
4 Interest income			
5a Ordinary dividends	1,008		
5b Qualified dividends	1,008	14 Foreign transactions	
6 Royalties			
7 Net short-term capital gain (loss)			
8a Net long-term capital gain (loss)	2,226		
8b Collectibles (28%) gain (loss)			
8c Unrecaptured section 1250 gain			
9 Net section 1231 gain (loss)			
10 Other income (loss)		15 Alternative minimum tax (AMT) items	
11 Section 179 deduction		16 Items affecting shareholder basis	cash distribution 150,000
12 Other deductions	charitable contribution 1,500		
		17 Other information	

* See attached statement for additional information.

For Privacy Act and Paperwork Reduction Act Notice, see Instructions for Form 1120S. Cat. No. 11520D Schedule K-1 (Form 1120S) 2004

Adjusting the Basis of S Corporation Stock

Shareholders make positive and negative adjustments to the basis in their S corporation stock in much the same way as partners adjust the basis in their partnership interests.[55] Specifically, shareholders increase the basis in their stock by their share of the corporation's income and gain for the year. Conversely, shareholders reduce the basis by their share of any corporate losses. Cash distributed by an S corporation to a shareholder is a nontaxable return of investment that reduces stock basis.[56]

[55] §1367(a).

[56] Salary payments to shareholder/employees have no effect on stock basis. If a shareholder receives a cash distribution that exceeds stock basis, the excess distribution is recognized as a capital gain. §1368.

EXHIBIT 9.6
(concluded)

Schedule K-1 (Form 1120S) 2004 Page **2**

This list identifies the codes used on Schedule K-1 for all shareholders and provides summarized reporting information for shareholders who file Form 1040. For detailed reporting and filing information, see the separate Shareholder's Instructions for Schedule K-1 and the instructions for your income tax return.

	Enter on
1. Ordinary business income (loss). You must first determine whether the income (loss) is passive or nonpassive. Then enter on your return as follows:	
Passive loss	See the Shareholder's Instructions
Passive income	Schedule E, line 28, column (g)
Nonpassive loss	Schedule E, line 28, column (h)
Nonpassive income	Schedule E, line 28, column (j)
2. Net rental real estate income (loss)	See the Shareholder's Instructions
3. Other net rental income (loss)	
Net income	Schedule E, line 28, column (g)
Net loss	See the Shareholder's Instructions
4. Interest income	Form 1040, line 8a
5a. Ordinary dividends	Form 1040, line 9a
5b. Qualified dividends	Form 1040, line 9b
6. Royalties	Schedule E, line 4
7. Net short-term capital gain (loss)	Schedule D, line 5, column (f)
8a. Net long-term capital gain (loss)	Schedule D, line 12, column (f)
8b. Collectibles (28%) gain (loss)	28% Rate Gain Worksheet, line 4 (Schedule D instructions)
8c. Unrecaptured section 1250 gain	See the Shareholder's Instructions
9. Net section 1231 gain (loss)	See the Shareholder's Instructions
10. Other income (loss)	
Code	
A Other portfolio income (loss)	See the Shareholder's Instructions
B Involuntary conversions	See the Shareholder's Instructions
C 1256 contracts & straddles	Form 6781, line 1
D Mining exploration costs recapture	See Pub. 535, Chap. 8
E Other income (loss)	See the Shareholder's Instructions
11. Section 179 deduction	See the Shareholder's Instructions
12. Other deductions	
A Cash contributions (50%)	Schedule A, line 15
B Cash contributions (30%)	Schedule A, line 15
C Noncash contributions (50%)	Schedule A, line 16
D Noncash contributions (30%)	Schedule A, line 16
E Capital gain property to a 50% organization (30%)	Schedule A, line 16
F Capital gain property (20%)	Schedule A, line 16
G Deductions—portfolio (2% floor)	Schedule A, line 22
H Deductions—portfolio (other)	Schedule A, line 27
I Investment interest expense	Form 4952, line 1
J Deductions—royalty income	Schedule E, line 18
K Section 59(e)(2) expenditures	See the Shareholder's Instructions
L Reforestation expense deduction	See the Shareholder's Instructions
M Preproductive period expenses	See the Shareholder's Instructions
N Commercial revitalization deduction from rental real estate activities	See Form 8582 Instructions
O Penalty on early withdrawal of savings	Form 1040, line 33
P Other deductions	See the Shareholder's Instructions
13. Credits & credit recapture	
A Low-income housing credit (section 42(j)(5))	Form 8586, line 5
B Low-income housing credit (other)	Form 8586, line 5
C Qualified rehabilitation expenditures (rental real estate)	Form 3468, line 1
D Qualified rehabilitation expenditures (other than rental real estate)	Form 3468, line 1
E Basis of energy property	Form 3468, line 2
F Qualified timber property	Form 3468, line 3
G Other rental real estate credits	See the Shareholder's Instructions
H Other rental credits	See the Shareholder's Instructions
I Undistributed capital gains credit	Form 1040, line 69, box a
J Work opportunity credit	Form 5884, line 3
K Welfare-to-Work credit	Form 8861, line 3
Code	Enter on
L Disabled access credit	Form 8826, line 7
M Empowerment zone and renewal community employment credit	Form 8844, line 3
N New York Liberty Zone business employee credit	Form 8884, line 3
O New markets credit	Form 8874, line 2
P Credit for employer social security and Medicare taxes	Form 8846, line 5
Q Backup withholding	Form 1040, line 63
R Credit for alcohol used as fuel	Form 6478, line 10
S Recapture of low-income housing credit (section 42(j)(5))	Form 8611, line 8
T Recapture of low-income housing credit (other)	Form 8611, line 8
U Recapture of investment credit	See Form 4255
V Other credits	See the Shareholder's Instructions
W Recapture of other credits	See the Shareholder's Instructions
14. Foreign transactions	
A Name of country or U.S. possession	Form 1116, Part I
B Gross income from all sources	Form 1116, Part I
C Gross income sourced at shareholder level	Form 1116, Part I
Foreign gross income sourced at corporate level	
D Passive	Form 1116, Part I
E Listed categories	Form 1116, Part I
F General limitation	Form 1116, Part I
Deductions allocated and apportioned at shareholder level	
G Interest expense	Form 1116, Part I
H Other	Form 1116, Part I
Deductions allocated and apportioned at corporate level to foreign source income	
I Passive	Form 1116, Part I
J Listed categories	Form 1116, Part I
K General limitation	Form 1116, Part I
Other information	
L Total foreign taxes paid	Form 1116, Part II
M Total foreign taxes accrued	Form 1116, Part II
N Reduction in taxes available for credit	Form 1116, line 12
O Foreign trading gross receipts	Form 8873
P Extraterritorial income exclusion	Form 8873
Q Other foreign transactions	See the Shareholder's Instructions
15. Alternative minimum tax (AMT) items	
A Post-1986 depreciation adjustment	See the Shareholder's Instructions and the instructions for Form 6251
B Adjusted gain or loss	
C Depletion (other than oil & gas)	
D Oil, gas, & geothermal properties—gross income	
E Oil, gas, & geothermal properties—deductions	
F Other AMT items	
16. Items affecting shareholder basis	
A Tax-exempt interest income	Form 1040, line 8b
B Other tax-exempt income	See the Shareholder's Instructions
C Nondeductible expenses	See the Shareholder's Instructions
D Property distributions	See the Shareholder's Instructions
E Repayment of loans from shareholders	See the Shareholder's Instructions
17. Other information	
A Investment income	Form 4952, line 4a
B Investment expenses	Form 4952, line 5
C Look-back interest—completed long-term contracts	See Form 8697
D Look-back interest—income forecast method	See Form 8866
E Dispositions of property with section 179 deductions	See the Shareholder's Instructions
F Recapture of section 179 deduction	See the Shareholder's Instructions
G Section 453(l)(3) information	See the Shareholder's Instructions
H Section 453A(c) information	See the Shareholder's Instructions
I Section 1260(b) information	See the Shareholder's Instructions
J Interest allocable to production expenditures	See the Shareholder's Instructions
K CCF nonqualified withdrawal	See the Shareholder's Instructions
L Information needed to figure depletion—oil and gas	See the Shareholder's Instructions
M Amortization of reforestation costs	See the Shareholder's Instructions
N Other information	See the Shareholder's Instructions

Basis Limitation on Loss Deductions

Objective 8
Contrast the basis limitation for S corporation losses with the basis limitation for partnership losses.

The tax law imposes the same limitation on S corporation losses as it does on partnership losses: Such losses are currently deductible only to the extent of the owner's investment. Under the limitation rule for S corporations, a shareholder can deduct an amount of loss that reduces his stock basis to zero.[57] If a shareholder also has basis in any debt obligation

[57] §1366(d)(1)(A).

from the S corporation, the shareholder may deduct additional loss to reduce the debt basis to zero.[58] In other words, a shareholder's investment that can be recovered through tax deductions includes both his equity investment *and* his investment as a corporate creditor.

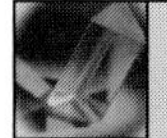

Nondeductible S Corporation Loss

Ms. Jentz owns 25 percent of the outstanding stock of SGM, a calendar year S corporation. At the beginning of 2004, Ms. Jentz's basis in her stock was $81,000. Several years ago, Ms. Jentz loaned $30,000 to SGM in return for its interest-bearing note. For 2004, SGM incurred a $500,000 operating loss. Although Ms. Jentz's Schedule K-1 reflects a $125,000 loss, Ms. Jentz can deduct only $111,000 of the loss on her Form 1040.

	Stock Basis	*Note Basis*
Beginning of year	$ 81,000	$30,000
Deductible loss	(81,000)	(30,000)
End of year	–0–	–0–
Nondeductible loss	$(14,000)	

Ms. Jentz's $14,000 nondeductible loss is carried forward into future years. If she creates basis by making an additional investment in SGM as either a shareholder or a creditor, she can deduct the loss to the extent of the additional basis. Alternatively, if SGM generates future income, Ms. Jentz's share of *undistributed* income will first increase the basis in her note to its $30,000 face amount and will then increase her stock basis.[59] Ms. Jentz can deduct her loss carryforward to the extent of her restored basis.

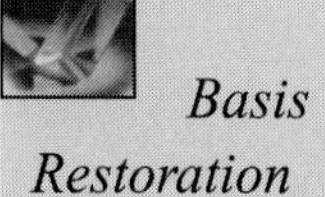

Basis Restoration

Ms. Jentz's 25 percent share of SGM's 2005 income is $50,000. The corporation made no cash distributions during the year. The undistributed income increases Ms. Jentz's investment basis and allows her to deduct the $14,000 loss carryforward from 2004 on her 2005 return.

	Stock Basis	*Note Basis*
Beginning of year	–0–	–0–
Share of income:		
Increase to note basis		$30,000
Increase to stock basis	$20,000	
	$20,000	$30,000
Loss carryforward from 2004	(14,000)	
End of year	$ 6,000	$30,000

Because of the deduction for her loss carryforward, Ms. Jentz's 2005 taxable income includes only $36,000 SGM income.

If SGM were to repay the $30,000 loan from Ms. Jentz before her basis in the note was restored to its face amount, the repayment is treated as an amount realized on sale of the

[58] §1366(d)(1)(B).

[59] §1367(b)(2).

note. Because the note is a capital asset to Ms. Jentz, she would recognize a capital gain equal to the excess of the repayment over her basis.[60]

Gain on Repayment of Debt

Change the facts in the previous example by assuming that SGM retired its debt to Ms. Jentz by paying her $30,000 (plus accrued interest) on June 30, 2005. Assume also that SGM distributed $50,000 cash to Ms. Jentz to match her $50,000 share of 2005 income. In this case, Ms. Jentz had no 2005 *undistributed* income to restore basis in either her SGM note or her SGM stock. Consequently, she must recognize a $30,000 long-term capital gain on repayment of the note and cannot deduct any of her 2004 loss carryforward.

Conclusion

In this chapter, we've examined the tax consequences of operating a business as a sole proprietorship or as a passthrough entity. In the case of a sole proprietorship, the business income is included in the owner's taxable income and taxed at the individual rates. In the case of a general or limited partnership, LLC, or S corporation, the business income is allocated to the owners of the entity. The income is taxed directly to the partners, members, or shareholders at their marginal rate. Many owners deliberately use these organizational forms to avoid paying an entity level tax on business income. This tax strategy is one of the topics covered in Chapter 11. Before we can evaluate this strategy, we must examine the tax consequences of operating a business as a regular corporation.

[60] §1271(a)(1) and Rev. Rul. 64-162, 1964-1 CB 304.

Key Terms

distributive share *237*
employee payroll tax *231*
employer identification number *230*
employer payroll tax *230*
general partnership *234*
guaranteed payment *237*
limited liability company (LLC) *244*
limited liability partnership (LLP) *234*
limited partnership *234*
partnership *233*
passthrough entity *235*
self-employment (SE) tax *232*
separately stated item *235*
sole proprietorship *226*
subchapter S corporation *245*

Questions and Problems for Discussion

1. Can a sole proprietorship be described as a passthrough entity?
2. Mrs. L owns a business as a sole proprietor. Near the end of her taxable year, she is evaluating a new opportunity that would generate $25,000 additional income for her business. What marginal tax rate should Mrs. L use to compute the tax cost of this opportunity?
3. This year, Mr. P's sole proprietorship generated a $17,000 net loss. Can Mr. P use this loss as an net operating loss carryback deduction?
4. This year, Firm Q, a cash basis taxpayer, remitted $26,800 FICA payroll tax to the federal government. However, the firm deducted only $13,400 FICA tax on its income tax return. Can you explain this apparent inconsistency?
5. Critique the employee payroll tax on the normative standards of convenience to the taxpayer and vertical equity.
6. Define the tax base for the self-employment tax. When do sole proprietors pay the self-employment tax to the federal government?
7. Why is only half of a sole proprietor's self-employment tax deductible in the computation of taxable income?

8. Mrs. G, Mr. Y, and Ms. N want to become co-owners of a business enterprise. Compare their personal liability for the debts incurred by the enterprise if they organize as:
   a. A general partnership.
   b. A limited partnership.
   c. An LLC.
   d. An S corporation.
9. Why are certain items of income, gain, deduction, or loss separately stated on a partnership or an S corporation tax return?
10. This year, Soya Partnership disposed of only one operating asset and recognized a \$22,000 loss on the disposition. Why must Soya report this net Section 1231 loss as a separately stated item rather than deducting the loss in the computation of ordinary business income?
11. Mr. A and Mr. Z are both sole proprietors. This year, each proprietorship generated \$85,000 net cash flow from business operations. Mr. A used the cash to expand his business, while Mr. Z used the cash to make the down payment on a new home for his family. Discuss how the different uses of cash affect each man's federal income tax for the year.
12. Four years ago, Mr. JB purchased 1,000 shares of UPF Inc. for \$10,000. These shares represent a 30 percent equity interest in UPF, which is an S corporation. This year, UPF defaulted on a \$120,000 unsecured debt to a major creditor.
    a. To what extent can the creditor demand repayment of the debt from Mr. JB?
    b. Would your answer change if UPF is a partnership in which Mr. JB is a 30 percent general partner?
    c. Would your answer change if UPF is a partnership in which Mr. JB is a 30 percent limited partner?
    d. Would your answer change if UPF is an LLC in which Mr. JB is a 30 percent member?
13. Mr. Y sold his interest in a business to an unrelated purchaser for \$500,000 cash. How does Mr. Y determine his adjusted basis for purposes of computing gain or loss realized on the sale if the business is:
    a. A sole proprietorship?
    b. A partnership?
    c. An S corporation?
14. Corporation ABC sold its 18 percent interest in KK Partnership on October 9 for \$150,000. KK Partnership uses a calendar year for tax purposes. Explain the reason why Corporation ABC cannot compute gain or loss realized on the date that the sale occurs.

Application Problems

1. Mrs. R is a self-employed professional singer. She resides in a rented apartment and uses one room exclusively as a business office. This room includes 172 of the 1,430 square feet of living space in the apartment. Mrs. R performs in recording studios and concert halls, but she conducts all of the administrative duties with respect to the business in her home office. This year, Mrs. R's apartment rent was \$36,000. She paid \$4,900 to a housekeeping service that cleaned the entire apartment once a week and \$1,130 for renter's insurance on the apartment furnishings. Compute Mrs. R's home office deduction assuming that:
   a. Her net profit from the business before the deduction was \$319,750.
   b. Her net profit from the business before the deduction was \$4,000.

2. Mr. C, a self-employed consultant, uses a room of his home as a business office. This room represents 10 percent of the home's square footage. This year, Mr. C incurred the following expenses in connection with his home.

Home mortgage interest	$12,980
Property tax on residence	2,200
Homeowner's insurance	1,475
Utilities	2,100
Furnace repairs	300

   Mr. C purchased the home in 1992 for $225,000. For MACRS depreciation purposes, he allocated $185,000 to the building and $40,000 to the land.

   a. If Mr. C's gross business income exceeded his operating expenses by $75,000, compute his net profit for the year.
   b. If Mr. C's gross business income exceeded his operating expenses by $1,800, compute his net profit for the year.

3. Mr. W is employed by BDF Inc. Compute BDF's 2005 employer payroll tax with respect to Mr. W assuming that:

   a. His annual compensation is $60,000.
   b. His annual compensation is $200,000.

4. Refer to the facts in the preceding problem. Assume that in the year 2006, the Social Security base amount increases to $96,000. Compute BDF's 2006 employer payroll tax with respect to Mr. W assuming that:

   a. His annual compensation is $60,000.
   b. His annual compensation is $200,000.

5. Mrs. S owns a profitable sole proprietorship. For each of the following cases, use a Schedule SE, Form 1040, to compute her 2004 self-employment tax and her income tax deduction for such tax.

   a. Mrs. S's net profit from Schedule C was $51,458. She had no other earned income.
   b. Mrs. S's net profit from Schedule C was $51,458, and she received a $50,000 salary from an employer.
   c. Mrs. S's net profit from Schedule C was $12,685, and she received a $94,000 salary from an employer.

6. This year, Ms. W's sole proprietorship, WW Bookstore, generated $120,000 net profit. In addition, Ms. W recognized a $17,000 gain on the sale of business furniture and shelving, all of which was recaptured as ordinary income. The business checking account earned $960 interest income.

   a. Which of these income items are subject to self-employment tax?
   b. Assuming that Ms. W's self-employment tax for the year is $14,300, compute her taxable income from her bookstore activity.

7. Ms. JC recently graduated from veterinary school and opened her own professional practice. This year, her net profit was $32,000. Compute Ms. JC's after-tax income from her practice assuming:

   a. Her self-employment tax is $4,522, and her marginal income tax rate is 25 percent.
   b. What percentage of the federal tax burden on Ms. JC's business income is represented by the self-employment tax?

8. Ms. J is a self-employed attorney. This year, her net profit exceeded $250,000, which put her in the 35 percent tax bracket. Early in the year, Ms. J hired Mr. B as a paralegal and paid him a $33,000 salary.
   a. Compute the employer payroll tax on Mr. B's salary.
   b. In addition to the employer payroll tax, Ms. J paid $400 unemployment tax on Mr. B's salary. The salary and tax expense reduced Ms. J's net earnings from self-employment, thereby saving $962 in self-employment tax. Compute Ms. J's after-tax cost of hiring Mr. B.
9. AB Corporation and YZ Corporation formed a partnership to construct a shopping mall. AB contributed $500,000 cash and YZ contributed land ($500,000 FMV and $430,000 basis) in exchange for a 50 percent interest in ABYZ Partnership. Immediately after its formation, ABYZ borrowed $250,000 from a local bank. The debt is recourse (unsecured by any specific partnership asset). Compute each partner's initial basis in its partnership interest, assuming that:
   a. AB and YX are both general partners.
   b. AB is a general partner, and YZ is a limited partner.
10. This year, FGH Partnership generated $600,000 ordinary business income. FGH has two equal partners: Triad LLC and Beta, an S corporation. Triad LLC has three members: Mr. T, who owns a 40 percent interest; Mrs. U, who owns a 35 percent interest; and V Inc., which owns a 25 percent interest. Beta has 100 shares of outstanding stock, all of which are owned by Ms. B. Identify the taxpayers who must pay tax on the partnership income and determine how much income must be reported by each.
11. KLMN Partnership's financial records show the following.

Gross receipts from sales	$670,000
Cost of goods sold	(460,000)
Operating expenses	(96,800)
Business meals and entertainment	(6,240)
Section 1231 loss on equipment sale	(13,500)
Charitable contribution	(1,500)
Distributions to partners	(10,000)

   Compute KLMN's ordinary business income for the year.
12. Refer to the facts in the preceding problem. Mr. T is a 10 percent general partner in KLMN. During the year, he received a $1,000 cash distribution from KLMN.
   a. Compute Mr. T's share of partnership ordinary income and separately stated items.
   b. If Mr. T's adjusted basis in his KLMN interest was $45,000 at the beginning of the year, compute his adjusted basis at the end of the year. Assume that KLMN's debt did not change during the year.
   c. How would your basis computation change if KLMN's debt at the end of the year was $28,000 more than its debt at the beginning of the year?
13. This year, individual X and individual Y formed XY Partnership. X contributed $50,000 cash, and Y contributed business assets with a $50,000 FMV. Y's adjusted basis in these assets was only $10,000. The partnership agreement provides that income and loss will be divided equally between the two partners. Partnership operations for the year generated a $42,000 loss. How much loss may each partner deduct currently, and what basis will each partner have in her interest at the beginning of next year?

14. AV Inc. is a member of an LLC. This year, AV received a Schedule K-1 reporting a $1,200 share of capital loss and a $4,000 share of Section 1231 gain. During the year, AV recognized a $5,000 capital loss on the sale of marketable securities and a $17,000 Section 1231 loss on the sale of business equipment. What effect do the LLC losses have on AV's taxable income?
15. Mr. B and Ms. G are equal general partners in BG Partnership. Mr. B receives a $4,000 monthly guaranteed payment for services. This year, BG generated $95,000 profit (before consideration of Mr. B's guaranteed payments).
    a. Compute each partner's distributive share of ordinary business income.
    b. Compute each partner's self-employment income.
    c. How would your answers change if BG's profit was only $32,000 instead of $95,000?
16. Mrs. Z owns a 60 percent general interest in YZ Partnership. At the beginning of 2003, the adjusted basis in her YZ interest was $95,000. For 2003, YZ generated a $210,000 business loss, earned $14,600 dividend and interest income on its investments, and recognized a $6,200 capital gain. YZ made no distributions to its partners and had no debt.
    a. How much of her share of YZ's loss can Mrs. Z deduct on her 2003 return?
    b. Compute Mrs. Z's adjusted basis in her YZ interest at the end of 2003.
    c. Would your answers change if Mrs. Z received a $5,000 cash distribution from YZ during 2003?
17. Refer to the facts in the preceding problem. In 2004, YZ generated $7,000 ordinary business income and $18,000 dividend and interest income. The partnership made no distributions. At the end of the year, YZ had $21,000 debt.
    a. How much partnership income will Mrs. Z report on her 2004 return?
    b. Compute Mrs. Z's adjusted basis in her YZ interest at the end of 2004.
18. At the beginning of 2004, Ms. P purchased a 20 percent interest in PPY Partnership for $20,000. Ms. P's Schedule K-1 reported that her share of PPY's debt at year-end was $12,000 and her share of 2004 ordinary loss was $28,000. On January 1, 2005, Ms. P sold her interest to another partner for $2,000 cash.
    a. How much of her share of PPY's loss can Ms. P deduct on her 2004 tax return?
    b. Compute Ms. P's recognized gain on sale of her PPY interest.
19. On January 1, 2004, Mr. L paid $15,000 for 5 percent of the stock in BLS, an S corporation. In November, he loaned $8,000 to BLS in return for a promissory note. BLS generated a $600,000 operating loss in 2004.
    a. How much of his share of the loss can Mr. L deduct on his 2004 tax return?
    b. Compute Mr. L's basis in his BLS stock and his BLS note at the beginning of 2005.
20. Refer to the facts in the preceding example. BLS generated $408,000 ordinary business income in 2005.
    a. How much of Mr. L's share of this income is included in his 2005 taxable income?
    b. Compute Mr. L's basis in his BLS stock and his BLS note at the beginning of 2006.
    c. How would your answers change if BLS's ordinary business income was only $220,000?
21. Refer to the facts in part *(c)* of the preceding problem. In 2006, BLS repaid its $8,000 debt to Mr. L before he restored any basis in the debt. What are the consequences of the loan repayment to Mr. L?

Issue Recognition Problems

Identify the tax issue or issues suggested by the following situations and state each issue in the form of a question.

1. Mrs. E has operated a sole proprietorship for six years during which net profit has been stable and Mrs. E's marginal tax rate has been a constant 25 percent. Mrs. E projects that her profit next year will be the same as this year. Consequently, she estimates her tax cost for next year based on a 25 percent rate. Late in the year, Mrs. E's husband graduated from law school and accepted an excellent offer of employment from a local firm.
2. Mr. J is a full-time employee of B Inc. and also operates a sole proprietorship. This year, his salary was $70,000 and his net earnings from self-employment were $60,000.
3. Mr. and Mrs. C file a joint income tax return. Mr. C reports the income from his full-time landscaping business on a Schedule C, which lists him as the sole proprietor. He also reports 100 percent of the net profit as his self-employment income and pays SE tax accordingly. During the last several years, Mrs. C has worked at least 20 hours per week in her husband's business. However, Mr. C does not pay her any salary or wage for her services.
4. Mr. T is a professional writer who maintains his business office in one room of his personal residence. The office contains Mr. T's desk, filing cabinets, personal computer and printer, copying machine, phone system, and fax machine. It also contains his family's library of video tapes, music CDs, popular novels, and the set of encyclopedias used by his three children for their schoolwork.
5. Ms. Y owns a 15 percent limited interest in AF Partnership, which uses a calendar year for tax purposes. On April 12, Ms. Y sold her entire interest to the R Corporation; consequently, she was a partner for only 102 days during the year. AF generated $845,000 ordinary business income this year and recognized a $70,000 capital gain on the November 13 sale of marketable securities.
6. Nine years ago, Mr. L paid $20,000 cash for a 2 percent limited interest in a very profitable partnership. Every year Mr. L has properly included his distributive share of partnership income in taxable income. This year, Mr. L sold his interest to an unrelated party for $80,000 and computed a $60,000 gain recognized on sale.
7. The 18 partners in KT Limited Partnership unanimously voted to convert their partnership to an LLC. To make the conversion, each partner will exchange his interest in KT for a membership interest in the newly formed LLC.
8. Four individuals are evaluating the tax cost of operating their business as an S corporation. They assume that the corporation will pay no tax on its annual business income. They plan to incorporate the business in a state with a 7 percent corporate income tax.
9. Mr. Y just sold his entire 20 percent interest in DK Partnership to an unrelated purchaser for $7,500. Mr. Y's adjusted basis in the interest was zero, and he had a $12,000 carryforward of DK loss.
10. Mrs. P's Schedule K-1 from an LLC reported a $12,000 share of ordinary loss and a $1,900 share of capital loss. Mrs. P's adjusted basis in her LLC interest before consideration of these losses was $6,200.
11. Mr. M, a cash basis individual, is a general partner in MNOP Partnership. Both Mr. M and MNOP use a calendar year for tax purposes. According to the partnership agreement, MNOP pays a $10,000 guaranteed payment to Mr. M on the last day of every calendar month. However, because of a bookkeeping error, the partnership did not pay (and Mr. M did not receive) his final guaranteed payment for 2005 until January 10, 2006.

12. Mr. D's Schedule K-1 from DES, an S corporation, reported $8,900 tax-exempt interest and $4,700 ordinary loss. Mr. D's adjusted basis in his stock before consideration of these items was $2,000.
13. Mr. and Mrs. W are the only shareholders in WW, an S corporation. This year, WW paid $21,000 to the caterers who provided food for the couple's silver wedding anniversary celebration.
14. The 100 shares of NS's outstanding stock are owned by seven unrelated individuals. NS has an S corporation election in effect. Late in the year, one individual announces to his fellow shareholders that he intends to give his NS shares to his son-in-law, who is a citizen and resident of Canada.
15. BR Inc. owns a 20 percent interest in a limited partnership. All the other partners are individual shareholders in BR. This year, BR sold land to the partnership for use in the partnership's business activity. BR's basis in the land was $400,000, and the selling price was $275,000. This price was determined by an independent appraiser.
16. JKL Partnership uses the calendar year for tax purposes. For 2005, the partnership generated $1 million ordinary business income. Corporation L, a 10 percent limited partner in JKL, uses a fiscal year ending June 30 as its tax year.
17. FG Inc. owned a 3 percent limited interest in a partnership that has been unprofitable for several years. The partnership recently informed its partners that they must contribute additional capital if the partnership is to survive. FG decided not to contribute any more money and sent written notification to the general partner relinquishing its equity interest. On the date of notification, FG's adjusted basis in the interest was $15,500.

Research Problems

1. Don Ferris and Lou Lindberg are the two partners in F&L Partnership. The partnership agreement provides that all income is allocated equally between Don and Lou but in no case shall the allocation to Don be less than $75,000 per year. (In other words, Don has a minimum guarantee of $75,000.) This year, F&L generated $107,200 net profit. Compute F&L's taxable income for the year and each partner's distributive share of that income.
2. Max Coen is employed as a full-time police officer by the Memphis Police Department. He is required to abide by the Department's rules of conduct, which apply whether he is on-duty or off-duty. With the Department's permission, Max "moonlights" as a security guard for several public school districts. While serving as a security guard, he is required to wear his police uniform and to carry police equipment (gun, handcuffs, etc.). The school districts pay security guards on an hourly basis and do not withhold income tax or payroll tax. This year, Max earned a $32,000 salary from the city of Memphis and $8,100 wages from the school districts. Do Max's wages constitute net earnings from self-employment on which he must pay SE tax?
3. Herold had been a calendar year S corporation since 1990. On October 10, 2005, Mrs. Hughes sold 18 shares of Herold stock to a foreign partnership, thereby terminating Herold's S election. Herold's taxable income for the entire 2005 calendar year was $592,030. Describe the federal tax returns that Herold must file for 2005, determine how much income must be reported on each, and compute any corporate income tax that Herold must pay.
4. At the beginning of 2005, Sandy Brewer had a zero basis in her 38 shares of stock in Lindlee, an S corporation, a zero basis in a $5,000 note from Lindlee, and a $7,400 carryforward of a 2004 ordinary loss from Lindlee that she was unable to deduct because of the basis limitation. Early in February 2005, Sandy was notified by Lindlee's

attorney that the corporation was bankrupt. Consequently, Lindlee was defaulting on its $5,000 debt to Sandy, and Sandy's 38 shares of stock were worthless. Describe the 2005 consequences to Sandy of the worthlessness of her Lindlee investments.

Tax Planning Cases

1. Mr. and Mrs. JW operate a restaurant business as a sole proprietorship. The couple has decided to purchase $85,000 of new kitchen equipment for the restaurant. They also want to buy two new automobiles—one for their personal use and one for their 19-year-old son's personal use. The two automobiles will cost $65,000. Mr. and Mrs. JW have $70,000 in a savings account that they can use to partially fund these purchases. They intend to borrow the additional $80,000 from a local bank at 7 percent annual interest. What steps should the couple take to minimize the after-tax cost of the borrowed funds?
2. On March 1, 2005, Mr. E and Ms. F each contributed $30,000 cash to the newly formed EF Partnership in exchange for a 50 percent general interest. The partnership immediately borrowed $50,000 from an unrelated creditor, a debt that it does not have to repay for two years. In November, the partners estimate with reasonable certainty that EF's operating loss for 2005 will be $100,000. However, EF's business has started to generate positive cash flow, and the partners also estimate that EF will be profitable in 2006, perhaps generating as much as $125,000 ordinary income. In anticipation of these future profits, Mr. E and Ms. F are considering withdrawing their initial cash contributions from EF before Christmas. Mr. E and Ms. F are both in the 35 percent tax bracket. What tax planning advice can you offer the partners?

Chapter Ten

The Corporate Taxpayer

Learning Objectives

After studying this chapter, you should be able to:

1. Identify the four primary legal characteristics of corporations.
2. Compute the corporate dividends-received deduction.
3. Prepare a reconciliation of book and tax income.
4. Compute the regular tax on corporate taxable income.
5. Discuss the purpose of the corporate alternative minimum tax.
6. Describe the corporate tax payment and return filing requirements.
7. Explain why corporate profits distributed as dividends are double taxed.
8. Discuss the incidence of the corporate income tax.

In the previous chapter, we studied business organizations that are not taxable entities: sole proprietorships, partnerships, limited liability companies (LLCs), and S corporations. These organizations are conduits of business income to the owners who are taxed directly on such income. In Chapter 10, we turn to the rules governing the taxation of business income earned by corporations.[1] In contrast to sole proprietorships and passthrough entities, corporations are taxpayers in their own right. The tax on corporate profits is determined without reference to the tax situations of the shareholders who own the corporation.

Chapter 10 begins with a discussion of the legal characteristics of corporations. The discussion then shifts to the computation of corporate taxable income and the reconciliation of that income with financial statement income. The corporate tax rate structure is examined, the function of tax credits is explained, and the corporate alternative minimum tax is introduced. The chapter concludes by analyzing the tax consequences of distributions of earnings to corporate investors.

[1] Corporations for which a subchapter S election is not in effect are referred to as regular corporations or C corporations. In this text, any reference to a corporation means the taxable, rather than the passthrough, variety.

LEGAL CHARACTERISTICS OF CORPORATIONS

Objective 1
Identify the four primary legal characteristics of corporations.

A corporation is an entity formed under state law to conduct a business enterprise. Ownership of the entity is represented by the outstanding shares of corporate stock. **Closely held corporations** are privately owned by a relatively small number of shareholders. These shareholders are often personally involved in the operation of the corporate business, and their ownership is stable over time. In contrast, the stock in **publicly held corporations** is traded on established securities markets such as the New York Stock Exchange or Nasdaq. The ownership of these corporations may be diffused over thousands of shareholders and may change on a daily basis.

Many entrepreneurs operate in the corporate form because of the advantageous legal and financial characteristics. One important legal characteristic is the **limited liability** of shareholders. The rights of corporate creditors and other claimants extend only to corporate assets and not to the personal assets of the corporation's owners. While this characteristic protects shareholders against many types of business risk, the scope of the protection is narrowed by two facts. First, financial institutions may refuse to lend money to closely held corporate businesses unless the shareholders personally guarantee repayment of the debt. Second, licensed professionals, such as physicians, attorneys, and CPAs, cannot avoid personal liability for their negligence or misconduct by operating in the corporate form. Even if they offer their services to the public as employees of a personal service corporation, professionals typically must protect themselves by carrying personal malpractice insurance.

Tax Talk
The corporate income tax, as a source of federal revenue, has been in decline since World War II, falling from 30 percent of tax revenues in 1946 to less than 10 percent by 2004.

A second attractive characteristic is the **unlimited life** of a corporation. Under state and federal law, corporations are persons separate and distinct from their owners. Consequently, their legal existence is not affected by changes in the identity of their shareholders. This characteristic gives corporations the vitality and stability so conducive to a successful enterprise. A related characteristic is the **free transferability** of equity interests in corporations. Stock in publicly held corporations is a highly liquid asset; investors can buy and sell this stock with maximum convenience and minimal transaction cost in a regulated market. As a result, publicly held corporations have access to millions of potential investors and can raise large amounts of venture capital.

In the context of closely held corporations, the characteristic of free transferability may be conspicuously absent. Shareholders are often family members or colleagues who want to protect the ownership of the business from outsiders. To this end, the stock in closely held corporations is usually subject to some type of **buy-sell agreement.** The agreement may prohibit the owner from disposing of the stock without approval of the other shareholders, or it may restrict the owner from transferring the stock to anyone but the existing shareholders or the corporation itself.

A fourth corporate characteristic is **centralized management.** Unlike a sole proprietorship or a general partnership, a corporation is not directly managed by its owners. Instead, managerial decisions are made by a board of directors appointed by and acting on behalf of the shareholders and by the officers who are hired by the board of directors. This characteristic is crucial to the efficient management of publicly held corporations with thousands of shareholders. In contrast, the shareholders of closely held corporations usually serve on the board of directors and are employed as corporate officers. In such case, the characteristic of centralized management has little significance.

Affiliated Groups

For various legal, financial, and managerial reasons, a single corporate entity may not be the best organizational form for a multifaceted enterprise. The enterprise may operate more efficiently if it is compartmentalized into several corporate entities that form an

affiliated group. Affiliated groups consist of a parent corporation that directly owns 80 percent or more of at least one subsidiary corporation plus all other subsidiaries that are 80 percent owned within the group.[2] Only taxable, domestic corporations are included in an affiliated group. The following diagram illustrates an affiliated group consisting of four corporations.

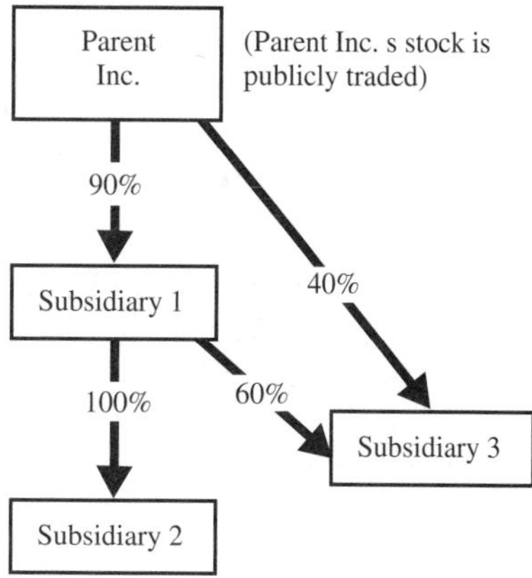

Parent Inc. is the parent corporation of the affiliated group because of its direct 90 percent ownership of Subsidiary 1. Subsidiaries 2 and 3 are also included in the group because 100 percent of each corporation's outstanding stock is owned within the group.

An affiliated group may consist of just two corporations or a conglomerate with hundreds of subsidiaries. Regardless of an affiliated group's size, the tax law treats it as one entity. For instance, an affiliated group may elect to file a **consolidated tax return**—one return reporting the combined results of the operations of all corporations in the group.[3] The major advantage of consolidated filing is that a net loss generated by one corporate member can offset the taxable income generated by other members.

Consolidated Return Filing

Refer to the affiliated group illustrated in the above diagram. This year, the separate operations of the group members resulted in the following.

	Net Income (Loss)
Parent Inc.	$960,000
Subsidiary 1	(750,000)
Subsidiary 2	225,000
Subsidiary 3	114,000

If the corporations file on a separate basis, Parent Inc., Subsidiary 2, and Subsidiary 3 report their incomes on their respective tax returns and Subsidiary 1 reports a $750,000 net operating loss on its tax return. This loss would generate an immediate tax benefit only to the extent that Subsidiary 1 could deduct it as an NOL carryback. If the group files a consolidated return, the taxable income on the return is $549,000 (combined net income and loss for the four members). Consequently, Subsidiary 1's loss generates an immediate tax benefit by reducing the affiliated group's taxable income by $750,000.

[2] §1504(a)(1).

[3] §1501.

Nonprofit Corporations

Many corporations are formed to conduct philanthropic, rather than profit-motivated, activities. As a general rule, these **nonprofit corporations** are nontaxable entities. Specifically, any corporation formed exclusively for "religious, charitable, scientific, testing for public safety, literary, or educational purposes, or to foster national or international amateur sports competition" is exempt from federal income taxation.[4] The IRS is generous in granting tax-exempt status to thousands of organizations devoted to some aspect of the public good. Nonetheless, a tax-exempt corporation that conducts a profitable sideline activity unrelated to its philanthropic purpose may find itself liable for the corporate tax on unrelated business taxable income.[5]

Unrelated Business Taxable Income

Phi Delta Theta is a national fraternity organized as a tax-exempt corporation. The fraternity published a quarterly magazine, *The Scroll,* that featured articles concerning the achievements of fraternity members and alumni. The publication costs were paid from the earnings from an endowment fund which generated over $100,000 annual investment income. The IRS determined that publication of *The Scroll* was incidental to the educational purpose that justified Phi Delta Theta's tax-exempt status. Consequently, the annual income from the endowment fund was unrelated business income on which the fraternity must pay tax.[6]

COMPUTING CORPORATE TAXABLE INCOME

Corporations report their taxable income and calculate the federal tax on that income on Form 1120 (U.S. Corporation Income Tax Return). The information on page 1, Form 1120, is essentially the corporation's income statement for tax accounting purposes.

Form 1120

Movement Plus Inc., a calendar year, accrual basis corporation, operates aerobics and dance studios. The first page of Movement Plus's Form 1120 is reproduced as Exhibit 10.1. The corporation recognized $822,000 gross profit from fees and memberships (lines 1c and 3) and $13,800 interest income from short-term investments of excess working capital (line 5). These two items represent Movement Plus's total income of $835,800 on line 11. The corporation's deductible operating expenses are listed on lines 12 through 26 and totaled to $510,860 on line 27. Movement Plus had a $6,700 NOL carryforward reported as a deduction on line 29c. The corporation's $318,240 taxable income is reported on line 30.

Corporations are allowed a deduction for charitable contributions. The annual deduction is limited to 10 percent of taxable income *before* the deduction. Contributions in excess of this limit are carried forward for five years as a deduction against future income.[7]

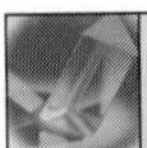

Limit on Contribution Deduction

Movement Plus Inc. contributed $40,000 to local charities. However, its deduction for the contribution is limited to $35,360, as shown on line 19, Form 1120. This limitation is computed as follows:

[4] §501(a) and (c)(3).

[5] §511 and §512.

[6] *Phi Delta Theta Fraternity* v. *Commissioner,* 887 F.2d 1302 (CA-6, 1989).

[7] §170(b)(2) and (d)(2). For purposes of this limitation, taxable income is computed without any dividend-received deduction or loss carrybacks into the year.

EXHIBIT 10.1

Form **1120** Department of the Treasury Internal Revenue Service

U.S. Corporation Income Tax Return

For calendar year 2004 or tax year beginning ...., 2004, ending ...., 20....
► See separate instructions.

OMB No. 1545-0123 **2004**

A Check if:
1 Consolidated return (attach Form 851) ☐
2 Personal holding co. (attach Sch. PH) ☐
3 Personal service corp. (see instructions) ☐
4 Schedule M-3 required (attach Sch. M-3) ☐

Use IRS label. Otherwise, print or type.

Name: Movement Plus INC.
Number, street, and room or suite no. If a P.O. box, see page 9 of instructions: 4800 Sun Valley Road
City or town, state, and ZIP code: Albuquerque N.M. 87131

B Employer identification number: 28 4288317
C Date incorporated: 1988
D Total assets (see page 8 of instructions): $ 642,212

E Check if: (1) ☐ Initial return (2) ☐ Final return (3) ☐ Name change (4) ☐ Address change

Income	1a	Gross receipts or sales 822,000 b Less returns and allowances c Bal ►	1c	822,000
	2	Cost of goods sold (Schedule A, line 8)	2	
	3	Gross profit. Subtract line 2 from line 1c	3	822,000
	4	Dividends (Schedule C, line 19)	4	
	5	Interest	5	13,800
	6	Gross rents	6	
	7	Gross royalties	7	
	8	Capital gain net income (attach Schedule D (Form 1120))	8	
	9	Net gain or (loss) from Form 4797, Part II, line 17 (attach Form 4797)	9	
	10	Other income (see page 11 of instructions—attach schedule)	10	
	11	**Total income.** Add lines 3 through 10 ►	11	835,800
Deductions (See instructions for limitations on deductions.)	12	Compensation of officers (Schedule E, line 4)	12	40,000
	13	Salaries and wages (less employment credits)	13	255,100
	14	Repairs and maintenance	14	16,900
	15	Bad debts	15	
	16	Rents	16	43,300
	17	Taxes and licenses	17	24,750
	18	Interest	18	
	19	Charitable contributions (see page 14 of instructions for 10% limitation)	19	35,360
	20	Depreciation (attach Form 4562) 20: 42,600		
	21	Less depreciation claimed on Schedule A and elsewhere on return 21a	21b	42,600
	22	Depletion	22	
	23	Advertising	23	12,200
	24	Pension, profit-sharing, etc., plans	24	
	25	Employee benefit programs	25	
	26	Other deductions (attach schedule) Insurance 19,250 utilities 21,400	26	40,650
	27	**Total deductions.** Add lines 12 through 26 ►	27	510,860
	28	Taxable income before net operating loss deduction and special deductions. Subtract line 27 from line 11	28	324,940
	29	**Less:** a Net operating loss deduction (see page 16 of instructions) 29a: 6,700; b Special deductions (Schedule C, line 20) 29b	29c	6,700
Tax and Payments	30	**Taxable income.** Subtract line 29c from line 28 (see instructions if Schedule C, line 12, was completed)	30	318,240
	31	**Total tax** (Schedule J, line 11)	31	107,364
	32	**Payments:** a 2003 overpayment credited to 2004 32a; b 2004 estimated tax payments 32b: 110,000; c Less 2004 refund applied for on Form 4466 32c ( ) d Bal ► 32d; e Tax deposited with Form 7004 32e; f Credit for tax paid on undistributed capital gains (attach Form 2439) 32f; g Credit for Federal tax on fuels (attach Form 4136). See instructions 32g	32h	110,000
	33	Estimated tax penalty (see page 17 of instructions). Check if Form 2220 is attached ► ☐	33	
	34	**Tax due.** If line 32h is smaller than the total of lines 31 and 33, enter amount owed	34	
	35	**Overpayment.** If line 32h is larger than the total of lines 31 and 33, enter amount overpaid	35	2,636
	36	Enter amount of line 35 you want: **Credited to 2005 estimated tax** ► 2,636 **Refunded** ►	36	

Sign Here Under penalties of perjury, I declare that I have examined this return, including accompanying schedules and statements, and to the best of my knowledge and belief, it is true, correct, and complete. Declaration of preparer (other than taxpayer) is based on all information of which preparer has any knowledge.

Signature of officer | Date | Title

May the IRS discuss this return with the preparer shown below (see instructions)? ☐ Yes ☐ No

Paid Preparer's Use Only Preparer's signature | Date | Check if self-employed ☐ | Preparer's SSN or PTIN
Firm's name (or yours if self-employed), address, and ZIP code | EIN | Phone no. ( )

For Privacy Act and Paperwork Reduction Act Notice, see separate instructions. Cat. No. 11450Q Form **1120** (2004)

Total income (line 11)	$835,800
Deductions *excluding* line 19 and *including* NOL deduction	(482,200)
Taxable income *before* charitable contribution deduction	$353,600
	.10
Charitable contribution deduction	$ 35,360

Movement Plus has a $4,640 contribution carryforward ($40,000 contribution – $35,360 contribution deduction) into next year.

The Dividends-Received Deduction

Objective 2
Compute the corporate dividends-received deduction.

The last deduction listed on the first page of Form 1120 (and described on line 29b as a special deduction) is the **dividends-received deduction.**[8] Corporations that receive dividends from other taxable, domestic corporations are entitled to this deduction. Note that dividends received from foreign corporations are generally not eligible for the deduction. The dividends-received deduction equals a percentage of the total dividends included in gross income. The percentage depends on the recipient corporation's investment in the corporation paying the dividend, as shown in the following schedule.

- If the recipient corporation owns *less than 20 percent* of the stock of the paying corporation, the deduction equals 70 percent of the dividends received.
- If the recipient corporation owns *at least 20 percent but less than 80 percent* of the stock of the paying corporation, the deduction equals 80 percent of the dividends received.
- If the recipient corporation owns *80 percent or more* of the stock of the paying corporation, the deduction equals 100 percent of the dividend received.

Dividends-Received Deduction

ABC Inc. owns 5 percent of the stock of Corporation X, 50 percent of the stock of Corporation Y, and 83 percent of the stock of Corporation Z. The three corporations in which ABC invested are taxable, domestic entities. ABC's gross income includes the following dividends.

Corporation X dividend	$ 24,000
Corporation Y dividend	8,000
Corporation Z dividend	90,000
	$122,000

ABC's dividends-received deduction is $113,200.

Deduction for Corporation X dividend ($24,000 × 70%)	$ 16,800
Deduction for Corporation Y dividend ($8,000 × 80%)	6,400
Deduction for Corporation Z dividend ($90,000 × 100%)	90,000
	$113,200

Because of the dividends-received deduction, only $8,800 of ABC's gross dividend income is included in taxable income. If ABC's marginal tax rate is 35 percent, the tax on this income is $3,080, and ABC's tax rate on its dividend income is only 2.5 percent ($3,080 ÷ $122,000). This low rate is not as generous as it first may seem. The dividends that ABC included in gross income represent after-tax dollars because Corporations X, Y, and Z already paid federal income tax on the earnings distributed as dividends to their investors (including ABC). As we will discuss in a later section of this chapter, ABC's dividends-received deduction simply prevents most of these earnings from being taxed again at the corporate level.

[8] §243. If corporate taxable income *before* the dividends-received deduction is less than the corporation's dividend income, the 70% and 80% deductions are limited to the respective percentages of such taxable income by §246(b)(1).

Reconciling Book Income and Taxable Income

Objective 3
Prepare a reconciliation of book and taxable income.

Because of differences between the measurement of income for federal tax purposes and the measurement of income under generally accepted accounting principles (GAAP), the taxable income reported on page 1, Form 1120, is usually not the same as the net income reported on the corporation's financial statements. The corporation must reconcile the two numbers so that the IRS can identify the differences between financial statement income and taxable income. Until 2004, all corporations provided this reconciliation on Schedule M-1, page 4, Form 1120. In 2004, the IRS developed a new reconciliation Schedule M-3 for use by corporations with total assets of $10 million or more. Schedule M-3 requires much more detailed information than Schedule M-1 and should make the book/tax reconciliation more transparent to revenue agents. According to the IRS, "the new schedule will enable us to focus our compliance resources on returns and issues that need to be examined and avoid those that do not." Schedule M-3 is included as Appendix 10–A to this chapter.

Corporations with total assets of less than $10 million may continue to provide their book/tax reconciliation on Schedule M-1. Here is an example of such reconciliation.

Book/Tax Reconciliation

Diamont Inc., which has total assets of $6.81 million, reported $343,093 net income after tax on its audited financial statements and $453,364 taxable income on its Form 1120. Here is Schedule M-1 reconciling these numbers:

Schedule M-1 **Reconciliation of Income (Loss) per Books With Income per Return (see page 24 of instructions)**

Line	Item	Amount
1	Net income (loss) per books	343093
2	Federal income tax per books	181474
3	Excess of capital losses over capital gains	20500
4	Income subject to tax not recorded on books this year (itemize): prepaid rent	8100
5	Expenses recorded on books this year not deducted on this return (itemize):	
a	Depreciation $	
b	Charitable contributions $	
c	Travel and entertainment $ 13909; bad debt 1300	15209
6	Add lines 1 through 5	568376

Line	Item	Amount
7	Income recorded on books this year not included on this return (itemize): Tax-exempt interest $; deferred gain on like-kind exchange	71200
8	Deductions on this return not charged against book income this year (itemize):	
a	Depreciation $ 43812	
b	Charitable contributions $	43812
9	Add lines 7 and 8	115012
10	Income (page 1, line 28)—line 6 less line 9	453364

- Diamont's net income per books is entered on line 1, and the federal income tax expense per books is entered on line 2.[9] This expense is not deductible in the computation of taxable income.
- Diamont realized a $20,500 net capital loss on the sale of investment securities and included the loss in financial statement income. This nondeductible loss is entered on line 3.
- Diamont received $8,100 prepaid rent that was recorded as a liability for unearned revenues for financial statement purposes. This taxable income is entered on line 4.
- Diamont incurred $27,818 meal and entertainment expense. The nondeductible half of this expense is entered on line 5(c).
- Diamont's addition to its allowance for bad debts exceeded its actual write-off of uncollectible accounts receivable by $1,300. This nondeductible excess is entered on line 5.

The total on line 6 is financial statement income increased by (1) taxable income items not included in book income and (2) expense items not deducted on the tax return.

[9] See the discussion of tax expense versus tax payable in Chapter 5.

- Diamont realized a $71,200 gain on an exchange of commercial real estate. The exchange involved like-kind properties so the realized gain was not recognized for tax purposes. The deferred gain is entered on line 7.
- Diamont's MACRS depreciation deduction exceeded its depreciation expense per books by $43,812. This excess is entered on line 8(a).

The total on line 9 equals (1) book income items not included in taxable income and (2) allowable deductions not reported as expenses for book purposes.

Line 10 is the final number in the reconciliation: taxable income reported on page 1, Form 1120, *before* any NOL deduction and dividends-received deduction. Diamont had neither of these special deductions this year. Consequently, it paid federal tax on $453,364 income.

COMPUTING THE REGULAR CORPORATE TAX

Objective 4
Compute the regular tax on corporate taxable income.

The final section on the first page of Form 1120 (Exhibit 10.1) is labeled "Tax and Payments." After the corporation has computed taxable income, it must calculate the federal tax on that income. The first step in the calculation is to determine the corporation's regular tax, which is based on the following rate schedule.[10]

If taxable income is:	The tax is:
Not over $50,000	15% of taxable income
Over $50,000 but not over $75,000	$7,500 + 25% of the excess over $50,000
Over $75,000 but not over $100,000	$13,750 + 34% of the excess over $75,000
Over $100,000 but not over $335,000	$22,250 + 39% of the excess over $100,000
Over $335,000 but not over $10,000,000	$113,900 + 34% of the excess over $335,000
Over $10,000,000 but not over $15,000,000	$3,400,000 + 35% of the excess over $10,000,000
Over $15,000,000 but not over $18,333,333	$5,150,000 + 38% of the excess over $15,000,000
Over $18,333,333	$6,416,667 + 35% of the excess over $18,333,333

Technically, this rate structure is progressive: Observe the 15 percent, 25 percent, and 34 percent rates on the first $100,000 of taxable income. The marginal rate increases to 39 percent on taxable income in excess of $100,000 but drops back to 34 percent for taxable income from $335,000 to $10 million. The additional 5 percent on income between $100,000 and $335,000 is actually a **surtax,** or extra tax, that recoups the benefit of the 15 percent and 25 percent rates on the first $75,000 of taxable income. This benefit equals $11,750, computed as follows.

Tax on $75,000 at 34%		$25,500
Tax on $50,000 at 15%	$7,500	
Tax on $25,000 at 25%	6,250	
		(13,750)
Benefit of 15% and 25% rates		$11,750

[10] §11(b)(1).

The maximum 5 percent surtax is \$11,750 (\$235,000 × 5 percent). Accordingly, corporations with taxable income between \$335,000 and \$10 million actually pay tax at a flat 34 percent rate.

Regular Tax Calculation

Corporation M's taxable income is \$4 million. Based on the corporate rate schedule, the regular tax on this income is \$1,360,000.

Taxable income	\$4,000,000
	(335,000)
Taxable income in excess of \$335,000	\$3,665,000
Marginal rate on excess	.34
	\$1,246,100
Tax on \$335,000 (from rate schedule)	113,900
	\$1,360,000

Because Corporation M's taxable income is between \$335,000 and \$10 million, its regular tax can be calculated by simply multiplying \$4 million by 34 percent.

Corporate taxable income in excess of \$10 million is taxed at 35 percent. A second surtax of 3 percent is levied on taxable income from \$15 million to \$18.33 million. The maximum 3 percent surtax is \$100,000 (\$3.33 million × 3 percent), which equals the difference between a 34 percent and a 35 percent rate on the first \$10 million of taxable income. Because of this second surtax, corporations with taxable income in excess of \$18.33 million pay tax at a flat 35 percent rate.

Regular Tax Calculation

Corporation R's taxable income is \$40 million. Based on the corporate rate schedule, the regular tax on this income is \$14 million.

Taxable income	\$ 40,000,000
	(18,333,333)
Taxable income in excess of \$18,333,333	\$ 21,666,667
Marginal rate on excess	.35
	\$ 7,583,333
Tax on \$18,333,333 (from rate schedule)	6,416,667
	\$ 14,000,000

Because Corporation R's taxable income exceeds \$18.33 million, its regular tax can be calculated by simply multiplying \$40 million by 35 percent.

Personal Service Corporations

Closely held corporations owned by individuals who perform services in the fields of health, law, engineering, architecture, accounting, actuarial science, performing arts, or consulting for the corporation's clientele are denied even the minimal progressivity of the corporate rate schedule. The income earned by these **personal service corporations** is taxed at a flat 35 percent rate.[11]

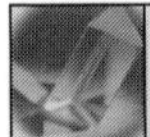

Health Care for Whom?

Creature Comforts Inc. operates a full-service pet care facility. The stock of the corporation is owned by four individuals, all of whom are licensed veterinarians. All four shareholders are employed by Creature Comforts to provide medical treatment to the dogs, cats, and other animals brought to the facility as patients. The corporation has six other employees who provide grooming, exercising, and boarding services, and who offer canine obedience courses. According to the IRS, the field of health includes the provision of veterinary care to animals. Consequently, Creature Comforts qualifies as a personal service corporation and must pay a 35 percent flat tax on its annual income.[12]

Reduced Tax Burden on Domestic Manufacturers

The current tax rate structure applies to corporate taxable income, regardless of the type of activity generating the income or the geographic location of the activity. Consequently, income from sales of tangible goods is taxed at the same statutory rate as income from the performance of services, and income from domestic activities is taxed at the same rate as income from foreign activities. In recent years, Congress has struggled to find a way to reduce the tax burden on domestic production activities because it believes that a lower tax on domestic manufacturers will improve their cash flow, stimulate investment in domestic facilities, and ultimately increase the number of manufacturing jobs in the United States.

Tax Talk
The ink was scarcely dry on the American Jobs Creation Act of 2004 when the Senate Finance Committee announced that Starbucks Corporation would not be eligible for the new U.S. production activities deduction for its coffee brewing activities in the United States. The Committee drew a distinction between "the roasting of coffee beans, which qualifies for the manufacturing tax break, and the brewing of coffee, which does not."

Acting on this belief, Congress enacted a radical new tax deduction as part of the American Jobs Creation Act of 2004. This deduction is available to any U.S. taxpayer deriving income from a qualified activity: the "lease, rental, license, sale, exchange, or other disposition" of tangible property, computer software, and sound recordings that are "manufactured, produced, grown, or extracted by the taxpayer in whole or in significant part within the United States."[13] This **U.S. production activities deduction** equals the following percentage of the *lesser* of the corporation's net income from the qualified activity or its taxable income computed before the deduction.

For taxable years beginning in:	
2005 and 2006	3 percent
2007, 2008, 2009	6 percent
2010 and later	9 percent

The amount of the deduction allowed for any taxable year cannot exceed 50 percent of the total compensation that the corporation pays to its U.S. workforce.

[11] §11(b)(2) and §448(d)(2).

[12] Rev. Rul. 91-30, 1991-1 CB 61.

[13] §199, effective for taxable years beginning after December 31, 2004. While this deduction is available to noncorporate taxpayers, it clearly was enacted as a corporate tax relief measure.

U.S. Production Activities Deduction

PeriProducts is a New York corporation engaged exclusively in the domestic manufacture and sale of electrical components. Assume that in 2010, it earns $800,000 net income from this qualified activity. Before the U.S. production activities deduction, its taxable income is also $800,000, and the compensation paid to its workforce is $219,675.

PeriProducts' U.S. production activities deduction for 2010 is $72,000 (9 percent × $800,000), which is less than 50 percent of total compensation paid. Therefore, the corporation's 2010 federal income tax is $247,520.

Taxable income before the deduction	$800,000
U.S. production activities deduction	(72,000)
Taxable income	$728,000
Tax rate	.34
Tax	$247,520

The U.S. production activities deduction is artificial in that it does not correspond to any expense, loss, or cash outflow incurred by the corporate taxpayer. Consequently, it is equivalent to a reduced tax rate on the income from any qualified activity. In our example, the $247,520 federal tax that PeriProducts pays on $800,000 net income equates to a 30.94 percent effective tax rate, even though its explicit tax rate is 34 percent.

TAX CREDITS

A corporate (or noncorporate) taxpayer's regular tax is offset by any tax credits for which the taxpayer is eligible. A **tax credit** is a direct reduction in tax liability. As a result, the value of a credit is greater than the value of a deduction of the same amount.

Deduction versus Credit

JHG Inc.'s taxable income is $600,000, and its regular tax (at 34 percent) is $204,000. If JHG is allowed an additional $50,000 deduction, the tax decreases to $187,000, and the tax savings from the deduction is $17,000 (34 percent of $50,000). In comparison, if JHG is entitled to a $50,000 tax credit, the tax decreases to $154,000, and the tax savings from the credit is $50,000.

	Deduction	*Credit*
Taxable income	$600,000	$600,000
Additional deduction	(50,000)	
Recomputed taxable income	$550,000	$600,000
	.34	.34
Precredit tax	$187,000	$204,000
Tax credit		(50,000)
Recomputed tax	$187,000	$154,000

Tax credits are generally nonrefundable, which means they can reduce current year tax to zero, but any credit in excess of precredit tax does not generate a refund from the

Treasury. However, the tax law may provide that an excess credit can be carried back or forward to reduce tax in a different year.

Because tax credits reduce the regular tax on business income, they are equivalent to a preferential tax rate. To be eligible for a particular credit, taxpayers must engage in very specific activities or transactions that Congress believes are worthy of government support. From this perspective, tax credits are instruments of fiscal policy and are enacted by Congress to increase the efficiency of the tax system as an agent of economic change. Currently, the tax law provides a **general business credit,** which is the sum of 19 different credits for the tax year.[14]

Most of these 19 credits are narrow in scope and are available to relatively few businesses. Moreover, the list of credits changes as Congress experiments with new credits and discards those that fail to produce the intended behavioral result. To learn how a tax credit can induce a certain behavior, we will look at the mechanics of just one credit.

Rehabilitation Credit

Taxpayers who renovate or reconstruct commercial buildings originally placed in service before 1936 or buildings certified as historic structures by the U.S. Department of the Interior are entitled to a **rehabilitation credit.**[15] The credit equals 10 percent of the rehabilitation costs of a qualifying commercial building and 20 percent of the rehabilitation costs of a certified historic structure. Congress designed this credit to encourage businesses to undertake urban renewal projects that might be financially unfeasible without the tax savings from the credit.

Rehabilitation Credit

Corporation QT must locate a suitable facility to house one of its regional offices and has narrowed its search to two buildings. One building is newly constructed and ready for occupancy. The second building was constructed in 1925 and is in need of extensive renovation. The purchase price of the first building is $10 million, while the purchase price of the second building is only $3 million. QT estimates that the rehabilitation costs for the second building would be $7.5 million. For tax purposes, QT's cost basis in either building ($10 million for the new building or $10.5 million for the old building) can be depreciated over the same 39-year recovery period.

Without the rehabilitation credit, the cost of the new building is less than that of the old building, and QT has no reason to invest in the older structure. However, the credit reduces the cost of the old building to $9,750,000.

Purchase price	$ 3,000,000
Rehabilitation cost	7,500,000
	$10,500,000
Tax savings from credit ($7,500,000 × 10%)	(750,000)
After-tax cost	$ 9,750,000

[14] §38. The general business credit that a taxpayer can use each year is limited to $25,000 plus 75 percent of precredit tax in excess of $25,000. §38(c). Any unused credit can be carried back one year and forward 20 years. §39(a).

[15] §47.

Because of the rehabilitation credit, QT minimizes its cost by purchasing the old building. Note that the tax savings from the credit is not a function of QT's marginal tax rate. But the savings calculation is based on the assumption that precredit tax is sufficient to allow full use of the credit in the current year. If this is not the case and QT must carry forward some of the credit for use in a future year, the present value of the carryforward might be insufficient to tip the scale in favor of the rehabilitation project.

Save a Building, Save Tax

The National Park Service released a report summarizing the positive effects of the rehabilitation credit on historic preservation. According to the report, 2,967 historic buildings were preserved in the last five years including Chicago office towers, Baltimore row houses, St. Louis warehouses, and Miami art deco hotels. The Park Service concluded that the tax credit "leverages private investment in depressed neighborhoods, creates jobs, promotes community preservation, fosters heritage education, enhances state and local tax revenues, and increases property values." Not bad for a tax credit![16]

ALTERNATIVE MINIMUM TAX

Objective 5
Discuss the purpose of the corporate alternative minimum tax.

The **alternative minimum tax (AMT)** is a second federal tax system parallel to the regular income tax system described throughout the text. Congress enacted the corporate AMT primarily for political reasons. Under the regular tax system, corporations with substantial economic income can occasionally take advantage of tax exclusions, deductions, or credits to dramatically reduce, or even eliminate, their tax. In past years, these occasions received a great deal of publicity and caused people to lose respect for a tax system so riddled with "loopholes" that huge companies can escape taxation altogether. In response to this embarrassing public perception, Congress created a backup system to ensure that every corporation pays a "fair share" of the federal tax burden.

Every newly formed corporation is exempt from AMT for its first taxable year. After the first year, a corporation is exempt from AMT for each year in which it passes a gross receipts test. The test is based on the corporation's average annual gross receipts for the three-year period (or portion thereof) *preceding* the test year. A corporation is exempt for its *first* test year if its average annual gross receipts for the testing period do not exceed $5,000,000. For all subsequent test years, the corporation is exempt if its average annual gross receipts for the testing period do not exceed $7,500,000. If a corporation fails the gross receipts test, it is subject to AMT for the test year and all subsequent years.[17]

AMT Exemption

Hermann Inc. was incorporated on January 1, 2000, and adopted a calendar year. It had the following gross receipts for its first five taxable years.

2000	$ 4,890,000
2001	6,520,000
2002	9,891,000
2003	10,037,000
2004	11,440,000

[16] "Tax Matters," *Journal of Accountancy*, September 2001, p. 107.

[17] §55(e).

Hermann was exempt from AMT for 2000 (its first taxable year). Thus, Hermann's first test year was 2001, and the testing period for that year was 2000. Because average annual gross receipts for the testing period ($4,890,000) did not exceed $5,000,000, it was exempt from AMT for 2001.

Hermann's second test year was 2002, and the testing period for that year was the two-year period 2000–2001. Average annual gross receipts for this period were $5,705,000 [($4,890,000 + $6,520,000) ÷ 2]. Because this average did not exceed $7,500,000, Hermann was exempt from AMT for 2002.

Hermann's third test year was 2003, and the testing period was the three-year period 2000–2002. Average annual gross receipts for this period were $7,100,333 [($4,890,000 + $6,520,000 + $9,891,000) ÷ 3]. Because this average did not exceed $7,500,000, Hermann was exempt from AMT for 2003.

Hermann's fourth test year was 2004, and the testing period was the three-year period 2001–2003. Average annual gross receipts for this period were $8,816,000 [($6,520,000 + $9,891,000 + $10,037,000) ÷ 3]. Because this average exceeded $7,500,000, Hermann was subject to AMT for 2004 and all subsequent taxable years.

Alternative Minimum Taxable Income

The base for the corporate AMT is **alternative minimum taxable income (AMTI).**[18] The computation of AMTI begins with taxable income for regular tax purposes. This income number is increased or decreased by a series of complicated **AMT adjustments** and increased by specific **tax preferences.** The computation of AMTI is presented in the following formula.

Taxable income for regular tax purposes
+ or − AMT adjustments
+ AMT tax preferences
Alternative minimum taxable income

To get a sense of the nature of AMT adjustments and preferences, let's examine three of the more common: the depreciation adjustment, excess percentage depletion, and the NOL adjustment.

Depreciation Adjustment

Under MACRS, business assets with a 3-year, 5-year, 7-year, or 10-year recovery period are depreciated under the 200 percent declining balance method. For AMT purposes, depreciation on these assets is computed under a 150 percent declining-balance method.[19] Consequently, the MACRS deduction with respect to these assets is greater than its AMT counterpart in the early years of an asset's life, and the excess MACRS becomes a positive adjustment in the AMTI computation. At some point in the asset's life, the situation reverses and AMT depreciation exceeds MACRS depreciation. At this point, the annual AMT adjustment becomes negative. Over the life of the asset, MACRS and AMT depreciation are equal, and the positive and negative AMT adjustments zero out.

[18] §55(b)(2).

[19] §56(a)(1). For property placed in service before January 1, 1999, AMT depreciation is based on the extended recovery periods under the alternative depreciation system (ADS) described in §168(g).

AMT Depreciation

JS Inc. owns two depreciable assets. This year, the MACRS depreciation, AMT depreciation, and AMT adjustment for each asset is:

	MACRS	AMT Depreciation	AMT Adjustment
Asset 1	$17,800	$12,000	$5,800
Asset 2	2,100	4,300	(2,200)
	$19,900	$16,300	$3,600

JS has a $5,800 positive AMT adjustment for Asset 1 (excess MACRS over AMT depreciation) and a $2,200 negative AMT adjustment for Asset 2 (excess AMT depreciation over MACRS). JS must add its $3,600 aggregate positive adjustment to regular taxable income in the computation of AMTI.

Excess Percentage Depletion

As we discussed in Chapter 6, the percentage depletion that corporations deduct over the productive life of a mine or well is not limited to the tax basis in the mineral property. If a corporation has recovered its entire basis and continues to deduct percentage depletion, the depletion deduction in excess of the zero basis is an AMT tax preference.[20]

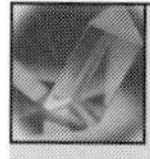

Depletion Preference

JS Inc. had $240,000 unrecovered basis in a mining property at the beginning of the year. The percentage depletion deduction with respect to this property for the year was $310,000. JS has $70,000 excess depletion and must add this preference to regular taxable income in the AMTI computation.

NOL Deduction

Even if a corporation generates a profit, it may have no taxable income because it has an NOL carryforward or carryback into the year. For AMT purposes, the NOL deduction is limited to 90 percent of AMTI.[21]

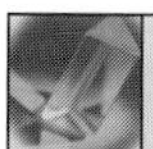

AMT NOL Deduction

JS Inc.'s taxable income before any NOL deduction is $2 million, and it has a $3 million NOL carryforward into the year. For regular tax purposes, JS can deduct $2 million of the carryforward, thereby reducing taxable income to zero. JS's AMTI before the NOL deduction is $2.4 million. Under the AMT rules, JS can deduct only $2.16 million of its NOL carryforward (90 percent of $2.4 million), resulting in $240,000 AMTI.

Calculating AMT

Calculation of the corporate AMT is a three-step process.[22] First, AMTI is decreased by any exemption to which the corporation is entitled. The basic exemption is $40,000. This

[20] §57(a)(1).

[21] §56(a)(4). Because the AMT NOL is calculated under the AMT system, the AMT NOL deduction can be different than the NOL deduction for regular tax purposes.

[22] §55 provides the rules for the AMT computation.

exemption is reduced by 25 percent of AMTI in excess of $150,000. Consequently, the exemption is reduced to zero for corporations with AMTI in excess of $310,000.

AMTI Exemption

IQP Corporations's AMTI is $293,000, and its exemption is $4,250.

AMTI	$ 293,000
	(150,000)
Excess AMTI	$ 143,000
	.25
Reduction in exemption	$ 35,750
Basic exemption	$ 40,000
	(35,750)
IQP's exemption	$ 4,250

In the second step of the AMT calculation, AMTI in excess of the exemption is multiplied by a flat 20 percent rate to compute **tentative minimum tax.** In the third step, the tentative minimum tax is compared to the corporation's regular tax. Any excess of tentative minimum tax over regular tax becomes AMT, which the corporation pays *in addition to* its regular tax.[23] The AMT calculation is demonstrated in the next example.

AMT Calculation

In 2004, Bantam Inc. has $5,000,000 taxable income and $9,750,000 AMTI. Bantam's tax is computed as follows.

AMTI	$ 9,750,000
Exemption	–0–
	$ 9,750,000
	.20
Tentative minimum tax	$ 1,950,000
Regular tax ($5,000,000 × 34%)	(1,700,000)
AMT	$ 250,000
Total tax (regular tax + AMT)	$ 1,950,000

Although Bantam's AMTI is almost twice its taxable income, its AMT is relatively small. Because the 20 percent AMT rate is so much less than the 34 percent or 35 percent regular tax rate, tentative minimum tax won't exceed regular tax unless AMTI is significantly greater than taxable income. Therefore, corporations with modest AMT adjustments and preferences escape the AMT. Nonetheless, the additional record keeping necessary to compute annual AMTI increases the tax compliance costs of these corporations.

[23] As a general rule, none of the tax credits available under the regular tax system reduce AMT. The major exception is the foreign tax credit, which is described in detail in Chapter 12.

Minimum Tax Credit

In the preceding example, the fact that Bantam's $1,950,000 tax bill consists of both regular tax and AMT may seem of little practical importance. Even so, corporations must keep careful track of their AMT because this tax payment is transformed into a **minimum tax credit.** This credit carries forward indefinitely and reduces the corporation's regular tax in subsequent years. However, the credit cannot reduce regular tax to less than the corporation's tentative minimum tax for the year.[24] The logic behind this credit is that the corporate AMT is not designed as a permanent tax increase. Instead, AMT merely accelerates the payment of tax into years when corporate taxable income is dramatically less than AMTI. To demonstrate the important function of the minimum tax credit, refer back to Bantam's situation.

Minimum Tax Credit

In 2005, Bantam has $7,500,000 taxable income and $8,000,000 AMTI. Bantam's tax is computed as follows.

AMTI	$8,000,000
Exemption	–0–
	$8,000,000
	.20
Tentative minimum tax	$1,600,000
Regular tax ($7,500,000 × 34%)	$2,550,000
AMT (regular tax *exceeds* tentative minimum tax)	–0–
Minimum tax credit from 2004	(250,000)
Total tax	$2,300,000

In this two-year example, the AMT affected only the timing and not the amount of Bantam's income tax. With or without AMT, Bantam pays $4,250,000 total tax for the two years.

Two-Year Summary for Bantam

	Total Tax with AMT	*Total Tax without AMT*
2004	$1,950,000	$1,700,000
2005	2,300,000	2,550,000
	$4,250,000	$4,250,000

The effect of the AMT over the two-year period was to accelerate $250,000 tax into the earlier year, not to permanently increase that tax. Realistically, AMT may take any number of years to reverse as minimum tax credits against regular tax. For growing businesses, each successive year's tentative minimum tax may exceed regular tax. In such case, use of the minimum tax credit is postponed indefinitely. Of course, regardless of the fact that a corporation may recoup AMT in a future year, that AMT always increases the corporation's tax cost in present value terms.

[24] §53.

PAYMENT AND FILING REQUIREMENTS

Objective 6
Describe the corporate tax payment and return filing requirements.

Corporations are required to pay their federal income tax for the year in four installments.[25] Each installment is 25 percent of the annual tax, and the installments are due by the 15th day of the 4th, 6th, 9th, and 12th months of the taxable year. Corporations that fail to make their required installment payments on a timely basis incur an **underpayment penalty.** If the total of the installment payments is less than the actual tax reported on Form 1120, the corporation must pay the balance due by the 15th day of the 3rd month following the close of the taxable year.[26] If the total is more than the actual tax, the corporation is entitled to a refund of the overpayment.

The required installment payments must total to 100 percent of the tax reported on Form 1120. Because corporations can't know their exact tax liability until after year-end, they must base their installment payments on their best estimate. Corporations that underestimate their tax incur the underpayment penalty. The law provides some leeway for small corporations (defined as corporations with less than $1 million taxable income). These corporations escape the underpayment penalty if their total installment payments equal 100 percent of the tax reported on the *previous* year's tax return.[27] This *safe harbor* provision is useful to newly formed corporations with rapidly growing businesses.

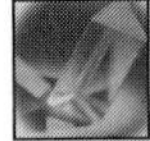
Safe Harbor Estimate

In 2003, Corporation DF's taxable income was $400,000, and its tax was $136,000. During 2004, DF made four $35,000 installment payments. Its 2004 taxable income was $930,000, and its tax was $316,200. Although DF paid only $140,000 tax during 2004, it did not incur an underpayment penalty because the payment exceeded 100 percent of its 2003 tax.

Corporations must file their annual income tax returns with the IRS by the 15th day of the 3rd month following the close of the taxable year.[28] Corporations that are unable to meet this filing deadline may request an automatic six-month extension of time to file their returns, and corporations routinely take advantage of this grace period.[29] It should come as no surprise that corporations that file delinquent returns may incur late-filing penalties.[30] An extension of the filing deadline does *not* extend the payment deadline for any balance of tax due for the year. Corporations must pay any estimated balance due by the 15th day of the third month after the close of the year even if they file an extended tax return.

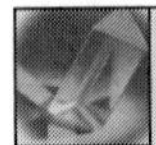
Payment and Filing Requirements

Keno, a calendar year corporation, filed a Form 7004 (Application for Automatic Extension of Time to File Corporation Income Tax Return) on March 3, 2005, on which it requested a six-month extension for its 2004 return. On the application, Keno reported that its estimated 2004 tax was $258,500 and its quarterly installment payments of that tax totaled $244,000.

[25] §6655.

[26] Corporations do not send tax payments directly to the IRS. Instead, they use the Electronic Federal Tax Payment System (EFTPS) or a Federal Tax Deposit Coupon to deposit their payments in a government account maintained by a qualified depositary, such as a commercial bank.

[27] Large corporations with highly fluctuating patterns of annual income may look to other statutory exceptions to the strict 100 percent requirement for relief from the underpayment penalty.

[28] §6072(b).

[29] Reg. §1.6081-3.

[30] §6651 describes the penalties for late filing. These penalties are discussed in more detail in Chapter 17.

Therefore, Keno paid its $14,500 estimated balance due with the Form 7004. Keno filed its 2004 return on August 29, 2005. The actual tax reported on the return was $255,039, which entitled Keno to a $3,461 refund of 2004 tax ($258,500 total payments − $255,039 actual tax).

DISTRIBUTIONS OF PROFITS TO INVESTORS

The corporate form of business organization allows an unlimited number of investors to contribute capital to the business. Investors can become creditors, either by lending money directly to the corporation in exchange for a promissory note or by purchasing the corporation's debt instruments traded on a public bond market. Alternatively, investors can become owners by contributing money or property directly to the corporation in exchange for shares of equity stock, purchasing shares from other shareholders, or purchasing shares traded on a public stock market.

Of course, both creditors and shareholders expect a return on their investment. Creditors receive interest income on their corporate notes or bonds. On the other side of the transaction, corporations can deduct the interest paid on their debt obligations. As a result, the business profit flowing through to investors as interest is not taxed at the corporate level but only to the investors. Corporate stockholders may receive a return on their investment in the form of dividends. Corporations *cannot* deduct dividend payments in the computation of taxable income. The business profit flowing through to investors as dividends is taxed both at the corporate level and again to the shareholders receiving the dividends.

Objective 7
Explain why corporate profits distributed as dividends are double taxed.

This double taxation of corporate earnings is one of the dominant characteristics of the federal income tax system. The fact that dividends are paid with after-tax dollars is a major consideration affecting the choice of organizational form—a consideration we will analyze in the next chapter. This fact also justifies the corporate dividends-received deduction. Without this deduction, business profit would be taxed over and over again as it is distributed through a chain of corporate investors before final distribution to individual shareholders for personal consumption.

From the corporate perspective, the nondeductibility of dividend payments creates a bias in favor of debt financing.[31] A corporation that raises capital by borrowing can deduct the interest paid on the debt. At a 35 percent tax rate, the after-tax cost of the capital is only 65 percent of the before-tax cost. In effect, the federal government pays 35 percent of the return on the creditors' investment. If the corporation raises capital by selling stock, the after-tax cost of the dividends paid on that stock equals the before-tax cost. Of course, the choice of debt financing has serious nontax implications, one of the more important of which is that interest and principal payments (unlike dividends paid on common stock) are not discretionary on the part of management. Corporations with high debt-to-equity ratios have more burdensome cash flow commitments and a greater risk of insolvency than corporations with less debt in their capital structures. Companies that break faith with their creditors suffer financial distress that may even lead to bankruptcy. In many situations, the nontax costs associated with debt financing outweigh the tax savings from the corporate interest deduction.[32]

[31] Richard A. Brealey and Stewart C. Myers, *Principles of Corporate Finance,* 5th ed. (New York: McGraw-Hill, 1996), p. 418.

[32] Ibid., p. 421.

Alternatives to Double Taxation

How could the present income tax system be reformed to eliminate the double taxation of corporate income? One alternative would be to treat corporations as passthrough entities by requiring them to allocate income to their shareholders on an annual basis. Shareholders would include share of corporate earnings in gross income and pay tax accordingly. This alternative would be administratively cumbersome, if not impossible, for publicly held corporations in which stock ownership changes daily. In addition, this alternative could cause cash flow problems for investors who find themselves owing tax on their share of corporate income but who did not receive a commensurate cash distribution from the corporation.

Another alternative is to make dividends nontaxable to individual investors so that the only tax on corporate income is at the entity level. Congress recently took an unprecedented step in this direction by enacting a 15 percent preferential tax rate for dividend income received by individuals. However, any preferential treatment of dividends is vulnerable to political attack as a tax break for the wealthy who receive much more dividend income than middle- and lower-income individuals. A variation on this alternative would be to allow corporations to deduct dividend payments (in the same way that they deduct interest payments) so that distributed corporate income would be taxed only at the shareholder level.

Still another alternative is a system in which individuals are allowed a tax credit for the corporate tax attributable to the dividends included in their gross income. For example, if a shareholder received a $6,500 dividend, representing $10,000 income on which the corporation already paid $3,500 tax, the shareholder would include the full $10,000 ($6,500 cash received grossed up by $3,500 tax) in income and compute his tax accordingly. The shareholder would then reduce that tax by a $3,500 credit. The end result is that $10,000 income is taxed only once at the individual's rate. Variations of this credit system are currently used in Canada and several western European nations.

Over the past decades, Congress and the Treasury have considered all these alternatives as solutions to the structural problem of double taxation. While the alternatives have theoretical merit, their implementation would result in significant revenue loss. Thus, it is unlikely that any of the alternatives will be enacted into law in the near future.

INCIDENCE OF THE CORPORATE TAX

Objective 8
Discuss the incidence of the corporate income tax.

Because corporations are taxpayers in their own right and yet have no human persona, they become easy political targets in any debate on tax reform. People don't enjoy paying taxes and often believe that their tax burden is too heavy because some other taxpayer's burden is too light. Impersonal corporate taxpayers are scapegoats as the hue and cry becomes "raise taxes on the corporate giants, not middle-class Americans." This sentiment ignores the fact that corporations are nothing more than a form in which people organize their business, and that an increase in the corporate tax represents an additional cost of conducting that business.

Just who does pay the corporate income tax? The answer to this question varies across corporations, depending on the nature of the markets in which they compete. In some markets, corporations may shift their tax costs directly to their customers as part of the price of goods and services. In markets in which price competition is fierce, management may offset tax costs by trimming production costs. In such case, the tax is passed on to the corporation's suppliers (smaller orders for materials), employees (lower compensation or workforce reductions), and even to consumers (lower quality). Still another possibility is that tax costs simply reduce the corporation's net income. In this case, the tax is paid by shareholders in the form of shrinking dividends or reduced market price for their stock. The question of the economic incidence of the corporate tax and whether that tax falls hardest on consumers, suppliers, labor, or capital has been researched and argued for decades without a definitive answer. Nonetheless, one conclusion is inescapable: Corporations do not pay taxes—people do.

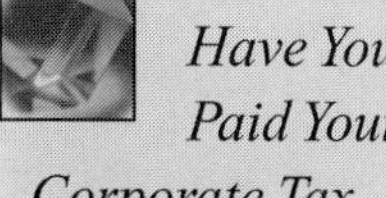

Have You Paid Your Corporate Tax Today?

According to a recent study, the per capita tax burden (local, state, and federal taxes attributable to each man, woman, and child in the United States) was $9,751 in 2004. This burden included $869 state and federal *corporate* income tax. The study explained: "The reason these taxes are rightly counted as part of the nation's tax burden is that taxes on businesses are ultimately passed on to consumers, employees, and shareholders in the form of higher prices, lower wages or employment levels, and lower share value."[33]

Conclusion

Corporations have many legal and financial characteristics that make them the entity of choice for many enterprises and the only option for publicly held companies. Corporations are taxable entities in their own right, paying tax at progressive rates ranging from 15 percent to 35 percent on annual income. When corporations distribute after-tax income as dividends to their shareholders, the income is taxed a second time. In the next chapter, we will consider the impact of this double taxation on the choice of business entity and the entire tax planning process.

[33] "America Celebrates Tax Freedom Day," *The Tax Foundation*, No. 129, April 2004, p. 9.

Sources of Book/Tax Differences

Permanent

- Dividends-received deduction
- U.S. production activities deduction

Temporary

- Corporate charitable contributions

Key Terms

affiliated group *263*
alternative minimum tax (AMT) *273*
alternative minimum taxable income (AMTI) *274*
AMT adjustments *274*
buy-sell agreement *262*
centralized management *262*
closely held corporation *262*
consolidated tax return *263*
dividends-received deduction *266*
free transferability *262*
general business credit *272*
limited liability *262*
minimum tax credit *277*
nonprofit corporation *264*
personal service corporation *270*
publicly held corporation *262*
rehabilitation credit *272*
surtax *268*
tax credit *271*
tax preferences *274*
tentative minimum tax *276*
underpayment penalty *278*
unlimited life *262*
U.S. production activities deduction *270*

Questions and Problems for Discussion

1. To what extent does the corporate characteristic of limited liability protect shareholder/employees who perform professional services for corporate clients?
2. The corporate form of business is characterized by centralized management. Describe this characteristic as it applies to publicly held corporations and closely held corporations.
3. The corporate form of business is characterized by free transferability of equity interests. Describe this characteristic as it applies to publicly held corporations and closely held corporations.
4. Mr. and Mrs. D and their six children own 100 percent of the stock in three family corporations. Do these corporations qualify as an affiliated group eligible to file a consolidated corporate tax return?
5. RP Inc. owns 59 percent of QV's voting stock. RP's board of directors elects the majority of the members of QV's board of directors and thereby controls QV's management. Are RP and QV an affiliated group eligible to file a consolidated corporate tax return?
6. Corporation L owns a national chain of retail music stores. The corporation wants to expand into a new, extremely competitive, and highly specialized business—the composition and production of rock music videos. Can you identify any nontax reasons why Corporation L may want to operate its new business through a controlled subsidiary corporation?
7. Corporations are allowed a dividends-received deduction for dividends from other domestic, taxable corporations. Why is this deduction not available for dividends from foreign corporations?
8. Corporations subject to the AMT are penalized because they took advantage of tax preferences during the year. If Congress doesn't want corporations to take advantage of a certain tax preference, why doesn't Congress simply repeal the preference?
9. For the last six years, Corporation V's AMTI has exceeded its regular taxable income, but it has never paid AMT. Can you explain this result?
10. In your own words, explain the conclusion that corporations do not pay tax—people do.

Application Problems

1. The stock of AB and YZ is publicly traded, and no shareholder owns more than a 1 percent interest in either corporation. AB owns 40 percent and YZ owns 60 percent of the stock of Alpha, which owns 90 percent of the stock of Beta. YZ and Beta each own 50 percent of the stock of Kappa. Which of the corporations identified in this problem form an affiliated group eligible to file a consolidated tax return?
2. Corporation P owns 93 percent of the outstanding stock of Corporation T. This year, the corporations' records provide the following information.

	Corporation P	*Corporation T*
Ordinary operating income (loss)	$500,000	$(200,000)
Capital gain (loss)	(8,300)	6,000
Section 1231 gain (loss)	(1,000)	5,000

   a. Compute each corporation's taxable income if they file separate tax returns.
   b. Compute consolidated taxable income if Corporation P and Corporation T file a consolidated tax return.

3. This year, Napa Corporation received the following dividends.

KLP Inc. (a taxable Delaware corporation in which Napa holds an 8% stock interest)	$ 55,000
Gamma Inc. (a taxable Florida corporation in which Napa holds a 90% stock interest)	120,000

   Napa and Gamma do not file a consolidated tax return. Compute Napa's dividend-received deduction.

4. This year, GHJ Inc. received the following dividends.

BP Inc. (a taxable California corporation in which GHJ holds a 2% stock interest)	$17,300
MN Inc. (a taxable Florida corporation in which GHJ holds a 52% stock interest)	80,800
AB Inc. (a taxable Canadian corporation in which GHJ holds a 21% stock interest)	17,300

   Compute GHJ's dividend-received deduction.

5. In its first year, Camco Inc. generated a $92,000 net operating loss, and it also made a $5,000 cash donation to a local charity. In its second year, Camco generated a $210,600 profit, and it also made a $10,000 donation to the same charity. Compute Camco's taxable income for its second year.
6. This year, Corporation EF made a $100,000 contribution to charity. In each of the following situations, compute the after-tax cost of this contribution assuming that EF uses a 6 percent discount rate to compute NPV.
   a. EF had $8 million taxable income before consideration of the contribution.
   b. EF had $490,000 taxable income before consideration of the contribution. Next year, EF's taxable income is $6 million, and it makes no charitable contributions.
   c. EF had $190,000 taxable income before consideration of the contribution. For the next five years, EF's annual taxable income is $130,000, and it makes no charitable contributions.
7. Hallick, a Michigan corporation, operates two facilities for the manufacture of tangible goods; one facility is located in Michigan and the other is located in Canada. In 2005, Hallick earned the following net income from these facilities.

	Michigan	***Canada***
Gross receipts from sales	$ 1,978,000	$ 1,642,000
Cost of goods sold	(1,233,000)	(1,001,000)
Gross manufacturing profit	$ 745,000	$ 641,000
Other deductible expenses	(316,000)	(298,000)
Net income	$ 429,000	$ 343,000

Hallick's total compensation paid to its U.S. workforce was $635,000, and total compensation paid to its Canadian workforce was $409,000. In addition to its manufacturing income, Hallick earned $39,400 taxable investment income in 2005.

a. Compute Hallick's 2005 taxable income.

b. How would your computation change if Hallick's Canadian facility generated a $112,700 loss instead of $343,000 net income?

8. EFG, a calendar year, accrual basis corporation, reported $479,900 net income after tax on its financial statements prepared in accordance with GAAP. The corporation's financial records reveal the following information.

   - EFG earned $314,800 from a qualified domestic production activity.
   - EFG earned $10,700 on an investment in tax-exempt municipal bonds.
   - EFG's allowance for bad debts as of January 1 was $21,000. Write-offs for the year totaled $4,400, while the addition to the allowance was $3,700. The allowance as of December 31 was $20,300.
   - On August 7, EFG paid a $6,000 fine to a municipal government for a violation of a local zoning ordinance.
   - EFG's depreciation expense per books was $44,200, and its MACRS depreciation deduction was $31,000.
   - This is EFG's second taxable year. In its first taxable year, it recognized an $8,800 net capital loss. This year, it recognized a $31,000 Section 1231 gain on the sale of equipment. This was EFG's only disposition of noninventory assets.
   - In its first taxable year, EFG capitalized $6,900 organizational costs for tax purposes and elected to amortize the costs over 180 months. For book purposes, it expensed the costs.
   - EFG's federal income tax expense per books was $241,589.

   a. Compute EFG's taxable income and regular tax.

   b. Prepare a Schedule M-1, page 4, Form 1120, reconciling EFG's book and tax income.

9. Corporation AB's marginal tax rate is 15 percent, and Corporation YZ's marginal tax rate is 35 percent.

   a. If both corporations are entitled to an additional $5,000 deduction, how much tax savings will the deduction generate for each corporation?

   b. If both corporations are entitled to a $5,000 tax credit, how much tax savings will the credit generate for each corporation? (Assume that each corporation's precredit tax exceeds $5,000.)

10. In each of the following cases, compute the corporation's regular tax.

    a. Corporation A, which produces motion pictures, has $160,000 taxable income.

    b. Corporation B, a personal service corporation providing medical care, has $160,000 taxable income.

    c. Corporation C, which develops and operates golf resorts, has $3.91 million taxable income.

    d. Corporation D, which drills oil wells, has $16.8 million taxable income.

    e. Corporation E, which manufactures farm equipment, has $57 million taxable income.

11. Refer to the cases in the preceding problem. In each case, identify the corporation's marginal tax rate, and compute its average tax rate.

12. Myamo was incorporated on January 1, 2002, and adopted a calendar year for tax purposes. It had the following gross receipts for its first three taxable years.

2002	$5,118,300
2003	3,520,000
2004	5,291,000

For which of these three years is Myamo exempt from AMT?

13. Northup was incorporated on January 1, 2000, and adopted a calendar year for tax purposes. It had the following gross receipts for its first six taxable years.

2000	$4,282,000
2001	8,418,000
2002	7,002,000
2003	9,668,000
2004	5,219,000
2005	3,843,000

For which of these years is Northup exempt from AMT?

14. PT Corporation's regular taxable income is $100,000, and it has positive AMT adjustments totaling $45,000 and a $22,000 AMT tax preference. Compute PT's AMT (if any).
15. RS Corporation's regular taxable income is $3,590,000, and it has positive AMT adjustments totaling $980,000 and AMT tax preferences totaling $315,000. Compute RS's AMT (if any).
16. GK Inc. has taxable income of $1.25 million before any NOL deduction. It has $2.8 million of NOL carryforwards but no other AMT adjustments or preferences. Compute GK's tax.
17. Corporation H was formed in 2001 and was exempt from AMT for that year. For 2002 through 2004, its regular tax and tentative minimum tax were as follows.

Year	*Regular Tax*	*Tentative Minimum Tax*
2002	$ 200,000	$ 160,000
2003	870,000	900,000
2004	1,500,000	1,820,000

a. Compute Corporation H's tax for 2002, 2003, and 2004.
b. Compute Corporation H's tax for 2005 if its regular taxable income is $9 million, and its AMTI is $11 million.
c. Compute Corporation H's tax for 2005 if its regular taxable income is $9 million, and its AMTI is $14.8 million.

18. In 2004, NB Inc.'s federal income tax was $242,000. Compute the required installment payments of 2005 tax in each of the following cases.

a. NB's 2005 taxable income is $593,000.
b. NB's 2005 taxable income is $950,000.
c. NB's 2005 taxable income is $1,400,000.

19. Mr. J, who is in the 35 percent marginal tax bracket, owns 100 percent of the stock of JJ Inc. This year, JJ generates $500,000 taxable income and pays a $100,000 dividend to Mr. J. Compute his tax on the dividend under each of the following assumptions.

a. The federal tax rules currently in effect apply to the dividend payment.
b. The federal tax system has been amended to allow shareholders to gross up dividend income by the corporate tax paid with respect to the dividend and credit this tax against their individual tax.

20. LFT Inc. manufactures laundry detergent and other cleaning products. This year, the government increased the corporate tax rate by 2 percent. The marketing department determined that LFT could not raise its prices and retain its market share. The production department concluded that manufacturing costs cannot be reduced by another penny. Consequently, LFT's before-tax profits remain constant, while after-tax profits decline by the full tax increase. The stock market reaction to the decline in earnings is a fall in LFT's stock price.
    a. Who bears the incidence of the increase in LFT's corporate tax?
    b. How would your answer change if LFT held its after-tax profit constant by shutting down the on-site day care center for its employees' preschool children and eliminating this operating cost from its budget?

Issue Recognition Problems

Identify the tax issue or issues suggested by the following situations, and state each issue in the form of a question.

1. Greentown Foundation is a nonprofit corporation exempt from federal income tax. Its purpose is to solicit volunteers to plant and tend public gardens and greenbelts located in inner cities. The board of directors is considering publishing a gardener's newsletter that Greentown could sell in retail bookstores to raise money for its various projects.
2. TK Enterprises, an accrual basis corporation, needs to raise capital. One idea is for TK to sell bonds to the public for $625 each. These bonds would have no stated rate of interest but would be redeemable from TK in five years for a redemption price of $1,000.
3. BB Corporation has not paid a dividend for six years. This year, the board of directors decides to declare a dividend. It hires a consultant to update the shareholder records so that the dividend can be distributed to the proper people. The consultant's fee for her services is $16,800.
4. M&M is a publicly held corporation, and its stock trades on Nasdaq. This year, M&M contributed 15,000 shares of its newly issued common stock to a local charity. At date of contribution, the stock was selling at $7.12 per share.
5. Twenty years ago, XZ Corporation developed, manufactured, and marketed Kepone, a chemical pesticide. As a result of manufacturing practices that violated state environmental standards, harmful levels of Kepone were discharged into the soil and groundwater. A state agency sued XZ for damages, and the corporation was indicted for criminal negligence for the unlawful discharge of toxic substances. The judge imposed a $1 million fine on XZ. After extensive meetings with the judge and prosecutors, XZ created the Midwest Environment Foundation, the purpose of which is to alleviate the effects of Kepone waste. XZ contributed $950,000 to this nonprofit organization, and the judge promptly reduced the fine to $50,000.
6. Several years ago, Corporation F purchased heavy machinery for $618,000. It sold the machinery this year for $500,000. Through date of sale, MACRS depreciation on the machinery was $320,000, while AMT depreciation was $198,000. Corporation F has paid AMT in three of its last five taxable years and expects to do so again this year.
7. In its first year of operations, Corporation TF incurred a $120,000 NOL. The director of tax projects that TF will generate $40,000 taxable income in each of the next three years.

Consequently, the director estimates that TF will pay no tax in these years because of the NOL carryforward deduction.

8. Corporation W is a calendar year taxpayer. For the past nine years, its taxable income has been stable, averaging $2 million per year. Through November of this year, its taxable income was $1.81 million. In April, June, and September, Corporation W made a $175,000 installment payment of tax. In December, it recognized a $5 million gain on the sale of investment land.

Research Problems

1. In 2004, Connor Inc. announced its intention to construct a manufacturing facility in the Shenandoah Valley. In order to persuade Connor to locate the facility in Augusta County, the county government contributed a six-acre tract of undeveloped county land to the corporation. The appraised FMV of the land at date of contribution was $280,000. Soon after accepting the contribution, Connor paid $3,300 to an attorney to do a title search to make sure that it had uncontested ownership of the land. Connor also paid $12,900 for a survey and site map of the six acres and $1,360 for two water wells drilled on the land. Did Connor recognize income because of the receipt of the land? What is the proper tax treatment of Connor's $17,560 expenditure with respect to the land?

   In 2005, Connor's attorney discovered that the Estate of Elsa Reynolds claimed title to the six acres and was preparing to file suit in Virginia state court to regain ownership and possession. The attorney advised Connor that the estate's claim appeared valid and would be upheld. Consequently, Connor informed Augusta County that it was renouncing all claim to the land and would build its new manufacturing facility 200 miles away in Rockingham County. Did Connor recognize a loss when it renounced its claim to the land?

2. On December 10, 2004, the representative of a national charitable organization contracted the CEO of Wilkie Inc., a calendar year accrual basis corporation, to solicit a $100,000 donation. The CEO presented the solicitation to Wilkie's board of directors on December 19, and the board unanimously authorized the donation. Pursuant to this authorization, Wilkie transferred ownership of 3,973 shares of Gydo Inc. common stock to the charity on March 20, 2005. Wilkie purchased the Gydo stock in 1997 for $71,800 and held it as an investment. On March 20, Gydo common was selling on the NYSE for $25.17 per share. Before consideration of this donation, Wilkie's taxable income for both 2004 and 2005 exceeded $8 million. In which year is Wilkie allowed a charitable deduction for this donation, and what is the amount of the deduction?

3. Barry and Lynette Majors own 36 percent of the outstanding stock of Echo Valley, which has approximately $5 million earnings and profits. Echo Valley owns 38 tracts of undeveloped land in central Colorado. Barry and Lynette want to acquire one of the tracts (tract D6) to develop as a campground and recreational park. The appraised FMV of tract D6 is $420,000 although the corporation's tax basis is only $211,000. At the most recent shareholder meeting, Barry and Lynette convinced the other shareholders to distribute tract D6 to them as a dividend. (The other shareholders would receive equivalent cash dividends proportionate to their stock ownership.) Would the distribution of tract D6 as a dividend be a taxable event to Echo Valley? How much dividend income would the Majors recognize, and what would be their tax basis in tract D6?

4. This year, Prewer Inc. received a $160,000 dividend on its investment consisting of 16 percent of the outstanding stock of TKS Inc., a taxable domestic corporation. Before considering this dividend, Prewer had a $43,500 operating loss for the year. It also had a $31,300 NOL carryover deduction from 2003. What is Prewer's taxable income this year?

Tax Planning Cases

1. Congress recently enacted a nonrefundable credit based on the cost of qualifying alcohol and drug abuse counseling programs provided by any corporate employer to its employees. The credit is limited to 50 percent of the total cost of the program. If a corporation elects the credit, none of the program costs are allowed as a deduction. Any credit in excess of current year tax may not be carried back or forward to another year.
   a. TMM Corporation spent $80,000 for a qualifying counseling program this year. If TMM has $500,000 taxable income before consideration of this expense, should it elect the credit or deduct the program's cost as an ordinary business expense?
   b. Would your answer change if TMM had only $70,000 taxable income before consideration of the expense?
2. A&Z Inc. averages $4 million taxable income a year. Because it needs an infusion of cash, the board of directors is considering two options: selling a new issue of preferred stock to the public for a total offering price of $500,000 or borrowing $500,000 from a local bank. The market dividend rate on preferred stock is only 5.6 percent, while the bank's interest rate is 9 percent. Which option minimizes the after-tax cost of the new capital?
3. In 2004, Corporation E paid both regular tax ($2,714,000) and AMT ($129,300). The director of tax forecasts that Corporation E will be in an AMT position for 2005 and 2006. However, its AMTI in 2007 will be significantly less than regular taxable income. Assuming a 6 percent discount rate, calculate the cost of the AMT in present value terms.

Appendix 10–A

Schedule M-3 for Reconciling Book and Taxable Income

SCHEDULE M-3 (Form 1120) Department of the Treasury Internal Revenue Service	**Net Income (Loss) Reconciliation for Corporations With Total Assets of $10 Million or More** ▶ Attach to Form 1120. ▶ See separate instructions.	OMB No. 1545-0123 **2004**
Name of corporation (common parent, if consolidated return)		**Employer identification number**

Part I **Financial Information and Net Income (Loss) Reconciliation**

1a Did the corporation file SEC Form 10-K for its income statement period ending with or within this tax year?
☐ **Yes.** Skip lines 1b and 1c and complete lines 2a through 11 with respect to that SEC Form 10-K.
☐ **No.** Go to line 1b.

b Did the corporation prepare a certified audited income statement for that period?
☐ **Yes.** Skip line 1c and complete lines 2a through 11 with respect to that income statement.
☐ **No.** Go to line 1c.

c Did the corporation prepare an income statement for that period?
☐ **Yes.** Complete lines 2a through 11 with respect to that income statement.
☐ **No.** Skip lines 2a through 10 and enter the corporation's net income (loss) per its books and records on line 11.

2a Enter the income statement period: Beginning ____/____/____ Ending ____/____/____

b Has the corporation's income statement been restated for the income statement period on line 2a?
☐ **Yes.** (If "Yes," attach an explanation and the amount of each item restated.)
☐ **No.**

c Has the corporation's income statement been restated for any of the five income statement periods preceeding the period on line 2a?
☐ **Yes.** (If "Yes," attach an explanation and the amount of each item restated.)
☐ **No.**

3a Is any of the corporation's voting common stock publicly traded?
☐ **Yes.**
☐ **No.** If "No," go to line 4.

b Enter the symbol of the corporation's primary U.S. publicly traded voting common stock . . . . ☐☐☐☐☐

c Enter the nine-digit CUSIP number of the corporation's primary publicly traded voting common stock . . . . ☐☐☐☐☐☐☐☐☐

4	Worldwide consolidated net income (loss) from income statement source identified in Part I, line 1	**4**	
5a	Net income from nonincludible foreign entities (attach schedule)	**5a**	( )
b	Net loss from nonincludible foreign entities (attach schedule and enter as a positive amount) . .	**5b**	
6a	Net income from nonincludible U.S. entities (attach schedule)	**6a**	( )
b	Net loss from nonincludible U.S. entities (attach schedule and enter as a positive amount) . . .	**6b**	
7a	Net income of other includible corporations (attach schedule)	**7a**	
b	Net loss of other includible corporations (attach schedule)	**7b**	( )
8	Adjustment to eliminations of transactions between includible corporations and nonincludible entities (attach schedule)	**8**	
9	Adjustment to reconcile income statement period to tax year (attach schedule)	**9**	
10	Other adjustments to reconcile to amount on line 11 (attach schedule)	**10**	
11	**Net income (loss) per income statement of includible corporations.** Combine lines 4 through 10	**11**	

For Privacy Act and Paperwork Reduction Act Notice, see the Instructions for Forms 1120 and 1120-A. Cat. No. 37961C **Schedule M-3 (Form 1120) 2004**

Schedule M-3 (Form 1120) 2004 Page **2**

Name of corporation (common parent, if consolidated return)	**Employer identification number**
Name of subsidiary (if consolidated return)	**Employer identification number**

Part II **Reconciliation of Net Income (Loss) per Income Statement of Includible Corporations With Taxable Income per Return**

	Income (Loss) Items	**(a)** Income (Loss) per Income Statement (optional)	**(b)** Temporary Difference	**(c)** Permanent Difference	**(d)** Income (Loss) per Tax Return (optional)
1	Income (loss) from equity method foreign corporations				
2	Gross foreign dividends not previously taxed				
3	Subpart F, QEF, and similar income inclusions				
4	Section 78 gross-up				
5	Gross foreign distributions previously taxed				
6	Income (loss) from equity method U.S. corporations				
7	U.S. dividends not eliminated in tax consolidation				
8	Minority interest for includible corporations				
9	Income (loss) from U.S. partnerships (attach schedule)				
10	Income (loss) from foreign partnerships (attach schedule)				
11	Income (loss) from other pass-through entities (attach schedule)				
12	Items relating to reportable transactions (attach details)				
13	Interest income				
14	Total accrual to cash adjustment				
15	Hedging transactions				
16	Mark-to-market income (loss)				
17	Inventory valuation adjustments				
18	Sale versus lease (for sellers and/or lessors)				
19	Section 481(a) adjustments				
20	Unearned/deferred revenue				
21	Income recognition from long-term contracts				
22	Original issue discount and other imputed interest				
23a	Income statement gain/loss on sale, exchange, abandonment, worthlessness, or other disposition of assets other than inventory and flow-through entities				
23b	Gross capital gains from Schedule D, excluding amounts from flow-through entities				
23c	Gross capital losses from Schedule D, excluding amounts from flow-through entities, abandonment losses, and worthless stock losses				
23d	Net gain/loss reported on Form 4797, line 18, excluding amounts from flow-through entities, abandonment losses, and worthless stock losses				
23e	Abandonment losses				
23f	Worthless stock losses (attach details)				
23g	Other gain/loss on disposition of assets other than inventory				
24	Disallowed capital loss in excess of capital gains				
25	Utilization of capital loss carryforward				
26	Other income (loss) items with differences (attach schedule)				
27	**Total income (loss) items.** Combine lines 1 through 26				
28	**Total expense/deduction items** (from Part III, line 36)				
29	Other income (loss) and expense/deduction items with no differences				
30	**Reconciliation totals.** Combine lines 27 through 29				

Note. Line 30, column (a), must equal the amount on Part I, line 11, and column (d) must equal Form 1120, page 1, line 28.

Schedule M-3 (Form 1120) 2004

Schedule M-3 (Form 1120) 2004 Page **3**

Name of corporation (common parent, if consolidated return)	**Employer identification number**
Name of subsidiary (if consolidated return)	**Employer identification number**

Part III **Reconciliation of Net Income (Loss) per Income Statement of Includible Corporations With Taxable Income per Return—Expense/Deduction Items**

	Expense/Deduction Items	**(a)** Expense per Income Statement (optional)	**(b)** Temporary Difference	**(c)** Permanent Difference	**(d)** Deduction per Tax Return (optional)
1	U.S. current income tax expense				
2	U.S. deferred income tax expense				
3	State and local current income tax expense				
4	State and local deferred income tax expense				
5	Foreign current income tax expense (other than foreign withholding taxes)				
6	Foreign deferred income tax expense				
7	Foreign withholding taxes				
8	Incentive stock options				
9	Nonqualified stock options				
10	Other equity-based compensation				
11	Meals and entertainment				
12	Fines and penalties				
13	Punitive damages				
14	Parachute payments				
15	Compensation with section 162(m) limitation				
16	Pension and profit-sharing				
17	Other post-retirement benefits				
18	Deferred compensation				
19	Charitable contribution of cash and tangible property				
20	Charitable contribution of intangible property				
21	Charitable contribution limitation				
22	Charitable contribution carryforward used				
23	Current year acquisition or reorganization investment banking fees				
24	Current year acquisition or reorganization legal and accounting fees				
25	Current year acquisition/reorganization other costs				
26	Amortization/impairment of goodwill				
27	Amortization of acquisition, reorganization, and start-up costs				
28	Other amortization or impairment write-offs				
29	Section 198 environmental remediation costs				
30	Depletion				
31	Depreciation				
32	Bad debt expense				
33	Corporate owned life insurance premiums				
34	Purchase versus lease (for purchasers and/or lessees)				
35	Other expense/deduction items with differences (attach schedule)				
36	**Total expense/deduction items.** Combine lines 1 through 35. Enter here and on Part II, line 28				

Schedule M-3 (Form 1120) 2004

Chapter **Eleven**

The Choice of Business Entity

Learning Objectives

After studying this chapter, you should be able to:

1. Explain the advantage of operating a business with start-up losses as a passthrough entity.
2. Calculate after-tax cash flow available to owners from passthrough entities and taxable corporations.
3. Describe how families can use partnerships or S corporations to shift income.
4. Define the term *constructive dividend.*
5. Explain why individuals no longer can use corporations as tax shelters.
6. Explain the purpose of the accumulated earnings tax and the personal holding company tax.
7. Apply the tax rates to income earned by a controlled corporate group.

In the two preceding chapters, we identified the basic forms of business organization and learned how the choice of form determines whether business income is taxed at the individual or corporate rates. These chapters concentrated on the tax rules and regulations applying to different business entities. In Chapter 11, we will build on this technical knowledge as we consider the tax planning implications of the choice of business entity. The first half of the chapter focuses on the advantages of conducting a business as a passthrough entity. The second half explains how business owners can control the tax cost of operating in the corporate form. Throughout the chapter, we will analyze how planning strategies affect after-tax cash flow available to the business owners.

No one organizational form is ideal for every business. The tax characteristics of one form may be advantageous in one case and disadvantageous in another. In some cases, a passthrough entity accomplishes the owners' tax objectives, while in other cases, a taxable corporation is the better option. Oftentimes, owners have compelling nontax reasons for operating their business in a particular form. As the business matures and the owners' financial situations evolve, the optimal form may change. Finally, business owners must reevaluate the form in which they conduct their business every time Congress amends the Internal Revenue Code. Even minor alterations in the law can affect the tax pros and cons of passthrough entities and taxable corporations.

TAX PLANNING WITH PASSTHROUGH ENTITIES

From Chapter 9, we know that businesses organized as partnerships, LLCs, and S corporations are not subject to federal income tax at the entity level. Instead, income passes through the entity to be reported by and taxed to the owners. If the business operates at a loss, the loss passes through and is reported as a deduction by the owners. Cash distributions from passthrough entities are generally nontaxable. These cash flows represent a return of the owners' investment in the business and do not affect the income or loss reported by the owners. For many individuals, this combination of rules helps them control tax costs and maximize the cash flow from their business.

Maximizing the Tax Benefit of Start-Up Losses

Objective 1
Explain the advantage of operating a business with start-up losses as a passthrough entity.

Organizers of a new business may expect to lose money during the start-up phase. If the business is organized as a passthrough entity, these initial losses can generate an immediate tax savings to the owners. If the business is organized as a corporation, the losses do not flow through but are trapped at the entity level as NOL carryforwards. As a result, the tax savings from the start-up losses are deferred until the corporation can deduct them against future income. The following example focuses on this important difference in timing.

Start-Up Losses

A group of individuals owns a business with the following income and deductions for its first three years.

Year	*Gross Income*	*Allowable Deductions*	*Net Income or Loss*
0	$ 420,000	$ (720,000)	$(300,000)
1	800,000	(920,000)	(120,000)
2	1,530,000	(1,000,000)	530,000

If the owners organized the business as a passthrough entity, they could deduct the operating losses in years 0 and 1.[1] In year 2, they paid tax on $530,000 business income. If the owners organized the business as a corporation, the losses in years 0 and 1 carried forward and resulted in $110,000 corporate taxable income in year 2. To isolate the tax effect of the timing difference, let's use a hypothetical 35 percent tax rate for both the individual owners and the corporation and a 5 percent discount rate.

Tax Savings and Costs

		Passthrough Entity		
Year	*(Deduction) or Taxable Income*	*Tax Savings or (Cost)*	*Discount Factor*	*Present Value of Tax Savings or (Cost)*
0	$(300,000)	$ 105,000		$ 105,000
1	(120,000)	42,000	.952	39,984
2	530,000	(185,500)	.907	(168,249)
		$ (38,500)		$ (23,265)

[1] If a passthrough loss exceeds the owner's other income for the year, the excess loss is a net operating loss. The owner can carry the NOL back as a deduction to the two preceding years or forward as a deduction for 20 years.

	Corporation			
Year	*(NOL Carryforward) or Taxable Income*	*Tax Savings or (Cost)*	*Discount Factor*	*Present Value of Tax Savings or (Cost)*
0	$(300,000)	–0–		–0–
1	(120,000)	–0–		–0–
2	110,000	$(38,500)	.907	$(34,920)
		$(38,500)		$(34,920)

In this simple case, the present value of the tax cost is minimized if the business was organized as a passthrough entity rather than as a corporation. The dramatic difference in tax cost is *entirely attributable* to the timing of the deduction for the first two years of losses. With a passthrough entity, these losses were deductible in the year incurred. Consequently, the owners received the tax savings from the deduction in years 0 and 1. With a corporate entity, the tax savings from the loss deduction were postponed until year 2, so the savings decreased in present value terms.

Avoiding a Double Tax on Business Income

Objective 2
Calculate after-tax cash flow available to owners from passthrough entities and taxable corporations.

People who own their own business often depend on the cash flow from the business to meet their family's consumption needs. Their basic financial strategy is to maximize the cash transferred from the business bank account to their personal checking account. This strategy usually dictates that they operate their business as a passthrough entity, rather than as a corporation, so that income is taxed only once.

Single versus Double Tax on Business Income

Mr. and Mrs. Gilbert are the sole shareholders in an S corporation that conducts a restaurant business.[2] The restaurant generates $100,000 taxable income annually and an equal cash flow. The corporation distributes all available cash to the Gilberts each year. Assuming a 28 percent individual tax rate, the after-tax cash flow from their business is $72,000.

Annual cash from operations	$100,000
Individual tax	
($100,000 taxable income × 28%)	(28,000)
After-tax cash flow	$ 72,000

If Mr. and Mrs. Gilbert had not elected subchapter S status for their corporation, the $100,000 income would be taxed at the entity level and the corporation itself would pay $22,250 tax. The cash available for distribution would be only $77,750. Moreover, the distribution would be a dividend to Mr. and Mrs. Gilbert, and the after-tax cash available for their personal consumption would be only $66,087.

Annual cash from operations	$100,000
Corporate tax	(22,250)
Cash distributed to shareholders	$ 77,750
Individual tax	
($77,750 dividend × 15%)	(11,663)
After-tax cash flow	$ 66,087

[2] To keep the example simple, assume that neither shareholder is an employee of the corporation.

In Mr. and Mrs. Gilbert's case, the double tax resulting from the corporate form would result in a 33.9 percent tax rate on their business income ($33,913 total tax ÷ $100,000 income). Clearly, Mr. and Mrs. Gilbert are minimizing their income tax and maximizing the money they can spend by operating their restaurant as a passthrough entity.

Income Shifting among Family Members

Objective 3
Describe how families can use partnerships or S corporations to shift income.

The creation of a family partnership or S corporation can be an effective way to divide business income among a number of taxpayers. To the extent that this division causes income to be taxed at a lower marginal rate, the total tax burden on the business shrinks. Let's illustrate this concept with a simple example.

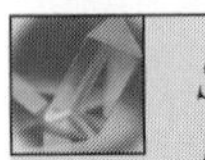

Shift of Business Income

Mrs. Alm owns a sole proprietorship generating $150,000 annual taxable income. Mrs. Alm is in the 35 percent tax bracket but has two children in the 25 percent tax bracket. If Mrs. Alm could convert her business into a passthrough entity in which she and her children are equal owners, the annual income would be allocated among three individual taxpayers. If the shift of $50,000 business income from Mrs. Alm to each child decreased the tax rate on the income from 35 percent to 25 percent, the tax savings would be $10,000.

Tax on $100,000 at 35%	$ 35,000
Tax on $100,000 at 25%	(25,000)
	$ 10,000

While Mrs. Alm should be impressed with this tax strategy, she must understand that the strategy will not just shift *income* to her children—it will shift *dollars* to them as well. As owners, the children are entitled to an equal share of any cash distributions from the business. When the business eventually terminates or is sold, each child will receive one-third of any remaining property or any amount realized on sale. In other words, if Mrs. Alm wants to shift two-thirds of the business income, she must part with two-thirds of the wealth represented by the business.

Statutory Restrictions

The tax savings achieved through income shifts to family members with low tax rates can be substantial. Not surprisingly, the Internal Revenue Code restricts the use of both partnerships and S corporations as income-shifting devices. Let's first consider the statutory rules pertaining to family partnerships.

If partnership income is primarily attributable to the work performed by individual partners rather than to the property owned by the partnership, any allocation of that income to nonworking partners is an unjustified assignment of earned income. Accordingly, a family member cannot be a partner in a personal service business unless he or she is qualified to perform services for the business.[3] In contrast, a family member can be a partner in a business in which property is a material income-producing factor.[4] Unlike a service partnership,

[3] *Commissioner* v. *Culbertson*, 337 U.S. 733 (1949).

[4] §704(e)(1). Property is a material income-producing factor if the business requires substantial inventories or a substantial investment in plant, machinery, or equipment. Reg. §1.704-1(e)(1)(iv).

the mere ownership of an equity interest in a capital-intensive partnership entitles a partner to a share of profits.

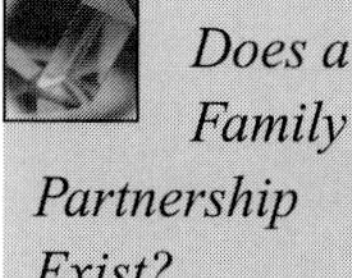

Does a Family Partnership Exist?

Elizabeth and Emerson Winkler, who lived on a farm in Illinois, had five children. Emerson was in poor health and was frequently hospitalized. Elizabeth and one or more of her children always drove Emerson to the hospital. During these trips, the family usually purchased three $1 lottery tickets at the gas station where they stopped for fuel. The money was contributed by any family member who happened to have a dollar bill, and Elizabeth kept all the tickets in her china cabinet. The family often joked about how they would spend their winnings from these "family" tickets. On one trip, Elizabeth used her own money to purchase the three tickets. That night, one of these tickets won $6.5 million. The family agreed that Elizabeth and Emerson should each receive 25 percent of the jackpot, while each child should receive 10 percent. Consequently, when Elizabeth received the $6.5 million, she paid $650,000 to each of her five children. The IRS contended that no family partnership existed among the Winklers, and that Elizabeth and Emerson made gifts (the lottery winnings) to the children on which they owed gift tax of over $116,000. But the federal court disagreed with the IRS. The court concluded that the Winklers formed a family partnership to purchase lottery tickets. Each family member contributed capital to the partnership when he or she spent a dollar to buy a ticket and each contributed services by going into the gas station to make the purchase. Consequently, the division of the jackpot was a distribution of profits to partners rather than a taxable gift from Elizabeth and Emerson to their children.[5]

Family partnerships are often created when a business owner makes a gift of an equity interest to a relative, thereby creating a partnership between donor and donee. Alternatively, the owner could sell the equity interest to the relative to create the partnership. In either case, the business income must be allocated among the partners based on their proportionate interests in partnership capital.[6]

Family Partnership

Refer to the earlier example involving Mrs. Alm and her two children. Mrs. Alm can convert her sole proprietorship to a family partnership only if capital is a material income-producing factor. In other words, if Mrs. Alm is a self-employed physician earning $150,000 from her medical practice, she can't make her children partners unless they are qualified to provide some type of service to the practice. On the other hand, if Mrs. Alm's business is a retail clothing store, she can transfer the business assets to a partnership and give her children a capital interest in the new entity. If each child receives a one-third interest, the partnership income can be allocated in equal shares to the partners. If Mrs. Alm gives each child only a 10 percent capital interest, only 10 percent of the income can be shifted to each child.

If the partner who gave away or sold an equity interest to a family member provides services to the partnership, the partner must receive a guaranteed payment as compensation.[7] The partnership is allowed to deduct the payment, and the remaining income is allocated in proportion to the capital interests.

[5] *Estate of Emerson Winkler,* TC Memo 1997-4.

[6] In nonfamily partnerships, the allocation of income does not have to be in proportion to each partner's ownership of capital. For example, the partnership agreement could provide that a partner who owns 50 percent of the capital is allocated 80 percent of the business income or loss.

[7] §704(e).

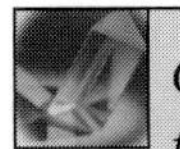

Compensation for Services Rendered to a Family Partnership

Refer to the preceding example and assume that Mrs. Alm formed a family partnership by giving a one-third equity interest in her retail clothing business to each of her two children. Mrs. Alm works 40 hours a week managing the business. If her services are reasonably worth $60,000 a year, the partnership must pay her a $60,000 guaranteed payment. If partnership income after deduction of this guaranteed payment is $90,000, the maximum allocation to each child is $30,000. Because of this allocation rule, Mrs. Alm can't increase the income shifted to her children by working for free on their behalf.

When a business is operated as an S corporation, annual income is allocated pro rata to the outstanding shares of corporate stock. Therefore, the percentage of income allocable to any one individual is based strictly on the number of shares owned. If Mrs. Alm converted her sole proprietorship to an S corporation and gave each child one-third of the stock, each child would be allocated one-third of the business income. If she gave each child only 10 percent of the stock, their pro rata share of the income drops to 10 percent. Before any corporate income is allocated to the shareholders, Mrs. Alm must receive a reasonable salary for any services performed for the corporation.[8]

Transaction Costs

Even with these statutory restrictions, partnerships and S corporations are a viable way to reduce the aggregate income tax burden on a family business. The potential tax savings must be compared to the transaction costs of forming the entity. If an individual creates a family partnership or S corporation by giving an equity interest in an established business to a family member, the donative transfer may be subject to the federal gift tax. This tax is based on the FMV of the transferred interest and must be paid by the *donor* (the individual making the gift). If the business has considerable value, the gift tax may represent a substantial transaction cost.[9] The various nontax transaction costs associated with the formation and operation of a separate legal entity should also be factored into the decision to create a family partnership or S corporation.

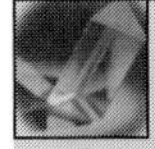

Transaction Costs of Partnership Formation

Refer back to the preceding example in which Mrs. Alm formed a family partnership by giving a one-third equity interest in her retail clothing business to each of her two children. Immediately before the formation, the business had an appraised FMV of $950,000. Consequently, the FMV of Mrs. Alm's gift to each child was $316,667, and her federal gift tax was $21,600. The partnership paid $2,750 to the attorney who drafted the partnership agreement and an $800 fee to transfer title in the business real estate to the partnership. Thus, the transaction costs of forming the family partnership totaled $25,150. The gift tax is a nondeductible personal expense. The attorney's fee is an organizational cost that the partnership can amortize over 60 months. The title transfer fee is capitalized to the partnership's basis in the real estate.[10]

Nontax Considerations

Entrepreneurs should carefully determine the extent to which the formation of a family-owned entity will dilute their control of the business. Many business owners who are willing to shift income and dollars to their relatives may be reluctant to give those relatives a

[8] §1366(e).

[9] The federal gift tax is discussed in more detail in Chapter 15.

[10] Reg. §1.709-2.

voice in management. A limited partnership in which the entrepreneur is the sole general partner can eliminate this concern. Another option is for the entrepreneur to create an S corporation capitalized with both voting and nonvoting stock. The entrepreneur can keep the voting stock and give the nonvoting stock to his family, thereby retaining complete control of the business.

Individuals who transfer equity interests to a family member should understand that the transfer must be complete and legally binding. The recipient becomes the owner of an intangible property right. Absent any restrictions, the recipient is free to dispose of this right, with or without the blessing of the other owners. *Buy-sell agreements* among the partners or shareholders are commonly used to restrict family members from selling or assigning their equity interest to an unrelated third party.

Still another important consideration is that the transfer of an equity interest must be irrevocable; the transferor can't simply change his mind and take the interest back. If the transferor becomes estranged from his family, an income-shifting arrangement could turn into a bitterly resented trap. A parent who has an ill-favored child can always disinherit the child. It is another matter entirely if the child owns stock in the family S corporation. A change in the relative economic circumstances of family members can also undermine an income-shifting strategy. Consider a situation in which a high-income taxpayer suffers a severe economic setback. An irreversible arrangement that shifts income away from this taxpayer could cause a personal financial crisis. These unhappy possibilities emphasize a point made earlier in the text: Tax strategies must be evaluated on the basis of flexibility. If a business owner is uneasy about her family's ability to cooperate, a family partnership or S corporation may be a bad idea.

A Family Partnership Gone Wrong

Refer one last time to the family partnership created by Mrs. Alm and her two children. Six years after the partnership was formed, one of the children died in an accident and his widow inherited his one-third interest in the partnership. The widow cannot get along with Mrs. Alm and the surviving child and contests every decision they make concerning the management of the retail clothing business. Because of the continual discord, the three partners finally discontinue the business and terminate the partnership.

PARTNERSHIP OR S CORPORATION?

Entrepreneurs who organize their business as a passthrough entity must choose between some type of partnership and an S corporation. The choice depends on the tax and nontax characteristics that differentiate these two organizational forms. In the next few paragraphs, we will identify the more important of these characteristics and examine how they enter into the decision-making process. Then we will analyze two planning cases.

Characteristics of Partnerships and S Corporations

Costs of Entity Formation and Operation

The transfer of cash or property to a new partnership or corporation in exchange for a controlling equity interest is a nontaxable exchange.[11] Consequently, forming a new business entity has no up-front income tax cost. The owners will incur legal, accounting, and professional fees incidental to the formation. If the owners form a corporation, they must file

[11] See the discussion of §721 and §351 in Chapter 8.

Tax Talk

The IRS's treatment of S corporations is increasingly taxpayer-friendly according to a survey of accountants and attorneys. Over the past five years, the IRS has made a deliberate effort to be more responsive to complaints and to ease restrictions on S corporations and their shareholders.

a timely subchapter S election with the IRS. In addition, they must incur the incremental cost of monitoring the ownership structure to ensure that their S corporation continues to meet the eligibility requirements. If an S corporation loses its eligibility and the election terminates, the corporation automatically reverts to a taxable entity. An S corporation may be more expensive to operate than a partnership because of state tax costs. Several states, including New York, Tennessee, and Texas, impose entity-level income or franchise taxes on S corporations. In contrast, partnerships are typically exempt from state tax at the entity level.

Flexibility of Income and Loss-Sharing Arrangement

Partnerships offer owners the maximum flexibility to tailor their business arrangement to fit their needs. The partnership agreement specifies the amount and type of capital each partner contributes to the business and can create special sharing ratios for different items of income, gain, deduction, and loss. Moreover, the partners can amend their agreement every year. S corporations offer less flexibility because of the statutory restrictions on capital structure. S corporations can have only a single class of stock, and each share must represent an identical claim on the income and assets of the business.

Owner Liability

Historically, an S corporation was the only choice for owners who wanted to pay a single tax on business income at the owner level and avoid unlimited personal liability for claims against the business. In contrast, the traditional partnership involved significant financial risk for general partners, who have unlimited liability for business debt. In recent years, traditional partnerships have been supplanted by LLPs and LLCs, both of which offer greater protection against financial risk. In an LLP, a partner is not personally liable for malpractice-related claims arising from the professional misconduct of another partner. In many states, professionals such as CPAs and attorneys organize their practices as LLPs to safeguard themselves against the negligent actions of any one individual partner. In an LLC, every member has limited liability for all debts of or claims against the business. Consequently, an LLC combines the tax advantages of a passthrough entity *and* the legal protection of the corporate form, without the costs or complications of the latter. The number of these organizations is growing at a phenomenal rate, and the LLC is now the entity of choice for most new businesses.

Two Planning Cases

To complete our discussion of the relative advantages and disadvantages of partnerships and S corporations, let's develop two cases in which differences between them are key variables in the planning process.

Leveraged Real Property Venture

Six individuals decide to form a company to purchase, rehabilitate, and manage a hotel. The hotel property is subject to a $3 million nonrecourse mortgage, and the owner is willing to sell his equity in the property for only $50,000. The commercial lender holding the mortgage has agreed to the conveyance of the hotel to the new company. The individuals will each contribute $20,000 cash in exchange for equal ownership interests, and the company will use the cash to buy the hotel and begin the necessary renovations. The individuals forecast that the company will generate a $264,000 tax loss for its first year. Most of this loss is from cost recovery deductions with respect to the hotel building and its furnishings.

The individuals intend to organize the company as a passthrough entity; consequently, each individual will be allocated $44,000 of the first-year loss. The individuals can deduct the loss only to the extent of the tax basis in their equity interest. If the company is organized as an S corporation, each individual's stock basis is $20,000—the cash contributed to the corporation. Therefore, each can deduct only $20,000 of the first-year loss.

If the company is organized as an LLC, the tax basis in each member's interest includes both the contributed cash *and* a portion of the LLC's debts. Because of the $3 million nonrecourse mortgage on the hotel, each individual has an initial basis of $520,000 ($20,000 cash + one-sixth of the mortgage). Because the LLC debt is included in basis, the individuals can deduct their entire shares of the first-year business losses.[12]

With respect to risk of financial loss, the individuals are indifferent between an LLC and an S corporation. In either case, the commercial lender can look only to the hotel property for satisfaction of the mortgage. The choice of entity should not affect the *total* business loss that each individual will eventually deduct. In the S corporation case, each shareholder can carry his $24,000 disallowed loss forward as a deduction against future income from the hotel business. The disadvantage of the S corporation is that the loss deduction is deferred. By operating their company as an LLC, the individuals can deduct the loss in the year incurred, thereby maximizing the value of the tax savings from the loss.

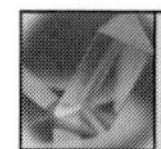

Transferring Equity to Successive Generations

Mr. and Mrs. Traub are approaching retirement age and want to begin transferring their business to their three children and, ultimately, to their seven grandchildren. The grandchildren range from 1 year to 18 years of age, and the adults agree that it would be premature to make any grandchild an owner. Mr. and Mrs. Traub could create a family partnership to give their children an ownership interest in the business. In this case, a legally drafted partnership agreement would create and define the equity interests of each family member. But what happens in four years when one partner wants to transfer a portion of her equity to the eldest grandchild, or in six years when Mr. Traub wants to withdraw from the business and divide his equity among his three children? Every time the family modifies the ownership structure, the partnership agreement must be amended and the partnership interests redefined—a procedure that may be both inconvenient and costly.

As an alternative, Mr. and Mrs. Traub could incorporate their business as an S corporation with a specified number of shares of stock. Each share would represent a pro rata interest in the business. Mr. and Mrs. Traub, and eventually their children, can modify the ownership structure of the corporation by simply giving shares to another relative. By choosing an S corporation rather than a partnership, Mr. and Mrs. Traub can minimize the transaction costs associated with a systematic transfer of ownership to their offspring.

TAX PLANNING WITH CLOSELY HELD CORPORATIONS

At some point in the life of a small business, the owners may decide to change from a passthrough entity to a corporation. Perhaps the organization has become so complex that the partnership form is unwieldy. Or perhaps the business has grown to the extent that the owners want to sell stock to the public, and the corporate form becomes a legal necessity. Regardless of the size or nature of the enterprise or the number of shareholders, the double taxation of income is the predominant tax problem associated with the corporate form. In this section of the chapter, we will discuss how the owners of closely held corporations cope with the problem.

[12] This statement assumes that the mortgage is qualified nonrecourse financing for at-risk purposes and the passive activity loss limitation is inapplicable. The passive activity loss limitation is discussed in Chapter 15.

Getting Cash Out of the Corporation

Owners of closely held corporations are aware that dividends have a high tax cost. Consequently, they can become very creative in devising ways to bail cash out of their corporations. The standard tactic is for an individual shareholder to assume an additional role with respect to the corporation. For instance, shareholders commonly serve as corporate officers or executives. In their role as employees, they are entitled to salaries that create cash flow to them and are deductible by the corporation. As a result, the business dollars paid as compensation are taxed only once at the individual level. Similarly, shareholders can become creditors by lending money to their corporations; the interest paid by the corporation on the debt is a deductible expense. Shareholders may lease property to their corporations for rent payments that the corporation can deduct. In all these cases, the cash received by the shareholder, whether as salary, interest, or rent, is taxable as ordinary income. The critical difference is at the corporate level where dividends are paid with after-tax dollars but salaries, interest, and rent are paid with before-tax dollars.

Prior to the enactment of the Jobs and Growth Tax Relief Reconciliation Act of 2003, individual shareholders paid tax on their dividends at the regular progressive rates. Beginning in 2003, dividends are taxed at a maximum 15 percent rate.[13] Because this new preferential rate decreases the double-tax burden on dividends, owners of closely held corporations now have less incentive to pay themselves salaries, interest, and rent instead of dividends.

Constructive Dividends

Objective 4
Define the term *constructive dividend.*

The IRS has no quarrel with shareholders who transact with their corporations if the transaction is based on reasonable terms comparable to those that would be negotiated between unrelated parties. Even so, the IRS understands that shareholders have an incentive to violate this arm's-length standard. When revenue agents audit closely held corporations, they pay special attention to any deductions for payments to shareholders. If an agent concludes that the payment is unreasonable in light of the facts and circumstances, the IRS may conclude that the unreasonable portion is a **constructive dividend.**

Unreasonable Compensation

Mr. Maupin, sole shareholder and chief executive officer of MP Inc., receives a $450,000 annual salary. If other companies comparable in size and function to MP pay salaries to their CEOs ranging from $400,000 to $500,000 and if Mr. Maupin has the talent and experience to merit such compensation, his salary appears reasonable, and MP can deduct it. Conversely, if the CEO salaries paid by comparable firms average only $300,000 and Mr. Maupin spends more time on the golf course than at corporate headquarters, the IRS may conclude that some portion of his salary is unreasonable.[14]

Let's build on the preceding example by assuming that the IRS decides that $150,000 of Mr. Maupin's annual salary is unreasonable and should be treated as a dividend. What are the tax consequences of this decision?

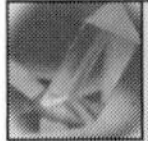

Constructive Dividend

The following table compares the net tax cost of a $450,000 payment from MP Inc. to Mr. Maupin when the entire payment is treated as salary with the net tax cost when only $300,000 is treated as salary and $150,000 is treated as a dividend. The table assumes that

[13] §1(h)(3)(B). The 15 percent rate drops to 5 percent for dividend income that would be taxed at 15 percent or less under the regular rate structure.

[14] The topic of reasonable compensation is discussed in more detail in Chapter 14.

Mr. Maupin's marginal rate on ordinary income is 35 percent and MP's marginal rate is 34 percent. (The comparison ignores the difference in payroll taxes under the two assumptions.)

	Salary	*Salary/ Dividend*
Mr. Maupin's salary	$450,000	$300,000
	.35	.35
Mr. Maupin's **tax cost** of salary	$157,500	$105,000
Mr. Maupin's dividend	-0-	$150,000
		.15
Mr. Maupin's **tax cost** of dividend		$22,500
MP's deduction for the payment	$450,000	$300,000
	.34	.34
MP's **tax savings** from the deduction	$153,000	$102,000
Net tax cost of payment **(tax costs less tax savings)**	$ 4,500	$ 25,500

Note that the reduction in Mr. Maupin's tax cost attributable to his 15 percent preferential rate on dividends is not enough to offset the reduction in MP Inc.'s tax savings attributable to payment of a nondeductible dividend. The $21,000 increase in the net tax cost when $150,000 of the $450,000 payment must be treated as a dividend falls squarely on Mr. Maupin as the sole owner of the corporation.

These next two examples illustrate constructive dividends in two other contexts.

Unreasonable Rent Payments

Mr. Serednesky rented office space from an unrelated third party for $8,000 annual rent, then subleased the office space to his wholly owned corporation for $16,604. The corporation deducted the $16,604 payment as rent expense on its tax return. The IRS determined that only $8,000 of the payment represented a reasonable, arm's-length rent, and that $8,604 of the payment was a nondeductible dividend.[15]

Shareholder Expenses

Mr. Leonard was the sole shareholder and employee of a personal service corporation. The corporation paid $1,663 of Mr. Leonard's personal travel and entertainment expenses and deducted the payment as a business expense. The IRS treated the payment as a nondeductible constructive dividend that Mr. Leonard had to include in his taxable income. The federal court agreed with the IRS's evaluation of the transaction. When Mr. Leonard protested that the tax consequences unfairly penalized him for operating a business in corporate form, the court replied, "The corporate bed may have lumps; once chosen, however, a taxpayer must endure a sleepless night every now and then."[16]

[15] *Social Psychological Services, Inc.*, TC Memo 1993-565.

[16] *Leonard*, TC Memo 1989-432.

Thin Capitalization

The organizers of closely held corporations usually understand that if they invest funds in exchange for a corporate debt obligation, the corporation can deduct the interest paid on the debt. Moreover, a loan is temporary, and the organizers will receive a return of their investment according to a fixed repayment schedule or even on demand. On the other hand, if they invest funds in exchange for equity stock, their investment is permanent, and any dividends paid on the investment are nondeductible. As a result, organizers are motivated to include as much debt as possible in their corporation's capital structure.

If the debt held by shareholders is excessive, the IRS may contend that some or all of the debt is disguised equity. As a result, interest payments are actually nondeductible dividends. Even worse, principal repayments may be reclassified as constructive dividends.[17] Because these repayments were nondeductible to the corporation, their reclassification doesn't affect the corporation's taxable income. However, the shareholders who believed they were receiving a nontaxable return of investment must recognize the repayments as income.

Disguised Equity

Mr. and Mrs. Vance formed V&V Inc. in 1997 by contributing $1,000 for 100 shares of common stock (the minimum capitalization under state law). The couple also loaned $25,000 to V&V in exchange for the corporation's note. The note had no fixed repayment schedule but did provide for annual interest. The corporation has never paid a dividend and paid no interest on the note from 1997 through 2002. Late in 2003, V&V distributed $36,250 to Mr. and Mrs. Vance. According to the corporate financial records, the distribution was a repayment of the 1997 loan plus $11,250 accrued interest. The corporation deducted the $11,250 interest on its tax return, and Mr. and Mrs. Vance reported $11,250 interest income on their tax return. The revenue agent who audited V&V's 2003 return concluded that Mr. and Mrs. Vance's loan was, in substance, an equity investment. Thus, the entire $36,250 distribution was a dividend—nondeductible to V&V and taxable to Mr. and Mrs. Vance.

The IRS is most likely to challenge the validity of shareholder debt when a closely held corporation is **thinly capitalized,** with an unusually high ratio of debt to equity. From the government's perspective, the debt-equity ratio is a measure of the business risk borne by the corporation's creditors. A capital structure can become so top heavy with debt that repayment depends on the corporation's continuing profitability rather than on the security of the underlying equity base. In such case, the purported debt has the economic characteristics of common stock. Although the tax law does not contain a safe harbor, a debt-equity ratio of 3 to 1 or less is generally considered immune from IRS attack.[18] Regardless of the corporate debt-equity ratio, shareholders should take care that any loan to their corporation has all the attributes of arm's-length debt. The loan should be evidenced by the corporation's written, unconditional promise to repay the principal by a specified date plus a fixed market rate of interest. Ideally, the debt should not be subordinated to other corporate liabilities, and the shareholders should not hold debt in the same proportion as they own the corporate stock. By respecting these formalities, shareholders can minimize the possibility that the IRS will question the capital structure of their corporation.

[17] This is typically the case when the debt held by the shareholders is in proportion to their stock interests. As a result, principal repayments are treated as distributions under §302(d) and are taxable as dividends to the extent of the corporation's earnings and profits.

[18] Boris I. Bittker and James S. Eustice, *Federal Income Taxation of Corporations and Shareholders,* 6th ed. (Boston: Warren Gorham Lamont, 1994), pp. 4–35.

The Decline of the Corporate Tax Shelter

A Historical Perspective

For most of the history of the federal income tax, the tax rates for individuals were significantly higher than the tax rates for corporations. For example, from 1965 through 1980, the top marginal rate for individuals was 70 percent, while the top marginal rate for corporations hovered around 48 percent. Business owners could take advantage of the rate differential by operating their businesses in the corporate form. Of course, this arbitrage strategy was effective only to the extent that the owners could do without annual dividends from their closely held corporations.

Individual shareholders who had their corporations *accumulate* (i.e., retain) after-tax earnings instead of distributing dividends did not permanently avoid the double tax on such earnings. The accumulated earnings increased the shareholders' equity and thus the value of the corporate stock. As long as shareholders held on to their stock, the unrealized appreciation in value was not taxed. But if and when a shareholder disposed of stock in a taxable transaction, the shareholder recognized the appreciation as capital gain and paid an indirect second tax on the corporation's accumulated earnings. Because this second tax was postponed until the year of the stock disposition, its cost was reduced in present value terms. Furthermore, the second tax was computed at the preferential capital gain rate instead of the regular rate on ordinary income. This combination of *deferral* and *conversion* (of ordinary income into capital gain) enhanced the attraction of the corporate tax shelter.

The Classic Corporate Tax Shelter

Many years ago, when the top individual tax rate was 70 percent and the top corporate tax rate was only 48 percent, Mr. and Mrs. Van Sant organized a new business as V&S Inc. For its first year (year 0), V&S generated $200,000 taxable income, paid $96,000 income tax, and accumulated $104,000. If the Van Sants had organized their business as a passthrough entity, their year 0 individual tax on $200,000 income would have been $140,000.

The Van Sants held their V&S stock until year 15 when they sold it to a competitor. Their capital gain on sale, which was taxed at a 20 percent preferential rate, reflected 15 years of appreciation in value attributable to V&S's accumulated earnings. Therefore, the indirect second tax on the $104,000 earnings accumulated in year 0 was $20,800. The NPV of this tax at an 8 percent discount rate was $6,552, and the double tax on the corporate income in present value terms totaled $102,552. By organizing their business as a corporation instead of a passthrough entity, the Van Sants saved $37,448 tax ($140,000 individual tax − $102,552 double tax) on their year 0 income.

The Current Environment

Objective 5
Explain why individuals no longer can use corporations as tax shelters.

In 1981, Congress began gradually to decrease the top marginal rates for both individual and corporate taxpayers and to diminish the spread between the rates. The Jobs and Growth Tax Relief Reconciliation Act of 2003 finally equalized the top marginal rates at 35 percent. As you learned in Chapter 10, only a minuscule amount of corporate income is taxed at the progressive rates below 34 percent. Consequently, in today's tax environment, the opportunity for individuals to exploit the differences between the individual and the corporate rate structures is exceedingly narrow.

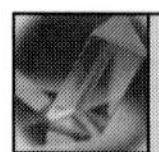

No More Shelter

What if the Van Sants were to begin their new business today? Could they save any tax by organizing as a corporation rather than a passthrough entity? Let's compare the tax outcomes under two different assumptions about the amount of 2005 income generated by the business.

If the business generates $200,000 income and is organized as a corporation, the 2005 corporate tax would be $61,250, and accumulated earnings would be $138,750. If the Van Sants sell their stock in 2020 (after 15 years), their indirect second tax on the $138,750 accumulated earnings at a 15 percent capital gains rate will be $20,813. The NPV of this tax at an 8 percent discount rate is $6,556, and the double tax on the corporate income in present value terms totals $67,806. But if the Van Sants organize their business as a passthrough entity, their 2005 tax on $200,000 *computed at the highest marginal rate* would be $70,000, which is a mere $2,194 more than the corporate alternative.

If the business generates $400,000 income and is organized as a corporation, the 2005 corporate tax would be $136,000, and accumulated earnings would be $264,000. If the Van Sants sell their stock in 2020, their indirect second tax on the $264,000 accumulated earnings at a 15 percent capital gains rate will be $39,600. The NPV of this tax at an 8 percent discount rate is $12,474, and the double tax on the corporate income in present value terms totals $148,474. But if the Van Sants organize their business as a passthrough entity, their 2005 tax on $400,000 *computed at the highest marginal rate* would be $140,000, which is $8,474 *less* than the corporate alternative!

This example demonstrates that entrepreneurs like the Van Sants can save tax by organizing their business as a corporation only if the business income is very small *and* if the entrepreneurs are willing to forgo cash flow (dividends) from the business for a long period of time. For most individuals, the corporate form offers no tax shelter whatsoever and a passthrough entity is the logical choice.

Penalty Taxes on Corporate Accumulations

Objective 6
Explain the purpose of the accumulated earnings tax and the personal holding company tax.

Prior to the equalization of the top individual and corporate rates, individuals could reduce their tax costs significantly by operating their businesses as corporations. Decades ago, Congress resolved to discourage the use of closely held corporations as tax shelters by enacting two penalty taxes on corporations that fail to distribute dividends to their individual shareholders. These two taxes, the accumulated earnings tax and the personal holding company tax, are still part of the tax law even though the glory days of corporate tax shelters are over. A corporation that finds itself liable for either tax must pay it *in addition to* its income tax for the year.

Accumulated Earnings Tax

The IRS can impose an **accumulated earnings tax** on any corporation "formed or availed of for the purpose of avoiding the income tax with respect to its shareholders by permitting earnings and profits to accumulate instead of being divided or distributed."[19] This tax avoidance purpose is presumed to exist when a corporation accumulates earnings beyond the reasonable needs of its business. The penalty tax equals 15 percent of the corporation's *accumulated taxable income* (roughly defined as taxable income less income tax and dividends paid). For example, a corporation with $660,000 after-tax income that pays no dividends and has no business justification to accumulate earnings could owe a $99,000 accumulated earnings tax ($660,000 × 15 percent).

The accumulated earnings tax is clearly intended to coerce corporations to pay dividends. The IRS's application of the tax is uncertain and subjective. Many corporations have accumulated millions of dollars, and their shareholders have never worried about the

[19] §532(a). Sections 531 through 537 describe the accumulated earnings tax.

penalty tax because they have documented reasons justifying the accumulation.[20] The corporate balance sheet may show that retained earnings financed the development of a new product line, the geographic expansion of the business, the retirement of long-term debt, or the construction of a new manufacturing facility. On the other hand, corporations vulnerable to the tax display two common traits. They have a history of minimal or no dividend payments, and their balance sheets reveal an overabundance of nonbusiness assets such as long-term certificates of deposit, marketable securities, investment real estate, and, most damning of all, substantial loans to shareholders.

The tax law gives newly incorporated businesses some leeway to retain after-tax income on a "no-questions-asked" basis. Specifically, every corporation can accumulate $250,000 without establishing business need and without exposure to the penalty tax.[21]

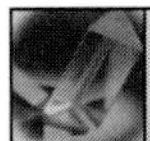

"No-Questions-Asked" Accumulation

Selby Inc., a calendar year corporate taxpayer, was formed in 2002. On December 31, 2002, Selby's accumulated earnings were $82,700. Consequently, Selby was immune to the accumulated earnings tax for 2002. By December 31, 2003, Selby's accumulated earnings had increased to $204,900. Because this accumulation was still less than $250,000, Selby's immunity continued for 2003. In 2004, Selby's after-tax earnings were $400,000, and the corporation did not pay any dividends. Shelby can accumulate only $45,100 ($250,000 − $204,900 prior years' accumulated earnings) in 2004 on a "no-questions-asked" basis. It must be able to demonstrate a reasonable business need for the additional $354,900 accumulation to avoid exposure to a 2004 accumulated earnings tax on these earnings.

Personal Holding Company Tax

Corporations qualifying as personal holding companies may be liable for a **personal holding company tax.**[22] The statutory definition of a **personal holding company** is technically complex—suffice it to say that personal holding companies are owned by a small number of individuals and earn primarily nonbusiness income such as dividends, interest, rents, and royalties. The penalty tax equals 15 percent of undistributed after-tax corporate income for the year. For example, a personal holding company with $2,450,000 undistributed after-tax income owes a $367,500 personal holding company tax ($2,450,000 × 15 percent). Personal holding companies that distribute 100 percent of after-tax earnings are not liable for any penalty tax.[23]

Congress enacted the personal holding company tax more than 60 years ago. Its purpose was to discourage individuals from incorporating their investment portfolios to take advantage of corporate tax rates that were 45 percentage points less than individual rates. Today, there is no difference between the highest corporate and individual rates, and individuals have no tax incentive to incorporate their portfolios. Nevertheless, a corporation qualifying as a personal holding company must attach a Schedule PH showing the computation of any additional penalty tax to its annual Form 1120.

[20] Publicly held corporations are normally immune to the accumulated earnings tax because their dividend policies are not controlled by their shareholders.

[21] Personal service corporations may accumulate only $150,000 without establishing reasonable business need.

[22] §541. Sections 541 through 547 describe the personal holding company tax.

[23] Personal holding companies are not subject to the accumulated earnings tax. §532(b)(1).

EXHIBIT 11.1
Controlled Corporate Groups

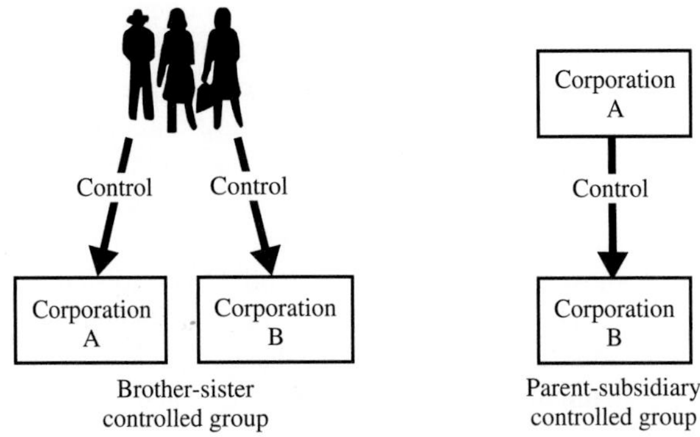

Controlled Corporate Groups

Objective 7
Apply the tax rates to income earned by a controlled corporate group.

The corporate tax rates are mildly progressive on taxable income up to $335,000, at which point the rate becomes a flat 34 percent. This rate applies until taxable income reaches $10 million, at which point the marginal rate increases to 35 percent. The rates again become slightly progressive until taxable income reaches $18,333,333, at which point the rate becomes a flat 35 percent. The owners of a corporate business might be tempted to take advantage of the progressivity in the tax rates by fragmenting their business into multiple corporate entities. For instance, if a business that generates $1 million annual income is organized as *one* corporation, its annual tax is $340,000. However, if that business could be splintered into *five* corporations, each reporting $200,000 taxable income, the annual tax would be reduced to $306,250 ($61,250 tax on $200,000 income × 5).

The law prevents this tax avoidance strategy through the rules applying to controlled groups of corporations. Specifically, a **controlled group** has only "one run" up the progressive rates because the rates apply to the group's aggregate taxable income instead of the taxable incomes of each group member.[24] Additionally, the controlled group as a whole can retain only $250,000 after-tax earnings without establishing a reasonable business need for the accumulation.[25]

The tax law identifies two types of controlled corporate groups. The first type is a brother-sister group consisting of two or more corporations controlled by the same set of individual shareholders. The second type is a parent-subsidiary group consisting of a parent corporation that owns one or more controlled subsidiaries. Both types of controlled groups are pictured in Exhibit 11.1.

Parent-subsidiary controlled groups often qualify as affiliated groups eligible to file a consolidated tax return.[26] Parent-subsidiary groups that elect to file on a consolidated basis compute the group's income tax based on consolidated taxable income. Similarly, the accumulated earnings tax rules apply with reference to consolidated after-tax earnings. Thus, the controlled group rules concern only those parent-subsidiary groups that file separate returns rather than a consolidated return. Brother-sister controlled groups, however, are not eligible to file consolidated tax returns. Consequently, the controlled group rules concern all brother-sister groups. While individual shareholders may create brother-sister corporate groups for good nontax reasons, they do not derive any tax advantage by doing so.

[24] §1561(a)(1).

[25] §1561(a)(2).

[26] See the discussion of consolidated tax returns in Chapter 10.

Conclusion

This chapter concludes our study of the five basic forms of business organization. Four of these forms—sole proprietorships, partnerships, LLCs, and S corporations—are not taxable entities for federal purposes. Individuals who use these forms pay a single tax on their business income. Only the fifth form—corporations—is taxed at the entity level, and shareholders pay a second tax when they receive dividends from the corporation. Business owners who want to engage in successful tax planning must understand the basic tax rules that differentiate passthrough entities and corporations. By taking advantage of these rules, the owners can control tax costs, maximize after-tax income available for personal consumption, and enhance the value of their investment in the business.

Key Terms

accumulated earnings tax *306*
constructive dividend *302*
controlled group *308*
personal holding company *307*
personal holding company tax *307*
thin capitalization *304*

Questions and Problems for Discussion

1. Mr. and Mrs. V are self-employed professional musicians. Their average annual income from performance fees and music lessons is $130,000. The couple wants to shift income to their two children, ages 19 and 22. Can Mr. and Mrs. V organize their music business as a family partnership and give each child a 25 percent interest?
2. Mr. and Mrs. B own a fast-food restaurant that generates $160,000 average annual income. The couple wants to shift some of this income to their two children, ages 19 and 22. Can Mr. and Mrs. B organize their restaurant as a family partnership and give each child a 25 percent interest?
3. Ms. J is eager to create a family partnership to generate income and cash flow for her three college-age children. She owns two businesses, either of which could be organized as a partnership. Ms. J established the first business 15 years ago. This business consists of operating assets with a $15 million FMV. Ms. J established the second business only 10 months ago. This business is growing rapidly and already is generating taxable income. However, its operating assets have only a $300,000 FMV. Which business is the better candidate for a family partnership? Explain your reasoning.
4. Discuss the tax and nontax reasons why the stock in an S corporation is typically subject to a buy-sell agreement.
5. Mr. ER operates an antique store located on the first floor of a four-story office building owned by Mr. ER. The top three stories are leased to business tenants. Mr. ER is considering giving a one-third interest in both the antique store and the building to each of his two grandchildren and operating the businesses in one passthrough entity. Mr. ER wants to receive 100 percent of the rent from his tenants for several years but is willing to distribute one-third of the net profit from the antique store to his grandchildren each year. On the basis of this objective, which form of organization should he choose?
6. Dr. Q, Dr. R, and Dr. T are dentists who practice as equal owners of QRT Dental Services. A patient of Dr. R's recently sued him for medical malpractice and was awarded a $500,000 judgment. Discuss each owner's personal liability for this judgment assuming that:
   a. QRT is a general partnership.
   b. QRT is an LLP.
   c. QRT is an LLC.

7. Refer to the facts in the previous problem. QRT purchased $30,000 of dental equipment on credit. When QRT failed to pay its bill, the seller took it to court and won a judgment for $30,000. Discuss each owner's personal liability for this judgment assuming that:
   a. QRT is a general partnership.
   b. QRT is an LLP.
   c. QRT is an LLC.
8. Mrs. T and Mrs. N each owns a small business that averages $80,000 annual income. Each woman is in the 35 percent marginal tax bracket. Mrs. T has decided to incorporate her business as a taxable corporation, while Mrs. N has decided to continue to operate as a sole proprietorship. Both decisions maximize the after-tax value of the business to its owner. How can you explain this apparent contradiction?
9. BNC, a closely held corporation, was organized in 1987. To date, it has accumulated over $10 million after-tax income. This year, BNC's taxable income is $750,000, and its federal tax is $255,000. Describe two different ways that BNC can avoid exposure to the accumulated earnings tax for the year.
10. Describe the FICA payroll tax implications when the IRS classifies a portion of a salary payment to a shareholder/employee as a constructive dividend.
11. When the IRS classifies a portion of a salary payment to a shareholder/employee as a constructive dividend, which party (corporation or shareholder) bears the economic burden of the tax consequences?
12. Ms. K recently loaned $20,000 to her closely held corporation, which needed the money for working capital. She sees no reason to document the loan other than as a "loan payable—shareholder" on the corporate balance sheet. She also sees no reason for her corporation to pay interest on the loan. What advice can you offer Ms. K concerning this related-party transaction?
13. Explain the logic of the tax rate for both the accumulated earnings tax and the personal holding company tax.
14. In what way does a corporate balance sheet provide information concerning the corporation's exposure to the accumulated earnings tax?
15. Why are publicly held corporations such as General Motors generally immune from the accumulated earnings tax?
16. How would the tax shelter potential of closely held corporations be affected by:
   a. An increase in the highest individual tax rate to 43 percent?
   b. A decrease in the preferential tax rate on individual capital gains to 5 percent?
   c. Repeal of the accumulated earnings tax?
17. Both brother-sister groups and parent-subsidiary groups are controlled groups for federal tax purposes. However, the qualification as a controlled group is more of an issue for brother-sister groups than for parent-subsidiary groups. Can you explain why?

Application Problems

1. Mr. T and Ms. U organized a new business as an LLC in which they own equal interests. The new business generated a $4,800 operating loss for the year.
   a. If Mr. T's marginal tax rate before consideration of the LLC loss is 35 percent, compute his tax savings from the first-year LLC loss.
   b. Assume that Ms. U has no taxable income for the year. However, her taxable income last year was enough to put her into the 28 percent tax bracket. Compute her tax savings from the LLC loss.

c. Assume that Ms. U has no taxable income for the year or for the two preceding years. Does she have any tax savings from the LLC loss?

2. Mr. and Mrs. LC and their two children (Ben and June) are the four equal partners in LCBJ Partnership. This year, LCBJ generated $36,000 ordinary income. Compute the tax cost for the business if Mr. and Mrs. LC's marginal rate is 33 percent, Ben's marginal rate is 28 percent, and June's marginal rate is 15 percent.
3. Ms. K owns a 10 percent interest in Carlton LLC. This year, the LLC generated $72,400 ordinary income. Mrs. K's marginal tax rate is 33 percent, and she does not pay SE tax on her LLC income.
   a. Compute the tax cost on Ms. K's share of Carlton's income assuming that she received a $35,000 cash distribution this year.
   b. Compute the tax cost on Ms. K's share of Carlton's income assuming that she received no cash distribution this year.
4. Mrs. FB, who is in the 35 percent tax bracket, owns a residential apartment building that generates $80,000 annual taxable income. She plans to create a family partnership by giving each of her two children a 20 percent equity interest in the building. (She will retain a 60 percent interest.) Mrs. FB will manage the building, and value of her services is $15,000 per year. If Mrs. FB's children are in the 15 percent tax bracket, compute the tax savings from this income-shifting arrangement.
5. WRT, a calendar year S corporation, has 100 shares of outstanding stock. At the beginning of the year, Mr. W owned all 100 shares. On September 30, he gave 25 shares to his brother and 40 shares to his daughter. WRT's ordinary income for the year was $216,000. What portion of this income must each shareholder include in income?
6. Mr. T, who is in the 35 percent tax bracket, is the sole shareholder of Toto, which manufactures greeting cards. Toto's average annual net profit (before deduction of Mr. T's salary) is $200,000. For each of the following cases, compute the income tax burden on this profit. (Ignore any payroll tax consequences.)
   a. Mr. T's salary is $100,000, and Toto pays no dividends.
   b. Mr. T's salary is $100,000, and Toto distributes its after-tax income as a dividend.
   c. Toto is an S corporation. Mr. T's salary is $100,000, and Toto makes no cash distributions.
   d. Toto is an S corporation. Mr. T draws no salary, and Toto makes no cash distributions.
   e. Toto is an S corporation. Mr. T draws no salary, and Toto makes cash distributions of all its income to Mr. T.
7. Mr. P and Mrs. Q are the equal shareholders in Corporation PQ. Both shareholders have a 35 percent marginal tax rate. PQ's financial records show the following.

Gross income from sales of goods	$880,000
Operating expenses	(410,000)
Interest paid on debt to Mr. P and Mrs. Q	(62,000)
Dividend distributions:	
Mr. P	(50,000)
Mrs. Q	(50,000)

   a. Compute the combined tax cost for PQ, Mr. P, and Mrs. Q.
   b. How would your computation change if the interest on the shareholder debt was $162,000, and PQ paid no dividends?

8. Ms. X, who is in the 35 percent tax bracket, is the sole shareholder and president of Xenon. The corporation's financial records show the following.

Gross income from sales of goods	$1,590,000
Operating expenses	(930,000)
Salary paid to Ms. X	(300,000)
Dividend distributions	(200,000)

a. Compute the combined tax cost for Xenon and Ms. X.

b. How would your computation change if Ms. X's salary was $500,000, and Xenon paid no dividends?

9. Mr. Z is the sole shareholder of TZ. He also owns the office building that serves as corporate headquarters. Last year, TZ paid $180,000 annual rent to Mr. Z for use of the building. TZ's marginal tax rate was 34 percent, and Mr. Z's marginal tax rate was 35 percent. The revenue agent who audited TZ's return concluded that the fair rental value of the office building was $125,000.

a. What effect does this conclusion have on Mr. Z's tax?

b. What effect does this conclusion have on TZ's tax?

10. In 1994, Mr. and Mrs. AD formed ADC by transferring $50,000 cash in exchange for 100 shares of common stock and a note from the corporation for $49,000. The note obligated ADC to pay 10 percent annual interest and to repay the $49,000 principal on demand. ADC has never declared a dividend nor made any interest payments on the note. Last year, it distributed $25,000 cash to Mr. and Mrs. AD as a principal repayment. When the IRS audited ADC's tax return, the revenue agent determined that this payment was a constructive dividend.

a. What is the effect of the constructive dividend on ADC's tax if its marginal tax rate was 34 percent?

b. What is the effect of the constructive dividend on Mr. and Mrs. AD's tax if their marginal tax rate was 35 percent?

11. During a recent IRS audit, the revenue agent decided that the FP family used their closely held corporation, Falco, to avoid shareholder tax by accumulating earnings beyond the reasonable needs of the business. Falco's taxable income was $900,000, it paid no dividends, and it had no business need to retain any income. Compute Falco's accumulated earnings tax assuming that:

a. It had accumulated $4 million after-tax income in prior years.

b. It had accumulated $129,000 after-tax income in prior years.

Issue Recognition Problems

Identify the tax issue or issues suggested by the following situations, and state each issue in the form of a question.

1. Mr. and Mrs. KK are in the highest marginal tax bracket. Their son, a freshman in college, earns minimal income from his summer job, and his marginal tax rate is 10 percent. Mr. and Mrs. KK are considering making their son an equal owner in a family business that generates over $200,000 taxable income each year. They believe that every dollar of income shifted to their son will save more than 25 cents of tax for the family.
2. Mr. J owns a 40 percent interest in newly formed JKL Partnership. The partners organized their business as a passthrough entity so that the start-up loss would generate an

immediate tax savings. Mr. J, however, had a substantial loss from another business and has no taxable income against which to deduct his share of the JKL loss.

3. Mr. and Mrs. B own 100 percent of the stock of BB Inc., which operates a temporary employment business. Late last year, Mr. B was short of cash in his personal checking account. Consequently, he paid several personal bills by writing checks on the corporate account and recorded the payments as miscellaneous expenses. Three months later he repaid the corporation in full.
4. REW Inc. is closely held by six members of the REW family. The corporation owns two vans that employees use for various business transportation purposes. However, for at least eight weeks during each year, the shareholders use the vans to take their families on extended vacation trips.
5. Eight years ago, Mr. and Mrs. L created a family partnership with their son, the son's wife, their daughter, and the daughter's husband. Each of these six individuals owns an equal interest in the partnership. This year, the son and his wife decide to divorce.
6. LSN, a calendar year S corporation, has 13 shareholders. Since its incorporation, LSN has retained over $800,000 income to reinvest in its business. Because LSN is a passthrough entity, the shareholders have paid tax on this undistributed income and increased their stock basis accordingly. The shareholders want to revoke the S election and operate LSN as a regular corporation. LSN has only $69,000 in its corporate bank account.
7. Last year, Mrs. K and Mrs. T each contributed the assets of their respective sole proprietorships to a new corporation. The shareholders believed that by combining their businesses, they could increase profitability. They were encouraged to do so because they could transfer their assets in exchange for stock without recognizing gain. Unfortunately, Mrs. K and Mrs. T discovered that they couldn't work together effectively. They agreed to part company by dissolving the corporation and taking back ownership of their respective assets (essentially just reversing the incorporation process).
8. Taha is closely held by eight family members. Taha purchased investment land 12 years ago for $100,000. The land was recently appraised at a FMV of $3 million. A buyer has offered to pay cash for the land. Because the shareholders need the cash, they plan to have Taha distribute the land to them as a dividend. They will then sell the land and recognize a capital gain taxable at the 15 percent preferential individual rate.
9. Mr. and Mrs. CR own 100 percent of the stock in CR Inc., which recently hired the couple's nephew at a $30,000 annual salary. The nephew, age 20, has been in several scrapes with the law and needs financial help, and the CR family agreed that a low-stress job with the family business is just what he needs for a year or two.
10. WQ Corporation, a closely held family business, has not paid a dividend for the last seven years. Each year, the minutes of the board of directors' December meeting state that WQ must accumulate after-tax income to pay for a new manufacturing facility. Until plans for construction are finalized, WQ has been investing its excess cash in marketable securities. This year, WQ curtails its manufacturing business and abandons its plan for the new facility.

Research Problems

1. Fifteen years ago, Mr. and Mrs. Boyer created Brovo, a regular corporation, through which to operate a service business. The Boyers own all of Brovo's 1,000 shares of stock with a $1.6 million aggregate tax basis. The corporate business has been extremely successful; at the beginning of the year, Brovo's balance sheet reflected over $2 million retained earnings. According to a recent appraisal, its stock is worth $2.5

million. The Boyers want to withdraw $500,000 cash from Brovo for their personal use, but they do not want Brovo to pay them a dividend. Instead, they plan to have Brovo distribute $500,000 in exchange for 200 shares of their stock. The Boyers believe that they will recognize a $180,000 gain on this redemption, which will qualify as capital gain. Are the Boyers correct in their analysis of the tax consequences of the redemption?

2. On March 1, Mr. and Mrs. Trent formed Trent Properties Inc. through which to operate a real estate management business. Both Mr. and Mrs. Trent worked full-time for modest, but reasonable, salaries. In early December, the Trents estimated that the corporation would incur a $325,000 net loss for its first 10 months of operation. They decided to adopt a calendar year for Trent Properties Inc. and make an S election so that they could deduct the loss on their individual tax return. Can the Trents make an S election for Trent Property Inc.'s first taxable year?
3. Fair View Inc. owns and operates a golf club, which includes two 18-hole courses, a driving range, a restaurant, and a pro shop. The club's facilities can be used only by its membership, which includes all the individual shareholders as well as nonshareholders. All the members are charged a green fee for each round of play plus an additional fee for use of a golf cart. However, the fees for shareholders are 30 percent less than the fees for nonshareholders. Shareholders also enjoy a 30 percent discount on the price of food and drink purchased in the club restaurant and merchandise purchased in the pro shop. Do these discounts have any income tax consequences to Fair View's shareholders?
4. Four years ago, Amy Huang contributed four acres of undeveloped land to Richter Company in exchange for a 12 percent equity interest in Richter. Amy's tax basis in the land was $275,000, and the land's appraised FMV on date of contribution was $430,000. The exchange of land for equity was nontaxable to both Amy and Richter. Since the exchange, Richter has held the land as a long-term investment. This year, Richter sold the land to an unrelated purchaser for $550,000. How much capital gain does Richter recognize on the sale? How much of this gain is allocated to Amy if Richter is an LLC? How much gain is allocated to Amy if Richter is an S corporation?

Tax Planning Cases

1. Mr. and Mrs. TE own a sizable investment portfolio of stock in publicly held corporations. The couple has four children, ages 20, 22, 25, and 27, with whom they want to share their wealth. Unfortunately, none of the children has demonstrated any ability to manage money. As a result, Mr. and Mrs. TE plan to transfer their portfolio to a new corporation in exchange for 20 shares of voting stock and 400 shares of nonvoting stock. They will give 100 nonvoting shares to each child. The couple will serve as the directors of the corporation, manage the investment portfolio, and distribute cash dividends when their children need money. They estimate that the portfolio will generate $72,000 annual dividend income.
   a. If the TE Family Corporation is operated as an S corporation, compute the annual income tax burden on the dividend income generated by the investment portfolio. Assume that Mr. and Mrs. TE are in the 35 percent tax bracket and each child is in the 15 percent tax bracket. To simplify the case, ignore any value of the couple's management service to the corporation.
   b. Compute the tax burden for the first year if TE Family Corporation does not have an S election in effect and distributes a $100 annual dividend per share.

2. Mr. Y operates a photography studio as a sole proprietorship. His average annual income from the business is $100,000. Because Mr. Y does not need the entire cash flow for personal consumption, he is considering incorporating the business. He will work as a corporate employee for a $40,000 annual salary, and the corporation will accumulate its after-tax income to fund future business expansion. For purposes of this case, assume that Mr. Y's marginal income tax rate is 33 percent and ignore any employment tax consequences.
   a. Assuming that the new corporation would not be a personal service corporation, would Mr. Y decrease the annual tax burden on the business by incorporating?
   b. How would your answer change if the new corporation would be a personal service corporation?

Chapter Twelve

Jurisdictional Issues in Business Taxation

Learning Objectives

After studying this chapter, you should be able to:

1. Define the term *nexus.*
2. Apportion corporate taxable income among states according to UDITPA.
3. Explain the significance of a permanent establishment for determining international tax jurisdiction.
4. Compute a foreign tax credit.
5. Compare the tax consequences of a foreign branch operation and a foreign subsidiary.
6. Compute a deemed paid foreign tax credit.
7. Explain how subpart F income earned by a CFC is constructively repatriated to the U.S. parent.
8. Describe the role of Section 482 in the international transfer pricing area.

Chapter 12 introduces the issues that arise when firms operate in more than one taxing jurisdiction. Firms that span territorial boundaries must understand that an overlap in jurisdictions can cause the same income to be taxed more than once. In this chapter, we will learn how firms can minimize the burden of such duplicative taxation. We will also discover how the differences in tax costs across jurisdictions create planning opportunities. Firms can implement many effective strategies to shift income away from jurisdictions with high tax costs. These strategies relate back to our maxim that tax costs decrease and cash flows increase when income is generated in a jurisdiction with a low tax rate.

Chapter 12 begins with an overview of state and local taxes as a cost of doing business, then focuses on the key issues involving state income taxation. The first issue concerns the states' right to tax interstate commerce and the federal restrictions on such right. The concept of income apportionment is introduced, and strategies for reducing the aggregate tax burden on multistate businesses are discussed. The remainder of the chapter deals with the taxation of international business. We will learn that the United States has a global tax system that can result in the double taxation of foreign source income. The major role of the foreign tax credit in mitigating double taxation and the limitations on the credit are covered in some detail. We will consider how U.S. firms can organize overseas operations to control the tax consequences of those operations. Finally, we will discuss how U.S. corporations use foreign subsidiaries to defer income recognition and reduce the tax cost of international business.

STATE AND LOCAL TAXATION

In the United States, even the smallest firm is subject to three taxing jurisdictions: local government, state government, and the federal government. Historically, firms concentrated their tax planning efforts at the federal level and devoted less attention to state and local tax costs. Recently, firms have become more aware of their state and local tax burden. In response to demand by the business community, public accounting firms have developed specialized state and local tax (SALT) practices to provide expert professional help. More than ever before, firms and their tax advisers are formulating strategies to minimize real and personal property taxes, unemployment taxes, and sales and use taxes.

In the first section of this chapter, we focus on planning opportunities in the area of state income taxation. As we learned in Chapter 1, most states impose both a personal (individual) and a corporate income tax. Consequently, business income is subject to state tax whether the business is organized as a passthrough entity or a corporation. For federal purposes, corporations are allowed to deduct state income tax in the computation of taxable income.[1] The tax savings from this deduction reduce the cost of the state tax.

Federal Deduction for State Income Tax

ZT Inc. paid $45,000 state income tax this year. If ZT's federal tax rate is 34 percent, the after-tax cost of the payment is only $29,700.

State tax paid	$(45,000)
Federal tax savings	
($45,000 deduction × 34%)	15,300
After-tax cost	$(29,700)

Nonetheless, ZT's aggregate tax burden is increased because it must pay income tax at both the state and federal level. If ZT's before-tax income is $900,000 and the state tax rate is 5 percent, ZT's tax rate for the year is 37.3 percent.

State tax ($900,000 taxable income[2] × 5%)	$ 45,000
Federal tax ($855,000 taxable income × 34%)	290,700
Total income tax	$335,700

$335,700 ÷ $900,000 before-tax income = 37.3%

[1] For individual taxpayers, the state tax on both business and nonbusiness income is allowed as an itemized deduction. See Chapter 16.

[2] State income tax payments are not deductible in the computation of taxable income for state purposes. Five states (Alabama, Iowa, Louisiana, Missouri, and North Dakota) allow corporations to deduct a limited amount of federal tax in the computation of taxable income for state purposes.

Constitutional Restrictions on State Jurisdiction

Objective 1
Define the term *nexus*.

A state has jurisdiction to tax all individuals who reside in the state and all corporations formed under the laws of the state. This jurisdiction extends to nonresident individuals and corporations conducting business within the state. Thus, firms engaged in interstate commerce may be subject to tax in any number of states. Given that thousands of U.S. companies conduct business in more than one state, if not all 50 states, some degree of national coordination is necessary to avert fiscal anarchy.

Tax Talk
The U.S. Court of Appeals for the Sixth Circuit ruled that Ohio's investment tax credit is unconstitutional because it gives preferential treatment to in-state development activities, thereby interfering with interstate commerce and hindering free trade among the states.

Article 1 of the U.S. Constitution grants the federal government the power to "regulate commerce with foreign nations, and among the several states, and with the Indian tribes." This **Commerce Clause** empowers Congress and the federal courts to establish ground rules for state tax laws. For a state tax to be constitutional, it must not discriminate against interstate commerce. For instance, an income tax with a 3 percent rate for resident corporations and a 6 percent rate for nonresident corporations would be blatantly unconstitutional. In addition, state taxes can be levied only on businesses having nexus with the state. **Nexus** means the degree of contact between a business and a state necessary to establish jurisdiction.

The Issue of Nexus

Let's examine the concept of nexus by considering the regional business conducted by Show-Me Inc., which is incorporated in Missouri. Show-Me's corporate headquarters are in St. Louis, and its two manufacturing plants are in Kansas and Arkansas. The corporation uses a common carrier to ship its products to customers in Missouri, Kansas, Arkansas, Iowa, Nebraska, and Oklahoma. Show-Me's business is illustrated in Exhibit 12.1.

EXHIBIT 12.1
Show-Me Inc.

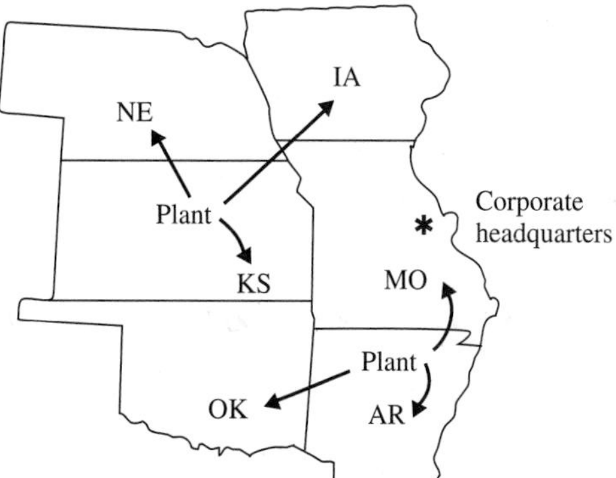

Because Show-Me is formed and protected under Missouri law and is commercially domiciled in the state, the corporation has nexus with Missouri. Show-Me has employees and owns real and personal property located in Kansas and Arkansas, and these states provide public benefits (fire and police protection, roads and highways, etc.) that add value to the corporation's business. Thus, Show-Me's physical presence in these two states creates nexus allowing both Kansas and Arkansas to tax the corporation.

But what about the other three states in Show-Me's region? According to the facts, Show-Me has no physical presence in Iowa, Nebraska, or Oklahoma. Under a long-standing federal statute, Public Law 86–272, firms do not establish nexus by simply selling tangible goods to customers residing in a state. Firms can even send traveling salespeople into a state to solicit orders for such goods without creating nexus.[3] Because of this federally mandated immunity, Show-Me is not subject to income tax in Iowa, Nebraska, and Oklahoma.

[3] 15 U.S.C. 381-384 (1959).

P.L. 86–272 does not pertain to business activities other than the sale of tangible goods. As a result, nonresident firms providing services (including the leasing of tangible property) or marketing intangible property to in-state residents are not immune to the state's taxing jurisdiction. Currently, the issue of nexus with respect to these in-state activities is unsettled. Several states have taken the aggressive position that any firm conducting a regular commercial activity within the state has established *economic* nexus. Accordingly, the state has jurisdiction to tax the firm regardless of the lack of physical presence in the state.[4] To date, Congress and the federal courts have remained silent on this controversial issue.[5]

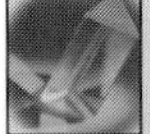

Economic Nexus

Show-Me's research division recently developed a manufacturing process that the corporation patented with the federal government. Show-Me licensed this patent to a number of companies, three of which operate in South Carolina. The companies pay an annual royalty for use of the patent. Although Show-Me has no physical presence (tangible property or employees) in South Carolina, it does earn revenue from marketing an intangible asset to South Carolina customers. On the basis of this economic nexus, South Carolina claims jurisdiction to tax Show-Me's royalty income.

The nexus issue is particularly uncertain for firms that sell goods and services over the Internet. Traditional nexus concepts make little sense when applied to business conducted in cyberspace. Consequently, many firms are hesitant about expanding their Internet operations for fear of inadvertently creating nexus with states in which they have no physical presence. In turn, state governments are concerned that the anticipated growth in electronic commerce will result in a loss of sales tax and income tax revenues from traditional commercial activities. The business community, the Internet industry, and state governments all acknowledge the need for a workable tax policy with respect to electronic commerce. Such policy should "facilitate, not impede, the growth of new technologies, while ensuring that no unfair tax advantage accrues to companies that develop or utilize such technologies."[6]

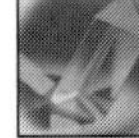

No Taxes in Cyberspace

On October 1, 1998, the Internet Tax Freedom Act went into effect. The act included a moratorium on new state and local taxes imposed on Internet access and a Congressional declaration that the Internet should be free of all international tariffs, trade barriers, and other restrictions. Supporters of the act maintain that the Internet is still in its infancy and must be protected against unbridled taxation. Critics claim that the act establishes the Internet as a giant tax shelter and that "for a bunch of nerds, computer types have proven to be very effective lobbyists."[7] On November 19, 2004, Congress voted to extend the Internet tax moratorium until November 1, 2007.

[4] The landmark case in this area is *Geoffrey, Inc.* v. *South Carolina Tax Commission,* 437 S.E.2d 13 (1993), *cert. denied,* 510 U.S. 992 (1993).

[5] A KPMG survey of corporate tax directors and CFOs revealed that nexus is the top state and local tax issue. "The uncertainty surrounding when an out-of-state corporation has sufficient contacts with a state to be subject to tax thwarts the compliance and planning effort and inhibits business." *Tax Adviser,* June 1996, p. 324.

[6] Houghton and Friedman, "Lost in [Cyber] Space?" 97 *State Tax Notes* 174-25.

[7] Lee Sheppard, "What Does 'No New Internet Taxes' Mean?" 97 *State Tax Notes* 141-51.

Apportionment of Business Income

The federal courts established the principle that states may tax only the income attributable to a firm's in-state business activity; the state may not tax income attributable to the firm's *extraterritorial value.* To comply with this principle, state law must provide a rational and fair method for determining the portion of a firm's total income subject to that state's tax.

In 1957, a National Conference of Uniform State Laws drafted the **Uniform Division of Income for Tax Purposes Act (UDITPA)** as a recommended method for apportioning income among multiple state jurisdictions. Today, most states use an apportionment formula modeled after UDITPA. Firms apply these formulas to derive an **apportionment percentage**, which determines the income taxable by each state. The UDIPTA formula is based on three equally weighted factors: the sales factor, the payroll factor, and the property factor.

$$\frac{\text{Sales factor} + \text{Payroll factor} + \text{Property factor}}{3} = \text{State apportionment percentage}$$

Objective 2
Apportion corporate taxable income among states according to UDITPA.

Each factor itself is a percentage computed as follows.

- The sales factor is the ratio of gross receipts from sales to in-state customers divided by total gross receipts from sales.
- The payroll factor is the ratio of compensation paid to employees working in-state divided by total compensation.
- The property factor is the ratio of the cost of real or tangible personal property located in-state divided by the total cost of such property.

To demonstrate the mechanics of income apportionment, let's examine the following data for Duo, a corporation conducting business in just two states, North Dakota and Montana.

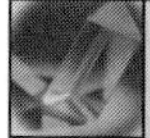

Apportionment Formulas

Duo's financial records provide the following information. (All numbers are in thousands of dollars.)

	North Dakota	*Montana*	*Total*
Gross receipts from sales	$ 8,200	$ 6,800	$15,000
Payroll expense	1,252	697	1,949
Property costs	18,790	10,004	28,794

Because both states use a three-factor UDITPA formula, each state's apportionment percentage is computed as follows.

	North Dakota	*Montana*
Sales factor	54.67% ($8,200 ÷ $15,000)	45.33% ($6,800 ÷ $15,000)
Payroll factor	64.24% ($1,252 ÷ $1,949)	35.76% ($697 ÷ $1,949)
Property factor	65.26% ($18,790 ÷ $28,794)	34.74% ($10,004 ÷ $28,794)

$$\text{North Dakota} \quad \frac{54.67\% + 64.24\% + 65.26\%}{3} = \underline{\underline{61.39\%}}$$

$$\text{Montana} \quad \frac{45.33\% + 35.76\% + 34.74\%}{3} = \underline{\underline{38.61\%}}$$

If Duo's annual income is $40 million, the portion taxable by North Dakota is $24.556 million (61.39 percent × $40 million) and the portion taxable by Montana is $15.444 million (38.61 percent × $40 million). Under these simple assumptions, exactly 100 percent of Duo's income is taxed. No income is taxed twice or escapes state taxation altogether.

Realistically, state apportionment methods never achieve this mathematical precision. One major reason is that 24 states now use a modified three-factor formula in which sales are *double-weighted* (the sales factor is counted twice and the factor total is divided by four). Another reason is that the definitions of the factors vary from state to state. For instance, the payroll factor under Virginia law includes compensation paid to corporate executive officers, while this compensation is excluded from North Carolina's payroll factor. Similarly, the definition of apportionable income is inconsistent across states. For instance, New Jersey law excludes interest and dividend income from the apportionment base, while New York law includes both as apportionable income. Clearly, states do not conform to a strictly uniform method of apportionment, and the federal courts have not required them to do so.[8] As a result, the division of taxable income among states inevitably results in some overlap or omission.

Tax Planning Implications

Multistate businesses can reduce their overall tax cost to the extent that they can shift income from a high-tax state to a low-tax state. This strategy often involves the manipulation of the state apportionment formulas. Let's refer back to our Duo example. Currently, North Dakota's tax rate on corporate income is 10.5 percent, while Montana's tax rate is 6.75 percent. Because of this rate differential, every $100 of income that Duo can shift from North Dakota's jurisdiction to Montana's jurisdiction saves $3.75 of tax.

Manipulating the Property Factor

Duo plans to build a new manufacturing plant at an estimated cost of $17 million. If the plant is built in Montana, the corporation's property factors will be revised as follows. (All numbers are in thousands of dollars.)

	North Dakota	Montana	Total
Property costs	$18,790	$10,004	$28,794
New manufacturing plant	-0-	17,000	17,000
Revised property costs	$18,790	$27,004	$45,794
Revised property factors	41.03%	58.97%	

[8] *Moorman Manufacturing Co. v. Bair, Director of Revenue of Iowa,* 437 U.S. 267 (1978).

Consequently, North Dakota's apportionment percentage will decrease, while Montana's apportionment percentage will increase.

North Dakota $\frac{54.67\% + 64.24\% + 41.03\%}{3} = \underline{\underline{53.31\%}}$

Montana $\frac{45.33\% + 35.76\% + 58.97\%}{3} = \underline{\underline{46.69\%}}$

Because Duo's decision to build a new plant in Montana increases that state's apportionment percentage, the decision shifts income from North Dakota to Montana and saves $121,200 state tax.[9]

Revised Apportionment

	Original Apportionment	
	North Dakota	**Montana**
Total taxable income	$40,000,000	$40,000,000
Apportionment percentage	.6139	.3861
State taxable income	$24,556,000	$15,444,000
	.105	.0675
State tax	$ 2,578,380	$ 1,042,470

	Revised Apportionment	
	North Dakota	**Montana**
Total taxable income	$40,000,000	$40,000,000
Apportionment percentage	.5331	.4669
State taxable income	$21,324,000	$18,676,000
	.105	.0675
State tax	$ 2,239,020	$ 1,260,630
Total state tax:		
Original apportionment	$ 3,620,850	
Revised apportionment	(3,499,650)	
Tax savings	$ 121,200	

Of course, the tax savings from the income shift is only one factor in the selection of the optimal site for the plant. Duo should certainly consider how its real and personal property tax costs will be affected by the geographic location of the plant. Nontax factors, such as the local cost of construction and the availability of a skilled workforce, are key elements in the selection process. While Duo may minimize its state income tax cost by locating its new manufacturing facility in Montana, this location is not necessarily the best choice for maximizing the value of the facility to the corporation.

[9] The Montana apportionment percentage will also reflect any increase in the Montana payroll factor attributable to the new manufacturing facility.

TAX CONSEQUENCES OF INTERNATIONAL BUSINESS OPERATIONS

In the current business environment, firms operating on a multinational level are becoming the rule rather than the exception. Globalization is creating exciting opportunities for U.S. businesses to expand into the emerging markets of eastern Europe, Africa, Asia, and South America. These opportunities are coupled with formidable obstacles. Firms with international aspirations must cope with differences across currencies, languages, technological sophistication, and cultural and political traditions.

Firms must be aware of the foreign tax implications of international operations. When a U.S. firm plans to expand its activities into another country, it should identify the taxes included in the country's fiscal structure. The firm's liability for these taxes will depend on the nature and extent of its activity within the country and whether such activity triggers the country's taxing jurisdiction. If the foreign country imposes a net income tax, its jurisdiction may depend on whether a tax treaty is in effect between the country and the United States.

Income Tax Treaties

Objective 3
Explain the significance of a permanent establishment for determining international tax jurisdiction.

An **income tax treaty** is a bilateral agreement between the governments of two countries defining and limiting each country's respective tax jurisdiction. The treaty provisions pertain only to individuals and corporations that are residents of either country and override the countries' general jurisdictional rules.[10] Under a typical treaty, a firm's income is taxable only by the country of residence (the home country) *unless* the firm maintains a **permanent establishment** in the other country (the host country). In this case, income attributable to the permanent establishment can be taxed by the host country. A permanent establishment is a fixed location, such as an office or factory, at which the firm carries on its regular commercial operations.[11] Because of this rule, a U.S. firm conducting business in a treaty country avoids that country's income tax if it does not maintain a fixed place of business in the host country.

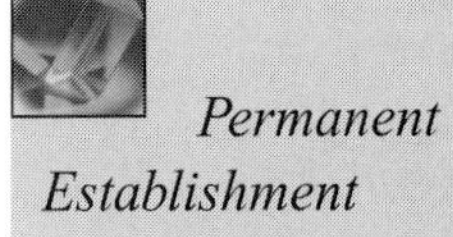

Permanent Establishment

Adam Inc., a U.S. manufacturer, sells its products to many major customers in Italy. The United States and Italy have an income tax treaty under which Italy does not have jurisdiction to tax Adam unless the corporation maintains a permanent establishment within Italy. If Adam maintains a permanent establishment (such as a sales office in Rome), Italy has jurisdiction to tax the portion of Adam's income attributable to such establishment.

If a U.S. firm conducts any business in a country that does not have an income tax treaty with the United States, the host country's jurisdiction depends on its unique tax laws. Consequently, the U.S. firm must research these laws to determine the level of activity that triggers jurisdiction. This determination is often subjective and results in considerable uncertainty for the firm. Moreover, the requisite level of business activity in nontreaty countries is often much less than the maintenance of a permanent establishment in the country.

U.S. Jurisdiction to Tax Global Income

The United States has a global tax system under which its citizens, permanent residents, and domestic corporations are taxed on *worldwide* income. In other words, when the United States is the home country, it claims jurisdiction to tax income regardless of where the income is earned. The United States does not surrender this primary jurisdiction when a U.S.

[10] The term *resident* includes individuals who are citizens or permanent residents of a country and corporations formed under the laws of the country or a political subdivision thereof.

[11] U.S. Treasury Department, Model Income Tax Treaty, article 5.

firm engages in **outbound transactions** with residents of other nations, even if the income from the transaction is taxed by a foreign government.[12] Thus, a fundamental issue confronting U.S. firms operating abroad is the potential double taxation of their income.

As we learned in Chapter 5, firms can deduct foreign income taxes paid or accrued during the taxable year. However, a deduction is an imperfect remedy for double taxation.

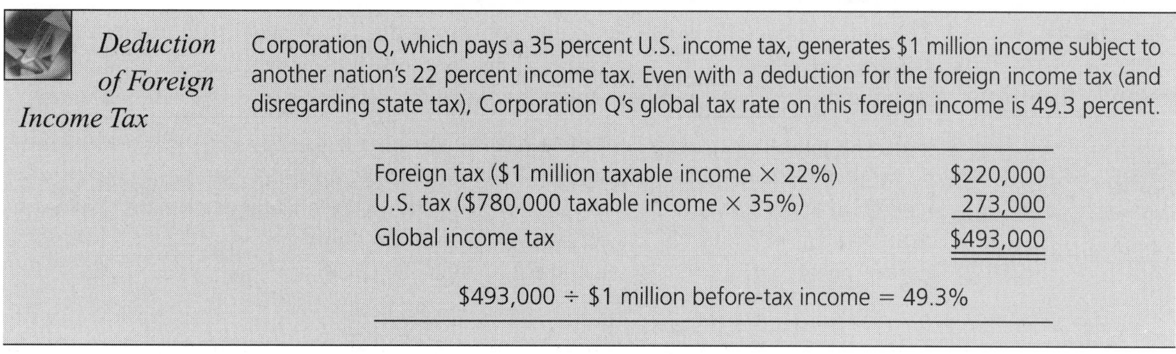

Deduction of Foreign Income Tax

Corporation Q, which pays a 35 percent U.S. income tax, generates $1 million income subject to another nation's 22 percent income tax. Even with a deduction for the foreign income tax (and disregarding state tax), Corporation Q's global tax rate on this foreign income is 49.3 percent.

Foreign tax ($1 million taxable income × 22%)	$220,000
U.S. tax ($780,000 taxable income × 35%)	273,000
Global income tax	$493,000

$493,000 ÷ $1 million before-tax income = 49.3%

The federal government understands that U.S. firms facing this tax burden could be at a competitive disadvantage in the global marketplace. Therefore, the tax law contains the powerful mechanism of a foreign tax credit to alleviate double taxation at the international level.

THE FOREIGN TAX CREDIT

U.S. citizens, residents, and domestic corporations may elect to credit foreign income tax paid or accrued during the year against their U.S. tax.[13] Taxpayers electing the credit are not allowed a deduction for foreign income taxes.[14] The **foreign tax credit** is available only for income taxes; foreign excise, value-added, sales, property, and transfer taxes are not creditable.[15] Let's refer back to the example involving Corporation Q to demonstrate the power of the foreign tax credit.

Credit for Foreign Income Tax

If Corporation Q does not deduct its $220,000 foreign tax payment and elects the tax credit, its U.S. tax decreases to $130,000, and its global tax rate decreases to 35 percent.

Precredit U.S. tax ($1 million taxable income × 35%)	$350,000
Foreign tax credit	(220,000)
U.S. tax	$130,000
Foreign tax ($1 million taxable income × 22%)	$220,000
U.S. tax	130,000
Global income tax	$350,000

$350,000 ÷ $1 million before-tax income = 35%

[12] The United States also taxes business income earned in this country by nonresident aliens and foreign corporations. §871(b) and §882. Any discussion of the tax rules applying to these *inbound transactions* is beyond the scope of this text.

[13] §901(a). The election to claim a foreign tax credit is made annually so that taxpayers can choose either the credit or the deduction on a year-to-year basis.

[14] §275(a)(4)(A).

[15] Firms either deduct or capitalize their noncreditable taxes relating to their foreign business activities.

By permitting Corporation Q to claim the foreign tax credit, the United States relinquished its taxing jurisdiction to the extent that another nation exercised its jurisdiction. In other words, the United States reduced its 35 percent rate by the 22 percent foreign rate so that Corporation Q paid only 13 percent U.S. tax on its foreign income.

Limitation on the Annual Credit

Objective 4
Compute a foreign tax credit.

The foreign tax credit is subject to a major limitation: The annual credit cannot exceed a specific percentage of the precredit U.S. tax for the year. This percentage is computed by dividing the taxpayer's **foreign source income** by taxable income.[16]

Foreign Tax Credit Limitation

In 2005, Corporation RH had $800,000 taxable income, $300,000 of which was generated by business activities in Country M. RH paid $123,900 foreign tax (at more than a 40 percent rate) to Country M.[17] Its U.S. income tax is computed as follows.

U.S. source income	$500,000	
Foreign source income	300,000	
Taxable income		$ 800,000
U.S. tax rate		.34
Precredit U.S. tax		$ 272,000
Foreign tax credit (limited)		(102,000)
U.S. tax		$ 170,000

RH's foreign tax credit is *limited* to the precredit U.S. tax of $272,000 multiplied by the ratio of foreign source income to taxable income.

$$\$272{,}000 \times \frac{\$300{,}000 \text{ foreign source income}}{\$800{,}000 \text{ taxable income}} = \$102{,}000$$

Even though RH paid $123,900 foreign income tax, only $102,000 is creditable against U.S. tax. Note that the limited credit equals the *entire precredit U.S. tax* on RH's foreign source income ($300,000 × 34 percent = $102,000). Note also that the U.S. tax equals 34 percent of $500,000 U.S. source income. Because of the foreign tax credit, RH pays no U.S. tax on its foreign source income. Because of the limitation on that credit, it pays the full U.S. tax on its *domestic* income.

Excess Credit Carrybacks and Carryforwards

When a firm is subject to the foreign tax credit limitation, the **excess foreign tax credit** (foreign tax paid but not credited) can be carried back one year and forward 10 years.[18] The firm can use its excess credits in a carryback or carryforward year, subject to the annual limitation.

[16] §904(a). The Internal Revenue Code contains elaborate and lengthy rules for distinguishing between foreign source and U.S. source income. See §861 through §865.

[17] The statement assumes that Country M and the United States use the same definition of taxable income. Actually, the definition of taxable income varies considerably from country to country.

[18] §904(c) as amended by the American Jobs Creation Act of 2004.

Excess Credit Carryback

In the preceding example, RH had a $21,900 excess credit ($123,900 foreign tax paid − $102,000 limited credit) in 2005. Its 2004 U.S. tax return showed the following.

U.S. source income	$350,000	
Foreign source income	250,000	
Taxable income		$ 600,000
U.S. tax rate		.34
Precredit U.S. tax		$ 204,000
Foreign tax credit (actual tax paid)		(77,500)
U.S. tax		$ 126,500

The credit limitation did not apply because the $77,500 foreign tax paid was less than the $85,000 limitation.

$$\$204{,}000 \times \frac{\$250{,}000 \text{ foreign source income}}{\$600{,}000 \text{ taxable income}} = \$85{,}000$$

Consequently, RH had a $7,500 excess limitation in 2004 ($85,000 limitation − $77,500 credited foreign tax). Because of the excess limitation, RH can carry back $7,500 of its 2005 excess credit and obtain a $7,500 refund of 2004 tax. The remaining $14,400 excess credit is available as a carryforward to 2006.

Cross-Crediting

If a firm's foreign source income is taxed by a foreign jurisdiction at a rate *lower* than the U.S. rate, its global rate on such income is the higher U.S. rate. In such case, the firm has an excess limitation equal to the U.S. tax paid on its foreign source income. If the foreign source income is taxed by a foreign jurisdiction at a rate *higher* than the U.S. rate, the global rate is the higher foreign rate. In this case, the firm pays no U.S. tax on its foreign source income. It will, however, have an excess foreign tax credit.

If a firm earns income in both low-tax and high-tax foreign jurisdictions, the excess credit from the high-tax income can be used to the extent of the excess limitation from the low-tax income. This **cross-crediting** reduces the firm's global tax rate on its foreign source income. Let's develop a case to illustrate this important result.

Cross-Crediting

CVB Inc. has the following taxable income.

U.S. source income	$350,000
Foreign source income:	
Country L	100,000
Country H	100,000
Taxable income	$550,000

Country L has a 15 percent income tax, and Country H has a 42 percent income tax. Thus, CVB paid $15,000 income tax to Country L and $42,000 income tax to Country H. Its U.S. tax is $130,000.

Taxable income	$550,000
U.S. tax rate	.34
Precredit U.S. tax	$187,000
Foreign tax credit (actual tax paid)	(57,000)
U.S. tax	$130,000

The credit limitation does not apply because the $57,000 foreign tax paid is *less* than the $68,000 limitation.

$$\$187{,}000 \times \frac{\$200{,}000 \text{ foreign source income}}{\$550{,}000 \text{ taxable income}} = \$68{,}000$$

In this example, CVB pays only $11,000 U.S. tax on its $200,000 foreign source income.

Foreign source income	$200,000
U.S. tax rate	.34
	$ 68,000
Foreign tax credit	(57,000)
U.S. tax on foreign source income	$ 11,000

Therefore, CVB's global rate on this income is 34 percent, even though the $100,000 earned in Country H was taxed at 42 percent. Because CVB blended low-tax and high-tax income in computing its foreign tax credit limitation, it reduced its U.S. tax bill by every dollar of foreign tax paid for the year.

ORGANIZATIONAL FORMS FOR OVERSEAS OPERATIONS

U.S. firms expanding internationally must decide on the form in which to operate their overseas activities. This section of the chapter surveys the basic organizational choices for foreign business ventures.

Branch Offices and Foreign Partnerships

Objective 5
Compare the tax consequences of a foreign branch operation and a foreign subsidiary.

U.S. firms wanting to establish a presence in a foreign country can open a branch office. A *branch office* is not a separate legal entity but is merely an extension of the U.S. firm. Any income or loss generated by the foreign branch is commingled with income and losses from the firm's other business activities. If the branch is profitable, its income is subject to U.S. tax. Any foreign tax paid on branch income is included in the computation of the foreign tax credit. The same tax consequences result if a U.S. firm becomes a partner in a foreign partnership. The firm reports its share of the partnership's foreign source income or loss and is entitled to a tax credit for its share of foreign income taxes paid by the partnership.

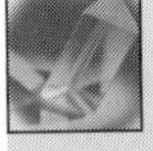

Foreign Partnership

SC, an Oklahoma corporation engaged in oil and gas drilling, owns a 60 percent interest in a partnership formed under South African law. This year, the foreign partnership generated $3 million income from its drilling activities in Africa and paid $420,000 income tax to various African jurisdictions. SC must include $1.8 million (60 percent × $3 million) foreign source income in its taxable income and may include $252,000 (60 percent × $420,000) of the African taxes paid by the partnership in computing its foreign tax credit.

Domestic Subsidiaries

U.S. corporations often create wholly owned subsidiaries to operate foreign businesses. Because of the parent's limited liability as a shareholder, this strategy confines the risks of the foreign operation to the subsidiary corporation. If the subsidiary is a domestic corporation, the tax consequences are virtually identical to those of a branch office. The parent and subsidiary can file a consolidated U.S. tax return so that profits and losses generated by the overseas business are combined with those of the parent and any other domestic subsidiaries.[19] The group can elect a consolidated foreign tax credit for income taxes paid by the subsidiary and any other corporation in the group.

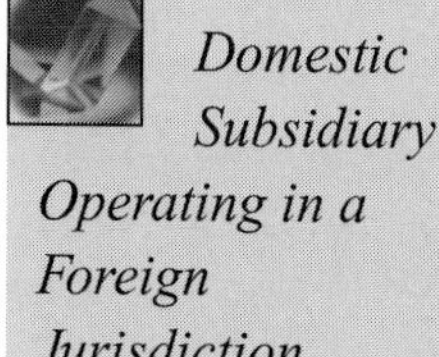

Domestic Subsidiary Operating in a Foreign Jurisdiction

SC, the Oklahoma corporation described in the preceding example, owns 100 percent of the outstanding stock of Pacifica, a California corporation. Pacifica conducts oil drilling activities in several countries in Southeast Asia. This year, Pacifica generated $14 million income and paid $3.1 million income tax to its host countries. SC files a consolidated federal tax return that includes Pacifica. Consequently, Pacifica's $14 million foreign source income is included in consolidated taxable income, and the $3.1 million foreign income tax paid by Pacifica is included in the computation of the SC consolidated group's foreign tax credit.

Foreign Subsidiaries

Another alternative is for a U.S. corporation to create a subsidiary under the laws of a foreign jurisdiction. In such case, the subsidiary is a foreign corporation, although it is completely controlled by a U.S. parent. The foreign jurisdiction is *both* home and host country to the subsidiary even though a U.S. shareholder owns the corporation. Multinational corporations typically have strong political and legal reasons for using foreign subsidiaries, such as the public image of the business in the host country or prohibitions against foreign ownership of real property located in the host country. When a U.S. corporation conducts business through a foreign subsidiary, the subsidiary's activities cannot be combined with those of the parent because foreign subsidiaries cannot be included in a U.S. consolidated tax return.[20] Thus, income generated by the subsidiary is not included in consolidated taxable income. Losses incurred by the subsidiary are isolated; the parent can't use these losses to shelter its own income from U.S. taxation. Depending on the tax laws of the foreign jurisdiction, the corporation may be allowed to carry the loss back or forward as a net operating loss deduction.

Foreign Subsidiary Operating in a Foreign Jurisdiction

SC, our Oklahoma oil and gas corporation, owns 100 percent of the outstanding stock of Latina, a Brazilian corporation. Latina conducts its business activities only in Brazil. This year, Latina generated $9 million income and paid $2.25 million Brazilian income tax. Although SC files a consolidated federal tax return with all its domestic subsidiaries, the return does not include Latina. Because Latina is a foreign corporation operating exclusively in a foreign jurisdiction, it does not pay U.S. income tax.

Dividends from Foreign Subsidiaries

When a U.S. corporation receives a dividend from another corporation (the payer), the dividend is included in the recipient's gross income. If the payer is a U.S. corporation, the recipient is allowed a dividends-received deduction. Consequently, little if any of the dividend

[19] See the discussion of consolidated corporate returns in Chapter 10.

[20] §1504(b)(3).

Tax Talk

The American Jobs Creation Act of 2004 created a one-year window of opportunity for U.S. multinationals to repatriate foreign earnings at a bargain tax rate. During the one-year period, cash dividends from foreign subs are eligible for an 85 percent dividends-received deduction.

is included in the recipient's taxable income.[21] If the payer is a foreign corporation, the recipient is not entitled to a dividends-received deduction.[22] The dividend is included in the recipient's taxable income, and the issue of double taxation again takes center stage.

Many countries (including the United States) impose a tax on dividends paid by resident corporations to foreign shareholders. The payer must withhold the tax from the dividend payment and remit it to the government. Consequently, the amount received by the shareholder is net of this **withholding tax.** The withholding tax rates vary across countries and are often specified in a country's income tax treaties. For example, Spain imposes a withholding tax on dividends paid by Spanish corporations to foreign shareholders, and the tax treaty between the United States and Spain specifies that the general withholding tax rate is 15 percent. A U.S. corporation that receives a dividend net of a foreign withholding tax is entitled to a foreign tax credit.

Credit for Foreign Withholding Tax

Domino, a U.S. corporation, owns about 2 percent of the stock of Carmela, a Spanish corporation. This year, Domino received a $265,000 dividend from Carmela net of the 15 percent Spanish withholding tax. Thus, Domino received only $225,250 *cash* ($265,000 dividend − $39,750 withheld foreign tax). The $265,000 dividend is included in Domino's foreign source taxable income, and the $39,750 withholding tax is a creditable foreign income tax.

Deemed Paid Foreign Tax Credit

Objective 6

Compute a deemed paid foreign tax credit.

A U.S. corporation's dividends received from a foreign corporation are included in taxable income and subject to U.S. tax. Regardless of whether the dividends are subject to a foreign withholding tax, they represent after-tax earnings if the foreign corporation had to pay income tax to its home country. If a U.S. corporation owns 10 percent or more of the voting stock of the foreign corporation, it is entitled to a **deemed paid foreign tax credit.**[23] This credit is based on the income tax paid by the foreign corporation and not on any tax paid directly by the U.S. corporation. The best way to explain the computation of the deemed paid foreign tax credit is through an example.

Deemed Paid Credit

YNK, a U.S. corporation, formed FC Inc. under the laws of Country F. In its first year of operation, FC generated $100,000 income and paid $25,000 tax to Country F. The foreign subsidiary distributed its $75,000 after-tax income to YNK as a dividend, which was not subject to any withholding tax by Country F. The preliminary step in the computation of YNK's deemed paid credit is to increase (gross up) this dividend by the foreign tax that FC paid. Because FC distributed its entire after-tax income, the $75,000 dividend is grossed up by the entire $25,000 Country F tax. Therefore, YNK reports a $100,000 grossed-up dividend as foreign source income.[24] YNK is now entitled to a credit for the $25,000 foreign tax deemed paid on YNK's behalf by FC. Because of this credit, YNK's U.S. tax on the dividend is only $10,000.

Foreign source income (grossed-up dividend)	$100,000
U.S. tax rate	.35
Precredit U.S. tax	$ 35,000
Deemed paid foreign tax credit	(25,000)
U.S. tax	$ 10,000

[21] See the discussion of the dividend-received deduction in Chapter 10. Intercompany dividends between members of an affiliated group filing a consolidated return are eliminated from consolidated taxable income. Reg. §1.1502-13(f)(2).

[22] §245 contains several exceptions to this general rule.

[23] §902(a).

[24] §78.

YNK's $25,000 credit is not limited because the 25 percent foreign tax rate is *less* than the U.S. tax rate. Because of the deemed paid credit, the global tax on the $100,000 foreign source income earned by YNK through FC is $35,000: $25,000 foreign tax paid by FC and $10,000 U.S. tax paid by YNK.

Now change the facts by assuming that FC distributed only $10,000 of its $75,000 after-tax income as a dividend. In this case, FC's tax attributable to the dividend is $3,333 ([$10,000 ÷ $75,000] × $25,000 Country F tax). The grossed-up dividend is $13,333, and YNK's U.S. tax on the dividend is $1,333.

Grossed-up dividend	$13,333
U.S. tax rate	.35
Precredit U.S. tax	$ 4,666
Deemed paid foreign tax credit	(3,333)
U.S. tax	$ 1,333

The global tax on the $13,333 foreign source income earned by YNK through FC is $4,666: $3,333 foreign tax paid by FC and $1,333 U.S. tax paid by YNK.

DEFERRAL OF U.S. TAX ON FOREIGN SOURCE INCOME

Foreign source income earned by a foreign corporation is not subject to U.S. tax unless and until the corporation pays a dividend to a U.S. shareholder. Accordingly, U.S. corporations that don't *repatriate* (bring home) the earnings of their foreign subsidiaries are deferring U.S. tax on such earnings. If a U.S. parent has no pressing need for cash from its overseas operations, this deferral can go on indefinitely. Let's develop a case that quantifies the value of such deferral.

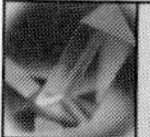

Deferral of U.S. Tax

RWB, a California corporation with a 35 percent U.S. tax rate, has two foreign operations, one organized as a branch office and the other organized as a foreign subsidiary. In year 0, both the branch and the subsidiary earned $500,000 income subject to a 20 percent foreign tax. Both operations reinvested their after-tax earnings in their respective businesses.

In year 0, RWB's U.S. tax on the $500,000 foreign source income earned by the branch is $75,000.

Foreign source income	$ 500,000
U.S. tax rate	.35
Precredit U.S. tax	$ 175,000
Foreign tax credit	(100,000)
U.S. tax	$ 75,000

RWB's global tax on the branch income is $175,000 ($100,000 foreign tax + $75,000 U.S. tax). In contrast, RWB's global tax on the $500,000 income earned by its foreign subsidiary is only $100,000, which is the tax paid by the subsidiary to its home country.

Note that RWB pays U.S. tax on the branch's income even though it did not withdraw any cash from the branch. If and when RWB does withdraw cash from the branch, the withdrawal will have no tax consequences. In contrast, RWB pays no U.S. tax on the income earned by the subsidiary *until* it withdraws cash (i.e., receives a dividend) from the subsidiary.

Tax Savings from Deferral

RWB's foreign subsidiary pays no dividends until year 6, when it distributes $400,000 to its parent. This distribution represents the after-tax income earned by the subsidiary in year 0. RWB's U.S. tax on this dividend is $75,000.

Dividend received	$400,000
Gross-up for tax paid by subsidiary	100,000
Foreign source income	$500,000
U.S. tax rate	.35
Precredit U.S. tax	$175,000
Deemed paid foreign tax credit	(100,000)
U.S. tax	$ 75,000

At a 9 percent discount rate, the present value of this tax in year 0 is $44,700, and the present value of RWB's global tax on the $500,000 income earned by its subsidiary in year 0 and repatriated in year 6 is $144,700.

Foreign tax paid by subsidiary in year 0	$100,000
Present value of U.S. tax paid in year 6 ($75,000 × .596 discount factor)	44,700
NPV of global tax	$144,700

This cost is $30,300 less than the $175,000 global tax on the year 0 income of the branch operation: a tax savings resulting entirely from the deferral of U.S. tax on foreign source income.

Tax deferral through foreign subsidiaries is possible only if the subsidiary's income is taxed at a foreign rate *less* than the U.S. rate. If a subsidiary operating in a high-tax country repatriates after-tax income as a dividend, the deemed paid foreign tax credit reduces the parent's U.S. tax on the dividend to zero. Thus, the parent's only tax on the foreign source income is the foreign income tax paid by the subsidiary in the year the income was earned.

Dividend from High-Tax Subsidiary

Vernon, a Georgia corporation with a 35 percent U.S. tax rate, has a foreign subsidiary subject to a 40 percent corporate income tax. The subsidiary distributed a $315,000 dividend that represents $525,000 before-tax income reduced by $210,000 foreign income tax. Vernon's U.S. tax on the dividend is zero.

Dividend received	$315,000
Gross-up for tax paid by subsidiary	210,000
Foreign source income	$525,000
U.S. tax rate	.35
Precredit U.S. tax	$183,750
Deemed paid foreign tax credit (limited)	(183,750)
U.S. tax	–0–

Although the subsidiary paid $210,000 foreign tax with respect to the earnings repatriated to Vernon, Vernon's credit for this tax is limited to the precredit U.S. tax on the dividend. Because of the limitation, Vernon has a $26,250 excess credit to use as a carryback or carryforward.

Controlled Foreign Corporations

U.S. corporations with foreign subsidiaries in low-tax countries (countries with tax rates less than the U.S. rate) can minimize tax by shifting as much income as possible to those subsidiaries. Before 1962, U.S. corporations routinely created subsidiaries in **tax haven** jurisdictions—countries with minimal or no corporate income tax. In many cases, the tax haven subsidiary existed only on paper, performing no function other than providing tax shelter. Consider the case of a U.S. manufacturer exporting its goods through a French subsidiary for retail sale in the European market. If the U.S. parent sold its goods directly to this marketing subsidiary at an arm's-length price, it would pay U.S. tax on the income from the outbound transaction. Furthermore, the subsidiary would pay French tax on the income from its retail sales of the goods. If, however, the U.S. parent also owned a subsidiary incorporated in the Cayman Islands, a Caribbean nation with no corporate income tax, the parent could sell its goods to this subsidiary for a very low price. The Cayman subsidiary could then sell the goods to the French subsidiary for a very high price. This three-party transaction is diagrammed in Exhibit 12.2.

EXHIBIT 12.2
Tax Haven Subsidiary

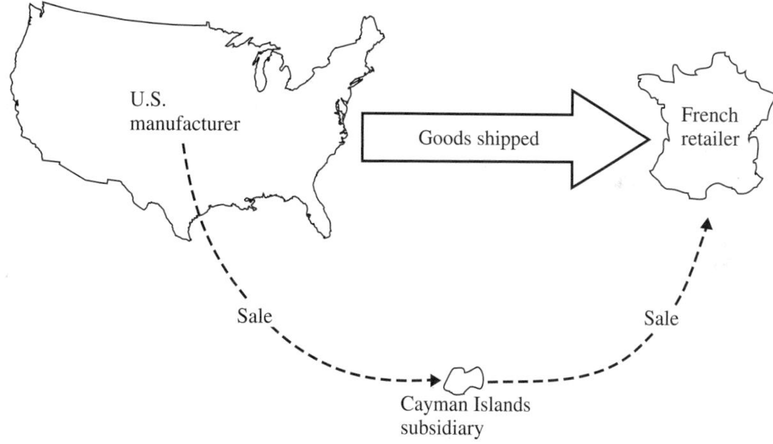

Even though the U.S. parent sold its goods to the Cayman subsidiary, it shipped the goods directly to the French subsidiary's warehouse outside of Paris. The Cayman subsidiary was not involved in the actual production or distribution process. Nevertheless, the subsidiary's intermediate legal title to the goods shifted most of the income from the outbound transaction to the Cayman corporation. Until such time as this corporation paid a dividend to its U.S. parent, no income taxes at all were levied on the income.

Objective 7
Explain how subpart F income earned by a CFC is constructively repatriated to the U.S. parent.

This classic tax avoidance scheme is just one example of the creative strategies used by international firms to divert income to tax haven jurisdictions. In 1962, Congress ended the most abusive strategies by enacting a set of "antideferral" rules applying to controlled foreign corporations. A **controlled foreign corporation (CFC)** is a foreign corporation in which U.S. shareholders own more than 50 percent of the voting power or stock value.[25] If

[25] §957(a).

a CFC earns certain types of income, the law treats such income as if it were immediately distributed to the CFC's shareholders.[26] Any U.S. shareholder with a 10 percent or more interest must pay tax on its pro rata share of this constructive dividend. These shareholders are entitled to increase the tax basis in their CFC stock by their constructive dividend.[27] If the CFC subsequently makes cash distributions to its shareholders, the distributions are nontaxable to the extent of any prior year constructive dividends and reduce the tax basis in the shareholder's CFC stock.[28]

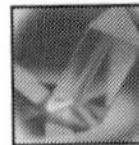

Deferral versus Constructive Dividends

In 2003, ABC created a wholly owned CFC, Flortez, in Country B. In 2003, 2004, and 2005, Flortez earned $20,000 income and paid $3,000 tax to Country B. Flortez paid no dividends in 2003 and 2004 and a $51,000 cash dividend in 2005.

The following chart reflects the tax consequences to ABC under two different assumptions. Under the "Deferral" assumption, ABC is not required to pay U.S. tax on Flortez's income until Flortez repatriates the income by paying a dividend. Under the "Constructive Dividend" assumption, ABC must recognize Flortez's $17,000 annual after-tax income as a constructive dividend in the year the CFC earns the income.

	Deferral	*Constructive Dividend*
2003:		
Cash received by ABC from Flortez	–0–	–0–
Dividend recognized by ABC	–0–	$17,000
Gross-up for Country B tax paid	–0–	3,000
ABC's foreign source income from Flortez	–0–	20,000
Increase in ABC's basis in Flortez stock	–0–	17,000
2004:		
Cash received by ABC from Flortez	–0–	–0–
Dividend recognized by ABC	–0–	$17,000
Gross-up for Country B tax paid	–0–	3,000
ABC's foreign source income from Flortez	–0–	20,000
Increase in ABC's basis in Flortez stock	–0–	17,000
2005:		
Cash received by ABC from Flortez	$51,000	$51,000
Dividend recognized by ABC	51,000	17,000
Gross-up for Country B tax paid	9,000	3,000
ABC's foreign source income from Flortez	60,000	20,000
Decrease in ABC's basis in Flortez stock	–0–	34,000

The only difference in the tax consequences under the two assumptions is the *timing* of ABC's recognition of its foreign source income from Flortez. Under both assumptions, ABC is entitled to a deemed paid foreign tax credit in the year it recognizes an actual or a constructive dividend from Flortez.

Subpart F Income

Not all foreign source income earned by a CFC must be constructively repatriated to its U.S. shareholders. Only narrowly defined categories of income (labeled **subpart F income** in the Internal Revenue Code) are treated as constructive dividends. Conceptually, subpart F

[26] §951(a)(1)(A).

[27] §961.

[28] §959.

income is artificial income because it has no commercial or economic connection to the CFC's home country. Subpart F income has many complex components, one of the more important of which is income derived from the sale of goods if (1) the CFC either buys the goods from or sells the goods to a related party and (2) the goods are neither manufactured nor sold for use within the CFC's home country.[29] In our Cayman Islands example, the Cayman CFC is related to both the U.S. manufacturer and the French distributor because all three corporations are members of one controlled group. Moreover, the goods described in the example never touched Cayman soil and have no connection to the country. Quite clearly, the Cayman subsidiary's entire taxable income is subpart F income on which the U.S. parent must pay current tax.

Subpart F Income

Petroni owns 100 percent of the stock of RYM, a CFC operating in Country M. This year, RYM earned $1 million taxable income, $700,000 of which related to RYM's commercial activities within Country M and $300,000 (30 percent) of which was subpart F income. RYM paid $100,000 income tax to Country M and made no cash distributions to Petroni. Nonetheless, Petroni must recognize a constructive dividend equal to RYM's after-tax earnings attributable to its subpart F income.

Petroni's constructive dividend from RYM (30% × RYM's $900,000 after-tax earnings)	$270,000
Gross-up for foreign tax paid by RYM	30,000
Petroni's foreign source income from RYM	$300,000
Petroni's deemed paid foreign tax	$ 30,000

Petroni can increase the basis in its RYM stock by the $270,000 constructive dividend.

Investment of CFC Earnings in U.S. Parent

Corporations can use CFCs to defer U.S. tax if three conditions are satisfied.

1. The CFC generates foreign source income in a jurisdiction with a tax rate *less* than the U.S. rate.
2. The foreign source income is not subpart F income.
3. The CFC accumulates after-tax earnings instead of paying dividends.

If the U.S. parent is content to reinvest the CFC's earnings in foreign activities, the third condition may not be an obstacle. But if the parent needs cash from its overseas operations, it may try to maneuver around this condition. An obvious strategy is for the parent to borrow money from or sell shares of its own stock to the CFC. Neither transaction results in taxable gain to the parent but both result in positive cash flow. Unfortunately for the parent, this strategy doesn't work. The tax law treats a CFC's debt or equity investment in its U.S. parent as a repatriation of earnings: a constructive dividend on which the parent must pay U.S. income tax.[30]

[29] Such income constitutes foreign base company sales income per §954(d)(1). Subpart F income is defined in §952 through §954.

[30] §951(a)(1)(B) and §956.

U.S. Investment of CFC Earnings

Dykeman owns 100 percent of the stock of FV, a CFC operating in a country with a 20 percent income tax. This year, FV earned $100,000 taxable income (none of which was subpart F income) and paid no dividends. However, FV paid $40,000 cash to Dykeman for 1,600 shares of newly issued Dykeman stock. Because of this "back door" repatriation of FV's earnings, Dykeman must recognize $50,000 foreign source income.

Dykeman's constructive dividend from FV (cash received in payment for stock)	$40,000
Gross-up for foreign tax paid by FV	10,000
Dykeman's foreign source income from FV	$50,000
Dykeman's deemed paid foreign tax	$10,000

Dykeman can increase the basis in its FY stock by the $40,000 constructive dividend.

Transfer Pricing and Section 482

Objective 8
Describe the role of Section 482 in the international transfer pricing area.

While the subpart F rules are potent, they do not extend to many types of foreign source income earned by CFCs. Consequently, U.S. parents benefit when they shift income to their foreign subsidiaries in low-tax jurisdictions. If a U.S. parent has subsidiaries in high-tax jurisdictions (such as Japan, France, Germany, and the United Kingdom), the tax strategy can be reversed. In such case, the parent wants to use its domestic subsidiaries as tax shelters.

Controlled groups of corporations can shift income among the members through their pricing structure for intercompany transactions. Consider the possibilities for income shifting if a U.S. parent owns an Irish subsidiary that manufactures consumer goods for worldwide export. Although the Irish subsidiary is a CFC, its profit from sales of goods manufactured in Ireland and sold to unrelated purchasers is not subpart F income. As a result, the income is subject only to the 10 percent Irish corporate tax until the CFC pays dividends to its parent. If the parent (or any domestic subsidiary) sells raw materials to the Irish subsidiary, the lower the price charged for the materials, the greater the income shifted to Ireland. If the U.S. parent provides administrative, marketing, or financial services to the Irish subsidiary, the parent could further inflate the subsidiary's profits (and deflate its own) by charging a nominal fee for the services rendered. Similarly, if the parent owns patents, copyrights, licenses, or other intangible assets that add value to the Irish manufacturing process, it could forgo royalty payments for the subsidiary's use of the intangible.

All the above pricing strategies shift income to the Irish subsidiary. Not surprisingly, the United States and most foreign countries, mindful of the income distortion resulting from artificial **transfer prices,** demand that related entities deal with each other in the same arm's-length manner as they deal with unrelated parties. Under federal tax law, Section 482 gives the IRS the authority to apportion or allocate gross income, deductions, or credits between related parties to correct any perceived distortion resulting from unrealistic transfer prices.[31]

[31] §482 was introduced in Chapter 5.

Section 482 Adjustment

BSX, a California corporation, owns a CFC that manufactures and sells goods in the Asian market. The CFC is incorporated in a country with no corporate income tax. Several years ago, BSX sent a team of system engineers to advise the CFC on improving inventory management. BSX did not charge the CFC a fee for this service. In the same year, BSX sold industrial equipment to the CFC for a price of $385,000. During its audit of BSX's tax return, the IRS determined that a reasonable transfer price for the advisory services was $150,000, and a reasonable transfer price for the equipment was $500,000. Consequently, the IRS allocated $265,000 gross income to BSX from its CFC and assessed U.S. tax on this Section 482 adjustment.

Over the past decades, the IRS has not hesitated to use its Section 482 power to ensure that domestic corporations pay U.S. tax on an appropriate amount of their international income. While corporations certainly can challenge the IRS in court, the prevailing judicial attitude is that the IRS's determination of an arm's-length transfer price should be upheld unless the corporation can demonstrate that the determination is "arbitrary, capricious, or unreasonable."[32] Clearly, multinational corporations are in a defensive posture concerning their transfer pricing practices and must be constantly aware of any Section 482 exposure created by their intercompany transactions.

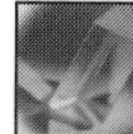

Transfer Pricing—An Issue of Global Proportion

Ernst & Young conducted a survey of the tax directors of over 450 multinational companies concerning transfer pricing issues. The survey results led to the following observations.

- Companies throughout the world regard transfer pricing as the most important international tax issue they will face in the future.
- Fiscal authorities in both developed and emerging markets are paying increased attention to transfer pricing compliance.
- Intercompany services are the transactions most susceptible to transfer pricing disputes.
- Nearly two-thirds of the companies surveyed report that their intercompany transactions have already been the target of a transfer pricing examination.
- Eight in ten multinationals expect to face a transfer pricing examination in the future.

Conclusion

In the preceding chapter, we discussed the tax implications when owners select a particular entity through which to conduct business. In this chapter, we added a new tax planning variable—the jurisdiction in which the entity is taxed. To the extent that owners can manipulate this variable by operating in low-tax jurisdictions, tax costs can be controlled. When a business stretches across jurisdictions, the owners run the risk that double taxation will erode their after-tax profits. If the competing jurisdictions are state governments, income is divided according to each state's apportionment rule. Businesses can often take advantage of anomalies in these rules and differences in state tax rates to reduce their tax burden. If the competing jurisdictions are the United States and a foreign government, the foreign tax credit is an invaluable mechanism for preventing double taxation.

Multinational U.S. corporations can achieve substantial tax savings by incorporating foreign subsidiaries in low-tax jurisdictions. As a general rule, the income earned by these subsidiaries is not subject to U.S. tax until it is repatriated. To take advantage of this deferral, U.S. parent corporations must carefully avoid the subpart F rules and be content with reinvesting their foreign earnings in overseas ventures. They must steer clear of transfer pricing disputes with the IRS and the tax enforcement agencies of other nations. Certainly, international tax planning is a complex and challenging specialty that will become more valuable as the global economy continues to develop.

[32] *Liberty Loan Corp.* v. *U.S.*, 498 F.2d 225 (CA-8, 1974), *cert. denied*, 419 U.S. 1089.

Sources of Book/Tax Differences

Permanent	Temporary
• Gross-up of foreign source dividends	• Constructive dividends from CFCs

Key Terms

apportionment *321*
Commerce Clause *319*
controlled foreign corporation (CFC) *333*
cross-crediting *327*
deemed paid foreign tax credit *330*
excess foreign tax credit *326*
foreign source income *326*
foreign tax credit *325*
income tax treaty *324*
nexus *319*
outbound transaction *325*
permanent establishment *324*
subpart F income *334*
tax haven *333*
transfer price *336*
Uniform Division of Income for Tax Purposes Act (UDITPA) *321*
withholding tax *330*

Questions and Problems for Discussion

In the questions, problems, and cases for Chapter 12, corporations are U.S. corporations unless otherwise stated.

1. Why does a corporation's state income tax cost depend on its marginal income tax rate for federal purposes?
2. NY is a New York corporation that manufactures office equipment in a factory located in New York. In which of the following cases does NY have nexus with Pennsylvania?
   a. NY owns two retail outlets for its products in Pennsylvania.
   b. NY owns no tangible property in Pennsylvania. It employs two salespeople who travel throughout Pennsylvania soliciting orders for office equipment from regular customers. NY fills the orders out of its New York factory and ships the equipment to the customers by common carrier.
   c. NY owns no tangible property in Pennsylvania and does not have any employees who work in the state. It does have Pennsylvania customers who order equipment directly from the New York factory by telephone or fax.
   d. Refer to the facts in (*c*) above. NY employs two technicians who travel throughout Pennsylvania providing repair and maintenance services to NY's customers.
3. Distinguish between the concepts of physical presence nexus and economic nexus.
4. Does the federal government require states to use a three-factor formula to apportion the income of an interstate business for state income tax purposes?
5. BNJ Inc. conducts a business that spans four states. Its total income for the year was $32 million. However, the total of the taxable incomes reported on BNJ's four state income tax returns was $34.8 million. Discuss the possible reasons for such discrepancy.
6. In what situation would a multistate business deliberately create nexus with a state so that the state has jurisdiction to tax a portion of the business income?
7. Distinguish between a home country and a host country in the international tax context.
8. What is the purpose of a bilateral income tax treaty between two countries?
9. LF Inc. sells its products to customers residing in Country X and Country Y. Both foreign jurisdictions have a 20 percent corporate income tax. This year, LF made more than $30 million of sales in both Country X and Country Y. However, it paid income tax only to Country X. What factors could account for this result?

10. Corporation PY plans to form a foreign subsidiary through which to conduct a new business in Country J. PY projects that this business will operate at a loss for several years.
    a. To what extent will the subsidiary's losses generate U.S. tax savings?
    b. To what extent will the subsidiary's losses generate a savings of Country J income tax?
11. HD Inc. operates its business in Country U through a subsidiary incorporated under Country U law. The subsidiary has never paid a dividend and has accumulated over $10 million after-tax earnings.
    a. Country U has a 45 percent corporate income tax. Describe the tax consequences to HD if it receives a $5 million dividend from the subsidiary.
    b. How would the tax consequences change if Country U's corporate income tax rate is only 20 percent?
12. TJ Inc. has a subsidiary incorporated in Country H, which does not have a corporate income tax. Which of the following activities generates subpart F income?
    a. The subsidiary buys woolen clothing products manufactured by a Swedish company and sells the products to unrelated wholesalers in the United States. TJ owns the Swedish company.
    b. The subsidiary buys coffee beans grown on plantations located in Country H and sells the beans to TJ, which makes coffee products.
    c. The subsidiary buys building materials from a Mexican company and sells the materials to construction companies operating in Country H. TJ owns the Mexican company.
13. Corporation BC has a subsidiary operating exclusively in Country A and a subsidiary operating exclusively in Country Z.
    a. Both subsidiaries were incorporated under Delaware law and are therefore U.S. corporations. Can Corporation BC use the losses from the Country A subsidiary to reduce the income from the Country Z subsidiary?
    b. Would your answer change if both subsidiaries are foreign corporations?
14. DF Partnership carries on business in the United States and four other countries. Explain why the ordinary income generated by the foreign business is a separately stated item on DF's Schedule K, Form 1065.
15. KS Inc. owns 100 percent of Sub 1 (a CFC in a country with a 50 percent corporate tax) and 90 percent of Sub 2 (a CFC in a country with a 10 percent corporate tax). KS sells goods and services to both CFCs. Is the IRS more interested in KS's transfer pricing for sales to Sub 1 or sales to Sub 2?
16. In what situation is the United States a tax haven for an international business operation?

Application Problems

1. This year, MN Inc.'s before-tax income was $9,877,000. It paid $419,000 income tax to Minnesota and $385,000 income tax to Illinois.
    a. Compute MN's federal income tax.
    b. What is MN's tax rate on its income?
2. OP Inc. conducts business in State M and State N, which both use the UDITPA three-factor formula to apportion income. State M's corporate tax rate is 4.5 percent, and State N's corporate tax rate is 7 percent. This year, OP had the following sales, payroll, and property (in thousands of dollars) in each state.

	State M	*State N*	*Total*
Gross receipts from sales	$3,000	$7,500	$10,500
Payroll expense	800	1,200	2,000
Property costs	900	1,000	1,900

If OP's before-tax income was $3 million, compute its State M and State N tax.

3. Refer to the facts in the preceding problem. Compute OP's State M and State N tax if State N uses an apportionment formula in which the sales factor is double-weighted.
4. Refer to the facts in Problem 2. Compute the state income tax savings if OP could relocate its personnel so that payroll expense in State M increased to $1,900 (thousand) and payroll expense in State N decreased to $100 (thousand).
5. AJ is a U.S. corporation. This year, it earned $8 million before-tax income and paid $450,000 income tax to jurisdictions other than the United States. Compute AJ's U.S. income tax assuming that:
   a. The other jurisdictions were the states of Montana, Colorado, California, and Arizona.
   b. The other jurisdictions were Italy and Spain, and AJ's foreign tax credit was not limited.
6. ZX Inc. has the following taxable income.

U.S. source income	$1,900,000
Foreign source income	240,000
Taxable income	$2,140,000

ZK paid $33,000 foreign income tax. Compute its U.S. income tax.

7. JHG Inc. has the following taxable income.

U.S. source income	$18,800,000
Foreign source income	2,690,000
Taxable income	$21,490,000

JHG paid $1,040,000 foreign income tax. Compute its U.S. income tax.

8. Corporation ABC has the following taxable income.

U.S. source income	$1,620,000
Foreign source income:	
Country A	550,000
Country B	2,000,000
Country C	2,900,000
Taxable income	$7,070,000

ABC paid $600,000 income tax to Country B and $1.3 million income tax to Country C. Country A does not have a corporate income tax. Compute ABC's U.S. income tax.

9. TT, an Ohio corporation, earned $700,000 U.S. source income from sales of goods to U.S. customers and $330,000 foreign source income from sales of goods to customers in Canada. Canada's corporate income tax rate is 40 percent, and the United States and Canada have a bilateral tax treaty.
   a. Compute TT's U.S. tax if it does not maintain a permanent establishment in Canada.
   b. Compute TT's U.S. tax if it does maintain a permanent establishment in Canada.
10. EQ, a South Carolina corporation, is a 20 percent partner in a Swiss partnership. This year, EQ earned $2 million U.S. source income and $190,000 foreign source income. It paid no foreign income tax. The Swiss partnership earned $1.73 million foreign source income and paid $660,000 income tax to Switzerland, France, and Austria. Compute EQ's U.S. tax.
11. The Trio affiliated group consists of Trio, a New Jersey corporation, and its three wholly owned subsidiaries. This year, the four corporations report the following.

	Net Income (Loss)
Trio	$ 412,000
Subsidiary 1	(180,000)
Subsidiary 2	389,000
Subsidiary 3	600,000

If Trio elects to file a consolidated return, compute consolidated taxable income assuming that:
   a. Subsidiary 1 is a domestic corporation, and Subsidiaries 2 and 3 are foreign corporations.
   b. Subsidiaries 2 and 3 are domestic corporations, and Subsidiary 1 is a foreign corporation.
12. CC operates solely within the United States. It owns two subsidiaries conducting business in the United States and several foreign countries. Both subsidiaries are U.S. corporations. This year, the three corporations report the following.

	Foreign Source Income	***U.S. Source Income***	***Foreign Income Tax Paid***
CC	–0–	$600,000	–0–
Sub 1	$3,500,000	150,000	$ 380,000
Sub 2	4,700,000	410,000	2,350,000

   a. If CC and its two subsidiaries file a consolidated U.S. tax return, compute consolidated income tax.
   b. How would the aggregate tax of the group change if the three corporations file separate U.S. tax returns?
   c. Identify the reason for the difference in the tax liability in (*a*) and (*b*) above.
13. VL Inc. began operations in 2004. For its first two taxable years, VL's records show the following.

	2004	2005
U.S. source income	$300,000	$270,000
Foreign source income	200,000	630,000
Taxable income	$500,000	$900,000
Foreign income tax paid	$ 82,000	$151,000

Compute VL's U.S. tax for both years.

14. Corporation RX's records show the following results for its first three years of operations.

	2002	2003	2004
U.S. source income	$180,000	$350,000	$ 800,000
Foreign source income	92,000	500,000	680,000
Taxable income	$272,000	$850,000	$1,480,000
Foreign tax paid	$ 21,000	$152,000	$ 224,400

In 2005, RX generated $2 million taxable income ($900,000 of which was foreign source) and paid $370,000 foreign income tax.

a. Compute RX's U.S. tax for 2002, 2003, and 2004.
b. Compute RX's U.S. tax for 2005.
c. Compute the refund generated by the carryback of the 2005 excess credit.

15. CS Inc. owns 100 percent of the stock in FS, a foreign corporation. All FS's income is foreign source, and its foreign income tax rate is 20 percent. This year, FS distributed a $50,000 dividend to CS.

a. Assuming that CS is in the 35 percent tax bracket, compute its U.S. tax on the dividend.
b. How would your computation change if the foreign income tax rate was 45 percent?

16. Dixie Inc., a Tennessee corporation, conducts business through branch offices in the United States, Mexico, and Canada. Dixie owns 100 percent of the stock of two foreign subsidiaries, Dix-Col Inc. and Dix-Per Inc., through which it conducts its South American business. This year, Dixie recognized the following items of taxable income.

U.S. source income from domestic branch	$4,922,000
Foreign source income from foreign branches	1,031,000
Cash dividends received from Dix-Col	249,000
Cash dividends received from Dix-Per.	186,000

During the year, Dixie paid $116,200 income tax to Mexico and $286,700 income tax to Canada. It paid no direct income taxes to any other foreign country. However, Dix-Col paid a 20 percent income tax to the country of Colombia, and Dix-Per paid a 37 percent income tax to the country of Peru.

a. Compute Dixie's taxable income.
b. Compute Dixie's U.S. tax.

17. JMT Inc., which has a 34 percent marginal tax rate, owns 40 percent of the stock of a CFC. At the beginning of 2004, JMT's basis in its stock was $660,000. The CFC's

2004 income was $1 million, $800,000 of which was subpart F income. The CFC paid no foreign income tax and distributed no dividends.

a. Does JMT have any 2004 tax consequences with respect to its investment in the CFC?
b. Compute JMT's basis in its CFC stock at the beginning of 2005.

18. Refer to the facts in the preceding problem. In 2005, the CFC's income was $600,000, none of which was subpart F income, and it distributed a $300,000 dividend to its shareholders ($120,000 to JMT). What is the tax consequence to JMT of this dividend?
19. Corporation YZ, which has a 35 percent marginal tax rate, owns 100 percent of Corporation QT, a foreign corporation in a country with a 15 percent corporate income tax. QT has never paid a dividend and has accumulated $18 million after-tax income (none of which is subpart F income). This year, QT lends $1 million to YZ. What is the tax consequence to YZ of this loan?
20. RKW, a Texas corporation, manufactures plastic components that it sells to AS, a Mexican corporation, for assembly into a variety of finished goods. RKW owns 60 percent of AS's stock. RKW's cost per component is $85, its selling price per component is $100, and it sold 70,000 components to AS this year. RKW's taxable income as reported on its Form 1120 was $900,000, and AS's taxable income as reported on its Mexican corporate income tax return was $1.2 million. Determine the effect on the taxable incomes of both corporations if the IRS determines that an arm's-length transfer price per plastic component is $108.

Issue Recognition Problems

Identify the tax issue or issues suggested by the following situations and state each issue in the form of a question.

1. State E wants to encourage the development of a local wine industry. Consequently, it decreased its excise tax rate on retail sales of locally produced wines to 3 percent. The state's excise tax on wines produced out-of-state but sold in-state is 10 percent.
2. ABC operates a meat and poultry business. The corporation distributes its products in six states and pays income tax to each based on the meat and poultry income apportionable to each. Last year, ABC invested in a motion picture. The picture was a commercial success, and ABC received a royalty check for $1,800,000 from the movie's producer.
3. Corporation NW is incorporated and has its commercial domicile in State N. This year, NW sold its manufactured products to customers in State N (61 percent of sales), State O (28 percent of sales), and State P (11 percent of sales). NW has nexus with State N and State O. However, it has no physical presence in State P and therefore is not taxed by that state. Both State N and State O use the three-factor UDITPA formula to apportion income.
4. The United States has a tax treaty with the United Kingdom that provides certain tax benefits to U.K. corporations conducting business in the United States. The United States does not have an income tax treaty with Chile. SA Company, a Chilean firm that exports goods to the United States, decides to operate its export business through a shell corporation formed under U.K. law.
5. BK is a consulting firm with its headquarters in New York City. This year, it entered into a consulting contract with a multinational corporation. Mrs. K, an employee, spent 33 days working at BK headquarters, 28 days in London, 50 days in Paris, and 14 days in Hong Kong performing the professional services specified in the contract. BK received a $1 million fee upon completion of Mrs. K's work.
6. Corporation HS operates a fleet of oceangoing cargo vessels. During the year, one HS vessel was docked at its home port in New Orleans for 55 days, on the high seas for

120 days, and docked at various foreign ports of call for the remaining 190 days. HS's net income from operation of this vessel was $620,000.

7. Corporation B conducts business in a foreign jurisdiction that imposes a 1 percent tax on gross receipts from sales within the jurisdiction. This year, Corporation B paid $750,000 gross receipts tax to the jurisdiction.
8. TY manufactures paper products in the United States and sells the products internationally. Because most of its foreign sales are in high-tax jurisdictions, TY has excess foreign credits from its paper business. This year, TY earned $8 million interest income on long-term bonds issued by Country NT, which has no income tax.
9. Corporation DL has a foreign subsidiary conducting a manufacturing business in Country Z, which has a 25 percent corporate income tax. The IRS recently challenged the transfer price at which DL performs managerial services for the subsidiary and used its Section 482 authority to reallocate $10 million income from the subsidiary to DL. The taxing authorities in Country Z maintain the transfer price was perfectly accurate.
10. Williams Inc. is a U.S. corporation that manufacturers toys in a factory located near Milwaukee, Wisconsin. Williams sells the toys to its foreign subsidiary, which is incorporated in Carnema, a Caribbean country with no corporate income tax. Williams actually ships the toys to a warehouse in Carnema, where the toys are sealed in protective plastic wrappings and labeled. The foreign subsidiary resells the sealed and labeled toys in the European market. This year, the foreign subsidiary's profit from toy sales will exceed $25 million.
11. HG owns a foreign subsidiary with over $8 million accumulated foreign source income (on which HG has never paid U.S. tax). The subsidiary recently purchased $500,000 worth of stock in a publicly held U.S. corporation with over 30,000 shareholders.

Research Problems

1. Visit the website for Federation of Tax Administrators **(www.taxadmin.org)** and use the Links button to go to the Illinois Department of Revenue website. Locate a copy of the Corporate Income and Replacement Tax Return (Form IL-1120), scrutinize Part II, and describe how Illinois's apportionment percentage is computed. Return to the FTA website and link to the Ohio Department of Taxation website. Locate a copy of the Ohio Corporation Franchise Tax Report (Form FT-1120), scrutinize Schedule D, and describe how Ohio's apportionment percentage is computed.
2. Endless Summer is a Florida corporation that operates a fleet of cruise ships. It offers two categories of cruises. The first category includes "round-trip" cruises on ships that depart from Miami, visit various Caribbean and South American ports, then return to Miami at the end of the cruise. The second category includes "one-way" cruises on ships that depart from Miami and travel to various South American ports. The passengers disembark and are responsible for arranging their return travel from the destination port. The ship then takes on a new group of passengers at the South American port for a one-way journey to Miami. This year, Endless Summer earned $4,912,000 from its round-trip cruises and $5,018,000 from its one-way cruises. How much of Endless Summer's $9,930,000 total transportation income is U.S. source income, and how much is foreign source income?
3. In 1995, Jenson Investments, a Delaware corporation with a 35 percent federal tax rate, formed Bestmark, a wholly owned German subsidiary. Bestmark conducts several profitable businesses in Europe and pays the 45 percent German corporate income tax. Bestmark has never paid a dividend to its U.S. parent and has accumulated $8.2 million after-tax earnings. Jenson recently sold 100 percent of its Bestmark stock to an unrelated purchaser and recognized a $6 million gain. Compute Jenson's U.S. tax on this gain.

Tax Planning Cases

1. Corporation TN wants to open a branch operation in eastern Europe and must decide between locating the branch in either Country R or Country S. Labor costs are substantially lower in Country R than in Country S. For this reason, the Country R branch would generate $700,000 annual income, while the Country S branch would generate only $550,000 annual income. However, Country R has a 20 percent corporate income tax, while Country S has a 10 percent corporate income tax. On the basis of these facts, in which country should Corporate TN locate its eastern European branch?
2. ETP Inc., which has a 35 percent U.S. tax rate, plans to expand its business into Country J. It could open a branch office, or it could create a foreign subsidiary in Country J. The branch office would generate $5,000,000 income in year 0. The foreign subsidiary would incur incremental legal costs and, as a result, would generate only $4,750,000 income in year 0. This income would be taxed at Country J's 18 percent corporate rate. ETP plans to defer repatriation of the subsidiary's year 0 after-tax earnings until year 4. Assuming a 6 percent discount rate, should ETP open the branch office or form the subsidiary to maximize the NPV of the year 0 foreign source income?
3. NMJ Corporation owns 100 percent of the stock of FJ, a foreign corporation conducting business in Portugal. FJ generates $100,000 before-tax annual income on which it pays a 30 percent Portuguese tax. FJ can reinvest its after-tax earnings for an indefinite time period in Europe at a 7 percent before-tax rate of return. Alternatively, FJ could distribute its after-tax earnings to NMJ, which could invest the funds in the United States at a 9 percent before-tax rate of return. Assuming that NMJ's U.S. tax rate is 35 percent, should it repatriate FJ's earnings to maximize its rate of return?

Comprehensive Problems for Part Four

1. Univex is a calendar year, accrual basis retail business. Its financial statements provide the following information for the year.

Revenues from sales of goods	$ 783,200
Cost of goods sold (FIFO)	(417,500)
Gross profit	$ 365,700
Interest income from certificates of deposit	1,300
Dividend income from IBM stock	6,720
Gain from sale of IBM stock purchased in 2000	8,615
Bad debt expense	3,900
Administrative salaries and wages	153,400
Business and employment taxes	31,000
Interest expense on debt incurred to buy inventory	5,100
Advertising	7,000
Meals and entertainment	3,780
Property insurance premiums	4,300
Depreciation	10,800
Repairs and maintenance	18,700
Supplies	4,120
Utilities	21,000
Contributions to charity	5,000

Univex's records reveal the following facts.

- Bad debt expense equals the addition to an allowance for bad debts. Actual write-offs of uncollectible accounts totaled $2,000.
- MACRS depreciation for the year was $21,240.
- Univex made no asset dispositions.
- The owners did not receive any compensation or withdraw any funds from Univex.

- Univex is entitled to an $1,800 general business credit.

a. Assume Univex is a sole proprietorship. Compute net profit on Schedule C, Form 1040, and identify the items from Univex's records that do not appear on Schedule C.

b. Assume Univex is an LLC. Compute ordinary income on page 1, Form 1065, and complete Schedule K, Form 1065.

c. Assume Univex is a corporation operating in a state without a corporate income tax. Univex made estimated federal tax payments totaling $23,500. Compute taxable income on page 1, Form 1120, calculate Univex's federal income tax, and complete page 1, Form 1120.

2. Dollin Inc. is incorporated under Virginia law and has its corporate headquarters in Richmond. Dollin is a distributor; it purchases tangible goods from manufactureres and sells the goods to retailers. It has a branch office through which it sells goods in the United Kingdom and owns 100 percent of a French corporation (French Dollin) through which it sells goods in France. Dollin's financial records provide the following information for the year.

Before-tax net income from sales:	
Domestic sales	$ 967,900
U.K. sales (foreign source income)	415,000
	$1,382,900
Dividend income:	
Brio Inc.	$ 8,400
French Dollin (foreign source income)	33,800

- Dollin pays state income tax in Virginia, North Carolina, and South Carolina. All three states tax their apportioned share of Dollin's net income from worldwide sales. Because Virginia is Dollin's commercial domicile, it also taxes Dollin's U.S. source (but not foreign source) dividend income net of any federal dividends-received deduction. The states have the following apportionment factors and tax rates.

	Apportionment Factor	***Tax Rate***
Virginia	43.19%	6.00%
North Carolina	11.02%	7.75%
South Carolina	8.52%	5.00%

- Dollin paid $149,200 income tax to the United Kingdom.
- Brio Inc. is a taxable U.S. corporation. Dollin owns 2.8 percent of Brio's stock.
- The $33,800 dividend from French Dollin is a distribution of after-tax earnings with respect to which French Dollin paid $17,000 French income tax.
- Dollin elects to claim the foreign tax credit rather than to deduct foreign income taxes.

Solely on the basis of the above facts, compute the following.

a. Dollin's state income tax for Virginia, North Carolina, and South Carolina.

b. Dollin's federal income tax. Assume that Dollin paid the state taxes during the year, and no state income tax is allocable to foreign source income.

The Individual Taxpayer

Chapter Thirteen

The Individual Tax Formula

Learning Objectives

After studying this chapter, you should be able to:

1. Determine an individual's filing status.
2. List the four steps in the computation of individual taxable income.
3. Explain the relationship between the standard deduction and itemized deductions.
4. Compute a personal exemption amount.
5. Compute the regular tax on ordinary income.
6. Explain why a marriage penalty exists in the federal income tax system.
7. Describe the child credit and dependent care credit.
8. Recognize the circumstances that may trigger the individual AMT.
9. Describe the individual tax payment and return filing requirements.

Parts Three and Four of *Principles of Taxation for Business and Investment Planning* are concerned with the taxation of business income. In Part Three, we learned how income is measured for federal tax purposes, and we identified the important differences between taxable income and financial statement income determined under generally accepted accounting principles (GAAP). In Part Four, we discovered that the computation of taxable income does not vary significantly across business entities, but the rate at which the income is taxed does depend on the type of entity. Income earned by a sole proprietorship or an S corporation is taxed at the individual rates. Income earned by a regular corporation is taxed at the corporate rates. Income earned by a partnership is allocated to either individual or corporate partners and taxed accordingly.

In Part Four, we observed that a corporation's business income is essentially equivalent to its taxable income. In contrast, an individual's business income is just one component of the total tax base reported on Form 1040 (U.S. Individual Income Tax Return). Unlike corporate taxpayers, people engage in many nonbusiness activities. If a person engages in a nonbusiness activity that results in an economic benefit, he or she may have to recognize the value of the benefit as income. If the activity involves an expense or loss, the person may be allowed to deduct it. Therefore, before we can compute individual taxable income and the federal tax on that income, we must turn our attention to the nonbusiness transactions in which people commonly engage.

Part Five of the text is devoted to the individual taxpayer. Chapter 13 lays the groundwork with an overview of the individual tax base and the individual tax computation. The chapter also describes the tax payment and return filing requirements for individuals. Chapter 14 concentrates on the tax implications of compensation arrangements from the perspective of both employer and employee. Chapter 15 turns to the tax consequences of investment activities, while Chapter 16 focuses on personal activities. Throughout Part Five, we will emphasize the planning opportunities and the cash flow consequences for individual taxpayers.

FILING STATUS FOR INDIVIDUALS

Tax Talk
Same-sex couples are prohibited from filing joint federal income tax returns even though they may be legally married under state law. The IRS says that the federal law is clear on the issue, with marriage restricted to a "legal union between a man and woman as husband and wife."

Every individual who is either a citizen or a permanent resident of the United States is a taxable entity who may be required to file a federal income tax return.[1] One of the first items of information that must be provided on this return is **filing status.** Filing status, which reflects an individual's marital and family situation, affects the calculation of taxable income and determines the rates at which that income is taxed.

Married Individuals and Surviving Spouses

An individual who is married on the last day of the taxable year can elect to file a **joint return** with his or her spouse.[2] A joint return reflects the combined activities of both spouses for the entire year. A husband and wife who file a joint return have **joint and several liability** for their tax bill. In other words, each spouse is responsible for paying the entire tax (not just one half).[3] With respect to a joint return, any reference to the taxpayer is actually a reference to two people.

Married Filing Jointly

Mr. and Mrs. Lane were legally married under Hawaiian law on December 12, 1990. For federal tax purposes, their marital status was determined on December 31. The newlyweds filed a joint return for 1990 that reported their combined incomes for the entire calendar year.

Objective 1
Determine an individual's filing status.

For the taxable year in which a married person dies, the widow or widower can file a joint return with the deceased.[4] If the widow or widower maintains a home for a dependent child, he or she qualifies as a **surviving spouse** for the two taxable years following the year of death.[5] A surviving spouse can use the married filing jointly tax rates for these two years.

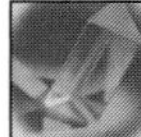
Surviving Spouse

Refer to the facts in the preceding example. Mrs. Lane died on September 14, 2002, and Mr. Lane has not remarried. Mr. Lane filed a 2002 joint return reflecting his deceased wife's activities from January 1 through September 14 and his activities for the entire year. The couple had two children, ages 6 and 10, who live with their father. Because Mr. Lane met the definition of surviving spouse, he was entitled to compute his tax for 2003 and 2004 using the married filing jointly rates.

[1] §7701(b) distinguishes between resident aliens and nonresident aliens. The former are subject to the same tax rules as U.S. citizens. Nonresident aliens are subject to federal income tax only if they earn U.S. source income.

[2] §6013.

[3] §6013(d)(3).

[4] §6013(a)(2).

[5] §2(a). A person does not qualify as a surviving spouse if he or she remarries within these two years.

As an alternative to joint filing, married individuals can file **separate returns** that reflect each spouse's independent activity and separate taxable income. In a few situations, individuals can derive some tax benefit by filing separately, but most couples who file separate returns do so for nontax reasons.

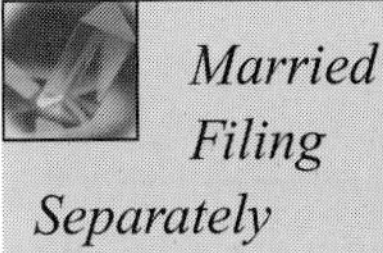

Married Filing Separately

Mr. and Mrs. Conrad have been legally separated for six years but have not divorced because of their religious faith. They live in different cities and have no joint financial dealings or obligations. Because the Conrads lead independent lives, they choose to file separate tax returns.

Unmarried Individuals

An individual who is unmarried on the last day of the year, who is not a surviving spouse, and who maintains a home that is the principal place of abode for a child or other dependent family member qualifies as a **head of household** for filing purposes.[6]

Head of Household

Refer back to our example involving Mr. Lane, a widower with two dependent children living at home. In 2003 and 2004, Mr. Lane filed his tax return as a surviving spouse. In 2005, his filing status changed to head of household. Mr. Lane will continue to qualify as a head of household until his children grow up and move out of his home or until he remarries.

An unmarried individual who is neither a surviving spouse nor a head of household files as a **single taxpayer.** Note that the tax law does not provide any special filing status for minor or dependent children. Regardless of age, children who earn income in their own name must file as single taxpayers, even if the income is collected and controlled by their parents.[7]

OVERVIEW OF THE TAXABLE INCOME COMPUTATION

A pragmatic way to approach the computation of individual taxable income is to observe how the computation is presented on Form 1040. In this section of the chapter we will do just that, concentrating on the basic structure of the computation without devoting much attention to its separate elements. In subsequent chapters, we will examine the more important of these elements in detail. This overview of the taxable income computation from a compliance perspective offers a practical benefit: It will help you to read and interpret your own Form 1040. The federal tax return is, after all, a legal document that individuals must sign. By doing so, they are attesting that they have examined the return and that the information on the return is "true, correct, and complete." Therefore, every person, even if he or she uses a professional tax return preparer, should understand the flow of information on a Form 1040.

The Four-Step Procedure

Objective 2
List the four steps in the computation of individual taxable income.

The computation of taxable income on an individual return follows four procedural steps contained on pages 1 and 2 of Form 1040.

[6] §2(b).

[7] §73.

Step 1: Calculate Total Income

As the first step, an individual must list all items of income recognized in the year on page 1, Form 1040. On the basis of the material in earlier chapters, we know that this list includes taxable income from any business in which the individual engaged. If the individual operated a sole proprietorship, the net profit (as computed on Schedule C) is carried to page 1. Similarly, if the individual conducted business through a partnership or owned stock in an S corporation, a share of the passthrough entity's income is carried from Schedule E to page 1. The list of income items also includes any salary or wage payments that the individual earned as an employee and any income from the individual's investments. The listed items are added together to result in the individual's **total income.**

Mr. and Mrs. Volpe: Step 1

In 2004, Mr. and Mrs. Volpe recognized three items of income.

Mr. Volpe's salary from his employer	$ 39,400
Interest income on certificates of deposit	8,600
Business income from Mrs. Volpe's sole proprietorship	56,730
Total income	$104,730

The first page of Mr. and Mrs. Volpe's Form 1040 on which these income items are listed is shown as Exhibit 13.1.

Step 2: Calculate Adjusted Gross Income

The second step is the calculation of the individual's adjusted gross income. **Adjusted gross income (AGI)** equals total income less the specific deductions listed on page 1, Form 1040.[8] One example is the deduction for one-half of any self-employment tax owed by the individual.[9] We will identify other so-called **above-the-line deductions** throughout the rest of the text.

While AGI represents an intermediate step in the computation of individual taxable income, it is an extremely important number in its own right. As we will soon discuss, many individual deductions and credits are limited by reference to the taxpayer's AGI. As a result, the amount of deduction or credit is a function of the AGI reported on the last line of page 1, Form 1040.

Mr. and Mrs. Volpe: Step 2

Mrs. Volpe's 2004 self-employment tax (computed on Schedule SE, Form 1040) is $8,016. One-half of this tax is deductible in the computation of AGI. In June, Mr. Volpe cashed in a one-year certificate of deposit after holding it for only 10 months. Because of the early withdrawal, the bank charged a $435 penalty. The Volpes are allowed to deduct this penalty in computing their AGI. Both these above-the-line deductions are reported on page 1, Form 1040 (Exhibit 13.1). Line 36 (the last line on page 1), reports that the couple's AGI is $100,287.

[8] §62 provides the list of above-the-line deductions that are subtracted in the AGI calculation.

[9] §164(f). See Chapter 9 for a discussion of SE tax.

EXHIBIT 13.1

Form **1040** Department of the Treasury—Internal Revenue Service
U.S. Individual Income Tax Return 2004 (99) IRS Use Only—Do not write or staple in this space.

For the year Jan. 1–Dec. 31, 2004, or other tax year beginning , 2004, ending , 20 — OMB No. 1545-0074

Label (See instructions on page 16.) Use the IRS label. Otherwise, please print or type.			
Your first name and initial: James L.	Last name: Volpe		Your social security number: 784 45 9042
If a joint return, spouse's first name and initial: Nancy J.	Last name: Volpe		Spouse's social security number: 617 38 0081
Home address (number and street). If you have a P.O. box, see page 16.: 10 St. Martin Circle		Apt. no.	▲ **Important!** ▲ You **must** enter your SSN(s) above.
City, town or post office, state, and ZIP code. If you have a foreign address, see page 16.: Exeter CN 04012			

Presidential Election Campaign (See page 16.) **Note.** Checking "Yes" will not change your tax or reduce your refund. Do you, or your spouse if filing a joint return, want $3 to go to this fund? ▶ You: ☒ Yes ☐ No Spouse: ☒ Yes ☐ No

Filing Status Check only one box.

1 ☐ Single
2 ☒ Married filing jointly (even if only one had income)
3 ☐ Married filing separately. Enter spouse's SSN above and full name here. ▶
4 ☐ Head of household (with qualifying person). (See page 17.) If the qualifying person is a child but not your dependent, enter this child's name here. ▶
5 ☐ Qualifying widow(er) with dependent child (see page 17)

Exemptions

6a ☒ **Yourself.** If someone can claim you as a dependent, **do not** check box 6a
b ☒ Spouse
Boxes checked on 6a and 6b: 2

c **Dependents:**

(1) First name	Last name	(2) Dependent's social security number	(3) Dependent's relationship to you	(4) ✓ if qualifying child for child tax credit (see page 18)
Sara	Volpe	249 98 1322	child	☑
Shana	Volpe	312 05 7886	child	☑
				☐
				☐

If more than four dependents, see page 18.

No. of children on 6c who: • lived with you: 2 • did not live with you due to divorce or separation (see page 18): — Dependents on 6c not entered above: —

d Total number of exemptions claimed — Add numbers on lines above ▶ 4

Income

Attach Form(s) W-2 here. Also attach Forms W-2G and 1099-R if tax was withheld.

If you did not get a W-2, see page 19.

Enclose, but do not attach, any payment. Also, please use **Form 1040-V**.

7	Wages, salaries, tips, etc. Attach Form(s) W-2	7	39,400
8a	**Taxable** interest. Attach Schedule B if required	8a	8,600
b	**Tax-exempt** interest. **Do not** include on line 8a — 8b		
9a	Ordinary dividends. Attach Schedule B if required	9a	
b	Qualified dividends (see page 20) — 9b		
10	Taxable refunds, credits, or offsets of state and local income taxes (see page 20)	10	
11	Alimony received	11	
12	Business income or (loss). Attach Schedule C or C-EZ	12	56,730
13	Capital gain or (loss). Attach Schedule D if required. If not required, check here ▶ ☐	13	
14	Other gains or (losses). Attach Form 4797	14	
15a	IRA distributions — 15a — b Taxable amount (see page 22)	15b	
16a	Pensions and annuities — 16a — b Taxable amount (see page 22)	16b	
17	Rental real estate, royalties, partnerships, S corporations, trusts, etc. Attach Schedule E	17	
18	Farm income or (loss). Attach Schedule F	18	
19	Unemployment compensation	19	
20a	Social security benefits — 20a — b Taxable amount (see page 24)	20b	
21	Other income. List type and amount (see page 24)	21	
22	Add the amounts in the far right column for lines 7 through 21. This is your **total income** ▶	22	104,730

Adjusted Gross Income

23	Educator expenses (see page 26)	23			
24	Certain business expenses of reservists, performing artists, and fee-basis government officials. Attach Form 2106 or 2106-EZ	24			
25	IRA deduction (see page 26)	25			
26	Student loan interest deduction (see page 28)	26			
27	Tuition and fees deduction (see page 29)	27			
28	Health savings account deduction. Attach Form 8889	28			
29	Moving expenses. Attach Form 3903	29			
30	One-half of self-employment tax. Attach Schedule SE	30	4,008		
31	Self-employed health insurance deduction (see page 30)	31			
32	Self-employed SEP, SIMPLE, and qualified plans	32			
33	Penalty on early withdrawal of savings	33	435		
34a	Alimony paid b Recipient's SSN ▶	34a			
35	Add lines 23 through 34a			35	4,443
36	Subtract line 35 from line 22. This is your **adjusted gross income** ▶			36	100,287

For Disclosure, Privacy Act, and Paperwork Reduction Act Notice, see page 75. Cat. No. 11320B Form **1040** (2004)

Step 3: Subtract the Standard Deduction or Itemized Deductions

Objective 3
Explain the relationship between the standard deduction and itemized deductions.

In the third step of the taxable income computation, AGI is reduced by the *greater of* a standard deduction or allowable itemized deductions.

Standard Deduction

The basic **standard deduction** is a function of filing status. The basic deductions for 2005 are:

EXHIBIT 13.1
(concluded)

Form 1040 (2004) Page **2**

Tax and Credits

Line	Description	Box	Amount
37	Amount from line 36 (adjusted gross income)	37	100,287
38a	Check if: ☐ **You** were born before January 2, 1940, ☐ Blind. ☐ **Spouse** was born before January 2, 1940, ☐ Blind. **Total boxes checked ▶ 38a**		
b	If your spouse itemizes on a separate return or you were a dual-status alien, see page 31 and check here ▶ 38b ☐		
39	**Itemized deductions** (from Schedule A) **or** your **standard deduction** (see left margin)	39	17,070
40	Subtract line 39 from line 37	40	83,217
41	If line 37 is $107,025 or less, multiply $3,100 by the total number of exemptions claimed on line 6d. If line 37 is over $107,025, see the worksheet on page 33	41	12,400
42	**Taxable income.** Subtract line 41 from line 40. If line 41 is more than line 40, enter -0-	42	70,817
43	Tax (see page 33). Check if any tax is from: a ☐ Form(s) 8814 b ☐ Form 4972	43	11,034
44	**Alternative minimum tax** (see page 35). Attach Form 6251	44	
45	Add lines 43 and 44 ▶	45	11,034
46	Foreign tax credit. Attach Form 1116 if required	46	
47	Credit for child and dependent care expenses. Attach Form 2441	47 870	
48	Credit for the elderly or the disabled. Attach Schedule R	48	
49	Education credits. Attach Form 8863	49	
50	Retirement savings contributions credit. Attach Form 8880	50	
51	Child tax credit (see page 37)	51 2000	
52	Adoption credit. Attach Form 8839	52	
53	Credits from: a ☐ Form 8396 b ☐ Form 8859	53	
54	Other credits. Check applicable box(es): a ☐ Form 3800 b ☐ Form 8801 c ☐ Specify	54	
55	Add lines 46 through 54. These are your **total credits**	55	2,870
56	Subtract line 55 from line 45. If line 55 is more than line 45, enter -0- ▶	56	8,164

Standard Deduction for—
- People who checked any box on line 38a or 38b **or** who can be claimed as a dependent, see page 31.
- All others:

Single or Married filing separately, $4,850

Married filing jointly or Qualifying widow(er), $9,700

Head of household, $7,150

Other Taxes

Line	Description	Box	Amount
57	Self-employment tax. Attach Schedule SE	57	8,016
58	Social security and Medicare tax on tip income not reported to employer. Attach Form 4137	58	
59	Additional tax on IRAs, other qualified retirement plans, etc. Attach Form 5329 if required	59	
60	Advance earned income credit payments from Form(s) W-2	60	
61	Household employment taxes. Attach Schedule H	61	
62	Add lines 56 through 61. This is your **total tax** ▶	62	16,180

Payments

Line	Description	Box	Amount
63	Federal income tax withheld from Forms W-2 and 1099	63 2,863	
64	2004 estimated tax payments and amount applied from 2003 return	64 15,000	
65a	**Earned income credit (EIC)**	65a	
b	Nontaxable combat pay election ▶ 65b		
66	Excess social security and tier 1 RRTA tax withheld (see page 54)	66	
67	Additional child tax credit. Attach Form 8812	67	
68	Amount paid with request for extension to file (see page 54)	68	
69	Other payments from: a ☐ Form 2439 b ☐ Form 4136 c ☐ Form 8885	69	
70	Add lines 63, 64, 65a, and 66 through 69. These are your **total payments** ▶	70	17,863

If you have a qualifying child, attach Schedule EIC.

Refund

Direct deposit? See page 54 and fill in 72b, 72c, and 72d.

Line	Description	Box	Amount
71	If line 70 is more than line 62, subtract line 62 from line 70. This is the amount you **overpaid**	71	1,683
72a	Amount of line 71 you want **refunded to you** ▶	72a	
▶ b	Routing number ▶ c Type: ☐ Checking ☐ Savings		
▶ d	Account number		
73	Amount of line 71 you want **applied to your 2005 estimated tax** ▶	73 1,683	

Amount You Owe

Line	Description	Box	Amount
74	**Amount you owe.** Subtract line 70 from line 62. For details on how to pay, see page 55 ▶	74	
75	Estimated tax penalty (see page 55)	75	

Third Party Designee Do you want to allow another person to discuss this return with the IRS (see page 56)? ☐ **Yes.** Complete the following. ☐ **No**

Designee's name ▶ Phone no. ▶ ( ) Personal identification number (PIN) ▶

Sign Here Under penalties of perjury, I declare that I have examined this return and accompanying schedules and statements, and to the best of my knowledge and belief, they are true, correct, and complete. Declaration of preparer (other than taxpayer) is based on all information of which preparer has any knowledge.

Joint return? See page 17. Keep a copy for your records.

Your signature: James L. Volpe — Date: 4/6/05 — Your occupation: Teacher — Daytime phone number: (641) 822-1050

Spouse's signature. If a joint return, **both** must sign.: Nancy J. Volpe — Date: 4/6/05 — Spouse's occupation: self-employed

Paid Preparer's Use Only

Preparer's signature ▶ Date — Check if self-employed ☐ — Preparer's SSN or PTIN

Firm's name (or yours if self-employed), address, and ZIP code ▶ — EIN — Phone no. ( )

Form **1040** (2004)

Married filing jointly and surviving spouses	$10,000
Married filing separately	5,000
Head of household	7,300
Single	5,000

An individual who has reached age 65 by the last day of the year is entitled to an additional deduction. An individual who is legally blind is also entitled to an additional deduction. For 2005, the additional deductions are:

Married filing jointly or separately and surviving spouse	$1,000
Head of household or single	1,250

Both the basic and the additional standard deductions are indexed for inflation and may change every year.[10]

Standard Deduction

Mr. and Mrs. O'Neil file a joint return and are 79 and 75 years of age, respectively. Mr. O'Neil is legally blind. Their standard deduction for 2005 is $13,0000.

Basic standard deduction	$10,000
Additional deductions for Mr. O'Neil:	
Age 65 or older	1,000
Legally blind	1,000
Additional deduction for Mrs. O'Neil:	
Age 65 or older	1,000
	$13,000

Tax Talk

According to a government report, more than 2 million people overpaid their 2002 tax by a collective total of almost $100 million because they claimed a standard deduction instead of itemizing.

Itemized Deductions

As a category, **itemized deductions** include any deduction allowed to an individual that cannot be subtracted in the calculation of AGI.[11] Individuals elect to itemize (i.e., subtract itemized deductions from AGI) only if their total deduction amount exceeds the standard deduction for the year. This situation is the exception rather than the rule; only about 30 percent of individual return filers elect to itemize.[12] Itemized deductions are reported on Schedule A, Form 1040.

Itemized deductions create a tax savings only if the individual elects to itemize. In a year in which the individual claims the standard deduction, any itemized deductions yield no tax benefit.

Election to Itemize

Assume that Mr. and Mrs. O'Neil in the preceding example accumulated $12,000 of itemized deductions in 2005. Because this total is less than their $13,000 standard deduction, they use the standard deduction to compute taxable income, and their itemized deductions yield no tax benefit.

Now assume that their itemized deductions totaled $15,000. In this case, they would elect to itemize by subtracting this amount from AGI. If their marginal tax rate is 28 percent, their itemized deductions save $4,200 in tax ($15,000 × 28 percent). However, the standard deduction would have saved $3,640 ($13,000 × 28 percent). Consequently, the incremental tax savings from the itemized deductions is only $560 ($2,000 excess itemized deductions × 28 percent).

This example leads to a key observation about individual tax deductions. A deduction listed as an above-the-line deduction *always* reduces taxable income. A deduction that must be itemized may have limited or even no effect on taxable income. Congress decides which

[10] §63(c) and (f).

[11] §63(d).

[12] "Individual Income Tax Returns: Selected Income and Tax Items for Specified Tax Years 1975–1996," Table 1, *Statistics of Income Bulletin,* Winter 1997/1998.

deductions are above-the-line and which deductions are itemized. The classification often reflects tax policy concerns and can change from year to year. For example, individuals are allowed to deduct attorney fees and other costs of lawsuits based on illegal discrimination by the individual's employer. Before the enactment of the American Jobs Creation Act of 2004, this deduction was an itemized deduction. The act reclassified it as an above-the-line deduction in order to improve the equity of the tax law for individuals involved in such lawsuits.

Bunching Itemized Deductions

People can often maximize the value of their itemized deductions through a tax planning technique called **bunching.** By controlling the timing of their deductible expenses, they can concentrate the deductions into one year. By doing so, they create a critical mass of itemized deductions, the total of which exceeds their standard deduction. The following example illustrates this technique.

Bunching of Itemized Deductions

Mr. Norris, a single taxpayer with a 35 percent marginal tax rate, routinely incurs $4,500 annual expenses qualifying as itemized deductions. This amount is less than his annual standard deduction. If his pattern of expenses is level from year to year, he will derive no benefit from the expenses. In contrast, if Mr. Norris can shift $1,500 of the expenses from 2005 to 2006, he can take his standard deduction in 2005 and elect to itemize in 2006.

	Level Pattern of Itemized Deductions	Bunched Deductions
2005:		
Itemized deductions	$4,500	$3,000
Standard deduction (single)	5,000	5,000
2006:		
Itemized deductions	$4,500	$6,000
Standard deduction (single)	5,000	(5,000)
Itemized deductions in excess of standard deduction		$1,000
		.35
Tax savings from bunching		$ 350

How can Mr. Norris shift deductible expenses from 2005 to 2006? As a cash basis taxpayer, he recognizes deductions in the year of payment. By *postponing* payment of an expense from December until January, he shifts the deduction to the next year. At the end of 2006, Mr. Norris may want to *accelerate* payment of deductible expenses that he normally would pay in 2007, when he will take the standard deduction under his cyclical bunching strategy.

Overall Limitation on Itemized Deductions

Individuals with AGI in excess of a threshold amount must reduce the total of certain itemized deductions by 3 percent of the excess AGI.[13] This reduction is limited to 80 percent of the total of these deductions. In other words, every individual regardless of income level can deduct at least 20 percent of the total. While this overall limitation diminishes the value of itemizing deductions to high-income taxpayers, it has no effect on the standard deduction. The technical details of the overall limitation are incorporated into an Itemized Deduction Worksheet included as Appendix 13–A to this chapter.

[13] §68. The overall limitation is scheduled to be phased out beginning in 2006.

EXHIBIT 13.2

SCHEDULES A&B (Form 1040) Department of the Treasury Internal Revenue Service (99)		Schedule A—Itemized Deductions (Schedule B is on back) ▶ Attach to Form 1040. ▶ See Instructions for Schedules A and B (Form 1040).			OMB No. 1545-0074 2004 Attachment Sequence No. 07
Name(s) shown on Form 1040		James L. and Nancy J. Volpe			Your social security number 784 48 9042
Medical and Dental Expenses		**Caution.** Do not include expenses reimbursed or paid by others.			
	1	Medical and dental expenses (see page A-2)	1		
	2	Enter amount from Form 1040, line 37 [2]			
	3	Multiply line 2 by 7.5% (.075)	3		
	4	Subtract line 3 from line 1. If line 3 is more than line 1, enter -0-		4	
Taxes You Paid (See page A-2.)	5	State and local **(check only one box):** a ☒ Income taxes, **or** b ☐ General sales taxes (see page A-2)	5	5,140	
	6	Real estate taxes (see page A-3)	6	1,920	
	7	Personal property taxes	7		
	8	Other taxes. List type and amount ▶	8		
	9	Add lines 5 through 8		9	7,060
Interest You Paid (See page A-3.)	10	Home mortgage interest and points reported to you on Form 1098	10	8,080	
	11	Home mortgage interest not reported to you on Form 1098. If paid to the person from whom you bought the home, see page A-4 and show that person's name, identifying no., and address ▶	11		
Note. Personal interest is not deductible.	12	Points not reported to you on Form 1098. See page A-4 for special rules	12		
	13	Investment interest. Attach Form 4952 if required. (See page A-4.)	13		
	14	Add lines 10 through 13		14	8,080
Gifts to Charity If you made a gift and got a benefit for it, see page A-4.	15	Gifts by cash or check. If you made any gift of $250 or more, see page A-4	15	1,930	
	16	Other than by cash or check. If any gift of $250 or more, see page A-4. You **must** attach Form 8283 if over $500	16		
	17	Carryover from prior year	17		
	18	Add lines 15 through 17		18	1,930
Casualty and Theft Losses	19	Casualty or theft loss(es). Attach Form 4684. (See page A-5.)		19	
Job Expenses and Most Other Miscellaneous Deductions	20	Unreimbursed employee expenses—job travel, union dues, job education, etc. Attach Form 2106 or 2106-EZ if required. (See page A-6.) ▶	20		
	21	Tax preparation fees	21		
(See page A-5.)	22	Other expenses—investment, safe deposit box, etc. List type and amount ▶	22		
	23	Add lines 20 through 22	23		
	24	Enter amount from Form 1040, line 37 [24]			
	25	Multiply line 24 by 2% (.02)	25		
	26	Subtract line 25 from line 23. If line 25 is more than line 23, enter -0-		26	
Other Miscellaneous Deductions	27	Other—from list on page A-6. List type and amount ▶		27	
Total Itemized Deductions	28	Is Form 1040, line 37, over $142,700 (over $71,350 if married filing separately)? ☒ **No.** Your deduction is not limited. Add the amounts in the far right column for lines 4 through 27. Also, enter this amount on Form 1040, line 39. ☐ **Yes.** Your deduction may be limited. See page A-6 for the amount to enter.	▶	28	17,070

For Paperwork Reduction Act Notice, see Form 1040 instructions. Cat. No. 11330X **Schedule A (Form 1040) 2004**

Mr. and Mrs. Volpe: Step 3

During 2004, Mr. and Mrs. Volpe incurred the following expenses that qualify as itemized deductions.

Connecticut personal income tax	$5,140
Real estate tax on the Volpes' personal residence	1,920
Home mortgage interest	8,080
Charitable donations	1,930

These deductions are listed on Schedule A (shown as Exhibit 13.2) and totaled on line 28. Note that the overall limitation on itemized deductions did not affect the Volpes because their AGI was *less* than the 2004 threshold ($142,700 for married filing jointly). Because the Volpes' $17,070 total itemized deductions exceeded their standard deduction, they elected to itemize by carrying the $17,070 total to line 39, page 2, Form 1040 (see Exhibit 13.1 on page 354).

Step 4: Subtract Personal Exemption Amount

Objective 4
Compute a personal exemption amount.

As the fourth and last step in the computation of taxable income, AGI is reduced by the individual's personal exemption amount. This amount equals the annual **personal exemption** ($3,200 for 2005) multiplied by the number of people in the individual's family.[14] The family consists of the taxpayer (two taxpayers on a joint return) plus any person qualifying as the taxpayer's **dependent.** Qualification is based on five requirements.

1. The person must have a familial relationship with the taxpayer (lineal ancestor, descendant, sibling, aunt or uncle, niece or nephew, or in-law) *or* reside in the taxpayer's home for the entire year.
2. The taxpayer must provide over half the financial support of the person for the year.
3. The person's gross income for the year must be less than the personal exemption. This requirement is waived for a child under age 19 or a child who is a full-time student under age 24.
4. The person must not file a joint return with a spouse.
5. The person must be a U.S. citizen or a resident of the United States, Mexico, or Canada.

A taxpayer may claim an exemption for any person meeting these five requirements. If a person who is claimed as a dependent is required to file his or her own tax return, the person may not claim an exemption on this return.

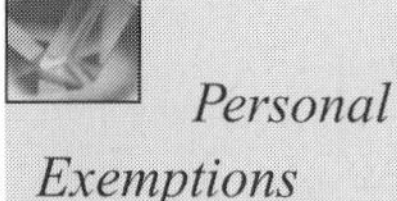

Personal Exemptions

In 2005, Mr. and Mrs. White provided 100 percent of the financial support of their three children who all live at home. The oldest child, age 18, has a part-time job and earned $5,641 during the year, which she saved for college. Although the child's gross income exceeded the exemption amount, she qualified as her parents' dependent because she is under age 19. Consequently, Mr. and Mrs. White's exemption amount was $16,000 ($3,200 × five family members).

The oldest child filed her own Form 1040 as a single taxpayer. She reported $5,641 wages and deducted a $5,000 standard deduction.[15] However, because Mr. and Mrs. White claimed her as a dependent, she could not claim a personal exemption on her return. Consequently, her taxable income was $641.

Exemption Phaseout

The personal exemption amount is gradually phased out for individuals with AGI in excess of a threshold amount.[16] This phaseout mechanism is conceptually similar to the limitation

[14] §151 and §152 contain the personal exemption rules.

[15] An individual who is claimed as a dependent on another person's return is entitled to a standard deduction on his or her own tax return. However, the standard deduction is limited to the *greater* of the person's earned income (wages, salary, or self-employment income) plus $250 or an inflation-adjusted base. The 2005 base is $800. The limited standard deduction may not exceed the regular standard deduction for that individual. §63(e)(5).

[16] §151(d)(3). The exemption phaseout is scheduled to be phased out beginning in 2006.

on itemized deductions because it diminishes the value of personal exemptions to high-income taxpayers. The major difference between the two is that the personal exemption amount can be decreased to zero. The details of this phaseout mechanism are incorporated into a Personal Exemption Amount Worksheet included as Appendix 13–B to this chapter.

Mr. and Mrs. Volpe: Step 4

Mr. and Mrs. Volpe have two daughters (ages 7 and 10) who live with their parents and are dependent on them for financial support. Mr. and Mrs. Volpe also provide about 80 percent of the annual financial support for Annie Jarvis, Mrs. Volpe's widowed mother (age 80). Mrs. Jarvis received $4,216 taxable interest from several savings accounts in 2004. The Volpes claimed exemptions for themselves and their two children on line 6, page 1, Form 1040 (Exhibit 13.1). They could not claim Annie Jarvis as a dependent because her gross income exceeded the $3,100 exemption amount. The Volpes' total exemption amount of $12,400 ($3,100 × 4) is reported on line 41, page 2, Form 1040 (Exhibit 13.1). The exemption phaseout did not affect them because AGI was *less* than the 2004 threshold ($214,050 for married filing jointly).

The Taxable Income Formula

The four-step procedure for computing individual taxable income can be summarized as follows.

Total income
(Above-the-line deductions)
Adjusted gross income
(Standard or itemized deductions)
(Personal exemption amount)
Taxable income

The AGI reported on Form 1040 is the closest gauge of individual disposable income. The standard deduction and exemption amount are not based on monetary expenses or economic losses and are unrelated to specific cash flows. The purpose of these two subtractions from AGI is to shelter a base amount of disposable income from tax. If a person's AGI is less than the tax-free threshold represented by the combined standard deduction and exemption amount, his taxable income is zero. Theoretically, such person must spend every dollar of AGI to buy the necessities of life and has no financial ability to pay income tax.

Mr. and Mrs. Volpe: Taxable Income

Pages 1 and 2 of Mr. and Mrs. Volpe's Form 1040 (Exhibit 13.1) reflect the following computation of taxable income.

Total income (line 22)	$104,730
Above-the-line deductions (line 35)	(4,443)
AGI (line 36)	$100,287
Itemized deductions (line 39)	(17,070)
Personal exemption amount (line 41)	(12,400)
Taxable income (line 42)	$ 70,817

COMPUTING INDIVIDUAL TAX

The tax on individual taxable income is computed under the rate schedule determined by the taxpayer's filing status.[17] These rate schedules are adjusted annually for inflation. Here are the 2005 rate schedules.

Individual Tax Rate Schedules

Married Filing Jointly and Surviving Spouse

If taxable income is:	The tax is:
Not over $14,600	10% of taxable income
Over $14,600 but not over $59,400	$1,460.00 + 15% of the excess over $14,600
Over $59,400 but not over $119,950	$8,180.00 + 25% of the excess over $59,400
Over $119,950 but not over $182,800	$23,317.50 + 28% of the excess over $119,950
Over $182,800 but not over $326,450	$40,915.50 + 33% of the excess over $182,800
Over $326,450	$88,320.00 + 35% of the excess over $326,450

Married Filing Separately

If taxable income is:	The tax is:
Not over $7,300	10% of taxable income
Over $7,300 but not over $29,700	$730.00 + 15% of the excess over $7,300
Over $29,700 but not over $59,975	$4,090.00 + 25% of the excess over $29,700
Over $59,975 but not over $91,400	$11,658.75 + 28% of the excess over $59,975
Over $91,400 but not over $163,225	$20,457.75 + 33% of the excess over $91,400
Over $163,225	$44,160.00 + 35% of the excess over $163,225

Heads of Household

If taxable income is:	The tax is:
Not over $10,450	10% of taxable income
Over $10,450 but not over $39,800	$1,045.00 + 15% of the excess over $10,450
Over $39,800 but not over $102,800	$5,447.50 + 25% of the excess over $39,800
Over $102,800 but not over $166,450	$21,197.50 + 28% of the excess over $102,800
Over $166,450 but not over $326,450	$39,019.50 + 33% of the excess over $166,450
Over $326,450	$91,819.50 + 35% of the excess over $326,450

Single

If taxable income is:	The tax is:
Not over $7,300	10% of taxable income
Over $7,300 but not over $29,700	$730.00 + 15% of the excess over $7,300
Over $29,700 but not over $71,950	$4,090.00 + 25% of the excess over $29,700
Over $71,950 but not over $150,150	$14,652.50 + 28% of the excess over $71,950
Over $150,150 but not over $326,450	$36,548.50 + 33% of the excess over $150,150
Over $326,450	$94,727.50 + 35% of the excess over $326,450

Objective 5
Compute the regular tax on ordinary income.

Each tax rate schedule consists of six income brackets with progressively higher rates. These brackets are listed in the left column. The right column gives the *cumulative* tax on

[17] Form 1040 instructions require individuals with taxable incomes less than $100,000 to use a Tax Table to compute tax. These tables are derived from the rate schedules and eliminate the arithmetic required to use the schedules.

the income in all lower brackets and the marginal rate for the bracket. To compute the tax on a given amount of income, refer to the left column to determine the income bracket and the *excess* taxable income over the bracket floor. Refer to the right column and multiply the *excess* by the marginal rate for the bracket. Add the result to the cumulative tax to equal the total tax on the income.

Tax Computation on Ordinary Income

Mr. and Mrs. Ames (married filing jointly), Mr. Boyd (head of household), and Ms. Croll (single) each report $160,000 taxable income for 2005. Their tax (rounding up to whole dollars) is computed as follows.

	Mr. and Mrs. Ames (Married Filing Jointly)	*Mr. Boyd (Head of Household)*	*Ms. Croll (Single)*
Taxable income	$ 160,000	$ 160,000	$ 160,000
Bracket floor	(119,950)	(102,800)	(150,150)
Excess over floor	$ 40,050	$ 57,200	$ 9,850
Bracket rate	.28	.28	.33
	$ 11,214	$ 16,016	$ 3,251
Cumulative tax	23,318	21,198	36,549
Tax	$ 34,532	$ 37,214	$ 39,800

Preferential Rates

The tax computation must take into account any preferential rate applying to dividends or capital gains included in taxable income. The complicated preferential rate structure is discussed in detail in Chapter 15. This next example illustrates the basic effect of a preferential rate on the tax computation.

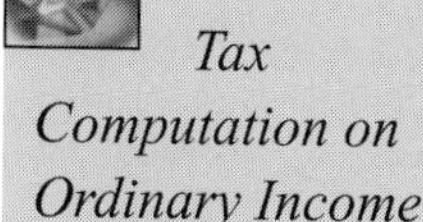

Tax Computation on Ordinary Income and Capital Gain

Assume that Ms. Croll recognized a $25,000 capital gain as part of her taxable income. This gain is eligible for a 15 percent preferential tax rate. Consequently, Ms. Croll's 2005 tax is computed as follows.

Taxable income	$160,000
Capital gain	(25,000)
Ordinary income portion of taxable income	$135,000
Bracket floor	(71,950)
Excess over floor	$ 63,050
Bracket rate	.28
	$ 17,654
Cumulative tax	14,653
Tax on ordinary income	$ 32,307
Tax on capital gain ($25,000 × 15%)	3,750
Tax	$ 36,057

The 15 percent capital gains rate reduced Ms. Croll's tax from $39,800 to $36,057 for a $3,743 tax savings

The Marriage Penalty Dilemma

Objective 6
Explain why a marriage penalty exists in the federal income tax system.

In our example in which a married couple (Mr. and Mrs. Ames) and a single individual (Ms. Croll) both had $160,000 ordinary taxable income, the couple's tax was $34,532, while the single's tax was $39,800. The rationale for this difference is straightforward: two people can't live as well as one on the same income. Mr. and Mrs. Ames presumably have less financial ability to pay than Ms. Croll and should pay less tax.

But now suppose that Mr. and Mrs. Ames are both employed and earn identical salaries. Assume that their separate returns would each reflect $80,000 taxable income (half their combined income). If they could use the rate schedule for single taxpayers, each would owe $16,907 tax, and their combined tax burden would be only $33,814. Based on a comparison of this number to their $34,532 joint tax, the couple could complain that they are paying a $718 penalty for being married.[18]

These comparisons show that the federal income tax system is not marriage neutral. However, in the Jobs and Growth Tax Relief Reconciliation Act of 2003, Congress provided some limited relief from the marriage penalty for lower-income individuals. Currently, the amount of income in the 10 percent and 15 percent brackets for married couples is exactly twice the amount of income in these brackets for single taxpayers. Furthermore, the standard deduction for married couples is exactly twice the standard deduction for single taxpayers.

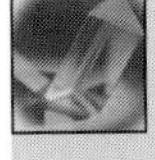

Marriage Penalty Relief

In 2005, Kelli Burns earned a $28,000 salary and her fiancé, Bob Tully, earned $17,300 wages. Here is a comparison of their combined tax burden if they marry before the end of the year or if they remain single.

	Married Filing Jointly		*Single (Kelli)*		*Single (Bob)*
AGI	$45,300		$28,000		$17,300
Standard deduction	(10,000)		(5,000)		(5,000)
Personal exemption	(6,400)		(3,200)		(3,200)
Taxable income	$28,900		$19,800		$ 9,100
Tax	$ 3,605	=	$ 2,605	+	$ 1,000

The couples' tax if they marry and file a joint return for 2005 would equal their combined tax if they do not marry and file as single taxpayers. Thus, the income tax is a neutral factor in their wedding plans.

Why can't Congress design an income tax system that is completely marriage neutral? The answer to this tax policy conundrum can be demonstrated by a simple set of facts. Assume that four people, A, B, C, and D, are taxed under a hypothetical system consisting of a 20 percent rate on income up to $30,000 and a 30 percent rate on income in excess of $30,000. The following table presents the relevant information if A, B, C, and D each file their own tax return.

[18] The couple can't avoid the marriage penalty by filing separately. Because of the married filing separately rate structure, the combined tax of the spouses equals their tax on a joint return.

Taxpayer	Taxable Income	Tax
A	$30,000	$ 6,000
B	30,000	6,000
C	10,000	2,000
D	50,000	12,000

Now assume that A marries B and C marries D. If the system requires the couples to file joint returns, the result is as follows.

Taxpayer	Taxable Income	Tax
AB	$60,000	$15,000
CD	60,000	15,000

As married couples, AB and CD have equal taxable incomes and equal tax. For couple AB, this tax is $3,000 more than their combined tax as single people. Because A and B aggregated their incomes on the joint return, $30,000 of that income was boosted out of the 20 percent bracket into the 30 percent bracket. As a result, the tax increased by $3,000. For couple CD, the tax on their joint return is $1,000 more than their combined single tax. In CD's case, the aggregation of their incomes boosted only $10,000 into the higher tax bracket.

The marriage penalties on AB and CD disappear if each spouse could file as a single taxpayer. Couple AB would file two returns, each reporting $6,000 tax, for a $12,000 combined tax burden. Couple CD would also file two returns, with C's return reporting $2,000 tax, and D's return reporting $12,000 tax. Couple CD's tax burden would be $14,000, *$2,000 more than Couple AB's tax burden.* Couple CD could certainly protest that this result is unfair because it violates the standard of horizontal equity. In our society, married couples are regarded as an economic unit, and their financial ability to pay tax should be a function of their aggregate income. Therefore, couples with the same aggregate income (such as AB and CD) should pay the same tax, regardless of which spouse earned the income. As this set of facts illustrates, a progressive income tax system that allows married couples to file joint returns can be marriage neutral or horizontally equitable—but not both.

The Elusive Marginal Tax Rate

The marginal tax rate is the percentage applying to the *next* dollar of taxable income. Obviously taxpayers must know their marginal rate to compute tax costs and after-tax cash flows from any income-generating transaction. Individuals can determine their apparent marginal rate by comparing their projected taxable income for the year to the applicable rate schedule. For instance, if a single taxpayer estimates that his 2005 income will be $160,000, he can refer to the rate schedule and observe that his statutory marginal rate is 33 percent. However, this apparent rate is not necessarily the actual marginal rate.

When an individual recognizes an additional dollar of income, AGI generally increases by one dollar. This increase changes the calculation of any deduction or credit limited by reference to AGI. In this chapter, we learned that both allowable itemized deductions and the personal exemption amount shrink as AGI climbs above a threshold level. In subsequent chapters, we will encounter more of these AGI-sensitive items. If an additional dollar of AGI triggers a decrease in one or more deductions or credits, taxable income will increase by *more* than one dollar.

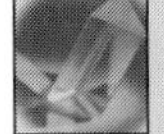

Increased AGI and Marginal Tax Rate

Ms. Grant, a single individual with an apparent 35 percent marginal rate, needs to calculate her after-tax cash flow from a transaction expected to generate $10,000 taxable cash flow. The $10,000 increase in her AGI will cause a certain itemized deduction to decrease by $700. Consequently, the $10,000 incremental income will result in $10,700 more taxable income and $3,745 more tax ($10,700 × 35 percent). Ms. Grant's actual marginal rate on the incremental income will be 37.45 percent, and her after-tax cash flow from the transaction will be $6,255 ($10,000 cash − $3,745 tax cost).

The lesson of this example is that the individual marginal tax rate can be an elusive number. The inverse relationship between AGI and certain deductions and credits can cause a hidden surtax not reflected by the apparent statutory rate. The only sure way to calculate the incremental tax from a proposed transaction is to "run the numbers" by incorporating the tax consequences of the transaction into a complete tax calculation.

Some Perspective on the Top Marginal Rate

Currently, the top statutory rate for the U.S. individual income tax is 35 percent. This rate compares favorably with the top rates in other industrialized countries. For instance, the top rate is 40 percent in the United Kingdom, 50 percent in Japan, 53 percent in Germany, and 54 percent in France. From a historical perspective, the 35 percent rate seems like a bargain compared to the top federal rate in 1951 (92 percent), 1964 (77 percent), and even 1981 (50 percent).

INDIVIDUAL TAX CREDITS

Individuals can reduce their tax by any tax credits for which they are eligible. People who conduct business as a sole proprietorship or in a passthrough entity are entitled to the general business credit discussed in Chapter 10. People who pay foreign income tax are entitled to the foreign tax credit discussed in Chapter 12. In addition to these credits, individuals may qualify for other credits, four of which are described in the following paragraphs.

Child Credit

Objective 7
Describe the child credit and dependent care credit.

Under current law, individuals can claim a $1,000 **child credit** for each dependent child under age 17 at the close of the year.[19] This credit phases out for high-income taxpayers. On a joint return, the total credit is reduced by $50 for every $1,000 increment (or portion thereof) of AGI in excess of $110,000. For single individuals and heads of households, the credit phaseout begins when AGI exceeds $75,000. For married individuals filing separate returns, the phaseout begins when AGI exceeds $55,000.

Child Credit

Mr. and Mrs. Dale reported $117,890 AGI on their Form 1040. They have four dependent children who were ages 18, 14, 12, and 10 on December 31. Mr. and Mrs. Dale's child credit is $2,600.

Adjusted gross income	$117,890
AGI threshold	(110,000)
Excess AGI	$ 7,890
Excess AGI divided by $1,000 and rounded up to nearest whole number	8

[19] §24. The child credit may be refundable for certain low-income families.

Maximum total credit ($1,000 × three children under age 17)	$ 3,000
Phaseout ($50 × 8)	(400)
Child credit	$ 2,600

Dependent Care Credit

Individuals with one or more dependents who are either under age 13 or physically or mentally incapable of caring for themselves may be eligible for a **dependent care credit.**[20] The credit is based on the cost of caring for these children or dependents. Such costs include compensation paid to caregivers who work in the home (nannies, housekeepers, and babysitters) and fees paid to child care or day care centers. The purpose of the credit is to provide tax relief to people who must incur these costs to be gainfully employed. Consequently, the annual cost on which the credit is based is limited to the taxpayer's earned income for the year. On a joint return, the limit is based on the *lesser* of the husband's or wife's earned income. The cost is further limited to $3,000 if the taxpayer has only one dependent and $6,000 if the taxpayer has two or more dependents.

The credit equals a percentage of dependent care costs (subject to the limitation described in the preceding paragraph). The percentage is determined by reference to AGI and equals 35 percent reduced by 1 point for each $2,000 (or fraction thereof) by which AGI exceeds $15,000. The percentage is reduced to a minimum of 20 percent (for all taxpayers with AGI over $43,000).

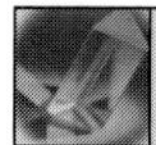

Dependent Care Credit

Mr. and Mrs. Axel spend $1,300 each year on child care for their six-year-old daughter. Their AGI is $25,400, and their dependent care credit percentage is 29 percent computed as follows.

AGI	$25,400
AGI floor	(15,000)
Excess AGI	$10,400
Reduction (excess AGI divided by $2,000)	5.2
Maximum credit percentage	35%
Reduction (rounded up to whole point)	(6)
Mr. and Mrs. Axel's percentage	29%

The Axels' dependent care credit is $377 ($1,300 cost × 29%).

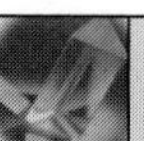

Mr. and Mrs. Volpe: Child and Dependent Care Credits

Refer back to page 2 of Mr. and Mrs. Volpe's Form 1040 (Exhibit 13.1) on page 354. Line 42 reports $70,817 taxable income and line 43 reports $11,034 tax computed on that income. During the year, Mr. and Mrs. Volpe paid $4,350 to an after-school camp program for their two young daughters. The dependent care cost was less than Mr. Volpe's $39,400 salary (the lesser of either spouse's earned income). The cost was also less than $6,000 (the limit for two dependents). Consequently, Mr. and Mrs. Volpe are entitled to an $870 dependent care credit

[20] §21.

($4,350 dependent care cost × 20 percent) reported on line 47. They are also entitled to a $2,000 child credit ($1,000 for each daughter) reported on line 51. Thus, Mr. and Mrs. Volpe's income tax is reduced to $8,164 on line 56.

Earned Income Credit

Many individuals pay no federal income tax because of the shelter provided by the standard deduction and the exemption amount. However, low-income families are not sheltered from the employee payroll tax, which is levied on the first dollar of wages or salary earned. In 1975, Congress enacted the **earned income credit** to offset the burden of the payroll tax on low-income workers and to encourage individuals to seek employment rather than to depend on welfare.

The credit is based on a percentage of the individual's earned income.[21] The percentage depends on whether the individual has no children, one child, or more than one child. For 2005, the maximum credit available to a family with two or more children is $4,400. If earned income exceeds a dollar threshold, the credit is phased out. For a married couple with two or more children, the 2005 phaseout threshold is $16,370, and the credit is reduced to zero when earned income reaches $37,263. The earned income credit differs from most other credits because it is *refundable:* Taxpayers may receive a refund of the credit that exceeds precredit income tax.

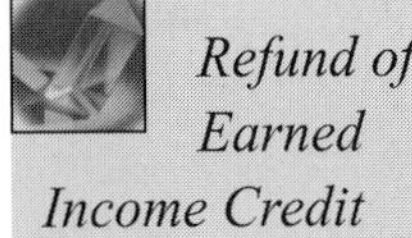

Refund of Earned Income Credit

Mr. and Mrs. Wong's precredit income tax for the year was $2,200. On the basis of the number of their children and their earned income, Mr. and Mrs. Wong claimed a $3,000 earned income credit. This credit reduced their income tax to zero and entitled them to an $800 refund from the Treasury.

The IRS estimates that 20 million families, the poorest fifth of this country's workforce, qualify for the earned income credit. The IRS computes the credit for those taxpayers who request such assistance when filing their income tax returns.

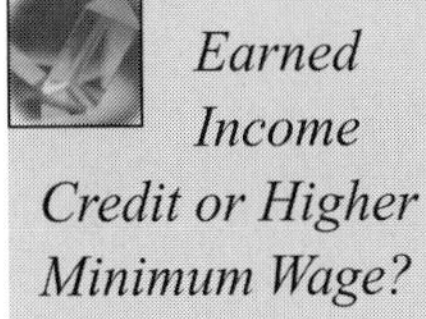

Earned Income Credit or Higher Minimum Wage?

Some economists believe that the earned income credit is a better alternative than a higher minimum wage to subsidize low-income families. An increase in the minimum wage raises the labor costs for companies that employ workers with limited skills. Thus, an increased minimum wage may reduce the number of entry-level jobs available. In contrast, the earned income credit does not adversely affect business costs and encourages people to accept entry-level jobs because they must work to receive the credit. The minimum wage does not always help impoverished families because workers who earn the minimum (such as teenagers) may belong to households with income well above the poverty line. The earned income credit, however, is a function of family, rather than individual, income.[22]

Excess Payroll Tax Withholding

The federal employee payroll tax equals 6.2 percent of an annual base amount of compensation plus 1.45 percent of total compensation. Employers are required to withhold this tax from their employees' paychecks and remit the withholding to the Treasury. When an

[21] §32.

[22] Gary Becker, "How to End Welfare As We Know It—Fast," *Business Week,* June 3, 1996.

employee changes jobs, the new employer must withhold payroll tax without regard to any tax withheld by any former employer. As a result, the employee may indirectly overpay his or her payroll tax for the year.

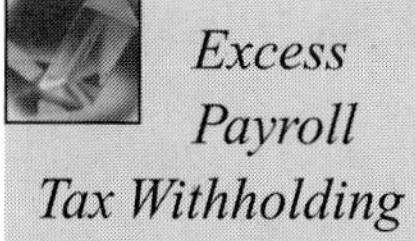

Excess Payroll Tax Withholding

Mrs. Vaughn worked for FM Inc. during the first nine months of 2004, then resigned to take a new position with CN Company. Her salary from FM was $98,000 from which FM withheld $6,871 employee payroll tax (6.2 percent of $87,900 base + 1.45 percent of $98,000). Her salary from CN was $42,000 from which CN withheld $3,213 (7.65 percent of $42,000). In computing this withholding, CN ignored the fact that FM had already withheld 6.2 percent on the annual base. Consequently, CN withheld $2,604 excess payroll tax from Mrs. Vaughn's salary.

Mrs. Vaughn's 2004 payroll tax:	
$87,900 × 6.2%	$ 5,450
$140,000 total salary × 1.45%	2,030
	$ 7,480
Payroll tax withheld:	
FM Inc.	$ 6,871
CN Company	3,213
	$10,084
Excess withholding ($10,084 − $7,480)	$ 2,604

Mrs. Vaughn claimed this **excess payroll tax withholding** as a credit against her 2004 income tax.[23] Her tax credit has no effect on the two firms that employed her during the year. Neither FM nor CN is entitled to any refund of the employer payroll tax on Mrs. Vaughn's compensation.

ALTERNATIVE MINIMUM TAX

Individuals are subject to the alternative minimum tax (AMT) system and may owe AMT in addition to their regular income tax.[24] The individual AMT is based on alternative minimum taxable income (AMTI), which is computed under the formula introduced in Chapter 10.

Taxable income for regular tax purposes
+ or − AMT adjustments
+ AMT tax preferences
Alternative minimum taxable income

Objective 8
Recognize the circumstances that may trigger the individual AMT.

Many AMT adjustment and preference items are common to both corporate and individual taxpayers. However, several items are unique to individuals. For instance, the standard deduction and personal exemption amount are AMT adjustments that must be added

[23] §31. The excess payroll tax withholding credit is refundable.
[24] §55.

back to taxable income in the AMTI computation.[25] The overall limitation on itemized deductions does not apply in the AMT world. Consequently, any reduction of itemized deductions because of this limitation is a negative AMT adjustment.[26] We will identify other individual AMT items in subsequent chapters.

Individuals can reduce their AMTI by an exemption based on filing status. However, the exemption is reduced by 25 percent of AMTI in excess of a threshold. The exemption, the AMTI threshold, and the AMTI at which the exemption is reduced to zero (AMTI maximum) are presented in the following table:

	Exemption	AMTI Threshold	AMTI Maximum
Married filing jointly and surviving spouses	$58,000	$150,000	$382,000
Married filing separately	29,000	75,000	191,000
Head of household or single	40,250	112,500	273,500

AMTI Exemption

Ms. Epps, a head of household, has $91,000 AMTI. Because her AMTI is below the threshold, her exemption is $40,250.

Mr. and Mrs. Floyd, who file a joint return, have $400,000 AMTI. Because their AMTI is greater than the AMTI maximum, their exemption is reduced to zero.

Mr. and Mrs. Gile, who file a joint return, have $215,000 AMTI, which falls in the phase-out range. Consequently, their exemption is $41,750, computed as follows:

AMTI	$ 215,000
AMTI threshold	(150,000)
AMTI in excess of threshold	$65,000
	.25
Reduction in exemption	$ 16,250
Exemption for married filing jointly	$ 58,000
Reduction	(16,250)
Exemption for Mr. and Mrs. Gile	$ 41,750

Individual tentative minimum tax is based on a rate structure consisting of two brackets:

- 26 percent on the first $175,000 AMTI in excess of the exemption ($87,500 for married filing separately).
- 28 percent of any additional excess AMTI.

If an individual's taxable income includes dividend income and capital gain taxed at a preferential rate (generally 15 percent), the same preferential rate applies in computing the tentative minimum tax on the dividend income/capital gain component of AMTI.[27]

[25] §56(b)(1)(E).

[26] §56(b)(1)(F).

[27] §55(b)(3).

Tentative AMT

Refer to the three taxpayers in the preceding example. Assuming their AMTI does not include any dividend income or capital gain, their tentative minimum tax is calculated as follows:

	Ms. Epps	*Mr. and Mrs. Floyd*	*Mr. and Mrs. Gile*
AMTI	$ 91,000	$400,000	$215,000
Exemption	(40,250)	–0–	(41,750)
AMTI in excess of exemption	$ 50,750	$400,000	$173,250
26% of first $175,000 excess AMTI	$ 13,195	$ 45,500	$ 45,045
28% of additional excess AMTI	–0–	63,000	–0–
Tentative minimum tax	$ 13,195	$ 108,500	$ 45,045

The individual AMT equals any excess of tentative minimum tax over the individual's regular income tax. Refer back to the preceding example in which Mr. and Mrs. Floyd have $108,500 tentative minimum tax. If their regular tax for the year is $97,200, the Floyds must pay $11,300 AMT *in addition to* the regular tax, bringing their total tax bill to $108,500. If their regular income tax is $110,075, the Floyds do not owe AMT, and their total tax bill is $110,075.

Individuals who pay AMT for a taxable year can carry some or all of the payment forward to be used as a credit against regular tax.[28] The amount of this *minimum tax credit* used in any future year is limited to the excess of regular tax over tentative minimum tax for that year.

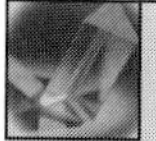

Minimum Tax Credit

To complete the example involving Mr. and Mrs. Floyd, assume that the couple does pay $11,300 AMT in 2005, all of which is carried forward as a minimum tax credit. In 2006, the Floyds' regular tax is $105,900, and their tentative minimum tax is only $100,400. In this case, the Floyds can use a $5,500 minimum tax credit to reduce their regular tax to $100,400. They have a remaining $5,800 minimum tax credit carryforward into 2007.

The AMT Trap

The original purpose of the individual AMT was to guarantee that high-income taxpayers who dramatically reduced their regular tax by overindulging in tax preferences would still pay a fair share of income tax. But in recent years, more and more middle-income taxpayers with modest amounts of AMT adjustments or preferences are finding themselves paying AMT. This trend is attributable to the fact that the regular income tax rates are adjusted annually for inflation but the AMT rates are not. As the regular rates on a given amount of income decrease and the AMT rates remain the same, the probability that the regular tax on that income will fall below the tentative minimum tax increases. In fact, this narrowing of the spread between the regular and AMT rates can trigger an AMT even for an individual with no AMT adjustments or preferences for the year.

[28] See §53 for the calculation of the precise amount of the minimum tax credit.

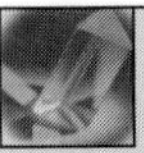

Blindsided by the AMT

In 2005, Mr. and Mrs. Booth's $385,000 taxable income consisted of $285,000 ordinary income and $100,000 dividends and capital gain. The couple had no AMT adjustments or preferences, so their AMTI also was $385,000, and their AMTI exemption was zero. To their complete surprise, the Booths owed a $1,658 AMT in 2005.

Tentative minimum tax:	
26% × $175,000 ordinary AMTI	$45,500
28% × $110,000 ($285,000 ordinary AMTI – $175,000)	30,800
15% × $100,000 dividends and capital gain	15,000
	$91,300
Regular tax:	
Regular tax (MFJ) on $285,000 ordinary income	$74,642
15% × $100,000 dividends and capital gain	15,000
Regular tax on taxable income	$89,642
AMT ($91,300 – $89,642)	$ 1,658

The AMT, which was designed to apply to a handful of wealthy people, is fast becoming a broad-based tax. Unless Congress makes major changes, the AMT will affect 33 million individuals by 2010: a number representing 37 percent of households with income between $50,000 and $75,000 and 73 percent of households with income between $75,000 and $100,000.[29]

PAYMENT AND FILING REQUIREMENTS

Objective 9
Describe the individual tax payment and return filing requirements.

Individuals are required to pay their income and self-employment tax to the federal government periodically over the course of the year. The income tax on compensation is paid automatically; employers are required to withhold income tax from each wage or salary payment and remit this withholding to the Treasury on their employees' behalf.[30] The tax on other income items, such as net profit from a sole proprietorship, distributive shares of partnership income, or investment income must be paid in four equal installments.[31] The first three of these installments are due on April 15, June 15, and September 15 of the current year, while the fourth installment is due on January 15 of the following year.

Individuals who fail to make timely payments of at least 90 percent of their current tax in the form of withholding and quarterly installments may incur an underpayment penalty.[32] Because of the uncertainty inherent in estimating the tax owed for the year in progress, the law provides a **safe-harbor estimate.** Individuals with AGI of $150,000 or less in the preceding year may pay current estimated tax equal to 100 percent of the preceding year's tax.[33] By doing so, they avoid any underpayment penalty, regardless of their actual current

[29] "Key Points on the Alternative Minimum Tax," *Urban-Brookings Tax Policy Center,* January 21, 2004.

[30] §3402. The withholding is based on the information concerning marital and family status provided by the employee to the employer on Form W-4. Employees can also specify a dollar amount of income tax to be withheld during the year.

[31] §6654(c).

[32] §6654(a) and (d)(1)(B)(i).

[33] §6654(d)(1)(B)(ii).

tax. The safe-harbor estimate for individuals with AGI *in excess* of $150,000 is 110 percent of the preceding year's tax.[34]

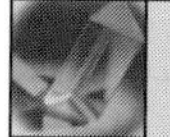

Safe-Harbor Estimate

Mrs. Ruiz works for a local corporation and knows that her income tax withholding for this year will be $14,000. Mr. Ruiz recently started a new business venture and doesn't know how much income it might generate. The couple knows that in the previous year their AGI was $92,000, and they paid $25,116 income and self-employment tax. Therefore, they can make a safe-harbor estimate for this year by paying in $25,116. If they make four installment payments of $2,779 each, their total installments plus Mrs. Ruiz's withholding will equal $25,116, and they are immune to penalty regardless of their actual tax for the year.

Form 1040 must be filed by the 15th day of the 4th month following the close of the taxable year; for calendar year taxpayers, this is the familiar April 15 due date.[35] If the tax paid throughout the year (withholding and quarterly installments) is *less* than the tax computed on the return, the taxpayer must pay the balance due with the return. If the prepayment is *more* than the tax, the return serves as a claim for refund of the overpayment.

Paying Taxes with Plastic

The IRS has arranged with private credit card companies to allow individuals to charge their federal tax. Individuals can now use American Express, Discover, or MasterCard to pay any balance of tax due for the year as well as to make their quarterly installment payments of estimated tax. While the IRS does not impose a fee for credit card payments, the credit card companies may impose convenience fees based on the tax amounts charged.

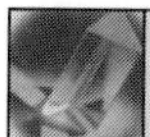

Undeliverable Refunds

The IRS is searching for 87,485 individuals whose 2003 refund checks were returned to the IRS by the U.S. Post Office because of an incorrect mailing address. These checks represent a total of about $73 million owed to people who should have left a forwarding address!

Individuals who are not ready to file a completed return by the due date may request an automatic extension of the filing deadline for four months (August 15 for a calendar year taxpayer).[36] This extension applies only to the return filing requirement; individuals who estimate that they still owe tax should pay the estimated balance due with the extension request to avoid interest and penalties.[37] If the four-month extension isn't enough extra time, individuals may request a second extension for two more months (until October 15). This second extension is not automatic, and the IRS grants approval only if unusual circumstances justify further delay.[38]

Mr. and Mrs. Volpe: Tax Refund

Refer back to page 2 of Mr. and Mrs. Volpe's Form 1040 (Exhibit 13.1) on page 354. Mrs. Volpe's $8,016 self-employment tax is reported on line 57. The couple's $16,180 total tax (income and self-employment) is reported on line 62. During the year, Mr. Volpe's employer withheld $2,863 income tax from Mr. Volpe's salary (line 63), and the couple made installment payments of estimated tax totaling $15,000 (line 64). Because the total payments

[34] §6654(d)(1)(C).

[35] §6072(a).

[36] See Form 4868 (Application for Automatic Extension of Time to File U.S. Individual Income Tax Return).

[37] Reg. §1.6081-4T.

[38] See Form 2688 (Application for Additional Extension of Time to File U.S. Individual Income Tax Return).

($17,863 on line 70) exceeded total tax by $1,683, the Treasury owed the Volpes a refund. The entry on line 73 shows that they decided to apply their refund to their 2005 estimated tax rather than to receive a cash refund.

Conclusion

Chapter 13 provides the "big picture" with respect to individual taxpayers. In this chapter, we developed the basic formula for the computation of taxable income and discussed the significance of AGI in this formula. We learned how to compute the regular tax on individual income, identified the most common individual tax credits, and considered the threat of the alternative minimum tax. The chapter closed with a synopsis of the payment and filing requirements for individual taxpayers.

In the next three chapters, we will explore the incredible variety of transactions that affect the computation of individual taxable income. Our discussions of the tax consequences of many specific transactions will reinforce your understanding of the individual tax formula and will lead to new tax planning ideas. Hopefully, the material in these chapters will also give you a real appreciation of the complexities and nuances that make the study of individual taxation so challenging and yet so fascinating.

Key Terms

above-the-line deduction *352*
adjusted gross income (AGI) *352*
bunching *356*
child credit *364*
dependent *358*
dependent care credit *365*
earned income credit *366*
excess payroll tax withholding *367*
filing status *350*
head of household *351*
itemized deduction *355*
joint and several liability *350*
joint return *350*
personal exemption *358*
safe-harbor estimate *370*
separate returns *351*
single taxpayer *351*
standard deduction *353*
surviving spouse *350*
total income *352*

Questions and Problems for Discussion

1. Discuss the extent to which adjusted gross income (AGI) is actually a net income number.
2. Describe the effect of an increase in AGI on:
   a. Total itemized deductions.
   b. Standard deduction.
   c. Personal exemption amount.
   d. Alternative minimum taxable income (AMTI).
   e. Dependent care credit.
3. Discuss possible tax policy reasons why individuals who are age 65 or older receive an additional standard deduction.
4. Individuals who are legally blind receive an additional standard deduction, while individuals with other disabilities, such as deafness or paralysis, are not entitled to an additional deduction. Is there a tax policy justification for the different treatment?
5. The overall limitation on itemized deductions and the personal exemption phaseout increase the tax burden on high-income individuals. Why does the tax law contain these two complicated provisions instead of a higher marginal tax rate for such individuals?

6. Identify the reasons why individual taxpayers benefit more from above-the-line deductions than from itemized deductions.
7. While checking the computations on his Form 1040, Mr. G realized he had misclassified a $2,700 expense as a business deduction on Schedule C. It should have been an itemized deduction on Schedule A. Mr. G did not correct the error because he assumed the correction would not affect taxable income. Is this assumption correct?
8. Individuals who plan to bunch itemized deductions into one year can either postpone the payment of expenses from an earlier year or accelerate the payment of expenses from a later year. Which technique is preferable from a cash flow standpoint?
9. Is AGI or taxable income a better gauge of an individual's disposable income for the year?
10. Under the current rate structure, a single person could pay more tax than a married couple on the same income. What economic circumstances might a single person cite to argue that his ability to pay tax is not necessarily greater than a married couple's ability to pay tax on the same income?
11. Single individuals S and Z were married this year and filed their first joint return. To what extent did this change in filing status affect the following?
    a. S and Z's aggregate standard deduction.
    b. S and Z's aggregate personal exemption amount.
    c. S and Z's aggregate child credit.
    d. S and Z's aggregate AMTI exemption.
12. Explain why an individual's combined standard deduction and personal exemption amount can be considered a bracket of income taxed at a zero rate.
13. Why is the formula for computing individual taxable income so much more complicated than the formula for computing corporate taxable income?
14. The tax law provides for both refundable and nonrefundable credits. What is the difference between the two types of credit?
15. Congress enacted the earned income credit to relieve the burden of the payroll tax on low-income workers. Why did Congress not accomplish this goal by providing a payroll tax exemption for a base amount of annual compensation paid by an employer to an employee?
16. When he accepted his job, Mr. MG instructed his employer to withhold substantially more federal income tax from his monthly paycheck than was indicated by his marital and family situation. As a result, he routinely overpays his tax and receives a refund each spring, which he invests in a mutual fund. Mr. MG views this strategy as an efficient means of enforced savings. Do you agree?
17. Ms. JR has been very ill since the beginning of the year and unable to attend to any financial matters. Her CPA advised that she request an automatic extension of time to file her prior year Form 1040. Ms. JR likes this idea because she believes the balance of tax due with the return will be at least $20,000, and she wants to avoid paying this tax for as long as possible. By requesting the extension, how long can Ms. JR delay paying the $20,000 to the Treasury?

Application Problems

For the following problems, assume the taxable year is 2005.

1. Determine Mr. J's filing status in each of the following cases.
    a. Mr. J and Mrs. J were legally divorced on November 18. Mr. J has not remarried and has no dependent children.

b. Mr. J and the first Mrs. J were legally divorced on April 2. Mr. J remarried the second Mrs. J on December 15. He has no dependent children.
c. Mrs. J died on July 23. Mr. J has not remarried and has no dependent children.
d. Mrs. J died on October 1, 2003. Mr. J has not remarried and maintains a home for one dependent child.
e. Mrs. J died on May 30, 2004. Mr. J has not remarried and has no dependent children.
f. Mr. J and Mrs. J were legally divorced on May 30, 2002. Mr. J has not remarried and maintains a home for his two dependent children.

2. Mr. and Mrs. K file a joint income tax return. Compute their standard deduction assuming that:
   a. Mr. K is age 68, and Mrs. K is age 60.
   b. Mr. K is age 70, and Mrs. K is age 68.
   c. Mr. K is age 70, and Mrs. K is age 68. Mrs. K is legally blind.
3. Mr. and Mrs. O file a joint income tax return. Determine if they can claim a personal exemption for any of the following individuals.
   a. Their son is age 22, unmarried, and a full-time graduate student at Indiana University. Mr. and Mrs. O provided 75 percent of his financial support for the year. During the year, the son earned $5,200 as a teaching assistant.
   b. Their daughter is age 26, unmarried, and unemployed. Mr. and Mrs. O provided 100 percent of her financial support for the year.
   c. Their daughter is age 26 and unemployed. Mr. and Mrs. O provided 75 percent of her financial support for the year. The daughter married in December and filed a joint return with her new spouse.
   d. Their nephew is age 18, unmarried, and a full-time high school student. Mr. and Mrs. O provided 60 percent of his financial support for the year. During the year, the nephew earned $3,650 from a part-time job.
4. Ms. G earned a $140,000 salary, and Mr. H earned a $70,000 salary. Neither individual had any other income and neither can itemize deductions.
   a. Compute Ms. G and Mr. H's combined tax if they file as single individuals.
   b. Compute Ms. G and Mr. H's tax if they are married and file a joint return.
5. Mr. P earned an $89,000 salary, and Mrs. P earned a $38,000 salary. The couple had no other income and cannot itemize deductions.
   a. Compute their combined tax if they file separate returns.
   b. Compute their tax if they file a joint return.
6. Mr. and Mrs. A had the following income items.

Mr. A's salary	$36,000
Mrs. A's Schedule C net profit	41,800
Interest income	1,300

Mrs. A's self-employment tax was $5,906. The couple had $4,150 itemized deductions and no children or other dependents. Compute their income tax on a joint return.

7. Mr. and Mrs. B had the following income items.

Mr. B's salary	$112,000
Mrs. B's salary	82,800
Ordinary partnership income	63,500

The couple had $19,700 itemized deductions (none of which were medical expense, investment interest expense, casualty, theft, or gambling loss). They have two dependent children over age 17. Using the worksheets in Appendixes 13–A and 13–B, compute their income tax on a joint return.

8. Mr. C, an unmarried individual, had the following income items.

Interest income	$ 14,200
Ordinary loss from an S corporation	(5,500)
Ordinary partnership income	179,000

He had $13,600 itemized deductions (none of which were medical expense, investment interest expense, casualty, theft, or gambling loss) and no dependents. Using the worksheets in Appendixes 13–A and 13–B, compute his income tax.

9. Mr. and Mrs. D had the following income items.

Dividend income eligible for 5% preferential rate	$ 3,400
Capital gain eligible for 5% preferential rate	2,900
Mrs. D's salary	28,000

Mr. D is age 66, and Mrs. D is age 58. Their itemized deductions totaled $5,200, and they have no dependents. Compute their income tax on a joint return.

10. Mr. RG, an unmarried individual, had the following income items.

Salary	$270,000
Interest income	19,700
Dividend income	31,000

He had $34,000 itemized deductions (none of which were medical expense or casualty, theft, or gambling loss). He has four dependent children (ages 5 through 15) and two dependent parents who live in his home. Using the worksheets in Appendixes 13–A and 13–B, compute his income tax.

11. Ms. E, a single individual, had $115,000 taxable income. Compute her income tax assuming that:

a. Taxable income includes no capital gain.
b. Taxable income includes $22,000 capital gain eligible for the 15 percent preferential rate.

12. On March 4, Mr. and Mrs. SP celebrated the birth of their third child. Compute the effect of this event on their taxable income, assuming that AGI on their joint return was:
 a. $72,000.
 b. $275,000.
 c. $450,000.
13. Mr. M's salary was $95,000, and Mrs. M's salary was $114,000. They had no other income items, no deductions, and no dependents.
 a. Compute their tax on a joint return.
 b. Compute their combined tax if they file separate returns.
 c. Compute their marriage penalty (excess of tax on a joint return over combined tax on two returns filed as single taxpayers).
14. Ms. NM, a single taxpayer, projects that she will incur $5,100 of expenses qualifying as itemized deductions in both 2005 and 2006. Assuming that her standard deduction is $5,000 in both years, compute the effect on taxable income for each year if she can shift $2,000 of expenses from 2005 to 2006.
15. Mrs. A is an unmarried taxpayer with one dependent child living in her home. Her AGI is $40,000, and she does not itemize deductions. The 18-year-old child earned $5,485 from a part-time job and incurred no deductible expenses.
 a. Compute Mrs. A's income tax.
 b. Compute her child's income tax.
16. Mr. LK had the following income items.

Salary	$35,000
Net income from a rental house	3,000

 He has custody of his four-year-old son, who attends a day care center while Mr. LK is at work. Mr. LK paid $2,100 to this center and has no itemized deductions. Compute his income tax.
17. Mr. and Mrs. OP have two dependent children. They paid $7,200 wages to a housekeeper to care for the children and $549 employer payroll tax on her wages. Mr. and Mrs. OP file a joint return. In each of the following cases, compute their dependent care credit.
 a. One child is age 10, and the other is age 15. Mr. OP's earned income is $75,000, and Mrs. OP has no earned income. Their AGI is $81,300.
 b. One child is age 2, and the other is age 6. Mr. OP's earned income is $45,000, and Mrs. OP's earned income is $28,000. Their AGI is $81,300.
18. Mr. and Mrs. Coulter have four dependent children, ages 1, 4, 7, and 11. Mr. Coulter's salary was $21,400, Mrs. Coulter's wages totaled $16,200, and the couple had no other income or any adjustments to their AGI this year. The Coulters paid $3,600 for day care and after-school child care.
 a. Compute the Coulters' child credit.
 b. Compute the Coulters' dependent care credit.
 c. Recompute the Coulters' child and dependent care credits if Mr. Coulter's salary was $100,000, Mrs. Coulter's wages totaled $32,000, and the couple earned $5,700 taxable interest income.

19. On March 31, Mr. R quit his job with MT Inc. and began a new job with PK Company. His salary from MT was $53,900, and his salary from PK was $70,000. Compute his excess payroll tax withholding credit.
20. Mr. and Mrs. K's AGI was $14,000. Their federal income tax withholding was $850. They had no itemized deductions and two dependent children, ages 17 and 18. If they are entitled to a $3,400 earned income credit, compute their tax refund.
21. In each of the following cases, compute AMT (if any). For all cases, assume that taxable income does not include any dividend income or capital gain.
    a. Mr. and Mrs. BH's taxable income on their joint return was $200,000, and their AMTI before exemption was $203,000.
    b. Mr. CK's taxable income on his single return was $76,000, and his AMTI before exemption was $98,000.
    c. Ms. W's taxable income on her head of household return was $181,000, and her AMTI before exemption was $200,000.
22. Jaclyn Biggs, who files as a head of household, never paid an AMT before 2005. In 2005, her $192,900 taxable income included $173,000 ordinary income and a $19,900 capital gain taxed at 15 percent. Her AMTI was $229,800.
    a. Compute Jaclyn's total income tax for 2005.
    b. In 2006, Jaclyn's $213,300 taxable income is all ordinary, and her AMTI is $216,500. *Using the 2005 tax rates,* compute Jaclyn's total income tax for 2006.
23. In January, Ms. NW projects that her employer will withhold $25,000 from her 2006 salary. However, she has income from several other sources and must make quarterly installments of tax. Compute the quarterly installments that result in a 2006 safe-harbor estimate assuming that:
    a. Her 2005 AGI was $176,000, and her tax was $47,200.
    b. Her 2005 AGI was $139,000, and her tax was $36,800.

Issue Recognition Problems

Identify the tax issue or issues suggested by the following situations and state each issue in the form of a question.

1. Mr. LR died on April 16. Mr. and Mrs. LR had been married for 29 years and had always filed a joint return. Mrs. LR remarried on December 21.
2. Mr. and Mrs. JC were married in 1985. This year they traveled to Reno, Nevada, immediately after Christmas and obtained a divorce on December 29. They spent two weeks vacationing in California, returned to their home in Texas on January 13, and remarried the next day.
3. Mr. GS, an unmarried individual, provides the entire financial support for his invalid mother. Until this year, she lived with Mr. GS. However, in March, he moved his mother to a nursing home so that she could receive full-time care.
4. Mr. T is a 20-year-old college student. This year he lived on campus for nine months and in his parents' home during the summer. His parents paid for all Mr. T's living expenses, but a scholarship paid for his $22,000 college tuition.
5. Mr. and Mrs. TB have an 11-year old child. The couple is divorced, and Mrs. TB has sole custody of the child. However, Mr. TB pays his former wife $1,200 child support each month.
6. Mr. G, age 90, lives in a nursing home. He has no gross income and is financially dependent on his four adult children, each of whom pays 25 percent of the cost of the home.

7. Mr. and Mrs. WQ both have full-time jobs. They employ Mrs. WQ's 18-year-old sister as an after-school babysitter for their 10-year-old son.
8. Mr. TJ, a self-employed attorney, has sole custody of his nine-year-old daughter. This year she spent eight weeks during the summer at a recreational camp. The total cost was $3,800.
9. During the first eight months of the year, Ms. V was self-employed and earned $40,000 net income. In September, she accepted a job with MW Company and earned $51,000 salary through the end of the year.
10. Mr. and Mrs. P own a sole proprietorship that generates approximately $60,000 annual net profit. This business is the couple's only source of income. In April, June, and September, they paid their quarterly installments of current year tax. In December, they won $250,000 in a state lottery.
11. In November, Mr. K discovered that his combined income tax withholding and quarterly installment payments would be less than his prior year tax and, therefore, would not be a safe-harbor estimate. He immediately requested that his employer withhold enough tax from his December paycheck to result in a safe-harbor estimate.
12. Mr. P's AGI includes an $8,700 dividend paid by a German corporation and $11,600 interest paid by a Canadian bank. He paid $3,000 foreign income tax this year.
13. Mr. and Mrs. CD engage a CPA to prepare their Form 1040. For the last two years, their itemized deductions totaled $10,230 and $10,664. The CPA estimates that $750 of his fee relates to the preparation of the Schedule A on which the itemized deductions are detailed.

Research Problems

1. Bob and Jane Kelso file a joint tax return. The couple's AGI averages $500,000. Consequently, their total exemption amount is completely phased out (reduced to zero), and they derive no tax benefit from their personal exemptions. The Kelsos provide about 90 percent of the financial support for their 20-year-old daughter, Brenda, who is a junior at San Diego State University. This year, their daughter had no earned income but received $6,491 interest and dividend income from an investment portfolio inherited from a grandparent. The Kelsos understand that Brenda qualifies as their dependent. But if they do not *claim* her as a dependent on their Form 1040, can Brenda claim a full standard deduction and a personal exemption on her own Form 1040 (thereby reducing her taxable income to zero)?
2. Bert Baker and Ernestine Moffet were never formally married but have lived together as husband and wife for the last 14 years. Bert and Ernestine reside in Washington, D.C., a jurisdiction that recognizes common law marriages as valid. Consequently, they filed both a joint district income tax return and a joint federal income tax return for the last eight years. Bert and Ernestine are planning to move their household to Frederick, Maryland, and become permanent residents of that state. Maryland does not recognize common law marriages. Will Bert and Ernestine's change in residence allow them to avoid the marriage penalty by filing as single individuals?
3. Tim Loker is the five-year-old godson of Mr. and Mrs. Bryant. Tim's parents died in an accident on December 18 of last year. Tim was seriously injured in the accident and remained hospitalized until July 12 of this year. After his discharge from the hospital, Tim moved into the Bryants' home. The Bryants have provided 100 percent of Tim's financial support since the accident and intend to raise him as their own child. Can the Bryants claim Tim as a dependent on this year's tax return?
4. Bill Young, a single taxpayer, reported the following information on his 2005 Form 1040.

Salary from part-time job	$16,600
Interest on savings account	400
Net loss from sole proprietorship	(22,100)
Alimony received	3,600
AGI	$ (1,500)
Standard deduction	(5,000)
Personal exemption	(3,200)
Taxable income	$ (9,700)

Does Bill have a net operating loss (NOL) that he can carry back or forward as a deduction in another taxable year?

Tax Planning Cases

1. Mr. and Mrs. WG's AGI averages $425,000, and they are in the 35 percent tax bracket. They support their 22-year-old son who is a full-time college student. Mr. and Mrs. WG are considering giving him a bond portfolio of marketable securities that generates $20,000 annual interest income. He could support himself with this income stream (he would be financially independent) and would file his own tax return. Compute the annual tax savings to the family resulting from this plan.
2. Mr. and Mrs. TP estimate that their AGI will be $260,000 and their itemized deductions will be $40,000. The couple has the opportunity to invest in a new business that should generate $20,000 additional ordinary income this year. Before they can make a decision concerning the investment, they must know the income tax cost with respect to the additional income. Compute the tax cost assuming that the couple files a joint return, has three dependent children, and has no AMT adjustments or preferences for the year.
3. Assume that the tax law allows individuals to claim an itemized deduction for the cost of music lessons for the taxpayer or any member of his family. Instead of this deduction, individuals may claim the first $1,000 of the cost as a nonrefundable tax credit (no carryforward or carryback of any excess credit). In each of the following situations, advise the taxpayer as to whether she should take the deduction or credit. In each situation the taxpayer is single.
   a. Ms. M has $95,000 AGI. Before consideration of the $5,000 cost of her music lessons, she has no itemized deductions.
   b. Ms. N has $27,000 AGI. Before consideration of the $5,000 cost of her music lessons, she has $5,100 itemized deductions.
   c. Ms. O has $95,000 AGI. Before consideration of the $5,000 cost of her music lessons, she has $7,200 itemized deductions.

THE COMPENSATION TRANSACTION

The payment of compensation is a transaction with tax consequences to two parties: the employer making the payment and the employee receiving the payment. The nature and amount of the compensation are determined by contractual agreement between these parties. The employer's objective in negotiating the contract is to minimize the after-tax cost of the compensation paid; the employee's objective is to maximize the after-tax value of the compensation received. High-ranking employees can usually negotiate with their employers on a personal basis. Because they are transacting in a private market, employer and employee can work together to achieve their objectives. Specifically, they can compare different compensation arrangements and evaluate the tax consequences to both parties. By doing so, employer and employee can design a package offering the greatest overall tax savings divided between them on a mutually satisfactory basis. In contrast, rank-and-file employees typically transact with their employers in an impersonal, public market. These employees can only accept or reject the compensation arrangement offered by the employer. In such case, both employee and employer must pursue their tax planning objectives independently.

EMPLOYEE OR INDEPENDENT CONTRACTOR?

Objective 1
Distinguish between employees and independent contractors.

The employer/employee relationship is characterized by the employer's right to direct and control how, when, and where the employee's duties are performed.[3] The relationship is continual because an **employee** works according to a regular schedule in return for periodic payments from the employer. The relationship is also exclusive because an employee provides services for one employer rather than the general public.

As an alternative to hiring an employee, a firm can engage an independent contractor to do the job. An **independent contractor** is a self-employed individual who performs services for monetary consideration and who controls the way the services are performed. The independent contractor's clients don't oversee his work but can only accept or reject the final product. The relationship between client and independent contractor is impermanent, and the contractor can have any number of clients at the same time.

Tax Consequences of Worker Classification

The distinction between employee and independent contractor is critical for tax purposes. As you learned in Chapter 9, employers must pay federal and state payroll taxes on the compensation paid to their employees. In addition, employers are required to withhold both employee payroll tax and federal, state, and local income tax from their employees' wages and salaries. At the end of the calendar year, employers must issue a Form W-2 (Wage and Tax Statement) to each employee.[4] This form provides detailed information about the various taxes withheld by the employer on the employee's behalf.

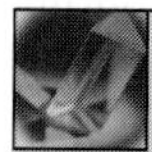

Form W-2

Robin Simms is employed by Crockett Products. During 2004, Robin earned a $111,000 salary. Her monthly "net" paycheck was $6,404, which equaled her $9,250 "gross" salary less federal income tax, federal Social Security and Medicare tax, and state income tax withheld by Crockett Products. Robin's Form W-2 is shown as Exhibit 14.1.

[3] Reg. §31.3401(c)-1(b).

[4] §6051(a). Employers must issue Form W-2s by January 31. If an employee who terminates employment during the year submits a written request for a Form W-2, the employer must issue the form within 30 days of receipt of the request.

EXHIBIT 14.1

a Control number	22222	Void ☐	For Official Use Only ▶ OMB No. 1545-0008

Field	Entry
b Employer identification number	87-4007325
c Employer's name, address, and ZIP code	Crockett Products P.O. Box 92252 Wilmington, DE 12899
d Employee's social security number	496-45-3150
e Employee's first name and initial / Last name	Robin L. Simms
f Employee's address and ZIP code	108 Brunswick Clayton, DE 12890
1 Wages, tips, other compensation	111,000
2 Federal income tax withheld	20,496
3 Social security wages	87,900
4 Social security tax withheld	5,450
5 Medicare wages and tips	111,000
6 Medicare tax withheld	1,610
7 Social security tips	
8 Allocated tips	
9 Advance EIC payment	
10 Dependent care benefits	
11 Nonqualified plans	
12a See instructions for box 12	
13 Statutory employee / Retirement plan / Third-party sick pay	☐ ☐ ☐
14 Other	
12b	
12c	
12d	

15 State	Employer's state ID number	16 State wages, tips, etc.	17 State income tax	18 Local wages, tips, etc.	19 Local income tax	20 Locality name
DE	400648	111,000	6,596			

Form **W-2** **Wage and Tax Statement** **2004**

Department of the Treasury—Internal Revenue Service

For Privacy Act and Paperwork Reduction Act Notice, see back of Copy D.

Copy A For Social Security Administration — Send this entire page with Form W-3 to the Social Security Administration; photocopies are **not** acceptable.

Cat. No. 10134D

When clients engage independent contractors, the fees paid are not subject to FICA payroll taxes, and clients are not required to withhold income tax. At the end of the year, clients must issue a Form 1099-MISC (Miscellaneous Income) to each independent contractor stating the annual compensation paid. Independent contractors who are sole proprietors (rather than in partnership with other individuals) report this compensation as business income on Schedule C, Form 1040. Independent contractors pay self-employment tax on the net profit from their business and make quarterly installments of both self-employment and federal income tax.

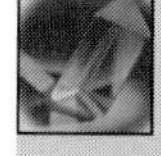

Form 1099-MISC

Sam Lincoln is an independent contractor who performs occasional professional services for Crockett Products. During 2004, Sam earned total fees of $34,700 from Crockett. His Form 1099-MISC on which these fees are reported is shown as Exhibit 14.2.

Business versus the IRS: Worker Classification Controversy

The classification of a worker as either employee or independent contractor depends on the facts and circumstances of each case.[5] The classification is usually straightforward. But occasionally, the nature of the working relationship does not clearly indicate whether the worker is an employee or an independent contractor.

The Firm's Viewpoint

When a firm hires a worker whose classification is ambiguous, it has a financial incentive to treat the worker as an independent contractor. By doing so, the firm avoids both the employer payroll tax and the administrative cost of the various withholding requirements. Moreover, it doesn't have to provide independent contractors with the fringe benefits available to its permanent workforce. The payroll cost for an employee includes both base

[5] In Rev. Rul. 87-41, 1987-1 CB 296, the IRS lists 20 factors for determining whether an individual is an employee or an independent contractor.

EXHIBIT 14.2

9595 ☐ VOID ☐ CORRECTED

PAYER'S name, street address, city, state, ZIP code, and telephone no.		1 Rents	OMB No. 1545-0115	**Miscellaneous Income**
CROCKETT PRODUCTS P. O. BOX 92252 WILMINGTON DE 12899		$ 2 Royalties $	**2004** Form **1099-MISC**	
		3 Other income $	4 Federal income tax withheld $	**Copy A** **For Internal Revenue Service Center**
PAYER'S Federal identification number 87-4007325	RECIPIENT'S identification number 165-39-2238	5 Fishing boat proceeds $	6 Medical and health care payments $	**File with Form 1096.**
RECIPIENT'S name Sam LINCOlN		7 Nonemployee compensation $ 34,700	8 Substitute payments in lieu of dividends or interest $	For Privacy Act and Paperwork Reduction Act Notice, see the **2004 General Instructions for Forms 1099, 1098, 5498, and W-2G.**
Street address (including apt. no.) 68 FERNglade #316		9 Payer made direct sales of $5,000 or more of consumer products to a buyer (recipient) for resale ► ☐	10 Crop insurance proceeds $	
City, state, and ZIP code WILMINGTON DE 12899		11	12	
Account number (optional)	2nd TIN not. ☐	13 Excess golden parachute payments $	14 Gross proceeds paid to an attorney $	
15		16 State tax withheld $ $	17 State/Payer's state no.	18 State income $ $

Form **1099-MISC** Cat. No. 14425J Department of the Treasury - Internal Revenue Service

compensation (wage or salary) and any benefits (medical and life insurance, paid vacation, sick leave, retirement pensions, etc.) for which the employee is eligible. If the firm can engage an independent contractor for the same base compensation, it eliminates the incremental cost of the benefits.

The IRS's Viewpoint

In theory, the federal government should be indifferent as to whether workers are employees or independent contractors. The IRS should collect the same employment tax on the worker's compensation, either as payroll tax or self-employment tax. Similarly, the compensation is subject to income tax in either case. Realistically, the IRS has a higher probability of collecting these taxes if the worker is an employee. In this case, the employer is legally responsible for remitting both the employment tax and the income tax on the compensation to the government.

If a firm classifies a worker as an independent contractor, the responsibility for paying tax shifts to the contractor. The IRS has determined that self-employed individuals as a group have a relatively low level of compliance, either because they fail to file a tax return or because they understate their business income.[6] For this reason, the IRS takes an aggressive stance with respect to worker classification. Firms that classify workers as independent contractors must be aware of the risk that a revenue agent may challenge this classification on audit. If the agent concludes that facts and circumstances tip the scales in favor of employee status, the firm may find itself liable for unpaid taxes, interest, and penalties because it failed to carry out its responsibilities as an employer.[7]

[6] See "Self-Employed Nonfilers, Post-Audit, Tax Year 1988," *Statistics of Income Bulletin,* Fall 1994, p. 123.

[7] From 1988 through 1995, the IRS reclassified 527,000 workers as employees and assessed their employers $830 million in back taxes, interest, and penalties. "Independent Contractor Legislation: Opportunity Knocks for Small Businesses," *Journal of Accountancy,* September 1996, p. 34.

Talking the Talk

Companies that use independent contractors may head off a dispute with the IRS by making sure that all written references to such contractors contain the proper terminology. For example, independent contractors are not "hired" or "fired" or paid "wages" or "salaries." Instead, they are "retained" or "discontinued" and paid "remuneration" or "fees." The company should never refer to itself as the "employer" but as the "principal" or "client." Finally, the department that deals with independent contractors should not be labeled "human resources" but "contractor relations."[8]

WAGE AND SALARY PAYMENTS

Tax Consequences to Employees

Employees typically are cash basis taxpayers who recognize wages or salary as income in the year in which payment is actually or constructively received. In terms of cash flow, payments are net of employee payroll tax and income tax withheld by the employer. While payroll tax withholding usually equals the individual's payroll tax liability, the income tax withholding is an approximate number. If the annual withholding exceeds the individual's actual income tax, the Treasury owes the individual a refund. Alternatively, withholding may be less than the actual tax, in which case the individual pays the balance due when she files her Form 1040 or extension request.

Tax Consequences to Employers

The employer's income tax consequences of wage or salary payments depend on the nature of the employee's services. If the employer is an individual and the services are *not* business related, the payment for such services is a nondeductible personal expense. For instance, people who employ private housekeepers, or gardeners, or nannies for their children can't deduct the compensation paid to these household employees. Of course, the fact that employees are performing domestic services does not excuse employers from their payroll tax obligations with respect to the compensation paid.[9]

For sole proprietorships, partnerships, and corporations that hire business employees, the compensation paid is either a deductible expense or a capitalized cost. This distinction depends on the nature of the service and the employer's method of accounting.

Accounting for Compensation Paid

Berring Corporation paid a $90,000 salary to its in-house attorney, an expense that it deducted in the computation of taxable income. It also paid $2,679,000 wages to workers on its production line, a direct labor cost that Berring capitalized to manufactured inventory.

If compensation is deductible, a cash basis firm takes the deduction in the year the compensation is paid, while an accrual basis firm takes the deduction in the year the liability for the compensation is incurred.[10]

[8] Daniel P. O'Meara and Jeffrey L. Braff, "A Preventative Approach to Using Independent Contractors," *Journal of Accountancy,* September 1997, p. 43.

[9] In 2005, household employers are not required to pay or withhold payroll tax unless they pay $1,400 or more in wages to an employee during the year. §3121(a)(7)(B) and (x). Household employers are not required to withhold federal income tax unless the employee requests it and the employer agrees. §3401(a)(3).

[10] An accrual basis firm that pays compensation to a related party who uses the cash method of accounting is not allowed a deduction until the year in which payment is made and the recipient recognizes the payment as income. §267(a)(2).

Tax Talk

In a recent Tax Court case, the judge concluded that the $20,642,485 annual compensation paid by Menard Inc., a publicly held corporation, to its CEO greatly exceeded the compensation of CEOs working for comparable businesses. The judge ruled that only $7,066,912 of the compensation was reasonable, and therefore deductible, by the corporate employer.

Reasonable Compensation

The tax law stipulates that only *reasonable* compensation for services rendered is deductible as a business expense. This stipulation is subjective: "Reasonable and true compensation is only such amount as would ordinarily be paid for like services by like enterprises under like circumstances."[11] The IRS generally assumes that compensation resulting from an arm's-length negotiation between employer and employee is reasonable. In other words, the IRS does not challenge compensation determined in the competitive marketplace. The law does limit the compensation *deduction* allowed to publicly held corporations.[12] These corporations can deduct no more than $1 million of the annual compensation paid to their chief executive officer and the four other most highly paid officers. This limitation is subject to a major exception: It does not apply to **performance-based compensation** paid solely because the corporate officer reached a performance goal established by a compensation committee consisting of outside members of the board of directors. The terms of the compensation arrangement, including the performance goal, must be disclosed to the shareholders who must approve the arrangement by a majority vote.

Compensation Packages for CEOs

The $1 million limit on the deduction for compensation paid to CEOs seems to have little practical effect. According to *Forbes* magazine's annual list of best-paid CEOs, Michael Dell of Dell Computer was paid a $926,000 base salary in 2003. However, he also received a $347,000 bonus and exercised stock options worth $81 million! Both the bonus and stock options qualified as performance-based compensation that was deductible by his employer.

Closely Held Corporations

The payment of compensation by a closely held corporation to an employee who is also a shareholder may not be an arm's-length transaction. To the extent the employee influences or even controls corporate policy in his capacity as a shareholder, salary negotiations occur in a fictitious market.[13] As a result, the IRS looks closely to determine if the compensation is reasonable. If it concludes that the compensation is unreasonably high, it will reclassify the unreasonable portion as a constructive dividend.[14]

Objective 2

List the factors determining reasonable compensation for a shareholder/employee.

Reasonable compensation is based on the facts and circumstances of each particular employer/employee relationship, and the federal courts have heard thousands of cases in which the IRS and a corporate employer disagreed on this issue. In a recent decision, the Second Circuit Court of Appeals described five factors relevant to the reasonableness of employee compensation.

1. The shareholder/employee's role in the corporate business, including the number of hours worked and the duties performed.
2. External comparisons with other companies: specifically, compensation paid to the employee relative to compensation paid to comparable employees by unrelated employers in a similar business.
3. The financial condition of the corporate employer, including sales, net income, capital value, and general economic fitness.
4. The employee's degree of control over dividend policy in his or her capacity as shareholder.

[11] Reg. §1.162-7(a)(3).

[12] §162(m).

[13] See the discussion of fictitious markets involving related parties in Chapter 3.

[14] See the discussion of constructive dividends in Chapter 11.

5. The internal consistency of the corporation's compensation system throughout the employee ranks.[15]

The appellate court pointed out that no single factor determines the issue and that it must "assess the entire tableau from the perspective of an independent investor—that is, given the dividends and return on equity enjoyed by a disinterested stockholder, would that stockholder approve the compensation paid to the employee?"[16] If unrelated shareholders acting in their economic self-interest would agree to the compensation paid to a shareholder/employee, that compensation should be considered reasonable.

$1 Million Man

William Choate founded Choate Construction Company in 1989. During the first three years, William worked 16 hours a day, seven days a week. He single-handedly wrote the corporation's business plans, training manuals, employee handbooks, and employment applications. He negotiated all its contracts, hired and trained its personnel, and was principally responsible for developing its business. In 1993, William was named Entrepreneur of the Year by a construction trade organization.

In 1992, Choate Construction Company paid a $1 million salary to William Choate and deducted the payment on its tax return. The IRS determined that $734,000 of this salary was unreasonable and reclassified this amount as a nondeductible dividend. The federal judge who heard the case sided with the corporation, concluding that William's service had been invaluable and was worth every penny of his salary.[17]

S Corporations

The IRS views the issue of reasonable compensation in an entirely different light when the employment relationship is between an S corporation and its sole shareholder. In this case, the entire corporate income is taxable to the individual who owns the corporation. With respect to the income tax, the individual is indifferent as to the salary he receives (and the corporation deducts). But the individual is not indifferent with respect to the federal payroll tax because every dollar of salary is taxed at the combined 15.3 percent FICA rate.[18] Therefore, the individual has an incentive for his corporation to pay an unreasonably *low* salary to minimize payroll tax cost. In several recent cases, the IRS successfully challenged this tax avoidance tactic by convincing the court that a portion of an S corporation's annual cash distributions should be reclassified as salary to the sole shareholder.[19]

Unreasonably Low Compensation

Mr. Petri is the sole shareholder and CEO of PML Inc., a calendar year S corporation. The IRS recently audited PML's 2002 tax return on which the corporation deducted a $35,000 salary paid to Mr. Petri as CEO. The corporation's 2002 taxable income was $741,240, and it distributed $400,000 cash to Mr. Petri as a shareholder. Mr. Petri reported both his salary and his 100 percent share of PML's taxable income on his 2002 Form 1040. After comparing Mr. Petri's salary with the salaries paid to CEOs of comparable corporate businesses, the IRS concluded that Mr. Petri's 2002 salary should have been $125,000. Consequently, it reclassified $90,000 of Mr. Petri's taxable income from PML as compensation and assessed Social Security and Medicare taxes accordingly.

[15] *Rapco, Inc.* v. *Commissioner,* 85 F.3d 950 (CA-2, 1996). See also *Exacto Spring Corporation* v. *Commissioner,* 196 F.3d 833 (CA-7, 1999).

[16] Ibid., p. 955.

[17] *Choate Construction Co.,* TC Memo 1997-495.

[18] S corporation shareholders do not pay self-employment tax on their share of the corporation's business income.

[19] See *Spicer Accounting, Inc.* v. *Commissioner,* 918 F.2d 90 (CA-9, 1990).

Family Members as Employees

While the tax law doesn't prohibit closely held businesses from hiring employees who are related to the owners, the compensation paid to these relatives must be reasonable for the services actually performed. Subject to this constraint, business owners can effectively shift income to family members who work in the business.

Family Members as Employees

Mrs. Young, who owns a sole proprietorship, is in the 35 percent tax bracket. She has two children, ages 14 and 17, who work for her after school and during the summer. The younger child performs clerical chores and runs errands for her mom, while the older child drives a delivery van. Mrs. Young pays her children a reasonable wage based on the actual number of hours worked each week. This year, the younger child earned $3,100, the older child earned $5,950, and the family saved $3,073 income tax.

Tax savings of business deduction to Mrs. Young ($9,050 wages paid × 35%)	$3,168	
Tax consequences to:	*Younger Child*	*Older Child*
Wage income	$ 3,100	$ 5,950
Standard deduction (single)	(3,100)	(5,000)
Taxable income	–0–	$ 950
Tax rate (single)		.10
Tax cost of compensation to children		$ 95
Tax savings to family:		
Mrs. Young's savings	$ 3,168	
Older child's cost	(95)	
	$ 3,073	

The income shift in this example had a second beneficial tax effect. The $9,050 business deduction reduced Mrs. Young's net earnings from self-employment and, therefore, her self-employment tax. However, wages paid to an employer's child under age 18 are not subject to FICA or unemployment tax.[20] Consequently, the wage payments to the two children did not create an additional payroll tax cost for the business.

Foreign Earned Income Exclusion

Before leaving the topic of wages and salaries, we should consider the special case of individuals who are U.S. citizens but who reside and work on an extended basis in another country. These individuals, referred to as **expatriates,** may face a higher cost of living because of their overseas assignment or may incur additional costs such as foreign income taxes. Because of these financial concerns, U.S. firms with international operations may have difficulty staffing their foreign offices. To help U.S. firms compete in the labor market and to encourage them to employ U.S. citizens to work abroad, the tax law allows expatriates to exclude foreign wages or salary from taxable income. This **foreign earned**

[20] §3121(b)(3)(A) and §3306(c)(5).

income exclusion is limited to $80,000 per year.[21] Expatriates may not claim a foreign tax credit for any foreign income tax paid on the excluded income.[22]

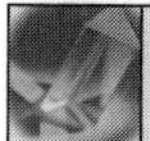

Foreign Earned Income Exclusion

PBG operates a branch office in Portugal, which is managed by Mr. Sims. Although Mr. Sims is a U.S. citizen, he has been a resident of Lisbon since 1994. His salary from PBG is $95,000, on which he paid $14,280 Portuguese income tax. In preparing his Form 1040, Mr. Sims may exclude $80,000 of his foreign earned income from taxable income. Consequently, only $15,000 of his salary is subject to U.S. tax. He may also claim a foreign tax credit based on the Portuguese income tax attributable to his *taxable* salary.

EMPLOYEE FRINGE BENEFITS

As a general rule, individuals are taxed on any economic benefit received as compensation for services rendered to their employers, even if the benefit does not result in any direct cash flow.[23] However, the tax law allows employees to exclude the value of certain statutorily defined **fringe benefits** from income. These fringe benefits not only escape the income tax but also are exempt from payroll tax. Firms that provide fringe benefits account for the cost of the benefits in the same manner as the base compensation paid. If the salary or wage paid to an employee is currently deductible, the cost of the employee's fringe benefits is also deductible.[24] This section of the chapter describes several important nontaxable fringe benefits and discusses how employers and employees include these benefits in their compensation arrangements to mutual advantage.

Health and Accident Insurance

Objective 3
Identify the most common nontaxable employee fringe benefits.

Employees can exclude the value of health and accident insurance coverage provided by their employers.[25] Hence, premiums that employers pay directly to insurance carriers on behalf of their employees are not taxable to the employees. Similarly, if an employer has a self-insured medical reimbursement plan, participating employees do not recognize the imputed value of their coverage under the plan as income. This fringe benefit has tremendous significance to the U.S. workforce. Millions of employees can't afford private medical insurance and rely on their employers for insurance protection. A worker's decision to accept or reject a job offer may depend on whether the prospective employer provides a comprehensive health and accident insurance plan. The tax law encourages employers to do so by making this form of compensation nontaxable. Such preferential treatment is costly; the Treasury loses over $120 billion of annual tax revenues because of the exclusion for employer-provided medical insurance, making it one of the largest items in the government's tax expenditures budget.

Group Term Life Insurance

Employees can exclude the value of term life insurance coverage provided under a group policy carried by their employers, but only to the extent the coverage does not exceed $50,000. If it exceeds $50,000, the employee is taxed on the cost of the excess. This cost is

[21] §911(a) and (b).

[22] §911(d)(6).

[23] Reg. §1.61-21.

[24] Reg. §1.263A-1(e)(3)(ii)(D).

[25] §106. This exclusion extends to the value of employer-provided long-term-care insurance. §213(d)(1)(D).

determined by reference to a uniform premium table provided by the Treasury rather than by reference to the actual insurance premiums paid by the employer.[26]

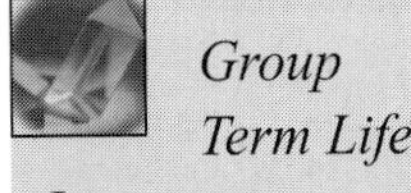

Group Term Life Insurance

Mr. Kung, a 46-year-old employee of ABC Corporation, has $200,000 life insurance coverage under ABC's group term plan. According to the Treasury's table, the cost of $1,000 of life insurance to a 46-year-old person is 15 cents a month. The annual cost of Mr. Kung's $150,000 excess coverage is $270 (150 × $.15 × 12 months). This amount is a taxable fringe benefit to Mr. Kung, and ABC must report $270 as part of Mr. Kung's compensation on his Form W-2.

Dependent Care Assistance Programs

Employees can exclude amounts paid or incurred by their employers for dependent care assistance.[27] Thus, employers may provide on-site day care for their employees' children (or other dependents) as a nontaxable fringe benefit. Alternatively, employers may contract with a third party to provide dependent care or may reimburse employees directly for their dependent care expenses. The annual exclusion is limited to $5,000 ($2,500 in the case of a separate return filed by a married individual). If the value of employer-provided dependent care exceeds $5,000, the employee must recognize the excess as taxable income.

Other Nontaxable Fringe Benefits

Most firms provide their employees with a variety of fringe benefits. The benefits that a particular firm offers depends on the nature of its business and the composition of its workforce. The list of possible benefits includes employee use of company cars, on-premise dining facilities, employer-provided parking and public transportation, moving expense reimbursements, business club memberships, professional dues and subscriptions, and company-sponsored picnics and Christmas parties. Each item on this list (as well as many other employee perks) can qualify as a nontaxable fringe benefit, but only if the item meets the detailed, and sometimes strict, requirements specified in the Internal Revenue Code and Treasury regulations.[28]

Fringe Benefits and Self-Employed Individuals

The tax-exempt status of many employee fringe benefits does not extend to benefits that a self-employed individual provides for himself. As a result, self-employed individuals must spend after-tax dollars to pay for certain commodities that employees can obtain with before-tax dollars (as nontaxable compensation). For example, if a self-employed person pays $750 to purchase a $50,000 life insurance policy to protect her family, the payment is a nondeductible personal expense. The same disadvantage applies to individual partners and shareholders in S corporations. If a partnership has a group term life insurance plan covering both employees and partners, the cost of a partner's insurance is a guaranteed payment that the partner must recognize as taxable income.[29] If an S corporation has a group term life insurance plan, the cost of a shareholder/employee's insurance is taxable compensation instead of a nontaxable fringe benefit.[30]

[26] Reg. §1.79-3. The employer's actual cost of group term life insurance is a §162 expense. Reg. §1.162-10 and Rev. Rul. 69-478, 1969-2 CB 29.

[27] §129.

[28] See §132 and accompanying regulations.

[29] Rev. Rul. 91-26, 1991-1 CB 184.

[30] §1372 prevents any shareholder who owns more than 2 percent of an S corporation's stock from excluding employee fringe benefits from taxable income.

Self-employed individuals, partners, and S corporation shareholders do receive special consideration with respect to medical and accident insurance for themselves and their families. These taxpayers are allowed an above-the-line deduction for the cost of this insurance.[31]

Deduction of Health Insurance Costs

Vernon LLC has 38 employees and five individual members who work for the LLC. The LLC provides a group medical insurance plan that covers both employees and members. The cost of the insurance is a nontaxable fringe benefit to Vernon's employees and taxable compensation to the members. In 2005, Mrs. George, an LLC member, recognizes the $2,650 cost of her medical insurance as an income item. However, she is allowed an above-the-line deduction of the same amount, so the net effect of this fringe benefit on her AGI is zero.

Compensation Planning with Fringe Benefits

Fringe benefits are an extremely popular form of compensation. One reason is that the employer's cost of providing the benefit is usually less than the benefit's value to the employee. This differential is attributable to the employer's economy of scale: The cost per person of providing a commodity such as health insurance or child care to a large group is less than the cost of the commodity to one individual.

Cost versus Value of Fringe Benefit

Contex Corporation, which has 1,200 employees, maintains a group medical plan with a commercial insurance company. Mr. Liu participates in this plan, and the annual cost of his coverage is $2,400. If Mr. Liu were not a participant, he would pay $3,600 per year for comparable private medical insurance. Contex operates an on-premise day care facility in which employees can enroll their preschool children at no charge. Contex's annual operating cost is $1,750 per child. Mr. Liu's son attends this facility. If the facility were not available, Mr. Liu would pay $2,100 per year to enroll his son in private day care. The aggregate value of these two fringe benefits to Mr. Liu is $5,700. Contex's cost to provide the benefits is only $4,150.

Cafeteria Plans

Because employees have varying financial needs and consumption preferences, each one places a different value on any noncash benefit offered by his or her employer.

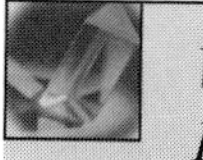

Valuing Fringe Benefits

In the preceding example, Mr. Liu placed a $2,100 value on the child care provided by Contex because he is willing to pay $2,100 for this commodity. Ms. Blane, another corporate employee, has no children. Therefore, Ms. Blane places a zero value on employer-provided child care. She would prefer a different fringe benefit or even additional salary from Contex rather than a worthless fringe benefit.

Employers can maximize the aggregate value of their fringe-benefit programs to their employees through a **cafeteria plan.** Under a cafeteria plan, each employee may select noncash benefits from a menu of benefit choices. In lieu of noncash benefits, employees may simply select additional taxable salary.[32] By participating in a cafeteria plan, employees can combine both nontaxable and taxable benefits to result in the greatest after-tax compensation based on their individual needs and preferences.

[31] §162(l).

[32] Cafeteria plans are described in §125.

Negotiating with Nontaxable Fringe Benefits

Employers are aware that employees may enjoy substantial tax savings because of nontaxable fringe benefits. By substituting nontaxable benefits for taxable compensation, employers can capture some portion of this savings for themselves and reduce the after-tax cost of the compensation. The examples that follow demonstrate this important point.

Salary Payment

Leyton Corporation is negotiating a one-year employment contract with Mrs. King, who begins the negotiation by requesting a $200,000 salary. Leyton's marginal tax rate is 35 percent, and Mrs. King's marginal tax rate is 33 percent. The after-tax cost of this salary to Leyton and the after-tax value of this salary to Mrs. King are computed as follows.

	Leyton	*Mrs. King*
Salary payment	$(200,000)	$ 200,000
Employer/employee payroll tax	(8,480)	(8,480)
Income tax savings (cost):		
Salary deduction × 35%	70,000	
Payroll tax deduction × 35%	2,968	
Salary income × 33%		(66,000)
After-tax (cost) value	$(135,512)	$ 125,520

Now assume that Leyton makes a counteroffer to Mrs. King. It will pay a $185,000 salary and provide complete medical and dental insurance coverage for her and her family, free parking in a convenient garage, and membership in its on-premises health spa. Assume that the value of these nontaxable fringe benefits to Mrs. King is $12,000, but their incremental cost to Leyton is only $9,000.[33]

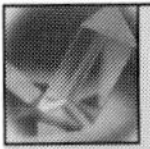

Reduced Salary plus Fringe Benefits

The after-tax cost of the compensation package (salary plus fringe benefits) to Leyton and the after-tax value of this package to Mrs. King are computed as follows.

	Leyton	*Mrs. King*
Salary payment	$(185,000)	$ 185,000
Fringe-benefit (cost) value	(9,000)	12,000
Employer/employee payroll tax	(8,263)	(8,263)
Income tax savings (cost):		
Salary deduction × 35%	64,750	
Fringe-benefit deduction × 35%	3,150	
Payroll tax deduction × 35%	2,892	
Salary income × 33%		(61,050)
After-tax (cost) value	$(131,471)	$ 127,687

[33] Employer-provided parking and on-premises athletic facilities can qualify as nontaxable fringe benefits. §132(f) and (j)(4).

The substitution of nontaxable fringe benefits for salary decreased Leyton's after-tax cost by $4,041 and increased Mrs. King's after-tax compensation by $2,167. Thus, both parties to this negotiation benefited from the inclusion of the nontaxable fringe benefits.

EMPLOYEE STOCK OPTIONS

Corporate employers often include stock options as a major component of the compensation package offered to key employees. A **stock option** is the right to purchase the corporation's stock for a stated price (the strike price) for a given period of time. From the employee's perspective, stock options are an opportunity to acquire equity at a bargain price. From the employer's perspective, stock options are a form of compensation that requires no cash outlay and, in fact, may eventually result in an infusion of capital. In addition, the option gives the employee a financial interest in the corporation's long-term success and a powerful incentive to contribute to that success in every way possible.

Stock Options for Everyone!

Stock options (once reserved for top executives) are filtering down to an increasing number of rank-and-file corporate employees. Since 1989, when pioneer PepsiCo granted every employee bonus options worth 10 percent of their salary, over 4,000 companies have instituted broad-based option plans with about 10 million participating employees. "Broad-based stock options are now the norm in high-technology companies and are becoming popular in many companies in other industries as part of an overall equity compensation strategy."[34]

Objective 4
Describe the tax consequences of stock options.

To analyze the tax consequences of compensatory stock options, consider the case of BRT and its employee, Mr. Bell. In year 1, BRT grants Mr. Bell an option to buy 2,000 shares of BRT stock for a strike price of $30 per share at any time during the next eight years. On the date of grant, BRT stock is selling for $28 per share. Because the strike price exceeds the market price, the option has no readily ascertainable value and Mr. Bell does not recognize income on receipt of the option.[35] The risk that Mr. Bell assumes in accepting the option is that the market price will not climb above $30 per share over the term of the option. In this case, the option is worthless, and Mr. Bell will simply let it lapse.

Mr. Bell's expectation is that the market price of BRT stock will increase over the option period. Suppose that by year 8, the stock is selling at $75 per share. Mr. Bell exercises the option by paying $60,000 cash to BRT for 2,000 shares with a market value of $150,000. Mr. Bell must recognize the $90,000 **bargain element** (excess of market value over cost) as ordinary income in year 8. These results are shown in Exhibit 14.3 in which the vertical axis is BRT stock price and the horizontal axis is the eight-year option period.

The shaded area in Exhibit 14.3 represents the value of Mr. Bell's option, which increased over time as the BRT stock price climbed from $28 to $75. Mr. Bell defers income recognition until he realizes this value by converting the option to actual shares of stock. Mr. Bell's tax basis in his 2,000 shares is $150,000: $60,000 out-of-pocket cost plus $90,000 income recognized on the exercise of the option.

Note that in year 8, Mr. Bell has *negative* cash flow; he must pay $60,000 for the stock plus both income and payroll tax on $90,000 compensation. Mr. Bell can generate cash by selling some of his BRT shares. This sale will not trigger additional income unless the selling

[34] Employment Policy Foundation, "The Economic Impact of Expensing Stock Options," September 17, 2002.

[35] Reg. §1.83-7.

EXHIBIT 14.3
Tax Consequences of Mr. Bell's Stock Option

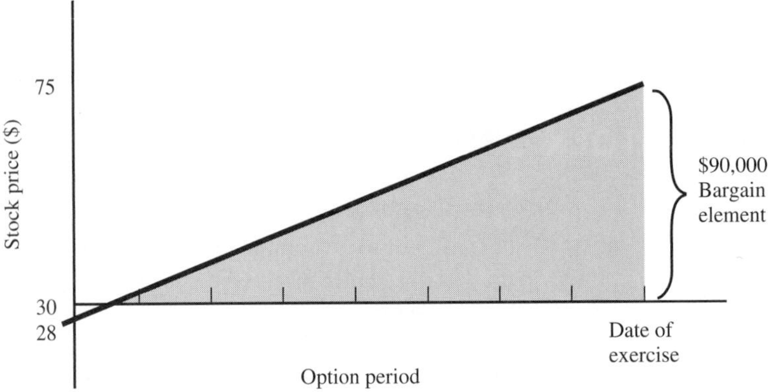

price exceeds Mr. Bell's $75 basis per share. On the other hand, BRT received $60,000 cash as paid-in capital when Mr. Bell exercised his stock option. Moreover, the corporation can deduct the $90,000 bargain element as compensation paid in year 8.[36]

Book/Tax Difference

The GAAP rules concerning the proper method of accounting for employee stock options are currently the subject of intense debate. Since 1995, the rules recommend but *do not require* corporations to record the estimated value of the options as an expense in the year of grant. However, most corporations have ignored the recommendation and merely disclose the pro forma effect of the unrecorded expense on net income in a footnote to their financial statements. In response to recent public concern about the reliability of financial statement information, many major corporations (including General Motors, Coca-Cola, and General Electric) have adopted the estimated value method, and the Financial Accounting Standards Board is in the process of changing the GAAP recommendation of this method to a requirement.

Employee stock options result in a difference between corporate book income and taxable income. Regardless of its book method of accounting for an option, a corporation can deduct the bargain element in the year the option is exercised. If the corporation did not report an expense in the year of grant, this deduction causes a permanent excess of book over taxable income.[37] If the corporation did expense the estimated value of the option, the expense caused a temporary excess of taxable over book income in the year of grant that reverses when the corporation takes the subsequent deduction in the year of exercise.

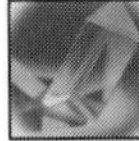

Book/Tax Difference from Stock Options

Four years ago, Perino Inc. granted stock options to its employees and expensed their $2,840,000 total estimated value on its income statement. This expense was nondeductible and resulted in a temporary excess of taxable over book income. This year, one of Perino's employees exercised an option and recognized the $103,100 bargain element (excess of market value over option price) as gross income. Perino's $103,100 deduction of the bargain element is a reversal of the original temporary difference.

[36] Reg. §1.83-6.

[37] Even though the tax savings from the deduction is permanent, it does not reduce income tax expense per books. Instead, the savings is booked as an increase to shareholders' equity.

Incentive Stock Options

The tax law creates a special type of employee stock option called an **incentive stock option (ISO).** The qualification requirements for ISOs are numerous and complex, but the preferential treatment of ISOs as compared to nonqualifying options is straightforward.[38] When an employee exercises an ISO, he does not recognize the bargain element as taxable income.[39] The tax basis in the purchased shares is the employee's out-of-pocket cost, and the employee recognizes no income with respect to these shares unless and until he disposes of them in a taxable transaction. Furthermore, any gain recognized on disposition is capital gain.

Refer back to the facts concerning Mr. Bell's option to purchase 2,000 shares of BRT common stock and assume that the option qualified as an ISO. In year 8, Mr. Bell does not recognize any income when he purchases 2,000 shares worth $150,000 for only $60,000. Suppose that Mr. Bell holds these shares until year 15, when he sells them for $225,000. Mr. Bell's capital gain on sale is $165,000 ($225,000 amount realized − $60,000 basis), $90,000 of which represents the untaxed bargain element on exercise of the option.

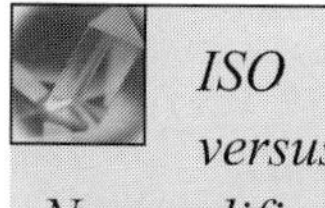

ISO versus Nonqualified Option

The following table contrasts Mr. Bell's income tax cost from this sequence of transactions to the tax cost if the stock option had not qualified as an ISO. The table assumes a 35 percent rate on ordinary income and a 15 percent rate on capital gain.

	ISO	*Nonqualified Option*
Year 8 (exercise of option):		
Ordinary income recognized	–0–	$ 90,000
Tax cost at 35%	**–0–**	**31,500**
Basis in 2,000 shares	$ 60,000	$ 150,000
Year 15 (sale of stock):		
Selling price	$225,000	$ 225,000
Basis	(60,000)	(150,000)
Capital gain recognized	$165,000	$ 75,000
Tax cost at 15%	**$ 24,750**	**$ 11,250**

This table shows the dual advantage of ISOs compared to nonqualified stock options: the extension of the tax-*deferral* period until the year of sale and the *conversion* of the option's bargain element from ordinary income to capital gain. However, individuals who are planning to exercise ISOs must be cautious. The untaxed bargain element is an alternative minimum tax (AMT) adjustment added to taxable income in the computation of alternative minimum taxable income (AMTI).[40] Accordingly, individuals may want to avoid exercising ISOs in a year in which they have any exposure to the AMT.

A negative feature of ISOs is that employers never receive a tax deduction for the option's bargain element. Consequently, they derive no tax benefit when an employee exercises an ISO.

[38] Incentive stock options are defined in §422(b).

[39] §421(a).

[40] §56(b)(3).

Corporate Deduction for Stock Options

The following table compares BRT's cash flow consequences of compensating Mr. Bell with an ISO rather than with a nonqualified stock option.

		ISO		*Nonqualified Option*
Year 8 (Mr. Bell's exercise of option):				
Paid-in capital from issuance of shares		$60,000		$60,000
Deduction for bargain element	–0–		$90,000	
BRT's marginal tax rate			.35	
Tax savings from deduction		–0–		31,500
Net cash flow in year 8		$60,000		$91,500

Mr. Bell's sale of his stock in year 15 has no effect on BRT.

EMPLOYMENT-RELATED EXPENSES

It is not unusual for individuals to incur out-of-pocket expenses relating to their employment. Common examples are union dues, subscriptions to professional or trade journals, uniforms, continuing education courses that maintain or improve job skills, and transportation costs incurred while conducting business for an employer. Employers routinely reimburse employees for employment-related expenses, thereby assuming the economic burden of the expense. In such case, the employee neither reports the cash reimbursement as income nor deducts the expense. The whole expense/ reimbursement transaction is a wash without any effect on the employee's taxable income.

The tax consequences of *unreimbursed* employment-related expenses are much less benign. Congress has expressed its belief that individuals should not be allowed to deduct such expenses. If the expenses are truly necessary to the successful performance of an employee's duties, the employer should be willing to provide reimbursement. Acting on this belief, Congress put employment-related expenses into the category of **miscellaneous itemized deductions,** which are deductible only to the extent that their total exceeds 2 percent of AGI.[41] Because of this limitation, many individuals derive no tax benefit from their unreimbursed employment-related expenses.

Unreimbursed Employment-Related Expenses

Ms. Jessup, who is employed by an advertising firm, spent $1,500 to attend a seminar on computer graphics. This unreimbursed employment-related expense is her only miscellaneous itemized deduction for the year. If Ms. Jessup's AGI is $69,400, she can deduct only $112 of the cost of the seminar.

Miscellaneous itemized deductions	$ 1,500
AGI threshold ($69,400 × 2%)	(1,388)
Allowable deduction	$ 112

[41] §67.

If Ms. Jessup's AGI equals or exceeds $75,000, her total miscellaneous itemized deductions fall short of the 2 percent AGI threshold. In such case, none of the employment-related expense is deductible, and her *after-tax* cost of the seminar is $1,500.

Moving Expenses

The tax law allows individuals to deduct unreimbursed moving expenses incurred in connection with "the commencement of work by the taxpayer as an employee or as a self-employed individual, at a new principal place of work."[42] **Moving expenses** include the cost of transporting household goods and personal belongings from the individual's former residence to a new residence. The costs of traveling to the new residence (with the exception of the cost of meals en route) also qualify as moving expenses. The moving expense deduction is an above-the-line deduction in the computation of AGI.

If an employee receives a moving expense reimbursement from his employer, the reimbursement is nontaxable to the extent of the moving expenses qualifying for the deduction. Any excess reimbursement is taxable compensation to the employee.

Moving Expenses

BV Corporation transferred its employee Mr. Carl from its San Diego office to its San Antonio office. Mr. Carl paid $3,800 to the moving company that transported his household goods from his California home to his new home in Texas. He also paid $2,400 to fly his family from California to Texas.

- If Mr. Carl did not receive any reimbursement from BV, he may deduct $6,200 in the computation of AGI.
- If Mr. Carl received a $5,000 reimbursement from BV, he may deduct $1,200 in the computation of AGI.
- If Mr. Carl received a $7,000 reimbursement from BV, he must recognize the $800 excess reimbursement as taxable compensation.

RETIREMENT PLANNING

At some point in their lives, most people confront the need to plan for retirement. Given the life expectancy for the average American, individuals who want to retire by age 65 know that they might live 20 to 30 years after leaving the workforce. They also know that they should take action now to maintain their standard of living during this postemployment period. Specifically, they must invest some portion of their current income in financial assets that will provide future income. In this section of the chapter, we will learn how the tax laws encourage people to save for retirement. By taking advantage of tax-favored retirement plans, individuals can maximize the future value of their investments and enhance their prospects for long-term security.[43]

[42] §217. Individuals must meet both a distance test and a duration-of-new-employment test to qualify for the deduction.

[43] While many people anticipate that they will receive Social Security benefits during their retirement years, they can't undertake any type of individualized tax planning to increase these benefits. Consequently, we will address the tax consequences of Social Security in Chapter 16 as part of our discussion of government transfer payments.

Retirement Planning Is Top Priority

On the basis of a survey of employee benefit specialists, retirement planning has replaced health care as the top priority for today's labor force. The "tidal wave of Baby Boomers" approaching retirement age is recognizing the need to evaluate the adequacy of retirement savings. Many firms have initiated investment education programs to help their employees assess their investment options and develop strategies to increase their retirement income. Better still, the value of these retirement planning services is a nontaxable fringe benefit to the employees.[44]

Tax Advantages of Qualified Retirement Plans

Objective 5
Compare the after-tax accumulated wealth in a qualified retirement plan and a nonqualified savings plan.

The tax law confers a generous set of advantages on an array of retirement savings plans, which are described generically as **qualified retirement plans.** While the statutory requirements and the financial and legal structures of the plans vary considerably, they all offer two basic benefits to the individuals who participate.

- Dollars of earned income contributed to the plan (or contributed by an employer on an employee's behalf) are not taxed currently.
- The plan itself is tax exempt, so that the earnings generated by the contributed dollars are not taxed currently.

The effect of these two benefits on the rate at which the contributed dollars grow over time is tremendous. The next example highlights this effect.

Qualified Retirement Plan Contributions

Mr. Quincy and Mrs. Russ, who are both in the 35 percent marginal tax bracket, have decided to contribute $20,000 annual compensation to a retirement fund. Both funds earn an annual 9 percent rate of return and involve the same financial risk. The only difference is that Mr. Quincy's fund is a qualified retirement plan while Mrs. Russ's fund is not. The following table shows the calculation of the balances in the two funds after 25 years.

	Mr. Quincy	*Mrs. Russ*
Annual compensation contributed to fund	$ 20,000	$ 20,000
Income tax cost of compensation	–0–	(7,000)
After-tax annual contribution	$ 20,000	$ 13,000
Before-tax rate of return on contributions	.09	.09
After-tax rate of return on contributions	.09	.0585
Fund balance after 25 years	$1,694,018	$698,353

The balance in Mr. Quincy's fund does not represent the disposable wealth available on retirement. The law allows him to *defer* the tax on his retirement savings—not to escape taxation entirely. When Mr. Quincy withdraws money from the fund, the withdrawals are fully taxable. In contrast, Mrs. Russ's fund balance consists of after-tax dollars that she may withdraw and spend at no further tax cost. The next example provides a final comparison of the two funds.

[44] "Benefit Specialists Identify Priorities for 1998," *Deloitte & Touche Review,* December 22, 1997. Qualified retirement planning services are a nontaxable fringe benefit per §132(a)(7).

Qualified Retirement Plan Withdrawals

At the end of 25 years, both Mr. Quincy and Mrs. Russ withdraw the balance from their retirement fund. Assume that Mr. Quincy pays 35 percent tax on the entire withdrawal.

	Mr. Quincy	*Mrs. Russ*
Fund balance after 25 years	$1,694,018	$698,353
Income tax cost of withdrawal	(592,906)	-0-
After-tax disposable wealth	$1,101,112	$698,353

This comparison of after-tax wealth is dramatic testimony to the power of tax deferral. Moreover, Mr. Quincy can prolong the deferral by liquidating his retirement fund gradually over a number of years rather than in a single lump sum. Depending on the type of plan, he may have the option of receiving the fund balance in the form of an annuity, a series of fixed payments over a specific period of time.[45] In such case, Mr. Quincy will pay tax on the retirement dollars received each year. The tax law does limit the duration of the deferral that people can achieve by investing in qualified retirement plans. Plan participants must begin receiving a statutorily defined **minimum distribution** no later than April 1 of the year following the year in which they reach the age of 70½.[46]

Premature Withdrawals

Objective 6
Calculate the tax cost of a premature withdrawal from a qualified plan.

When Congress decided to allow individuals to defer income tax through participation in qualified plans, the intent was that participants use the plans to save for retirement. To discourage people from withdrawing funds before retirement, the Internal Revenue Code imposes a 10 percent penalty on any **premature withdrawal** from a qualified plan.[47] Generally, a withdrawal is premature unless the participant has reached the age of 59½ by the date of withdrawal. This rule is subject to a number of important exceptions. For instance, the penalty is waived if the owner is totally or permanently disabled; if the owner has reached age 55 and has terminated employment with the plan sponsor; or if the withdrawal is made by the owner's estate or beneficiary after the owner's death.

The 10 percent penalty applies only to the portion of a withdrawal included in the participant's income. Individuals who withdraw funds from a qualified plan can avoid both the income tax and any premature withdrawal penalty by rolling over the funds to *another* qualified plan (including an IRA) within 60 days of the withdrawal.

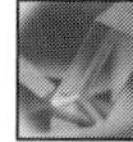

Rollover of Withdrawal

Mrs. Harris, age 48, participated for 14 years in a qualified retirement plan sponsored by her employer, Acton Inc. This year, she resigned from Acton to accept a new job with Zuma Inc. Because of her termination of employment, she received a cash distribution of the $35,000 balance in her Acton plan. Mrs. Harris spent $12,000 to buy a new car and made a **rollover contribution** of the $23,000 remainder to Zuma's qualified retirement plan. Consequently,

[45] An annuity can last for a specified number of months or years or for the lifetime (or lifetimes) of the annuitant (annuitants).

[46] §401(a)(9) and §408(a)(6). Participants who fail to receive the minimum distribution must pay a 50 percent excise tax on the undistributed amount. §4974. In the case of employer-sponsored retirement plans, employees who continue to work after reaching age 70½ may postpone receiving distributions until they retire.

[47] §72(t).

she recognized only $12,000 of the distribution as taxable income subject to her 25 percent marginal rate. The total tax cost of the withdrawal was $4,200.

Income tax ($12,000 × 25%)	$3,000
Premature withdrawal penalty ($12,000 × 10%)	1,200
Total tax cost	$4,200

TYPES OF QUALIFIED PLANS

Qualified retirement plans fall into three categories.

1. Plans that employers provide for their employees.
2. Plans available to self-employed individuals (Keogh plans).
3. Individual retirement accounts (IRAs) available to any person who recognizes compensation or earned income.

This section of the chapter describes the plans included in each category. As you will observe, qualified plans come in a variety of shapes and sizes. But regardless of the differences in structure or operation, qualified retirement plans share a common characteristic: They all are vehicles for tax-deferred savings.

Employer-Provided Plans

One of the more common fringe benefits offered to employees is participation in one or more retirement plans sponsored and maintained by their employer. For an **employer-provided plan** to be qualified for federal tax purposes, it must satisfy a formidable list of statutory requirements.[48] These requirements reflect two underlying policy objectives. The first objective is that *employer-provided plans should carry minimum risk for participating employees.* To meet this objective, the law requires that:

- Qualified plans must be written, permanent arrangements and must be administered in trust form so that the plan assets are invested by an independent trustee for the exclusive benefit of the employees and their families.
- Qualified plans must be funded; annual contributions made to a plan by an employer on behalf of the employees must consist of cash or other valuable property.
- Employees must have a nonforfeitable (vested) right to 100 percent of their retirement benefits under a qualified plan after no more than seven years of service with the employer.

The second objective is that *employer-provided plans should provide benefits in an equitable manner to all participating employees.* Accordingly, plans may not discriminate in favor of officers, owner-employees, or highly compensated employees. In other words, rank-and-file employees must be entitled to participate in qualified retirement plans on essentially the same basis as the chief executive officer.

[48] §401 through §415.

Defined-Benefit Plans

Employer-provided plans may take the form of a pension plan under which participating employees are promised a targeted or defined benefit when they retire. Firms make annual contributions to their pension plans based on the actuarially determined cost of funding the future retirement benefits to which the current workforce is entitled.[49] These contributions are deductible payroll expenses, even though the employees do not recognize the contributions as income.[50] For tax purposes, firms must comply with a minimum funding standard for their qualified pension plans.[51] Because of this standard, a firm may be required to make contributions to the retirement trust in years in which it operates at a loss or experiences cash flow difficulties. For this reason, employers should regard employee pension plans as long-term financial obligations.

Funding a Defined-Benefit Plan

BN Inc. provides a qualified defined-benefit plan for its employees. This year, an independent actuary determined that BN must contribute $4.28 million to the retirement trust to fund the future pension benefits to which its workforce is entitled. The contribution does not represent taxable compensation to the employees participating in the plan. However, BN can deduct the $4.28 million contribution on its Form 1120.

The annual pension that employers can provide through a qualified **defined-benefit plan** is limited to the *lesser* of 100 percent of the retiree's average compensation for her three highest compensation years or an inflation-adjusted base amount.[52] In 2005, the base amount is $170,000. Firms wanting to provide more generous pensions must do so through nonqualified retirement plans. The tax consequences of nonqualified plans are discussed later in this section.

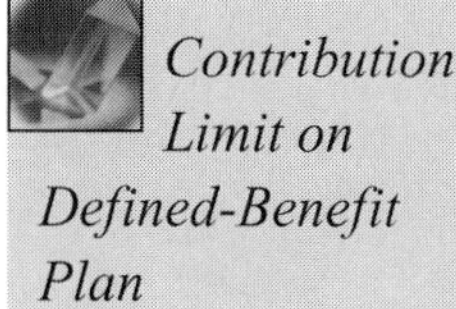

Contribution Limit on Defined-Benefit Plan

Mr. Underwood, a corporate officer of BN Inc., earns a $150,000 salary and anticipates a salary increase every year until his retirement. He participates in BN's qualified pension plan. Although Mr. Underwood's average compensation for his three highest compensation years is projected to be at least $200,000, BN's 2005 plan contribution on his behalf is limited to the amount necessary to fund an annual pension benefit of only $170,000.

Defined-Contribution Plans

Employer-provided plans may be structured as **defined-contribution plans** under which the retirement trust maintains a separate account for each participating employee. Each year, the employer contributes a specified amount to each account. The yearly contribution for each employee is limited to the *lesser* of 100 percent of annual compensation or an inflation-adjusted base amount.[53] In 2005, this base amount is $42,000. Employers may deduct their yearly contributions even though these contributions are not taxable to the employees.

[49] In 1974, Congress created the Pension Benefit Guaranty Corporation (PBGC) to insure defined benefit plans and to guarantee that participating employees receive their promised pension, even if the plan is underfunded or is terminated by the employer. Qualified plans must pay annual premiums to the PBGC for such insurance.

[50] Employer contributions to qualified plans are not subject to FICA payroll tax. §3121(a)(5).

[51] §412 contains the minimum funding standards that employers must satisfy every year for qualified defined-benefit plans.

[52] §415(b).

[53] §415(c).

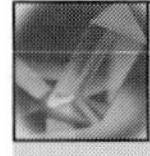

Contribution Limit on Defined-Contribution Plan

Ms. Lewis, a midlevel manager with JH Corporation, earned a $110,000 salary in 2005 and participates in JH's qualified defined-contribution plan. JH's 2005 contribution to Ms. Lewis's plan account is limited to $42,000.

Profit-sharing plans under which firms contribute a percentage of current earnings to a retirement trust are a common type of defined-contribution plan. A firm has no obligation to contribute to the trust in a year in which it operates at a loss. As a result, profit-sharing plans are favored by new companies with volatile earnings and uncertain cash flows. From the employees' perspective, these plans require them to share the risk associated with their employer's business because the retirement savings available to each employee depends on the long-term success of that business.

Tax Talk

Sears, the retailing giant, is phasing out its pension plan as part of a strategy to compete with retailers such as Wal-Mart that offer less costly benefits to employees. Sears employees under age 40 will be shifted from the traditional pension plan to a self-funded Section 401(k) plan.

Employee stock ownership plans (ESOPs) are a second type of defined-contribution plan that gives corporate employees a vested interest in their employer's long-term financial success. Employer contributions to ESOPs are invested primarily in the employer's own common stock.[54] Consequently, employees who participate in ESOPs become shareholders, and the value of their retirement benefits depends on the market value of their employer's stock. When participants retire, they receive distributions of the stock held in their ESOP accounts. Such distributions represent taxable income only to the extent of the ESOP's aggregate basis in the stock. Any excess of the stock's market value over basis is excluded from the recipient's income.[55]

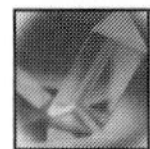

Participation in an ESOP

Mr. Kemp was employed by BD Inc. for 29 years during which BD made annual contributions to an ESOP on his behalf. Mr. Kemp retired this year and received a lump-sum distribution of the balance in his retirement account: 14,987 shares of BD common stock. The ESOP's aggregate basis in the shares was $79,250, and the market value of the shares at date of distribution was $299,600. Mr. Kemp recognized $79,250 ordinary income because of the distribution and took a $79,250 basis in his BD shares. He will not recognize any of the $220,350 unrealized appreciation in the shares until he sells them.

Section 401(k) plans, also described as *salary reduction plans* or *cash-or-deferred arrangements,* are another popular qualified plan. Under these plans, each participating employee defines his or her own contribution by authorizing the employer to divert some amount of current salary or wage to the employee's retirement account. The compensation diverted to the account is tax deferred to the employee even though it is deductible by the employer.[56] In 2005, the maximum compensation that employees can contribute to a Section 401(k) plan is $14,000.[57] Employers often agree to make additional contributions or even match their employees' contributions to Section 401(k) plans.

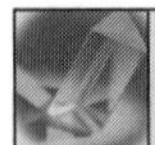

Section 401(k) Plan Contribution

Mrs. Toley, a financial analyst with PW Inc., received a $92,000 salary in 2005. She elected to contribute the $14,000 maximum to PW's Section 401(k) plan. Consequently, only $78,000 of her salary was taxable. PW's policy is to match each employee's elective contribution (subject to the yearly limitation on contributions to defined-contribution plans). So PW

[54] §409.

[55] §402(e)(4)(B).

[56] This compensation is subject to payroll tax in the year of contribution. §3121(v)(1)(A).

[57] §402(g)(1)(B).

contributed another $14,000 to Mrs. Toley's retirement account, increasing the total tax-deferred contribution to $28,000.

Nonqualified Deferred-Compensation Plans

Objective 7
Explain why employers use nonqualified deferred-compensation plans.

Qualified retirement plans seem to offer a win-win outcome. Employers can deduct contributions made to the plans on their employees' behalf, while employees defer income recognition until they receive distributions from the plans at retirement. But as we learned in our discussion of pension plans, profit-sharing plans, and Section 401(k) plans, the dollar amount of compensation that employers can offer on a tax-deferred basis is limited. Moreover, because of the nondiscrimination requirements, employers can't be overly selective as to the employees who may participate in a qualified retirement plan. Finally, most employers need professional help to cope with the morass of federal rules and regulations governing qualified plans. Hence, these plans can be expensive to maintain, even for the smallest employer.

These negative aspects of qualified plans have prompted many employers to establish nonqualified retirement plans. Employers can use these plans to offer unlimited **deferred compensation** to key employees, such as highly paid corporate executives, without extending the benefits of the plan to other employees. In their simplest form, deferred-compensation plans are nothing more than contractual arrangements under which an employer agrees to pay some portion of the employee's compensation at a specified future date. The arrangement is unfunded: The employer accrues its liability for the deferred compensation but does not set aside any cash or property to secure the liability.

Employees who agree to this arrangement don't recognize their deferred compensation as income because they are not in actual or constructive receipt of any payment.[58] These employees will recognize income in the future year in which their employer makes good on its obligation to pay the deferred compensation. On the employer's side of the arrangement, the accrued liability for deferred compensation is a current expense for financial statement purposes. However, employers are not allowed to deduct deferred compensation until the year of payment when the employee includes the compensation in income.[59]

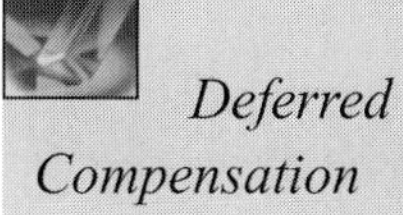

Deferred Compensation

Mr. Jarvis, age 49 and NY's chief financial officer, received a $300,000 salary in 2005. At its December meeting, NY's board of directors awarded Mr. Jarvis a $150,000 bonus to be paid in three annual installments, beginning in the year he retires at age 60. NY did not set aside any cash or property to fund the deferred compensation but accrued a $150,000 liability on its balance sheet. Mr. Jarvis did not recognize the deferred compensation as 2005 income nor did NY deduct the deferred compensation expense on its 2005 Form 1120. Mr. Jarvis will recognize income and NY will claim a deduction over the three years during which the compensation is actually paid.

Employees who consider saving for retirement through a deferred-compensation plan must weigh the tax advantages against the financial risk inherent in the plan. In the case of an unfunded plan, the employee is an unsecured creditor of the employer with respect to the deferred compensation. If the employer is financially secure, the employee's retirement is

[58] Rev. Rul. 60-31, 1960-1 CB 174.

[59] §404(a)(5). Deferred-compensation plans typically require the employer to accrue interest on its liability to the employee. Employers may not deduct this interest until the year it is actually paid to the employee. *Albertson's Inc.* v. *Commissioner,* 42 F.3d 537 (CA-9, 1994), *cert. denied,* 516 U.S. 807 (1995).

equally secure. But if the employer's business should fail and the employer defaults on its liabilities, the employee may discover that her right to deferred compensation has little or no value as a source of retirement income.

Keogh Plans for Self-Employed Individuals

Objective 8
Describe the tax benefit of a Keogh plan to a self-employed individual.

Individuals who earn self-employment income can make annual payments to a **Keogh plan** (named after the congressman who sponsored the legislation that created this qualified plan).[60] These payments are deductible as an above-the-line deduction in the computation of AGI. Thus, individuals pay no income tax on the business earnings invested in their Keogh plans.[61] Because Keogh plans are qualified retirement plans, the earnings generated by the financial assets held in the plan are tax exempt. Accordingly, sole proprietors and partners can take advantage of Keogh plans to accumulate tax-deferred savings in the same way that employees take advantage of their employer-provided plans.

Like employer-provided plans, Keogh plans must be administered by an independent trustee. Commercial banks, credit unions, brokerage firms, and other financial institutions typically serve as trustees for the prototype Keogh plans they maintain and manage for their individual clients. While Keogh plans can be either defined-benefit or defined-contribution plans, the latter type is more popular. Individuals who own defined-contribution Keogh plans can invest the *lesser* of 20 percent of self-employment income or an inflation-adjusted base amount ($42,000 in 2005) each year. For purposes of computing this limitation, self-employment income is reduced by the deduction for one-half of the individual's self-employment tax.

Keogh Plan Contribution

Mr. Abeg's sole proprietorship generated $63,000 net profit in 2005 on which he paid $8,902 self-employment tax. He deducted $4,451 (one-half) of the SE tax in the computation of AGI. His self-employment income is computed as follows.

Net profit from sole proprietorship	$63,000
SE tax deduction	(4,451)
Self-employment income	$58,549

Mr. Abeg's 2005 contribution to his Keogh plan is limited to the lesser of 20 percent of his self-employment income or $42,000. Therefore, his maximum deductible contribution to the plan is $11,710 (20 percent of $58,549).

Keogh plans have a potentially serious downside for self-employed individuals who hire employees to work in their business: The plan must provide retirement benefits to such employees on a nondiscriminatory basis. In other words, the owner can't use a Keogh plan to defer tax on her own earnings unless the plan allows her employees to do the same with respect to their compensation. The owner's tax savings from the Keogh plan are eroded by the incremental cost of including employees in the plan. Clearly, the self-employed person with no employees is the ideal candidate for a Keogh plan.

[60] §401(c) and §404(a)(8).

[61] They do, however, pay self-employment tax on this income. *Gale* v. *United States,* 768 F. Supp. 1305 (ND Ill., 1991).

Individual Retirement Accounts

Objective 9
Describe the tax consequences of IRA contributions and withdrawals.

Every person who earns employee compensation or self-employment income may save for retirement on a tax-deferred basis through an **individual retirement account (IRA).** People establish IRAs with commercial banks or other financial institutions that serve as trustee of the account.[62] IRAs are tax exempt. As a result, income generated by the financial assets in the account is not taxed until the owner withdraws the income at retirement. In 2005, individuals can contribute up to $4,000 to their IRAs, and those who have reached age 50 by the end of the year can make an additional $500 *catch-up* contribution.[63] The annual contribution is generally limited to 100 percent of the individual's compensation\ self-employment income. For married couples filing jointly, this limit is based on their combined compensation/self-employment income.[64]

IRA Contributions

In 2005, Mr. Gupta (age 53 and single) earned a $64,300 salary and contributed the $4,500 maximum to his IRA. Mr. Swazer (age 26 and single) earned $2,810 self-employment income and contributed the $2,810 maximum to his IRA. Mr. Rollin (age 35) earned a $38,500 salary, and Mrs. Rollin (age 30) earned $2,400 wages from her part-time job. Because the Rollins file a joint return and their combined compensation is over $8,000, they each could contribute the $4,000 maximum to their IRAs.

Deduction of IRA Contributions

IRA contributions may be fully deductible in the computation of AGI, nondeductible, or partially deductible. If the individual making the contribution is an *active participant* in any other qualified retirement plan (an employer-provided or Keogh plan), the above-the-line deduction is computed by reference to AGI before the deduction. The 2005 computational rules can be summarized as follows.[65]

If AGI is less than:
$70,000 (Married filing jointly) $50,000 (Single or head of household) **IRA contributions are fully deductible**
If AGI is more than:
$80,000 (Married filing jointly) $10,000 (Married filing separately)[66] $60,000 (Single or head of household) **IRA contributions are nondeductible**

[62] §408 contains the qualification requirements for IRAs.

[63] §219(a). The contribution limit is $4,000 for 2005 through 2007 and $5,000 for 2008. After 2008, the $5,000 limit will be adjusted annually for inflation in $500 increments. The annual catch-up contribution will increase to $1,000 beginning in 2006. §219(b)(5).

[64] §219(c).

[65] §219(g). The AGI thresholds in these rules are scheduled to increase every year through 2007.

[66] Married individuals filing separate returns who live apart at all times during the year are considered single taxpayers under the IRA rules. §219(g)(4).

If AGI is between:
$70,000 and $80,000 (Married filing jointly) –0– and $10,000 (Married filing separately) $50,000 and $60,000 (Single or head of household) **IRA contributions are partially deductible. The deduction is phased out proportionally as AGI increases through the $10,000 phaseout range.**

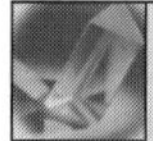

Phaseout of Deduction for IRA Contribution

In 2005, Mr. and Mrs. Howard each made the $4,000 maximum contribution to their IRAs. Both spouses are active participants in their respective employer's profit-sharing plan. Before any deduction for their IRA contributions, the AGI on their joint return is $76,900. Because this AGI falls in the phaseout range, their IRA contributions are partially deductible.

AGI before IRA deduction	$76,900
Phaseout threshold for married filing jointly	(70,000)
AGI in phaseout range	$ 6,900

$6,900 ÷ $10,000 = .69 phaseout percentage

Each spouse's IRA contribution	$4,000
	.69
Deduction phaseout	$2,760

Consequently, Mr. and Mrs. Howard can deduct $1,230 of each IRA contribution, and their AGI is $68,440.

AGI before IRA deduction		$76,900
Each spouse's IRA contribution	$4,000	
Deduction phaseout	(2,760)	
Deductible contribution	$1,240	
	2	
IRA deduction		(2,480)
AGI		$74,420

IRA Deduction for Nonparticipants

If an individual who contributes to an IRA is *not* an active participant in any other qualified retirement plan, the contribution is fully deductible, subject to one major exception. If that individual's *spouse* on a joint return is an active participant in another plan, the individual's deduction is phased out proportionally as AGI increases through a $10,000 phaseout range that begins at $150,000.[67]

[67] §219(g) (7).

IRA Deduction for a Nonparticipant Spouse

In 2005, Mr. and Mrs. Dowd (both age 60) each make the $4,500 maximum contribution to an IRA. Mr. Dowd is an active participant in a Keogh plan, but Mrs. Dowd is not an active participant in any other qualified plan. The couple files a joint return.

- If their AGI is $42,000 before any IRA deduction, it is below the phase-out range for married individuals filing jointly. Consequently, each spouse's contribution is fully deductible, and their AGI is $33,000 ($42,000 − $9,000 IRA deduction).
- If their AGI is $92,000 before any IRA deduction, it is above the phaseout range for married individuals filing jointly. Therefore, Mr. Dowd's contribution is nondeductible because he is an active participant. Mrs. Dowd's contribution is fully deductible because she is not an active participant. Their AGI is $87,500 ($92,000 − $4,500 IRA deduction).
- If their AGI is $200,000 before any IRA deduction, it is above the phaseout range for married individuals with a spouse who is an active participant. Consequently, neither spouse's contribution is deductible, and their AGI is $200,000.

Withdrawals from IRAs

High-income individuals who are active participants in other qualified plans can't deduct their IRA contributions. Such individuals invest in IRAs to take advantage of the tax deferral on the earnings generated by the account. When a person retires and begins to withdraw funds from an IRA, any portion of the withdrawal attributable to nondeductible contributions is a nontaxable return of investment rather than tax-deferred income. The nontaxable withdrawal is based on the ratio of the person's unrecovered investment at the beginning of the year to the current year value of the IRA. The *current year value* is defined as the year-end IRA balance *plus* current year withdrawals.[68]

IRA Withdrawals

Mr. Potter owns an IRA to which he made $44,000 of contributions, $19,000 of which were nondeductible. In 2004, Mr. Potter retired at age 63 and made a $15,000 withdrawal from his IRA. The account balance at year-end was $73,220. In 2005, he withdrew $17,500 from the IRA. The account balance at year-end was $60,200. (Note that the IRA continued to earn tax-exempt income during both years.) The yearly withdrawals that Mr. Potter must recognize as taxable income are computed as follows.

		2004		2005
Year-end balance in IRA		$73,220		$60,200
Plus withdrawals during the year		15,000		17,500
Current year value of IRA		$88,220		$77,700
Nondeductible contributions	$19,000		$19,000	
Prior year recoveries	(–0–)		(3,231)	
Unrecovered investment	$19,000		$15,769	
Ratio of unrecovered investment to current year value	.2154		.2029	
Withdrawal during the year		$15,000		$17,500
		.2154		.2029
Nontaxable recovery of investment		$ 3,231		$ 3,551
Taxable income: (Withdrawal − nontaxable recovery)		$11,769		$13,949

[68] §408(d).

As Mr. Potter continues to withdraw funds from his IRA, he will treat a portion of each withdrawal as a nontaxable return of investment. By the time he completely liquidates the account, he will have recouped his $19,000 nondeductible contributions on a tax-free basis.

As a general rule, owners who make withdrawals from their IRAs before reaching age 59½ must pay the 10 percent penalty described earlier in the chapter. However, this penalty is waived in a number of situations. For instance, an individual can withdraw funds from an IRA to pay higher education expenses (tuition, fees, books, supplies, and equipment). An individual who qualifies as a "first-time homebuyer" can withdraw up to $10,000 to finance the acquisition of a home. While some or all of the withdrawal must be included in the owner's taxable income, the taxable portion escapes the premature withdrawal penalty.[69]

Roth IRAs

The Tax Reform Act of 1997 created a new type of savings vehicle labeled a **Roth IRA** (named for Senator William V. Roth, Jr., who championed the legislation in Congress).[70] Basically, a Roth IRA works like a regular IRA with two major differences. First, contributions to a Roth IRA are nondeductible in every case. Second, *qualified* withdrawals from a Roth IRA are completely tax free. To qualify, a withdrawal must be made:

- On or after the date on which the owner reaches age 59½ (or after the owner's death or permanent disability) or
- To finance the acquisition of a home by a first-time homebuyer (subject to the $10,000 maximum).

In addition, a qualified withdrawal must occur after the five-year period beginning with the year in which the owner made the initial contribution to the Roth IRA.

This tax-favored investment is not available to everyone. The maximum annual contribution to a Roth IRA is reduced proportionally over an AGI phaseout range. For married individuals filing jointly, the $10,000 phaseout range is between $150,000 and $160,000 AGI. For married individuals filing separately, the $15,000 phaseout range is between zero and $15,000 AGI.[71] For single individuals or heads of household, the $15,000 phaseout range is between $95,000 and $110,000 AGI.

Roth IRA

Mr. Tran (age 52 and single) wants to make a contribution to a Roth IRA. Because his AGI is $101,670, the amount of his contribution is limited to $2,497.

AGI	$101,670
Phaseout threshold (single)	(95,000)
AGI in phaseout range	$ 6,670

$6,670 ÷ $15,000 = .445 phaseout percentage

Maximum contribution	$4,500
	.445
contribution phaseout	$2,003
Limited contribution ($4,500 - $2,003)	$2,497

Alternatively, Mr. Tran could make a $4,500 nondeductible contribution to a regular IRA.

69 §72(t)(2)(E) and (F).

70 §408A contains the tax rules governing Roth IRAs.

71 §See footnote 65.

Individuals who are eligible to make deductible contributions to a regular IRA or nondeductible contributions to a Roth IRA must determine which investment vehicle will maximize their after-tax retirement income. The comparison of these investment options is complicated and requires assumptions about the individual's tax situation at retirement. However, individuals who cannot make *deductible* contributions to a regular IRA should always contribute to a Roth IRA to take advantage of the tax-exempt (rather than tax-deferred) earnings.

Conclusion

In Chapter 14, we've explored the tax consequences of compensation arrangements between employer and employee. These arrangements can consist of a mix of cash payments and noncash fringe benefits, many of which are excluded from the recipient's income. Corporate employers frequently include stock options and ISOs in the compensation packages offered to key employees. By understanding both the economic implications and the tax consequences of the various forms of compensation, employers and employees can negotiate to improve their respective after-tax positions.

No area of the tax law offers a better opportunity for effective long-term planning than qualified retirement plans. The tax deferral available through these plans is one of the surest routes toward wealth maximization. Young adults who are just beginning their careers should take immediate advantage of any pension or profit-sharing plans sponsored by their employers. Entrepreneurs who own their own businesses should consider making regular contributions to a qualified Keogh plan. And every working person, regardless of age, who can afford to save even a few dollars each year toward retirement should consider an IRA.[72]

[72] In 2001, Congress enacted still another inducement for individuals to save for retirement: a nonrefundable tax credit for low- and middle-income taxpayers. The credit equals a percentage of the taxpayer's *elective* contributions to a qualified retirement plan (including a Section 401(k) plan or an IRA). The maximum annual contribution eligible for the credit is $2,000, and the maximum credit percentage is 50 percent. This credit is available through 2006. §25B.

Sources of Book/Tax Differences

Permanent

- Deduction for stock option exercise (no expense at date of grant)
- Nondeductible compensation

Temporary

- Deduction for stock option exercise (expense at date of grant)
- Nonqualified deferred compensation

Key Terms

bargain element *395*
cafeteria plan *393*
deferred compensation *405*
defined-benefit plan *403*
defined-contribution plan *403*
employee *384*
employee stock ownership plan (ESOP) *404*
employer-provided plan *402*
expatriate *390*
foreign earned income exclusion *390*
fringe benefits *391*
incentive stock option (ISO) *397*
independent contractor *384*
individual retirement account (IRA) *407*
Keogh plan *406*
minimum distribution *401*
miscellaneous itemized deductions *398*
moving expenses *399*
performance-based compensation *388*
premature withdrawal *401*
profit-sharing plan *404*
qualified retirement plans *400*
rollover contribution *401*
Roth IRA *410*
Section 401(k) plan *404*
stock option *395*

Questions and Problems for Discussion

1. Discuss how the presence of a strong labor union may change the nature of the market in which rank-and-file employees negotiate with their employer.
2. Discuss the difference in the relationship between an employer and employee and a client and an independent contractor.
3. Mr. U accepted an engagement to perform consulting services for MK Company. The engagement will last at least 18 months. Identify any reasons why Mr. U might prefer to be classified as an MK employee rather than as an independent contractor.
4. Discuss the practical reasons why the tax law authorizes the IRS to collect unwithheld employee payroll tax from the employer rather than the employees who were liable for the tax.
5. A reasonable compensation problem for the sole shareholder of a regular corporation is quite different from the reasonable compensation problem for the sole shareholder of an S corporation. What is the difference?
6. Mr. B owns 10 percent of the stock of ABC Inc. and is the corporation's director of marketing. ABC has a medical insurance plan for its employees. This year, it paid $1,400 of premiums to the insurance carrier for Mr. B's coverage. Contrast the treatment of this payment to Mr. B if ABC is a regular corporation or an S corporation.
7. This year, publicly held Corporation DF paid its CEO a $1.4 million salary, only $1 million of which was deductible. It also accrued a $200,000 liability for deferred compensation payable in the year 2013 (when the CEO must retire). To what extent does either transaction result in a difference between DF's book income and taxable income? Is the difference permanent or temporary?
8. Discuss how employees who routinely incur unreimbursed employment-related expenses can maximize the tax benefit of the expenses by bunching them into one year.
9. Mr. Z was recently promoted to an executive position by his corporate employer. The corporation now requires him to entertain clients much more frequently, and Mr. Z expects to incur at least $1,000 out-of-pocket business entertainment expenses each month. The corporation will either reimburse him directly for these expenses or give him a salary bonus at year-end that indirectly covers his annual expenses. Which option should Mr. Z choose and why?
10. Six years ago, Corporation AT granted a stock option to employee N to purchase 1,000 shares of AT stock for $15 per share. At date of grant, AT stock was selling for $14.10 per share. Over the last six years, the market price has steadily declined to $11.80 per share. What are the tax consequences to employee N when the option lapses?
11. Two years ago, Corporation WZ granted a stock option to employee R to purchase 2,500 shares of WZ stock for $30 per share. Since the date of grant, the market price of the stock has risen steadily and reached $31 just days ago. However, the option period is 10 years. Should R exercise the option immediately to minimize the income he must recognize or should he wait for eight more years before exercising the option?
12. Explain the basic difference between a defined-benefit plan and a defined-contribution plan.
13. How does the fact that employees have a vested right to their benefits reduce the risk of participating in an employer-sponsored qualified retirement plan?
14. How does the fact that an employer-sponsored qualified retirement plan is administered by an independent trustee reduce the employees' risk of participating in the plan?

Application Problems

For the following problems, assume the taxable year is 2005.

1. Trent Inc. needs an additional worker on a multiyear project. It could hire an employee for a $50,000 annual salary. Alternatively, it could engage an independent contractor for a $53,000 annual fee. On the assumption that Trent's marginal income tax rate is 35 percent, which option minimizes the after-tax cost of obtaining the worker?
2. DPO, a publicly held corporation with a 35 percent marginal tax rate, is negotiating a compensation package with its CEO. In each of the following cases, determine DPO's after-tax cost of the compensation. In making your calculation, ignore the employer payroll tax.
   a. DPO will pay its CEO an annual salary of $1.5 million.
   b. DPO will pay its CEO an annual salary of $900,000 plus a $750,000 year-end bonus if its gross revenues increase by at least 5 percent during the year. This bonus qualifies as performance-based compensation.
3. Mr. and Mrs. Soon are the sole shareholders of SW Inc. For the last three years, SW has employed their son as a sales representative and paid him a $30,000 annual salary. During a recent IRS audit, the revenue agent discovered that the son has never made a sale and spends most of his time playing saxophone in a jazz band. Compute the potential tax cost of this discovery to Mr. and Mrs. Soon under the following assumptions. In making your calculations, ignore any payroll tax implications.
   a. Mr. and Mrs. Soon are in the 35 percent tax bracket, and SW is an S corporation.
   b. Mr. and Mrs. Soon are in the 35 percent tax bracket, and SW is a taxable corporation in the 35 percent tax bracket.
4. Mr. F is a U.S. citizen who has been stationed at his employer's Tokyo office for the last six years.
   a. Compute Mr. F's AGI if his only item of income was his $65,000 salary.
   b. Compute Mr. F's AGI if his only item of income for the year was his $122,500 salary.
   c. Under Japanese law, Mr. F is a permanent resident and must pay Japanese income tax on his salary. Assuming that the Japanese individual tax rates exceed the U.S. rates, will Mr. F owe U.S. tax on any portion of his salary?
5. Mrs. O, age 61, participates in the group-term life insurance plan sponsored by her corporate employer. According to Treasury tables, the cost of $1,000 of life insurance for a 61-year-old person is 66 cents per month. Determine the taxable income that Mrs. O must recognize assuming that:
   a. The plan provides $40,000 coverage to Mrs. O.
   b. The plan provides $300,000 coverage to Mrs. O.
6. Mrs. ST's corporate employer has a cafeteria plan under which its employees can receive a $3,000 year-end Christmas bonus or enroll in a qualified medical reimbursement plan that pays up to $3,000 of annual medical bills. Mrs. ST is in a 28 percent tax bracket, and her medical bills average $2,300 each year.
   a. Should Mrs. ST choose the cash bonus or the nontaxable fringe benefit? (Ignore any payroll tax implications.)
   b. Does your answer change if Mrs. ST is in the 15 percent tax bracket?
7. Mr. N and Mr. R are employed by HD Inc., which provides its employees with free parking. If the parking were not available, Mr. N would pay $35 a month to a city garage. Mr. R uses public transportation to commute. HD offers a complete family medical plan to its employees in which both Mr. N and Mr. R participate. Mr. N's family consists of five

Research Problems

1. Curtis Bedford, age 73, is a professor of English at a private university. He holds a tenured position, which represents a lifetime employment contract. The university has offered Curtis a $75,000 lump-sum payment if he will retire from the faculty. If Curtis accepts the payment, he must give up any legal claim against the university for age discrimination and must forfeit all of his privileges as a faculty member. If Curtis accepts the university's offer, will the $75,000 payment represent compensation that is subject to employer and employee payroll (Social Security and Medicare) tax?
2. Helene Toolson, age 67, is an avid collector of historical documents and signatures. Her collection is worth over $300,000 and, by any measure, is an excellent investment. Helene also owns an IRA with First State Bank. She recently learned that a letter written by Thomas Jefferson was available for purchase out of a private collection. As a result, she met with a bank vice president to discuss having her IRA acquire the letter. The vice president determined that state banking laws would not prohibit such an acquisition by an IRA. The asking price of the letter is $32,500. Would the purchase of the letter by her IRA have any adverse tax consequence to Helene?
3. Marion Kline was recently elected mayor of a large Midwestern city that furnishes its mayor with an official residence for occupancy during the term of office. The residence (house and gardens) is owned and maintained by the city, and the mayor does not pay any rent. Marion and her family are required to live in the residence so that she can carry out the many social and ceremonial obligations of her office. Many of these obligations occur in the evenings and on weekends. The fair rental value of the mayoral residence is $60,000 annually. Must Marion recognize the value of her employer-provided housing as taxable compensation?
4. Early this year, Scott Lowe, age 54, became dissatisfied with the service he was receiving from the broker who managed his IRA. He requested a distribution of the $48,200 balance in the account and received a check for this amount from the broker on May 23. Scott planned to roll the distribution over into a new IRA with a different broker. Before he could do so, he received news that his son-in-law had died in a hunting accident. Scott immediately traveled to his daughter's home to console her and his grandchildren. During this period of trauma and confusion, Scott wrote a check for $48,200 to his new broker but failed to instruct the broker to put the money into an IRA. Instead, the broker invested it in a taxable money market account. Scott and his broker did not discover the mistake until late December. Must Scott include the $48,200 withdrawal in his gross income and pay a $4,820 premature withdrawal penalty?

Tax Planning Cases

1. This year, Mr. Joss (age 26 and in the 28 percent marginal tax bracket) accepted a job with BL Inc. He intends to work for only eight years, then start his own business. He has two options for accumulating the money he will need for this business.
   - *Option 1:* He is eligible to participate in BL's Section 401(k) plan and can afford to save $5,000 of his salary each year by diverting it to this plan. The plan earns 10 percent a year. Consequently, his plan balance in eight years will be $57,179 ($5,000 for eight years compounded at 10 percent).
   - *Option 2:* He can take his entire salary in cash, pay income tax, and save $3,600 ($5,000 less $1,400 tax) in an investment fund that earns 10 percent a year. Because the annual earnings are taxable, his savings in the fund will grow at only 7.2 percent a year. Consequently, his fund balance in eight years will be $37,202 ($3,600 for eight years compounded at 7.2 percent).

Assuming a constant 28 percent tax rate, which option results in the greatest after-tax cash for Mr. Joss to begin his business?

2. Mr. and Mrs. B, ages 64 and 65, are both retired and live on Social Security plus the interest and dividends from several investments. Their taxable income averages $25,000 a year. Mrs. B owns an IRA that she funded entirely with deductible contributions. The couple plans to withdraw $70,000 from the IRA to make some much needed improvements to their home. How should they time the withdrawal (or series of withdrawals) to maximize the cash available from the IRA?
3. Mr. RS is entitled to a $5,200 bonus this year (year 0). His employer gives him two options. He can either receive his $5,200 bonus in cash, or the employer will credit him with $4,500 deferred compensation. Under the deferral option, the employer will accrue 6 percent annual interest on the deferred compensation. Consequently, the employer will pay $8,059 ($4,500 plus compounded interest) to Mr. RS when he retires in year 10. Which option has the greater NPV under each of the following assumptions? In making your calculations, use a 5 percent discount rate.
   a. Mr. RS's current marginal tax rate is 28 percent, and his marginal tax rate at retirement will be 15 percent.
   b. Mr. RS's current marginal tax rate is 28 percent, and his marginal tax rate at retirement will be 28 percent.

Chapter Fifteen

Investment and Personal Financial Planning

Learning Objectives

After studying this chapter, you should be able to:

1. Determine the tax consequences of interest and dividend income.
2. Explain how life insurance policies and annuity contracts defer taxable income.
3. Compute gain or loss recognized on security transactions.
4. Compute the tax on short-term and long-term capital gains.
5. Describe the tax benefit of qualified small business stock and Section 1244 stock.
6. Determine the deduction for investment interest expense.
7. Apply the passive activity loss limitation.
8. Compute a taxable gift by applying the annual and lifetime exclusions.
9. Determine a decedent's taxable estate.

Chapter 15 focuses on the tax consequences of investment activities involving the acquisition, holding, and disposition of income-producing property. Individuals engage in investment activities expecting them to be profitable. In financial terms, they expect the investment to yield a positive return on capital. This return can take the form of current income (and cash flow) generated by the property or appreciation in the property's value. This chapter explores the tax consequences of both types of returns. Of course, not every investment is profitable, and Chapter 15 also deals with the tax consequences of investment losses.

Many individuals who accumulate significant wealth through their business and investment activities want their children and grandchildren to benefit from their good fortune. These individuals must develop personal financial planning strategies to achieve this goal in the most cost-effective manner. In the final section of this chapter, we will discover that the federal gift and estate taxes are serious impediments in this planning process. However, we will also consider some basic techniques by which people can minimize these taxes and maximize the wealth available to their younger-generation family members.

BUSINESS VERSUS INVESTMENT ACTIVITIES

The tax consequences of investment activities can be very different from the tax consequences of business activities. Individuals engage in the two types of activities for the same purpose: to make a profit. The distinction between business and investment activities lies in the extent of the individual's personal involvement in the activity. An individual engaging in a business activity commits time and talent to the activity on a regular basis, and the business profit is partially attributable to this personal involvement.[1] In contrast, an individual engaging in an investment activity takes a passive role as the owner of income-producing property. The profit from the activity is primarily attributable to the invested capital rather than to the owner's personal involvement. For tax purposes, this distinction holds true even when individuals devote substantial time to managing income-producing property. "A taxpayer who merely manages his investments seeking long-term gain is not carrying on a trade or business. This is so irrespective of the extent or continuity of the transactions or the work required in managing the portfolio."[2]

INVESTMENTS IN FINANCIAL ASSETS

Financial assets are legal claims on the real assets owned by a business entity or other organization. Financial assets include equity interests such as common and preferred corporate stock and creditor interests such as savings accounts, certificates of deposit, notes, bonds, and other debt instruments. These types of financial assets are commonly referred to as **securities.** Financial assets are intangible property rights. They have no intrinsic value; their worth depends on the underlying value of the real assets subject to their claim. Financial assets may be publicly traded on an established market or may be privately placed.

Individuals who invest in financial assets can own the assets directly or indirectly through a mutual fund. A **mutual fund** is a diversified portfolio of securities owned and managed by *a regulated investment company (RIC)*. RICs sell shares in their funds to the public—specifically to purchasers wanting to diversify their financial holdings and take advantage of the professional expertise of the fund managers. A mutual fund portfolio can consist of equity stocks, debt instruments, or a combination of both, depending on the investment objectives of the particular fund. Currently, more than 80 million people, or one out of two households in America, hold over $7 trillion of financial assets in mutual funds, making them the most popular investment vehicle on the market.

Dividend and Interest Income

Objective 1
Determine the tax consequences of interest and dividend income.

Individuals who invest in securities usually expect a return on their investment in the form of dividends or interest. As cash basis taxpayers, individuals recognize dividend or interest income in the year in which they actually or constructively receive payment. Investors in stocks and mutual funds often have a dividend reinvestment option under which their dividends are used to purchase additional shares for their account. Even though shareholders who elect this option receive no cash payments, they are in constructive receipt of the dividends reinvested on their behalf.

[1] In capital-intensive businesses, profit is attributable to the assets as well as to the personal involvement of the business owners.

[2] *Moller* v. *United States,* 721 F.2d 810, 814 (CA FC, 1983).

Historically, individual investors recognized both dividends and interest as ordinary income taxed at the regular rates. However, the Jobs and Growth Tax Relief Reconciliation Act of 2003 created a new 15 percent preferential tax rate for qualified dividend income earned by noncorporate (individual) shareholders. The preferential rate drops to 5 percent for any qualified dividend income that would be taxed at 15 percent or less under the regular rate structure. **Qualified dividend income** is broadly defined as dividends received from taxable domestic corporations and certain qualified foreign corporations.[3]

Organizations that pay dividends or interest issue annual Forms 1099-DIV (Dividends and Distributions) and Forms 1099-INT (Interest Income) to inform investors of their total payments for the year. The IRS receives copies of these forms and cross-checks to make sure that the payment reported on each form matches the income reported on Schedule B of the investor's Form 1040. Investors must pay careful attention to the detailed information on their Form 1099s to determine the correct tax treatment of their payments. For example, corporations occasionally make cash distributions to their shareholders that are tax-free returns of capital rather than taxable dividends. These distributions, which are identified on Form 1099, are not included in the recipient's gross income but instead reduce the recipient's tax basis in the corporate stock.

Corporate Distributions

Rocko Inc., a New York corporation, distributed $935,700 cash to its shareholders this year. Rocko's tax department determined that only $894,100 (95.55 percent) of the distribution was a dividend paid from corporate earnings. The $41,600 remainder was a return of corporate capital.

Mr. Jude Isley received a $44,800 cash distribution from Rocko. According to his Form 1099, only $42,806 (95.55 percent) of his distribution was qualified dividend income, while the $1,994 remainder was a nontaxable reduction in the basis of Mr. Isley's Rocko stock.

Dividend distributions from mutual funds actually represent a flow through of the various types of income generated by the fund's investment portfolio. Consequently, a mutual fund dividend could include a **capital gain distribution** of the net long-term capital gain recognized by the fund on sales of securities. It could also include a **qualified dividend distribution** of the dividends generated by the fund's portfolio of equities. Form 1099s issued by mutual funds must report any capital gain and qualified dividend distributions for the year so that individual investors can benefit from the preferential rates on these types of income.

Mutual Fund Dividend

Stargaze Mutual Fund manages a diversified portfolio consisting of 60 percent stock in taxable domestic corporations, 35 percent corporate bonds, and 5 percent cash. This year, Stargaze received $8 million of dividends and $3.6 million of interest and recognized a $1.9 million net long-term capital gain on security sales. Stargaze distributed a $13.5 million cash dividend to its investors that consisted of an $8 million qualified dividend distribution, a $3.6 ordinary dividend, and a $1.9 million capital gain distribution.

Ms. Cindy Jung received a $9,930 cash distribution from Stargaze. According to her Form 1099, $5,884 was a qualified dividend distribution, $2,648 was an ordinary dividend, and $1,398 was a capital gain distribution.

[3] §1(h)(3)(B) and (h)(11).

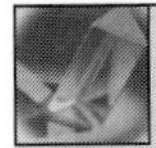

Mr. and Mrs. David: Schedule B

Mr. and Mrs. David, who file a joint return, own a $75,000 certificate of deposit with Second Union Bank and a $100,000 bond issued by Tryton Inc. This year, they earned $4,712 interest on the CD and $6,200 interest on the bond. Shortly after year-end, they received a Form 1099-INT from each payor on which their annual interest income was reported. They entered this information on Part I of their Schedule B (shown as Exhibit 15.1). Their $10,912 total interest (line 4) was carried as an income item to page 1, Form 1040.

At the beginning of the year, Mr. and Mrs. David owned 5,122 shares of Prime Growth mutual fund. They elected to reinvest their annual dividends in additional Prime Growth shares. Consequently, they received no cash from the mutual fund during the year. Mr. and Mrs. David received a Form 1099-DIV from Prime Growth containing the following information.

Ordinary dividend	$ 2,316
Qualified dividend distribution	4,775
Capital gains distribution	5,383
Gross distribution	$12,474
Shares owned on January 1	5,122
Additional shares purchased for investor's account	
(198 shares at $63 per share = $12,474)	198
Shares owned on December 31	5,320

Mr. and Mrs. David also own 16,780 shares of Mortimer Industries common stock. At the beginning of the year, their cost basis in these shares was $59,000. During the year, they received cash distributions totaling $19,000 from Mortimer. Their Form 1099-DIV contained the following information.

Qualified dividend income	$17,980
Nontaxable distribution	1,020
Gross distribution	$19,000

Mr. and Mrs. David entered their ordinary dividends from Prime Growth and Mortimer on Part II, Schedule B. The capital gains distribution was reported on Schedule D for inclusion with their other capital gains and losses. The nontaxable distribution reduced the tax basis in the Mortimer stock to $57,980. Their $25,071 total ordinary dividends (line 6) was carried as an income item to page 1, Form 1040.

Tax-Exempt Interest

The public security markets offer thousands of financial assets that individuals can select to meet their particular investment needs. In making their selection, investors should consider their overall tax situation, as well as any preferential tax characteristics of the assets under consideration. One such characteristic is the tax-exempt status of interest on certain debt instruments.

State and Local Bonds

For federal tax purposes, interest income earned on investments in debt instruments issued by state and local governments, including the District of Columbia, is excluded from income.[4] The interest rate on these tax-exempt bonds is typically lower than the rate on tax-

[4] §103. This exclusion extends to any portion of a mutual fund dividend attributable to the fund's investment in tax-exempt bonds.

EXHIBIT 15.1

Schedules A&B (Form 1040) 2004 — OMB No. 1545-0074 — Page **2**

Name(s) shown on Form 1040. Do not enter name and social security number if shown on other side. Ronald and Janet David

Your social security number 498 : 31 : 1240

Schedule B—Interest and Ordinary Dividends

Attachment Sequence No. **08**

Part I Interest

(See page B-1 and the instructions for Form 1040, line 8a.)

Note. If you received a Form 1099-INT, Form 1099-OID, or substitute statement from a brokerage firm, list the firm's name as the payer and enter the total interest shown on that form.

			Amount
1	List name of payer. If any interest is from a seller-financed mortgage and the buyer used the property as a personal residence, see page B-1 and list this interest first. Also, show that buyer's social security number and address ▶		
	CD - Second Union Bank	1	4,712
	6.2% Tryton bonds		6,200
2	Add the amounts on line 1	2	10,912
3	Excludable interest on series EE and I U.S. savings bonds issued after 1989. Attach Form 8815	3	
4	Subtract line 3 from line 2. Enter the result here and on Form 1040, line 8a ▶	4	10,912

Note. If line 4 is over $1,500, you must complete Part III.

Part II Ordinary Dividends

(See page B-2 and the instructions for Form 1040, line 9a.)

Note. If you received a Form 1099-DIV or substitute statement from a brokerage firm, list the firm's name as the payer and enter the ordinary dividends shown on that form.

			Amount
5	List name of payer ▶		
	Prime Growth dividend	5	2,316
	Prime Growth qualified dividend		4,775
	Mortimer Ind. qualified dividend		17,980
6	Add the amounts on line 5. Enter the total here and on Form 1040, line 9a ▶	6	25,071

Note. If line 6 is over $1,500, you must complete Part III.

Part III Foreign Accounts and Trusts

(See page B-2.)

	You must complete this part if you **(a)** had over $1,500 of taxable interest or ordinary dividends; or **(b)** had a foreign account; or **(c)** received a distribution from, or were a grantor of, or a transferor to, a foreign trust.	Yes	No
7a	At any time during 2004, did you have an interest in or a signature or other authority over a financial account in a foreign country, such as a bank account, securities account, or other financial account? See page B-2 for exceptions and filing requirements for Form TD F 90-22.1		
b	If "Yes," enter the name of the foreign country ▶		
8	During 2004, did you receive a distribution from, or were you the grantor of, or transferor to, a foreign trust? If "Yes," you may have to file Form 3520. See page B-2		

For Paperwork Reduction Act Notice, see Form 1040 instructions. **Schedule B (Form 1040) 2004**

able bonds with a comparable degree of risk; investors who purchase tax-exempt bonds pay an implicit tax equal to this rate differential.[5] Moreover, state and local bond interest may be taxed by the state or locality in which the investor resides. Finally, the interest on tax-exempt **private activity bonds** issued by any state or local government after August 7, 1986, is a preference item for alternative minimum tax (AMT) purposes.[6] Because of these

[5] See the discussion of implicit tax in Chapter 4.

[6] §57(a)(5). The proceeds from private activity bonds are used for nongovernmental purposes, such as industrial development.

variables, even individuals in high marginal tax brackets can't assume that they will benefit by buying tax-exempt bonds until they evaluate the investment on an after-tax basis.

U.S. Debt Obligations

The U.S. government issues a variety of debt instruments for investors. Treasury bills are issued on a discount basis and are payable at a fixed maturity date not exceeding one year from date of issue. Treasury notes have maturity periods ranging from 2 to 10 years, while Treasury bonds have maturity periods in excess of 10 years. Both are issued at face value and bear a stated rate of interest, payable at six-month intervals. **Series EE savings bonds** are long-term debt instruments issued at a discount. The interest on all these debt instruments is subject to federal income tax. However, the interest is completely exempt from income tax levied by any state or local government. Because state and local tax rates are generally much lower than federal rates, exemption from such taxes may result in only a modest benefit. Nonetheless, investors should be aware of this preferential tax characteristic of U.S. debt obligations.

Deferred Interest Income

The tax law offers investors a few narrow opportunities to defer the recognition of interest income. For instance, cash basis taxpayers who purchase short-term debt obligations at a discount do not recognize income until the obligation matures.[7]

Interest Deferral

In July 2004, Mrs. Webb bought a $50,000 U.S. Treasury bill for $48,900; the bill matured 26 weeks after date of issue. She reported no 2004 income from this investment, even though most of the interest on the bill accrued in 2004. When Mrs. Webb redeemed the bill in January 2005 for $50,000, she recognized the entire $1,100 interest income.

Individuals can achieve the same type of deferral if they purchase Series EE savings bonds. Even though these discount bonds may have maturity periods of 10 years or longer, individuals postpone recognition of any interest income until they cash in the bonds. In the unusual case in which an investor prefers to take the discount into annual income on an accrual basis, he may elect to do so by reporting the accrued interest on Schedule B.

Market Discount

Cash basis investors who purchase bonds *in a market transaction* at a price lower than the bond's stated redemption value at maturity are not required to accrue the **market discount** as interest income over the life of the bond.[8] Instead, they recognize the discount as interest in the future year in which they sell the bond or the bond is redeemed.[9]

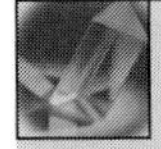

Deferral of Market Discount

Mr. Barry bought a publicly traded corporate bond through his broker for $21,300. Although the bond is redeemable at maturity for $25,000, it traded at a discounted price because the stated interest rate (6 percent) was below the market rate (8 percent). Mr. Barry will include the 6 percent interest payments in his annual income but will not include any portion of the market discount. If he holds the bond until maturity, Mr. Barry will recognize the entire

[7] See §454 and §1271(a)(3) and (4). Short-term debt obligations have fixed maturity periods of one year or less.

[8] §1278(a). However, investors may elect to do so under §1278(b).

[9] This recognition rule extends to any market discount on state and local bonds. While the periodic interest payments on these bonds are tax exempt, the accrued discount is fully taxable as ordinary income.

$3,700 excess of the $25,000 redemption proceeds over his $21,300 cost basis as ordinary income in the year of redemption.[10]

Original Issue Discount

Investors who purchase *newly issued* corporate debt instruments at a discount can't defer recognition of the interest income represented by the original issue discount. **Original issue discount (OID)** equals the excess of the bond's stated redemption value at maturity (face value) over the issue price. Even cash basis investors must recognize accrued income by amortizing this discount over the life of the bond.[11]

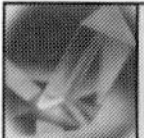

Amortization of OID

Jacks Inc. made a new public offering of 15-year bonds with a stated interest rate of only 1.5 percent of face value. Mr. Barry, our investor in the previous example, bought $50,000 of these bonds for their discounted issue price of $27,000. Mr. Barry's return on his investment consists of the $750 yearly interest payments *plus* the $23,000 difference between his cost and the cash he will collect when the bonds mature. Every year, Jacks sends Mr. Barry the following.

- Form 1099-INT reporting the $750 interest payment.
- Form 1099-OID reporting the amortized discount he must recognize as additional interest income.[12]

Over the 15-year term of the bonds, Mr. Barry will recognize $23,000 OID income with no corresponding cash flow. However, he will not recognize any additional income when he redeems the bonds at maturity for $50,000.

Life Insurance Policies and Annuity Contracts

Life Insurance Policies

Objective 2
Explain how life insurance policies and annuity contracts defer taxable income.

A life insurance policy is a legal contract between a purchaser (the owner) and a commercial insurance company. The owner pays a premium or series of premiums for the company's commitment to pay a specific sum of money (death benefit) on the death of the person whose life is insured. The owner has the right to name the beneficiary (the person or organization that will receive the death benefit). An individual purchases insurance on his or her own life primarily to provide financial protection for dependent family members. However, many life insurance contracts offer both protection against premature death and an investment element. The investment element is called the **cash surrender value,** which increases every year that the policy remains in effect. The owner does not recognize this annual increase in value, called the **inside buildup,** as taxable income. If the owner eventually decides that his family no longer needs insurance protection, he may liquidate the policy for its cash surrender value. In this case, the owner recognizes the *excess* cash surrender value over his investment in the policy (total premiums paid) as ordinary income.[13]

[10] While the tax law permits Mr. Barry to defer the recognition of the discount, this discount is not converted to capital gain. See §1276.

[11] §1272(a). This income recognition rule does not apply to tax-exempt state and local obligations.

[12] The annual OID income on debt instruments issued after July 1, 1992, is based on the instrument's constant yield to maturity. §1272(a)(3). This calculation results in increasing annual OID income over the life of the instrument. Corporations may take an annual interest deduction for amortized OID. §163(e)(1).

[13] §72(e)(2).

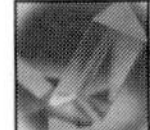

Liquidation of Life Insurance Policy

Twenty years ago, Mr. Wilde purchased an insurance policy on his own life. The policy provided a $350,000 death benefit payable to Mr. Wilde's wife and children. To date, Mr. Wilde has paid $38,000 of premiums. Because his wife predeceased him and his children are financially independent, Mr. Wilde liquidated the policy for its $42,800 cash surrender value. The insurance company sent Mr. Wilde a Form 1099-R reporting $4,800 ordinary income ($42,800 − $38,000 aggregate premiums).[14]

The deferral of tax on the inside buildup certainly makes life insurance contracts a tax-preferred investment. The tax consequences are even more favorable if the policy is held until it matures on the death of the insured. In this case, the beneficiary excludes the death benefit from income, and the accumulated return on the owner's investment in the life insurance contract escapes tax entirely.[15]

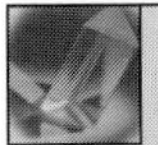

Life Insurance Proceeds

Twenty years ago, Mrs. Muzo purchased an insurance policy on her own life. The policy provided a $350,000 death benefit payable to Mrs. Muzo's children. Mrs. Muzo paid $38,000 of premiums, and the policy's cash surrender value was $42,800. Mrs. Muzo died on May 4 with the policy still in effect. On September 3, her children received $350,000 from the insurance company and excluded the entire payment from their taxable income.

This highly advantageous tax treatment also applies to **accelerated death benefits:** payments made under the contract to insured individuals who are terminally or chronically ill.[16] Such individuals may be forced to draw against or even liquidate their life insurance policies to pay medical expenses resulting from an extended illness. The tax law alleviates this financial hardship by classifying these premature payments as nontaxable death benefits.

Annuity Contracts

Individuals purchase annuity contracts from commercial insurance companies to provide themselves with a fixed stream of income for a future period of time. The owner pays a premium or series of premiums that the insurance company invests on the owner's behalf. The owner is not taxed on the yearly inside buildup in the value of her investment. Instead, tax is deferred until the owner begins receiving periodic payments under the contract. The portion of each annuity payment representing a distribution of accumulated earnings is taxed as ordinary income, while the portion representing a return of the owner's investment is nontaxable.

Annuity Payments

Mrs. Water purchased an annuity for a $75,000 single premium when she was 51 years old. This year, Mrs. Water reached age 65 and began receiving annuity payments. Under the terms of her contract, she will receive $1,100 per month for the rest of her life. The portion of each payment representing a return of her investment is based on the ratio of that investment to the expected return under the contract.[17] Based on life expectancy tables provided in Treasury regulations, Mrs. Water can expect to receive 240 payments ($264,000). Consequently, her exclusion ratio is 28.41 percent.

[14] Form 1099-R reports distributions from insurance contracts, annuities, and pension, profit sharing, IRA and other retirement plans.

[15] §101.

[16] §101(g). Accelerated death benefits include the proceeds of the sale or assignment of a contract to a *viatical settlement provider,* which is a company licensed to engage in the business of purchasing life insurance contracts from the terminally or chronically ill.

[17] §72(b)(1).

$$\frac{\$75{,}000 \text{ investment (single premium)}}{\$264{,}000 \text{ expected return}} = .2841$$

Mrs. Water received eight monthly payments totaling $8,800 this year, and her nontaxable return of investment is $2,500.

Total annuity payments received	$8,800
Exclusion ratio	.2841
	$2,500

Mrs. Water must recognize the remaining $6,300 of the total payments as ordinary income.

Each year Mrs. Water will apply the exclusion ratio to determine the nontaxable portion of her total payments until she recovers her entire $75,000 investment. Any additional payments will be fully taxable.[18] If Mrs. Water dies before recovering her investment, the unrecovered portion is allowed as an itemized deduction on her final Form 1040.[19]

Nontax Considerations

People buy life insurance policies to protect against dying too soon and annuity contracts to protect against living too long. In addition to their protection element, both assets offer a tax-deferred financial return. However, life insurance policies and annuity contracts may have lower before-tax rates of return and higher transaction costs than investment opportunities that are not tax favored. For instance, life insurance policies have the highest commission charges of any financial product—typically more than 50 percent of the first-year premium paid by the investor. Annuity contracts routinely charge an annual fee and impose early-surrender charges on individuals who liquidate their investment in the contract before the annuity starting date. These nontax costs can overwhelm the benefit of tax deferral, particularly for individuals in the lower tax brackets or who aren't prepared to commit to these investments for the long haul.

GAINS AND LOSSES FROM SECURITY TRANSACTIONS

A key principle of federal tax law is that *unrealized* gains and losses are not taxed. Increases or decreases in the value of property over time are not recognized until an external transaction triggers gain or loss realization. Accordingly, individuals who invest in financial assets defer paying tax on any appreciation in value until they dispose of the assets in a taxable transaction. In this section of the chapter, we will examine the tax rules that apply to dispositions of securities. By paying attention to these rules, individuals can control their tax costs and enhance the after-tax return on such investments.

Computing Gains and Losses

Objective 3
Compute gain or loss recognized on security transactions.

Realized gain from the sale of securities equals the excess of the amount realized over the seller's basis in the securities. Realized loss equals the excess of basis over amount realized. Amount realized is the sum of any money plus the fair market value (FMV) of any property received by the seller. Investors who sell securities through a broker receive a Form 1099-B

[18] §72(b)(2).

[19] §72(b)(3) and §67(b)(10).

(Proceeds from Broker and Barter Exchange Transactions) reporting the gross sales price. If the investor incurred any selling expenses, such as brokerage fees and commissions, these expenses reduce the amount realized on sale. A seller's basis in a security depends on the transaction in which the security was acquired. Securities acquired by purchase have a cost basis including both the price of the securities plus any front-end fees or load charges.

Tracking Security Basis

Individuals should keep careful record of the initial cost of the securities in their investment portfolios and the effect of any subsequent transactions on such basis. For instance, if an investor elects to reinvest dividends in additional shares of stock or a mutual fund, the dividend becomes the cost basis in the new shares. If an investor receives a nontaxable distribution with respect to shares of stock, the basis in the shares must be reduced by this return of capital. Investors who own long-term debt instruments with original issue discount should increase their basis in the securities by the OID income accrued each year. Failure to keep track of these common basis adjustments results in overstatement or understatement of gain or loss realized on the eventual disposition of the securities.

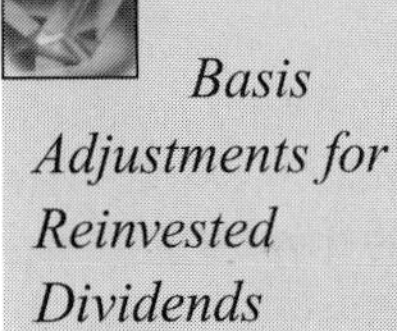

Basis Adjustments for Reinvested Dividends

Nine years ago, Ms. Farley paid $25,000 for 3,400 shares of Fastrack mutual fund. She elected to reinvest her dividends in additional shares. As of June 4, Ms. Farley had recognized $19,100 dividend income (without any corresponding cash flow) and acquired 2,816 additional shares. On June 4, she sold all 6,216 shares for $58,000. Her realized gain is computed as follows.

Amount realized on sale		$ 58,000
Adjusted basis:		
Cost of 3,400 shares	$25,000	
Cost of 2,816 shares (reinvested dividends)	19,100	
		(44,100)
Gain realized on sale		$ 13,900

Identifying Basis on Sale

When an investor sells a specific security with an identifiable basis, gain or loss is determined with reference to such basis. However, investment portfolios often contain identical securities acquired at different times and for different prices. If the investor sells some of the securities but can't identify which specific ones were sold, the basis is determined by a first-in, first-out (FIFO) method.[20] In other words, the investor is presumed to have sold the securities with the earliest acquisition date. Individuals who sell mutual fund shares can also use an average basis method for calculating gain or loss. Under the simplest version of this method, the basis of each mutual fund share equals the aggregate basis of all shares divided by the total number of shares.

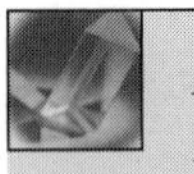

Average Basis Method

At the beginning of the year, Mr. Yao owned 1,000 shares of TNT Mutual Fund with a $52,000 aggregate basis. Every month, he invested $1,000 in the fund. Because of fluctuations in the market price of TNT shares, he acquired a different number of shares with a

[20] Reg. §1.1012-1(c).

different cost basis each month. By September, Mr. Yao owned 1,155 shares with a $60,000 aggregate basis. On September 9, he sold 300 shares for $56 per share ($16,800 total price). He can determine his basis in the 300 shares as follows.

$60,000 aggregate basis ÷ 1,155 shares = $51.948 basis per share

300 shares sold × $51.948 basis per share = $15,584

Consequently, Mr. Yao's gain on sale is $1,216 ($16,800 amount realized − $15,584 basis), and his aggregate basis in his 855 remaining shares is $44,416 ($60,000 − $15,584).

Worthless Securities and Nonbusiness Bad Debts

Securities are capital assets in the hands of individual investors. Therefore, gains and losses realized on security sales are capital gains and losses subject to the special tax rules presented in the next section of the chapter. According to the general statutory definition, capital gains and losses result from the sale or exchange of capital assets.[21] The Internal Revenue Code provides that two other events result in capital loss. If an individual owns a security that becomes worthless, the event is treated as if the individual sold the security on the last day of the year for an amount realized of zero.[22] In other words, the individual recognizes his unrecovered basis in the security as a capital loss. The second event occurs when an individual who loaned money to another party determines that the debt is uncollectible. In such case, the individual recognizes the unpaid balance of the **nonbusiness bad debt** as a capital loss.[23]

Nonbusiness Bad Debt

Two years ago, Mr. Jared loaned $25,000 to PT Partnership in exchange for PT's interest-bearing note. PT has repaid $9,000 of the debt. However, Mr. Jared recently learned that PT is hopelessly insolvent and cannot pay any of its creditors. He can recognize his $16,000 nonbusiness bad debt as a capital loss.

Nontaxable Exchanges of Securities

As a general rule, the exchange of one security for another security is a taxable event. For instance, if an investor exchanges stock in Corporation A for a long-term bond issued by Corporation Z, the investor recognizes the difference between his amount realized (FMV of the bond) and the basis of the stock as capital gain or loss. The tax law does contain several nontaxable exchange provisions applying to security transactions. No gain or loss is recognized on the exchange of one class of common stock for a different class of common stock *in the same corporation.* Similarly, preferred stock can be exchanged for preferred stock *in the same corporation* at no current tax cost.[24] If an investor exchanges stock or securities in one corporation for stock or securities in a different corporation, no gain or loss is recognized only if the exchange is pursuant to a **reorganization** involving the two corporations.[25]

[21] §1222.

[22] §165(g).

[23] §166(d). If an individual lends money or extends credit *as part of his business,* any resulting bad debt is a deductible business expense.

[24] §1036.

[25] Reorganizations are a set of very precisely defined transactions in which one corporation acquires another, one corporation divides into two corporations, or one corporation changes its capital structure. Reorganizations are defined in §368.

In each of these nontaxable exchanges, the investor's basis in his newly acquired security equals the basis of the security surrendered. Because of this substituted basis rule, gain or loss realized on the exchange is merely deferred, not eliminated.[26]

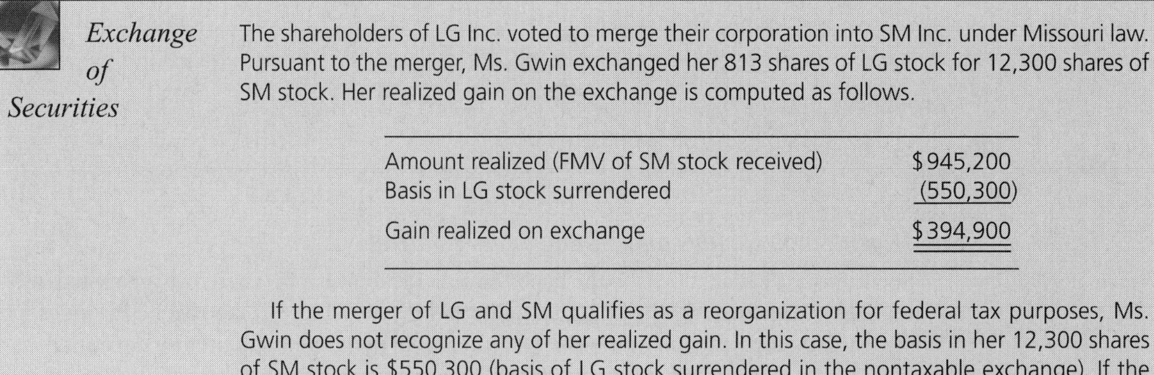

Exchange of Securities

The shareholders of LG Inc. voted to merge their corporation into SM Inc. under Missouri law. Pursuant to the merger, Ms. Gwin exchanged her 813 shares of LG stock for 12,300 shares of SM stock. Her realized gain on the exchange is computed as follows.

Amount realized (FMV of SM stock received)	$945,200
Basis in LG stock surrendered	(550,300)
Gain realized on exchange	$394,900

If the merger of LG and SM qualifies as a reorganization for federal tax purposes, Ms. Gwin does not recognize any of her realized gain. In this case, the basis in her 12,300 shares of SM stock is $550,300 (basis of LG stock surrendered in the nontaxable exchange). If the merger does not qualify as a reorganization, Ms. Gwin must recognize a $394,900 taxable gain on the exchange. In this case, the basis in her 12,300 shares of SM stock is their $945,200 cost (FMV of LG stock surrendered).

TAX CONSEQUENCES OF CAPITAL GAINS AND LOSSES

Individuals who recognize both capital gains and losses during the year can deduct the losses to the extent of the gains. In other words, individuals can combine their capital gains and losses to result in either a net gain or a net loss. A net gain is included in adjusted gross income and may be taxed at a preferential rate (or rates). A net loss results in a limited deduction in the AGI computation. Before we can focus on these outcomes, we must examine the rules governing the netting of capital gains and losses.

Netting Capital Gains and Losses

Capital gains and losses are reported on Schedule D, Form 1040. Each gain and loss is classified as short-term or long-term.[27]

- **Short-term capital gains or losses** result from the sale or exchange of capital assets owned for one year or less. The capital loss from a nonbusiness bad debt is classified as a short-term loss, regardless of the time period of the debt.
- **Long-term capital gains or losses** result from the sale or exchange of capital assets owned for more than one year. There is a narrow subcategory of long-term gains and losses, described as **28 percent rate gains or losses** that includes recognized gains and losses from the sale or exchange of **collectibles** (tangible assets such as works of art, antiques, gems, stamps, and coins) and the taxable gain recognized on the sale of qualified small business stock.[28]

The gains and losses in each class are combined to result in a net gain or loss for that class.

[26] See the discussion of generic nontaxable exchanges in Chapter 8

[27] See §1222.

[28] §1(h)(5) and (6). When an individual sells or exchanges a collectible held for personal use (rather than as an investment), a realized gain is recognized (taxable) but a realized loss is not recognized (nondeductible). For further discussion, see Chapter 16. Qualified small business stock is discussed on page 438.

Mr. and Mrs. Dixon: Schedule D

During 2004, Mr. and Mrs. Dixon made the following three sales.

	Date Acquired	*Date Sold*	*Tax Basis*	*Sales Price*
110 shares of BN stock	11/8/96	10/2	$ 4,200	$13,900
42 shares of EF stock	6/29/98	10/14	19,000	17,100
118 shares of Oslo Mutual Fund	2/14/04	12/6	15,000	16,400

Shortly after year-end, the Dixons received a Form 1099-DIV from Oslo Mutual Fund reporting a $7,800 capital gain distribution. They recorded their capital transactions on Schedule D (shown as Exhibit 15.2). This schedule provides the following information.

Net short-term capital gain (line 7)	$ 1,400
Net long-term capital gain (line 15)	15,600

The next step is to combine the short-term and long-term positions to compute the total capital gain or capital loss. In the previous example, Mr. and Mrs. Dixon had a total capital gain of $17,000 ($1,400 net short-term gain + $15,600 net long-term gain) included in taxable income. The following examples illustrate two other combinations that result in total capital gain.

Total Short-Term Gain

Mr. Boin's Schedule D reflects a $12,200 net short-term gain and a $4,700 net long-term loss. Because the loss can be deducted (netted) against the gain, he has a $7,500 total short-term capital gain included in taxable income.

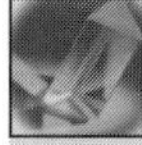

Total Long-Term Capital Gain

Ms. Coller's Schedule D reflects an $8,500 net short-term loss and a $20,000 net long-term gain ($12,000 of which is a 28 percent rate gain). Because the loss can be deducted (netted) against the gain, she has an $11,500 total long-term capital gain included in taxable income. Under the netting rules, a short-term loss reduces 28 percent rate gain *before* other long-term gain. Consequently, Ms. Coller's $11,500 total gain consists of $3,500 28 percent rate gain ($12,000 28 percent rate gain − $8,500 short-term loss) and $8,000 other long-term gain.

Preferential Rates on Long-Term Capital Gains

Objective 4
Compute the tax on short-term and long-term capital gains.

If individual taxable income includes capital gain, any short-term portion is taxed at ordinary rates, while any long-term portion is taxed at the following preferential rates.[29]

- A 28 percent rate gain is taxed at a *maximum* rate of 28 percent. Thus, this rate is beneficial only if the ordinary rate that would apply to such gain exceeds 28 percent.
- Other long-term gain is taxed at a 15 percent rate. However, any portion of such gain that would be taxed at 15 percent or less under the ordinary rate structure is taxed at only 5 percent. This dual rate structure ensures that every individual benefits from the preferential long-term capital gains rate, regardless of his or her marginal rate on ordinary income.[30]

[29] §1(h).

[30] The Jobs and Growth Tax Relief Reconciliation Act of 2003 reduced the preferential rate structure from 20 percent/10 percent to 15 percent/5 percent for gains recognized after May 5, 2003.

EXHIBIT 15.2

SCHEDULE D (Form 1040) Department of the Treasury Internal Revenue Service (99)	**Capital Gains and Losses** ▶ Attach to Form 1040. ▶ See Instructions for Schedule D (Form 1040). ▶ Use Schedule D-1 to list additional transactions for lines 1 and 8.	OMB No. 1545-0074 **2004** Attachment Sequence No. **12**
Name(s) shown on Form 1040	Mark and Sue Dixon	Your social security number 512 22 4061

Part I **Short-Term Capital Gains and Losses—Assets Held One Year or Less**

	(a) Description of property (Example: 100 sh. XYZ Co.)	(b) Date acquired (Mo., day, yr.)	(c) Date sold (Mo., day, yr.)	(d) Sales price (see page D-6 of the instructions)	(e) Cost or other basis (see page D-6 of the instructions)	(f) Gain or (loss) Subtract (e) from (d)
1	118 sh. Oslo MF	2-14-04	12-6-04	16,400	15,000	1,400

2	Enter your short-term totals, if any, from Schedule D-1, line 2	2		1,400
3	**Total short-term sales price amounts.** Add lines 1 and 2 in column (d)	3	16,400	
4	Short-term gain from Form 6252 and short-term gain or (loss) from Forms 4684, 6781, and 8824	4		
5	Net short-term gain or (loss) from partnerships, S corporations, estates, and trusts from Schedule(s) K-1	5		
6	Short-term capital loss carryover. Enter the amount, if any, from line 8 of your **Capital Loss Carryover Worksheet** on page D-6 of the instructions	6		( )
7	**Net short-term capital gain or (loss).** Combine lines 1 through 6 in column (f)	7		1,400

Part II **Long-Term Capital Gains and Losses—Assets Held More Than One Year**

	(a) Description of property (Example: 100 sh. XYZ Co.)	(b) Date acquired (Mo., day, yr.)	(c) Date sold (Mo., day, yr.)	(d) Sales price (see page D-6 of the instructions)	(e) Cost or other basis (see page D-6 of the instructions)	(f) Gain or (loss) Subtract (e) from (d)
8	110 sh. BN Inc.	11-8-96	10-2-04	13,900	4,200	9,700
	42 sh. EF Inc.	6-29-98	10-14-04	17,100	19,000	(1,900)

9	Enter your long-term totals, if any, from Schedule D-1, line 9	9		
10	**Total long-term sales price amounts.** Add lines 8 and 9 in column (d)	10	31,000	
11	Gain from Form 4797, Part I; long-term gain from Forms 2439 and 6252; and long-term gain or (loss) from Forms 4684, 6781, and 8824	11		
12	Net long-term gain or (loss) from partnerships, S corporations, estates, and trusts from Schedule(s) K-1	12		
13	Capital gain distributions. See page D-1 of the instructions	13		7,800
14	Long-term capital loss carryover. Enter the amount, if any, from line 13 of your **Capital Loss Carryover Worksheet** on page D-6 of the instructions	14		( )
15	**Net long-term capital gain or (loss).** Combine lines 8 through 14 in column (f). Then go to Part III on the back	15		15,600

For Paperwork Reduction Act Notice, see Form 1040 instructions. Cat. No. 11338H **Schedule D (Form 1040) 2004**

Let's refer back to the preceding three examples to illustrate how these various tax rates apply.

Mr. and Mrs. Dixon: Short-Term and Long-Term Gain

Mr. and Mrs. Dixon's taxable income included $17,000 capital gain consisting of the following:

Short-term gain	$ 1,400
Long-term gain	15,600
Total capital gain included in taxable income	$17,000

Their marginal rate on ordinary income was 35 percent. Consequently, $1,400 of their total capital gain was taxed at 35 percent, and $15,600 was taxed at 15 percent.

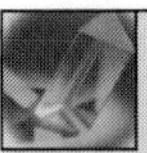

Short-Term Gain

Mr. Boin's taxable income includes $7,500 short-term capital gain. This gain is taxed at the ordinary rates that apply to his other income items.

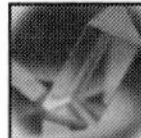

Long-Term Gain

Ms. Coller's taxable income includes $11,500 long-term capital gain consisting of the following.

28 percent rate gain	$ 3,500
Other long-term gain	8,000
Long-term gain	$11,500

Her marginal rate on ordinary income is 35 percent. Consequently,

- $3,500 of her capital gain is taxed at 28 percent.
- $8,000 of her capital gain is taxed at 15 percent.

Now change the facts by assuming that Ms. Coller's taxable income is low enough that her marginal ordinary rate is only 10 percent, so the maximum rate on 28 percent rate gain is inapplicable. Consequently,

- $3,500 of her capital gain is taxed at 10 percent.
- $8,000 of her capital gain is taxed at 5 percent.

Even though Ms. Coller is in the lowest tax bracket, she benefits from the preferential capital gain rate, which reduces her tax bill by $400 (5 percent of $8,000).

Unrecaptured Section 1250 Gain

Real property used in a business (including rental real estate) and held for more than one year is a Section 1231 asset rather than a capital asset. When an individual sells or exchanges business or rental realty, recognized gain is subject to the partial depreciation recapture rule discussed in Chapter 7. Any additional gain (subject to the Section 1231 netting process) is treated as long-term capital gain. Such long-term gain is taxed according to the following rules.

- Any unrecaptured Section 1250 gain is taxed at a *maximum* rate of 25 percent. **Unrecaptured Section 1250 gain** is defined as Section 1231 gain that would be recaptured as ordinary income under the full depreciation recapture rule.[31]
- Any remaining gain is treated as other long-term capital gain.

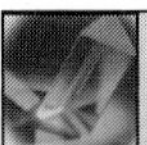

Unrecaptured Section 1250 Gain

Mr. Lilley sold two tracts of real estate, Property A and Property B, both of which he held for more than one year. He did not sell any other capital or Section 1231 asset, and his marginal tax rate on ordinary income is 35 percent.

[31] §1(h)(7).

	Property A		Property B	
Sale price		$800,000		$475,000
Original cost	$950,000		$440,000	
Depreciation (straight-line)	(190,000)		(32,000)	
Adjusted basis		(760,000)		(408,000)
Gain recognized		$ 40,000		$ 67,000

Because Mr. Lilley used the straight-line method to compute depreciation, the partial recapture rule is inapplicable, and the gain recognized on both sales is Section 1231 gain. However, the $40,000 gain recognized on the sale of Property A is less than the accumulated depreciation. Consequently, the entire gain is classified as unrecaptured Section 1250 gain. The $67,000 gain recognized on the sale of property B includes only $32,000 unrecaptured 1250 gain (equal to accumulated depreciation). Thus, Mr. Lilley's real estate sales resulted in $72,000 unrecaptured Section 1250 gain (taxed at 25 percent) and $35,000 Section 1231 gain treated as long-term capital gain (taxed at 15 percent).[32]

Even simple examples of the various preferential capital gains rates reflect the complexity of this tax rate structure. Individuals who must use the capital gains rates to compute their tax can follow the procedure contained in Part III of Schedule D. Use of this procedure is illustrated in the Comprehensive Schedule D Problem included as Appendix 15–A to this chapter.

Policy Reasons for a Preferential Rate

Tax Talk

As individual taxable income rises, so does the percentage of dividend income and capital gain included in income. For individuals with AGI less than $50,000, only 3 percent of their 2002 income consisted of dividends and capital gains. For individuals with AGI between $100,000 and $500,000, 11.5 percent of their income consisted of dividends and capital gains. For individuals with AGI over $10 million, 61.4 percent of their income consisted of dividends and capital gains.

What is the theory justifying a preferential tax rate on capital gains? This tax policy question is relevant in assessing the vertical equity of the income tax system because capital gains are recognized most frequently by high-income individuals who engage in significant investment activities. Supporters of the preferential rate observe that individuals don't pay tax on capital gain each year as the gain accrues but only in the year in which the gain is realized. This bunching effect could cause the gain to be taxed at a higher rate than if it were taxed in annual increments. Critics of the preferential rate respond that the bunching problem is mitigated by the deferral of tax on the capital gain until the year of realization.

A second argument is that the preferential rate on long-term gains counteracts the effect of inflation. An investor's tax basis in capital assets is not adjusted for changes in the purchasing power of the dollar. If an investor holds an asset for a long time, the dollars realized on sale may exceed the historical basis of the asset, but some or even all the realized gain may be inflationary rather than real. The counterargument is that a preferential rate on all long-term gains, regardless of the duration of the investor's holding period, is a crude solution to this problem. Congress periodically considers indexing the tax basis of assets to reflect changes in the value of the dollar but has backed away from this theoretically appealing solution because of the complexity it would add to the tax law.

Many economists contend that the preferential rate on capital gains encourages the mobility of capital. Without a tax break on realized gains, individuals owning appreciated assets might be unduly reluctant to liquidate or convert such assets because of the tax cost. This locking-in effect distorts financial decision making and retards the efficiency of the stock and bond markets. A variation on this argument is that the preferential rate reduces

[32] Net short-term capital loss or net 28 percent rate loss is netted against unrecaptured Section 1250 gain before other long-term gain.

the risk of financial investments and thereby increases the supply of venture capital to the economy. The counterargument is that the rate applies to all capital gains irrespective of the risk inherent in the underlying investment.

Capital Loss Limitation

If an individual's capital losses exceed capital gains for the year, only $3,000 of the net capital loss can be entered on page 1, Form 1040, as an above-the-line deduction in the computation of AGI.[33] The nondeductible portion of the loss is carried forward indefinitely to be combined with the individual's future capital gains and losses. Carryforwards retain their character as short-term or long-term loss. A long-term capital loss carryforward is netted against 28 percent rate gain before other long-term gain.

Net Capital Loss

Ms. Nash sold four blocks of securities this year with the following result.

Sale 1: Short-term capital loss	$ (4,000)
Sale 2: Short-term capital gain	6,100
Sale 3: Long-term capital loss	(11,500)
Sale 4: Long-term capital gain	1,250

She has a $2,100 net short-term gain and a $10,250 net long-term loss that net to an $8,150 long-term loss. She can deduct $3,000 of this loss in the computation of AGI; the $5,150 nondeductible portion is a long-term capital loss carryforward.

The netting of capital gains and losses on Schedule D reflects the basic rule that capital losses are deductible to the extent of capital gains. Thus, the tax savings from a capital loss depend on the amount of capital gain recognized during the year.

Tax Savings from Capital Losses

Refer to the facts in the preceding example. Ms. Nash's capital losses sheltered $6,100 short-term capital gain, $1,250 long-term capital gain, and $3,000 ordinary income from tax. If Ms. Nash's marginal tax rate is 35 percent, the losses saved $3,373 tax.

Tax savings on:	
Short-term gain ($6,100 × 35%)	$2,135
Long-term gain ($1,250 × 15%)	188
Ordinary income ($3,000 × 35%)	1,050
	$3,373

Ms. Nash's $5,150 capital loss carryforward will save tax in future years to the extent she can deduct it against capital gains or ordinary income.

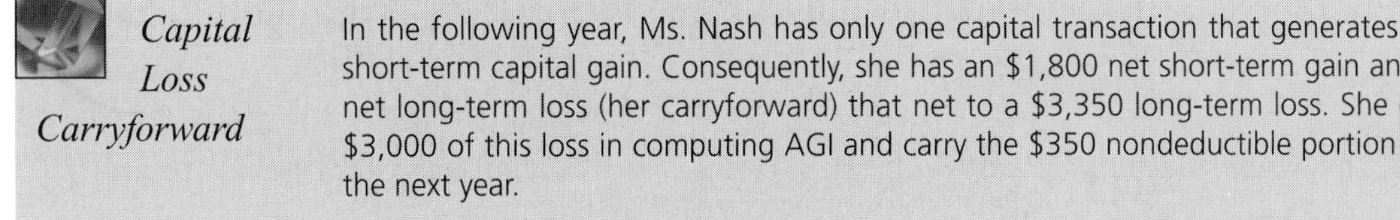

Capital Loss Carryforward

In the following year, Ms. Nash has only one capital transaction that generates an $1,800 short-term capital gain. Consequently, she has an $1,800 net short-term gain and a $5,150 net long-term loss (her carryforward) that net to a $3,350 long-term loss. She can deduct $3,000 of this loss in computing AGI and carry the $350 nondeductible portion forward to the next year.

[33] §1211(b). If the net capital loss consists of both short-term and long-term loss, the $3,000 deduction is attributed to the short-term loss first. §1212(b).

In present value terms, the tax savings from a capital loss diminish with each year that the investor must wait to deduct it. The obvious tax planning strategy is for the investor to generate capital gains to absorb the loss as soon as possible. Of course, even without capital gains, individuals can deduct their capital losses at the rate of $3,000 per year. But for investors who suffer large losses, the value of this stream of annual deductions may be negligible.

INVESTMENTS IN SMALL CORPORATE BUSINESSES

Objective 5
Describe the tax benefit of qualified small business stock and Section 1244 stock.

Investments in small corporate businesses that are struggling to grow are riskier than investments in well-established corporations with proven track records. To encourage individuals to accept this higher level of risk, the tax law contains two preferential provisions for investments in small corporate businesses.

Qualified Small Business Stock

Individuals who realize capital gain on the sale or exchange of **qualified small business stock** held for more than *five years* may exclude 50 percent of such gain from income.[34] The remaining capital gain is classified as 28 percent rate gain.[35] The stock must have been issued directly to the individual in exchange for money, property, or services rendered to the issuing corporation. In other words, individuals cannot purchase qualified small business stock from other shareholders. Moreover, the stock must be issued after August 10, 1993. Because of the five-year holding requirement, 1998 was the first year in which individuals could take advantage of this preference.[36]

Gain on Qualified Small Business Stock

In November 1996, Ms. Hock contributed $200,000 to QB Inc. in exchange for 1,000 shares of stock. QB is a qualified small business. This year, Ms. Hock sold her QB shares for $560,000, realizing a $360,000 gain. She may exclude $180,000 of this gain from income. The $180,000 long-term capital gain included in income is 28 percent rate gain.

A qualified small business is a regular corporation with no more than $50 million of gross assets immediately after the qualified stock was issued. The corporation must conduct an active trade or business other than a financial, leasing, real estate, farming, mining, hospitality, or professional service business.[37]

Section 1244 Stock

Individuals who realize a loss on the disposition of **Section 1244 stock** may deduct a limited portion as ordinary, rather than capital, loss. Married couples filing jointly are limited to an annual $100,000 ordinary deduction, while unmarried individuals or married individuals filing separate returns are limited to an annual $50,000 ordinary deduction. Any loss in excess of these limits retains its character as capital loss.[38]

[34] §1202. For any tax year, the gain eligible for this exclusion is limited to the *greater* of (1) 10 times the aggregate basis in the stock disposed of during the year or (2) $10 million reduced by eligible gain recognized in prior taxable years. If an individual disposes of stock in more than one qualified small business during a year, the limitation applies separately with respect to each business.

[35] §1(h)(7).

[36] An amount equal to 7 percent of the excluded gain is an AMT tax preference that must be added to taxable income in the calculation of the individual's AMTI. §57(a)(7).

[37] See §1202(d) and (e) for the complete definition of a qualified small business.

[38] §1244(a) and (b).

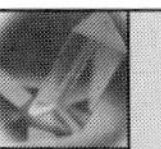

Loss on Section 1244 Stock

Six years ago, Mr. and Mrs. Phipp contributed $200,000 to NW Inc. in exchange for 1,000 shares of stock, which qualified as Section 1244 stock. This year, they sold all 1,000 shares for $30,000. This was their only asset sale. Their salary, interest, and dividend income totaled $319,000, and the AGI on their joint return is $216,000.

Salary, interest, dividends	$319,000
Maximum Section 1244 loss	(100,000)
Capital loss deduction	(3,000)
AGI	$216,000

Mr. and Mrs. Phipp can carry their $67,000 nondeductible long-term capital loss ($170,000 recognized loss − $100,000 Section 1244 loss − $3,000 deductible capital loss) forward to next year.

As a general rule, the first $1 million of stock issued by a corporation that derives more than 50 percent of its annual gross receipts from the conduct of an active business qualifies as Section 1244 stock.[39] This special character applies only to stock issued directly by the corporation to an individual investor in exchange for money or property. Stock issued for services rendered to the issuing corporation does not qualify as Section 1244 stock. The Section 1244 label has no downside. If the fledgling corporate venture is a success and the investor eventually sells the stock at a gain, that gain is characterized as capital gain. On the other hand, if the investor sells the stock at a loss or if the stock becomes worthless, a significant portion (if not all) of the loss yields an immediate benefit as a deduction in the computation of AGI.

INVESTMENT EXPENSES

Object 6
Determine the deduction for investment interest expense.

Individuals are allowed to deduct ordinary and necessary expenses paid or incurred for the management, conservation, or maintenance of investment property.[40] Such expenses include the cost of subscriptions to investment publications and newsletters, investment management fees, and the rental of a safety deposit box to hold securities or investment-related documents. The deduction for investment expenses is classified as a miscellaneous itemized deduction and thus often fails to result in any tax benefit.[41]

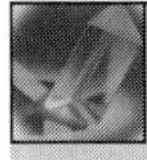

Investment Expenses

Mrs. Guss owns a portfolio of investment securities. This year, she paid $825 to attend a two-day seminar entitled "Asset Allocation Strategies for the Senior Investor." She also paid a $445 subscription fee to *The Wall Street Journal*. Mrs. Guss itemized deductions and reported her $1,270 total investment expenses as her only miscellaneous deductions. Because her AGI was $65,072, she could not actually deduct any of these expenses.

[39] §1244(c).

[40] §212.

[41] Miscellaneous itemized deductions are allowed only to the extent that their total exceeds 2 percent of AGI. §67.

Miscellaneous itemized deductions	$1,270
AGI threshold ($65,072 × 2%)	(1,301)
Allowable deduction	–0–

Investment Interest Expense

An important set of rules governs the deductibility of interest that individuals pay on debt incurred to purchase investment property. If the property is tax-exempt state and local bonds, the interest is nondeductible.[42] The logic of this rule is apparent: Congress doesn't want the tax law to subsidize the purchase of investments yielding nontaxable income. If an individual incurs debt to purchase other investment property, the interest on the debt is an itemized deduction but only to the extent of the debtor's net investment income.[43] The nondeductible portion of the interest expense is carried forward to future taxable years.

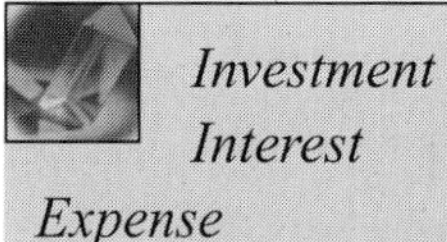

Investment Interest Expense

Mr. Guss borrowed $40,000 at 9 percent and invested the loan proceeds in a mutual fund that paid a $5,000 dividend. He paid $3,600 of **investment interest expense** for the year. Because his net investment income exceeded $3,600, the entire interest payment is an itemized deduction.

Now assume that Mr. Guss used the loan proceeds to purchase common stock in a corporation that did not pay a dividend. His only investment income was $750 interest earned on a savings account. In this case, he can deduct only $750 investment interest expense. The $2,850 nondeductible expense carries forward to next year, when Mr. Guss can deduct it subject to the net investment income limitation.

Net Investment Income

Investment income is generated by property held for investment purposes and includes income, dividends, annuity payments, and capital gain on the sale of investment assets. **Net investment income** equals total investment income less any expenses (other than interest) directly connected with the production of the income. If an individual recognizes income that is taxed at a preferential rate (qualified dividend income and net long-term capital gain), the tax law offers an interesting choice. The individual may elect to treat such income (or any portion thereof) as investment income, thereby securing a deduction for investment interest. But by making this election, the individual forfeits any preferential tax rate on the income.[44] This election prevents investors from enjoying a double benefit. Their dividends and long-term capital gains can increase the investment interest expense deduction or be taxed at a preferential rate, but not both.

Election to Treat Capital Gain as Investment Income

Ms. Small paid $5,000 investment interest this year. She did not earn any interest, dividend, or other investment income. She did, however, recognize a $6,000 net long-term capital gain from the sale of investment assets. Ms. Small can elect to treat $5,000 of this gain as investment income so she can deduct her investment interest expense. If she makes the election, only $1,000 of the $6,000 long-term capital gain included in taxable income is eligible for the 15 percent preferential rate.

[42] §265.

[43] §163(d).

[44] §1(h)(2).

INVESTMENTS IN REAL PROPERTY

As an alternative to financial assets, individuals may put their money into real estate. In this section of the chapter, we will examine the tax consequences of investing in real property.

Undeveloped Land

Individuals who invest in undeveloped land expect a return in the form of appreciation in value because land typically does not generate any significant revenue or cash flow.[45] However, owners may incur out-of-pocket expenses with respect to their land. Real property taxes can be a considerable annual expense; these tax payments are itemized deductions.[46] If the owner financed the purchase of the land through a mortgage, the interest payments are investment interest, deductible to the extent of the owner's net investment income. Instead of treating property taxes and interest as current expenses, the owner may make an annual election to capitalize these carrying charges to the basis of the land.[47] Another important consideration is that undeveloped land may be a very illiquid asset. All in all, land may be a poor investment choice for individuals who want ready access to cash.

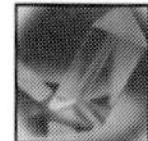

Capitalized Interest and Tax

Ms. Jamison recently purchased a 15-acre tract of undeveloped land as a long-term investment. She financed the purchase through a mortgage. This year, she paid $1,780 interest on the mortgage and $492 local property tax on the land. Ms. Jamison took the standard deduction on her income tax return and, therefore, derived no tax benefit from any itemized deductions, including her mortgage interest and property tax. So she elected to capitalize the interest and tax, thereby increasing her basis in the land by $2,272. In any future year in which she itemizes deductions, Ms. Jamison can deduct the mortgage interest and property tax paid during such year instead of making the annual election.

The tax advantage of holding investment land is that appreciation in value is not recognized as income until the owner disposes of the land in a taxable transaction.[48] Moreover, any gain recognized on the sale of land held for at least a year qualifies for a preferential tax rate. This conclusion, of course, presumes that the land was a capital asset in the owner's hands. Individuals who make periodic sales of land run the risk that the IRS may treat this activity as a business and the land as an inventory asset held primarily for sale to customers. In such case, the gains recognized on the sale are ordinary income rather than capital gain.

The question of whether an individual who sells land is engaging in an investment or a business is subjective; the answer depends on the facts and circumstances of each case. When called on to decide the issue, the federal courts consider the number, frequency, and regularity of the sales and the extent to which the individual actively solicited buyers, either through advertising or a real estate agent. In cases in which the individual added substantial improvements to the land, such as roads and drainage ditches, or subdivided a single tract of land into smaller parcels, the courts have generally agreed with the IRS that the individual engaged in a business.[49]

[45] Owners might receive revenues from grazing, hunting, mineral, or crop leases.

[46] §164(a)(1).

[47] §266.

[48] Individuals frequently enter into like-kind exchanges of investment real property. See the discussion of these nontaxable exchanges in Chapter 8.

[49] See, for example, *W. R. Royster,* TC Memo 1985-258.

Rental Real Estate

Developed real estate consists of land with some type of building or structure permanently attached. Individuals who own developed real estate receive rents paid by tenants or lessees who occupy the property. In many respects, rental real estate is treated as a business for tax purposes. The owner recognizes the rents as ordinary income and deducts operating and maintenance expenses.[50] These items are reported on Schedule E, Form 1040. Consequently, only net profit from the rental activity is included in the owner's AGI. Rental real estate is a Section 1231 asset, and the building component is depreciable property with either a 27.5-year or a 39-year MACRS recovery period. Therefore, the owner can recover his investment in the building through annual depreciation deductions.

Mr. and Mrs. David: Schedule E

Mr. and Mrs. David own residential real estate that they have leased to the same tenant since 1995. In 2004, their revenue and expenses were as follows:

Rents received ($2,250 per month)	$27,000
Monthly yard maintenance	1,480
Property and liability insurance	2,880
Interest on mortgage	1,720
Repairs and painting	4,140
Local property tax	2,075
Monthly utilities	2,900
Legal fee for consultation on zoning restriction	675

MACRS depreciation for the year was $6,400. This information is summarized on their Schedule E, shown as Exhibit 15.3. Their $4,730 net income (line 26) was carried as an income item to page 1, Form 1040.

While rental real estate activities have many business characteristics, they actually fall into the special class of *passive activities*.[51] This classification in no way affects the tax consequences of profitable rental activities. But as we will learn in the next section, the classification has major tax consequences for rental activities operating at a loss.

INVESTMENTS IN PASSIVE ACTIVITIES

Objective 7
Apply the passive activity loss limitation.

Individuals can own equity interests in business entities without rendering any personal services to the business. Many partners and shareholders have no involvement in the business conducted by their partnership or S corporation. Nevertheless, these owners are allocated a share of business income. Even the owner of a sole proprietorship might choose to leave the business operation entirely in the hands of employees. But regardless of such lack of participation, net profits belong to the proprietor. In these situations, the income to which the partner, shareholder, or sole proprietor is entitled is primarily a return on invested capital. Although such income retains its ordinary business character when reported on the owner's individual tax return, it is economically equivalent to investment income.

If an individual owns an interest in a business but does not materially participate in that business, the interest is a **passive activity** for federal tax purposes. **Material participation**

[50] Reg. §1.212-1.

[51] §469(c)(2).

EXHIBIT 15.3

SCHEDULE E (Form 1040)
Department of the Treasury Internal Revenue Service (99)

Supplemental Income and Loss
(From rental real estate, royalties, partnerships, S corporations, estates, trusts, REMICs, etc.)
▶ Attach to Form 1040 or Form 1041. ▶ See Instructions for Schedule E (Form 1040).

OMB No. 1545-0074
2004
Attachment Sequence No. 13

Name(s) shown on return: Ronald and Janet David
Your social security number: 498 31 1240

Part I **Income or Loss From Rental Real Estate and Royalties** **Note.** If you are in the business of renting personal property, use **Schedule C** or **C-EZ** (see page E-3). Report farm rental income or loss from **Form 4835** on page 2, line 40.

	1 List the type and location of each **rental real estate property:**	2 For each rental real estate property listed on line 1, did you or your family use it during the tax year for personal purposes for more than the greater of: • 14 days **or** • 10% of the total days rented at fair rental value? (See page E-3.)		Yes	No
A	1412 West Reeder Avenue Omaha, Nebraska 51102		A		✓
B			B		
C			C		

Income:		Properties A	Properties B	Properties C		Totals (Add columns A, B, and C.)
3 Rents received	3	27,000			3	27,000
4 Royalties received	4				4	
Expenses:						
5 Advertising	5					
6 Auto and travel (see page E-4)	6					
7 Cleaning and maintenance	7	1,480				
8 Commissions	8					
9 Insurance	9	2,880				
10 Legal and other professional fees	10					
11 Management fees	11					
12 Mortgage interest paid to banks, etc. (see page E-4)	12	1,720			12	1,720
13 Other interest	13					
14 Repairs	14	4,140				
15 Supplies	15					
16 Taxes	16	2,075				
17 Utilities	17	2,900				
18 Other (list) ▶ legal expense	18	675				
19 Add lines 5 through 18	19	15,870			19	15,870
20 Depreciation expense or depletion (see page E-4)	20	6,400			20	6,400
21 Total expenses. Add lines 19 and 20	21	22,270				
22 Income or (loss) from rental real estate or royalty properties. Subtract line 21 from line 3 (rents) or line 4 (royalties). If the result is a (loss), see page E-4 to find out if you must file **Form 6198**	22					
23 Deductible rental real estate loss. **Caution.** Your rental real estate loss on line 22 may be limited. See page E-4 to find out if you must file **Form 8582.** Real estate professionals must complete line 43 on page 2	23	( )	( )	( )		
24 **Income.** Add positive amounts shown on line 22. **Do not** include any losses					24	4,730
25 **Losses.** Add royalty losses from line 22 and rental real estate losses from line 23. Enter total losses here					25	( )
26 **Total rental real estate and royalty income or (loss).** Combine lines 24 and 25. Enter the result here. If Parts II, III, IV, and line 40 on page 2 do not apply to you, also enter this amount on Form 1040, line 17. Otherwise, include this amount in the total on line 41 on page 2					26	4,730

For Paperwork Reduction Act Notice, see Form 1040 instructions. Cat. No. 11344L **Schedule E (Form 1040) 2004**

means that the individual is involved in day-to-day operations on a regular, continual, and substantial basis.[52]

Passive Activity

JKL Partnership consists of three equal individual partners. Mr. Jett and Ms. Kyle are general partners who work full-time in JKL's business, while Mr. Lamb is a limited partner who has no personal involvement at all. For the two general partners, their interest in JKL is clearly a

[52] §469(c)(1). Reg. §1.496-5T provides several objective tests for determining material participation.

business activity. Because Mr. Lamb does not materially participate in the business, his interest in JKL is a passive activity.[53]

The classification of an interest as a passive activity does not affect how the *income* is taxed. Assume that JKL Partnership generated $129,000 business income. Each of the three partners received a Schedule K-1 reporting a $43,000 share of this income. All three included this share as ordinary income on their Form 1040 and paid tax accordingly. The fact that Mr. Lamb's share was passive activity income had no effect on the computation of his tax on the income.

Passive Activity Loss Limitation

The classification of business interest as a passive activity has profound tax consequences if the business operates at a loss. Specifically, the owner of the passive activity can deduct the loss only to the extent of income generated by other passive activities.[54] Any disallowed loss is carried forward as a suspended passive activity loss. Suspended losses are deductible in any future year to the extent of the owner's passive activity income in that year.[55]

Passive Activity Loss Limitation

Refer to the facts in the preceding example and assume that JKL Partnership generated a $90,000 operating loss. Each partner received a Schedule K-1 reporting a $30,000 share. Mr. Jett and Ms. Kyle, the general partners who work in the business, can deduct their loss in the computation of AGI.[56] Mr. Lamb, the limited partner, is subject to the passive activity loss limitation. If his JKL interest is his only passive activity, he cannot deduct any of his $30,000 loss. If he owns another passive activity that generated income, he can deduct the loss to the extent of such income. Any disallowed loss is carried forward as a suspended passive activity loss. Mr. Lamb can deduct the suspended loss in a future year to the extent he recognizes income from either JKL Partnership or any other passive activity.

Rental Activities

The term *passive activity* includes any **rental activity** in which revenues are principally derived from the lease of tangible property for an extended period of time.[57] Activities in which revenues are principally derived from the provision of customer services are not rental activities. For instance, the operation of a hotel is a business rather than a rental activity. Similarly, businesses providing short-term use of property such as automobiles, tuxedos, or videocassettes are not rental activities. If an individual owns a rental activity, that activity is passive, *regardless of the extent of the owner's participation in the activity.*

As mentioned earlier in the chapter, rental real estate activities are passive activities.[58] Accordingly, individuals who invest in rental real estate can deduct losses only to the extent

[53] The statute creates a presumption that a *limited* partnership interest is a passive activity. §469(h)(2).

[54] §469(a)(1) and (d)(1).

[55] §469(b).

[56] This statement presumes that the partners have sufficient basis in their partnership interests to absorb their loss. See Chapter 9.

[57] Reg. §1.469-1T(e)(3).

[58] Real estate professionals who devote more than one-half of their work effort each year and at least 750 hours annually to a real property business are engaged in an active business rather than a passive rental activity. A real property business includes the development, redevelopment, construction, reconstruction, acquisition, conversion, rental, operation, management, leasing or brokering of real property. §469(c)(7).

of their passive activity income. However, the law provides an important exception under which individuals can deduct up to $25,000 annual loss from rental real estate without regard to the passive activity loss limitation.[59] To qualify for the full $25,000 exception, the individual's AGI (before consideration of any rental loss) must not exceed $100,000. If AGI exceeds this threshold, the $25,000 exception is reduced by 50 percent of the excess. Thus, the exception shrinks to zero for taxpayers with AGI over $150,000.

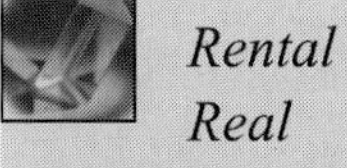

Rental Real Estate Exception

Mr. and Mrs. Ennis own and manage three duplexes that they rent to college students. They do not own any other passive activities. The duplexes generated a $31,000 loss this year. Before deduction of this loss, the couple's AGI was $95,000. Because of the rental real estate exception, they can deduct $25,000 of the rental loss to reduce AGI to $70,000. The $6,000 excess loss is a nondeductible passive activity loss that carries forward to next year.

If Mr. and Mrs. Ennis's AGI before deduction of their rental loss was $141,000, their exception is reduced to $4,500.

AGI before loss	$141,000
AGI threshold	(100,000)
Excess AGI	$ 41,000
	.50
Reduction in $25,000 exception	$ 20,500

Consequently, they can deduct $4,500 of their rental loss to reduce AGI to $136,500. The $26,500 excess loss is a nondeductible passive activity loss that carries forward to next year.

Dispositions of Passive Activities

The passive activity loss limitation is not a *permanent* loss disallowance rule. When an investor disposes of her entire interest in a passive activity in a taxable transaction (generally a sale or exchange), any suspended losses with respect to the interest are fully deductible in the year of disposition. As a result, the investor finally reaps a tax benefit from every dollar of loss disallowed in an earlier year. Of course, in present value terms, the tax savings from the deferred deduction are less than the savings from a deduction in such earlier year.

Planning with Passive Activity Losses

Suppose that Mrs. Queen, a practicing attorney, paid $50,000 to buy stock in an S corporation operating a chain of Mexican restaurants. Because she does not materially participate in the S corporation's business, Mrs. Queen's interest is a passive activity. On her first Schedule K-1, she is allocated a $9,000 ordinary business loss, which reduces the basis in her stock to $41,000.[60] She owns no other passive activities and therefore recognized no passive activity income this year. Consequently, she can't deduct her $9,000 loss in computing AGI. Stated another way, Mrs. Queen's passive activity loss doesn't shelter the income generated by her legal practice (or any other income) from tax.

[59] §469(i). The individual must own at least a 10 percent interest in the real estate and must be significantly involved in its management.

[60] §1367(a).

Sale of a Passive Activity

What are Mrs. Queen's options with respect to her $9,000 suspended loss? Given that the restaurant business apparently is losing money, her best option may be to sell the stock as quickly as possible! Suppose that early in the next year, Mrs. Queen finds a buyer who offers $30,000 for her shares. If she sells, she will recognize an $11,000 capital loss *and* can deduct her $9,000 suspended passive activity loss as an ordinary business loss.[61] The total of the two losses ($11,000 capital loss + $9,000 ordinary loss) corresponds to her $20,000 economic loss on this unfortunate investment. The only effect of the passive activity loss limitation was to defer the deduction of the ordinary loss (and the tax benefit therefrom) for one year.

Purchase of a PIG

If Mrs. Queen believes that the restaurant business is a solid long-term investment, her second option is to find a source of passive activity income. Perhaps the restaurant will become profitable so that Mrs. Queen eventually can deduct her suspended loss against her share of the S corporation's future taxable income. If this possibility is too uncertain, she could invest in a moneymaking passive activity (dubbed a **passive income generator [PIG]** by the financial press). For instance, if she buys an interest in a profitable commercial office building, she can deduct her suspended loss from the S corporation to the extent of her rental income from the PIG.

WEALTH TRANSFER PLANNING

Individuals who engage in successful business and investment activities inevitably accumulate wealth in the process. At some point in their lives, individuals begin to think about transferring wealth to other parties—usually to their children and grandchildren. The decision to part with property can be intensely personal; the property owner may be more concerned with private family matters than with the financial implications of the decision. However, once the decision is made, most people are eager to adopt financial strategies to maximize the wealth available to younger-generation family members. As we will learn in this final section of Chapter 15, the federal transfer taxes are a primary consideration in the development of such strategies.

Good News, Bad News for Baby Boomers

Over the next decade, the largest transfer of property in U.S. history will take place as baby boomers inherit their parents' wealth. Economists estimate that boomers will inherit $4.8 trillion through the year 2015. The bad news is that the majority of individuals over age 65 have not considered the effect of the federal estate tax on their accumulated wealth.[62]

The Transfer Tax System

The federal transfer tax system has three components: the gift tax, the estate tax, and the generation-skipping transfer tax (which we will not discuss in this text). Congress enacted the original estate tax in 1916 as a way to redistribute some of the enormous fortunes amassed by society's richest families to the public domain. Historically, only a tiny fraction

[61] This calculation of loss is based on Mrs. Queen's basis in the stock on January 1 without adjustment for any pro rata share of the corporation's income or loss for the year of sale.

[62] Douglas D. Wilson, "Providing Guidance to Executors and Trustees," *Journal of Accountancy*, October 1997.

Tax Talk
William H. Gates Sr., co-chairman of the Bill and Melinda Gates Foundation, has publicly criticized the repeal of the estate tax during wartime. "There is something unseemly about Congress's obsession with repealing the estate tax, the nation's most equitable tax on accumulated wealth, at a time when life and death are at stake. The American history of estate and inheritance taxes is wound together with mobilizations for war."

of the population had any exposure to the federal transfer taxes. However, in recent decades, these taxes have applied to increasing numbers of individuals and have become politically unpopular. In 2001, Congress took the bold step of repealing the estate tax and generation-skipping transfer taxes (but *not* the gift tax). However, the repeal is not effective until 2010, and many commentators are skeptical that the repeal will actually occur. In the meantime, affluent individuals and their tax advisers must continue to deal with the federal transfer tax system.

Structure of the Gift and Estate Taxes

The federal gift tax is imposed on property transfers that individuals make during life **(inter vivos transfers),** while the federal estate tax is imposed on final property transfers occurring at death **(testamentary transfers).**[63] In both cases, the tax base is the FMV of the property transferred, and both taxes are computed with reference to the same rate schedule. The transfer tax rate schedule is progressive, with a 47 percent top marginal rate in 2005.[64] This schedule is included as Appendix 15–B to this chapter.

The gift and estate taxes have a unique feature in that they are not computed on an annual basis. Instead, the taxes are based on the *cumulative* FMV of taxable transfers made over a lifetime. As a result, each successive transfer (including the last transfer at death) is boosted higher in the rate brackets and has a greater tax cost.

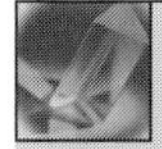

Cumulative Taxable Transfers

Mr. Tang made his first taxable transfer in 1995: a $1 million cash gift to his children. He made a second taxable transfer in 1999: a gift of property with a $1 million FMV to his grandchildren. Mr. Tang died in 2005. His taxable estate had a $1 million FMV. Exhibit 15.4 shows that the three transfers of equal value were taxed at progressively higher rates because each successive transfer was "stacked" on the cumulative value of the earlier transfers.

Annual Gift Tax Exclusion

Objective 8
Compute a taxable gift by applying the annual and lifetime exlusions.

Any transfer of property for which the transferor does not receive adequate consideration in money or money's worth is a gift for federal tax purposes.[65] The **donor** making the gift is usually motivated by generosity or affection toward the **donee** receiving the gift. In other words, a gift occurs in a personal, rather than a business, context. Not every gift is subject

EXHIBIT 15.4
Cumulative Nature of Federal Transfer Taxes

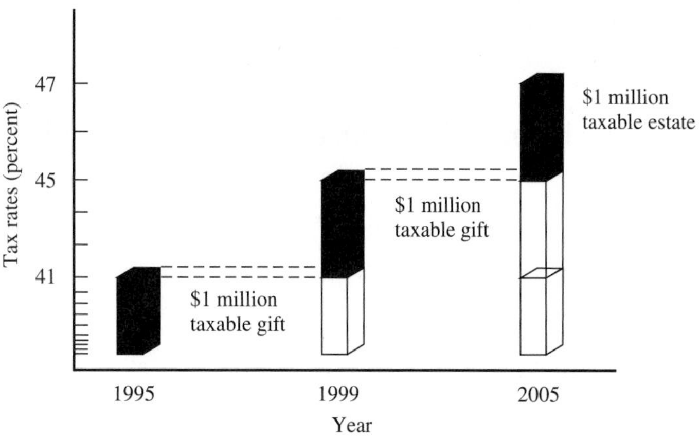

[63] Married couples do not file joint transfer tax returns.

[64] §2001(c).

[65] §2512(b).

to the federal gift tax. Donors can give away unlimited property to qualified charities or to their spouse and can pay tuition to an educational institution or medical expenses for another person without incurring a gift tax.[66]

Every donor can give a *de minimis* amount to each donee that is excluded from the donor's tax base for the year. In 2005, the amount is $11,000 per donee.[67] This **annual gift tax exclusion** removes most routine birthday, graduation, and Christmas presents from the gift tax base. Married couples can elect to treat a gift made by either spouse as a gift made in equal portions by both spouses. By making this gift-splitting election, the couple doubles the 2005 exclusion to $22,000 per donee.[68] The first rule of transfer tax planning is that individuals should take full advantage of this annual exclusion.

Annual Gift Tax Exclusion

Mr. and Mrs. Archer have two adult children, who are both married, and six unmarried grandchildren. In 2005, they gave $22,000 to each of 10 donees (children, children-in-law, and grandchildren), thereby transferring $220,000 of property without making a taxable gift. When the grandchildren marry and produce great-grandchildren, Mr. and Mrs. Archer plan to add them to their list of annual donees, systematically bestowing wealth on their younger-generation family members at no tax cost.

Lifetime Gift Tax Exclusion

If the FMV of a gift exceeds the annual exclusion, the excess is a taxable gift. However, a donor does not pay gift tax until the cumulative amount of taxable gifts exceeds the donor's **lifetime gift tax exclusion.** Currently, this exclusion is $1 million.[69]

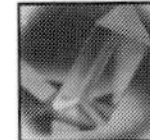

Lifetime Gift Tax Exclusion

Ms. Wood, an unmarried individual, made her first taxable gift in 2002 by transferring marketable securities to her niece. The FMV of the securities was $145,000, and the taxable gift was $134,000 ($145,000 FMV − $11,000 annual exclusion). Because the taxable gift was less than the $1 million lifetime exclusion, Ms. Wood owed no gift tax in 2002.

In 2003, Ms. Wood gave real estate to her godson. The FMV of the real estate was $750,000, and the taxable gift was $739,000 ($750,000 FMV − $11,000 annual exclusion). Because her $873,000 cumulative taxable gifts ($134,000 2002 gift + $739,000 2003 gift) were less than the $1 million lifetime exclusion, she owed no gift tax in 2003.

In 2005, Ms. Wood gave $400,000 cash to her niece and $400,000 cash to her godson. The taxable gift was $778,000 ($800,000 FMV − $22,000 annual exclusions for two donees). Ms. Wood must pay gift tax on the $651,000 excess of her cumulative taxable gifts ($134,000 2002 gift + $739,000 2003 gift + $778,000 2005 gift) over the $1 million lifetime exclusion.

Income Tax Consequences of Gifted Property

When a donor gives property to a donee, the donor's adjusted basis in the property carries over to become the donee's basis.[70] Because of this carryover basis rule, unrealized appreciation in the value of the property is shifted from donor to donee.

[66] §2503(e), §2522, and §2523.

[67] §2503(b). The annual exclusion is indexed for inflation.

[68] §2513.

[69] §2505(a)(1). The exclusion is actually accomplished by a tax *credit* that offsets the gift tax on the lifetime exclusion amount.

[70] §1015 governs the income tax basis of gifted property. If the donor pays a gift tax, the carryover basis is increased by the tax attributable to the appreciation in the gifted property. If the FMV of gifted property is less than the donor's basis, the donee's basis is limited to FMV, and the donor's unrealized loss in the property disappears. As a result, donors avoid giving away devalued property.

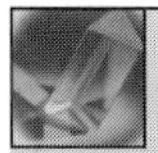

Carryover Basis

Six years ago, Mr. Roy transferred marketable securities with a $2,400 basis and a $10,000 FMV to his 15-year-old grandson, Steve. Because of the annual exclusion, Mr. Roy paid no gift tax on the transfer. Steve's carryover basis in the securities was $2,400. He received $900 annual dividends and sold the securities for $16,000 this year. His capital gain on sale was $13,600.

Let's summarize the tax consequences of this transfer.

- Mr. Roy gave valuable property to Steve without incurring any transfer tax.
- Steve, rather than Mr. Roy, recognized the income from the property after the transfer.
- Steve, rather than Mr. Roy, recognized the unrealized appreciation in the value of the property as capital gain.

If Steve's marginal rate was less than Mr. Roy's marginal rate, the income shift from the gift resulted in a tax savings for the family.

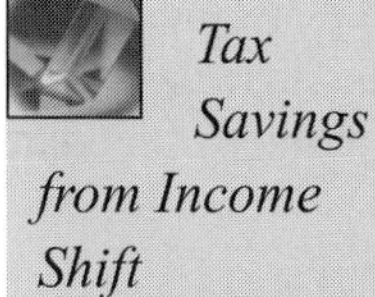

Tax Savings from Income Shift

Assume that during the six years that Steve owned the securities, his marginal tax rate on ordinary dividends was 5 percent, while Mr. Roy's marginal rate was 15 percent. The following table compares Steve's total tax on the shifted dividends and capital gain with Mr. Roy's tax cost if he had not made the gift.

	Steve	*Mr. Roy*
Dividend income ($900 for six years)	$ 5,400	$ 5,400
Tax rate	.5	.15
Tax on dividends	$ 270	$ 810
Capital gain	$13,600	$13,600
Preferential tax rate	.05	.15
Tax on capital gain	$ 680	$ 2,040
Total tax	$ 950	$ 2,850

Because of the difference in marginal rates, Mr. Roy's gift to Steve saved $1,900 tax for the family.

Kiddie Tax

The Internal Revenue Code severely limits the tax savings from a transfer of income-producing property to a child under the age of 14 years. The investment income from the property is reported on the child's tax return. However, the child's *unearned* taxable income in excess of an inflation-adjusted base amount ($800 in 2005) is taxed at the marginal rate from the child's *parents'* return.[71] Moreover, if the child is claimed as a dependent by another taxpayer, the child's standard deduction is limited to the *greater* of $800 or earned income plus $250.[72]

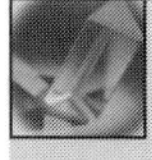

Kiddie Tax

Mr. Roy, our grandfather in the preceding example, gave corporate bonds to his nine-year-old granddaughter, Kim. In 2005, Kim received $4,000 interest income, which was her only income item. Her parents' marginal tax rate was 35 percent, so Kim's tax was $920.

[71] §1(g).

[72] §63(c)(5). The $250 add-on to earned income is adjusted annually for inflation.

Interest income	$4,000
Standard deduction	(800)
Taxable income	$3,200
Unearned taxable income	$3,200
Base	(800)
Income taxed at parents' rate	$2,400
Kim's tax:	
$2,400 × 35%	$ 840
$800 × 10%	80
	$ 920

While this **kiddie tax** certainly reduces the benefit of income shifts to young children, families can avoid it by giving assets that yield deferred rather than current income. For instance, children can be given stock in a growth corporation that doesn't pay dividends. Similarly, children can be given Series EE savings bonds that won't generate interest income until the year of redemption.

The Taxable Estate

Objective 9
Determine a decedent's taxable estate.

Wealthy individuals who choose not to transfer property as gifts are postponing the inevitable. No one can avoid the final transfer of property that must occur at death. The federal estate tax is levied on the FMV of a deceased individual's taxable estate.[73] The **taxable estate** includes all assets owned by the decedent and transferred under a valid will or state intestacy statute. These assets constitute the decedent's **probate estate.** The taxable estate may also include other property transferred because of the decedent's death. For instance, a decedent may have participated in a retirement plan that pays a death benefit to the surviving family members. Or the decedent may have owned an insurance policy on his life that pays proceeds to the beneficiary named in the policy. Neither the death benefit nor the insurance proceeds are part of the probate estate, but both amounts are included in the taxable estate.[74]

The taxable estate is reduced by the decedent's debts, funeral expenses, and any administrative costs of settling the estate.[75] It is also reduced by bequests to religious, charitable, educational, government, or other nonprofit organizations.[76] Thus, a person could leave her entire fortune to public causes and avoid the estate tax altogether. Lastly, the taxable estate is reduced by the FMV of property transferred to a surviving spouse.[77] Because of this **unlimited marital deduction,** the estate tax on the wealth accumulated by a married couple can be deferred until both spouses are deceased.

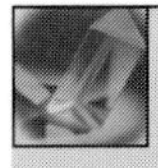

Taxable Estate

Mr. Webb died on May 3, and was survived by his wife and two children from a previous marriage. At date of death, he owned assets with a $7,270,000 aggregate FMV and had $938,000 of debts. The funeral expenses and legal fees relating to the estate totaled

[73] §2031.

[74] §2039 and §2042.

[75] §2053.

[76] §2055.

[77] §2056.

$94,300. In his will, Mr. Webb left his art collection worth $1.8 million to the Metropolitan Museum, marketable securities worth $2.5 million to his widow, and the rest of his property in equal shares to his children. His taxable estate is computed as follows.

FMV of property owned by decedent	$ 7,270,000
Decedent's debts	(938,000)
Funeral and administrative costs	(94,300)
Net estate	$ 6,237,700
Deductible charitable bequest	(1,800,000)
Deductible marital bequest	(2,500,000)
Taxable estate	$ 1,937,700

Estate Tax Exclusion

The estate tax is scheduled for repeal in 2010. For 2002 through 2009, every estate is entitled to an exclusion to reduce the amount subject to tax.[78] Here are the exclusion amounts:

For Estates of Decedents Dying in:	Exclusion
2002 and 2003	$1,000,000
2004 and 2005	1,500,000
2006, 2007, and 2008	2,000,000
2009	3,500,000

These annual exclusions must be decreased by any lifetime gift tax exclusion used by the decedent.

Estate Tax Exclusion

Let's determine how much of Mr. Webb's taxable estate is actually taxed under three different assumptions.

Assumption 1: Mr. Webb did not make any taxable gifts and therefore did not use any of his lifetime gift tax exclusion. His date of death was May 3, 2002.

Taxable estate	$1,937,700
2002 exclusion	(1,000,000)
Estate subject to tax	$ 937,000

Assumption 2: Mr. Webb made $400,000 taxable gifts and used $400,000 of his lifetime gift tax exclusion to avoid paying gift tax. His date of death was May 3, 2002.

[78] §2010(c). The exclusion is actually accomplished by a tax *credit* that offsets the estate tax on the exclusion amount.

Taxable estate	$1,937,700
2002 exclusion:	
($1,000,000 – $400,000)	(600,000)
Estate subject to tax	$1,337,000

Assumption 3: Mr. Webb made $400,000 taxable gifts and used $400,000 of his lifetime gift tax exclusion to avoid paying gift tax. His date of death was May 3, 2005.

Taxable estate	$1,937,700
2004 exclusion:	
($1,500,000 – $400,000)	(1,100,000)
Estate subject to tax	$ 837,000

Basis of Property Transferred at Death

When property is transferred at death, the new owners take a tax basis equal to FMV at date of death.[79] Consequently, any unrealized appreciation in the property's value simply vanishes and is never recognized as income.

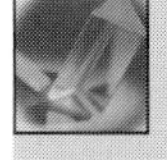

Basis Step-Up to FMV

Mrs. Webb inherited marketable securities that had a $2,500,000 FMV at the date of Mr. Webb's death. His aggregate tax basis in these securities was only $420,000. If Mr. Webb had sold the securities immediately before his death, he would have recognized a $2,080,000 taxable gain. If Mrs. Webb sells the securities immediately after his death, she recognizes no gain because the tax basis is *stepped-up* to FMV ($2,500,000) on the transfer from the decedent.

This extremely favorable income tax result will be repealed when the estate tax is repealed. Beginning in 2010, the basis of property transferred at death will be a carryover basis (just like the basis of property transferred by gift). As a result, any unrealized appreciation in value will survive to be recognized as income when the new owner disposes of the property in a taxable transaction.

Conclusion

Millions of individuals work conscientiously to provide financial comfort for their families. They pay close attention to the income tax consequences of their business and investment decisions and implement strategies to minimize income tax cost. Unfortunately, many of these same individuals give little thought to long-range transfer tax planning. They have no idea the size of the tax bill that would be triggered by their death. Such shortsightedness can have disastrous financial consequences, particularly in cases of unexpected and untimely death.[80] The moral of this story should be clear. People with wealth should consult a tax professional to determine their exposure to the federal transfer tax. In virtually every case, the application of fundamental planning principles can reduce that exposure and guarantee a brighter financial future.

[79] §1014.

[80] A case in point: When Joe Robbie (former owner of the Miami Dolphins) died, his estate was hit with a $47 million tax bill. The estate had insufficient liquid assets, and the family was forced to sell both the football team and the Dolphins' stadium to raise cash to pay the tax.

Key Terms

accelerated death benefits *428*
annual gift tax exclusion *448*
capital gain distribution *423*
cash surrender value *427*
collectibles *432*
donee *447*
donor *447*
inside buildup *427*
inter vivos transfer *447*
investment interest expense *440*
kiddie tax *450*
lifetime gift tax exclusion *448*
long-term capital gain or loss *432*
market discount *426*
material participation *442*
mutual fund *422*
net investment income *440*
nonbusiness bad debt *431*
original issue discount (OID) *427*
passive activity *442*
passive income generator (PIG) *446*
private activity bonds *425*
probate estate *450*
qualified dividend distribution *423*
qualified dividend income *423*
qualified small business stock *438*
rental activity *444*
reorganization *431*
Section 1244 Stock *438*
securities *422*
Series EE savings bonds *426*
short-term capital gain or loss *432*
taxable estate *450*
testamentary transfer *447*
28 percent rate gain or loss *432*
unlimited marital deduction *450*
unrecaptured Section 1250 gain *435*

Questions and Problems for Discussion

1. Contrast the income tax consequences of the yields on the following investments.
   a. U.S. Treasury bonds
   b. Bonds issued by the State of Illinois.
   c. Bonds issued by a publicly held corporation at their face value.
   d. Bonds issued by a publicly held corporation at a discounted value.
   e. Preferred stock issued by a publicly held corporation.
   f. Shares issued by a mutual fund.
2. Term life insurance has no investment element and no cash surrender value. As a result, a term policy represents pure insurance protection. What are the tax consequences when the owner lets a term policy lapse by discontinuing premium payments?
3. Mrs. SD, age 74, has $50,000 in a certificate of deposit paying 6 percent annual interest. In addition to this interest income, she receives Social Security and a modest pension from her former employer. Her marginal tax rate is 10 percent. Mrs. SD lives independently, but she anticipates that in several years she will need to liquidate the certificate of deposit to buy into an assisted-living retirement home. She recently read a magazine article on the benefits of tax-deferred annuities and wonders if she should transfer her $50,000 savings into an annuity. Discuss whether this tax planning strategy is advisable for Mrs. SD.
4. As of November, Ms. B had $12,000 capital losses and no capital gains. She owns 4,900 shares of GG stock with a $15 basis and a $45 FMV per share. Ms. B plans to hold her stock for three more years before selling it and using the proceeds to buy a home. However, she could easily sell 400 shares to trigger a $12,000 capital gain and then immediately repurchase them. If her marginal tax rate is 35 percent, should she implement this strategy?
5. What is the logic for the presumption that a limited interest in a business partnership is a passive activity?
6. Mrs. K is a shareholder in TK, an S corporation. What fact would be the strongest indicator that she materially participates in TK's business?

7. Discuss the potential effect of the passive activity loss limitation on the market value of *profitable* rental real estate activities.
8. Identify the structural similarity between the investment interest expense limitation, the capital loss limitation, and the passive activity loss limitation.
9. Mr. and Mrs. FB each own 30 percent of the voting common stock of FB Inc. Four unrelated investors each own 10 percent. Based on a recent appraisal, FB's net worth is $10 million. Discuss the *valuation* issue suggested if:
   a. Mr. and Mrs. FB give their combined 60 percent stock interest to their son.
   b. An unrelated investor gives her 10 percent stock interest to her son.
10. Mr. and Mrs. T have never made a taxable gift, but they want their five children and dozen grandchildren to enjoy their wealth after they are both gone. Mr. and Mrs. T each have a will that leaves their entire property to the other so there will be no estate tax when the first spouse dies. Can you identify the problem with this strategy?
11. Mr. and Mrs. B earn a combined annual salary of $150,000. What *two* basic economic choices do they have with respect to this income (i.e., what can they do with their money)? Now assume that Mr. and Mrs. B own property worth $2 million. What *three* basic economic choices do they have with respect to this wealth?

Application Problems

For the following problems, assume the taxable year is 2005.

1. At the beginning of the year, Mr. S paid $15 per share for 620 shares of Carmel stock. He received cash distributions totaling $840. His Form 1099-DIV reported that $700 was an ordinary dividend and $140 was a nontaxable distribution. Compute his basis in his 620 shares at year-end.
2. Mrs. Z, a resident of Virginia, paid $50,000 for a bond issued by Pennsylvania that paid $3,400 interest this year. Her marginal state income tax rate is 6 percent. Under Virginia law, interest on debt obligations issued by another state is taxable. Mrs. Z can deduct state income tax on her Form 1040, and her marginal federal income tax rate is 35 percent. Compute her after-tax rate of return on the bond.
3. In 2003, Mrs. U paid $80,000 for a corporate bond with a $100,000 stated redemption value. Based on the bond's yield to maturity, amortization of the $20,000 discount was $1,390 in 2003 and $1,480 in 2004. Mrs. U sold the bond for $83,250 in 2005. What are her tax consequences in each year assuming that:
   a. She bought the newly issued bond from the corporation?
   b. She bought the bond in the public market through her broker?
4. In 2003, Mr. DP paid $47,600 for 3,400 shares of GKL Mutual Fund and elected to reinvest dividends in additional shares. In 2003 and 2004, he received Form 1099s reporting the following.

	Dividends Reinvested	Shares Purchased	Price per Share	Total Shares Owned
2003	$5,070	312	$16.25	3,712
2004	5,780	340	17.00	4,052

   a. If Mr. DP sells his 4,052 shares for $18 per share, compute his recognized gain.
   b. If he sells only 800 shares for $18 per share and uses the FIFO method to determine basis, compute his recognized gain.
   c. If he sells only 800 shares for $18 per share and uses the average basis method, compute his recognized gain.

5. Sixteen years ago, Ms. U purchased a $400,000 insurance policy on her own life and named her son as sole beneficiary. She paid a total of $21,900 premiums to keep this policy in force.
   a. This year, she liquidates the policy for its $27,200 cash surrender value. Does she recognize any income on the liquidation?
   b. Now assume that Ms. U is terminally ill. The insurance policy provides that a person with a life expectancy of less than one year can liquidate the policy and receive 80 percent of the death benefit. She does so and receives a $320,000 accelerated death benefit. Does she recognize any income on the liquidation?
6. Fifteen years ago, Mr. F paid $50,000 for a single-premium annuity contract. This year, he began receiving a $1,300 monthly payment that will continue for his life. Based on his age, he can expect to receive $312,000. How much of each monthly payment is taxable income to Mr. F?
7. Refer to the facts in the preceding problem. Assume that on January 1, 2020, Mr. F's unrecovered investment in the annuity is $1,875.
   a. How much of his total 2020 annuity payments ($15,600) are taxable?
   b. Assume that he dies in February 2020 after receiving only one $1,300 payment. What are the tax consequences on his final Form 1040?
8. Ten years ago, Mr. L paid $8 per share for 1,800 shares of Drago stock. Mr. L learned that Drago is in bankruptcy and can pay only 30 percent of its debt. What are the tax consequences to Mr. L of Drago's bankruptcy?
9. Three years ago, Mrs. B loaned $10,000 to Mr. J in return for his interest-bearing note. She made the loan to enable him to begin his own business. This year, Mr. J informed Mrs. B that his business had failed and that he was unable to repay the debt. Mrs. B decided not to take legal action to enforce the debt. What are her tax consequences of this bad debt?
10. CVF owned 2,000 shares of Jarvis nonvoting common stock with a $225,000 basis. In each of the following cases, determine CVF's recognized gain or loss on the disposition of this stock.
    a. CVF exchanged it for 1,300 shares of Jarvis voting common stock worth $387,000.
    b. CVF exchanged it for U.S. long-term bonds worth $317,500.
    c. CVF exchanged it for 900 shares of Newton common stock worth $280,000. This exchange was not pursuant to a corporate reorganization involving Jarvis and Newton.
    d. CVF exchanged it for 900 shares of Newton common stock worth $280,000. This exchange was pursuant to a corporate reorganization involving Jarvis and Newton.
11. Refer to the preceding problem. For each case, determine CVF's tax basis in the security received in the exchange.
12. Before considering capital gains and losses, Mr. and Mrs. R had $128,000 AGI. For each of the following cases, compute their AGI.
    a. On May 8, they recognized a $8,900 short-term capital gain. On June 25, they recognized a $15,000 long-term capital loss.
    b. On February 11, they recognized a $2,100 long-term capital gain. On November 3, they recognized a $1,720 long-term capital loss.
    c. On April 2, they recognized a $5,000 long-term capital loss. On September 30, they recognized a $4,800 short-term capital loss.
    d. On January 12, they recognized a $5,600 short-term capital loss. On July 5, they recognized a $1,500 long-term capital gain.

13. Refer to the preceding problem. Determine which of the four cases results in a capital loss carryforward for Mr. and Mrs. R. What is the amount and character of each carryforward?
14. Mr. J, a single taxpayer, recognized a $70,000 long-term capital gain, a $10,000 short-term capital gain, and a $45,000 long-term capital loss. Compute J's tax if his taxable income before consideration of his capital transactions is $400,000.
15. In 1994, Ms. EJ, a head of household, contributed $50,000 in exchange for 500 shares of Seta stock. Seta is a qualified small business. This year, she sold all 500 shares for $117,400. Her only other capital transaction resulted in an $8,600 long-term capital gain. Her taxable income before consideration of her two capital transactions is $191,000.
    a. Compute her tax for the year.
    b. How would the computation change if Ms. EJ acquired the Seta stock in 2002 instead of 1994?
16. In 1996, Mr. EF, a single taxpayer, contributed $45,000 in exchange for 500 shares of DB stock. In 2000, he paid $40,000 to another shareholder to purchase 1,000 more DB shares. All DB's stock qualified as Section 1244 stock when it was issued. This year, Mr. EF sold all 1,500 DB shares for $16 per share. His only income item was his $80,000 salary.
    a. Compute Mr. EF's AGI.
    b. How would AGI change if he recognized a $20,000 capital gain on the sale of other securities?
17. This year, Mr. and Mrs. MS earned $78,000 combined salaries and recognized $890 interest income, a $1,000 short-term capital gain, and a $7,200 long-term capital gain. They incurred $6,400 investment interest expense and $9,500 other itemized deductions. They have no dependents and file a joint return. Should they elect to treat $4,510 of their long-term capital gain as investment income?
18. Mr. D, who is in a 35 percent marginal tax bracket, recognized a $15,000 capital loss in 2005. Compute the tax savings from this loss assuming that:
    a. He also recognized an $18,000 short-term capital gain.
    b. He also recognized an $18,000 long-term capital gain.
    c. He also recognized an $18,000 28 percent rate gain.
    d. He recognized no capital gain in 2005 and does not expect to recognize capital gain in 2006 through 2009. Mr. D uses a 5 percent discount rate to compute NPV.
19. Mr. and Mrs. MH own a grocery store as a sole proprietorship. Their net profit and other relevant items for the year are:

Grocery store net profit	$44,000
SE tax on net profit	6,217
Dividends and interest income	5,700
Loss from a rental house	(1,900)
Loss from a limited partnership interest	(2,600)

    Compute Mr. and Mrs. MH's AGI.
20. Mr. V owns stock in VP and in BL, both of which are S corporations. This year, he had the following income and loss items.

Salary	$62,300
Business income from VP	19,000
Business loss from BL	(25,000)

Compute Mr. V's AGI under each of the following assumptions.

a. He materially participates in VP's business but not in BL's business.
b. He materially participates in BL's business but not in VP's business.
c. He materially participates in both corporate businesses.
d. He does not materially participate in either corporate business.

21. Ms. TN owns a one-half interest in an apartment complex, which is her only passive activity. The complex operated at a $60,000 loss this year. In addition to her share of this loss, Ms. TN had the following income items.

Salary	$59,000
Interest and dividends	4,400

a. Compute her AGI.
b. How would AGI change if her salary was $128,000 rather than $59,000?
c. How would AGI change if her salary was $200,000 rather than $59,000?

22. Ms. A owns an interest in ABCD Partnership, which is a passive activity. At the beginning of the year, she projects that her share of ABCD's business loss will be $13,000, and that she will have the following items.

Net profit from her consulting business	$75,000
SE tax on net profit	10,597
Interest and dividends	1,500

Ms. A plans to buy a rental house that should generate $8,000 income this year. Compute her AGI and the tax cost of her projected rent income.

23. Mr. D earned an $85,000 salary and recognized a $12,000 loss on a security sale and a $14,000 gain on the sale of a limited partnership interest. His share of the partnership's business income through date of sale was $2,100. (Both the gain and the business income are passive activity income.) Mr. D was allocated a $13,900 passive activity loss from an S corporation. Compute his AGI.

24. Mr. JS died on June 19 when the total FMV of his property was $10 million and his debts totaled $789,000. His executor paid $13,000 funeral expenses and $82,600 accounting and legal fees to settle the estate. Mr. JS bequeathed $500,000 to the First Lutheran Church of Milwaukee and $1 million to Western Wisconsin College. He bequeathed his art collection (FMV $2.4 million) to his wife and the residual of his estate to his three children. Compute Mr. JS's taxable estate.

25. Mrs. WP owns investment land with a $138,000 basis and a $200,000 FMV. Compute the after-tax sale proceeds in each of the following cases.

a. She sells the land herself. Her taxable income before considering the long-term gain on sale is $310,000.
b. She gives a 25 percent interest in the land to each of her four single adult grandchildren (without incurring a gift tax) who immediately sell it. Each grandchild's taxable income before considering the gain on sale is $8,000.
c. She dies while still owning the land. Her single daughter inherits the land and immediately sells it. The daughter's taxable income before considering the gain on sale is $79,000.

Issue Recognition Problems

Identify the tax issue or issues suggested by the following situations and state each issue in the form of a question.

1. Mr. X invests in Series EE savings bonds. He projects that his sole proprietorship will generate a sizable loss, and he wants to accelerate income from other sources to offset it. He could elect to recognize $28,000 accrued interest on the savings bonds he now owns. However, he does not want to recognize current income on the bonds he will purchase in future years.
2. At the beginning of the year, Ms. A owned 2,900 shares of SBS stock with a basis of $32 per share. SBS paid a 50 percent stock dividend, and Ms. A received 1,450 additional SBS shares. Before this dividend, the market price per share was $90. After the dividend, the price fell to $65.
3. In 1993, Mr. L paid $18,000 for a newly issued BN bond with a $30,000 stated redemption value. He has recognized $6,000 of the original issue discount (OID) as ordinary interest income. This year, BN went bankrupt and informed Mr. L that his bond was worthless.
4. Mr. and Mrs. G paid $53,000 for a corporate bond with a $50,000 stated redemption value. They paid the $3,000 premium because the bond's annual interest rate is higher than the market interest rate.
5. Three years ago, Mrs. B purchased 1,000 shares of NN stock from an unrelated party for $12 per share. After her purchase, the value of the shares steadily declined. Two weeks ago, an unrelated party offered to buy the shares for 30 cents per share. Mrs. B declined the offer and immediately mailed her shares to NN's secretary-treasurer with a note declaring her intention to abandon them.
6. Two years ago, Ms. X loaned $3,500 to her 20-year-old daughter, who used the loan proceeds to buy a used car. This year, the daughter informed her mother that she could not repay the debt.
7. Mr. O was a 25 percent partner in MNOP Partnership, which operated a gift and souvenir shop. He materially participated in the partnership business. Several years ago, Mr. O loaned $10,000 to MNOP in return for a written, interest-bearing note. Unfortunately, MNOP went bankrupt before the loan was repaid.
8. This year, Ms. T had a $29,000 capital loss carryforward and a $8,200 suspended passive activity loss carryforward. He died on September 12 and did not recognize any capital gain or passive activity income during the year.
9. Ms. N has $60,000 suspended passive activity losses from her interest in the EZ Limited Partnership. In December, she sold this interest to N Inc., a regular corporation in which she is the sole shareholder.
10. Mr. B has a $7,900 adjusted basis in his limited interest in PKO Partnership. He also has $22,000 suspended passive activity losses from PKO. Mr. B recently sent a letter to PKO's corporate general partner formally abandoning his equity in the partnership.
11. Mr. OG, a 66-year-old divorced individual, has two children with his former wife. He recently married a 45-year-old woman with no property of her own. Therefore, Mr. OG plans to change his will to provide that when he dies, his fortune will be placed in a trust. His new wife will receive the income for as long as she lives, but she has no direct ownership in the trust property. When she dies, Mr. OG's two children will inherit everything.
12. Mr. D died on March 8. His taxable estate includes an individual retirement account (IRA) with a $140,000 balance. Mr. D's contributions to this IRA were fully deductible. His son is the beneficiary of the IRA.

13. Mrs. AS died on June 1. She and her surviving husband were co-owners of real property with a \$200,000 adjusted basis and a \$1.6 million FMV. Mr. AS inherited his wife's half of the property.

Research Problems

1. Mrs. Evelyn Baker sued her stockbroker for mismanagement of her account. The broker ultimately settled the case by paying her \$250,000. The payment represented the loss in value of Mrs. Baker's stock portfolio attributable to the mismanagement. Because the payment was made with respect to capital assets, Mrs. Baker could report the payment as a \$250,000 capital gain (rather than ordinary income) on her Form 1040. Her legal fees for the lawsuit totaled \$70,000. Can Mrs. Baker treat the fees as a capital loss by simply offsetting them against the settlement and thereby include only \$180,000 net capital gain in her AGI?
2. Todd Zimler, who files a joint income tax return with his wife, Stella, owns 85 percent of the outstanding stock of Zimler Manufacturing. In January of last year, Todd transferred a tract of investment land to the corporation in exchange for 600 shares of nonvoting preferred stock, which qualified as Section 1244 stock. At date of transfer, Todd's basis in the land was \$185,000, and the land's FMV was \$60,000. The exchange of land for stock was nontaxable under Section 351. Consequently, Todd recognized no loss and took a \$185,000 substituted basis in the 100 shares of stock. In May of this year, Todd sold the 100 shares to an unrelated investor for \$62,000. What is the character of Todd's \$123,000 recognized loss?
3. Rachel Sanchez is a limited partner in HN Partnership, which operates a souvenir shop, and a member in Jams-n-Jellies LLC, which makes specialty food items and sells them at retail. Rachel has no involvement in the partnership business, but she handles all the advertising for the LLC. The LLC compensates her at the rate of \$45 per hour, and she billed the LLC for 592 hours of work during 2005. Rachel's only other income-generating activity is her part-time employment as a librarian.

   Rachel's 2005 Schedule K-1 from HN Partnership reported that her share of ordinary business loss was \$3,810. Her 2005 Schedule K-1 from Jams-n-Jellies LLC reported that her share of ordinary business income was \$15,082. How much of her share of the partnership loss can Rachel deduct on her 2005 Form 1040?

Tax Planning Cases

1. Ms. K, who is in the 35 percent marginal tax bracket, acquired the following blocks of stock in KDS, a closely held corporation.

July 12, 1995	1,400 shares at \$41 per share
December 3, 2000	800 shares at \$46 per share
September 30, 2002	2,000 shares at \$49 per share*
October 2, 2005	750 shares at \$53 per share

*Qualified small business stock.

   In November 2005, Ms. K agreed to sell 1,000 KDS shares to Mr. N for \$60 per share. Which shares should she sell to maximize her after-tax cash from the sale?
2. Ms. EH is the owner and beneficiary of a \$150,000 insurance policy on her mother's life. Ms. EH has paid \$46,000 premiums, and the policy is fully paid up (no more premiums are due). She needs money and is considering cashing in the policy for its \$95,000 cash surrender value. Alternatively, she can borrow \$70,000 against the policy

from the insurance company. She will pay 5 percent annual interest (a nondeductible personal expense) and repay the loan from the death benefit. Ms. EH's mother is in poor health and should live no more than 10 years. Ms. EH's marginal tax rate is 25 percent. Assuming a 6 percent discount rate, should she cash in the policy or borrow against it?

3. Mr. and Mrs. KQ are evaluating an investment in undeveloped land. The year 0 cost is \$100,000, and they can borrow \$60,000 of the purchase price at 8 percent. They will pay interest only in years 1 through 5. The annual property tax on the land will be \$1,200 in years 1 through 5. Mr. and Mrs. KQ project that they can sell the land in year 5 for \$160,000 and repay the \$60,000 loan from the sales proceeds. They have a 35 percent marginal tax rate and use a 9 percent discount rate to compute NPV. Determine if they should make this investment under the following assumptions.
   a. They have enough net investment income and other itemized deductions so that the \$6,000 annual carrying charge (interest plus property tax) is deductible in years 1 through 5.
   b. Because they do not itemize deductions, they elect to capitalize the annual carrying charge to the basis of the land.
4. Mr. and Mrs. U's taxable income is \$260,000. Mr. U plans to exercise incentive stock options with a \$65,000 bargain element. In addition to this bargain element, the couple has approximately \$10,000 positive AMT adjustments and preferences. They want to invest \$50,000 excess funds and could purchase either a corporate bond paying 10 percent or a newly issued private activity tax-exempt bond paying 7.5 percent. Both bonds have identical risk. Which investment yields the greater after-tax cash flow?
5. Ms. ZH is evaluating two investment opportunities with identical risk. Investment A will generate \$7,200 income and cash flow in years 0 through 2. Investment P will generate a \$25,000 passive activity loss in years 0 and 1 and no cash flow. In year 2, Investment P will generate \$73,000 taxable income and \$23,000 cash flow. After three years, both investments will return her initial cash contribution. Ms. ZH uses an 8 percent discount rate to compute NPV. Determine the superior investment under each of the following assumptions.
   a. Her marginal tax rate over the investment period is 25 percent, and she owns no other passive activities.
   b. Her marginal tax rate over the investment period is 35 percent, and she owns rental property generating \$40,000 annual income.
6. Ms. BB purchased a limited interest in Quinnel Partnership in 2004. Her share of the partnership's 2004 business loss was \$5,700. Unfortunately, Ms. BB could not deduct this loss because she had no passive activity income, so she is carrying it forward into 2005. Quinnel Partnership projects that it will operate at breakeven (no income or loss) for several years. However, Ms. BB believes that her partnership interest is a solid long-term investment, and she has no plans to sell it.

   On January 1, 2005, Ms. BB must decide between two new investments that are comparable in terms of risk and liquidity. She could invest \$100,000 in TNB Limited Partnership, and her share of the partnership's 2005 business income would be \$8,000. Alternatively, she could invest \$100,000 in a high-yield bond fund that promises a 10 percent return (Ms. BB would receive \$10,000 interest income in 2005). Which investment would result in a better after-tax return for 2005, assuming that:
   a. Ms. BB is in a 25 percent marginal tax bracket?
   b. Ms. BB is in a 35 percent marginal tax bracket?

Appendix **15–A**

Comprehensive Schedule D Problem

Mr. and Mrs. Lowell made the following stock sales.

	Date Acquired	Date Sold	Tax Basis	Selling Price
1,782 shares ZT common	1/28/93	9/3	$14,900	$36,900
119 shares MN preferred	2/11/97	9/12	9,000	7,050
2,040 shares GG common	5/14/99	10/6	18,000	22,400
45 shares Pluto mutual fund	8/3/04	12/30	3,100	3,500

- Mrs. Lowell is a limited partner in Cohen LP. Her Schedule K-1 reported a $7,610 share of long-term capital gain.
- The Lowells received a Form 1099 from Pluto mutual fund reporting a $700 long-term capital gain distribution.
- In 2001, Mrs. Lowell loaned $4,250 to a friend who needed the money for a new business venture. The friend recently declared personal bankruptcy, and Mrs. Lowell decided not to pursue collection of the $4,250 debt in court.
- The Lowells have a $1,200 long-term capital loss carryforward.
- Their taxable income (Form 1040, line 42) is $166,332, which includes $6,200 qualified dividend income (line 9b).

The above information and the calculation of Mr. and Mrs. Lowell's regular tax are shown on the following Schedule D and worksheet.

SCHEDULE D (Form 1040)
Department of the Treasury Internal Revenue Service (99)

Capital Gains and Losses

▶ Attach to Form 1040. ▶ See Instructions for Schedule D (Form 1040).
▶ Use Schedule D-1 to list additional transactions for lines 1 and 8.

OMB No. 1545-0074
2004
Attachment Sequence No. **12**

Name(s) shown on Form 1040: MR. and MRS. Lowell
Your social security number: 416 01 1921

Part I Short-Term Capital Gains and Losses—Assets Held One Year or Less

(a) Description of property (Example: 100 sh. XYZ Co.)	(b) Date acquired (Mo., day, yr.)	(c) Date sold (Mo., day, yr.)	(d) Sales price (see page D-6 of the instructions)	(e) Cost or other basis (see page D-6 of the instructions)	(f) Gain or (loss) Subtract (e) from (d)
1 45 sh. Pluto MF	8·3·04	12·30·04	3,500	3,100	400
Nonbusiness bad debt	see attached explanation				(4,250)

2 Enter your short-term totals, if any, from Schedule D-1, line 2	2		
3 **Total short-term sales price amounts.** Add lines 1 and 2 in column (d)	3	3,500	
4 Short-term gain from Form 6252 and short-term gain or (loss) from Forms 4684, 6781, and 8824		4	
5 Net short-term gain or (loss) from partnerships, S corporations, estates, and trusts from Schedule(s) K-1		5	
6 Short-term capital loss carryover. Enter the amount, if any, from line 8 of your **Capital Loss Carryover Worksheet** on page D-6 of the instructions		6	( )
7 **Net short-term capital gain or (loss).** Combine lines 1 through 6 in column (f)		7	(3,850)

Part II Long-Term Capital Gains and Losses—Assets Held More Than One Year

(a) Description of property (Example: 100 sh. XYZ Co.)	(b) Date acquired (Mo., day, yr.)	(c) Date sold (Mo., day, yr.)	(d) Sales price (see page D-6 of the instructions)	(e) Cost or other basis (see page D-6 of the instructions)	(f) Gain or (loss) Subtract (e) from (d)
8 1,782 sh. ZT common	1·28·93	9·3·04	36,900	14,900	22,000
119 sh. MN preferred	2·11·97	9·12·04	7,050	9,000	(1,950)
2,040 sh. GG common	5·14·99	10·6·04	22,400	18,000	4,400

9 Enter your long-term totals, if any, from Schedule D-1, line 9	9		
10 **Total long-term sales price amounts.** Add lines 8 and 9 in column (d)	10	66,350	
11 Gain from Form 4797, Part I; long-term gain from Forms 2439 and 6252; and long-term gain or (loss) from Forms 4684, 6781, and 8824		11	
12 Net long-term gain or (loss) from partnerships, S corporations, estates, and trusts from Schedule(s) K-1		12	7,610
13 Capital gain distributions. See page D-1 of the instructions		13	700
14 Long-term capital loss carryover. Enter the amount, if any, from line 13 of your **Capital Loss Carryover Worksheet** on page D-6 of the instructions		14	(1,200)
15 **Net long-term capital gain or (loss).** Combine lines 8 through 14 in column (f). Then go to Part III on the back		15	31,560

For Paperwork Reduction Act Notice, see Form 1040 instructions. Cat. No. 11338H **Schedule D (Form 1040) 2004**

Schedule D (Form 1040) 2004 Page 2

Part III **Summary**

16	**Combine lines 7 and 15 and enter the result. If line 16 is a loss, skip lines 17 through 20, and go to line 21. If a gain, enter the gain on Form 1040, line 13, and then go to line 17 below** . .	**16**	27,710
17	**Are lines 15 and 16 both gains?** ☒ **Yes.** Go to line 18. ☐ **No.** Skip lines 18 through 21, and go to line 22.		
18	**Enter the amount, if any, from line 7 of the 28% Rate Gain Worksheet on page D-7 of the instructions** . . . . . . ▶	**18**	0
19	**Enter the amount, if any, from line 18 of the Unrecaptured Section 1250 Gain Worksheet on page D-8 of the instructions** . . . . . . ▶	**19**	0
20	**Are lines 18 and 19 both zero or blank?** ☒ **Yes.** Complete Form 1040 through line 42, and then complete the **Qualified Dividends and Capital Gain Tax Worksheet** on page 34 of the instructions for Form 1040. **Do not** complete lines 21 and 22 below. ☐ **No.** Complete Form 1040 through line 42, and then complete the **Schedule D Tax Worksheet** on page D-9 of the instructions. **Do not** complete lines 21 and 22 below.		
21	If line 16 is a loss, enter here and on Form 1040, line 13, the **smaller** of: • The loss on line 16 or • ($3,000), or if married filing separately, ($1,500) . . . . . . **Note.** When figuring which amount is smaller, treat both amounts as positive numbers.	**21**	( )
22	Do you have qualified dividends on Form 1040, line 9b? ☐ **Yes.** Complete Form 1040 through line 42, and then complete the **Qualified Dividends and Capital Gain Tax Worksheet** on page 34 of the instructions for Form 1040. ☐ **No.** Complete the rest of Form 1040.		

Schedule D (Form 1040) 2004

Qualified Dividends and Capital Gain Tax Worksheet—Line 43

Keep for Your Records 

Before you begin:
- √ See the instructions for line 43 on page 33 to see if you can use this worksheet to figure your tax.
- √ If you do not have to file Schedule D and you received capital gain distributions, be sure you checked the box on line 13 of Form 1040.

Line	Description	Inner column	Middle column	Right column
1.	Enter the amount from Form 1040, line 42		1. 166,332	
2.	Enter the amount from Form 1040, line 9b	2. 6,200		
3.	Are you filing Schedule D? ☒ **Yes.** Enter the **smaller** of line 15 or 16 of Schedule D, but do not enter less than -0- ☐ **No.** Enter the amount from Form 1040, line 13	3. 27,710		
4.	Add lines 2 and 3	4. 33,910		
5.	If you are claiming investment interest expense on Form 4952, enter the amount from line 4g of that form. Otherwise, enter -0-	5. 0		
6.	Subtract line 5 from line 4. If zero or less, enter -0-		6. 33,910	
7.	Subtract line 6 from line 1. If zero or less, enter -0-		7. 132,422	
8.	Enter the **smaller** of: • The amount on line 1, or • $29,050 if single or married filing separately, $58,100 if married filing jointly or qualifying widow(er), $38,900 if head of household.		8. 58,100	
9.	Is the amount on line 7 equal to or more than the amount on line 8? ☒ **Yes.** Skip lines 9 through 11; go to line 12 and check the "No" box. ☐ **No.** Enter the amount from line 7		9.	
10.	Subtract line 9 from line 8		10.	
11.	Multiply line 10 by 5% (.05)			11.
12.	Are the amounts on lines 6 and 10 the same? ☐ **Yes.** Skip lines 12 through 15; go to line 16. ☒ **No.** Enter the **smaller** of line 1 or line 6		12. 33,910	
13.	Enter the amount from line 10 (if line 10 is blank, enter -0-)		13. 0	
14.	Subtract line 13 from line 12		14. 33,910	
15.	Multiply line 14 by 15% (.15)			15. 5,087
16.	Figure the tax on the amount on line 7. Use the Tax Table or Tax Computation Worksheet, whichever applies			16. 27,036
17.	Add lines 11, 15, and 16			17. 32,123
18.	Figure the tax on the amount on line 1. Use the Tax Table or Tax Computation Worksheet, whichever applies			18. 36,530
19.	**Tax on all taxable income.** Enter the **smaller** of line 17 or line 18. Also include this amount on Form 1040, line 43			19. 32,123

Appendix 15–B

Federal Transfer Tax Rates (2005)

The following rate schedule can be used to compute the federal gift or estate tax before reduction for the Section 2505 or Section 2010 unified credit.

If the taxable transfer is:	The precredit tax is:
Not over $10,000	18% of the taxable transfer
Over $10,000 but not over $20,000	$1,800 + 20% of the excess over $10,000
Over $20,000 but not over $40,000	$3,800 + 22% of the excess over $20,000
Over $40,000 but not over $60,000	$8,200 + 24% of the excess over $40,000
Over $60,000 but not over $80,000	$13,000 + 26% of the excess over $60,000
Over $80,000 but not over $100,000	$18,200 + 28% of the excess over $80,000
Over $100,000 but not over $150,000	$23,800 + 30% of the excess over $100,000
Over $150,000 but not over $250,000	$38,800 + 32% of the excess over $150,000
Over $250,000 but not over $500,000	$70,800 + 34% of the excess over $250,000
Over $500,000 but not over $750,000	$155,800 + 37% of the excess over $500,000
Over $750,000 but not over $1,000,000	$248,300 + 39% of the excess over $750,000
Over $1,000,000 but not over $1,250,000	$345,800 + 41% of the excess over $1,000,000
Over $1,250,000 but not over $1,500,000	$448,300 + 43% of the excess over $1,250,000
Over $1,500,000 but not over $2,000,000	$555,800 + 45% of the excess over $1,500,000
Over $2,000,000	$780,800 + 47% of the excess over $2,000,000

Chapter Sixteen

Tax Consequences of Personal Activities

Learning Objectives

After studying this chapter, you should be able to:

1. Identify personal receipts that are taxable income.
2. Describe the tax consequences of divorce settlements.
3. Identify personal expenses and losses that result in itemized deductions.
4. Describe the tax treatment of revenues and expenses from a hobby.
5. Compute the itemized deduction for home mortgage interest.
6. Describe the preferential tax treatment of gain from the sale of a personal residence.
7. Identify the itemized deductions that are limited or disallowed for AMT purposes.

To this point, Part Five has focused on the tax consequences of profit-motivated activities. We learned how to compute taxable income from business, employment, and investment activities and discovered many effective techniques for reducing the tax on such income. Chapter 16 introduces a new topic: the tax consequences of activities in which people engage for personal reasons. The first section of this chapter discusses the taxation of economic benefits that are not derived from business, employment, or investment activities.

The second section of the chapter concentrates on the tax rules for personal expenses or losses and identifies the limited circumstances under which they result in a tax savings. The third section explains the significant tax advantages of home ownership, while the last section integrates the material introduced in Chapter 16 into the alternative minimum tax (AMT) system.

GROSS INCOME FROM WHATEVER SOURCE DERIVED

Section 61 of the Internal Revenue Code states that gross income means all income from whatever source derived. This statement creates a presumption that any receipt of an economic benefit that increases an individual's net worth is subject to income tax. The context in which the receipt occurred or the source of the receipt is irrelevant.[1] The tax law does make exceptions to this inclusive rule, and we will identify a number of them in this chapter. Nevertheless, an individual who receives an economic benefit should assume that it is taxable income, even if it was derived from a purely personal or private activity.

Property Tax Abatements for Senior Volunteers

More than 50 Massachusetts cities have adopted a state-sponsored program under which senior citizens who perform voluntary civic services receive local property tax abatements of up to $500. The IRS ruled that the amount of the abatements is gross income to the senior citizens for federal tax purposes because no exception to the general rule of inclusion applies to this particular economic benefit.[2]

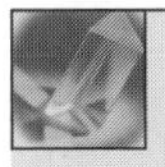

Holocaust Victim Restitution

Many victims of the Nazi regime who were persecuted because of their race or religion are entitled to restitution from European governments or other institutions for property that was stolen or otherwise lost to them during World War II. Federal law specifically provides that such restitution payments to Holocaust victims (or their heirs) are not included in the recipient's gross income for tax purposes.[3]

Personal Receipts

Objective 1
Identify personal receipts that are taxable income.

People who receive prizes or awards must recognize them as taxable income.[4] This general rule applies to awards based on achievement or merit such as the Nobel and Pulitzer prizes. It also applies to academic and athletic awards. However, students who are degree candidates at educational institutions may exclude scholarship or fellowship awards to the extent the award pays for tuition, fees, books, supplies, and equipment.[5]

Scholarships

Mary Dillon received a four-year scholarship from the University of Kansas that pays her $12,250 annual tuition (including all fees and books) plus her $10,300 annual room and board. She also received a $2,000 alumni association scholarship that she used to buy her college wardrobe. Mary can exclude the tuition scholarship but must include the $12,300 other scholarship awards in taxable income.

The general rule of taxability also applies to receipts attributable entirely to good luck, such as lottery jackpots, raffle or door prizes, and gambling winnings. The prize or award need not consist of cash; the game show contestant who wins a trip to Paris must include the value of the trip in taxable income.[6]

The major exception to the rule that personal receipts are taxable applies to gifts and inheritances.[7] Individuals who receive gifts of cash or property from a donor or who inherit cash or property from a decedent don't report the receipt as income on Form 1040. Simi-

[1] This presumption applies to receipts derived from unlawful activities such as embezzlement or extortion. Consequently, even illegal income is subject to income tax. *James* v. *United States*, 366 U.S. 213 (1961).

[2] Chief Counsel Advice Memorandum 200227003 (January 15, 2002).

[3] §803(a) of the Economic Growth and Tax Relief Reconciliation Act of 2001.

[4] §74. The law provides a narrow exception for certain employee achievement awards to the extent the award consists of tangible property worth no more than $1,600. This is called *the gold watch exception.*

[5] §117.

[6] *Reginald Turner*, TC Memo 1954–38.

[7] §102.

larly, life insurance proceeds are nontaxable. The beneficiary of a life insurance policy does not include the death benefit in taxable income.[8]

Personal Receipts

This year, Ms. Hardy received the following items.

Birthday gift of cash from her dad	$ 1,500
Set of dishes won at a church raffle (retail value)	600
Pearl ring inherited from her grandmother (appraised FMV)	2,600
Insurance proceeds from a policy on her grandmother's life	50,000

The only item that she must report on her Form 1040 is the $600 raffle prize.

Gift or Compensation Income

Reverend Lloyd Goodwin received an annual salary plus the use of a parsonage from the church at which he served as pastor. The church held three "special occasion" Sundays each year when the congregation was invited to make anonymous cash contributions to their pastor and his family. For the three tax years in question, the contributions totaled $42,250, and Reverend Goodwin did not report them on his tax return. The IRS concluded that the contributions represented employment compensation and should be included in taxable income. Members of the congregation who testified on behalf of Reverend Goodwin described the contributions as gifts made out of "love, respect, and admiration" for him. The court, however, concluded that the contributions were regular payments made by persons to whom Reverend Goodwin provided professional services and, therefore, were taxable compensation rather than nontaxable gifts.[9]

Legal Settlements

Individuals may receive economic benefits under legal agreements or settlements. For instance, a person who suffered an injury or detriment because of the fault of another party may be awarded damages by a court of law. The general rule is that legal damages are taxable income unless they represent compensation for physical injury or illness.[10]

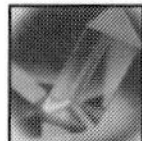

Legal Damages

Mrs. Spears was walking along a city sidewalk when she was struck by falling debris from a construction project. She sued the construction company for negligence and was awarded a $300,000 settlement: $100,000 for her physical pain and trauma plus $200,000 punitive damages (damages intended to punish a defendant for extreme misconduct). Mrs. Spears may exclude $100,000 of this settlement from income but must report and pay tax on the $200,000 punitive damages.[11]

Divorce

Objective 2
Describe the tax consequences of divorce settlements.

The divorce of a married couple is a personal event that may have profound economic consequences. The divorce decree, which specifies the rights and obligations of the divorcing parties, may require one party to transfer ownership of valuable property to the other. For

[8] §101(a).

[9] *Goodwin* v. *Commissioner*, 67 F.3d 149 (CA-8, 1995).

[10] §104(a)(2).

[11] Mrs. Spears's legal fees allocable to the taxable punitive damages are a miscellaneous itemized deduction. See Reg. §1.212-1(k) and *Benci-Woodward,* TC Memo 1998-395.

income tax purposes, this transfer is treated as a gift, regardless of any affection or animosity underlying the transfer.[12] As a result, the transferor recognizes no gain or loss on the disposition of the property. The transferee recognizes no income on receipt of the property and takes a carryover tax basis from the transferor.

The divorce decree may require one party to pay alimony to the other. Alimony consists of a series of payments by which a person discharges a legal obligation to support an ex-spouse. The recipient must include the alimony in income, while the payer may deduct it above-the-line in computing adjusted gross income (AGI).[13] If the divorcing couple has dependent children, the parent who surrenders custody may be required to pay child support to the custodial parent. Child support payments (in contrast to alimony) are not taxable income to the recipient and are nondeductible by the payer. Child support raises the question of which parent can claim the personal exemption and child tax credit for a dependent child. Regardless of the support involved, the custodial parent is entitled to the exemption and credit *unless* he or she signs a written declaration granting them to the noncustodial parent.[14]

Payments Pursuant to a Divorce

Mr. and Mrs. Watson recently divorced. Under the terms of the divorce decree, Mr. Watson transferred $600,000 worth of marketable securities to Mrs. Watson as a property settlement. His basis in the securities was $319,000. He is also required to pay $1,500 a month to his ex-wife: $900 alimony and $600 child support for their five-year-old daughter, who lives with Mrs. Watson.

Mr. Watson did not recognize taxable gain on disposition of the appreciated securities, and Mrs. Watson did not recognize income on their receipt. She has a $319,000 basis in the securities. Mrs. Watson recognizes the $900 monthly alimony payment as income, and Mr. Watson is allowed a corresponding deduction. Mrs. Watson is entitled to claim a personal exemption and child tax credit for the daughter on her Form 1040 unless she grants the exemption and credit to Mr. Watson.

Government Transfer Payments

People who receive need-based payments from a local, state, or federal government agency may exclude the payments from income.[15] Consequently, benefits provided through public assistance programs such as school lunches, food stamps, and welfare are nontaxable. In contrast, people who are entitled to receive government transfer payments irrespective of any demonstrated economic need must include the payments in income. For instance, unemployed workers must pay federal income tax on unemployment compensation received from their state government.[16]

Social Security

The question of whether Social Security benefits should be taxable is controversial. One political camp argues that these benefits should be taxed because they are not based on financial need. The opposing camp argues that Social Security benefits should be immune to the income tax. After all, aren't retirees entitled to their benefits because they paid nondeductible employee payroll tax or self-employment tax during their working years? The

[12] §1041. The transfer is not subject to gift tax.

[13] §71 requires the income inclusion, while §215 and §62(a)(1) allow the deduction. While legal fees paid in connection with a divorce are generally nondeductible, any fee properly attributable to the collection of alimony is a miscellaneous itemized deduction. Reg. §1.262-1(b)(7).

[14] §152(e) and §24(c)(1)(A).

[15] See Rev. Rul. 71-425, 1971-2 CB 76.

[16] §85.

federal government's complicated approach to taxing Social Security benefits reflects a cautious compromise between these polar positions. In very general terms:

- Married couples with less than $32,000 and single individuals with less than $25,000 of modified AGI are not required to pay tax on their benefits.
- Married couples with modified AGI between $32,000 and $44,000 and single individuals with modified AGI between $25,000 and $34,000 may have to pay tax on 50 percent of their benefits.
- Married couples with more than $44,000 and single individuals with more than $34,000 of modified AGI may have to pay tax on 85 percent of their benefits.[17]

The complete details of the computation are incorporated into a Social Security Worksheet included as Appendix 16–A to this chapter.

Gains on Sales of Personal Assets

Most personal assets fall into the category of *consumer durables*—tangible assets that people buy for their private use and enjoyment. Individuals can't recover the cost of these assets through depreciation. Thus, the initial cost basis of consumer durables is not adjusted downward, even though the market value of such goods invariably decreases over time. For this reason, people who sell consumer durables usually realize a loss on the transaction. As we will discuss later in the chapter, these personal losses are nondeductible.

People occasionally hold personal assets that do not wear out, break down, or become outdated but that actually increase in value. Collectibles such as postage stamps and antiques are good examples. If an individual does realize a gain on the sale of a collectible, the gain is either short-term capital gain or 28 percent rate gain, depending on the holding period of the asset.[18]

Collect for Love, Not for Money

According to a representative of Christie's East, a New York auction house, the first rule of investing in collectibles is to purchase items that give you pleasure and don't plan on making money on your collection. "We don't preach that art, for example, is a good investment. We preach that you buy art because you want to wake up in the morning and see it and enjoy it." If a collectible happens to increase in value, chalk it up to good luck. If a collectible decreases in value, you can still love it.[19]

Gain on Sale of Collection

During the last 15 years, Boyd Lovett purchased over 700 bottles of French wine, which he stored in his personal wine cellar. This year, Boyd moved to a small apartment and sold his entire wine collection to a local restaurant for $112,500. Boyd's cost basis in the collection was $73,600. Therefore, he recognized a $38,900 long-term capital gain on which he paid $10,892 federal income tax ($38,900 × 28%).

[17] §86. For purposes of this general summary, modified AGI includes one-half of any Social Security benefits received and any tax-exempt interest earned during the year.

[18] According to §1221(3), literary, musical, or artistic compositions, letters, and memoranda are not capital assets in the hands of either the individual who created the property or any individual who received such property as a gift from the creator. These individuals recognize ordinary income if they sell such assets at a gain.

[19] "Collect for Love, Not for Money," *Dallas Morning News,* August 4, 1998.

PERSONAL EXPENSES

The Internal Revenue Code states that no deduction is allowed for personal, living, or family expenses.[20] Accordingly, the everyday costs of managing a household, raising a family, pursuing social or civic interests, and enjoying leisure time do not result in any tax benefit. Even expenses with a tangential connection to a business or employment activity, such as the cost of a professional wardrobe, the daily commute to work, or routine noonday lunches, are inherently personal in nature and thus nondeductible.

Business or Personal Expenses?

Jeffrey Stone operated an appliance repair business out of a shop located about eight miles from his home. On the Schedule C on which he computed business income, he reported several thousand dollars of miscellaneous expenses. The IRS discovered that the miscellaneous expenses included payments for his children's birthday parties, Christmas presents to his nephews, trips to visit Mrs. Stone's parents, family trips to baseball tournaments, a fishing license, subscriptions to *People, Ladies' Home Journal,* and *Family Circle* magazines, and veterinary bills for the family dog and cat. The judge who tried Mr. Stone's case agreed with the IRS that his miscellaneous expenses were clearly nondeductible. "In differentiating between personal and business expenses, there may be some 'grey' areas, but the expenditures here do not fall within those areas, at least not without a Herculean effort of delusion."[21]

The tax law bends the no-deduction rule for three major categories of personal expenses: medical expenses; local, state, and foreign tax payments; and charitable contributions. Individuals who incur such expenses may be entitled to an itemized deduction on Schedule A.

Medical Expenses

Objective 3
Identify personal expenses and losses that result in itemized deductions.

Individuals may claim an itemized deduction for the unreimbursed cost of medical care for themselves and their family.[22] Deductible expenses include payments to health care practitioners (doctors, dentists, chiropractors, etc.) and treatment facilities (outpatient clinics, hospitals, and long-term-care facilities), certain travel expenses related to medical treatment, the cost of medical aids (eyeglasses, hearing aids, crutches, wheelchairs, etc.) and prescription drugs. Premiums paid to purchase health, accident, and long-term-care insurance also qualify as medical expenses.[23]

The medical expense deduction is limited to the excess of total unreimbursed expenses over 7.5 percent of AGI.

Medical Expense Deduction

Mr. and Mrs. Chester incurred $4,400 of medical expenses (including insurance premiums) during the year. They received a $1,800 payment from their insurance company in partial reimbursement of these expenses. If their AGI is $30,000, they can claim a $350 itemized deduction.

Medical expenses	$4,400
Insurance reimbursement	(1,800)
Unreimbursed expenses	$2,600
AGI threshold ($30,000 AGI × 7.5%)	(2,250)
Medical expense deduction	$ 350

[20] §262.

[21] *Jeffrey C. Stone,* TC Memo 1998-437.

[22] §213.

[23] Medical insurance reimbursements are excluded from gross income under §105(b).

If AGI exceeds $34,667, the 7.5 percent threshold exceeds unreimbursed expenses, and the Chesters have no medical expense deduction this year.

Tax Talk
Even though about one-third of individual taxpayers elect to itemize deductions, less than 6 percent of individuals actually benefit from a medical expense deduction.

As this example demonstrates, the AGI limitation restricts the number of taxpayers who actually receive a tax benefit from their medical expenses. Only those unfortunate families that bear extraordinary health care costs receive any tax relief from this particular itemized deduction.

Local, State, and Foreign Tax Payments

Individuals may deduct real or personal property taxes paid on personal assets (such as their home or family automobile). They may elect to deduct *either* state and local sales taxes *or* state and local income taxes (but not both!). This election is particularly beneficial to residents of the seven states that have a sales tax but no individual income tax (Alaska, Florida, Nevada, South Dakota, Texas, Washington, and Wyoming).[24] Individuals who pay income tax to a foreign jurisdiction may either deduct such tax or (as generally is the case) claim a foreign tax credit.

Several common taxes that individuals pay are not deductible for federal income tax purposes. Gift and estate taxes, employee payroll taxes, and employment taxes paid for household employees are all nondeductible personal expenses.[25] Of course, the federal income tax itself is a nondeductible expense. But interestingly, the tax law authorizes a miscellaneous itemized deduction for "expenses paid or incurred in connection with the determination, collection, or refund of any tax, whether the taxing authority be Federal, State, or municipal."[26] Because of this rule, fees paid to tax practitioners for return preparation and professional advice are deductible.

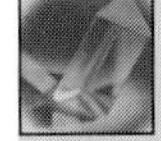

Taxes and Tax Return Preparation Fee

This year, Ruthie Green paid an estimated $10,000 Louisiana sales tax, $15,119 Louisiana income tax, $2,899 federal gift tax, and $1,290 employer payroll tax on the wages paid to her housekeeper. Ruthie also paid a $3,100 fee to the CPA who prepared her various tax returns. Ruthie elected to report her state income tax (instead of her sales tax) as an itemized deduction, and she reported her tax return preparation fee as a miscellaneous itemized deduction subject to the 2 percent AGI limitation. Her gift tax and payroll tax payments are nondeductible.

Charitable Contributions

People who contribute money or property to nonprofit organizations that have been granted tax-exempt status by the IRS can claim the contribution as an itemized deduction.[27] The policy rationale is that this deduction encourages private citizens to support worthy causes that benefit society as a whole. By allowing the charitable contribution deduction, the federal government indirectly subsidizes thousands of social, civic, cultural, religious, scientific,

[24] §164. The election to deduct either income tax or sales tax is effective for 2004 and 2005. The IRS will provide tables that individuals can use to estimate their general sales tax for the year based on AGI.

[25] §275.

[26] Reg. §1.212-1(l).

[27] §170. Contributions of $250 or more to a single charity must be substantiated by a written acknowledgment from the charity. §170(f)(8).

environmental, and educational institutions. This subsidy represents a tax expenditure of over $30 billion annually. There are broad limits on the charitable contribution deduction. In general, the annual deduction for contributions to public charities cannot exceed 50 percent of AGI. Any contribution in excess of such limit is carried forward as an itemized deduction for five years.

Charitable Contribution Limitation

In 1996, First Lady Hillary Rodham Clinton earned $742,000 royalties from her book *It Takes a Village,* kept $152,000 to pay state and federal tax on the income, and donated the $590,000 remainder to charity. However, because the Clintons' AGI on their joint return was $1,065,101, their charitable contribution deduction was limited to $532,551.

When an individual contributes property to charity, the amount of the deduction depends on the character of the property.[28] If the property is a long-term capital asset to the contributor, the deduction generally equals FMV. As a result, individuals who own highly appreciated capital assets enjoy a significant tax benefit if they give the assets to charity.

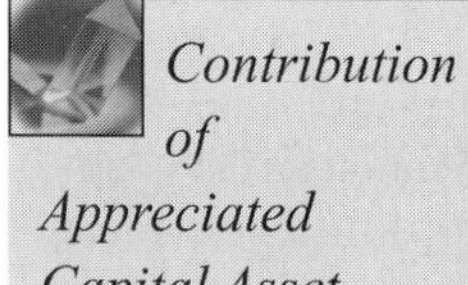

Contribution of Appreciated Capital Asset

Mr. Nelke, who is in the 35 percent marginal tax bracket, owns an oil painting that he bought 15 years ago for $50,000. The painting's value was recently appraised at $400,000. If Mr. Nelke gives this painting to the Metropolitan Museum of Art, his itemized deduction is $400,000, and his tax savings is $140,000 (35 percent of $400,000). Most of the savings is attributable to the $350,000 appreciation in the painting's FMV, an unrealized gain on which Mr. Nelke never paid income tax.

If an individual contributes property that is not a capital asset to charity, the deduction is limited to the *lesser* of FMV or the contributor's basis in the property. In this case, the contributor does not enjoy a deduction for any unrealized appreciation in the property.

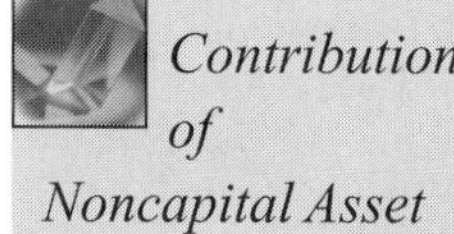

Contribution of Noncapital Asset

Ms. Holk owns and operates a pet store. She contributed 5,000 bags of cat and dog food from her inventory to the local Society for Prevention of Cruelty to Animals. Her cost basis in the pet food was $6,300, and its FMV (retail) was $9,500. Ms. Holk's itemized deduction for this contribution is limited to $6,300.

Tax Subsidies for Education

The costs incurred by individuals for their own education and the education of their children are nondeductible personal expenses. However, Congress has enthusiastically subsidized the cost of education through a profusion of tax incentives available to low-income and middle-income families. Here is a bullet-point summary of the major education incentives. Students who want more details should refer to IRS Publication 970 *Tax Benefits for Education.*

- Individuals can exclude the interest earned on the redemption of qualified Series EE savings bonds (**education savings bonds**) to the extent of tuition and fees paid to a post-secondary educational institution. This exclusion is phased out for high-income taxpayers.[29]
- Individuals can report **qualified tuition expenses** as an above-the-line deduction.[30] Qualified tuition expenses include tuition and fees paid for post-secondary education. In

[28] See §170(e).

[29] §135.

[30] §222.

2005, this deduction is available only to taxpayers with less than $130,000 AGI (married filing jointly) or $65,000 AGI (single or head of household), and the maximum deduction is $4,000. Individuals can also report interest paid on **qualified education loans** as an above-the-line deduction.[31] This deduction is limited to $2,500 and is phased out for high-income taxpayers.

- Individuals can claim a **Hope Scholarship Credit** based on qualified tuition expenses paid during the first two years of post-secondary education.[32] The maximum annual credit is $1,500 per eligible student. Alternatively, individuals may claim a **Lifetime Learning Credit** based on 20 percent of their qualified tuition expenses. The maximum annual credit is $2,000. Individuals cannot claim both a deduction and a credit for the same qualified tuition expenses, and both credits are phased out for high-income taxpayers.
- Individuals can contribute a maximum of $2,000 every year to a tax-exempt **Coverdell education savings account** established for a beneficiary (typically a child or grandchild) under the age of 18. Withdrawals from the account are nontaxable to the extent of the beneficiary's elementary, secondary, and higher education expenses. The maximum contribution is phased out for individuals with AGI in excess of $190,000 (married filing jointly) and $95,000 (single individuals and heads of household).[33]
- Individuals can contribute to tax-exempt **qualified tuition programs** sponsored by states or by private post-secondary educational institutions. Distributions from qualified tuition programs are nontaxable to the extent used to pay higher education expenses.[34]

PERSONAL LOSSES

Losses on Sales of Personal Assets

In earlier chapters of this text, we learned that individuals can deduct losses realized on the disposition of business or investment assets. While the capital loss and passive activity loss limitations may defer recognition of such losses to future years, sooner or later the losses reduce AGI and result in a tax savings. If an individual realizes a loss on the disposition of a personal asset, the general rule is that such loss is nondeductible. In many instances, this rule has little economic significance. Suppose a person pays $1,500 for a new refrigerator, uses it for eight years, then sells it at a garage sale for $200. The $1,300 realized loss ($200 amount realized less $1,500 cost basis) is nondeductible, and the sale of the personal asset is a nonevent for tax purposes.

Nondeductible Personal Loss

Mr. Rooker purchased a membership in a private country club for $20,000. During the last 13 years, he was assessed $7,000 for the cost of capital improvements to the club's swimming pool, tennis courts, and golf course. This year, he sold his membership to an unrelated party for $15,000. The IRS acknowledged that the club membership was a capital asset and that Mr. Rooker realized a $12,000 loss on the sale ($15,000 amount realized − $27,000 original cost plus assessments). However, the IRS ruled that the loss was nondeductible because he held the membership primarily for personal use rather than for investment purposes.[35]

[31] §221.

[32] §25A.

[33] §530.

[34] §529. Distributions from qualified tutition programs sponsored by private colleges and universities were not fully excluded from gross income until 2004.

[35] This example is based on IRS Letter Ruling 8205045.

A loss realized on the sale of a personal residence can result in severe economic distress. For many people, their residence is their most valuable asset, and they consider it as a long-term investment. Even so, owner-occupied housing is a personal rather than an investment asset for tax purposes, and a loss on sale is nondeductible.

Loss on Sale of Personal Residence

Mr. and Mrs. Zuma purchased their family home in Colorado Springs for $278,000 in 1995. This year, the Zumas had to relocate to Minnesota. Because of the depressed housing market in their locality, they sold their home for only $210,000. Their $68,000 loss realized on the sale is a nondeductible personal loss.

Casualty and Theft Losses

Individuals can claim an itemized deduction for personal property losses arising from casualty or theft.[36] A casualty is a sudden and unexpected event such as a fire, hurricane, earthquake, automobile accident, or vandalism that damages or destroys property. For tax purposes, the loss is the *lesser* of the tax basis in the property or the decrease in value from the casualty or theft.[37]

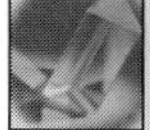

Casualty Losses

Mrs. Ober owns a sailboat that was damaged during a recent hurricane. Her basis in the boat is $27,000, but the decrease in value is only $5,000. Accordingly, the casualty loss is $5,000.[38]

Mrs. Ober owned a motorcycle that was totally destroyed in a traffic accident. Her basis in the motorcycle was $18,000, and its value immediately before the accident was $20,000. Even though the decrease in value is $20,000, the casualty loss is limited to her $18,000 basis.

A casualty or theft loss is reduced by any insurance proceeds so that only the *unreimbursed* loss is deductible.[39] Furthermore, the loss from each casualty or theft is reduced by a $100 floor. Finally, only the aggregate loss in excess of 10 percent of AGI is deductible.[40]

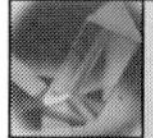

Casualty Loss Deduction

Mrs. Ober received nothing from her insurance company for the damaged sailboat and $7,200 for the destroyed motorcycle. If she suffered no other casualty or theft losses for the year, her aggregate loss is $15,600.

	Sailboat	*Motorcycle*
Casualty loss	$5,000	$18,000
Insurance proceeds	–0–	(7,200)
Unreimbursed loss	$5,000	$10,800
$100 floor per casualty	(100)	(100)
	$4,900	$10,700

[36] §165(c)(3).

[37] Reg. §1.165-7(b).

[38] The decrease in value can be determined by independent appraisal or measured by the cost of repairs necessary to restore the property to its original condition. Reg. §1.165-7(a)(2).

[39] If the insurance proceeds exceed the basis of the property, the owner may defer recognition of such gain by replacing the property. See the discussion of involuntary conversions in Chapter 8.

[40] §165(h)(1) and (2).

Aggregate loss: $4,900 + $10,700 = $15,600

If Mrs. Ober's AGI is $68,000, her itemized deduction for this loss is $8,800. If her AGI is $130,000, her deduction is only $2,600. If her AGI is $200,000, she has no itemized deduction at all.

	AGI		
	$68,000	*$130,000*	*$200,000*
Aggregate casualty loss	$15,600	$15,600	$15,600
10% AGI threshold	(6,800)	(13,000)	(20,000)
Casualty loss deduction	$ 8,800	$ 2,600	–0–

Hobby and Gambling Losses

Objective 4
Describe the tax treatment of revenues and expenses from a hobby.

Activities in which people engage primarily for personal enjoyment may generate revenues. Consider the case of Dr. Cox, a practicing physician, who breeds toy poodles as his hobby. Not only does he exhibit his own animals in local and regional dog shows, but he also sells puppies and shows poodles owned by other people. In a good year, Dr. Cox might earn as much as $3,000 from his canine-related activities. His annual expenses, such as dog food, veterinary fees, and travel to shows average $5,000. What are the tax rules concerning his annual **hobby loss**? Because of the inclusive rule for income recognition, he must report his annual revenues as miscellaneous income on page 1, Form 1040. He is allowed a deduction for his expenses but only to the extent of his revenues.[41] Moreover, it is a miscellaneous itemized deduction subject to the 2 percent AGI limitation.

Hobby Loss

Dr. Cox's revenues from his dog-breeding activities totaled $2,980, while his related expenses totaled $5,300. His AGI (which includes the $2,980 miscellaneous income) is $86,300. He may report $2,980 expenses as a miscellaneous item on Schedule A. However, if this is his only miscellaneous item, the deduction is limited to $1,254.

Total miscellaneous items	$2,980
AGI threshold ($86,300 × 2%)	(1,726)
Miscellaneous itemized deduction	$1,254

This is a very unsatisfactory result for Dr. Cox. His hobby expenses exceeded his revenues by $2,320, but his taxable income from the hobby is $1,726 ($2,980 income less $1,254 itemized deduction). Furthermore, this result assumes that he can itemize deductions for the year. If he claims the standard deduction, the $2,980 poodle revenue is fully taxable, and he receives no tax benefit at all from the poodle expenses.

The tax consequences would be much more favorable if Dr. Cox could treat his dog-breeding activity as a business. In such case, he would account for revenues and expenses on a Schedule C and could deduct his $2,320 net loss in the computation of AGI. To do so,

41 §183.

he must demonstrate that he breeds poodles with the "actual and honest objective" of making a profit rather than for recreation.[42] To this end, he should operate in a businesslike manner by maintaining a separate bank account and proper accounting records. He should actively seek out customers by advertising in the appropriate trade journals and should charge the market rate for his products and services. Of course, the best way for Dr. Cox to demonstrate a profit motive is to actually make a profit. The tax law establishes a *presumption* that any activity generating net income (gross income over deductible expenses) in three out of five consecutive years is a business. In such case, the IRS must prove that the activity is a hobby, and it rarely tries to do so.

For tax purposes, gambling activities are treated very much like hobbies. Individuals must report their winnings as income and may deduct their losses only to the extent of such winnings. The itemized deduction for gambling losses, however, is not categorized as a *miscellaneous* itemized deduction and is not subject to the 2 percent AGI limitation.[43]

TAX CONSEQUENCES OF HOME OWNERSHIP

Even though an owner-occupied residence is a personal asset, the Internal Revenue Code contains several preferential rules that can make such residence a fine investment. In fact, one of the greatest economic advantages of home ownership is that the tax law treats owner-occupied real property as a nonproductive personal asset. Consider the relative economic situations of Mr. Hicks and Mr. Gray. Neither individual owns his own home, and each pays $8,000 a year to rent a dwelling. These rent payments are nondeductible personal expenses. This year, each man inherits $100,000. Mr. Hicks uses the money to buy a home, while Mr. Gray invests his money in a financial asset yielding 8 percent a year. What are the cash flow implications of their respective purchases?

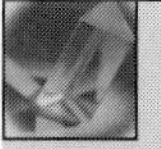

Comparative Cash Flows

Mr. Hicks now lives in his own home and no longer pays rent. Consequently, his annual after-tax cash outflow decreases by $8,000. Mr. Gray continues to pay rent but also receives $8,000 income on his investment. If Mr. Gray is in a 28 percent marginal tax bracket, his after-tax cash outflow decreases by only $5,760.

	Mr. Hicks	*Mr. Gray*
Cash outflow before purchase:		
Rent expense	$(8,000)	$(8,000)
Cash outflow after purchase:		
Rent expense	–0–	$(8,000)
Taxable income from investment	–0–	8,000
Tax cost of income	–0–	(2,240)
	–0–	$(2,240)
Decrease in cash outflow	$(8,000)	$(5,760)

How can the purchase of a personal asset have a better financial result than the purchase of income-producing investment property? Observe that Mr. Hicks's personal residence

[42] *Ronnen*, 90 TC 74, 91 (1988). For recent cases, see *Zdun v. Commissioner*, 229 F.3d 1161 (CA-9, 2000) and *Lucian T. Baldwin III*, TC Memo 2002-162.

[43] See §165(d) and §67(b)(3).

provides an $8,000 annual benefit—the rent he avoids paying. Economists refer to this benefit as the **imputed income from owner-occupied housing.** The federal tax system has never required homeowners to include such imputed income in their tax base. This preferential treatment creates an economic incentive for people to purchase a home. In our example, both Mr. Hicks and Mr. Gray invested $100,000 in assets yielding an 8 percent before-tax return. Because Mr. Hicks's return consists of nontaxable imputed income, his after-tax return is also 8 percent, making his purchase of a personal residence the superior investment.

Home Mortgage Interest Deduction

Objective 5
Compute the itemized deduction for home mortgage interest.

Individuals who incur debt to finance a personal expenditure cannot deduct the interest paid on the debt.[44] The major exception to this rule applies to **qualified residence interest,** which individuals may claim as an itemized deduction.[45] Qualified residence interest includes interest paid on both acquisition debt and home equity debt.

- **Acquisition debt** is incurred to acquire, construct, or substantially improve a personal residence. Acquisition debt must be secured by the residence and is limited to $1 million ($500,000 for married filing separately).
- **Home equity debt** is any other debt secured by a personal residence to the extent it does not exceed the owner's equity. Home equity debt is limited to $100,000 ($50,000 for married filing separately).

Individuals may take into account the interest paid with respect to their principal residence *and* one other personal residence in computing their deduction for qualified residence interest.[46]

Qualified Residence Interest

Mr. and Mrs. Tabor financed the construction of their home through a mortgage from their local bank. Last year, they took out a second mortgage from another lending institution and used the proceeds to purchase new furniture and to pay their three children's college tuition.

This year, the average balance of the first mortgage was $600,000, and the average balance of the second mortgage was $140,000. The Tabors paid $52,540 interest on these mortgages, only $49,700 of which is qualified residence interest.[47]

Acquisition debt	$600,000
Home equity debt (limited)	100,000
Qualifying debt	$700,000

$$\frac{\$700{,}000 \text{ qualifying debt}}{\$740{,}000 \text{ total debt}} \times \$52{,}540 \text{ total interest} = \$49{,}700$$

Therefore, Mr. and Mrs. Tabor can claim $49,700 as an itemized deduction. Because they used the proceeds of the home equity debt for personal expenditures, the remainder of the interest payment is nondeductible.

[44] §163(h)(1).

[45] §163(h)(3).

[46] §163(h)(4).

[47] IRS Publication 936 *Home Mortgage Interest Deduction* contains a worksheet for computing qualified residence interest when an individual's acquisition or home equity debt exceeds the $1 million or $100,000 limit.

Vacation Homes

Many people own more than one personal residence. In addition to their **principal residence** (the home in which they reside for most of the year and consider their permanent address), they may own a **vacation home** for occasional use. Owners of vacation homes often rent the property to other individuals for some limited period of time. In such case, they can deduct the expenses of maintaining the home (utilities, homeowners insurance, repairs, etc.) allocable to the rental period on a Schedule E.[48] They are also allowed a depreciation deduction based on the number of days of rental usage. The aggregate of these deductions is limited to the gross rents less any mortgage interest or property taxes allocable to the rental period.[49]

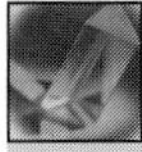

Vacation Home

Ms. DeSilva owns a vacation home on Cape Cod. She and her family use the home on weekends and during June and July. During August and September, she rents the home to tourists. This year, this rental activity resulted in the following.

Rent revenue	$6,400
Mortgage interest and real property tax for August and September[50]	3,505
Maintenance expenses for August and September	3,760
MACRS depreciation for August and September	1,200

Ms. DeSilva reports this rental activity on a Schedule E as follows.

Gross rents	$6,400
Interest and property tax deduction	(3,505)
	$2,895
Deductible maintenance expenses	(2,895)
MACRS depreciation deduction	-0-
Net rental income	-0-

Ms. DeSilva can carry the $865 disallowed maintenance expenses and the $1,200 disallowed depreciation forward and include them in future calculations of her Schedule E deductions.[51] While such deductions may decrease or even eliminate the rental revenue included in Ms. DeSilva's AGI, they can never generate a net rental loss.

Exclusion of Gain on Sale of Principal Residence

Objective 6
Describe the preferential tax treatment of gain from the sale of a personal residence.

Individuals who realize gain on the sale (or exchange) of a home can exclude the gain from income if the home was owned and used as the principal residence for periods aggregating at least two years during the five-year period ending on the date of sale.[52] The exclusion applies to only one sale every two years. The amount of the exclusion is limited to $250,000

[48] §280A(e)(1). If an owner rents a personal residence for less than 15 days during a year, the revenue is nontaxable and the related expenses are nondeductible. §280A(g).

[49] §280A(c)(5).

[50] The mortgage interest allocable to the other 10 months of the year may be deductible as qualified residence interest. Property tax allocable to this 10-month period is an itemized deduction.

[51] §165(c)(5).

[52] §121.

for each sale. The maximum exclusion is doubled (to $500,000) for a married couple filing jointly if *either* spouse meets the two-out-of-five-year ownership requirement and *both* spouses meet the two-out-of-five-year use requirement for the residence.

Maximum Exclusion

Mr. and Mrs. Sutton, who file a joint tax return, purchased a principal residence as cotenants in 1983 and have lived there ever since. On October 6, 2004, they realized a $618,000 gain on sale of the residence. Because they meet the ownership/use requirement and did not sell another principal residence within the two-year period prior to the sale, they may exclude $500,000 of the gain from income. The $118,000 recognized gain is long-term capital gain taxed at 15 percent.

A person who realizes a gain on sale of a principal residence but fails to meet the ownership/use requirement or violates the two-year/one-sale rule may be eligible for a reduced exclusion. If the person sold the residence because of a change in place of employment, for health reasons, or because of unforeseen circumstances, the allowable exclusion equals the maximum exclusion multiplied by a reduction ratio. The numerator of the ratio equals the *shorter* of (1) the aggregate time period of ownership/use of the residence or (2) the time period between the earlier sale of a residence for which gain was excluded and the current sale. The denominator of the ratio is two years.

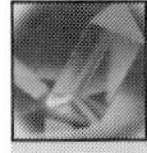

Reduced Exclusion

Mr. and Mrs. Sutton purchased and moved into a new principal residence on December 13, 2004. In June 2005, Mr. Sutton suffered a major heart attack. To accommodate his physical condition, the couple sold their new residence on August 10, 2005, and moved into an assisted-living apartment. The gain realized on this sale was $15,200. Mr. and Mrs. Sutton owned *and* occupied their new residence for only 240 days and sold it just 308 days after the sale of their former residence. Consequently, they fail the ownership/use requirement *and* violate the two-year/one-sale rule. However, because they sold the new residence for health reasons, they are eligible for a reduced exclusion of $164,384.

$$\$500{,}000 \times \frac{\text{240 days of ownership/use}}{\text{730 days (two years)}} = \$164{,}384$$

Consequently, they may exclude the entire $15,200 gain on the second sale from income.

ITEMIZED DEDUCTIONS AS AMT ADJUSTMENTS

Tax Talk
Every year, the IRS releases a list of the 20 most serious problems confronting taxpayers and threatening our country's voluntary compliance system. This year, the individual AMT is the number one problem on the list!

Before leaving the topic of personal activities, we should integrate the material introduced in the chapter into the alternative minimum tax (AMT) system. None of the personal income or gain items triggers an AMT adjustment or preference. However, certain personal itemized deductions are limited or disallowed in the computation of alternative minimum taxable income (AMTI).[53]

- Medical expenses are deductible only to the extent they exceed 10 percent of AGI.
- The itemized deduction for tax payments is disallowed.
- Miscellaneous itemized deductions (including investment and employment-related expenses) are disallowed.
- Qualified residence interest paid on home equity debt is disallowed.

[53] §56(b)(1).

Objective 7
Identify the itemized deductions that are limited or disallowed for AMT purposes.

Our last two examples illustrate the computation of these AMT adjustments and their effect on AMT.

AMT Itemized Deductions

Mrs. Keil had $75,000 AGI and the following itemized deductions in 2005.

Unreimbursed medical expenses	$10,500	
AGI threshold ($75,000 × 7.5%)	(5,625)	$ 4,875
State income tax		4,000
Local property tax on personal residence		3,100
Charitable contributions		5,500
Qualified residence interest:		
Acquisition debt		9,200
Home equity debt		6,800
Miscellaneous itemized deductions	$ 2,400	
AGI threshold ($75,000 × 2%)	(1,500)	900
Itemized deductions		$34,375

In computing her AMTI, Mrs. Keil must make the following *positive* adjustments to taxable income.

Unreimbursed medical expenses	$10,500	
AMT/AGI threshold ($75,000 × 10%)	(7,500)	
	$ 3,000	
Regular medical expense deduction		$ 4,875
AMT medical expense deduction		(3,000)
AMT adjustment for medical expenses		$ 1,875
Disallowed state income tax		4,000
Disallowed local property tax on personal residence		3,100
Disallowed interest on home equity debt		6,800
Disallowed miscellaneous itemized deductions		900
Positive AMT adjustments		$16,675

Computing AMT

Assume that Mrs. Keil is a head of household with two dependent children, ages 18 and 19. Her 2005 tentative minimum tax was calculated as follows.

	Regular Tax	*Tentative Minimum Tax*
AGI	$75,000	
Itemized deductions	(34,375)	
Exemption amount ($3,200 × 3)	(9,600)	
Taxable income	$31,025	$31,025

AMT adjustments for:	
Itemized deductions	16,675
Exemption amount	9,600
AMTI	$57,300
Exemption (head of household)	(40,250)
Tax base	$17,050
Tax rate	.26
Tentative minimum tax	$ 4,433

Mrs. Keil's total 2005 tax is calculated as follows.

Regular tax on $31,025 taxable income	$4,131
AMT ($4,433 tentative minimum tax − $4,131)	302
Total tax	$4,433

Conclusion

Even when people engage in personal transactions with no connection to any business, employment, or investment activity, they should be sensitive to tax implications. Of course, most personal transactions are nonevents for tax purposes. But, occasionally, a personal transaction will have significant tax consequences. If any transaction results in an economic benefit, the individual must consider the prospect that such benefit is taxable. He or she should also determine if the transaction can be structured so that part or all of the benefit escapes taxation. If a transaction involves an expense or loss, the individual might be entitled to deduct some or even the entire expense or loss. Through an awareness of this possibility, the individual can plan to maximize the deduction and minimize his tax bill.

Key Terms

acquisition debt *477*
Coverdell education savings account *473*
education savings bonds *472*
hobby loss *475*
home equity debt *477*
Hope Scholarship Credit *473*
imputed income from owner-occupied housing *477*
Lifetime Learning Credit *473*
principal residence *478*
qualified education loan *473*
qualified residence interest *477*
qualified tuition expenses *472*
qualified tuition program *473*
vacation home *478*

Questions and Problems for Discussion

1. Contrast the general rule concerning the recognition of income from personal activities with the general rule concerning the deductibility of personal expenses and losses.
2. Discuss the tax policy reasons why gifts and inheritances are not taxable income.
3. In what way does the tax law give preferential treatment to the divorced spouse with custody of the children?
4. Why are welfare payments from a state social services agency nontaxable to the recipient while state unemployment benefits are taxable?

5. A basic principle of federal tax law is that a return of investment is nontaxable. Discuss the application of this principle to Social Security payments.
6. If an individual purchases property insurance on business equipment, the premiums are deductible, but if that same individual purchases property insurance on his home, the premiums are nondeductible. Can you explain this inconsistent tax treatment?
7. Mr. M is a passionate stamp collector. His collection is so valuable that he keeps it in a safety deposit box in a local bank, which charges him $25 a month. Can he deduct this expense?
8. Assume that Congress amended the tax law to limit the itemized deduction for charitable contributions to 5 percent (rather than 50 percent) of AGI. Discuss the incidence of the tax increase represented by this expansion of the tax base.
9. People frequently hold garage sales to sell used appliances, old furniture and clothing, books, toys, and other personal goods. Should these people recognize the cash proceeds from such sales as taxable income?
10. Last year, both the M family and the N family incurred $8,000 unreimbursed medical expenses. Mr. and Mrs. M deducted $6,000 of their expenses, while Mr. and Mrs. N were unable to deduct any of their expenses. How do you explain this apparently inequitable result?
11. Wealthy individuals can reduce their taxable estate by donating property to charity either during life or at death. Discuss the reasons why an inter vivos charitable donation is the preferable option for tax planning purposes.
12. Mrs. Q's profession is dentistry, but she has quite a reputation as a master gardener. Last year she won $990 in prize money from entering her roses in competitions and earned $800 in lecture fees from garden clubs. Because she did not itemize deductions, none of the expenses associated with her hobby were deductible. Should Mrs. Q pay self-employment tax on her prize money and fees?
13. Discuss the similarities and differences in the structure of the hobby loss rule and the vacation home rule.

Application Problems

1. Marcy Tucker received the following items this year. Determine to what extent each item is included in her AGI.
   a. A $25,000 cash gift from her parents.
   b. A $500 cash award from the local Chamber of Commerce for her winning entry in a contest to name a new public park.
   c. $8,000 alimony from her former husband.
   d. $3,700 unemployment compensation from the state of Michigan.
2. Will and Sandra Emmet were divorced this year. As part of the property settlement, Sandra transferred marketable securities to Will. Her basis in the securities was $89,800, and their FMV was $135,000. Four months after the divorce, Will sold the securities for $142,000.
   a. How much income does Will recognize on receipt of the securities from Sandra?
   b. How much gain does Will recognize on the sale of the securities?
   c. Does Sandra recognize any gain on the transfer of the securities to Will?
3. Ms. Q, age 21, is a full-time college student with an athletic scholarship that provides the following annual benefits.

Tuition payment	$12,800
Fees and books	3,500
Room and board	10,000

Ms. Q works in the athletic department as a trainer for a $4,200 salary. She also receives a $6,000 annual allowance from her grandmother. Compute Ms. Q's AGI.

4. Four years ago, Lyle Mercer was injured in a railroad accident and sued the railroad for damages. The jury required the railroad to pay $600,000 compensation for his physical injuries, $150,000 for lost wages during his long recuperation, and $1,000,000 punitive damages. How much of the $1,750,000 settlement is taxable income to Lyle?
5. Mr. and Mrs. T have major medical and dental insurance provided by Mrs. T's employer. This year, they incurred the following *unreimbursed* expenses:

Routine office visits to doctors and dentists	$940
Emergency room visits	415
Disposable contact lenses for Mr. T	360
Prescription drugs	500

Compute their itemized deduction for medical expenses if AGI is:

a. $25,000.

b. $50,000.

6. Mr. AB paid the following professional fees.

To CPA for preparation of Form 1040 ($2,500 for preparation of Schedule C for sole proprietorship)	$4,200
To CPA for preparation of federal gift tax return	900
To attorney for drafting Mr. AB's will	7,800
To attorney for estate tax planning advice	3,000
To attorney for advice concerning custody of Mr. AB's minor grandson	750
To attorney for settling a dispute concerning a neighbor's barking dog	400

To what extent (if any) can Mr. AB deduct each of these payments?

7. Mr. CC paid the following taxes.

Federal income tax	$50,789
Federal gift tax	285
Federal employer payroll tax for housekeeper	920
Indiana income tax	3,710
Indiana sales tax on consumer goods and services	2,040
Local property tax on:	
Principal residence	4,800
Vacation home	1,800
Two automobiles	900

To what extent (if any) can Mr. CC deduct each of these payments?

8. Diane Bauman, a professional artist with AGI in excess of $75,000, made the following donations. Determine to what extent each donation is deductible on her Schedule A.
   a. $2,000 cash to the First Methodist Church of Chicago.
   b. $50 cash to a homeless vagrant.
   c. One of Diane's own oil paintings to the local chapter of Meals on Wheels, a tax-exempt charity. The charity sold the painting for $3,900 at a silent auction.
   d. $10,000 cash to the Democratic political party.
   e. Used household furniture to the Salvation Army. Diane's original cost was $6,800, and the furniture was reasonably worth $1,200.
9. Conrad Smith, a business executive, is an avid collector of vintage comic books. In February, he sold a 1938 Superman comic for $3,700 that he had purchased six years ago for $625. In December, Conrad sold a 1950 Donald Duck comic for $575 that he had purchased two years ago for $900. What is the effect of these two sales on Conrad's AGI?
10. Mrs. PL made the following interest payments. Determine the extent to which she can deduct each payment.
    a. $21,000 on a $280,000 mortgage incurred to construct (and secured by) her personal residence.
    b. $3,000 on a $34,000 second mortgage secured by her personal residence. She used the proceeds to pay off her credit card debt.
    c. $2,290 on credit card debt.
    d. $15,000 on a $200,000 bank loan incurred to purchase inventory for her sole proprietorship.
    e. $1,610 on a bank loan incurred to purchase a car for her son.
    f. $1,750 on a bank loan incurred to purchase mutual fund shares that generated $1,900 dividend income this year.
11. Ms. KP has been unlucky this year. On a business trip to Boston, her wallet (which contained $900 cash) was stolen. Her new automobile ($24,000 basis and FMV) was completely destroyed by a fire, and she received only $17,500 from the insurance company. A tornado wiped out a grove of ornamental trees growing near her home. She paid $6,100 to replace the trees and received no insurance reimbursement. Compute Ms. KP's casualty loss deduction if her AGI is:
    a. $53,000.
    b. $210,000.
12. Ms. K wants to create a scholarship in honor of her parents at the law school from which she received her degree. She could endow the scholarship with $500,000 cash or with $500,000 worth of marketable securities with a cost basis of $318,000. If her AGI is $1.8 million, compare the after-tax cost of the two endowment options.
13. A burglar broke into Mr. and Mrs. V's home and stole an oil painting purchased 15 years ago for $89,000. This theft was their only property loss, and their AGI was $125,000. Describe the tax consequences of the theft under each of the following circumstances.
    a. The painting was insured for $200,000, which they used to purchase another painting by the same artist.
    b. The painting was insured for $200,000, which they used to purchase marketable securities.
    c. The painting was insured for $50,000, which they used to purchase marketable securities.
    d. The painting was uninsured.
14. Mr. MC is a self-employed computer consultant who earns over $100,000 each year. He also is an enthusiastic artist. This year, he spent $4,900 on oil paints, canvasses,

supplies, and lessons at a local studio. He made several trips to the National Gallery in Washington, D.C., to attend lectures on painting technique. His total travel costs were $3,350. Describe the tax treatment of Mr. MC's painting revenue and expenses under each of the following assumptions.

a. Mr. MC earned $13,290 from sales of his paintings. This was the sixth consecutive year that the painting activity generated a profit.

b. Mr. MC earned $2,000 from sales of his paintings. The painting activity has never generated a profit.

c. Mr. MC earned $2,000 from sales of his paintings. The painting activity also generated a net loss four years ago, but was profitable in each of the past three years.

15. Mr. and Mrs. KG own a principal residence and a vacation home. Each residence is subject to a mortgage. The mortgage on the principal residence is acquisition debt, while the mortgage on the vacation home is home equity debt. This year, the mortgage holders provided the following information.

	Mortgage Interest Paid	*Average Balance of Mortgage*
Principal residence	$28,000	$513,500
Vacation home	21,700	340,000

Compute Mr. and Mrs. KG's qualified residence interest.

16. On January 12, 2003, Mr. and Mrs. PS moved out of their old residence (where they had lived for 22 years) and into a new residence purchased on January 3. They finally sold their old residence on June 7, 2003, for a $278,000 realized gain.

a. How much gain did they recognize on sale of their old residence?

b. On February 26, 2005, Mr. and Mrs. PS sold their new residence for a $48,000 realized gain and moved into a nearby house with a swimming pool. How much gain did they recognize?

c. How much gain did they recognize if they sold the new residence because Mrs. PS accepted a job in a different state, and the family had to relocate?

17. Mrs. JM, a widow, paid $148,000 for her home 20 years ago. She recently sold this home and moved in with her son on a permanent basis. Describe the tax consequences of the sale assuming that her amount realized was:

a. $140,000.

b. $262,500.

c. $467,000.

18. Mr. and Mrs. B file a joint return on which they claim their three children (all over age 14) and Mr. B's mother as dependents. Their 2005 AGI is $112,200, and they have the following itemized deductions.

State income tax	$ 6,925
Local real and personal property taxes	4,122
Qualified interest on a home equity loan	1,377
Charitable contributions	5,330
Miscellaneous itemized deductions	769
	$18,523

Based on these facts, compute Mr. and Mrs. B's 2005 AMT.

Issue Recognition Problems

Identify the tax issue or issues suggested by the following situations and state each issue in the form of a question.

1. A local radio station offers a $5,000 reward for information leading to the arrest of vandals and other petty criminals. Mr. J received the reward for identifying three people who spray-painted graffiti on a public building.
2. Mr. SA, a real estate broker, just negotiated the sale of a home for a wealthy client. Two days after the sale closed, he received a beautiful leather briefcase from the client with a card reading: "In grateful appreciation of your efforts over the past year."
3. Mr. TL was a contestant on a game show and won a vacuum cleaner with a retail price of $365. Three months later, he sold the unused appliance in a garage sale for $275.
4. The pilots of Skyway Airlines have been on strike for four months. Ms. BG received a $2,700 benefit from her union, the Airline Pilots Association International. The union funded the benefits for Skyway pilots through a solicitation from union members flying for other airlines.
5. Ms. LS, a bartender and aspiring actress, won a statewide beauty pageant and was awarded a $15,000 cash scholarship to further her education and career goals. She used the money to pay for private acting lessons.
6. On a recent scuba dive, Mr. UW located a shipwreck and recovered a Spanish sword inlaid with precious stones. The sword's appraised value is $11,500. Mr. UW mounted the sword over his fireplace.
7. Mrs. OP, age 60, won an age discrimination suit against her former employer. The court awarded her $100,000 in damages for mental anguish and $200,000 for the violation of her civil rights.
8. Zachary and Stella Hernandez divorced this year. The divorce agreement reads "Zachary Hernandez shall pay Stella Hernandez $1,750 every month. This payment is in complete satisfaction of Mr. Hernandez's legal obligation to his former wife and their two children, Tony and Kristen Hernandez." The agreement provides no other information concerning the nature of the monthly payments.
9. Mrs. N, who is a self-employed author, paid $3,200 for a new computer system. She uses the system to write her books, and her two children use it for their schoolwork.
10. In honor of her 50th birthday, Mrs. VV treated herself to a complete face-lift. The $8,900 cost of the cosmetic surgery was not covered by her medical insurance policy.
11. Mr. S suffers from severe arthritis. His physician advised him to swim for at least one hour every day in a heated pool. Because such a facility is not conveniently located in his area, he paid $25,000 to build a heated lap pool in his backyard.
12. Mrs. PM's daughter is undergoing physical therapy for injuries sustained in a bike accident. Every two weeks, mother and daughter drive 170 miles to a regional hospital where the daughter is treated. Then they spend the night in a motel before driving home.
13. Mr. R, a CPA who charges $150 per hour for his professional services, keeps the financial records for a local charity. Although he spends at least 10 hours each month at this task, he does not charge the charity a fee for his services.
14. Mr. and Mrs. FP bought $500 worth of Girl Scout cookies from their godchild. Because they don't eat sweets, they gave away every box to various friends and family members.
15. Ms. DS owns a diamond ring worth $12,000 that she has worn on her right hand for 12 years. While washing her hands two days ago, she noticed that the ring was missing. She searched her home, her car, and her place of business but has been unable to locate the ring.

16. Mr. D borrowed $600,000 to purchase 62 acres of undeveloped land and secured the debt with the land. He converted a three-room log cabin on the land to his principal residence. This year, he paid $39,910 interest on the mortgage.
17. For the past 10 years, Mr. Y lived on his sailboat for eight months of the year and spent the other four months in his daughter's home. This year, he realized a $35,200 gain on sale of the boat and moved into his own apartment.
18. Ms. SE paid $155,000 for a house that she occupied as her principal residence until February 1, when she moved out and converted the house to rental property. The appraised FMV of the house was $140,000. She leased the house to tenants who purchased it on November 18. Her realized loss on the sale was $24,700, computed as follows.

Amount realized		$ 125,000
Original cost basis	$155,000	
MACRS depreciation during rental period	(5,300)	
Adjusted basis		(149,700)
		$ (24,700)

19. Mr. and Mrs. AQ purchased their home one year ago. This year, a local government attempted to seize the home because the former residents had failed to pay their property taxes for 12 years. Mr. and Mrs. AQ paid $1,700 to an attorney who resolved the dispute in their favor.

Research Problems

1. Mr. Clark Besson is undergoing extensive chemotherapy treatment for cancer. His oncologist recommended that he ingest marijuana to relieve the painful side effects. However, possession or use of marijuana is illegal in Mr. Besson's state of residence. Therefore, he makes a weekly trip to a neighboring state in which the medically prescribed use of marijuana is legal. Since beginning his treatment, he has spent $2,730 to buy marijuana. Is this a deductible medical expense?
2. Mr. and Mrs. Lukert own a sole proprietorship and have no other source of income. This year, they paid $11,674 Massachusetts income tax, all of which is attributable to their business profit. Can they deduct their state income tax as a business expense on Schedule C, or must they report it as an itemized deduction on Schedule A?
3. Betsy and Larry Lorch own and reside in an apartment in midtown Manhattan. They left the city to avoid the uproar surrounding New Year's Eve and spent a long holiday with Larry's parents in upstate New York. They sublet their apartment to a German couple who wanted to join the throng in Times Square. They paid the Lorches $500 per night ($11,000 total) to stay in the apartment from December 21 through January 11. What are the tax consequences of this rental arrangement?
4. Eighteen months ago, Barry Shelton won a $2 million Maryland state lottery jackpot and chose to receive it as $120,000 annual annuity for the rest of his life. This year his brothers persuaded him to sell the annuity to a financial institution for $1.79 million and invest the sales proceeds in a new family business. How much gain did Barry recognize on sale of his annuity, and is it ordinary income or long-term capital gain?
5. Howard Wilson, a single individual, sold his principal residence in Cleveland eight months ago and excluded his entire $148,000 gain on the sale from gross income. He purchased and moved into a new home in a suburb of Chicago. Shortly thereafter,

Howard's 20-year-old son moved in with him. The son was on probation from a prison sentence for drug dealing and assault with a deadly weapon. Howard's neighbors learned about the son's criminal record and have organized protests against the son's presence in the community. Howard has received several verbal and written threats, and his house has been spray painted with graffiti. The atmosphere has become so hostile that Howard has decided to sell his new home and relocate in a different city. Will he be eligible to exclude any of his gain on this second sale?

Tax Planning Cases

1. Ms. JL is a successful attorney in the 35 percent marginal tax bracket. During the past several years, she provided legal services to her great uncle, who is 78 years old and in failing health. Although the uncle offered to pay for her work, she refused any compensation, requesting instead that her uncle remember her appropriately in his will. The uncle recently added a codicil providing for a $250,000 cash bequest to Ms. JL. The remainder of his estate will pass to his two children and seven grandchildren.
   a. What tax planning objective may Ms. JL have accomplished through her request of her uncle?
   b. Can you identify both the opportunity cost and the risk inherent in her plan?
2. Mr. and Mrs. TB are going through an amicable divorce. Mrs. TB, who is a full-time homemaker, will have custody of their two children, ages 2 and 4. She suggested that Mr. TB pay $4,000 child support each month. He countered by offering to pay $1,600 child support and $3,000 alimony each month if he can claim their two children as dependents. In either case, Mrs. TB will qualify as a head of household. Mr. TB's AGI averages $140,000, putting him in the 28 percent marginal tax bracket.
   a. Compute Mr. TB's after-tax cost and Mrs. TB's after-tax cash flow if he pays her $4,000 monthly child support and she claims their children as dependents.
   b. Compute Mr. TB's after-tax cost and Mrs. TB's after-tax cash flow if she accepts his counterproposal.
3. Mr. and Mrs. JM, ages 68 and 66, always claim the standard deduction on their joint return. They own a local restaurant, the Shoreline Grill, as a sole proprietorship. They are both graduates of State University and make regular donations to their alma mater. Their method for doing so is a bit unusual. At the beginning of each State University home football game, the public address system informs the crowd that the Shoreline Grill will contribute $50 to the athletic scholarship fund for every first down the home team makes. As a result of this commitment, Mr. and Mrs. JM contributed $4,950 to State University this year. What tax planning objective may they have accomplished by structuring their donation in this manner?
4. Mr. Z, who is in the 33 percent marginal tax bracket and itemizes deductions, recently inherited $30,000. He is considering three alternative uses for this windfall.
   - He could buy shares in a mutual bond fund paying 11 percent interest a year.
   - He could pay off a $30,000 personal debt to a local bank on which he pays $2,350 interest each year.
   - He could pay off $30,000 of the mortgage incurred to buy his home. This principal repayment would decrease his annual home mortgage interest expense by $2,900.

   Which alternative would you recommend and why?

Comprehensive Problems for Part Five

1. Blake and Valerie Meyer (both age 30) are married with one dependent child (age 5). Based on the following information, compute the Meyers' federal income tax on their joint return.
   - Blake's salary from his corporate employer was $70,000.
   - Valerie's salary from GuiTech, an S corporation, was $29,400.
   - Valerie owns 16 percent of GuiTech's outstanding stock. Her pro rata share of GuiTech's ordinary business income was $13,790, her pro rata share of GuiTech's net loss from rental real estate was $8,100, and she received a $12,000 cash distribution from GuiTech.
   - Blake received a $50,000 cash gift from his grandmother.
   - Valerie won $6,400 in the Maryland state lottery.
   - The Meyers received a distribution from their investment in Pawnee Mutual Fund that consisted of a $712 qualifying dividend and a $3,020 long-term capital gain.
   - Blake paid $12,000 alimony to a former spouse.
   - The Meyers paid $14,200 home mortgage interest and $2,780 property tax on their personal residence.
   - The Meyers paid $7,000 state income tax and $4,200 state and local sales tax.
   - Valerie contributed $945 to the First Baptist Church.
2. Mrs. Cora Yank (age 42) is divorced and has full custody of her 10-year-old son, William. Based on the following information, compute Mrs. Yank's federal income tax and the amount due with her Form 1040 *or* the refund she should receive.
   - Mrs. Yank works as a medical technician in a Chicago hospital. Her salary was $38,400, from which her employer withheld $3,412 federal income tax and $2,938 employee FICA tax.
   - Several years ago, Mrs. Yank was seriously injured in a traffic accident caused by another driver's negligence. This year, she received a $25,000 settlement from the driver's insurance company: $20,000 as compensation for her physical injuries and $5,000 for lost wages during her convalescent period. Because she was unable to work for the first seven weeks of the year, she collected $1,400 unemployment compensation from the state of Illinois.
   - Mrs. Yank earned $629 interest on a savings account. She contributed $800 to a regular IRA. She is not an active participant in any other qualified retirement plan.
   - Mrs. Yank paid $10,800 rent on the apartment in which she and William live. She received $1,600 alimony and $2,350 child support from her former husband.
   - Mrs. Yank is covered under her employer's medical reimbursement plan. However, this year's medical bills exceeded her reimbursement limit by $1,630.
   - Mrs. Yank paid $2,062 income tax to Illinois.
   - Mrs. Yank spent $470 on hospital shoes and uniforms. Her employer did not reimburse her for this expense.
   - Mrs. Yank paid $1,300 for after-school child care for William.
3. Tom and Allie Benson (ages 53 and 46) are residents of Fort Worth, Texas, and file a joint federal income tax return. They provide the entire support for their three children, ages 19, 18, and 14. Based on the following information, compute Mr. and Mrs. Benson's federal income and SE tax and the amount due with their Form 1040 *or* the refund they should receive.

- Mr. Benson is an attorney who practices in partnership with 18 other attorneys. His ordinary income was $278,300, and his net earnings from self-employment were $257,010 (92.35 percent of $278,300). The Bensons made estimated tax payments totaling $58,000 to the IRS and a $28,500 contribution to the qualified Keogh plan maintained by the partnership.
- The Bensons earned $10,160 interest income and $13,790 qualified dividend income from their investment portfolio. They also received a $4,218 long-term capital gain distribution from a mutual fund. They have a $9,723 capital loss carryforward from last year.
- The Bensons received a Schedule K-1 from an S corporation in which they own 6 percent of the stock. Their share of the corporation's business loss was $4,930. The S corporation operates a mink farm in Maine.
- Mrs. Benson received a $50,000 cash inheritance from her great aunt.
- The Bensons moved from San Antonio to Fort Worth in April so that Mr. Benson could manage the Fort Worth office. The cost of moving their household goods was $11,260. The law firm reimbursed Mr. Benson for $10,000 of this expense.
- The Bensons paid $33,890 interest on their home mortgage, $7,400 property taxes on their personal residence, and $2,920 homeowners insurance.
- The Bensons made $21,980 cash donations to various qualified charities.

Appendix **16–A**

Social Security Worksheet (Adapted from IRS Publication 915)

1. Social Security benefits received	________
2. One-half of line 1	________
3. Adjusted gross income (AGI) (without Social Security benefits)	________
4. Tax-exempt interest income	________
5. Add lines 2, 3, and 4	________
6. Enter: $32,000 (married filing jointly) $25,000 (single or head of household) –0– (married filing separately)*	________
7. Subtract line 6 from line 5	________
If line 7 is zero or less, the Social Security benefits are nontaxable.	
8. Enter: $12,000 (married filing jointly) $9,000 (single or head of household) –0– (married filing separately)	________
9. Subtract line 8 from line 7. If zero or less, enter zero	________
10. Enter the lesser of line 7 or line 8	________
11. Enter one-half of line 10	________
12. Enter the lesser of line 2 or line 11	________
13. Multiply line 9 by 85 percent	________
14. Add line 12 and line 13	________
15. Multiply line 1 by 85 percent	________
16. Enter the lesser of line 14 or line 15	________
Line 16 is the taxable portion of the Social Security benefits.	

1. Social Security benefits received	14,400
2. One-half of line 1	7,200
3. Adjusted gross income (AGI) (without Social Security benefits)	43,000
4. Tax-exempt interest income	600
5. Add lines 2, 3, and 4	50,800
6. Enter: $32,000 (married filing jointly) $25,000 (single or head of household) –0– (married filing separately)*	32,000
7. Subtract line 6 from line 5	18,800
If line 7 is zero or less, the Social Security benefits are nontaxable.	
8. Enter: $12,000 (married filing jointly) $9,000 (single or head of household) –0– (married filing separately)	12,000
9. Subtract line 8 from line 7 If zero or less, enter zero	6,800
10. Enter the lesser of line 7 or line 8	12,000
11. Enter one-half of line 10	6,000
12. Enter the lesser of line 2 or line 11	6,000
13. Multiply line 9 by 85 percent	5,780
14. Add line 12 and line 13	11,780
15. Multiply line 1 by 85 percent	12,240
16. Enter the lesser of line 14 or line 15	11,780
Line 16 is the taxable portion of the Social Security benefits.	

* Married individuals filing separate returns who live apart at all times during the year are considered single for purposes of this computation.

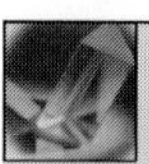

Example Mr. and Mrs. PB received $14,400 Social Security benefits this year. The AGI on their joint return before considering these benefits was $43,000, and they received $600 tax-exempt interest. The taxable portion of their Social Security benefits is $11,780.

The Tax Compliance Process

Chapter Seventeen

The Tax Compliance Process

Learning Objectives

After studying this chapter, you should be able to:

1. Compute a late-filing and late-payment penalty.
2. Describe the statute of limitations for a tax return.
3. Identify the three types of IRS audits.
4. Describe the circumstances in which the IRS imposes a negligence or a civil fraud penalty.
5. Identify the three judicial levels in the tax litigation process.
6. Define the term *transferee liability.*
7. Explain the purpose of the innocent spouse rule.

The federal income, payroll, self-employment, and transfer taxes are all self-assessed taxes. The Internal Revenue Code requires persons liable for any of these taxes to compute the tax due, file the proper return, and maintain adequate records supporting the calculations presented on the return.[1] As a practical matter, the tax laws are sufficiently complex that the majority of taxpayers engage a tax practitioner to assist in the preparation of their returns. Nevertheless, even taxpayers who rely entirely on professional help remain responsible for complying with the law and must bear the consequences of failure to comply.

This final chapter of *Principles of Taxation for Business and Investment Planning* is an overview of the federal tax compliance system. The procedural rules for payment of tax and filing of income tax returns and the IRS's audit process are explained. Your rights as a taxpayer in dealing with the IRS, as well as the penalties the IRS may impose, are described. The chapter ends with a discussion of the judicial process by which both individuals and corporations may challenge the outcome of an IRS audit in federal court.

[1] See §6001 and §6011.

FILING AND PAYMENT REQUIREMENTS

Most individuals report income on the basis of a calendar year and are required to file their Form 1040 for the current year by April 15 of the following year. The few individuals who have adopted a fiscal year must file their returns by the 15th day of the 4th month following the close of the taxable year. Corporations, which report on the basis of either a calendar year or a fiscal year, must file their Form 1120 by the 15th day of the 3rd month following the close of their taxable year. The law permits both individual and corporate taxpayers to request automatic extensions of time to file their annual income tax returns.[2]

Paperless Tax Returns

The IRS e-file program offers taxpayers a totally paperless experience in which they can prepare, sign, and file their returns electronically, then either receive a refund or pay the balance of tax due through a wire transfer to or from their bank account. The IRS received 53 million e-filed returns during the 2003 filing season, about 40 percent of total returns filed. The e-file program's long-term goal is that by 2007, 80 percent of returns will be filed electronically.

As a general rule, both individuals and corporations must pay their tax by the *unextended* filing date of the return for the year. From the government's perspective, taxpayers who are late in paying any portion of their tax received a loan from Uncle Sam. Accordingly, the IRS bills these taxpayers for interest based on the period of time from the required payment date to the date the delinquent tax is actually paid.[3] The annual interest rate (underpayment rate) equals the federal short-term rate plus three percentage points; interest is compounded daily, and the rate is adjusted quarterly.[4]

Millions of taxpayers overpay their annual income tax in the form of excess withholding or quarterly installment payments. In theory, these individuals and corporations loaned money to the federal government. However, the government is not required to pay interest on any tax overpayment refunded within 45 days after the filing date for the return.[5] As a result, taxpayers who routinely receive their refund checks within this statutory grace period do not earn interest on the refund. In the rare case when the IRS fails to mail a refund check on a timely basis, the government must pay interest to the taxpayer. The annual overpayment rate for individuals equals the federal short-term rate plus three percentage points. For corporations, the rate equals the short-term rate plus only two percentage points.[6]

Late-Filing and Late-Payment Penalty

Objective 1
Compute a late-filing and late-payment penalty.

If a taxpayer fails to file an income tax return on a timely basis, the IRS may impose a **late-filing and late-payment penalty,** the calculation of which is quite complicated. Basically, this combined penalty equals 5 percent of the balance of tax due with the return for each month (or portion thereof) that the return is delinquent. The 5 percent penalty runs only for five months (until the penalty equals 25 percent of the balance due). After five months the penalty rate drops to one-half percent of the balance of tax due. This reduced penalty can run for an additional 45 months.[7]

[2] §6081. Individuals may request an automatic four-month extension, and corporations may request an automatic six-month extension.

[3] §6601.

[4] §6621(a)(2) and §6622.

[5] §6611(e)(1).

[6] §6611(a) and §6621(a)(1). In the case of a corporate overpayment that exceeds $10,000, the government's interest rate equals the short-term rate plus one-half percent.

[7] §6621.

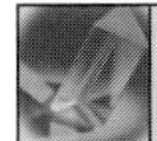

Late-Filing and Late-Payment Penalty

Mr. Toomey failed to request an extension of time to file his 2004 return and didn't file his Form 1040 until July 29, 2005. The return showed $45,890 tax and $42,000 withheld by his employer. Mr. Toomey enclosed a check for the $3,890 balance due with his late return. Because the tax due was not paid by April 15, the IRS charged him interest on $3,890 from April 16 through July 28. Because his return was not filed on a timely basis, the IRS also assessed a $778 penalty.

Balance of tax due on late return		$3,890
Delinquency period:		
April 16–May 15	.05	
May 16–June 15	.05	
June 16–July 14	.05	
July 15–July 28	.05	
		.20
		$ 778

The IRS may agree to waive this penalty (but not the interest) if Mr. Toomey can show reasonable cause for his tardiness.

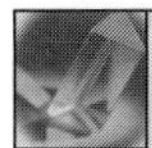

Reasonable Cause for a Delinquent Return?

David McMahan, an investment broker, engaged James Russell, a tax attorney, to file his individual income tax return. Mr. Russell filed an automatic extension and subsequently told his client that he had also filed a second extension request for additional time. Months later, Mr. McMahan discovered that his attorney had neglected to file the second extension request. The IRS assessed a $141,028 late filing and late payment penalty which he contested in court. Mr. McMahan argued that his reliance on a tax professional to file an extension request was reasonable cause for the delinquent return. The court was not persuaded by his argument, observing that a "taxpayer has an affirmative nondelegable duty to ensure that the appropriate forms—whether a tax return or an extension request—are actually filed by the statutory deadline." Consequently, Mr. McMahan was liable for the penalty.[8]

One interesting feature of the late-filing penalty deserves mention. The penalty is based on the balance of tax due with a delinquent return. If a taxpayer overpaid his tax, his return will show a refund due instead of a balance due. In this case, the government cannot assess any penalty if such return is filed after the due date. Of course, for as long as the return is delinquent, the government is enjoying an interest-free loan from the taxpayer that it does not repay until the taxpayer finally decides to file.[9]

Return Processing

Each year more than 135 million income tax returns are filed with the IRS by individuals, corporations, partnerships, and fiduciaries.[10] These returns pour into the 10 IRS service centers located throughout the country. The service centers are information-processing facilities

[8] *McMahan* v. *Commissioner,* 114 F.3d 366 (CA-2, 1997).

[9] Individuals who overpaid their income tax and want to file a return to claim their refund have a limited period of time to do so. Generally, they must file their claim within three years after the date on which the tax return was due. §6511(a).

[10] Terry Manzi, "Projections of Returns to Be Filed in Calendar Years 2002–2009," *SOI Bulletin,* Winter 2002–2003, p. 127.

where each return is checked for mathematical accuracy and logged into the IRS's computer system. This system cross-checks each return against information returns filed with respect to the taxpayer, such as Form W-2s filed by employers; Form 1099s filed by payers of interest, dividend, rents, or other types of income; and such Schedule K-1s filed by partnerships and S corporations. If a return reflects a math error or a discrepancy with an information return, the service center mails a letter to the taxpayer explaining the problem and calculating the additional tax or refund. The service centers are responsible for depositing personal checks or money orders with the U.S. Treasury and for authorizing refund checks to be mailed.

Objective 2
Describe the statute of limitations for a tax return.

Statute of Limitations. Many taxpayers place unjustified significance on the fact that the government cashed their check or punctually mailed their refund. While these events prove that their tax return was processed, they do not mean that the IRS has accepted the accuracy of the return. A **statute of limitations** gives the IRS three years from the later of the statutory due date (April 15th for calendar year individuals) or the date on which the return was actually filed to examine that return for mistakes and to assess any additional tax.[11]

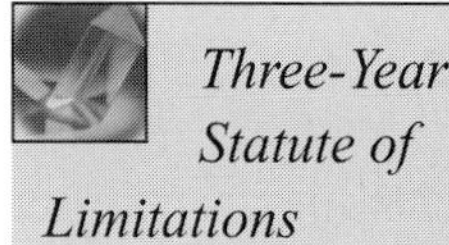

Three-Year Statute of Limitations

Mr. and Mrs. Epps filed their 2004 Form 1040 on March 16, 2005. The IRS has until April 15, 2008, to audit this return and assess any additional tax. Mr. Procter requested an extension of time to file his 2004 return and actually filed the return on August 2, 2005. In his case, the IRS has until August 2, 2008, to audit the return and assess additional tax.

If a taxpayer files a return and omits an amount of gross income exceeding 25 percent of the gross income reported on the return, the normal three-year statute of limitations is extended to six years. If the IRS determines that a return is fraudulent (a concept discussed later in this chapter), the return remains open (subject to audit) indefinitely.

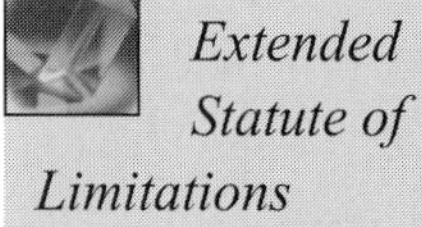

Extended Statute of Limitations

Ms. Yang, a self-employed consultant, failed to include a $13,200 business receipt in the income reported on her 2004 return, which she filed on April 8, 2005. The gross income on the return was $52,000, and the omitted income was more than 25 percent of this income.

$13,200 > $13,000 ($52,000 gross income × 25%)

Consequently, Ms. Yang's return remains open until April 15, 2011. If the IRS determines that her omission of income constituted fraud, it can audit the return and assess additional tax at any time.

Because of the possibility of audit, taxpayers should keep all supporting paperwork such as receipts and canceled checks for at least three years after the return is filed. Records substantiating the tax basis of property, any legal documents containing tax information (closing statement on a property sale, divorce decree, etc.), and a copy of the return should be retained permanently.

THE AUDIT PROCESS

The IRS selects corporate tax returns for audit primarily on the basis of the magnitude of the business, measured in terms of taxable income and net worth as reported on Form 1120. Individual returns are usually selected by a highly classified computer program that

[11] §6501.

analyzes the contents of each return and assigns a **discriminate function system (DIF) score.** This score theoretically measures the return's potential for generating additional tax revenue on audit. The higher the score, the greater the likelihood that the return contains an error causing an understatement of tax. Obviously, returns with the highest DIF scores are chosen for examination. Although the details of the DIF selection process are a closely guarded secret, tax practitioners generally assume that highly speculative investment activities, unusually large itemized deductions, and deductions that are prone to manipulation or abuse (travel and entertainment expenses, nonbusiness bad debts, losses generated by a secondary business, etc.) inflate DIF scores. Similarly, high-income returns are much more likely to be selected for audit than returns reflecting modest incomes.

Audit Coverage

According to the 2003 IRS Data Book, the IRS audited 849,296 of the 130 million individual returns filed in 2002, an audit coverage rate of .65 percent. The rate for returns reporting taxable income between $25,000 and $50,000 was only .30 percent, while the rate for returns with income in excess of $100,000 was .98 percent. The audit coverage rate for Form 1040s containing a Schedule C with gross receipts in excess of $100,000 was 1.47 percent.

Types of Audits

Objective 3
Identify the three types of IRS audits.

Routine audits are conducted by personnel working out of the IRS district offices located throughout the United States. The simplest audit, called a **correspondence examination,** may be handled entirely by telephone or through the mail. More complex audits take place at a district office (an **office examination** conducted by a tax auditor) or at the taxpayer's place of business (a **field examination** conducted by a revenue agent). Office audits focus on a few questionable items on a return. Field audits are broader in scope and may involve a complete analysis of the taxpayer's books and records for the year or years under investigation.

If the IRS requests a personal interview with a taxpayer or if the taxpayer requests an interview during an audit, the IRS must schedule the interview at a reasonable time and a convenient location. Individuals who must deal with the IRS can represent themselves or authorize an attorney, certified public accountant, or enrolled agent to represent them. While attorneys and CPAs are licensed to practice by state boards or agencies, **enrolled agents** receive certification to practice before the IRS by passing an exam on tax law written and administered by the IRS itself.

Assessments of Deficiencies and Interest

Individuals who are notified that they are being audited may panic unnecessarily. Any person who made a good faith effort to comply with the laws in preparing the return and has maintained adequate records has nothing to fear. In a best case scenario, the audit will be concluded promptly with no change in tax, or even with a refund (plus interest) due to the taxpayer. Of course, the return was selected for audit because of its high probability of error. Consequently, the probable outcome is that the IRS will decide that the return contains a mistake that resulted in an understatement of tax. In this case, the taxpayer is assessed a **deficiency** (the additional tax owed), plus interest based on the number of days between the time the return was filed and the date the deficiency is paid.

Corporations may deduct the interest paid on federal income tax deficiencies as a business expense. However, Treasury regulations state that interest paid by an individual on a federal income tax deficiency is nondeductible personal interest "regardless of the source of the income generating the tax liability."[12]

[12] Reg. §1.163-9T(b)(2)(i)(A).

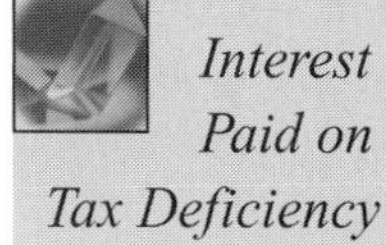

Interest Paid on Tax Deficiency

Maria Cardona owns a sole proprietorship that makes custom-designed patio furniture. This year, Maria received a deficiency notice from the IRS informing her that she owed $42,760 additional income tax for 2002 plus $6,157 interest. The entire deficiency resulted from an understatement of net profit on Maria's 2002 Schedule C. Nonetheless, she must treat her $6,157 interest payment as a nondeductible personal expense.[13]

Your Rights as a Taxpayer

In 1989, Congress enacted the **Taxpayer Bill of Rights,** which requires the IRS to deal with every citizen and resident in a fair, professional, prompt, and courteous manner and to provide the technical help needed by taxpayers to comply with the law. The IRS publishes over 100 free information booklets, one of which, IRS Publication 910 *Guide to Free Tax Services,* is a catalog describing the many types of assistance offered. The Taxpayer Bill of Rights ensures personal and financial confidentiality. If the IRS requests information, the taxpayer has the right to know how the information will be used and the nature of any consequences if the taxpayer refuses to provide the information. However, the bill contains an important disclaimer: The IRS can share tax return information with state tax agencies, the Department of Justice, other federal agencies, and foreign governments under tax treaty provisions.

In 1996, Congress enacted Taxpayer Bill of Rights 2, which expanded on the 1989 legislation. The IRS Reform and Restructuring Act of 1998 included the massive Taxpayer Bill of Rights 3, described as the "most extensive taxpayer-protective provisions ever enacted in a single setting."[14] The 1998 legislation created the office of National Taxpayer Advocate, the purpose of which is to assist taxpayers in resolving problems and to help taxpayers who suffer hardship because of IRS actions. The National Taxpayer Advocate heads a team of local Taxpayer Advocates who operate independently of the IRS's audit, assessment, and collection functions.

IRS Mission Statement

As part of its ongoing public relations effort, the IRS adopted the following mission statement: "Provide America's taxpayers top-quality service by helping them understand and meet their tax responsibilities and by applying the tax law with integrity and fairness to all."

Noncompliance Penalties

Negligence

Objective 4
Describe the circumstances in which the IRS imposes a negligence or a civil fraud penalty.

During the course of an audit, a revenue agent may conclude that the taxpayer did not make a good faith effort to compute the correct tax. In such case, the IRS may impose an administrative penalty on the taxpayer. The Internal Revenue Code contains dozens of penalties, each one designed to discourage a particular type of misconduct. One of the more frequently imposed is the **negligence** penalty, which equals 20 percent of any tax underpayment caused by the taxpayer's failure to make a reasonable attempt to comply with the law or the taxpayer's intentional disregard of rules and regulations.[15]

[13] *Edward A. Robinson III,* 119 TC 44 (2002).

[14] Gerald A. Kafka, "Restructuring and Reforming the IRS and the Code—Congress Takes a Quantum Leap," *Journal of Taxation,* September 1998, p. 134.

[15] §6662(a) and (b)(1).

Negligence

The IRS agent who audited Ms. Purl's Form 1040 discovered three errors that collectively resulted in a $45,000 understatement of her tax. The agent believed that two of the errors were attributable to her misunderstanding of the law but that she had no legitimate excuse for the third error. The portion of the understatement caused by the third error was $13,000. The agent could impose a negligence penalty of $2,600 (20 percent of $13,000). Ms. Purl must pay this penalty *in addition to* the $45,000 deficiency and the interest thereon.

The distinction between an honest mistake and negligence is nebulous. An individual's exposure to the negligence penalty depends on subjective factors such as the complexity of the issue in question, the individual's education and business experience, the existence of supporting documentation, and the individual's degree of cooperation during the audit. Individuals who follow the advice of tax practitioners are much less likely to incur a negligence penalty than individuals who rely on their own judgment, although reliance on professional advice is not a guaranteed defense. When the IRS imposes the negligence penalty and the taxpayer challenges it in court, the IRS has the *burden of production* in the litigation. In other words, the IRS must present a *preponderance of evidence* establishing negligence before the court will sustain the penalty.[16]

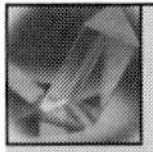

An Unlikely Story

Benjamin Smith was a teacher for the New York State Board of Education and a licensed attorney. On his 1992 and 1993 tax returns, he reported $8 gross receipts and deducted $57,938 business expenses in connection with his law practice. When the IRS requested written substantiation of these expenses, Mr. Smith explained that he kept his business records and receipts in a U-Haul trailer. Unfortunately, the trailer had unhitched from his car and had overturned, destroying all its contents. After he failed to provide any evidence of this accident, the IRS disallowed his business deductions and slapped him with a negligence penalty. The Tax Court observed that "Petitioner is an attorney. He claims he had been in private practice for several years. Although petitioner contends that he lacks any proficiency with regard to the tax matters, we believe that as a member of the legal profession, he should have recognized the importance of substantiating his expenses. Petitioner was given ample time and opportunity to procure and reconstruct the necessary records. Petitioner chose not to do so." The Tax Court agreed with the IRS that Mr. Smith acted in bad faith in filing his tax returns and was guilty of negligence.[17]

Civil Fraud

The harshest administrative penalty that the IRS may impose is the **civil fraud** penalty, which equals 75 percent of the portion of a tax underpayment attributable to fraud.[18] Fraud can be defined as the intent to cheat the government by deliberately understating tax. Fraud is characterized by the systematic omission of substantial amounts of income from the tax return or by the deduction of nonexistent expenses or losses. Revenue agents often assess a fraud penalty when they discover that a taxpayer keeps two sets of financial records: one for tax purposes and one reflecting the taxpayer's true income. The fact that a taxpayer altered or destroyed business records and documents, concealed assets, or cannot account for large cash receipts or deposits is a strong indication of fraud.

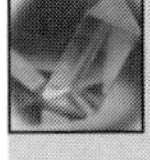

Civil Fraud

The IRS agent who audited Mr. Lowe's Form 1040 discovered that he made large monthly cash deposits to a bank account under a fictitious name. He told the agent that he received

[16] §7491(c).

[17] *Benjamin H. Smith,* TC Memo 1998-33.

[18] §6663.

the cash as a gift from a friend. When asked to reveal the friend's identity, Mr. Lowe became verbally abusive and refused to answer. After further investigation, the agent discovered that the cash represented $62,000 unreported income from his lawn service business on which he owed $23,220 federal tax. Because the agent concluded that Mr. Lowe intended to cheat the government by failing to report the income, the IRS assessed a $17,415 fraud penalty (75 percent of $23,220).

Because of the severity of the penalty, the burden of proof in establishing fraud falls on the IRS.[19] To sustain a fraud penalty, the IRS must have more than just a preponderance of evidence; it must show by *clear and convincing evidence* that the fraud occurred.[20]

A Clear Case of Fraud

Mr. William Tully conducted seminars in which he encouraged people to establish tax-exempt organizations through which (according to Mr. Tully) they could conduct all their financial transactions at no tax cost. While Mr. Tully did not charge for the seminars, he did charge a $3,000 fee to form a tax-exempt organization for those people who acted on his advice. Mr. Tully operated this business through his own tax-exempt organization. Thus, he did not report $620,500 business profit on his own Form 1040. The IRS discovered this omission of income, assessed a deficiency for the income tax on the business earnings, and imposed a civil fraud penalty equal to 75 percent of the deficiency. The court upheld the penalty because the facts of the case "constitute clear and convincing evidence that petitioner, fraudulently and with the intent to evade taxes known to be owing, omitted more than 90 percent of his income earned during 1992 and that the underpayment of tax required to be shown on his 1992 income tax return is due to fraud."[21]

Criminal Fraud

Tax Talk
The IRS is struggling to enforce the tax laws at a time when more people than ever are deliberately ignoring those laws. According to the IRS Oversight Board, as many as one in five taxpayers now believe that cheating on their tax return is acceptable behavior.

If a revenue agent uncovers a particularly egregious incident of fraud, the IRS may turn the matter over to its Criminal Investigation branch. Criminal Investigation will assign a **special agent** to determine if the government has enough evidence to indict the taxpayer for **criminal fraud,** also known as tax evasion. **Tax evasion** is a felony offense, punishable by severe monetary fines (up to $100,000 in the case of an individual and $500,000 in the case of a corporation) and by imprisonment in a federal penitentiary.[22] A person must be convicted of tax evasion in a court of law, and the prosecution must establish guilt *beyond a reasonable doubt.*[23] If Criminal Investigation decides that the case against the taxpayer does not meet this strict evidential standard and is too weak to prosecute, the IRS may have to settle for the civil fraud penalty.

Tax Return Preparer Penalties

The Internal Revenue Code imposes penalties on income tax return preparers who fail to comply with certain statutory rules of professional conduct.[24] The term **income tax return preparer** refers to any person who prepares returns (or who employs other people to prepare returns) for compensation, regardless of whether such person is a licensed attorney, certified public accountant, or enrolled agent. Preparers are required to:

[19] §7454(a).

[20] *McGirl,* TC Memo 1996-313.

[21] *William J. Tully,* TC Memo 1997-310.

[22] §7201.

[23] *Bonansinga,* TC Memo 1987-586.

[24] §6694 through §6696. The American Bar Association and the American Institute of Certified Public Accountants also have standards of professional conduct for their members in tax practice.

- Sign the tax returns prepared for their clients.
- Include their identifying number on such returns.
- Furnish clients with copies of their completed returns.
- Retain copies of all returns or a list of the names and identifying numbers of all clients.

In addition, preparers are prohibited from endorsing or negotiating tax refund checks. Violation of any of these procedural rules without reasonable cause results in a monetary penalty. For instance, a preparer who fails to sign a tax return may be assessed $50 for each failure. The maximum penalty with respect to returns filed during any calendar year is limited to $25,000.

If a preparer takes a position on an income tax return resulting in an understatement of tax and the preparer knows (or should know) that such position has no realistic possibility of being sustained on its merit, the IRS may assess a $250 penalty with respect to the return. If the position represents an intentional disregard of rules and regulations, the penalty increases to $1,000. Clearly, these penalties are intended to discourage tax advisers from taking overly aggressive positions on behalf of their clients. Even though the monetary penalties are modest, they can result in adverse publicity that may seriously damage an income tax return preparer's professional reputation.

CONTESTING THE RESULT OF AN AUDIT

Taxpayers who disagree with all or any part of the outcome of an audit (including penalties) may appeal the disputed issue to a regional Appeals Office of the IRS. An appeal leads to an administrative conference between the taxpayer (or more typically, the taxpayer's representative) and a specially trained IRS appeals officer. The purpose of the conference is to resolve the controversy in a fair and impartial manner. Appeal officers have broad latitude in settling disputes and may negotiate a compromise between the contestants on questionable issues. IRS Publication 5, *Your Appeal Rights and How to Prepare a Protest If You Don't Agree,* explains a taxpayer's appeal rights and the appeals procedure in detail.

Litigation

Trial Court

When a taxpayer and the government fail to resolve their differences in an administrative conference, the taxpayer can take the case to federal court for judicial review. In federal tax matters, one of three trial courts has original jurisdiction. A taxpayer may refuse to pay the deficiency determined by the IRS and file a petition with the **U.S. Tax Court** to hear the case. Alternatively, the taxpayer may pay the deficiency, then immediately sue the government for a refund in either the local **U.S. District Court** or the **U.S. Court of Federal Claims** located in Washington, D.C. The tax litigation process is illustrated in Exhibit 17.1.

The selection of the appropriate judicial forum is an important matter of strategy for the taxpayer's legal counsel. Each of the courts is different in operation, and one may be more advantageous than the others depending on the nature of the controversy. The Tax Court adjudicates only federal income, gift, and estate tax issues and is comprised of judges who are acknowledged experts in the tax law. In contrast, judges in the district courts and Court of Federal Claims preside over cases involving many legal issues and typically have no special expertise in the tax area.

Taxpayers who want a jury trial must take their case to district court. In both the Tax Court and Court of Federal Claims, a single judge or a panel of judges tries the case and renders a verdict. If the controversy is one of fact rather than the technical application of the law, the taxpayer's attorney may recommend that the matter be put to a jury in the hope that the

EXHIBIT 17.1
The Tax Litigation Process

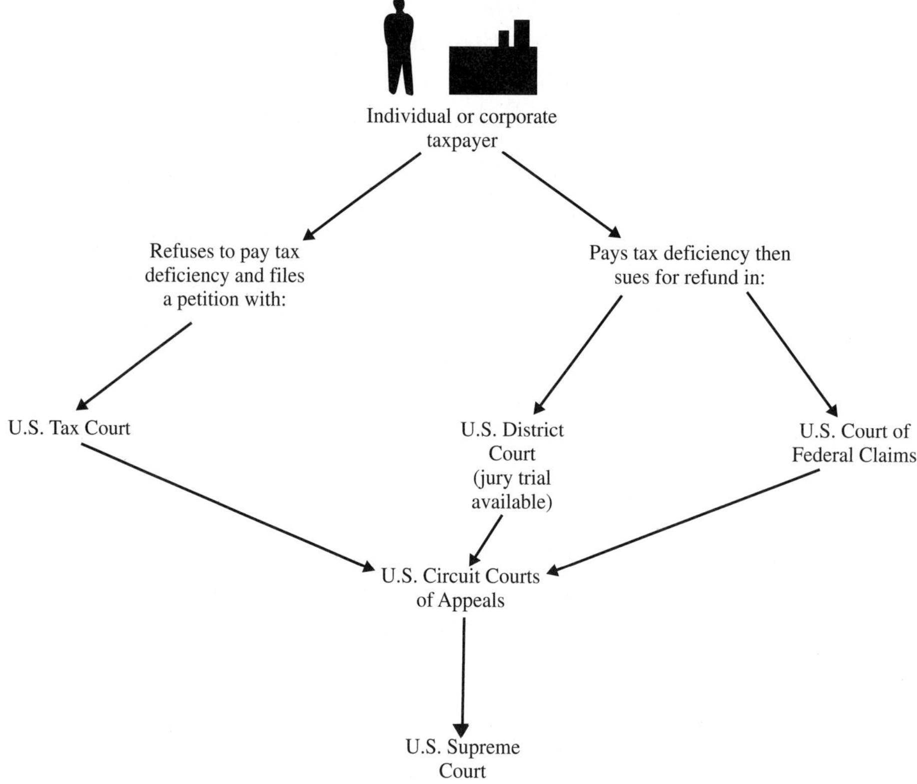

jury panel (who, after all, are taxpayers themselves) may be sympathetic. Of course, the viability of this strategy depends on the particular issue at hand. For instance, if the parent of a chronically ill child is arguing that the cost of a nontraditional treatment should qualify as a deductible medical expense, a jury trial seems a wise choice. However, if a businessman is trying to prove that a $350,000 salary from his closely held corporation is reasonable compensation, he may be better off pleading his case before a Tax Court judge.

Appellate and Supreme Court

Objective 5
Identify the three judicial levels in the tax litigation process.

The losing party at the trial court level (taxpayer or government) may appeal the verdict to one of 13 **U.S. Circuit Courts of Appeals.** The geographic location of the trial court determines which appellate court has jurisdiction. These courts generally do not review findings of fact by a lower court, but they will consider if the lower court properly applied the relevant law to the facts. After the appellate court has either affirmed or reversed the trial court's decision, the losing party may appeal the case to the **U.S. Supreme Court.** This Court may agree to hear the case *(grant certiorari)* or refuse to hear it *(deny certiorari).* When the Supreme Court denies certiorari, the decision of the appellate court is final. During an average term, the Supreme Court hears no more than a dozen federal tax cases, which are selected either because the Court believes that the case involves a significant principle of law or because two or more appellate courts have rendered conflicting opinions on the proper resolution of a tax issue.

A Case History: *Lori Williams* v. *United States*

To summarize our discussion of the tax litigation process, consider the sequence of events in which Ms. Lori Williams took her case to the Supreme Court.

Facts of the Case

During Lori Williams's marriage to Jerrold Rabin, he failed to pay $41,000 of federal employment tax related to his business. The government assessed a deficiency for the unpaid tax against Mr. Rabin and placed a lien on all his property, including the personal residence jointly owned with his wife. However, just one month before the lien was recorded, Mr. Rabin transferred his interest in the residence to Lori Williams as part of a divorce settlement. Nine months later, she contracted to sell the residence. Although Ms. Williams was not personally liable for her former husband's $41,000 tax deficiency, she paid it under protest. Her payment was the only way to remove the government's lien on the residence so that she could convey clear title to the purchasers.

Trial Court Decision

After paying her former husband's tax bill, Ms. Williams filed a claim for refund, arguing that the government had "erroneously or illegally assessed or collected" the tax. The IRS refused to even consider her claim, responding that Ms. Williams could not seek a refund of tax assessed against another person, even though she paid the tax. Ms. Williams then brought suit against the United States for her refund in district court.[25] The district court accepted the government's argument and held that Ms. Williams lacked standing to seek a refund. In making its decision, the district court relied on precedent established in decisions by the Fifth and Seventh Circuit Courts of Appeals.[26]

Lori Williams's Appeal

Lori Williams appealed the trial court's verdict to the Ninth Circuit Court of Appeals. This court analyzed a very similar case decided in the taxpayer's favor by the Fourth Circuit Court.[27] The Ninth Circuit Court was persuaded by the Fourth Circuit Court's reasoning and decided that Lori Williams had the right to seek a refund, thereby reversing the district court's verdict.[28]

The Government's Appeal

Now it was the government's turn to appeal the case to the Supreme Court, which granted certiorari to resolve the conflict among the appellate courts. In a decision in which six justices concurred and three justices dissented, the Court affirmed the Ninth Circuit Court's decision by holding that any person who pays a tax has the right to seek a refund of such tax.[29] Justice Ruth Bader Ginsburg, writing for the majority, concluded that federal statute does not expressly restrict refund claims to those persons against which the tax was assessed. Ms. Williams had no realistic alternative to paying the tax assessed against her former husband if she ever wanted to sell the residence. Congress did not intend to leave people in Ms. Williams's predicament without legal remedy, and equity demands that the IRS consider her claim.

Making the Legal System More Taxpayer Friendly

While every taxpayer who disagrees with the IRS has a right to his day in court, many people are reluctant to bear the emotional and financial cost of litigation. To make the legal

[25] *Lori Rabin Williams* v. *United States,* Civil No. 91-5286 WMB (DC CA, September 2, 1992).

[26] *Snodgrass* v. *United States,* 834 F.2d 537 (CA-5, 1987) and *Busse* v. *United States,* 542 F.2d 421 (CA-7, 1976).

[27] *Martin* v. *United States,* 895 F.2d 992 (CA-4, 1990).

[28] *Williams* v. *United States,* 24 F.3d 1143 (CA-9, 1994).

[29] *United States* v. *Williams,* 514 U.S. 527 (1995).

system a bit more accessible to the average person, Congress established a **Small Tax Case Division** of the Tax Court.[30] A taxpayer who is disputing a deficiency of $50,000 or less may request an informal hearing presided over by an officer of the court. The filing fee for such hearing is only $60, and the taxpayer may plead his own case without an attorney. After the presiding officer has heard the taxpayer's side of the story and rendered judgment, the matter is settled—neither taxpayer nor government may appeal the case to any other court.

Taxpayers who win their tax case may be entitled to recover litigation expenses from the government.[31] Such expenses include court costs, attorney fees, fees paid to expert witnesses, and payments for technical studies, analyses, tests, and reports necessary for the preparation of the taxpayer's case. Taxpayers are reimbursed for these expenses unless the IRS can convince the court that its position in the case was substantially justified. If the IRS failed to follow any of its own published rules, regulations, and procedures during the taxpayer's audit, the legal presumption is that the IRS's position was unjustified. Another factor that the courts consider is whether the IRS pursued the litigation to harass or embarrass the taxpayer or out of political motivation.

Recovery of Litigation Expenses

St. David's Health Care System is a nonprofit corporation that provides medical services to the public. The IRS challenged St. David's charitable purpose and attempted to revoke its tax-exempt status, and the corporation fought the revocation in court. The Texas district court sided with the corporation by concluding that "There is absolutely no issue as to whether St. David's has a charitable purpose, and any argument to the contrary appears at least mildly disingenuous."[32] The court then ordered the federal government to pay the corporation's $950,000 of litigation expenses because the IRS's position in the case was not substantially justified.

The existence of the Small Tax Case Division and the right of taxpayers to recover litigation costs reflect congressional sympathy for individuals who sincerely believe that they are right and the IRS is wrong. On the other hand, Congress has little tolerance for people who waste federal time and money by initiating foolish lawsuits against the IRS. The Internal Revenue Code authorizes the Tax Court to impose a monetary penalty up to $25,000 on a taxpayer who takes a frivolous or groundless position before the court or institutes a case primarily for delay.[33]

A Frivolous Deduction

In December 1996, Douglas Riley filed delinquent income tax returns for 1992 through 1995 which reported AGI of $53,029, $60,406, $7,154, and $16,399. Each return included a Schedule A reporting a casualty loss deduction of $50,729, $58,056, $4,704, and $13,899. He described his casualty as the loss of a "nonviable fetus" resulting from his wife's termination of a pregnancy in either 1974 or 1975. After the IRS disallowed the deductions, Mr. Riley took his case to Tax Court. After sustaining the IRS, the Tax Court chided him for claiming "utterly groundless" deductions that he obviously calculated to offset his taxable income. "Notwithstanding the Court's warning that such claims appeared frivolous, petitioner proceeded to trial. Petitioner has wasted the time and resources of this Court and the respondent [IRS]. We will accordingly exercise our discretion to require petitioner to pay a penalty to the United States of $1,000."[34]

30 §7463.

31 §7430. Taxpayers may also be entitled to recover reasonable administrative costs incurred when dealing with the IRS.

32 *St. David's Health Care System Inc.* v. *United States,* 90 AFTR 2d 2002-6878 (DC TX, 2002).

33 §6673.

34 *Douglas Michael Riley,* TC Memo 1999-363.

IRS Collection Procedures

Taxpayers who have exhausted every avenue of appeal must finally pay their tax deficiency (including interest and penalties) to the government. The IRS is authorized to collect the deficiency by whatever means necessary, including seizing the taxpayer's assets and selling them at auction, levying bank accounts, and garnishing the taxpayer's salary or wage. Nonetheless, the IRS knows that it can't get blood out of a stone. If a taxpayer has insufficient financial means to pay a tax deficiency and is willing to cooperate, the IRS may negotiate a settlement (referred to as an **offer in compromise**) for some lesser amount. Alternatively, the IRS may allow the taxpayer to pay off the debt over time on an installment basis.

Objective 6
Define the term *transferee liability*.

A question sometimes arises as to which person is legally responsible for the payment of a federal tax deficiency. If the taxpayer is a corporation, the deficiency must be satisfied with corporate assets; shareholders are not liable for their corporation's unpaid taxes. A major exception to this limited shareholder liability arises when the corporation no longer exists. In this case, the shareholders have **transferee liability** for the corporation's unsatisfied debts, including federal taxes, to the extent of the value of any assets received on liquidation of the corporation.[35]

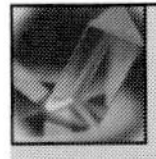

Transferee Liability

Ms. Morgan owned 30 percent of the stock of KLM, which was dissolved under state law in 2003. Ms. Morgan received a $55,000 cash distribution from KLM in complete liquidation of her equity interest. The IRS audited KLM's tax returns for 2001, 2002, and 2003, and determined that it underpaid its income tax by $114,800. The IRS can assess $55,000 of this deficiency against Ms. Morgan.

The Innocent Spouse Rule

Objective 7
Explain the purpose of the innocent spouse rule.

When individuals sign their Form 1040s, they become liable for any tax deficiency with respect to that return. In the case of a joint return, both husband and wife must sign, thereby becoming jointly and severally liable.[36] As a result, the IRS may assess either person for the entire deficiency determined on subsequent audit of the return. Occasionally this rule can work a real hardship on a person who is liable for unpaid taxes on a joint return that he or she signed without any knowledge of the information on the return. Such a person may be relieved of liability under the **innocent spouse rule.**[37] Such relief is dependent on three conditions:

1. The deficiency must be attributable to erroneous items (such as omitted income or bogus deductions) of the person's spouse.
2. The person must establish that in signing the return he or she did not know, and had no reason to know, that the return understated the correct tax.
3. Taking into account all the facts and circumstances, it is inequitable to hold the person liable for the deficiency.

One factor that the courts weigh very heavily in analyzing the third condition is whether the person significantly benefited, directly or indirectly, from any income omitted from the return. If a court concludes that a significant benefit existed, innocent spouse relief is denied, even if the person was clearly ignorant of the omission. Normal spousal support is not considered a significant benefit, but an unusually lavish or extravagant lifestyle may indicate that both spouses enjoyed the omitted income. Another factor that the courts consider is whether the person seeking relief has been deserted by or is divorced from his or her spouse.

[35] §6901.

[36] §6013(d)(3).

[37] §6015.

Innocent Spouse Relief

Mr. and Mrs. Vriner married in 1989 and divorced in 1997. They filed joint tax returns for 1989 through 1995 that reported no taxable income. During the marriage, Mr. Vriner worked at a restaurant owned by his parents. Mrs. Vriner never saw a paycheck, and her husband told her that the restaurant was none of her business. Mrs. Vriner was not employed. The couple did not have a joint checking account; Mr. Vriner paid their bills with cash or money orders. They resided in an old neighborhood and lived modestly, seldom dining out or traveling.

In 1995, federal narcotic agents arrested Mr. Vriner for drug trafficking. Mrs. Vriner learned of her husband's illegal activities from reading the newspaper after his arrest. The IRS subsequently determined that Mr. Vriner failed to report any income from his drug trafficking and assessed a $36,417 tax deficiency for 1994 and 1995. The Tax Court decided that Mrs. Vriner was entitled to relief as an innocent spouse. She had no actual knowledge of the tax understatement and no reason to know, given her lack of education and her exclusion from family finances. The court concluded that it would be inequitable to hold Mrs. Vriner liable for the deficiency because she received very little, if any, benefit from the income that gave rise to the deficiency.[38]

Conclusion to the Text

Chapter 17 has provided a brief summary of the tax compliance process. After reading this chapter, you should have a much better sense of the rights and responsibilities of corporate and individual taxpayers. You should be aware that noncompliance with the tax laws can result in monetary penalties and, in extreme cases, criminal prosecution. Finally, you should understand the roles played by the IRS and the federal courts in administering our nation's tax laws. The information contained in this chapter, which culminates our study of the federal tax system, should serve you in good stead in your role as a taxpaying citizen or resident of the United States.

To bring *Principles of Taxation for Business and Investment Planning* to its conclusion, let's briefly revisit the three objectives established in the introduction to the text. The first objective was to familiarize readers with tax policy issues. If the text has been successful in meeting this objective, you should be confident of your ability to evaluate tax laws based on the characteristics of sufficiency, ease of administration, economic efficiency, and equity. You should be able to form rational opinions concerning the strengths and weaknesses of the system—opinions based on knowledge rather than popular misconceptions or political bombast. Perhaps you even have some definite ideas as to how the tax system can be improved through the democratic process.

The second objective of the text was to bridge the gap between finance and tax. Hopefully, you now understand that these two subjects are inextricably related and that business managers cannot make good financial decisions without considering tax consequences. In our many discussions of the tax implications of business and investment transactions, we've analyzed transactions in terms of after-tax cash flows. We've observed how the net present value of cash flows can increase when tax costs are minimized or tax savings are maximized. You have worked hard to develop an aptitude for recognizing tax planning opportunities to improve financial outcomes.

The third objective of the text was to teach the basic framework of the federal income tax. Throughout the text, we have concentrated on core concepts rather than technical details. You now understand how the income tax relates to the business, employment, investment, and even personal activities in which you will engage throughout your life. Almost certainly, you have concluded that the income tax system deserves its reputation for complexity. But

[38] *Barbara A. Vriner,* TC Memo 1995-465.

if the text has achieved its third objective, you also appreciate the reasons for much of the complexity. In addition, you now have a theoretical framework in place. As you continue to learn about taxes and tax systems, either in the classroom or through experience, you can integrate your new knowledge into this framework. If you do this, the lessons learned from *Principles of Taxation for Business and Investment Planning* will create value for many years to come.

Key Terms

civil fraud *501*
correspondence examination *499*
criminal fraud *502*
deficiency *499*
discriminate function system (DIF) score *499*
enrolled agent *499*
field examination *499*
income tax return preparer *502*
innocent spouse rule *507*
late-filing and late-payment penalty *496*
negligence *500*
offer in compromise *507*
office examination *499*
Small Tax Case Division *506*
special agent *502*
statute of limitations *498*
tax evasion *502*
Taxpayer Bill of Rights *500*
transferee liability *507*
U.S. Circuit Courts of Appeals *504*
U.S. Court of Federal Claims *503*
U.S. District Court *503*
U.S. Supreme Court *504*
U.S. Tax Court *503*

Questions and Problems for Discussion

1. Discuss the policy reasons for a statute of limitations for tax returns.
2. Historically, about 1 percent of Form 1040s are audited. Why does a Form 1040 reflecting \$31,000 AGI and a standard deduction have much *less* than a 1 percent chance, while a Form 1040 reflecting \$235,000 AGI and \$85,790 itemized deductions have a much *greater* than 1 percent chance of audit?
3. Which has the greater chance of audit: a Form 1040 with \$200,000 AGI, all of which is salary income, or a Form 1040 with \$200,000 AGI, all of which is net profit from a sole proprietorship?
4. Mrs. NM received a letter from the IRS asking her to submit written substantiation of a \$1,500 charitable contribution deduction. Discuss the probable tax consequences to Mrs. NM if:
   a. She sends the IRS copies of her canceled check for \$1,500 made out to the charitable organization and the thank-you letter in which the organization acknowledged her contribution.
   b. She ignores the IRS request because she has no substantiation.
5. Is it easier for the IRS to determine that an individual omitted an income item from a return or overstated deductions?
6. Corporation VL's net worth exceeds \$160 million, its stock is publicly traded, and a national CPA firm audits its financial statements. Corporation TT's net worth also exceeds \$160 million. However, it is closely held by members of the TT family. Discuss the reasons that the IRS might choose to audit Corporation TT rather than Corporation VL.
7. NK and CS are both closely held corporations. NK's tax returns for the last five years reflect average taxable income of \$90 million. CS's tax returns for the same period reflect average taxable income of \$90,000. Discuss the reasons that the IRS might choose to audit NK rather than CS.

8. During an IRS audit, Ms. H provided the revenue agent with a meticulous set of records substantiating every number on the return. The agent actually complimented her on the quality of her preparation. Nevertheless, Ms. H did make an error in her favor. When she received formal notification that she owed an additional $4,350 tax, she was dismayed that the IRS also billed her for $920 interest on the deficiency. She doesn't understand why she must pay interest when she obviously made a good faith effort to comply with the tax law. Can you explain why?
9. Discuss the burden of proof as it relates to the penalties for:
   a. Negligence
   b. Civil fraud
   c. Criminal fraud
10. During a field examination of GNT's income tax returns for 2003 and 2004, the revenue agent discovered that the treasurer had systematically omitted substantial income items and inflated deductions to minimize the corporation's tax. The agent suspects that the treasurer adopted this deliberate course of action as early as 1992. Can the IRS initiate an audit of GNT's tax returns all the way back to 1992? Explain briefly.
11. Mr. JY, a commercial artist, engaged Mr. DE, a local attorney, to prepare his income tax return. Mr. JY provided the attorney with his check register, deposit slips, receipts, and pertinent financial documents, and read through the completed return before signing it. This year, the return was selected for audit. The IRS agent discovered that Mr. DE incorrectly deducted certain of Mr. JY's personal living expenses. Consequently, the tax was understated by $8,900. The agent decided that the deduction represented an unrealistic position with no reasonable basis in the law.
   a. Is Mr. JY liable for payment of the $8,900 tax deficiency plus interest?
   b. Could the IRS impose a negligence penalty on Mr. JY?
   c. Could Mr. DE be penalized because of the error made in preparing Mr. JY's income tax return?
   d. Would your answer to the preceding questions change if Mr. DE were Mr. JY's brother-in-law who prepared the return as a favor rather than for compensation?
12. Mr. NG is an enrolled agent in tax practice. Last year, the IRS imposed a $750 preparer penalty on him, and he immediately hired an attorney to contest the penalty. Mr. NG's legal fee was $7,900. Was he acting irrationally by spending so much money to avoid the penalty?
13. Mr. and Mrs. BL filed a joint tax return reporting $24,000 AGI. During the year, Mr. BL was extremely ill and was hospitalized for four months. Mrs. BL, desperate for funds to pay her husband's medical bills, took a night job as a bartender. She earned approximately $7,000 of tips, none of which she reported on the return. Mr. BL had no idea his wife had gone to such lengths on his behalf. After auditing this return, the IRS notified Mr. BL that he owed a $1,100 deficiency plus interest because of the unreported tip income. Can he avoid liability as an innocent spouse? Explain your conclusion.
14. Mrs. QE has decided to contest a $28,650 tax deficiency. She understands that she can initiate the litigation in district court or the Tax Court. Identify any reasons why she might prefer one trial court over the other.

Application Problems

1. Mr. TH prepared and signed last year's tax return on April 3. However, he forgot to mail the return until the morning of April 18. He enclosed his check for the $8,048 balance of tax due with the return. Compute his late-filing and late-payment penalty.

2. Ms. CP did not request an extension of time to file last year's income tax return and did not mail the completed return to the IRS until July 2. She enclosed a check for $2,380, the correct balance of tax due with the return.
   a. Assuming that she cannot show reasonable cause for filing a delinquent return, compute the late-filing and late-payment penalty.
   b. How would your answer change if she did not mail her return until November 21?
3. Mr. DD filed a delinquent tax return on July 27. The return reflected $3,700 total tax, $4,000 withholding, and a $300 refund due. Compute his late-filing penalty.
4. LZ uses a fiscal year ending November 30. The controller filed LZ's Form 1120 for the year ending November 30, 2004, on December 23, 2004.
   a. What is the last day on which the IRS may assess additional tax for this fiscal year?
   b. How would your answer change if LZ's return was timely filed on its extended due date of August 15, 2005?
5. Mrs. FG, who is divorced, failed to include $28,000 alimony on her 2003 Form 1040. The only income she reported was her $78,000 salary. She filed her return on January 19, 2004.
   a. What is the last date that the IRS can assess additional tax for 2003?
   b. Would your answer change if Mrs. FG also reported $37,500 dividend income on her 2003 Form 1040?
6. Collin Products received notice of a $21,000 income tax deficiency plus $4,300 interest. The deficiency related to an incorrect method of accounting for business inventory. Compute the after-tax cost of the $4,300 interest payment assuming that:
   a. Collin Products is a corporate taxpayer with a 35 percent marginal tax rate.
   b. Collin Products is a sole proprietorship owned by Leslie Collin. Leslie's marginal tax rate on her Form 1040 is 35 percent.
7. A revenue agent determined that Ms. PH understated her tax by $48,100 and concluded that $9,200 was caused by her inadequate record keeping while the remainder was caused by her misapplication of a complex rule of law. Compute the negligence penalty that the revenue agent can impose on Ms. PH.
8. Mr. GH has an MBA degree from Stanford University and has been in business for himself for 18 years. The revenue agent who audited his Form 1040 discovered a glaring error resulting in a $16,200 understatement of tax. When the agent questioned him about the error, Mr. GH just shrugged his shoulders and offered no logical explanation.
   a. If the error resulted from Mr. GH's intentional disregard of a tax rule, compute the negligence penalty.
   b. Should the fact of Mr. GH's education and business experience influence the agent's decision to impose the negligence penalty?
9. During the audit of Mr. and Mrs. J's 2003 and 2004 tax returns, the revenue agent learned that they kept two sets of books for their sole proprietorship. A comparison of the two revealed that Mr. and Mrs. J earned over $80,000 unreported income. The tax deficiency on the unreported income was $32,000.
   a. Compute the civil fraud penalty the IRS may impose.
   b. Describe the procedural steps the IRS must take to charge the couple with criminal fraud.
   c. Why might the IRS decide to impose a civil fraud penalty on Mr. and Mrs. J but not charge them with criminal fraud?

10. The IRS assessed a $32,800 income tax deficiency plus $4,015 interest against Mr. and Mrs. OE because of an alleged understatement of investment income. They refused to pay and took their case to the U.S. Tax Court. They incurred $7,829 attorney fees and other costs of the litigation. Determine their after-tax cost assuming that:
    a. They won their case, and the IRS failed to demonstrate that its position was substantially justified.
    b. They won their case, but the IRS convinced the court that its position was substantially justified.
    c. They lost their case.
11. Ms. TY is a professional tax return preparer. Three years ago, she prepared the return for MK Limited Partnership, which has 42 individual partners. The IRS discovered that she incorrectly deducted $67,000 expenses, which resulted in an understatement of each partner's share of income. Compute the preparer penalty if the IRS concludes that:
    a. Ms. TY should have known that the deduction had no realistic possibility of being sustained on its merit if the partnership return was audited.
    b. Ms. TY willfully attempted to understate the partners' tax by claiming the erroneous deduction on the partnership return.
12. Two years ago, LT's shareholders voted to dissolve the corporation. Pursuant to the dissolution, LT sold all its assets, paid off its outstanding debts, and distributed $789,000 remaining cash to its shareholders in complete liquidation of their equity. This year, the IRS determined that LT underpaid its corporate income tax for its last three years. The tax deficiency totaled $1.4 million.
    a. To what extent can the IRS collect the deficiency from the former LT shareholders?
    b. MN Partnership was a 5 percent LT shareholder. How much tax can the IRS collect from MN partnership?

Issue Recognition Problems

Identify the tax issue or issues suggested by the following situations and state each issue in the form of a question.

1. On April 3, Mr. and Mrs. BR traveled to Japan. They made the trip because their son, who lives in Tokyo, was injured in an accident and needed their care. After nursing their son back to health, they returned home on June 11. On June 17, Mrs. BR mailed their delinquent Form 1040 and remitted the $18,262 balance of tax due with the return.
2. On July 2, Mrs. N received a notice assessing a $10,861 tax deficiency plus $1,900 interest (computed through the date the IRS mailed the notice). She was short of funds, so she did not pay her tax bill within 10 days as required by the notice. Instead, she waited until September 29 to mail a check for $12,761 to the IRS.
3. On April 13, Mr. LP filed a request for an automatic extension of time to file his Form 1040. He estimated that the balance of tax due was $3,800, which he paid with the extension request. He filed his return on June 20. The actual balance of tax due was $6,900, so he paid an additional $3,100 with the return.
4. Mr. B, a self-employed consultant, charged a client a $15,000 fee plus $3,900 reimbursable business expenses. The client paid the $18,900 bill and sent a Form 1099 reporting $18,900 income. When Mr. B prepared his Schedule C, he simply reported $15,000 income from the client. He did not report the $3,900 reimbursement or deduct the expenses.

5. Mrs. LK died on February 12 and left her entire estate (including her marketable securities) to her son. After the end of the year, the son received 14 Form 1099s showing his mother's name and Social Security number. These 1099s reported $29,788 dividend income that the son simply reported on his Form 1040.
6. Mr. T has not paid income tax or filed a tax return for the last eight years. He believes that the IRS can no longer assess any back taxes for the first five of those years.
7. KP, a calendar year corporation, filed its 2001 return on March 8, 2002. On February 19, 2005, it filed an amended 2001 return reflecting $2.61 million *less* taxable income than the original return and requesting a $913,000 tax refund.
8. Corporation N, a calendar year taxpayer, incurred a net operating loss in 2004 that it carried back as a deduction against 2002 income. Corporation N's treasurer filed a claim for a $712,600 refund of 2002 tax and expects to receive a check from the government any day now.
9. Mr. MK died and left all his property to his only grandson. After the estate was settled, the grandson received his $942,000 inheritance. Nine months later, the IRS audited Mr. MK's final Form 1040 and discovered that he underpaid his income tax by $18,450.

Research Problems

1. Using an electronic tax library that contains IRS publications, determine the purpose of Publication 334, Publication 504, and Publication 907.
2. Locate information on the procedure by which an individual taxpayer can request a photocopy of a prior-year federal income tax return. What is the number of the form to request a photocopy? Does the IRS charge a fee for this service? How many days will it take to receive the copy from the IRS?
3. Using an electronic tax library, locate a recent judicial decision involving taxpayer negligence and a different decision involving taxpayer fraud. Describe the actions of the taxpayers that resulted in these penalties.

Tax Planning Cases

1. Mr. JR's tax situation for the year is very complicated. He engaged in several high-dollar investment transactions involving unresolved tax issues. He has instructed his accountant to take the most aggressive position possible with respect to these transactions. Mr. JR also wants to take a home office deduction for one of his business activities. The deduction would be only $1,293. Can you suggest any strategic reason why he should forgo the home office deduction?
2. The IRS recently assessed a $290,800 income tax deficiency on CMP Corporation. The deficiency is attributable to a complicated accounting issue involving CMP's investment in a controlled foreign corporation. CMP plans to contest the deficiency in court. CMP is located in the Third Circuit. Neither the local district court, the Tax Court, nor the Third Circuit Court of Appeals has considered the accounting issue. The Court of Federal Claims and the Eighth Circuit Court of Appeals have decided the issue in favor of the government. However, the Ninth and Tenth Circuit Courts of Appeals have decided the identical issue in favor of the taxpayer. Discuss CMP's litigation strategy in selecting a trial court.

Glossary

abandonment loss The unrecovered basis in an abandoned asset. Abandonment losses with respect to business assets are ordinary deductions.

abatement A property tax exemption granted by a government for a limited period of time.

ability to pay Economic resources under a person's control from which he or she can pay tax.

above-the-line deduction An allowable deduction for an individual taxpayer that can be subtracted from total income to compute AGI.

accelerated death benefits Payments made under a life insurance contract to insured individuals who are terminally or chronically ill.

accrual method of accounting An overall method of accounting under which revenues are realized in the year the earnings process is complete and expenses are matched against revenues in the year the liability for the expense is incurred.

accumulated earnings tax A penalty tax levied on corporations accumulating income beyond the reasonable needs of the business to avoid paying dividends to their shareholders. The tax is levied in addition to the regular income tax.

acquisition debt Debt incurred to acquire, construct, or substantially improve a personal residence. The debt must be secured by the residence and is limited to $1 million ($500,000 for married filing separately).

activity-based tax A tax imposed on the results of an ongoing activity in which persons or organizations engage.

ad valorem tax A tax based on the value of property.

adjusted basis The initial tax basis of an asset reduced by cost recovery deductions allowable with respect to the basis.

adjusted gross income (AGI) Total income less adjustments as computed on page 1, Form 1040. AGI is an intermediate step in the calculation of individual taxable income.

affiliated corporation For purposes of the tax rules governing worthless securities, any 80 percent or more controlled domestic subsidiary that has always derived more than 90 percent of annual gross receipts from the conduct of an active business.

affiliated group A parent corporation and its 80 percent or more controlled subsidiaries.

all-events test The test for determining if an accrued expense is deductible. For most routine accruals, the test is satisfied if the liability on which the accrued expense is based is fixed, and the amount of the liability is determinable with reasonable accuracy.

allowance method The GAAP method for computing bad debt expense. The expense is based on the estimated losses from current year receivables.

alternative minimum tax (AMT) A second federal tax system parallel to the regular tax system. Congress enacted the AMT to ensure that every individual and corporation pays at least a minimal tax every year.

alternative minimum taxable income (AMTI) The tax base for the AMT: regular taxable income increased or decreased by AMT adjustments and increased by AMT tax preferences.

amortization The ratable deduction of the capitalized cost of an intangible asset over its determinable life.

amount realized The sum of any money plus the fair market value of any property received by a seller on the sale or exchange of property.

AMT adjustments Increases or decreases to regular taxable income in the computation of AMTI.

annual gift tax exclusion The annual amount that a donor can give to each donee that is excluded from taxable gifts.

annualized income The taxable income reported on a short-period return mathematically inflated to reflect 12 months of business operations.

annuity A cash flow consisting of a constant dollar amount for a specific number of time periods.

apportionment A method of dividing a firm's taxable income among the various states with jurisdiction to tax the firm's business activities.

arm's-length transaction A transaction occurring between unrelated parties who are dealing in their own self-interest.

assignment of income doctrine Income must be taxed to the entity that renders the service or owns the capital with respect to which the income is paid.

average rate The tax rate determined by dividing total tax liability by the total tax base.

bargain element The excess of fair market value over cost of stock acquired on exercise of a stock option.

boot Cash or other nonqualifying property included as part of a nontaxable exchange.

bracket The portion of a tax base subject to a given percentage rate in a graduated rate structure.

bunching A tax planning technique to concentrate itemized deductions into one year so that the total exceeds the standard deduction for the year.

business purpose doctrine A transaction should not be effective for tax purposes unless it is intended to achieve a genuine and independent business purpose other than tax avoidance.

buy-sell agreement A binding agreement that restricts the conditions and terms under which shareholders may dispose of corporate stock.

cafeteria plan A compensation plan under which employees may choose among two or more benefits, including both cash and noncash items.

calendar year The 12-month period from January 1 through December 31.

capital asset Any asset that does not fall into one of eight statutory categories of noncapital assets. Most business assets (accounts receivable, supplies, inventories, tangible personalty, realty, and purchased intangibles) are noncapital assets.

capital gain distribution A distribution of long-term capital gain recognized by a mutual fund to investors in the fund.

capital gain or loss Gain or loss realized on the sale or exchange of a capital asset. Capital gain may be eligible for a preferential tax rate.

capitalization An accounting requirement that an expenditure be charged to a balance sheet account rather than against the firm's current income.

carryover basis The basis of transferred property in the hands of the recipient equal to the basis of the property in the hands of the transferor.

cash method of accounting An overall method of accounting under which revenue is accounted for when payment is received and expenses are accounted for when payment is made.

cash surrender value The amount paid to the owner of a life insurance policy on the liquidation of the policy.

centralized management A legal characteristic of the corporate form of business: Corporations are managed by a board of directors appointed by and acting on behalf of the shareholders.

child credit A credit based on the number of the taxpayer's dependent children under age 17.

civil fraud The intention to cheat the government by deliberately understating tax liability.

closely held corporations Corporations privately owned by a relatively small number of shareholders.

collectibles Tangible capital assets such as works of art, antiques, gems, stamps, and coins.

Commerce Clause Article 1 of the U.S. Constitution that grants the federal government the power to regulate interstate commerce.

consolidated tax return A single Form 1120 reporting the combined results of the operations of an affiliated group of corporations.

constructive dividend A distribution by a corporation to a shareholder that the corporation classifies as salary, interest, rent, or some other type of payment but that the IRS classifies as a dividend.

constructive receipt The point at which a taxpayer has unrestricted access to and control of income, even if the income item is not in the taxpayer's actual possession.

controlled foreign corporation (CFC) A foreign corporation in which U.S. shareholders own more than 50 percent of the voting power or stock value.

controlled group A brother-sister group of corporations owned by the same individual shareholders or a parent-subsidiary group of corporations.

convenience The second standard for a good tax. A tax should be convenient for the government to administer and for people to pay.

correspondence examination The simplest type of audit that can be handled entirely by telephone or through the mail.

cost basis The purchase price of an asset including any sales tax paid by the purchaser and any incidental costs related to getting the asset in place and into production.

cost depletion The method for recovering the capitalized cost of an exhaustible natural resource. Cost depletion equals unrecovered basis in the resource (mine or well) multiplied by the ratio of units of production sold during the year to the estimated total units of production at the beginning of the year.

cost of goods sold The capitalized cost of inventory sold during the taxable year and subtracted from gross receipts in the computation of gross income.

Coverdell education savings account An investment account through which individuals can save for education expenses on a tax-exempt basis.

criminal fraud A felony offense involving the willful attempt to evade or defeat any federal tax.

cross-crediting Crediting the excess foreign tax paid in high-tax jurisdictions against the excess limitation attributable to income earned in low-tax jurisdictions.

Cumulative Bulletin (CB) Semiannual compilation of weekly Internal Revenue Bulletins.

declining marginal utility of income The theory that the financial importance associated with each dollar of income diminishes as total income increases.

deduction An offset or subtraction in the calculation of taxable income.

deemed paid foreign tax credit A credit available to U.S. corporations that receive dividends from a foreign subsidiary. The credit is based on foreign income tax paid by the subsidiary.

deferred compensation A nonqualified plan under which an employer promises to pay a portion of an employee's current compensation in a future year.

deferred tax asset The excess of tax payable over tax expense per books resulting from a temporary difference between book income and taxable income.

deferred tax liability The excess of tax expense per books over tax payable resulting from a temporary difference between book income and taxable income.

deficiency An underpayment of tax determined on audit and assessed by the IRS.

defined-benefit plan A qualified plan under which participants are promised a targeted benefit, usually in the form of a pension, when they retire.

defined-contribution plan A qualified plan under which an annual contribution is made to each participant's retirement account.

dependent A member of a taxpayer's family or household who receives more than half of his or her financial support from the taxpayer.

dependent care credit A credit based on the taxpayer's cost of caring for dependents either under age 13 or physically or mentally incapable of caring for themselves.

depreciation The systematic deduction of the capitalized cost of tangible property over a specific period of time.

depreciation recapture Recapture computed with reference to depreciation or amortization deductions claimed with respect to property surrendered in a sale or exchange.

direct write-off method The method for determining a bad debt deduction required by the tax law. Only receivables that are written off as uncollectible during the year are deductible.

discount rate The rate of interest used to calculate the present value of future cash flows.

discriminate function system (DIF) score A numeric score assigned to individual tax returns that measures the return's potential for generating additional tax on audit.

distributive share A partner's share of any item of income, gain, deduction, or loss recognized by the partnership. Distributive shares are usually expressed as a percentage and specified in the partnership agreement.

dividends-received deduction A corporate deduction equal to a percentage of dividend income received from other taxable, domestic corporations.

donee An individual or organization that receives a gift.

donor An individual who makes a gift.

dynamic forecast A projection of revenue gain or loss resulting from a tax rate change that assumes that the change will affect the tax base.

earmarked tax A tax that generates revenues for a designated project or program rather than for the government's general fund.

earned income credit A refundable income tax credit that offsets the impact of the payroll tax on low-income workers.

economic performance A requirement of the all-events test for nonrecurring, extraordinary accruals. Economic performance means that all activities necessary to satisfy the accrued liability have been completed.

education savings bonds Qualified Series EE savings bonds that can be redeemed tax-free to pay for certain education expenses.

efficiency The third standard for a good tax. Classical economic theory holds that an efficient tax is neutral and has no effect on economic behavior. In contrast, Keynesian theory holds that an efficient tax is a fiscal policy tool by which the government can affect economic behavior.

employee An individual who performs services for compensation and who works under the direction and control of an employer.

employee payroll tax The FICA tax (Social Security and Medicare tax) levied on employees who receive compensation during the year.

employee stock ownership plan (ESOP) A qualified defined contribution plan in which contributions are invested primarily in the corporate employer's common stock.

employer identification number A number assigned to an employer by the IRS to identify the employer for employment tax purposes.

employer payroll tax The FICA tax (Social Security and Medicare tax) levied on employers that pay compensation during the year.

employer-provided plan A retirement plan sponsored and maintained by an employer for the benefit of the employees.

employment tax A tax based on wages, salaries, and self-employment income. Federal employment taxes are earmarked to fund Social Security and Medicare.

enrolled agent A tax practitioner certified by the IRS to represent clients in IRS proceedings.

event- or transaction-based tax A tax imposed on the occurrence of a certain event or transaction.

excess foreign tax credit Foreign tax paid or accrued during the year but not credited against U.S. tax because of the foreign tax credit limitation.

excess payroll tax withholding An overpayment of employee payroll tax allowed as a credit against income tax.

excise tax A tax levied on the retail sale of specific goods or services. An excise tax may be in addition to or instead of a general sales tax.

expansion costs Costs of enlarging the scope of operations of an existing business.

expatriate An individual who is a U.S. citizen and resides and works for an extended period in a foreign country.

explicit tax An actual tax liability paid directly to the taxing jurisdiction.

field examination An audit conducted by a revenue agent at the taxpayer's place of business.

FIFO The inventory costing convention under which the first goods manufactured or purchased are assumed to be the first goods sold.

filing status A classification for individual taxpayers reflecting marital and family situation and determining the rate schedule for the computation of tax liability.

firm A generic business organization. Firms include sole proprietorships, partnerships, limited liability companies, Subchapter S and regular corporations, and any other type of arrangement through which people carry on a profit-motivated activity.

fiscal year Any 12-month period ending on the last day of any month except December.

flat rate A single percentage that applies to the entire tax base.

foreign earned income exclusion An annual amount of foreign source earned income on which expatriates are not required to pay federal income tax.

foreign source income Taxable income attributable to a U.S. firm's business activities carried on in a foreign jurisdiction.

foreign tax credit A credit against U.S. tax based on foreign income tax paid or accrued during the year.

free transferability A legal characteristic of the corporate form of business: Shareholders can buy and sell corporate stock with maximum convenience and minimal transaction cost.

fringe benefits Any economic benefit subject to valuation received by an employee as additional compensation.

general business credit The aggregate of numerous different tax credits available to business enterprises.

general partnership A partnership in which all the partners have unlimited personal liability for the debts incurred by the partnership.

generally accepted accounting principles (GAAP) The set of accounting rules developed by the Financial Accounting Standards Board (FASB) and adhered to by the public accounting profession.

going-concern value Value attributable to the synergism of business assets working in coordination.

goodwill Value created by the expectancy that customers will continue to patronize a business.

graduated rates Multiple percentages that apply to specified brackets of the tax base.

gross income Realized increases in wealth from whatever source derived. In the business context, gross profit from sales of goods, performance of services, and investments of capital.

gross profit percentage The ratio of gain realized to total contract price in an installment sale.

guaranteed payment A distribution from a partnership to a partner to compensate the partner for ongoing services performed for the partnership.

half-year convention Property placed in service on any day of the taxable year is treated as placed in service halfway through the year for MACRS purposes.

head of household Filing status for an unmarried individual who maintains a home for a child or dependent family member.

hobby loss Excess of expenses over revenue from a personal activity not engaged in for profit.

home equity debt Debt secured by a personal residence to the extent the debt does not exceed the owner's equity in the residence. Home equity debt is limited to $100,000 ($50,000 for married filing separately).

Hope Scholarship Credit An individual tax credit based on qualified tuition expenses paid during the first two years of post-secondary education.

horizontal equity One aspect of the fourth standard of a good tax: A tax is fair if persons with the same ability to pay (as measured by the tax base) owe the same tax.

hybrid method of accounting An overall method of accounting that combines the accrual method for purchases and sales of inventory and the cash method for all other transactions.

implicit tax The reduction in before-tax rate of return that investors are willing to accept because of the tax-favored characteristics of an investment.

imputed income from owner-occupied housing The nontaxable economic benefit (fair rental value) derived by the owner of a home.

incentive stock option (ISO) A qualified stock option for federal tax purposes. Individuals do not recognize the bargain element as income on the exercise of an ISO.

incidence The ultimate economic burden represented by a tax.

income effect A behavioral response to an income tax rate increase: taxpayers engage in more income-producing activities to maintain their level of disposable income.

income tax A tax imposed on the periodic increases in wealth resulting from a person's economic activities.

income tax return preparer Any person who prepares returns (or who employs other people to prepare returns) for compensation and who is subject to tax return preparer penalties.

income tax treaty A bilateral agreement between the governments of two countries defining and limiting each country's respective tax jurisdiction.

independent contractor A self-employed individual who performs services for compensation and who retains control over the manner in which the services are performed.

individual retirement account (IRA) An investment account through which individuals with compensation or earned income can save for retirement on a tax-deferred basis.

innocent spouse rule The rule of law under which a person who filed a joint return with a spouse is not held liable for any deficiency of tax with respect to the return.

inside buildup Annual increase in value of a life insurance or annuity contract.

installment sale method A method of accounting for gains realized on the sale of property when some part of the amount realized consists of the buyer's note. Under the installment sale method, gain recognition is linked to the seller's receipt of cash over the life of the note.

intangible drilling and development costs (IDC) Expenses such as wages, fuel, repairs to drilling equipment, hauling, and supplies associated with locating and preparing oil and gas wells for production. IDC are deductible for federal tax purposes.

inter vivos transfer A transfer of property occurring during the life of the property owner.

Internal Revenue Bulletin (IRB) The IRS's weekly publication containing revenue rulings and revenue procedures.

Internal Revenue Code of 1986 The compilation of statutory tax laws written and enacted by the Congress of the United States.

Internal Revenue Service (IRS) The subdivision of the U.S. Treasury Department responsible for the enforcement of the federal tax laws and the collection of federal taxes.

investment interest expense Interest paid by an individual on debt incurred to purchase or carry investment property.

involuntary conversion The receipt of insurance or condemnation proceeds with respect to property destroyed by theft or casualty or taken by eminent domain.

itemized deduction An allowable deduction for an individual taxpayer that cannot be subtracted in the calculation of AGI.

joint and several liability Each spouse on a joint tax return is individually liable for the entire tax for the year.

joint return A return filed by husband and wife reflecting their combined activities for the year.

jurisdiction The right of a government to levy tax on a specific person or organization.

Keogh plan A qualified retirement plan for self-employed individuals.

key-person life insurance policies Insurance purchased by a firm on the life of a high-level employee. The firm is the beneficiary of the policy.

kiddie tax The tax on a child's unearned income based on the child's parents' marginal rate.

late-filing and late-payment penalty The penalty imposed on taxpayers who fail to file their returns and pay the balance of tax due on a timely basis.

leasehold costs Up-front costs incurred to acquire a lease on tangible business property.

leasehold improvements Physical improvements made by a lessee to leased real property.

leverage The use of borrowed funds to create tax basis.

lifetime gift tax exclusion The $1 million cumulative amount of taxable gifts that an individual can make without incurring federal gift tax.

Lifetime Learning Credit An individual tax credit based on 20 percent of qualified tuition expenses.

LIFO The inventory costing convention under which the last goods manufactured or purchased are assumed to be the first goods sold.

like-kind property Qualifying business or investment property that can be exchanged on a nontaxable basis.

limited liability A legal characteristic of the corporate form of business: Corporate shareholders are not personally liable for the unpaid debts of the corporation.

limited liability company (LLC) A form of unincorporated business organization in which the members have limited liability for business debt. LLCs are generally treated as partnerships for federal tax purposes.

limited liability partnership (LLP A partnership in which the general partners are not personally liable for malpractice-related claims arising from the professional misconduct of another general partner.

limited partnership A partnership in which one or more partners are liable for partnership debt only to the extent of their capital contributions to the partnership. Limited partnerships must have at least one general partner.

long-term capital gain or loss Gain or loss resulting from the sale or exchange of a capital asset owned for more than one year.

marginal rate The tax rate that applies to the next dollar of taxable income.

market A forum for commercial interaction between two or more parties for the purpose of exchanging goods or services.

market discount The excess of a bond's stated redemption value over the price paid for the bond in a market transaction.

material participation An owner's regular, continual, and substantial involvement in the day-to-day operation of an active business.

method of accounting A consistent system for determining the point in time at which items of income and deduction are recognized for tax purposes.

midmonth convention Property placed in service on any day of a month is treated as placed in service at the midpoint of the month for MACRS purposes.

midquarter convention Property placed in service on any day of a quarter is treated as placed in service at the midpoint of the quarter for MACRS purposes.

minimum distribution The annual withdrawal an individual must make from a qualified retirement plan beginning no later than April 1 of the year following the year in which he reaches age 70½.

minimum tax credit AMT liability carried forward indefinitely as a credit against future regular tax liability.

miscellaneous itemized deductions Itemized deductions that are deductible only to the extent their total exceeds 2 percent of AGI.

Modified Accelerated Cost Recovery System (MACRS) The statutory and regulatory rules governing the computation of depreciation for tax purposes.

moving expenses The cost of transporting household goods and personal belongings and travel costs incurred in connection with an employment-related move. Moving expenses are an adjustment in computing AGI.

mutual fund A diversified portfolio of securities owned and managed by a regulated investment company.

negative externality An undesirable by-product of the free enterprise system.

negligence Failure to make a prudent attempt to comply with the tax law or the intentional disregard of tax rules and regulations.

net capital gain The excess of current year capital gains over capital losses.

net capital loss The excess of current year capital losses over capital gains.

net cash flow The difference between cash received and cash disbursed.

net investment income Income from investment assets reduced by expenses directly related to the production of investment income.

net long-term gain or loss Aggregate gain or loss from the sale or exchange of capital assets owned for more than a year.

net operating loss (NOL) An excess of allowable deductions over gross income.

net present value (NPV) The sum of the present values of all cash inflows and outflows relating to a transaction.

net short-term gain or loss Aggregate gain or loss from the sale or exchange of capital assets owned for a year or less.

nexus The degree of contact between a business and a state necessary to establish the state's jurisdiction to tax the business.

NOL carryback A net operating loss allowed as a deduction in the two years prior to the year of loss.

NOL carryforward A net operating loss allowed as a deduction in the 20 years following the year of loss.

nonbusiness bad debt An uncollectible debt held by an individual creditor that is unrelated to the individual's business.

nonprofit corporation A corporation formed for philanthropic purposes and, as a result, exempt from the federal income tax.

nonrecourse debt A debt secured by specific collateral for which the debtor is not personally liable.

nontaxable exchange A transaction resulting in realized gain or loss that is not recognized (in whole or part) in the current year.

offer in compromise A negotiated settlement with the IRS in which the taxpayer pays less than the entire deficiency.

office examination An audit conducted by a tax auditor at an IRS district office.

ordinary gain or loss Any realized gain or loss that is not a capital gain or loss.

ordinary income Any income that is not capital gain. Ordinary income is taxed at the regular individual or corporate tax rates.

organizational costs Expenditures incurred in connection with the formation of a partnership or corporate entity.

original issue discount (OID) The excess of a bond's stated redemption value over the issue price.

outbound transaction A transaction by which a U.S. firm engages in business in a foreign jurisdiction.

partnership An unincorporated association of two or more persons to conduct business as co-owners.

passenger automobiles Four-wheeled vehicles manufactured primarily for use on public roads with an unloaded gross vehicle weight of 6,000 pounds or less.

passive activity An individual's interest in (1) an active business in which the individual does not materially participate or (2) a rental activity.

passive income generator (PIG) An interest in a profitable passive activity.

passthrough entities Business entities that are not taxable entities. The income, gains, deductions, and losses recognized by a passthrough entity are reported by the entity's owners and taxed only once at the owner level.

percentage depletion An annual deduction based on the gross income generated by a depletable property multiplied by a statutory depletion rate.

performance-based compensation Compensation paid solely because the recipient employee attained a performance goal established by a compensation committee of outside members of the corporate board of directors.

permanent difference A difference between financial statement income and taxable income that does not reverse over time.

permanent establishment A fixed location at which a firm carries on its regular commercial activities. For income tax treaty purposes, a country has no jurisdiction to tax a foreign business entity unless the entity maintains a permanent establishment in the country.

personal exemption A dollar amount allowed as a deduction from AGI for each taxpayer and qualifying dependent. The personal exemption is indexed annually for inflation.

personal holding company A corporation owned by a small number of individuals that receives taxable income consisting primarily of nonbusiness income such as dividends, interest, rents, and royalties.

personal holding company tax A penalty tax levied on personal holding companies in addition to the regular corporate income tax.

personal service corporations Closely held corporations owned by individuals who perform services in the fields of health, law, engineering, architecture, accounting, actuarial science, performing arts, or consulting for the corporation's clientele. Personal service corporations are subject to a flat 35 percent tax rate.

personalty Any asset that is not realty.

premature withdrawal A withdrawal from a qualified retirement plan made before the individual reaches age 59½.

principal residence The home in which an individual resides for most of the year and considers his permanent address.

private activity bonds Tax-exempt bonds issued by state or local governments for nongovernmental purposes such as industrial development.

private letter ruling The IRS's written response to a taxpayer's inquiry as to how the tax law applies to a proposed transaction.

private market A market in which the parties deal directly with each other and can customize the terms of their agreement to meet their respective objectives.

probate estate Property owned by a decedent and disposed of according to the terms of a valid will or state intestacy laws.

profit-sharing plan A defined-contribution plan under which an employer regularly contributes a percentage of current earnings to the employees' retirement accounts.

progressive rate structure A graduated rate structure with rates that increase as the base increases.

property similar or related in service or use Qualifying replacement property in a nontaxable involuntary conversion.

proportionate rate structure A rate structure with a single, or flat, rate.

public market A market in which the parties deal indirectly through an intermediary such as a broker or a financial institution.

publicly held corporations Corporations with outstanding stock traded on an established securities market.

qualified dividend distribution A distribution of qualified dividend income received by a mutual fund to investors in the fund.

qualified dividend income Dividends received from taxable domestic corporations and certain qualified foreign corporations eligible for a preferential individual tax rate.

qualified education loan Any debt incurred to pay higher education expenses.

qualified residence interest Interest paid on acquisition debt or home equity debt allowed as an itemized deduction.

qualified retirement plans Retirement plans that meet certain statutory requirements and that allow participants to save for retirement on a tax-deferred basis.

qualified small business stock Stock in a corporate business that meets certain statutory requirements. Individuals who recognize gain on the sale of qualified small business stock may be eligible to exclude 50 percent of the gain from income.

qualified tuition expenses Tuition and fees required for enrollment in a post-secondary educational institution.

qualified tuition program A savings program sponsored by a state or private educational institution in which individuals can invest to pay future college expenses.

qualifying property The specific property eligible for a particular nontaxable exchange.

real property tax A tax levied on the ownership of realty and based on the property's assessed market value.

realization Income is taken into account when the earnings process with respect to the income is complete and an event or transaction occurs that provides an objective measurement of the income.

realized gain or loss The positive or negative difference between the amount realized on the disposition of property and the adjusted basis of the property.

realty Land and whatever is erected or growing on the land or permanently affixed to it.

recapture Recharacterization of Section 1231 or capital gain as ordinary income.

recognition Inclusion of an item of income or deduction in the computation of taxable income.

recognized gain or loss Realized gain or loss taken into account for tax purposes in the current year.

recourse debt A debt for which the debtor is personally liable.

recovery period The number of years prescribed by statute over which the basis of tangible business property is depreciated under MACRS.

regressive rate structure A graduated rate structure with rates that decrease as the base increases.

rehabilitation credit A business credit equal to a percentage of the cost of rehabilitating commercial buildings placed in service before 1936 or certified historic structures.

related party transaction A transaction between parties who share a common economic interest or objective and who may not be dealing at arm's length.

rental activity An activity where payments are principally for the use of tangible property for an extended period of time. Rental activities are passive activities.

reorganization A statutorily defined transaction in which one corporation acquires another, one corporation divides into two corporations, or a corporation changes its capital structure.

research and experimental expenditures A preferential deduction for costs of basic research designed to encourage businesses to conduct such research.

revenue Total tax collected by the government and available for public use.

revenue rulings and revenue procedures Published pronouncements explaining how the IRS applies current tax law to a particular set of facts and circumstances.

rollover contribution A distribution from one qualified plan contributed to another qualified plan within 60 days.

Roth IRA An investment account through which individuals with compensation or earned income can save for retirement on a tax-exempt basis.

safe-harbor estimate Estimated current year tax payments based on the preceding year's tax liability that protect the taxpayer from the underpayment penalty.

sales tax A general tax levied on the retail sale of goods and services.

section Numerically labeled subdivision of the Internal Revenue Code. Each section contains an operational, definitional, or procedural rule relating to one of the federal taxes.

Section 401(k) plan A defined-contribution plan under which employees elect to contribute a portion of current year compensation to an employer-provided retirement plan.

Section 179 election The election under which firms can expense a limited dollar amount of the cost of tangible personalty placed in service during the taxable year.

Section 1231 asset Real or depreciable property used in a trade or business (including rental real estate) and intangible business assets subject to amortization held by the owner for more than one year.

Section 1244 stock The first $1 million of stock issued by a corporation for cash or property. Some portion of the loss on the disposition of Section 1244 stock is ordinary to individual investors.

securities Financial instruments including equity interests in business organizations and creditor interests such as savings accounts, notes, and bonds.

self-employment (SE) tax Employment tax levied on an individual's net earnings from self-employment.

seller-financed sale A sale transaction in which the seller accepts the purchaser's debt obligation as part of the sale price.

separate return A return filed by a married individual reflecting his or her independent activity and tax liability for the year. The tax liability is based on the married filing separately rate schedule.

separately stated item An item of income, gain, deduction, or loss recognized by a passthrough entity that retains its character as it flows through to the owners. Separately stated items are not included in the computation of the entity's ordinary business income or loss.

Series EE savings bonds Long-term debt instruments issued by the U.S. government at a discount.

short-period return A tax return for a taxable year consisting of less than 12 months.

short-term capital gain or loss Gain or loss resulting from the sale or exchange of a capital asset owned for one year or less.

single taxpayer An unmarried individual who is neither a surviving spouse nor a head of household.

Small Tax Case Division A division of the U.S. Tax Court that holds informal hearings of disputes involving tax deficiencies of $50,000 or less.

sole proprietorship An unincorporated business owned by one individual.

special agent A revenue agent who handles criminal fraud investigations.

specific identification method An accounting method under which cost of goods sold includes the actual cost of specific items of inventory sold during the year.

standard deduction A deduction from AGI based on filing status. The standard deduction amounts are indexed annually for inflation.

start-up expenditures Up-front costs of investigating the creation or purchase of a business and the routine expenses incurred during the preoperating phase of a business.

static forecast A projection of revenue gain or loss resulting from a tax rate change that assumes that the change will have no effect on the tax base.

statute of limitations The statutory limit on the time period after a tax return is filed during which the IRS can audit the return and assess additional tax.

step transaction doctrine The IRS can collapse a series of intermediate transactions into a single transaction to determine the tax consequences of the arrangement in its entirety.

stock option The right to purchase corporate stock for a stated price (the strike price) for a given period of time.

subchapter S corporation A corporation with a subchapter S election in effect. The corporation is a passthrough entity for federal tax purposes and does not pay federal income tax.

subpart F income A category of foreign source income earned by a CFC constructively distributed to U.S. shareholders in the year earned. Conceptually, subpart F income is artificial income in that it has no commercial or economic connection to the country in which the CFC is incorporated.

substance over form doctrine The IRS can look through the legal formalities to determine the economic substance (if any) of a transaction and to base the tax consequences on the substance instead of the form.

substituted basis The basis of qualifying property received in a nontaxable exchange determined by reference to the basis of the property surrendered in the exchange.

substitution effect A behavioral response to an income tax rate increase: Taxpayers engage in fewer income-producing activities and more non-income-producing activities.

sufficiency The first standard for a good tax. A tax should generate enough revenue to pay for the public goods and services provided by the government levying the tax.

supply-side economic theory A decrease in the highest income tax rates should stimulate economic growth and ultimately result in an increase in government revenues.

surtax In the corporate context, the extra 5 percent or 3 percent tax imposed to recoup the benefit of the progressive corporate tax rates.

surviving spouse Filing status that permits a widow or widower to use the married filing jointly rate schedule for two taxable years following the death of a spouse.

tax A payment to support the cost of government. A tax is nonpenal but compulsory and is not directly related to any specific benefit provided by the government.

tax assessor An elected or appointed government official responsible for deriving the value of realty located within a taxing jurisdiction.

tax avoidance The implementation of legal strategies for reducing taxes.

tax base An item, occurrence, transaction, or activity with respect to which a tax is levied. Tax bases are usually expressed in monetary terms.

tax basis A taxpayer's investment in any asset or property right and the measure of unrecovered dollars represented by the asset.

tax cost An increase in tax liability for any period resulting from a transaction.

tax credit A direct reduction in tax liability.

tax evasion The willful and deliberate attempt to defraud the government by understating a tax liability through illegal means. Also see *Criminal fraud.*

Tax Expenditures Budget Part of the federal budget that quantifies the annual revenue loss attributable to each major tax preference.

tax haven A foreign jurisdiction with minimal or no income tax.

tax law The body of legal authority consisting of statutory laws, administrative pronouncements, and judicial decisions.

tax planning The structuring of transactions to reduce tax costs or increase tax savings to maximize net present value.

tax policy A government's attitude, objectives, and actions with respect to its tax system.

tax preferences In the general context, provisions included in the federal tax law as incentives to encourage certain behaviors or as subsidies for certain activities; in AMT context, specific items added to regular taxable income in the computation of AMTI.

tax savings A decrease in tax liability for any period resulting from a transaction.

taxable estate The aggregate fair market value of property owned by a decedent or transferred because of the decedent's death reduced by allowable deductions.

taxable income Gross income minus allowable deductions for the taxable year.

taxpayer Any person or organization required by law to pay tax to a governmental authority.

Taxpayer Bill of Rights Part of the federal law requiring the IRS to deal with every citizen and resident in a fair, professional, prompt, and courteous manner.

temporary difference A difference between financial statement income and taxable income that reverses over time.

tentative minimum tax AMTI in excess of the exemption multiplied by the AMT rates. Any excess of tentative minimum tax over regular tax is the AMT for the year.

testamentary transfer A transfer of property occurring on the death of the property owner.

thin capitalization A corporate capital structure with a high ratio of debt to equity.

time value of money A dollar available today is worth more than a dollar available tomorrow because the current dollar can be invested to start earning interest immediately.

total income The sum of the income items recognized by an individual during the year and listed on page 1, Form 1040.

transfer price In the international area, the price at which goods or services are exchanged between controlled corporations operating in different taxing jurisdictions.

transfer tax A tax levied on the transfer of wealth by gift or at death and based on the market value of the transferred assets.

transferee liability Liability of a recipient of property (transferee) for the unpaid tax of the transferor of the property.

Treasury regulation The official interpretation of a statutory tax rule written and published by the U.S. Treasury.

28 percent rate gain or loss Long-term capital gain or loss from the sale or exchange of collectibles or qualified small business stock.

underpayment penalty The penalty imposed by the Internal Revenue Code on both individuals and corporations that fail to make required installment payments of current tax on a timely basis.

unemployment tax A tax levied by both the federal and state governments on compensation paid by employers to their employees. Unemployment taxes are earmarked to fund the national unemployment insurance program.

uniform capitalization (unicap) rules The set of tax rules governing the type of current expenditures that must be capitalized to inventory.

Uniform Division of Income for Tax Purposes Act (UDITPA) A model act describing a recommended method for apportioning a firm's taxable income among multiple state jurisdictions.

U.S. Circuit Courts of Appeals Thirteen federal courts that hear appeals of trial court decisions.

U.S. Court of Federal Claims A federal trial court located in Washington, D.C., in which taxpayers can sue the government for a refund of tax.

U.S. District Courts Federal trial courts in which taxpayers can sue the government for a refund of tax.

U.S. production activities deduction A tax preference deduction for U.S. manufacturers equal to a percentage of net income from a qualified domestic activity.

U.S. Supreme Court The highest federal court. The Supreme Court hears appeals of circuit court decisions.

U.S. Tax Court A federal court that tries only federal income, gift, and estate tax cases.

unlimited life A legal characteristic of the corporate form of business: A corporation's legal existence is not affected by changes in the identity of its shareholders.

unlimited marital deduction A deduction in the computation of a decedent's taxable estate equal to the value of property transferred to the decedent's surviving spouse.

unrecaptured Section 1250 gain Section 1231 gain on the sale of business realty that would be recaptured as ordinary income under the full recapture rule.

use tax A tax levied on the ownership, possession, or consumption of goods if the owner did not pay the jurisdiction's sales tax when the goods were purchased.

vacation home A personal residence other than the owner's principal residence.

value-added tax (VAT) A tax levied on firms engaged in any phase of the production or manufacture of goods and based on the incremental value added by the firm to the goods.

vertical equity One aspect of the fourth standard of a good tax: A tax is fair if persons with a greater ability to pay (as measured by the tax base) owe more tax than persons with a lesser ability to pay.

wash sale A sale of marketable securities if the seller reacquires substantially the same securities within 30 days after (or 30 days before) the sale.

withholding tax A tax on dividends paid to foreign shareholders that is withheld by the corporation paying the dividend.

Appendixes

A Present Value of $1

B Present Value of Annuity of $1

C Tax Research

Appendix A

Present Value of $1

Periods	3%	4%	5%	6%	7%	8%	9%
1	.971	.962	.952	.943	.935	.926	.917
2	.943	.925	.907	.890	.873	.857	.842
3	.915	.889	.864	.840	.816	.794	.772
4	.888	.855	.823	.792	.763	.735	.708
5	.863	.822	.784	.747	.713	.681	.650
6	.837	.790	.746	.705	.666	.630	.596
7	.813	.760	.711	.665	.623	.583	.547
8	.789	.731	.677	.627	.582	.540	.502
9	.766	.703	.645	.592	.544	.500	.460
10	.744	.676	.614	.558	.508	.463	.422
11	.722	.650	.585	.527	.475	.429	.388
12	.701	.625	.557	.497	.444	.397	.356
13	.681	.601	.530	.469	.415	.368	.326
14	.661	.577	.505	.442	.388	.340	.299
15	.642	.555	.481	.417	.362	.315	.275
16	.623	.534	.458	.394	.339	.292	.252
17	.605	.513	.436	.371	.317	.270	.231
18	.587	.494	.416	.350	.296	.250	.212
19	.570	.475	.396	.331	.277	.232	.194
20	.554	.456	.377	.312	.258	.215	.178

Periods	10%	11%	12%	13%	14%	15%	20%
1	.909	.901	.893	.885	.877	.870	.833
2	.826	.812	.797	.783	.769	.756	.694
3	.751	.731	.712	.693	.675	.658	.579
4	.683	.659	.636	.613	.592	.572	.482
5	.621	.593	.567	.543	.519	.497	.402
6	.564	.535	.507	.480	.456	.432	.335
7	.513	.482	.452	.425	.400	.376	.279
8	.467	.434	.404	.376	.351	.327	.233
9	.424	.391	.361	.333	.308	.284	.194
10	.386	.352	.322	.295	.270	.247	.162
11	.350	.317	.287	.261	.237	.215	.135
12	.319	.286	.257	.231	.208	.187	.112
13	.290	.258	.229	.204	.182	.163	.093
14	.263	.232	.205	.181	.160	.141	.078
15	.239	.209	.183	.160	.140	.123	.065
16	.218	.188	.163	.141	.123	.107	.054
17	.198	.170	.146	.125	.108	.093	.045
18	.180	.153	.130	.111	.095	.081	.038
19	.164	.138	.116	.098	.083	.070	.031
20	.149	.124	.104	.087	.073	.061	.026

Appendix B

Present Value of Annuity of $1

Periods	3%	4%	5%	6%	7%	8%	9%
1	.971	.962	.952	.943	.935	.926	.917
2	1.913	1.886	1.859	1.833	1.808	1.783	1.759
3	2.829	2.775	2.723	2.673	2.624	2.577	2.531
4	3.717	3.630	3.546	3.465	3.387	3.312	3.240
5	4.580	4.452	4.329	4.212	4.100	3.993	3.890
6	5.417	5.242	5.076	4.917	4.767	4.623	4.486
7	6.230	6.002	5.786	5.582	5.389	5.206	5.033
8	7.020	6.733	6.463	6.210	5.971	5.747	5.535
9	7.786	7.435	7.108	6.802	6.515	6.247	5.995
10	8.530	8.111	7.722	7.360	7.024	6.710	6.418
11	9.253	8.760	8.306	7.887	7.499	7.139	6.805
12	9.954	9.385	8.863	8.384	7.943	7.536	7.161
13	10.635	9.986	9.394	8.853	8.358	7.904	7.487
14	11.296	10.563	9.899	9.295	8.745	8.244	7.786
15	11.938	11.118	10.380	9.712	9.108	8.559	8.061
16	12.561	11.652	10.838	10.106	9.447	8.851	8.313
17	13.166	12.166	11.274	10.477	9.763	9.122	8.544
18	13.754	12.659	11.690	10.828	10.059	9.372	8.756
19	14.324	13.134	12.085	11.158	10.336	9.604	8.950
20	14.877	13.590	12.462	11.470	10.594	9.818	9.129

Periods	10%	11%	12%	13%	14%	15%	20%
1	.909	.901	.893	.885	.877	.870	.833
2	1.736	1.713	1.690	1.668	1.647	1.626	1.528
3	2.487	2.444	2.402	2.361	2.322	2.283	2.106
4	3.170	3.102	3.037	2.974	2.914	2.855	2.589
5	3.791	3.696	3.605	3.517	3.433	3.352	2.991
6	4.355	4.231	4.111	3.998	3.889	3.784	3.326
7	4.868	4.712	4.564	4.423	4.288	4.160	3.605
8	5.335	5.146	4.968	4.799	4.639	4.487	3.837
9	5.759	5.537	5.328	5.132	4.946	4.772	4.031
10	6.145	5.889	5.650	5.426	5.216	5.019	4.192
11	6.495	6.207	5.938	5.687	5.453	5.234	4.327
12	6.814	6.492	6.194	5.918	5.660	5.421	4.439
13	7.103	6.750	6.424	6.122	5.842	5.583	4.533
14	7.367	6.982	6.628	6.302	6.002	5.724	4.611
15	7.606	7.191	6.811	6.462	6.142	5.847	4.675
16	7.824	7.379	6.974	6.604	6.265	5.954	4.730
17	8.022	7.549	7.120	6.729	6.373	6.047	4.775
18	8.201	7.702	7.250	6.840	6.467	6.128	4.812
19	8.365	7.839	7.366	6.938	6.550	6.198	4.843
20	8.514	7.963	7.469	7.025	6.623	6.259	4.870

Appendix C

Tax Research

Tax research is the process of determining the most probable tax consequences of a course of action undertaken by an individual or organization. Because of the complexity of state, local, and federal tax laws, most taxpayers are unable to conduct research on their own behalf. Consequently, they engage professionals such as certified public accountants (CPAs) or attorneys to investigate the tax consequences of their business, investment, and financial transactions. Taxpayers expect to receive fair value in return for the substantial fees paid to their tax advisers. Specifically, they expect their advisers to provide accurate, useful, and complete tax information on a timely basis.

A client may engage a tax adviser to research a transaction (or series of transactions) that has already occurred. In such case, the adviser must identify the consequences of the transaction and the proper reporting of the transaction on the client's tax return. Because the transaction is complete, the facts surrounding the transaction are a matter of record and are no longer subject to the client's control. The tax consequences of such a closed-fact transaction can't be changed, even if they are not to the client's liking. Thus, the adviser is limited to providing a tax compliance service to the client.

Alternatively, a client may engage a tax adviser to research a transaction that the client proposes to undertake at some future date. In this case, the adviser not only can determine the tax consequences of the prospective transaction but also can suggest ways in which the transaction can be modified to result in a more favorable outcome. The facts surrounding a prospective transaction have yet to be established and, therefore, are subject to the client's control. In such an open-fact transaction, the adviser can help the client create facts that will influence the tax consequences. Clearly, this tax planning service can be extremely valuable to clients who want to maximize the after-tax value of their transactions.

Purpose of This Appendix

Tax research is an intellectual skill that is developed through both education and experience. Men and women who enter the tax profession have completed many hours of formal study as part of their undergraduate and graduate education. During their careers, they will devote many more hours to maintaining the currency of their technical tax knowledge. Tax professionals also learn by doing. As with any skill, proficiency comes with practice, and tax professionals become more proficient with every research project they undertake.

Students enrolled in an introductory tax class are struggling to learn the rudiments of the tax law. Their knowledge of the subject is limited and they have no professional experience on which to draw. Nonetheless, even beginning tax students can benefit from an introduction to the tax research process. By studying this process, students gain insight into the nature of the work performed by tax professionals. They learn how CPAs and attorneys identify tax problems, solve those problems, and communicate the solutions to their clients. They gain an appreciation of the expertise necessary to perform these tasks. Finally, students start to develop their own analytic framework for determining the tax consequences of business, investment, and financial transactions.

Many tax textbooks include entire chapters on tax research, and several textbooks are devoted entirely to the subject. Most graduate accounting and law programs offer a course on tax research. Obviously, this appendix provides only a brief discussion of the fundamentals of a complex subject. However, after reading this appendix, students should be ready to try their hand at solving the Research Problems provided at the end of the chapters. Students who do so will enjoy an intellectual challenge that will increase their understanding of the fascinating subject of taxation.

The Tax Research Process

The tax research process can be broken down into six steps. This appendix provides a description of each research step, followed by an example of the application of the step to a research case. Students who are just starting to develop their research skills should focus on and complete each distinct step in sequence. By doing so, students will establish good research "habits." As they become more proficient, students will gradually integrate the steps into a seamless research process. Those students who become accomplished researchers will automatically perform the six steps for every research project they undertake.

Step 1: Understand the Client's Transaction and Ascertain the Facts Before a researcher can analyze the tax consequences of a transaction, she must thoroughly understand the transaction itself. Specifically, the researcher should discuss the details of the transaction with her client to ascertain the client's motivation. What are the client's economic objectives in undertaking the transaction? What does the client foresee as the desired outcome? What risks has the client identified? By asking these types of questions, the researcher acquaints herself with the nontax features of the transaction before considering any tax implications.

The researcher must discover all the facts concerning the client's transaction. Like a newspaper reporter, the researcher should question the client about the precise "who, when, where, why, and how" of the transaction. The researcher should not assume that the client's initial summary of the transaction is factually accurate and complete. Perhaps the client hasn't determined all the facts that the researcher needs. Or the client may have discounted the significance of certain facts and omitted them from the initial summary. The researcher should encourage the client to be objective in stating the facts. Oftentimes a client will unwittingly present the researcher with the client's subjective conclusions about the facts rather than with the facts themselves.

When a researcher is working with a client to uncover the relevant facts, the researcher must take into account the level of the client's tax knowledge. If the client has some knowledge of the tax law, the researcher can ask questions that presume such knowledge. On the other hand, if the client is unsophisticated in tax matters, the researcher should ask only questions that the client can answer without reference to the tax law.

Applying Step 1. Sara Colter, a professional photographer, is a new client who has engaged your accounting firm to determine the tax consequences of a proposed transaction: Sara's sale of a 12-acre tract of land to CCM Inc. Sara provides the following facts in her initial summary of the transaction.

- *Sara purchased the land from Mr. and Mrs. Bianca in 1994 for $400,000 cash.*
- *Sara and CCM Inc. have reached a tentative agreement under which CCM will pay $325,000 cash for the land and will pay all transaction expenses.*

As a tax professional, you know that the tax consequences of a transaction may depend on whether the parties involved are "related parties" for federal tax purposes. You also know that the tax consequences of the sale of an asset depend on the classification of the asset as capital or noncapital. Because Sara is unsophisticated in tax matters, you cannot ask her directly if she and CCM Inc. are related parties. Nor can you ask Sara if the land is a capital asset. Because of her lack of tax knowledge, such questions would be meaningless to your client. Accordingly, you decide to ask Sara the following series of questions.

- *Do you have any personal relationship with Mr. and Mrs. Bianca? Did you know them in any capacity other than as the sellers of the land that you purchased in 1994?*
- *What was your reason for purchasing the land? Have you made any improvements to the land since 1994? Have you purchased or sold any other real estate during the last ten years?*
- *How did you and CCM Inc. reach an agreement that the land is worth only $325,000? Why has the land declined in value since you purchased it?*
- *Do you own any stock in CCM Inc.? Who are CCM Inc.'s stockholders?*

In response to your questions, Sara provides the following additional facts.

- *She has no personal relationship with the Biancas and did not know them prior to her purchase of their land. The purchase was arranged through a professional real estate broker.*
- *She purchased the land because she thought that its value would increase over time and she could eventually sell it at a profit. She has not made any improvements to the land; it is in exactly the same condition today as the day she purchased it. She has never purchased nor sold any other real estate other than her personal residence.*
- *Two months ago, Sara obtained two independent appraisals of the value of the land. The appraisals both concluded that the current market value of the land is $325,000. CCM Inc. performed its own appraisal that confirmed this value. The $75,000 decline in value is attributable to local zoning restrictions on the land that were put in place in 1997.*
- *Sara does not own any CCM Inc. stock. Twenty-four individual stockholders own the 1,000 outstanding CCM shares. Two of these stockholders are Sara's brother Jack and Jack's son Robert. Sara is not acquainted with any of the other stockholders.*

Step 2: Identify the Tax Issues, Problems, or Opportunities Suggested by the Facts and Formulate Specific Research Questions After a researcher is satisfied that she understands her client's transaction and knows all the relevant facts, she can proceed to the second step in the research process. In this step, the researcher identifies the tax issue or issues suggested by the transaction. The ability to recognize tax issues is the product of technical education and professional experience. Consequently, this step is usually the most challenging for students in an introductory tax course.

The identification of issues leads to the formulation of tax research questions. The tax researcher should be as precise as possible in formulating questions. A precise question is narrowly stated and provides clear parameters for the remaining steps in the research process. An imprecise question that is vague or overly broad in scope may provide insufficient parameters and result in wasted time and effort.

If the tax issues suggested by a transaction lead to multiple research questions, the researcher must determine the order in which the questions should be answered. In our complex tax system, the answer to a question often depends on the answer to one or more preliminary questions. Tax researchers who understand the hierarchy of their research questions can address each question in the right order and conduct their research with maximum efficiency.

Applying Step 2. After studying the facts, you conclude that Sara's proposed transaction involves one basic tax issue: Will Sara's sale of the land to CCM Inc. result in a loss that she can deduct on her individual income tax return? This issue suggests four research questions, which you decide to address in the following order.

Will Sara realize a loss on the sale of her land to CCM Inc?

Can Sara recognize her realized loss?

What is the character of any recognized loss?

Given the character of the loss, to what extent can Sara deduct the loss in the computation of taxable income for the year of sale?

Students should note that the research problems provided at the end of the chapters do not require students to perform the first two steps in the tax research process. These problems are deliberately written to contain all the facts necessary to solve the problem. Moreover, the problems provide the specific research question or questions for students to answer. Such is the nature (and weakness) of textbook research problems! But in the real world of tax practice, the first two tasks are not performed by anyone but the researcher. If the researcher fails to ascertain the key facts, identify the important issues, and ask the right questions, all her subsequent efforts are futile.

Step 3: Locate Relevant Tax Law Authority As the third step in the research process, the researcher heads for a tax library. Her mission is to locate authority providing answers to the research questions. Traditional libraries consist of shelves filled with books, looseleaf binders, magazines, and other published materials containing all the technical minutiae of the tax law. Today, traditional libraries are disappearing as professional tax advisers gain access to the electronic libraries available on CD-ROM or the Internet. One obvious advantage of electronic libraries is the speed at which researchers can access sources of authority and move among the sources. A second advantage is the ease with which electronic databases can be updated to include current developments. A third advantage is that an electronic library is portable. A tax researcher with a laptop computer can access the library at any time and from any location.

Regardless of whether a tax researcher is working in a traditional or electronic library, she must be knowledgeable about the content and organization of the reference materials in that library. The researcher must know how to locate references pertaining to the problem at hand. The researcher must also be able to distinguish between the two main categories of reference materials: sources of authority and sources of information.

Chapter 1 of this text includes a discussion of the three sources of authority that comprise the federal tax law: statutory law (the Internal Revenue Code), Treasury regulations and IRS pronouncements, and judicial decisions. These primary legal sources are not particularly user-friendly and can be intimidating even to seasoned professionals. Consequently, many researchers prefer to begin their task with a source of information about the tax law, rather than with the law itself. Sources of information include textbooks (like *Principles of Taxation for Business and Investment Planning*), treatises, guides, and professional journals. Commercial tax services, such as RIA (Research Institute of America) Federal

Tax Coordinator 2d, CCH (Commerce Clearing House) Federal Tax Service, and Tax Management, Inc. Portfolios are excellent sources of information. These services function much like encyclopedias. They are organized by topic and provide detailed explanations of literally thousands of technical rules.

Tax researchers who rely on sources of information should always keep in mind that they are reading another person's opinion about the tax law. While that person might be an expert on the subject at hand, a good researcher should not be satisfied until she goes beyond the source of information to analyze the underlying source of authority. Researchers who discipline themselves to read the Internal Revenue Code, Treasury regulations, IRS pronouncements, and judicial decisions will discover that their comprehension of these complex materials increases with each effort.

Applying Step 3. To begin your search for authority, you turn to Chapter 7 in this text and review the section entitled "Computation of Gain or Loss Recognized." The text states that a seller of property realizes a loss equal to the excess of the seller's adjusted basis in the property over the amount realized on sale. The text also reminds you of the general rule that losses are recognized in the year realized. The footnotes in the text lead you to Section 1001(a) and (c) of the Internal Revenue Code, which provides the statutory authority for these statements. Further reading in Chapter 7 leads you to Section 267, which provides that a taxpayer cannot recognize a loss realized on a sale to a related party.

Step 4: Analyze Relevant Authority and Answer the Research Questions Regardless of whether a researcher is reading from a printed page or a computer screen, she must have the skill to interpret and evaluate the authority at hand. In some cases, the authority may provide an unambiguous answer to the researcher's question. In other cases, the answer may be equivocal because the authority is inconclusive or subject to interpretation. Or perhaps different sources of authority provide conflicting answers. In these cases, the researcher must bring her judgment to bear in analyzing the authority and answering the question.

As part of the analytic process, the researcher should decide if the authority requires her to make a factual judgment or an evaluative judgment. In making a factual judgment the researcher compares the authority to a set of facts. Assuming that the facts are complete and accurate, the researcher can provide a definitive answer to the research question. For example, consider the following research problem.

> Mr. Johnson provides 100 percent of the financial support for Ms. Lewis, who is Mr. Johnson's sister-in-law. Does Ms. Lewis qualify as Mr. Johnson's dependent?

Section 152 provides the relevant statutory authority for this research question.

> Sec. 152. Dependent defined
>
> (a) General definition
>
> For purposes of this subtitle, the term "dependent" means any of the following individuals over half of whose support, for the calendar year in which the taxable year of the taxpayer begins, was received from the taxpayer:
>
> (1) A son or daughter of the taxpayer, or a descendant of either,
> (2) A stepson or stepdaughter of the taxpayer,
> (3) A brother, sister, stepbrother, or stepsister of the taxpayer,
> (4) The father or mother of the taxpayer, or an ancestor of either,
> (5) A stepfather or stepmother of the taxpayer,
> (6) A son or daughter of a brother or sister of the taxpayer,
> (7) A brother or sister of the father or mother of the taxpayer,

(8) A son-in-law, daughter-in-law, father-in-law, mother-in-law, brother-in-law, or sister-in-law of the taxpayer, or
(9) An individual (other than an individual who at any time during the taxable year was the spouse, determined without regard to section 7703, of the taxpayer) who, for the taxable year of the taxpayer, has as his principal place of abode the home of the taxpayer and is a member of the taxpayer's household.

By comparing the facts of this research problem to the relevant authority, a researcher can conclude that Ms. Lewis qualifies as Mr. Johnson's dependent. Therefore, the answer to the research questions is an unqualified yes.

Researchers are required to make evaluative judgments when the relevant authority relates to a conclusion inferred from a set of facts, rather than to the facts themselves. By definition, conclusions are subjective; different observers may draw different conclusions from the same facts. A researcher who must draw a conclusion to complete a research project can never be sure that such conclusion will go unchallenged by the IRS. Therefore, the researcher should never give an unqualified answer to a research question requiring an evaluative judgment. This point is illustrated by the following research problem.

Mrs. Clancy operates a business as sole proprietorship. Last week, she traveled to New York for an important meeting with a major client. Mrs. Clancy paid $2,615 for a first-class airline ticket and paid $340 per night for her hotel room. Can Mrs. Clancy deduct these business expenses on her Schedule C, Form 1040?

Section 162 provides the relevant statutory authority for this research question.

Sec. 162. Trade or business expenses

(a) In general
There shall be allowed as a deduction all the ordinary and necessary expenses paid or incurred during the taxable year in carrying on any trade or business, including—
(1) a reasonable allowance for salaries or other compensation for personal services actually rendered;
(2) traveling expenses (including amounts expended for meals and lodging other than amounts which are lavish or extravagant under the circumstances) while away from home in the pursuit of a trade or business.

This authority requires the researcher to evaluate the circumstances surrounding Mrs. Clancy's travel expenses. If the expenses were not lavish and extravagant, the entire amount is deductible. However, if some amount was lavish or extravagant, such amount is nondeductible. Note that the term "lavish or extravagant" is a matter of opinion, and reasonable persons might disagree as to whether the term describes Mrs. Clancy's expenses. If the researcher believes that the facts and circumstances support a conclusion that the travel expenses were not lavish or extravagant, the researcher could advise Mrs. Clancy to deduct the expenses. But the researcher should qualify this advice by explaining the risk that an IRS agent might draw the opposite conclusion and disallow the deduction.

Applying Step 4. On the basis of your reading of Section 1001(a), you determine that Sara will realize a $75,000 loss if she sells her land to CCM Inc. for $325,000 cash. According to the general rule of Section 1001(c), realized losses are recognized "except as otherwise provided in this subtitle." Therefore, Sara can recognize the loss and report it on her tax return for the year of sale unless Section 267 disallows the loss. The portions of Section 267 that seem applicable to Sara's case read as follows:

Sec. 267. Losses, expenses, and interest with respect to transactions between related taxpayers

(a) In general

(1) Deduction for losses disallowed

No deduction shall be allowed in respect of any loss from the sale or exchange of property, directly or indirectly, between persons specified in any of the paragraphs of subsection (b).

(b) Relationships

The persons referred to in subsection (a) are:

(2) An individual and a corporation more than 50 percent in value of the outstanding stock of which is owned, directly or indirectly, by or for such individual;

(c) Constructive ownership of stock

For purposes of determining, in applying subsection (b), the ownership of stock—

(2) An individual shall be considered as owning the stock owned, directly or indirectly, by or for his family;

(4) The family of an individual shall include only his brothers and sisters (whether by the whole or half blood), spouse, ancestors, and lineal descendants; and

(5) . . . stock constructively owned by an individual by reason of the application of paragraph (2) or (3) shall not be treated as owned by him for the purpose of again applying either of such paragraphs in order to make another the constructive owner of such stock.

According to Section 267(a)(1), Sara cannot recognize her realized loss if she and CCM Inc. are related parties. According to Section 267(b)(2), Sara and CCM Inc. are related parties if Sara directly or indirectly owns more than 50 percent in value of CCM's outstanding stock. You know that Sara does not own any CCM stock directly, but you are uncertain as to whether she owns any stock indirectly. Section 267(c)(2) provides that Sara is considered to own any CCM stock owned by her "family." When you refer to the facts you established during your first meeting with Sara, you discover that you do not know how many shares of CCM stock are owned by Sara's brother Jack and nephew Robert.

Step 5: Repeat Steps 1 through 4 as Many Times as Necessary! At some point in the research process, even an expert may discover that she failed to ascertain all the facts necessary to complete the analysis of the client's transaction. In such case, the researcher must repeat Step 1 by obtaining additional information from the client. Oftentimes the additional information suggests additional tax issues and research questions that the researcher must address. A researcher may have to repeat Steps 1 through 4 several times before she is satisfied with the analysis.

Applying Step 5. You contact Sara to ask one more question: How many shares of CCM stock do Jack and Robert each own? She replies that Jack owns 350 shares and Robert owns 200 shares of the 1,000 outstanding shares of CCM stock. With this additional fact, you can complete your analysis of Section 267 as it applies to Sara's proposed sale.

According to Section 267(c)(2), Sara's family includes her brother Jack but does not include her nephew Robert. Therefore, Sara indirectly owns the 350 CCM shares directly owned by Jack. However, Jack also indirectly owns the 200 CCM shares owned by his son Robert. Section 267(c)(5) states that Jack's indirect ownership of these shares is disregarded for the purpose of determining Sara's ownership. On the basis of these statutory rules, you conclude that Sara directly and indirectly owns only 350 (35 percent) of CCM's 1,000 outstanding shares of stock. Thus, she and CCM Inc. are not related parties, Section 267(a) will not apply to her sale of the land to the corporation, and Sara can recognize her $75,000 realized loss.

You continue to analyze sources of information and sources of authority that pertain to your last two research questions. You ultimately conclude that Sara's $75,000 recognized *loss will be characterized as a long-term capital loss. She can deduct this loss in the year of sale to the extent of any capital gains recognized during the year. If the capital loss exceeds her capital gains, Sara is allowed to deduct $3,000 of the excess in the computation of adjusted gross income. Any nondeductible loss becomes a long-term capital loss carryforward into subsequent taxable years.*

Step 6: Document Your Research and Communicate Your Conclusions The tax researcher's task is to find an accurate, useful, and complete answer to the research question(s) concerning the client's situation. This task is not finished until the researcher documents her work by preparing a written summary of the research process. Such summary usually takes the form of a research memo that includes (1) a statement of the pertinent facts, (2) an analysis of the relevant sources of authority, (3) an explanation of the researcher's conclusions, and (4) the details of any advice given to the client as part of the research engagement. This memo becomes a permanent record of the research process—a record to which the researcher (or any other professional) can refer at a future date.

The researcher also must communicate her conclusions to the client. Typically, the researcher writes a client letter containing information similar to that in the research memo. In writing the letter, the researcher should tailor both the contents and the writing style to accommodate the client. For example, a letter to a client who has extensive tax knowledge may contain technical references that would be inappropriate in a letter to a client with minimal tax knowledge. Similarly, a letter to an individual who has been both a client and friend for many years may be written in an informal style that would be inappropriate for a letter to the chief financial officer of a new corporate client.

Applying Step 6. After writing a research memo for your permanent record, you write the following letter to Sara Colter.

March 5, 2005

Ms. Sara Colter
1812 Riverbend Place
Kirkwood, Missouri 62119

Dear Ms. Colter:

This letter is in response to your inquiry concerning the tax consequences of a proposed sale of 12 acres of undeveloped land to CCM Inc. Before stating my conclusions, I'd like to summarize the facts of your case. You purchased the land in 1994 as a long-term investment. The purchase price was $400,000 and the sellers of the property, Mr. and Mrs. Bianca, are unrelated to you. You have not improved the land in any way since date of purchase and have neither purchased nor sold any other real estate with the exception of your personal residence. CCM Inc. is a closely held corporation with 1,000 shares of outstanding stock. Although you do not own any shares, your brother Jack Colter and his son Robert Colter own 350 and 200 shares, respectively. You are not acquainted with any other CCM stockholders. The accuracy of my conclusions depends entirely on my understanding of these facts. Consequently, if the statement of facts is in any way incorrect or incomplete, please notify me immediately.

If you sell your land to CCM Inc. for the proposed contract price of $325,000, you will realize a $75,000 loss. This loss equals the excess of your $400,000 investment in the land over the $325,000 cash you will receive at closing. You are allowed to report this loss on your individual tax return in the year of sale unless you and CCM Inc. are "related parties" within the meaning of the tax law. According to my research, you and CCM Inc. do not meet the statutory definition of "related parties," even though your brother and nephew own an aggregate 55 percent interest in CCM Inc. Therefore, you can report your $75,000 loss for tax purposes. Because you held the land for investment and owned it for more than one year, the loss is classified as a long-term capital loss. You can deduct a long-term capital loss to the extent of your capital gains for the year. If your capital loss exceeds your capital gains, you can deduct only $3,000 of the excess loss against other sources of income.

Thank you for giving my firm the opportunity to advise you in this matter. If you have any questions about my conclusions, please don't hesitate to call me. If you proceed with your plans to sell the land, I would be glad to meet with you to develop a strategy to maximize your deduction for the projected $75,000 capital loss.

Sincerely,

Bridget McGuffin

Index